THE CAPACITY TO JUDGE:
PUBLIC OPINION AND DELIBERATIVE DEMOCRACY IN UPPER CANADA, 1791–1854

JEFFREY L. McNAIRN

The Capacity to Judge

Public Opinion and Deliberative Democracy in Upper Canada, 1791–1854

UNIVERSITY OF TORONTO PRESS
Toronto Buffalo London

© University of Toronto Press Incorporated 2000
Toronto Buffalo London
Printed in Canada

ISBN 0-8020-4360-7 (cloth)

Printed on acid-free paper

Canadian Cataloguing in Publication Data

McNairn, Jeffrey L., 1967–
    The capacity to judge : public opinion and deliberative democracy
    in Upper Canada, 1791–1854

    Includes bibliographical references and index.
    ISBN 0-8020-4360-7

    1. Representative government and representation – Ontario –
    History – 19th century.   2. Constitutional history – Ontario.
    3. Ontario – Politics and government – 19th century.   4. Public opinion –
    Political aspects – Ontario – History – 19th century.   I. Title.

    FC3071.2.M36 2000   971.3'02   C00-930420-7
    F1058.M36 2000

University of Toronto Press acknowledges the financial assistance to its
publishing program of the Canada Council for the Arts and the Ontario
Arts Council.

This book has been published with the help of a grant from the Humanities
and Social Sciences Federation of Canada, using funds provided by the
Social Sciences and Humanities Research Council of Canada.

University of Toronto Press acknowledges the financial support for its
publishing activities of the Government of Canada through the Book
Publishing Industry Development Program (BPIDP).

Revolutions do not arise from what men suffer, but from what they think.

William Lyon Mackenzie, 1837

Contents

Preface

It has become increasingly common, even fashionable, to lament the poverty of public debate in Canada and to complain about the seeming inability or unwillingness of our political institutions and leaders to respond to public opinion. Such comments betray a number of assumptions: that widespread public debate is a vital sign of national health; that a sizeable number of Canadians are able and willing to engage in reasoned and informed debate; that such debate contributes to resolving political and social conflict; and that, once such debate has taken place, constitutional, legal, and political structures ought to reflect its conclusions. Whatever the current practice, such assumptions remain at the core of our democratic beliefs. They are, however, of relatively recent origin. What we are prone to take for granted as obvious and widely shared assumptions were once highly contested propositions; dismissed as risible or denounced as revolutionary.

Understanding how these assumptions developed is vital to assessing their continued relevance and reminds us why they were once thought so important. Focusing on the colony that became Ontario, this book asks what made widespread public debate possible; why it came to be seen as desirable, even essential; and how it was integrated into the province's constitutional and social identity. Despite fits of forgetfulness, we remain heirs of this story.

In the text that follows, I have tried to let contemporaries speak for themselves. Aware of the processes they participated in, they cared passionately about politics. As a result, I have used direct quotations extensively. Faithful to their meaning, I have not always retained their punctuation or littered my transcriptions with square brackets and the often patronizing *sic.* Emphasis in quotations is from the original unless otherwise indicated.

The ideals of public reasoning that defined democracy in early Ontario were modelled on those of the Republic of Letters, a term used to describe the community of scholars since the seventeenth century. Modern academe, where this project began as a doctoral dissertation, is another descendant. Substituting for the aristocratic patrons who sustained most early-modern scholars, the generous support of the Social Science and Humanities Research Council, the Ontario Graduate Scholarship program, and the University of Toronto gave me the time and resources to proceed.

The project would have been equally inconceivable without the many scholars whose works are cited in the footnotes and the staff of various archives and libraries, including the Archives of Ontario, the National Archives of Canada, the Baldwin Room of the Toronto Reference Library, and the Thomas Fisher Rare Book Room. Special thanks to the staff of the Robarts Research Library, especially its Microtext Reading Room. Preserving and disseminating the printed sources of Canada's early history, the Canadian Library Association's Newspaper Microfilming Project and the Canadian Institute for Historical Microreproductions (CIHM) too often go unacknowledged.

My apprenticeship in the Republic of Letters owes most to Arthur Silver. I won't risk embarrassing him by listing the numerous ways in which he has contributed as thesis supervisor and friend. I do, however, want to remind him of his response to my first, rather confused, draft 'chapter.' After managing to find his way through its tangled mass, he asked, 'What do you make of all of these references to public opinion? Have you read Habermas?' At last, I have an answer. Its strength probably owes more than I care to admit to another historian who attended my first conference presentation on 'public opinion.' Deprecating intellectual history, he kindly suggested a couple of alternative dissertation topics. I have worked hard to justify ignoring his advice.

Far more numerous and supportive were the suggestions, bits of good counsel, and words of encouragement from committee members Carl Berger and Ian Radforth. Allan Greer and A.B. McKillop were exemplary thesis examiners. All four asked questions that helped me to see what I was, and was not, trying to do. I hope they find the answers in the pages that follow more cogent than the ones they heard at my thesis defence. Long before, Terry Copp showed me why I wanted to be a historian.

The roller-coaster ride of historian-in-training was made more exhilarating, but also less harrowing, by sharing it with Adam Crerar, Jane Harrison, Julia Roberts, Jane Thompson, and Deborah Van Seters. Over much coffee and tea, et cetera, they have shared references, read drafts, listened to self-indulgent whining, laughed at jokes, organized much-needed distractions, and proffered good advice. During the thesis-to-book stretch, Adam, Jane H., and Julia read the entire manuscript. The end product would be better had I found the energy to engage their suggestions more fully. Also valuable at this stage were the reports of two anonymous readers.

Everyone at the University of Toronto Press has earned my gratitude. For his enthusiasm for the project, even in its earliest days as dissertation-in-progress, and for his calming responses to my less calm e-mails, I thank Gerry Hallowell. Jill McConkey and Frances Mundy guided the book through its various phases in ways that made it appear effortless to a novice and, as copy-editor, John St James identified my more opaque constructions and saved me from a number of embarrassing blunders. All those that remain are my own. Earlier versions of chapter 6 and part of chapter 3 have appeared in the *Canadian Historical Review* and the *Journal of Canadian Studies*. I thank them for permission to reprint here.

When I first met Paul de Figueiredo, he was working on his own, very different, public sphere. He has made a significant contribution to my work on this one without reading a word. My parents paid for the map. This book is dedicated to them for all the more profound debts I owe them.

Jeffrey L. McNairn
Toronto, Summer 1999

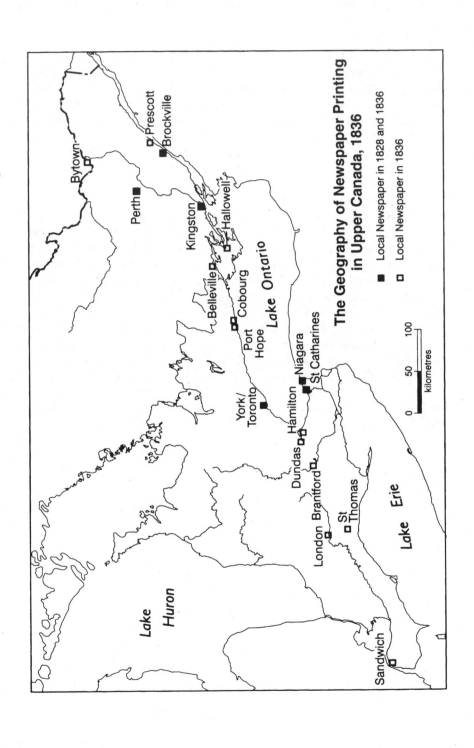

The Geography of Newspaper Printing
in Upper Canada, 1836

■ Local Newspaper in 1828 and 1836
□ Local Newspaper in 1836

Bytown
Prescott
Brockville
Perth
Kingston
Hallowell
Belleville
Cobourg
Port Hope
Lake Ontario
York/Toronto
Hamilton
Niagara
St Catharines
Dundas
Brantford
London
St Thomas
Sandwich
Lake Huron
Lake Erie

0   50   100
kilometres

THE CAPACITY TO JUDGE:
PUBLIC OPINION AND DELIBERATIVE
DEMOCRACY IN UPPER CANADA,
1791–1854

Introduction

'I will not be silent.' Writing to a Kingston newspaper in the spring of 1834, this mechanic added his 'voice, however feeble it may be,' to discussions of the relative merits of candidates for the upcoming election. 'I cannot any longer remain a mere idle spectator ... and not be moved to say something.' What he said disabused the town's commanding few of the notion that they could expect deference from those of more humble station. On behalf of his fellow mechanics, he bluntly told a prominent local lawyer and prospective candidate that 'we are as capable of judging on a point which concerns our interests, either as citizens or mechanics, as well as he; we will not be led by the nose, by any interested set of men.'[1] Those who presumed that their superior social standing, wealth, formal education, or connections entitled them to define the community's interests arrogated to themselves what belonged to all. With their judgment open to question, their claims to direct public affairs crumbled. This anonymous mechanic declared his *intellectual* independence – one of the many now-forgotten Upper Canadians who refused to remain silent. *Political* independence followed.

It was just this sort of independence that Dr Robert Douglas Hamilton had urged on his audience at a Scarborough public meeting two years before: '... do not trust either my propositions or conclusions, examine for yourselves, read fully and think freely; for there is a great difference between a taught and an acquired belief, and since the mind of man imbibes falsehood as readily as truth, let me admonish you never to place implicit confidence in any man, however commanding his talents

---

1 'A True Irishman,' *British Whig*, 11 Mar. 1834

may be, for authority is not proof, and assertions are not arguments, never therefore surrender your own reason to that of another man, however small you may reckon your own, when compared with his; for you cannot think in borrowed wisdom, nor understand by another man's knowledge.'[2]

Whatever separated tradesman from medical doctor, letter from speech, declaration from exhortation, these two Upper Canadians spoke for the same idea – that intellectual independence was something to be earned, valued, and put to good use. The place of this idea in Upper Canada's constitutional and political history – how and by whom it was earned, valued, and used – is the subject of this book.

'*Enlightenment*,' according to the German philosopher Immanuel Kant, '*is man's emergence from his self-incurred immaturity. Immaturity* is the inability to use one's own understanding without the guidance of another ... Have the courage to use your own understanding!'[3]

Kant blamed fear and laziness for keeping most people unenlightened. It was easier to surrender one's own judgment to a minority who presumed to think for others and, having little interest in giving up their monopoly, 'soon see to it that by far the largest part of mankind (including the entire fair sex) should consider the step forward to maturity not only as difficult but also as highly dangerous.' Thus 'only a few, by cultivating their own minds, have succeeded in freeing themselves from immaturity.' By cultivating their minds together, greater hope of enlightenment lay with 'the entire public.' Promoted by a few who had achieved intellectual maturity, collective enlightenment was 'almost inevitable, if only the public concerned is left in freedom ... freedom to make public use of one's reason in all matters.'

Such public reasoning was modelled on scholarship: '*as a man of learning* addressing the entire *reading public.*' The printing press allowed individuals to transcend their particular roles as citizen, military officer, clergyman, government official, or teacher to become, instead, authors speaking to 'the entire reading public.' An individual, like part of a machine, had to obey the military officer, cleric, or tax-gatherer, but he could also be 'a member of a complete commonwealth or even of cos-

---

2 Guy Pollock [Hamilton], *Courier of Upper Canada* copied in *Western Mercury*, 22 Mar. 1832
3 Kant, 'An Answer to the Question: "What Is Enlightenment?"' *Kant: Political Writings*, 54–60

mopolitan society,' free to use his own reason, to address other individu-als in his writings, and to submit 'these to his public for judgement.' In print, arguments travelled without their authors, creating a truly free and rational space for intellectual exchange. The hierarchies of society, church, and state were transcended by a commonwealth of authors judging arguments in print.

Enlightenment was achieved when all matters of common concern were debated by a reading public that, though informed by men of learning, was itself the ultimate judge. For Kant, the invention of the printing press, greater political freedom, and a growing desire on the part of individuals to think for themselves were enlarging the public and bringing more matters before it. 'Eventually,' he concluded, 'it even influences the principles of governments, which find that they can themselves profit by treating man, who is *more than a machine*, in a man-ner appropriate to his dignity.' Kantian enlightenment was realized by a government grounded in the reasoned deliberations of its citizens.

Dr Hamilton, whose oratory has already been sampled, was a good exam-ple of Kant's 'man of learning.' Doctor and scientific researcher, essayist and novelist, and founder of a local library, he also wrote frequently on political topics for the *Courier of Upper Canada* under the nom de plume 'Guy Pollock, a local blacksmith.'[4] Hamilton did not speak as a doctor or community leader. He claimed neither expertise nor elevated social standing. There was no hint that readers were to pay more or less heed to his arguments because they were purportedly those of an artisan.

Hamilton's clarion call for individual enlightenment – for others to emulate his own intellectual independence – arose from the conviction that his audience would then ignore the claims of those who insisted that Upper Canada suffered under a tyrannical and corrupt govern-ment. If only Upper Canadians reasoned for themselves, rather than blindly heeding the 'harangues' of self-interested 'agitators,' they would actively support the existing constitution. Agitators would have no one to agitate. Yet these same critics of the status quo, including the anony-mous Kingston mechanic with whom we began, called for intellectual independence precisely because they believed that the existing political order could not withstand public scrutiny. If only Upper Canadians rea-soned for themselves, they would sweep away a rotten system sustained

---

4 Charles G. Roland, 'Hamilton, Robert Douglas,' *Dictionary of Canadian Biography*, 8 (Toronto: University of Toronto Press 1985), 357–9

only by a coterie of profit-seeking office-holders and the ignorant or apathetic. Confident in the truth of their own case, each called for wider, better informed, and more critical discussion of matters of state. Upper Canada's constitution was forged by those discussions.

Enlightenment, in the Kantian sense, became a virtue, or at least an unavoidable necessity, for Upper Canadians across the spectrum of opinion and experience. Newspaper editors, commentators, officials, and vocal citizens came to it at different times, by different routes, for different reasons, and with different degrees of enthusiasm – but come to it they did. Once they arrived, Upper Canada was no longer the polity it had been. The idea that authoritative decisions about the common good could and should be generated by critical discussion among private persons outside the control of traditional authorities or the most privileged was revolutionary. Complete with contradictions and unfulfilled promises, it marked the birth of the modern political order.

Scarborough's most articulate blacksmith supported pre-existing constitutional principles, but by calling for a more robust reasoning public he helped rewrite the social contract. He advanced the process by which Upper Canadians came to understand authority and themselves in new ways. This book traces part of that process. For those caught up in it, the Kantian enlightenment had arrived in the backwoods of North America. For those left at its margins, much of the vocabulary and mechanisms by which they would demand and gain inclusion were established.

Heralding this new social contract, the concept of 'public opinion' was increasingly invoked. Not widely used in Europe until well into the eighteenth century,[5] the concept meant something quite different from our most common understanding. Public opinion was not the mere aggregate of individuals' episodic opinions, unreflective preferences, initial reactions, or longstanding prejudices. This is largely the definition of the twentieth century, of marketers and pollsters armed with survey questionnaires and probability samples. As its foremost historian puts it, 'public opinion came to be what the polls measured.' Ironically, this current definition suggests that 'public opinion' exists at any time in any community. While defying precise quantification until our own

---

5 Precise dating remains controversial, but for an emphasis on the 1730s see J.A.W. Gunn, 'Public Opinion,' in Terence Ball, James Farr, and Russell L. Hanson, eds., *Political Innovation and Conceptual Change* (Cambridge: Cambridge University Press 1989), 249–50. The *Oxford English Dictionary* found the first use of 'publick Opinion' in 1735.

century, the existence of individual opinions that could, in principle, be aggregated is conceivable across time and space.[6]

Intellectual history is at its best when it excavates the past meanings of such concepts and tries to understand the conditions under which they developed and mutated. It allows us to better appreciate and more critically assess current manifestations in light of these other, now lost, possibilities.[7] In the present case, rather than an aggregate of individual opinions, 'public opinion' of the Kantian enlightenment was a collective entity – the outcome of prolonged public deliberation among diverse individuals listening to and participating in the free, open, and reasoned exchange of information and argument. Such deliberation gave rise to conclusions that participants accepted as rational, preferred, and representative.

The process resulted in a different 'public opinion' from that often captured by today's polls. To begin with, it neither assumed that every point expressed was of equal weight nor that individuals had preexisting answers waiting only to be captured, expressed numerically, and tabulated. Classical public opinion required the collective search for the best possible answer. Participants, not their opinions, were equal. The weight of an opinion was its merit as an answer to the question at hand as determined by participants themselves during their deliberations. Moreover, individual opinions were formulated during those deliberations and altered by their educational effect – the experience of ongoing exchanges of information and argument with diverse others. This meant that the 'public' of classical public opinion could only be those with the requisite inclination, skills, and information to partake in its deliberations, not everyone in a given community. Finally, since modern polling captures individual opinions, the resulting aggregation or 'public opinion' can be expressed as any set of percentages adding up to one hundred. Since it was the result of sustained delibera-

---

6 J.A.W. Gunn, '"Public Opinion" in Modern Political Science,' in James Farr, John S. Dryzek, and Stephen T. Leonard, eds., *Political Science in History: Research Programs and Political Traditions* (Cambridge: Cambridge University Press 1995), 99–122 is excellent on differences among conceptions of public opinion; quotation at 100. Historians of Upper Canada have referred to 'public opinion' on a given issue or have used election returns as an admittedly crude measure. They have not seen the concept itself as problematic. See esp. Graeme H. Patterson, 'Studies in Elections and Public Opinion in Upper Canada,' PhD thesis, University of Toronto 1969.

7 Quentin Skinner, *Liberty before Liberalism* (Cambridge: Cambridge University Press 1998), 109–20

tion intended to define the best possible answer, classical public opinion tended to be expressed as approaching consensus – the collective answer of the public – or it was as yet inconclusive or divided. Typical references to 'almost all,' 'nine-tenths,' or 'the vast majority' reflect more than the absence of modern survey techniques. They reflect another understanding of public opinion itself.

These two ways of understanding public opinion correspond to competing archetypes of democracy. The modern public opinion of pollsters fits neatly with an economic model of democracy. Individuals are consumers who form a market, compete and bargain with each other, and 'purchase' personnel and policies from political parties to optimize their aggregate interests. It is not coincidental that public-opinion polling grew out of market research and customer surveys.[8] Classical public opinion as it developed in the eighteenth and nineteenth centuries corresponds to what is now referred to as 'deliberative democracy.' As the name implies, individuals are citizens who form a discursive community in which they exchange information and arguments while learning more about each other and the process of deliberation. Their goal is to arrive at the best possible means of advancing their common project – the collective good of their community. Educational, civic, and collective rather than mechanical, private, and aggregative, the concept of deliberative democracy is enjoying something of a renaissance. The introduction to a recent anthology calls it 'an exciting development in political theory' emerging 'in the last two decades.'[9] The label may be new, but the idea is not. Classical 'public opinion' was the public's post-deliberation verdict. To the extent that governments were responsive to those verdicts, as in the case of Upper Canada by the 1850s, they were deliberative democracies.

Neither 'public opinion' nor 'deliberative democracy' are timeless normative standards. The process of deliberation upon which they were based was possible only under certain conditions that did not exist in much of Europe until into the eighteenth century or in Upper Canada

---

8 Gunn, '"Public Opinion" in Modern Political Science,' 107 and Daniel J. Robinson, *The Measure of Democracy: Polling, Market Research, and Public Life, 1930–1945* (Toronto: University of Toronto Press 1999)

9 James Bohman and William Rehg, 'Introduction,' in *Deliberative Democracy: Essay on Reason and Politics* (Cambridge, Mass.: MIT Press 1997), ix. For the other extreme – that 'the idea of deliberative democracy ... [is] as old as democracy itself' – see Jon Elster, 'Introduction,' in *Deliberative Democracy* (Cambridge: Cambridge University Press 1998), 1.

until the second quarter of the nineteenth. In *The Structural Transformation of the Public Sphere,* Jürgen Habermas provides the most influential account of those conditions. Indebted to Kant, Habermas offers a sociological-historical investigation of the creation and destruction of the social domain in which private individuals could come together to exercise their reason in public. Habermas insists that the emergence of public opinion cannot be understood apart from the constellation of forces that made this social domain or 'public sphere' possible. Broadly conceived, these included the expanding norms and mechanisms by which relevant information and judgments were gathered, transmitted, discussed, assessed, and assimilated. The much-debated specifics of Habermas's work are less important here than the essential insight: debates about the nature and power of public opinion were not only matters of political rhetoric; they were also part of people's experience of concrete social, economic, and cultural change.[10] In this sense, 'the Enlightenment' cannot be limited to a small canon of famous writers and texts.

Historians of Upper Canada are not accustomed to portraying the colony as a participant in the Enlightenment in any sense. As Frank Underhill put it, 'We never had an eighteenth century of our own. The intellectual life of our politics has not been periodically revived by fresh drafts from the invigorating fountain of eighteenth-century Enlightenment ... All effective liberal and radical democratic movements in the nineteenth century have had their roots in this fertile eighteenth-century soil.'[11] As European historians move away from the works of 'a few great men' to the full range of printed texts and the mechanisms that sustained their circulation and discussion, historians of other communities are invited to pose similar questions. Neither the concept of public opinion nor the norms and institutions that made it credible were confined to Western Europe. How the concept developed in Upper Canada has not been studied. A pivotal chapter in the province's engagement with liberal democracy is missing.

Of course, Upper Canada's intellectual and constitutional past has not been ignored. Two areas, in particular, have produced considerable insight. First, the mental framework of government officials, leading clerics, and their supporters has received sustained attention, largely in an

---

10 Jürgen Habermas, *The Structural Transformation of the Public Sphere: An Inquiry into a Category of Bourgeois Society,* trans. Thomas Burger (Cambridge, Mass.: MIT Press 1989)

11 Frank Underhill, 'Some Reflections on the Liberal Tradition in Canada,' in *In Search of Canadian Liberalism* (Toronto: Macmillan 1960), 12

attempt to map a distinctive Upper Canadian political culture. Second, constitutional development – the workings of the colonial government, the rise of opposition to it, and the gradual development of autonomy within the British Empire – has been studied as part of a national narrative of increasing self-determination and territorial expansion.

The first area owes most to the elegant and stimulating essays of S.F. Wise. Broadly, they contend that an entrenched conservative elite in church and state held that Upper Canada had a providential mission to preserve the British Empire and its monarchical, hierarchical, and communal values in North America against the republican, egalitarian, and individualistic values of the United States. Acting on its beliefs, this articulate elite had a lasting impact on Ontario's political culture, including a heightened willingness to use the state to advance economic and other collective goals, thereby reinforcing differences with the neighbouring republic. Recent contributions have elaborated and modified, more than challenged, Wise's interpretative vision in a field that continues to probe the forging of a coherent, largely anti-American, political culture.[12]

Despite important variations in emphasis, the general thrust in this field remains away from highlighting enlightenment, liberal, or democratic antecedents. Upper Canada was formed in reaction to the American and French revolutions. Its leaders are typically described by a number of reinforcing labels often presented, incorrectly, as synonyms:

---

12 S.F. Wise, *God's Peculiar Peoples: Essays on Political Culture in Nineteenth Century Canada,* ed. A.B. McKillop and Paul Romney (Ottawa: Carleton University Press 1988). Besides the editors' valuable introduction, see Colin Read, 'Conflict to Consensus: The Political Culture of Upper Canada,' *Acadiensis* 19, no. 2 (Spring 1990), 169–85. For recent contributions indebted to Wise, see esp. David Mills, *The Idea of Loyalty in Upper Canada, 1784–1850* (Kingston and Montreal: McGill-Queen's University Press 1988), Curtis Fahey, *In His Name: The Anglican Experience in Upper Canada, 1791–1854* (Ottawa: Carleton University Press 1991), and Jane Errington, *The Lion, the Eagle, and Upper Canada: A Developing Colonial Ideology* (Kingston and Montreal: McGill-Queen's University Press 1987). As this book does, Mills emphasizes the importance of attitudes towards opposition and conflict, although our discussions are organized around different concepts and our categorization of key players is occasionally at odds. While containing much of value on Anglicanism, Fahey's insistence that Upper Canada was closed-minded and rigidly counter-revolutionary, anti-American, and eighteenth-century 'Tory' is less convincing than Wise's own treatment. Errington's book, arguing that the early elite was neither monolithic nor entirely hostile to everything American, was particularly helpful in conceptualizing chapter 6. For other work, see Paul Romney, 'From the Rule of Law to Responsible Government: Ontario Political Culture and the Origins of Canadian Statism,' Canadian Historical Association *Historical Papers,* 1988, 86–199.

'conservative,' 'Tory,' 'monarchical,' 'anti-American,' and 'British.' Much of this work appears motivated, in part, by a desire to differentiate English Canada from the United States. Consciously or not, the result has been to turn Upper Canada into something of an anomaly, largely standing apart from the broader intellectual trends of the Western world or at least those outside of the British mainstream. The colony was not so parochial. This study, heavily indebted to work in this field, nonetheless insists on placing Upper Canada firmly in that broader world. It is also preoccupied with the form and content of political debate rather than the more elusive and problematic concept of political culture.

Canada's constitutional and institutional trajectory has been a second focus of scholarship. The steps from imperial outpost to colonial responsible government, to transcontinental Dominion, to autonomous member of the British Commonwealth have been well traced. That they were taken, for the most part, without revolution, widespread violence, or the severing of all ties to Britain reinforces interpretations that stress English Canada's conservative and 'un-American' nature. While the emphasis of the profession has moved away from Colonial Office despatches and disputes between British-appointed officials and local leaders, historians of the British Empire, especially Phillip A. Buckner and Ged Martin, remind us how much such sources and disputes can still teach us.[13] This study concerns many of the same players and episodes, but seeks to shift attention away from formal structures to changes in the principles that legitimated authority within the colony and thus dictated changes to those structures.

Alongside these two long-standing concerns, there are at least three newer strands of relevant scholarship. First, some have returned to the study of the state and its processes, less to understand the arguments made about them and certainly not to celebrate their democratization or increasing autonomy from Britain, but to investigate the ways in which they impinged upon the lives of Canadians.[14] Of course, those

---

13 E.g., Phillip A. Buckner, *The Transition to Responsible Government: British Policy in British North America, 1815–1850* (Westport, Conn.: Greenwood Press 1985) and 'Whatever Happened to the British Empire?' *Journal of the Canadian Historical Association* 4 (1993), 3–32. As well as Ged Martin's many cogent articles see *Britain and the Origins of Canadian Confederation, 1837–1867* (Vancouver: UBC Press 1995).

14 See esp. Bruce Curtis, *Building the Educational State: Canada West, 1836–1871* (London, Ont.: Althouse Press 1988), Allan Greer and Ian Radforth, eds., *Colonial Leviathan: State Formation in Mid-Nineteenth Century Canada* (Toronto: University of Toronto Press 1992), and J.I. Little, *State and Society in Transition: The Politics of Institutional Reform in*

interested in state formation have much to discuss with students of the principles that shaped state power by (de)legitimating specific practices and institutions. A second strand has placed early Canada's political discourse in broader perspective by applying the categories and rich insights of British and American scholarship on the struggle between 'civic republicanism' and 'liberalism' or 'court' and 'country.'[15] Constituting the beginnings of a third strand, several scholars have begun to point out that despite being largely excluded from the electorate and office-holding, women were not irrelevant to public life in the colony.[16]

Engaging aspects of these strands, this book also advances a fourth: that the form and distribution of arguments and information, the institutions that fostered the skills and norms to evaluate them, and the nature and number of sites where they could be read and discussed are vital to understanding their meaning and consequences. Aware of these factors, contemporaries frequently debated the extent and importance of public debate. Thus we will pursue 'public opinion' down two intersecting paths: as a subject of public debate and as something contemporaries felt as a real, sociological force.

Leaving aside public debate as a window onto an underlying 'political culture' or as a jumble of insults encoded with particular status, gender, or other identities, the focus here is on the specifics of public debate. Highlighting the relationship between those specifics and constitutional theory pushes us away from a narrative of the rise of 'responsible government' and towards an emphasis on competing assessments of individuals' ability to reason in public. Such a focus also reveals the pragmatic eclecticism with which contemporaries constructed a case.[17] Rather than

---

the Eastern Townships, 1838–1852 (Montreal and Kingston: McGill-Queen's University Press 1997).

15 Several key essays have been collected in Janet Ajzenstat and Peter J. Smith, eds., Canada's Origins: Liberal, Tory or Republican? (Ottawa: Carleton University Press 1995). See also the editors' earlier works and Gordon T. Stewart, The Origins of Canadian Politics: A Comparative Approach (Vancouver: UBC Press 1986).

16 For Upper Canada, the most ambitious monograph is Cecilia Morgan, Public Men and Virtuous Women: The Gendered Languages of Religion and Politics in Upper Canada, 1791–1850 (Toronto: University of Toronto Press 1996), but see also Katherine M.J. McKenna, A Life of Propriety: Anne Murray Powell and Her Family, 1755–1849 (Montreal and Kingston: McGill-Queen's University Press 1994).

17 I am indebted to Eckhart Hellmuth, '"The palladium of all other English liberties": Reflections on the Liberty of the Press in England during the 1760s and 1770s,' in Hellmuth, ed., The Transformation of Political Culture in England and Germany in the Late Eighteenth Century (Oxford: Oxford University Press 1990), 469–71.

highly abstract and coherent paradigms, traditions, or languages (such as 'civic republicanism'), what emerges is contemporaries' ability to choose vocabularies and arguments from a broad and rich repertoire. Participants shifted, manipulated, and merged their choices to fashion the most effective argument possible. The importance and flexibility of this process are lost by relying too heavily on terms like 'ideology' and 'discourse,' or by too readily assuming that words meant to function strategically in specific contexts can be swept into a few tidy compartments.

For Immanuel Kant, enlightenment was achieved when even questions about the structure and justification of the state were determined by public opinion. Part 1 of this study analyses the key forces that helped to create and lend credence to the concept of public opinion. Part 2 shows contemporaries grappling with the consequences of this new form of authority as they tried to refashion the constitutional, political, and social identity of their province. While these issues were central to Upper Canada's emergence as a liberal democracy, legal, religious, and economic forces also made important contributions that can only be acknowledged here.

Within the British common-law tradition, the rule of law entailed norms and procedures similar to those of the later public sphere. Most important was impartiality or equality under the law. Participants' ascribed characteristics were, in theory, wholly subservient to the legal merits of the case. Also crucial was trial by jury, whereby a group of peers deliberated and reached verdicts based upon evidence and arguments that emerged from the adversarial clash of competing claims. The use of judicial terms such as 'court' or 'tribunal' to describe public opinion was not coincidental.

The relationship between law and public opinion went further. First, colonial grand juries often acted as vehicles for local sentiment. Second, prominent political protagonists frequently confronted each other in the colony's courtrooms as well as in its newspapers and legislative institutions. Third, Paul Romney has emphasized the connection between the perceived mal-administration of justice by those closely associated with the constitutional status quo and growing demands for greater political accountability to the local population.[18] Finally, the relation-

---

18 Esp. Romney, 'From Type Riot to Rebellion: Elite Ideology, Anti-Legal Sentiment, Political Violence, and the Rule of Law in Upper Canada,' *Ontario History* 79, no. 2 (June 1987), 113–43 and *Mr Attorney: The Attorney General for Ontario in Court, Cabinet,*

ship was also manifest when the law was used to try to control expressions of political opinion (in cases of seditious libel, for instance), or to deal with politically motivated violence (as in the destruction of the print shop of William Lyon Mackenzie, one of the government's fiercest critics).[19]

There was also a multifaceted connection between the public sphere and religious ideas and institutions. Upper Canadians, though overwhelmingly Christian, were divided into numerous denominations, sects, faiths, and traditions. Relations among them, and between them and the state, provided some of the most divisive issues and personalities in colonial politics and helped mould its political groupings. The beliefs and behaviour of each denomination might also promote or hinder the development of the public sphere: the emphasis on equality within its ranks or among denominations; the preferred relationship between it and the state; the role assigned to reason and intellect; the relative weight accorded to individual interpretation of the printed word, collective ceremony, or more intimate and emotional connections to religious truth; the presence or absence of conscious attempts to reinforce or undercut non-religious hierarchies; laity's role in its government; the degree of concern with individuals' public behaviour; and, finally, the extent to which it used tracts, newspapers, and voluntary associations to influence society.

More broadly, George Rawlyk and Nancy Christie argue that early evangelicalism was culturally democratic. Yet its emphasis on the emotional aspects of conversion allowed its Anglican and Presbyterian critics to present themselves as the religion of moderation and reason.[20] Neither type led to the public sphere in any straightforward way, but it is

---

and Legislature, 1791–1899 (Toronto: University of Toronto Press 1986), esp. 62–157. See also Robert L. Fraser, '"All the privileges which Englishmen possess": Order, Rights, and Constitutionalism in Upper Canada,' in Provincial Justice: Upper Canadian Legal Portraits from the Dictionary of Canadian Biography (Toronto: University of Toronto Press 1992), xxi–xci.

19 Aspects of the connection between law and the public sphere are discussed in chapter 3 and in Murray Greenwood and Barry Wright, eds., Canadian State Trials: Law, Politics, and Security Measures, 1608–1837 (Toronto: University of Toronto Press 1996).

20 George A. Rawlyk, The Canada Fire: Radical Evangelicalism in British North America, 1775–1812 (Montreal and Kingston: McGill-Queen's University Press 1994), esp. chaps. 7–8, and Nancy Christie, '"In These Times of Democratic Rage and Delusion": Popular Religion and the Challenge to the Established Order, 1760–1815,' in Rawlyk, ed., The Canadian Protestant Experience, 1760–1990 (Montreal and Kingston: McGill-Queen's University Press 1990), 9–47.

probably not accidental that the development of the public sphere coincided with an emerging Protestant consensus in the province. The connection requires additional study.[21]

Further, the concept of public opinion required reasoned debate across denominational and political lines. Like threats of coercion, an appeal to God's will as a reason for a claim was not legitimate participation in the public sphere. Rather, it was an attempt to supersede or short-circuit conversation; an attempt to trump or ignore the arguments of others by appealing to an ultimate, if contested, source of authority outside the public sphere itself. Thus, one sign of the growth of a public sphere, not fully explored here, was the waning of explicit and strictly denominational appeals in political debate in favour of secular or vaguely Judaeo-Christian sentiments and idioms. This study says little about the origins, religious or otherwise, of the arguments and assumptions used in public debate. Only a more biographical approach could draw persuasive links between public argument and religious conviction or experience. Individuals' participation in the public sphere may have been shaped by religion,[22] but, when talking to other Upper Canadians from competing traditions, they needed to translate their claims into other terms. In sum, successful claims had to be framed to engage, not exclude or silence.

As with law and religion, there were links between evolving economic practices and vocabulary and the public sphere. Habermas explicitly ties the rise of the eighteenth-century public in Europe to particular economic interests and forms. Ironically, those French historians most indebted to him have largely ignored this aspect of his work, preferring to emphasize broadly political and cultural factors.[23] Nonetheless, there

---

21 William Westfall, *Two Worlds: The Protestant Culture of Nineteenth Century Ontario* (Montreal and Kingston: McGill-Queen's University Press 1989) argues for convergence as evangelicalism shed its more populist characteristics, becoming more institutionalized and concerned with respectability, while Anglicanism abandoned much of its insistence on social deference and direct ties to the colonial state. Michael Gauvreau, *The Evangelical Century: College and Creed in English Canada from the Great Revival to the Great Depression*, (Montreal and Kingston: McGill-Queen's University Press 1991) also emphasizes the connection between evangelical consensus and English Canadian culture, highlighting the complex relationship between reason and faith in the nineteenth century.

22 Michael Gauvreau, 'Protestantism Transformed: Personal Piety and the Evangelical Social Vision, 1815–1867,' in *Canadian Protestant Experience*, esp. 86–92, calls for more attention to the impact of evangelical religion on colonial politics.

23 Dale K. Van Kley, 'In Search of Eighteenth-Century Parisian Public Opinion,' *French Historical Studies* 19, no. 1 (Spring 1995), 216

are likely, if complex and still not sufficiently understood, connections between the public sphere and trends in economic thought and behaviour. Classical public opinion and some versions of the market economy shared the ideas that individuals could be informed and act rationally, that they were formally equal, and that stable and optimum outcomes could arise from unplanned mutual exchange. The currency of exchange, however, was different – arguments about the common good in one realm and economic, private self-interest in the other.[24]

Integrating the rise of the public sphere with related legal, religious, and economic themes would be to undertake an analysis of Upper Canada's emergence into the liberal democracy of the nineteenth century. Less ambitious, this study draws on the long-standing interest in the colony's intellectual and political past to add a neglected, but crucial, dimension: the emergence of 'public opinion' as a new form of authority.

This new authority developed within the context of Upper Canada's founding constitution. Understood as a replica of Britain's mixed or balanced monarchy, the colonial constitution assumed that the vast majority of inhabitants were not sufficiently rational or informed to judge public measures by themselves. Against a background of political theories and cultural assumptions that warned against unlimited political discussion, social entities other than 'the people' and political institutions other than the people's representatives were seen as essential to good government and a healthy society. Yet this constitutional order did provide for regular elections to a deliberative legislative chamber, the rule of law, and other political and legal mechanisms that made it an example of what contemporaries called 'free government.' It was not, however, compatible with the robust concept of public opinion developing in its midst. To understand the credibility of that concept we need to look beyond the constitution to voluntary associations, the periodical press, and the dynamics of political conflict.

Voluntary associations were schools for the public sphere. They brought individuals together to pursue common projects, instructing them in the public use of their reason. The nature, distribution, and

---

24 We lack an intellectual history of the colonial economy, but E.A. Heaman, *The Inglorious Arts of Peace: Exhibitions in Canadian Society during the Nineteenth Century* (Toronto: University of Toronto Press 1999) is a good place to start. As Read, 'Conflict to Consensus,' 184–5 notes, historians argue that shifts in Upper Canada's political culture 'stemmed from a deep structural change, the development of capitalism. Oddly, none really explore that key notion.'

content of colonial newspapers ensured that this public reasoning was based upon adequate information. Developments in the colony's associational and print life ensured that officials, legislators, and the most privileged no longer held a monopoly on the ability to reason in public. Those who gained entry into that life earned the capacity and right to judge.

Political conflict also fuelled appeals to 'public opinion.' By the 1830s, an increasing range of commentators claimed that authoritative decisions about the common good could and should be generated by critical discussion among private persons. What began as the flimsy rhetoric of the politically marginalized became the common stance of political actors. All were forced to appeal to and try to mould 'the public' and thus helped to create and invest it with authority. By the early 1840s, the public sphere had become both political ideal and approximate social reality.

Not everyone, of course, gained equal purchase in this new social space. Voluntary associations, newspapers, and political conflict created and lent credence to the space by diffusing its norms and political information. The 'many' gained what had once been the province of the 'few,' but the many – the public – was not everyone. Part of diffusing the capacity to judge was the simultaneous need to distinguish it from other forms of behaviour and those deemed most likely to practise them. The more weight placed upon public reasoning, the more information, reason, and judgment had to be distinguished from ignorance, passion, and prejudice. None of these terms were entirely unproblematic. The rise of the public sphere erased older boundaries only by drawing its own.

The increasing credibility of 'public opinion' required a new understanding of good government and a heathy social structure. The constitutional and social arguments of the early 1840s swept away the original understanding of Upper Canada's constitution, establishing deliberative democracy in its stead. Over the next decade, a number of alternative mechanisms for actualizing this democracy were canvassed. Parliamentary or responsible government was accepted in preference to both American-style republicanism and radical or populist democracy as the best institutional means for fostering and guiding 'public opinion' and for translating its verdicts into laws. Paradoxically, many of the formal mechanisms of parliamentary government have persisted longer than the classical sense of 'public opinion' that legitimated them.

To investigate the form, content, and mechanisms of public discussion, this book relies upon contemporary publications. In the colonial period, this largely means newspapers: their commentary and editorials, announcements and advertisements, letters to the editor, the proclamations and official documents they copied, the legislative debates and public meetings they reported, and the pamphlets and broadsheets produced on their presses and often serialized in their columns. Given their centrality, it was necessary to move beyond the words of the colony's best-known editors to examine more than seventy newspapers from numerous towns and villages; that is, to most for which a significant number of issues have survived. They originated in every part of the province and expressed a broader range of opinion than the handful of their better-known contemporaries. Closer inspection might reveal local or regional variation, but the focus here is on provincial debate. Indeed, the development of a political public sphere helped create a provincial community. Explaining the sheer mass of this evidence and its overwhelming preoccupation with provincial politics is part of the task of this study.

As the number of newspapers attests, Upper Canada grew rapidly from its founding in 1791 to the 1850s, when public opinion was the acknowledged foundation of its constitution. By 1812, when war broke out between Great Britain and the United States, the colony's settler population approached 80,000, about 60 per cent of whom were recent immigrants from the United States. The United Empire Loyalists and their descendants made up an additional 20 per cent. The capital, York (renamed Toronto in 1834), had fewer than seven hundred inhabitants. Post-war Upper Canada was transformed by three major waves of British emigration, the second of which ended abruptly with the outbreak of armed rebellion in 1837. Responding to failed rebellions in both Upper and Lower Canada, the British parliament united them as the Province of Canada in 1841. The population of what contemporaries still referred to as Upper Canada (a convention I have adopted) had surpassed 400,000. It reached one million in the early 1850s, spurred by Irish famine migration.

By the census of 1851–2, the population of Toronto was over 30,000, greater than the combined total of the two next largest towns, Hamilton to the west and Kingston to the east.[25] Nonetheless, thirty-seven newspa-

25 Much of the information in this section is derived from Douglas McCalla, *Planting the Province: The Economic History of Upper Canada, 1784–1870* (Toronto: University of Toronto Press 1993), esp. 67–115, 220, quotations at 76 and 113.

pers were published outside Toronto in 1845; a further ten in the city itself. Most of the thirty-one towns of at least 1000 had their own newspaper, but together they accounted for only 14 per cent of the population. Upper Canada remained overwhelmingly rural, with agriculture its dominant occupation. As Douglas McCalla emphasizes, the substantial economic growth of the three decades before 1851 was primarily extensive – the result of population increase, more family farms and businesses, and the cultivation of more land – rather than intensive – the product of significant urbanization or industrialization.

This was, however, 'a commercial frontier.' Family farms sought a degree of independence, but were still integrated into networks of capital and credit primarily organized by local merchants. Beyond their own subsistence, they produced a marketable surplus sufficient to support a substantial non-agricultural population of merchants, professionals, artisans, and labourers. Without slighting developments in the larger centres, McCalla concludes that artisans and non-agricultural labourers were primarily rural, spread throughout the province, worked in non-specialized, relatively small enterprises, frequently owned or cultivated small plots of land, and were 'closely integrated into the rural economy.' In short, throughout the period of this study, Upper Canada remained a pre-industrial society undergoing a process of settlement that, despite impressive growth and important exceptions, continued to see itself as predominantly home to small, petty producers concerned with the ongoing struggle for family independence.

In broadest outline, 'the rise of public opinion' was not unique to this society. No precedence, chronological or otherwise, is claimed. Without detailed studies of other North American communities, its precise peculiarities remain matters for speculation. More comparative work is needed. What is clear is that Upper Canada participated fully in this international process and that it developed the requisite forces indigenously. Our goal is, first, to learn more about this conceptual revolution and the conditions that made it possible; and second, to return to well-worn, if now neglected, topics in Upper Canadian constitutional history with new questions and fresh perspective. Upper Canada was not a somnolent backwater of conservatism whose ideas and politics have nothing more to say to us.

PART ONE

Creating a Public

To a representative democracy this unofficial, unpaid, and incorruptible judicatory is an instrument of support; and in regard to it, the object and endeavour will be to maximize the rectitude of the decisions given by it ... To every other form of government, it is by correspondent causes rendered an object of terror and anxiety, though the magnitude of its power is universally acknowledged among them.

Jeremy Bentham, 1827

CHAPTER I

'The very image and transcript': Transplanting the Ancient Constitution

This province is singularly blessed, not with a mutilated Constitution, but with a Constitution which has stood the test of experience, and is the very image and transcript of that of Great Britain, by which she has long established and secured to her subjects as much freedom and happiness as it is possible to be enjoyed under the subordination necessary to civilized Society.[1]

With these carefully crafted words, Lieutenant-Governor John Graves Simcoe closed the first session of Upper Canada's parliament at Newark in October 1792. His depiction of the colonial constitution as 'the very image and transcript' of the British became the most repeated phrase in colonial politics. For some, it served as Simcoe had intended, as a call for unstinting gratitude for an inestimable gift freely offered and fully bestowed. For others, it was a powerful reminder of unfulfilled promise, a useful benchmark from which to measure the shortcomings of constitutional practice. The phrase was used with such mind-numbing regularity by government officials, legislators, commentators, and ordinary Upper Canadians to advance such a bewildering array of causes that it now appears as a kind of unthinking mantra or formula devoid of substance.

Incessant reference to the British (or occasionally just the English) constitution lends a cramped and derivative tone to constitutional thinking in Upper Canada. Disputations about the meaning of British constitutional precedents ring far less nobly and sound far less indepen-

---

1 Simcoe, *Journals of the House of Assembly*, 15 Oct. 1792, 18

dent-minded than stirring affirmations of 'We the People' or 'the inherent and inalienable rights of man.' In this case, appearances are deceiving. Upper Canadians were no strangers to serious discussions of the nature of good government. Over time, the content, form, and extent of those discussions created 'public opinion' as a new form of authority that in turn gave new meaning to Simcoe's words. To appreciate this process, we must begin by trying to understand how Simcoe and his audience understood the British constitution. Next we need to explain the longevity of that understanding in the face of considerable political conflict in the colony and, finally, its eventual inadequacy.

What, precisely, was being transplanted to this colonial outpost in North America? The 1791 Constitutional Act divided the old province of Quebec into Upper and Lower Canada and gave each the basic institutions to enact local laws: first, an elective representative assembly; second, another deliberative chamber, the legislative council, composed of men the Crown appointed for life or ennobled with a hereditary seat; and, third, a governor representing the monarch and imperial government as the head of the colonial executive. The governor participated formally in the legislative process by granting or withholding royal assent to bills passing both the assembly and legislative council or by reserving them until the wishes of the imperial government were known. As a British official new to the colony, he was assisted by a loosely defined body of local advisers, the executive council.

The formal symmetry between this skeletal structure and Britain's King, Lords, and Commons was apparent and intended. Both had a bicameral legislature composed of an elective and non-elective branch. Both were headed by a constitutional monarch. Unlike many previous colonial constitutions, the executive and legislative councils of the Canadas were formally distinct bodies rather than a single body performing two sets of functions. Greater assimilation to the Westminster model was part of the reaction against the American Revolution. A separate legislative council, as an independent upper house like the British House of Lords, was to offer effective support for royal governance against possible encroachments by elected assemblies.[2] The leader of the British government, William Pitt, defended the provision for ennobling Canadians with a hereditary seat in the legislative council on the grounds that 'an

---

2 W.L. Morton, 'The Local Executive in the British Empire, 1763–1828,' *English Historical Review* 78 (1963), 446, 450–1

aristocratical principle being one part of our mixed Government, he thought it proper there should be a council in Canada as was provided for by the bill.'[3] Though pithy, Pitt's defence made two key points: that the Canadian constitutions were modelled on Britain's and that the latter was mixed.

At least since Aristotle, classical authors divided all constitutions into three basic types: monarchy, aristocracy, and democracy, or rule by the one, the few, and the many. Each had a particular virtue: rule by one was thought strong and decisive, the few were the wisest and most independent, and the many had no partial or minority interest to pursue. The fate of the republics of classical Greece and Rome was thought to prove that each form, left to its own devices, degenerated: monarchy into despotism, aristocracy into oligarchy, and democracy into anarchy. Each degenerate form was an example of tyranny. Oppression, it seemed, arose from a reliance on a single form of government and so classical authors reasoned that a mixture of all three forms could avoid the otherwise inevitable slide towards tyranny. The benefits of each form could be preserved while staving off its peculiar vice by incorporating the other two forms. Tyranny, at least temporarily, could be rendered impossible.

The notion that England (and later Britain) had achieved this mixture or balance had a long and tenacious grip on the imagination, not only of those who lived under it, but of numerous admirers from afar. In 1642, Charles I's *Answer to the Nineteen Propositions* equated England's parliament of King, Lords, and Commons with the classical republican notion of a balance or mixture of the three forms of government.[4] More than a century later, William Blackstone's authoritative *Commentaries on the Laws of England* explained that

> herein indeed consists the true excellence of the English government, that all parts of it form a mutual check upon each other. In the legislature, the people are a check upon the nobility, and the nobility a check upon the people, ... while the sovereign is a check upon both, which preserve the executive power from encroachments. And this executive power is again checked, and kept within due bounds by the two houses ... Thus every branch of our civil polity supports and is supported, regulates and is regu-

---

3 [Pitt], *Constitution of the Canadas,* 40

4 J.G.A. Pocock, *The Machiavellian Moment: Florentine Political Thought and the Atlantic Republican Tradition* (Princeton: Princeton University Press 1975), 361ff.

lated, by the rest ... Like three distinct powers in mechanics, they jointly impel the machine of government in a direction different from what either, acting by themselves, would have done; but at the same time in a direction partaking of each, and formed out of all; a direction which constitutes the true line of liberty and happiness of the community.

More succinctly, another legal textbook, William Paley's *Principles of Moral and Political Philosophy* (1785), defined British government as 'a combination of the three regular species of government ... to unite the advantages of the several simple forms, and to exclude the inconveniences.' British government united decisiveness, wisdom, and honesty and prevented despotism, oligarchy, and anarchy by combining, mixing, or balancing monarchy, aristocracy, and democracy. Each of these powers corresponded to a social entity – the monarch, nobles, and populace – that provided the basis for the political institution thought to embody its particular virtues and vices.[5] Essentially, mixed monarchy was a form of limited or constitutional government whereby any two of its branches could prevent a usurpation of power by the third.

In 1776, two works challenged the correlation of the British constitution with a tripartite balance. In January, Thomas Paine's explosive *Common Sense* argued that whatever freedom Britons enjoyed arose from their right to elect the House of Commons. The monarch and House of Lords were not two of three essential estates, but 'the base remains of two ancient tyrannies' best disposed of. In April, Jeremy Bentham's *A Fragment on Government* ridiculed Blackstone's contention that the British constitution, by uniting monarchy, aristocracy, and democracy united strength, wisdom, and honesty. From one of his trademark mathematical proofs, Bentham deduced that 'after the same manner it may be proved to be *all-weak, all-foolish,* and *all-knavish.*'[6] Such attempts to decouple the British constitution from a mixture of monarchy, aristocracy, and democracy failed. Few read Bentham. Despite Paine's popularity, most Britons, radicals included, continued to think about government more in terms of the ancient constitution and a tripartite legislature than natural rights or utilitarianism.[7] In its broadest outlines, the theory of mixed monarchy was the intellectual property of every

---

5 Blackstone, *Commentaries,* v. 1, 123, 125–7 and Paley, *Works,* v. 1, 214

6 Paine, *Political Writings,* 6 and Bentham, *A Fragment on Government,* 83–4

7 James A. Epstein, 'The Constitutionalist Idiom,' in *Radical Expression: Political Language, Ritual, and Symbol in England, 1790–1850* (New York: Oxford University Press 1994), 3–28

educated person in the North Atlantic world – a commonplace distillation of British theory and practice.

Yet by the 1830s, if not the 1790s, it was obvious that the British constitution was undergoing significant, if still contested, change: the development of political parties and an informed and critical public; the mounting influence of ministers of the Crown in the House of Commons; the increasing inability of the monarch to choose or dispose of advisers freely; the declining use of the legislative veto by the House of Lords; and numerous other real or apprehended alterations. The language of mixed monarchy persisted, in part, because it was flexible enough to accommodate the early manifestations of these developments. The clarity of the mechanical metaphor was deceptive. It accommodated strikingly different interpretations of where the balance lay, what threatened it, and how it could be preserved.[8] More corrosive to the theory of mixed monarchy than the frontal assault of a Paine or Bentham was the long and ultimately frustrating process of trying to make sense of changing political reality in its terms.

The theory of mixed monarchy persisted in Upper Canada as well. The Constitutional Act of 1791 had reduced the complex and evolving nature of the British constitution to its most elemental form: three legislative bodies representing the one, the few, and the many. Imperial authorities were well aware that Upper Canada, a colony and loose collection of frontier agricultural settlements, could not possess precisely the same constitution as Britain. They did, however, think it possible to transplant the basic form and principles of the tripartite legislature. It was this form, with its attendant view of society, that informed the policies of Lieutenant-Governor Simcoe.[9] A half-century later, when the Constitutional Act of 1791 was superseded by the reunion of Upper and

---

8 J.A.W. Gunn, 'Influence, Parties and the Constitution: Changing Attitudes, 1783–1832,' *The Historical Journal* 17, no. 2 (1974), 301–28, Gunn, *Beyond Liberty and Property: The Process of Self-Recognition in Eighteenth-Century Political Thought* (Kingston and Montreal: McGill-Queen's University Press 1983), and Mark Francis with John Morrow, 'After the Ancient Constitution: Political Theory and English Constitutional Writings, 1765–1832,' *History of Political Thought* 9, no. 2 (Summer 1988), 283–302, though the last emphasizes discontinuity.

9 S.J.R. Noel, *Patrons, Clients, and Brokers: Ontario Society and Politics, 1791–1896* (Toronto: University of Toronto Press 1990), 46–8 and, in general, A.F. Madden, '"Not for Export": The Westminster Model of Government and British Colonial Practice,' *Journal of Imperial and Commonwealth History* 8, no. 1 (October 1979), 18–19

Lower Canada, the semi-official organ of one of Simcoe's successors went to considerable lengths to reassure readers that 'the general principles of our Government remain the same as they have ever been ... We still have the three estates, with their distinct, and independent powers, and their mutual relations, checks and balances.'[10]

Summaries of the genius of the British constitution appeared regularly in addresses to the colonial electorate. A candidate in 1808 assured potential supporters, 'I am a British born subject, I have lived under the Government, I have *read* that great and wonderful *production*, the Constitution, and admire it ... The *three* estates, or *regal power*, when *united*, are like *three pillars* set apart at the *bottom*, and all joined at the *top*, the one supports the other.'[11] Silent on the practical application of any of this to Upper Canada, the candidate merely affirmed his admiration for a constitution composed of three independent social parts that together formed the sovereign power.

Twenty years later, another candidate promised 'to watch over the finely balanced powers of that Constitution ... That Constitution, Gentlemen, teaches us that certain rights and powers belong to the three branches of the Legislature respectively, and that if the one should successfully encroach on the rights and powers of the other, the balance and equi-poise of the machine is destroyed – and that disorder must be the inevitable consequence.'[12] Again, the evolving, uncodified British constitution had been reduced to its tripartite legislature. Overtly, the address was neutral about who was doing the encroaching. Its audience, aware of the candidates and recent political history, undoubtedly heard something more contentious.

During the same election, Jesse Ketchum, an American-born government critic often ridiculed for a lack of intellectual refinement, addressed the Freeholders of the County of York:

Having always heard the British Constitution spoken of with commendation, its great excellence appears to consist in its dividing and compounding the several parts so as to make and preserve a whole, more perfect in its operation than the constitution of the sorrounding nations. The democratic part keeps the prerogative of the Crown within due limits ... while in return, the active energy of the regal prerogative prevents the democratic

---

10 'Policy of the Government,' *Monthly Review* 1, no. 1 (January 1841), 1–14
11 Robert Henderson, *York Gazette*, 30 Apr. 1808 in *Town of York*, 189
12 Captain McKenzies, *Kingston Chronicle*, 26 July 1828

branch of government from degenerating into licentiousness – and the Aristocracy, gives stability and permanence to both; acting as a salutary check upon the royal power, and also opposing the encroachments of the Commons. The system not only looks beautiful in theory but also works well, as is confirmed by the page[s] of British history, in which it appears that when the three estates have preserved their constitutional powers unimpaired, good government has been the uniform and certain result.

As a leading critic of the colonial status quo, Ketchum concluded from his able summary that 'a departure from the true principles of the Constitution seems to be the chief cause of all the evils which exist in these provinces.'[13]

Why did a leading reformer rely on the theory of mixed monarchy? Why did he trace the 'evils' he diagnosed to 'a departure from the true principles' of the British constitution? Why did the theory of mixed monarchy continue to structure political debate long after Simcoe had left the colony?[14]

There are good reasons why it might not have. On closer inspection, the analogy between the colonial and British constitutions appears superficial. How could a temporary imperial appointee reporting to the Colonial Office be equated with an hereditary monarch? How could an ancient peerage sitting by hereditary right in the House of Lords be compared with a handful of office-holders, clerics, and men of business appointed to the legislative council? How could complex British conventions that had developed over centuries be frozen in time and transplanted to a population that was largely North American–born? British emigration increased over time, but there is no reason to assume that those who left Ireland, Scotland, or England were particularly enamoured with the British constitution as they had experienced it.

The questions multiply: How could a colony have the same constitution as the empire? How could practices informed by the British social structure be made relevant to a few scattered settler communities? Different distributions of land ownership alone were enough to make any analogy tenuous. Of course, Simcoe and those who thought like him hoped that Upper Canada would come to resemble Britain over time. They devised administrative, cultural, and legal measures, such as a land-granting

13 *Colonial Advocate,* 10 July 1828
14 I'm indebted for these questions to Epstein, 'The Constitution Idiom.'

system meant to encourage inequality, to push it in that direction. Many failed to produce the desired results or were abandoned.

A correspondent in the *Kingston Chronicle* feigned incomprehension when the *Montreal Herald* argued that without a monarch or aristocracy the 'internal tendencies of our society [are] at variance with those of Great Britain.'[15] Such dismissals were convenient, if hardly convincing. Nine years later, the pro-government or conservative *Patriot* echoed Montesquieu: 'Political institutions of every people must have a close reference to their peculiar state & habits, religious beliefs & sentiments, modes of thinking and feeling, manners, &c. – in short, that the government of every individual country or nation must be a transcript as near as may be, of the national character and manners.' The *Patriot*'s declaration, in the same article, that 'the social or political structure of the British Constitution, must be considered as identical with those of her Canadian colony,' could hardly be taken literally.[16] Why 'must' two very different polities be 'identical?' Such stubborn insistence on the analogy between Britain and Upper Canada was more a desperate act of faith than a realistic assessment. Wish was expressed as fact.

Much of the emphasis American historian Jack Greene places on the psychological predisposition of early American colonists to mimic imperial forms holds for Upper Canada. Isolated geographically and culturally from Britain, colonial elites framed their legislative politics in the vocabulary and history of the British constitution. Doing so 'gave them an enlarged purpose that transcended the narrow bounds of their several localities and, by investing their actions with national – not to say, universal – meaning ... gave them a more secure sense of who and what they were.'[17] Most Upper Canadian legislators held tight to the notion of constitutional assimilation with Britain because it cast them in the great epic drama of British liberty and justice played out in the ongoing struggles of King, Lords, and Commons, rather than as petty disputants in some colonial backwater.

---

15 John Bull jun., *Kingston Chronicle*, 13 May 1825
16 *Patriot*, 21 Oct. 1834. The term 'conservative' was not generally used before the rebellion. It refers here to those who generally supported the government and who did not see themselves or were not seen as 'reformers.' It does not always refer to a coherent body of doctrine. 'Tory' is used sparingly, as explained in note 36 below and because it was more often a term of abuse than of self-identification.
17 Jack P. Greene, 'Political Mimesis: A Consideration of the Historical and Cultural Roots of Legislative Behaviour in the British Colonies in the Eighteenth Century,' *American Historical Review* 75, no. 2 (December 1969), 351

The theory of mixed monarchy could continue to play such a role because it was open to different interpretations and was thus useful in the pursuit of different ends and in different social settings. The 'British constitution' was a complex and evolving collection of institutions, statutes, conventions, historical events, and cultural symbols from which a variety of prescriptive meanings could be fashioned. As J.A.W. Gunn points out, King, Lords, and Commons 'might be simultaneously perceived as orders of the population, branches of the legislature, and organs of government performing different functions.' The result was numerous interpretations and much confusion.[18] The language of mixed monarchy could be sociological – an argument for a Canadian aristocracy or hierarchical social structure. It could be institutional and thus preoccupied with the form of three independent legislative branches. It could also be functional. The monarch headed the executive as well as being part of the legislature. The House of Lords played an important judicial as well as legislative role. Thus, demands for the further separation or blending of executive, legislative, and judicial functions could be expressed in terms of the relationship among King, Lords, and Commons.

Perhaps the most important reason for the persistence of the theory of mixed monarchy was its compatibility with certain forms of opposition. Jesse Ketchum had no need to search for alternative ways to express his discontent. According to an essayist in the *Kingston Chronicle*, the constitutional system divided people into 'those who incline to the privileges of the People, and those who incline to the prerogatives of the Crown: those who have popular, and those who have aristocratical and monarchical notions.' Bestowing sovereignty on the King-in-Parliament, a collective entity combining identifiable elements, ensured that 'the two divisions of men I have alluded to exist to this hour, and can only cease with the Constitution itself.'[19] Indeed, by framing their opposition as intended to maintain or restore the balance of the three estates, reformers could portray themselves as the true patriots. The term 'reform' itself implies a return to lost purity.

The *Chronicle*'s essayist divided people into two basic camps, but the theory of mixed monarchy offered multiple targets for criticism. The personnel, structure, and behaviour of the governor, executive council,

---

18 Gunn, 'Influence, Parties and the Constitution,' 301 and M.J.C. Vile, *Constitutionalism and the Separation of Powers* (Oxford: Oxford University Press 1967), 1–118

19 'Points in History: The English Constitution,' *Kingston Chronicle*, 6 Nov. 1830

legislative council, and assembly could all be questioned employing the terms of mixed monarchy. The perceived source of grievance changed over time without requiring a change in constitutional paradigm.

Much of the dynamic generated by the politics of analogy was evident in two pamphlets published during the colony's first fully public constitutional dispute. One, published in 1809 by John Mills Jackson, praised the British parliament for 'bestowing [on Upper Canada] a constitution nearly an epitome of the British.' For Jackson, the root of colonial ills was what he portrayed as the growing and arbitrary power of the lieutenant-governor. 'Armed with the executive and judicial authority' and able to distribute Crown lands for political purposes or appropriate public funds without the consent of the assembly, the lieutenant-governor was too powerful. Such concentration thwarted Britain's noble intentions.[20] Jackson's critique did not refer to the social aspects of mixed monarchy, preferring to point to its division of power and separation of functions.

Abandoning Jackson's qualification 'nearly,' one of the governor's defenders began from the premise that the colony had 'an exact epitome of the British constitution.' Jackson's charges must, therefore, be unfounded. Even if the governor harboured ill intentions, he could not act outside the law. Every law required the consent of 'the third branch of the Legislature ... composed of the yeomanry of the country ... wholly of that class of people who have a strong interest in preserving their own independence.' By equating a social entity (the yeomanry) with a particular virtue (independence) and incorporating it into one of the three estates (the assembly), mixed monarchy prevented tyranny.[21]

This early exchange typifies the framework of much constitutional debate in the colony. Demands for change were presented in terms of implementing the British constitution granted in 1791 but perverted in practice. The usual rejoinder argued that the British constitution was already in place and that problems, if any existed, could be traced to other sources. Far less typical, this early exchange focused on the lieutenant-governor. His status as representative of both the British monarch and the imperial government heightened the risks of opposition. Such attacks were easily portrayed as disloyal. Other targets made more sense.

The weakest part of the constitutional analogy between Upper Canada and Britain was in the correspondence between the legislative

---

20 Jackson, *View of the Political Situation*, 2, 6, 31
21 Anon., *To the Right Honorable Lord Castlereagh*, 12–13

council and the House of Lords. The latter, steeped in ancient tradition and spectacle, was composed of a large number of members, most of whom attended by hereditary right. The constitutional provision for the creation of Canadian peers was never used. Instead, the legislative council was made up of a handful of men selected for life by the governor and confirmed by the Colonial Office. While their seats in the council were secure, many remained dependent on other offices held only at the pleasure of the Crown. Further, they appeared to represent no social category not already present in the assembly.

The legislative council was attacked from several angles, all compatible with the theory of mixed monarchy. For instance, critics could accept the utility of an aristocratic or independent second chamber but doubt whether a body of executive appointees could fulfil such a role. Marshall Spring Bidwell, reform leader in the assembly, advocated an elective legislative council. Echoing countless colleagues, he told the assembly that 'the Legislative Council could not with propriety be compared with the British House of Lords – the lords were an hereditary race, the descendants of the most illustrious and renowned men, that had ever adorned the English nation. Can this be said of the Legislative Council?'[22] Conservatives were suspicious of Bidwell's professed reverence for the British aristocracy, but the more the Lords were praised as noble, independent, and ancient, the more the legislative council paled by comparison.

Conservatives felt acutely vulnerable on this point. Some advocated the creation of a local aristocracy to reinforce the analogy. Others advocated the appointment of non-office-holders of various political persuasions and nationalities or tried to publish the council's deliberations to increase its standing. Conservative dissatisfaction with the council was widespread, checked only by their fear of lending additional support to demands for more radical change, particularly direct election, which most believed would seriously undermine monarchical government and the imperial connection.[23]

---

22 Bidwell and letter to the *Observer* copied in *Patriot*, 19 Feb. 1836
23 On the need for a local aristocracy see One of the People [A. Burwell], *Kingston Chronicle*, 17 Dec. 1831. Allan MacNab rejected demands for an elective legislative council, but admitted that 'the gentlemen who composed the Legislative Council were almost all appointed from one side of the question in politics, which he thought was not judicious, and certainly very unsatisfactory.' MacNab also rejected the solicitor general's idea that the upper house should be a court of appeal like the House of Lords. It was too small, too dominated by office-holders living at Toronto, and too much under the

The council was also attacked for rejecting a far greater proportion of the bills from the assembly than the Lords rejected from the Commons. Worse, when the majority of the people's representatives opposed the administration, the assembly's measures fared even more poorly in a council dominated by office-holders.[24] The *Cobourg Reformer* thought a system of checks among three estates admirable, but 'the model is a clumsy piece of workmanship ... The teeth of the checks are so made that they will turn only one way.' The assembly was checked but if it attempted 'to check the Council it immediately comes into collision with an irresponsible body of life legislators.' In turn, 'far from the Council being a check on the Governor it may be controlled by him and may be made a scapegoat to bear all his sins. With respect to the balances we cannot conceive where they will be found in our inimitable model.'[25]

Similarly, in an editorial entitled 'The Balance of Power,' the *St Thomas Liberal* expressed its growing impatience with this expression 'lugged in in all political discussions, whether relevant to the question in agitation or not. It is, in fact the Shibboleth of the party, and is pronounced with the greatest *flippancy* by every one of the favoured few.' Yet the *Liberal* was unwilling to abandon the idea of balance to its opponents, readily agreeing with them 'that the peculiar excellencies of the British Government, consist in the powers delegated to each branch being nicely balanced.' After all, 'as every one knows,' that government

---

influence of John Beverley Robinson. MacNab, *Correspondent & Advocate*, 9 and 23 Apr. 1835 and 28 Jan. 1836. A correspondent for the conservative *Cobourg Star*, 21 Jan. 1835, offered a compromise whereby the governor would choose councillors from popularly elected nominees and suggested that the council might become elective when education was more widely diffused. The *Star* thought the plan 'eminently deserving attention' and, on 20 Apr. 1836, admitted the need for reform. The *Port Hope Gazette*, copied in *Correspondent & Advocate* 28 Dec. 1836, had supported the government during the recent election, but once the contest was concluded admitted that the council was not independent of the executive; 'a monstrous innovation on the British Constitution.' Likewise, with the defeat of the 'republicans,' the *Courier of Upper Canada*, 7 Dec. 1836, felt it was now safe for those committed to the British constitution to undertake the necessary reforms of the council. The *Courier*'s editor had called for changes much earlier in the *Gore Gazette*, 4 Oct. 1828. See also *Niagara Gleaner*, 14 Apr. 1828, 19 Jan. 1829, and 13 Feb. 1830.

24 Swift [Mackenzie], *A New Almanack*, 16 estimated that 134 bills were vetoed between 1824 and 1833. The *Dundas Weekly Post*, 5 April 1836, counted a total of 127 bills between 1829 and 1835.

25 *Reformer*, 7 April, also copied in *Brockville Recorder*, 17 Apr. 1835

'consists of three distinct forms or branches of government – a monarchy, an aristocracy, and a democracy.' The problem was that 'there is
not the smallest resemblance between the speculating, stock-jobbing
monopolizing Legislative Council of this Province and the English
House of Lords.' Further, the majority of the assembly, which the *Liberal*
also opposed, 'is under the complete controul of the other branches –
this is the Balance of power that has so many enthusiastic admirers in
this Province ... It is an insult to the understanding.' Robert Davis's exasperation soon led him to rebellion: 'Talk of mixed government indeed!
The *three* estates!! yes, we have three estates – a *tory*, an *aristocracy*, and
an *oligarchy*, the compound of which is pure DESPOTISM!!!'[26] Thus, opponents in the elective assembly, as well as those in the appointive executive and legislative councils, could be attacked in the terms of mixed
monarchy. The notion that Upper Canada possessed such a mixture
could be ridiculed without challenging its virtues.

From its inception, William Lyon Mackenzie's *Colonial Advocate* argued
that the assembly, despite the analogy to the British House of Commons,
was powerless. Mackenzie knew well that 'there is a parade about "Three
distinct sections of government," but constitutionally to speak, the whole
power is lodged in the executive.' It acted independently or hid behind
the 'pompous impotent screen' of a legislative council it controlled.[27]
Overlapping personnel between the legislative and executive councils
ensured that legislative and executive powers were concentrated in the
same hands – a standard definition of tyranny.[28] As a result, the assembly,
the only estate responsible to Upper Canadians, was powerless. Its members were bought by executive patronage, or elections were unfair, or its
most popular measures were vetoed by the legislative council, the governor, or the imperial government.

Such complaints did not, however, lead to the abandonment of the
analogy with the British constitution. They only seemed to invite its
more insistent application so that the assembly could claim all the powers and privileges of the British House of Commons. The analogy could,
however, be worked the other way. When radicals demanded a
reformed legislative council on the grounds that it 'bears no analogy to

---

26 *St Thomas Liberal,* 1 Aug. 1833 and Davis, *Canadian Farmer's Travels,* 70
27 *Colonial Advocate,* 29 July 1830 and Mackenzie, *Correspondent & Advocate,* 16 Apr. 1835.
   See also *Advocate,* 30 Dec. 1824 and 7 May 1829.
28 Mackenzie, *Sketches of Canada,* 405–10 and *Reformer* copied in *Correspondent & Advocate,*
   22 Oct. 1835

the British House of Lords, neither in numbers, wealth, influence, or intelligence,' the point could be conceded while asking 'what analogy the Canadian House of Assembly bears of the British House of Commons in numbers, wealth, influence and intelligence?' More bluntly, another opponent of an elective legislative council insisted that radicals also 'contrast the enlightened House of Commons of England with the illiterate insensible majority here.'[29] If the legislative council was more active than the Lords in checking the people's representatives, it was because 'the numbers, wealth, influence and intelligence' of those elected in Britain made such vigilance unnecessary. In short, despite shared constitutional theory, good government required something different in Upper Canada than it did in Britain.

The theory of mixed monarchy accommodated expressions of discontent from various quarters aimed at various institutions. It could also justify radical remedies. The *Reformer*, adopting a common Chartist contention, asserted that 'universal suffrage [like annual elections] has been exercised by the people of England long before and after John signed Magna Charta ... It was wrested from them by such tyrannic monarchs as Henry VI.' This is only one example of the routine transAtlantic use of historical narratives of the British constitution. By plotting local issues in a larger story, such narratives identified and enlarged their significance, prompted readers to see their constitution as the outcome of ongoing confrontation and struggle, and, by pointing to possibilities for change, further empowered readers as active agents in that contest. Some critics, like the *Reformer*, posited a mythical golden age that, while currently lost, could be redeemed through renewed effort.[30] Most, as we shall soon see, achieved the same effect by projecting into

---

29 A Canadian [Egerton Ryerson], 'Letters on the Canadas No. VI,' *Patriot*, 20 Sept. 1836, and anon., *Observer* copied in *Patriot*, 19 Feb. 1836. See also the *Upper Canada Herald*, 22 Sept. 1835.

30 Besides Epstein, 'The Constitutional Idiom,' see John Belchem, 'Republicanism, Popular Constitutionalism and the Radical Platform in Early Nineteenth-Century England,' *Social History* 6, no. 1 (January 1981), 1–32, James Vernon, *Politics and the People: A Study in English Political Culture, c. 1815–1867* (Cambridge: Cambridge University Press 1993), 295–330, Vernon, ed., *Re-reading the Constitution: New Narratives in the Political History of England's Long Nineteenth Century* (Cambridge: Cambridge University Press 1996), and Patrick Joyce, *Democratic Subjects: The Self and the Social in Nineteenth-Century England* (Cambridge: Cambridge University Press 1994), 192–204. British radicals appear to have relied rhetorically more on recovering a golden age than did their Upper Canadian counterparts, who more often stressed ongoing evolution.

the future a linear narrative of constitutional progress. In this particular example, restoring the purity of the ancient constitution meant the rights of universal suffrage and annual parliaments. To head off the rejoinder that British liberties were protected by the three estates of mixed monarchy, the *Reformer* had carefully placed these rights in 'the people' (not, pointedly, in the vaunted British yeomanry) independent of the demands of the barons at Runnymede or King John's assent in 1215. Further, these rights had been lost through the unconstitutional actions of other, albeit more successfully 'tyrannic,' monarchs. They could, however, be recovered by the collective popular action the *Reformer* was attempting to incite.

American republicanism, with its separation of President, Senate, and House of Representatives, could also be presented as 'essentially British.' Three estates could exist in North America, but only if each was elective. 'Here, say our tories, republicanism shows its cloven foot! Say you so?' asked the *Reformer*. Britain had a monarch and an aristocracy, but the colonies had neither.[31] In such different social circumstances, mixed monarchy required elective institutions. If political institutions merely reflected social 'reality,' as here suggested, emphasizing the sociological aspects of the theory of mixed monarchy limited human agency. Yet, as already evident from discussions of the legislative council, the obvious differences between Upper Canadian and British society opened up wide-ranging possibilities for constitutional change framed as attempts to preserve functional similarity in the face of social difference.

The analogy to Britain could even justify rebellion. A month before one broke out, John Kent, a frequent contributor to the conservative press, offered his 'Reasons against Rebellion.' He began, however, by conceding that 'every lover of British liberty will readily admit, that there are certain cases in which resistance to constituted authorities is sanctioned.' With the example of the Glorious Revolution before them, supporters of the British constitution were hard pressed to deny the right of resistance, only its relevance to current circumstance. As Kent understood, reasons had to be given. Thus, a couple of weeks later, another conservative pleaded with those contemplating rebellion to read conservative newspapers, convinced that 'a fair trial of balance' would convince them to uphold mixed monarchy. Moreover, no matter how hedged by qualifications, the right of resistance implied that ulti-

---

31 *Reformer*, 3 Mar. and 7 Apr. 1835

mate sovereignty was vested in society. Since those who exercised political authority were only trustees, loyalty was, by definition, conditional.[32]

British constitutionalism was also useful in advocating less radical remedies than universal suffrage, elective institutions, or resistance. As a response to charges that any reform of Upper Canada's constitution was an attack on mixed monarchy, it helped to point out instances when the British constitution itself had been altered. The *Canadian Correspondent* listed the Protestant Reformation, the end of feudalism, the rise of the House of Commons, the Glorious Revolution, the Septennial and Union Acts, and the Reform Bill of 1832. 'Any man having the slightest acquaintance with English history cannot be ignorant that the British constitution is the result of successive improvements advancing with the intelligence of the people.'[33] There was no reason to believe that history had ended abruptly in 1791.

The *Correspondent*'s list of improvements was such that conservatives could not disagree. In 1830 Justice Macaulay invited a grand jury 'to review the energies of a great people gradually emerging from a state of servility and ignorance, to one of freedom and intelligence.' Their constitution had 'from age to age unfolded' and 'in the maturing progress of time' had 'become the proud boast – the valued inheritance of all.'[34] By historicizing the British constitution, Macaulay opened the possibility of continued evolution.

Other conservatives, well versed in the progressive narrative of that constitution, attempted to foreclose it. One thought the British constitution had reached its apotheosis at the Glorious Revolution of 1688 and the Bill of Rights in 1689. Although fairly standard Whig strategy, this could hardly stand as the last word. As the author was forced to admit, important constitutional developments had occurred since 1689.[35] In fact, the adoption of what was arguably the most important, the Reform Bill of 1832, was urged by every conservative newspaper in Upper Canada, save one. Reform of the franchise, in this instance, was seen as a

---

32 Alan Fairford [John Kent], *Patriot,* 7 Nov. and A Conservative, *London Gazette,* 18 Nov. 1837. On the conditional nature of loyalty see letter to the ed., *Upper Canadian Guardian,* 27 Aug. 1807 in National Archives of Canada, MG11 CO42, 350. See also Kathleen Wilson, *The Sense of the People: Politics, Culture and Imperialism in England, 1715–1785* (Cambridge: Cambridge University Press 1995), 216.
33 *Canadian Correspondent,* 18 Oct. 1834 and *Correspondent & Advocate,* 25 Jan. 1836. See also 'Canadian Institutions,' *Reformer* copied in *St Thomas Liberal,* 18 July 1833.
34 Macaulay, *Brockville Recorder,* 2 Nov. 1830
35 'General Union: Letter IX, The British Constitution,' *Cobourg Star,* 20 Mar. 1839

means of maintaining the balance of the British constitution from the combined threat of an overgrown aristocracy and radical demagogues. This is one reason why the label 'Tory' was more a reformer's jeer than an illumination of colonial arguments. As those writing for a British audience had to point out, many colonial conservatives would not be considered Tories in Britain.[36] It was, of course, easier to support reforms at a distance than those that struck at cherished structures of local power. Nonetheless, the near unanimity of editorial support for the Reform Bill was a recognition that the British constitution was neither static nor incapable of improvement. For the most part, however, conservatives were largely satisfied with the basics of the existing constitution and thus talked of it as something to be preserved. Reformers, less satisfied, tended to talk of the British constitution as something to be restored, purified, or allowed to evolve.[37] Both, however, spoke the same constitutionalist idiom and could, when occasion demanded, switch sides.

One final factor helps account for the longevity of the theory of mixed monarchy – its compatibility with rights-based language. Tidy distinctions between reasoning from British history and from natural rights were not made. As James A. Epstein argues, 'There was a structured interdependence between these two modes of reasoning within English political discourse since certain rights "inherent in the People" had been either fully or partially realized historically.'[38] Thus, furious at what it considered an arbitrary act by the Colonial Office, the conservative *Patriot* asked, 'What is the British Constitution? Why it is the *beau ideal* of the full Rights of Man in civilization?'[39] Likewise, the radical *Correspondent & Advocate* argued that 'the inhabitants of the Province, as British subjects, have an inherent right, co-existent with birth, to the rights and

---

36 *Courier of Upper Canada* copied in *Western Mercury*, 27 June 1833. The exception was the *Brockville Gazette*. See also *Niagara Gleaner*, 10 Nov. 1832 and 15 June 1833. Many conservatives also opposed privileges for the Anglican church. On travellers' need to emphasize the differences from Britain see John Thurston, '"The Dust of Toryism": Monarchism and Republicanism in Upper Canadian Travel and Immigration Texts,' *Journal of Canadian Studies* 30, no. 4 (Winter 1995–6), 80–4. Increasing hostility to Whig colonial policy in the 1830s did not always translate into support for everything 'Tory.' Neither did a decided preference for mixed monarchy; see *Courier* copied in *Canadian Emigrant*, 24 Jan. 1835.
37 Epstein, 'The Constitutional Idiom,' 27
38 Ibid., 21
39 *Patriot*, 3 May 1833

liberties of their fellow subjects in England.'[40] No one disagreed. The problem was defining those rights and applying them locally. The inherent rights of British subjects embodied in the principles of the British constitution were not natural or human rights, but if they included (as William Lyon Mackenzie contended)[41] the right to change one's form of government, it was a distinction without a difference.

The longevity of mixed monarchy as a way of talking about and understanding the constitution can be explained, in part, by the concept's flexibility, its allowance for criticism, its ability to accommodate various targets for that criticism, its compatibility with both radical and moderate reforms, and its partial affinity with rights-based reasoning. In these respects, mixed monarchy served reformers well. There was little need to resort to other idioms. When repudiating it was equated with disloyalty to Britain and empire and when the government used the courts and other means to silence opponents, it made sense to critique constitutional structures using the theory that legitimated them. Moreover, arguments in the language of mixed monarchy might mobilize those who were dissatisfied with colonial governance but believed in the superiority of the British constitution or feared independence. Overt appeals to republicanism or natural rights were neither needed nor helpful.

Occasionally, its strategic value lent a high degree of instrumentality to uses of the theory of mixed monarchy. The *Reformer*'s discussion of the executive council referred to the British Privy Council, 'as we must ever seek for analogies in the English constitution, though this resembles ours less than a puppy is like a dog, or a calf like an ox.'[42] Some shared the frustration, but the use of alternative idioms was inconsistent and minimal.

Paradoxically, colonial status made the theory of mixed monarchy more, not less, resilient in Upper Canada. In a North American outpost feeling threatened externally by a republican neighbour and internally by a population largely American-, Canadian-, and Irish-born, social and political leaders often seemed insecure – their appeals to 'Britishness'

---

40 *Correspondent & Advocate*, 11 Apr. 1836. See also *St Catharines Journal*, 22 Oct. 1835 and
   St Thomas Liberal, 18 Feb. 1836. Imperial membership could be quite useful to radicals.
41 *Colonial Advocate*, 15 July 1830. Mackenzie followed Richard Price rather than Edmund
   Burke by arguing that 'the British nation have acquired [in 1688] three fundamental
   rights: 1. To choose their own rulers and governors. 2. To cashier them for misconduct. 3. To frame a government for themselves, suitable to their wants and necessities.'
42 *Reformer* copied in *Correspondent & Advocate*, 22 Oct. 1835

helped to solidify their identity as participants in a broader British civilization. Any alternative, especially one drawing positively from the American experience, threatened that identity.

The perceived social differences between Upper Canada and Britain could also strengthen, rather than weaken, support for mixed monarchy. Colonial conservatives could not rely on large land-owners with a dependent tenantry, extensive disparities in wealth, widespread social deference, an established church, long-standing indigenous traditions, or the cultural baggage of many emigrants. Formal legislative structures became the last bulwark against such hostile circumstances. Only the theory of mixed monarchy could guarantee the rule of gentlemen under a hereditary monarch.[43] It provided a rationale for non-elective institutions and offices and ensured that those in positions of authority as appointees of the Crown were not entirely dependent upon Upper Canadians or their elected representatives. Such a theory was valuable indeed. 'Who ever heard of a tory,' asked the St Thomas Liberal, 'who was not a pretended stickler for the constitution; this is their text on all occasions: to justify their measures, our ears are stunned by their sickening senseless rant of the glorious and inimitable, the sublime, immaculate and never-to-be-sufficiently-praised constitution.'[44]

Differences between Upper Canada and Britain helped entrench the theory of mixed monarchy in a third, less obvious, way. It was clear to observers that the power of the British House of Commons was growing while aristocratic families and the executive had considerable influence over who was elected to it. These developments led several influential Whig thinkers, particularly Francis Jeffrey of the Edinburgh Review, to argue that the balance of King, Lords, and Commons no longer occurred primarily among three independent branches but within the House of Commons itself. Monarchy and aristocracy were felt in the Commons through those elected to it by their influence. Thus, such influence, far from undermining the independence of the Commons, preserved constitutional balance. Further, since measures that passed in the Commons already reflected the views of the three estates, there was no need for the Crown or Lords to exercise their legislative veto. Such

---

43 Robert L. Fraser, '"All the privileges which Englishmen possess": Order, Rights, and Constitutionalism in Upper Canada,' in Provincial Justice: Upper Canadian Legal Portraits from the Dictionary of Canadian Biography (Toronto: University of Toronto Press 1992), xxxvi
44 St Thomas Liberal, 2 Nov. 1832

an approach justified the pre-eminence of the Commons, the declining use of the veto by the Lords, and the influence of the ministers of the Crown in the Commons.

This transitional form of the balanced constitution was not unknown in Upper Canada. In 1834 the *Patriot* used it to justify supporting a parliamentary candidate who already held executive office. Since the Commons 'is de facto, an exact epitome or reflected image of the whole three branches of the legislature embodied,' the Crown needed to be represented in the Commons by its officers just as the peerage was by its younger sons. Despite demonstrating awareness of evolving Whig doctrine, this editorial was almost its sole use in the colony.[45]

The rarity of references to these newer Whig ideas of balance is easily accounted for. Upper Canada had no aristocracy to get its younger sons elected and there were neither closed boroughs nor sufficient executive patronage to ensure the election of the governor's advisers. More important, Upper Canada had no need for the doctrine. It became popular in British Whig circles to preserve the image of the balanced constitution while recognizing that the Crown no longer – and the Lords only rarely – vetoed measures. In Upper Canada, by contrast, the legislative council frequently rejected measures from the assembly. The governor was also in less need of indirect methods such as securing the election of individual favourites. He headed the executive in a far more real sense than did the British monarch and could also influence, delay, or veto legislation as the representative of the imperial government. The governors of Upper Canada exercised far more visible legislative authority than British monarchs had for a century. In Upper Canada, three differently constituted branches of government assented to or rejected proposed legislation. The tripartite legislature was more real to Upper Canadians – it better explained what they saw of their law-making process – than it was to nineteenth-century Britons.[46]

---

45 *Patriot*, 21 Oct. 1834. The only other example might be *Mirror*, 28 July 1838. For Britain, see Vile, *Constitutionalism and the Separation of Powers*, 216–20, Gunn, 'Influence, Parties and the Constitution,' 319–20, and Biancamaria Fontana, *Rethinking the Politics of Commercial Society: The Edinburgh Review, 1802–1832* (Cambridge: Cambridge University Press 1985), 147–60.

46 Further, if, as Francis and Morrow argue, 'After the Ancient Constitution,' 287–8, the unity of action demanded by the concept of parliamentary sovereignty led theorists away from the notion of a balance of three estates, the same pressure did not exist in Upper Canada. Colonial institutions established by ordinary British statute could not easily consider themselves sovereign in the same sense as the imperial King-in-Parliament.

Finally, and again unlike the original model, a tripartite legislature was enshrined in an actual text. Borrowing from Thomas Paine, Mackenzie might ask the governor, 'Did Your Excellency ever see the British Constitution in print?'[47] but in 1833 the printer of the *Hallowell Free Press* published *The Constitution of the Canadas*. The Constitutional Act was Upper Canada's written and codified charter to be preserved, restored, or adjusted. In sum, the theory of mixed monarchy made more sense of constitutional reality in Upper Canada than in Britain.

From at least 1828 William Warren Baldwin and his son, Robert, publicly advocated something else they called 'responsible government,' whereby the Crown's advisers in Upper Canada, the executive council, would form a cabinet of ministers and retain office only as long as they enjoyed the support of the majority of the people's elected representatives. When the government removed one of its critics, John Walpole Willis, from the Court of the King's Bench in 1828, the elder Baldwin addressed a large public meeting at York. The resulting petition began with the usual pledge of support for the Constitutional Act of 1791 before complaining about executive influence on the legislative council. Instead of proceeding to demand reform of the legislative council, the petition traced the problem to the executive council. The latter's power was augmented by its control of the former. The result was 'the practical irresponsibility of Executive Counsellors and other official advisers of your Majesty's representative, who have hitherto with impunity both disregarded the laws of the land, and despised the opinions of the public.' They were not responsible to anyone, least of all to public opinion.

The principal remedy was 'a legislative act ... made in the Provincial Parliament, to facilitate the mode in which the present constitutional responsibility of the advisers of the local government may be carried practically into effect; not only by the removal of these advisers from office, when they lose the confidence of the people, but also by impeachment for the heavier offenses chargeable against them.' Baldwin, with rather a perverse view of British history, portrayed this not as an innovation (which may account for why he thought provincial legislation could achieve it), but merely as the final implementation of what the British parliament had recognized as the rights of Upper Canadians

---

47 'Letter to Sir J. Colborne,' *Colonial Advocate*, 15 July 1830 and also 3 Jan. 1828

in 1791.[48] The analogy to Britain was to be retained even if the theory of mixed monarchy was to be modified or abandoned.

The consequences and desirability of 'responsible government' were hotly debated, but as Graeme Patterson has noted, the concept remained highly ambiguous. It 'became a sort of ideological nucleus around which revolved a whole constellation of opposing ideas.' To many, 'it simply meant the opposite of arbitrary government.'[49] At its most general, it meant that power should not be entrusted to those who were not answerable for its use and, further, that such accountability could only be effective if it was to those most directly affected. Despite protestations to the contrary by some of its advocates, responsible government was simply local self-government. It could be direct (making institutions and officers subject to popular election) or indirect (making them accountable to the people's representatives). It could be judicial (as in impeachment for 'heavier offenses') or political (as in dismissal for not acting in accordance with the wishes of the people or their representatives). The Baldwins, among others, typically used the term in the more limited sense of ministerial responsibility, defined in 1834 by the *British American Journal* as having 'the Executive Council changed as often as they shall find themselves in a minority in the Commons House of Assembly.' This deceptively simple formula did violence to the ambiguities and subtleties of current British practice. The British House of Commons had yet to establish a clear and binding constitutional convention that a ministry had to resign upon losing its ability to command a majority in the Commons.[50]

Even so, the demand for responsible government did not dominate the opposition agenda in Upper Canada before 1836. It was frequently

---

48 Baldwin, *Canadian Freeman*, 11 July 1828 and Paul Romney, *Mr Attorney: The Attorney General for Ontario in Court, Cabinet, and Legislature, 1791–1899* (Toronto: University of Toronto Press 1986), 145–6, 151

49 Graeme H. Patterson, 'An Enduring Canadian Myth: Responsible Government and the Family Compact,' in J.K. Johnson and Bruce G. Wilson, eds., *Historical Essays on Upper Canada: New Perspectives* (Ottawa: Carleton University Press 1991), 500–1. See also G.M. Craig, 'The American Impact on the Upper Canadian Reform Movement before 1837,' *Canadian Historical Review* 29, no. 4 (December 1948), 334. The term's various meanings continue to plague attempts at dating and genealogy.

50 *British American Journal*, 15 Apr. 1834 and Peter Burroughs, 'The Determinants of Colonial Self-Government,' *Journal of Imperial and Commonwealth History* 6, no. 3 (May 1978), 319–20. After all, in 1834 a monarch (though admittedly for the last time) summarily dismissed his ministers against their wishes and those of parliament.

coupled with other reforms, especially an elective legislative council. Upon his arrival in Upper Canada, the new lieutenant-governor, Sir Francis Bond Head, attempted to conciliate opposition opinion by appointing two reformers, Robert Baldwin and John Rolph, to the executive council. The entire council resigned in March 1836, claiming that Head had often failed to seek their advice or heed it when offered. Robert Baldwin insisted that 'what the constitution required was that there should be persons within this country itself who could be made responsible to the provincial parliament here for the administration of the internal affairs of the province.' However this contention might relate to current British practice or Baldwin's desires for Upper Canada, it was certainly not what the Constitutional Act of 1791 had required. Nevertheless, the reform majority in the assembly rallied behind the ex-councillors and refused to grant supplies. Head dissolved parliament and led the 'Constitutionalist' forces in the ensuing election. The nature of this crisis, discussed further in chapter 4, focused debate on the executive council as almost never before.[51] The Baldwinite panacea of ministerial responsibility temporarily dominated the constitutional agenda of reformers. Robert Baldwin insisted that this agenda was 'nothing more than the principles of the British Constitution applied to that of this Province.' By interpreting British constitutional developments since 1791 in a particular fashion, Baldwin preserved the analogy to the British constitution while seeking local self-government in terms not obviously indebted to American republicanism.

Head did not challenge Baldwin's reading of current British practice. Instead, he cautioned that Upper Canada's constitution 'resembles, but is not identical with, the Constitution of the Mother Country.' Some form of ministerial responsibility existed in Britain, but Head insisted that this evolution should not be mimicked in the colony. The governor was not a hereditary monarch but an officer of the imperial government. He, not his advisers, was responsible for executive acts. If, as reformers were often reminded, the colonial executive was responsible to the colonial parliament rather than to the imperial government, there would be no effective institutional link between colony and empire. Upper Canada's colonial status was not, however, Head's key

---

51 The language of the 'Family Compact' often gave prominence to executive councillors but usually encompassed all major office-holders. As well, most proposed remedies involved the judiciary and the legislative council or were intended to strengthen the assembly's independence.

rationale. Rather, he emphasized that 'the difference between the Constitution of the Mother Country and that of its Colony,' in particular the persistence of an independent governor and legislative council, was 'highly advantageous to the latter.' More than in Britain, in 'small communities, private interests, and party feeling must unavoidably be conflicting.' A responsible ministry in a community of petty factions without disinterested statesmen would become little more than 'an oligarchy composed of a few dominant families, shielded by secrecy' and capable of uniting legislative and executive authority in their own hands. The people were better served by a governor independent of the assembly to whom they could appeal directly for redress.[52] Mixed monarchy had been safely modified in Britain, but it remained the best form of government for Upper Canada.

Head's theme was taken up by colonial opponents of responsible government. The *Kingston Spectator* agreed that an independent governor was preferable to 'a body of irresponsible functionaries with a domineering power, who have their own interests to promote, and their own prejudices to revenge.' Whatever current British practice, the *Spectator* thought mixed monarchy better suited to Upper Canada than cabinet government. Likewise, by insisting that the executive council was analogous to the British Privy Council, rather than the cabinet (for which it argued there was no colonial equivalent), the *Brantford Sentinel* left the colony with the three independent branches of the balanced constitution. The *Kingston Chronicle* also doubted that cabinet government would benefit the province, but if Baldwin and others sincerely disagreed, they should petition for a new constitution – not hide the innovation behind empty invocations of the 'British constitution.' More broadly, the *Cobourg Star* thought it 'unreasonable to suppose it at all practicable for us, as a new and dependent country, to possess an Executive government upon terms of equality with that of the Mother Country, containing *a highly cultivated and dense population!* Our constitution is assimilated to that of Great Britain, as is expedient for our interests, and safe for the parent state. As we advance in population and improvement, we may look forward to every necessary modification of our constitutional laws.'[53] Canada's constitution would evolve with its own

---

52	Head's reply to his former councillors, *Patriot,* 18 Mar. 1836. See also his reply to resolutions of a public meeting, *Patriot,* 29 Mar. 1836.
53	'Spirit of the Upper Canadian Journals,' *Patriot,* 8 Apr. and *Cobourg Star,* 23 Mar. 1836. For another reference to the executive council as Upper Canada's Privy Council, not

society, not because the original constitutional model had been altered to reflect developments in Britain. The nature of good government in Upper Canada, not the analogy with Britain, was at issue. If Baldwin preserved the analogy with the British constitution by abandoning mixed monarchy, Head and his supporters were willing to sacrifice the analogy to preserve that form of government.[54]

Of course, these discursive strategies fit nicely with the situation of their advocates. The theory of mixed monarchy justified a power structure that colonial conservatives usually found congenial; one that welcomed democratic input while retaining effective limits on it. Likewise, Baldwinite responsible government promised more power to those whose support was primarily electoral and local self-government without the taint of American republicanism. British history provided much (but by no means all) of the evidence for the merits of both options. Not surprisingly, it was used selectively. While their arguments were often couched in terms of competing interpretations of the British constitution, Upper Canadians debated the best form of government.

To convince Upper Canadians that mixed monarchy was worth preserving, it was not helpful to emphasize that the theory carried several meanings or that the analogy to Britain helped advance the speaker's own interests. Public debate required a different order of justifications.

---

cabinet, see A British Emigrant to Head, *Patriot*, 10 May 1836. Compare with the view that conservatives held to a kind of empty legal formalism in the face of reform appreciation for the 'real' British constitution, in Paul Romney, 'From Constitutionalism to Legalism: Trial by Jury, Responsible Government, and the Rule of Law in the Canadian Political Culture,' *Law and History Review* 7, no. 1 (Spring 1989), 151–4.

54 Indeed, in 1818 it was the legislative council that was most selective with British precedents. When the assembly resisted the council's attempt to amend money bills, the council responded that the two bodies 'are co-ordinate branches of a limited legislature constituted by the statute' of 1791. Their powers derived from that act, not from British history or its constitution. Since the council 'does not assume the power, authority and privileges of the upper house of parliament grown out of the practice of ages, and unsuitable to the circumstances of this country,' the assembly should not claim all the 'power, authority and privileges' of the House of Commons. Both systems incorporated coordinate legislative bodies, but their relationship should take colonial status and social structure into account. The assembly rejected this argument unanimously. When, at the same time, Robert Gourlay used the dissimilarities between the two polities to advocate reforms he undoubtedly reminded conservatives of the dangers of relaxing the analogy. For the council's resolutions see *Niagara Spectator*, 9 Apr. 1818 and for the need to maintain the analogy in the face of Gourlay's agitation, see A U.E. Loyalist, *Kingston Chronicle*, 11 June 1819.

Three seemed most promising: that mixed monarchy was essential to imperial membership; that it was constitutive of being British; or, as Head insisted in 1836, that mixed monarchy was the best form of government. In the long term, only the last was viable.

The argument that membership in the British empire entailed local mixed monarchy was rarely heard. Some institutional link to Britain was required, but this need not determine how local laws were made. In 1841, Lord Sydenham's *Monthly Review* argued that 'while Great Britain continues to rule her Colonies, it is both natural and necessary that she should rule them according to her own model; because, if otherwise, the Government would have no unity of character, purpose or action.'[55] Put so bluntly, this line of argument was exceedingly rare. It also wasn't true. The British empire encompassed an array of constitutional structures while British statesmen were frequently more wary of analogies to the Westminster model than were colonists.[56] Moreover, far from contributing to public debate, such an argument was a blatant attempt to short-circuit it. It offered Upper Canadians no reason to be sincerely attached to the British constitution. If, as the price of imperial membership, they could not alter their constitution, it was irrelevant whether it was good or bad. It failed to justify the British constitution in Upper Canada – it transformed it into an imperial fiat.

A second, related approach relied on cultural, rather than juridical, ties to Britain. The 1820s saw heightened anxiety over the cultural identity of Upper Canada as a British colony with a predominantly American-born population. Arguments often fell into a pattern: mixed monarchy is British, Upper Canada is British, therefore Upper Canada must maintain mixed monarchy. Thus, John Beverley Robinson thought it only natural that those born in the United States preferred the republicanism they had grown accustomed to, but they 'should acquiesce in institutions which they found established here, and which were congenial to our form of government.' On the same grounds, future British immigrants would expect Upper Canada's institutions to resemble those they were accustomed to.[57]

While there were numerous examples of this approach, especially in the 1820s, it was deeply flawed. Robinson's call for acquiescence was hardly ennobling. It was likely to alienate and galvanize, rather than co-

---

55 'Policy of the Government,' *Monthly Review* 1, no. 1 (January 1841), 1–14
56 Madden, '"Not for Export"'
57 Robinson, *Canadian Freeman*, 1 Dec. 1825

opt, those being read out of the political nation based on their place of birth and presumed untrustworthiness.[58] The argument broke down when demands for reform came from the British-born, as they frequently did, or when it was impossible not to see that Britons were searching for alternative understandings of their own constitution. Finally, this approach did not identify the essential aspects of the British constitution or show how (or even if) they could be transplanted to North America. A competing theory, ministerial responsibility, was being sold in part on the grounds that it better embodied the cultural connection to Britain. Successful appeals to a diversity of Upper Canadians had to rest on the argument that something was the best – not just that it was British.

Edward Allen Talbot informed prospective readers of his newspaper that 'we are by birth – by education – from reason – and from reflection, attached firmly and unalterably to the British constitution.' The list seems reasonable. As an Irish gentleman and Anglican, Talbot was predisposed to the British constitution. Reason and reflection had confirmed its superiority, without precluding criticism of those who administered it. Talbot could then appeal to all Upper Canadians to support their colonial copy (which he was not alone in thinking superior to the original).[59] Born outside Britain, the editor of a radical newspaper could not share in 'that excessive veneration for British institutions, which some pretend to.' He had, however, 'studied the distinguishing features of different constitutional governments' and had 'not the least hesitation, early prejudice aside, in giving a decided preference to the limited monarchy of England, with its mixed government of King, Lords and Commons.'[60]

Upper Canadians were indeed called upon to 'venerate' the British constitution, implying awe-struck reverence more than critical judgment. Yet faced with opposition, conservatives' celebration of that consti-

---

58 See more broadly David Mills, *The Idea of Loyalty in Upper Canada, 1784–1850* (Kingston and Montreal: McGill-Queen's University Press 1988).

59 Prospectus, *London Sun*, in H. Orlo Miller, 'The History of the Newspaper Press in London, 1830–1875,' Ontario Historical Society *Papers and Records* 22 (1937), 118. For a similar list, see *Niagara Gleaner*, 13 Nov. 1824. Commentators pointed to the absence of a state church and tithing or (esp. in 1832) to the broader basis of representation as key advances of the colonial imitation over the original. See A U.E. Loyalist, *Kingston Chronicle*, 11 June 1819, A British Subject, *Patriot*, 21 Feb. 1832, John Bull to *Kingston Chronicle*, 7 Apr. 1832, and *Canadian Freeman*, 22 Mar. 1832.

60 *British American Journal*, 28 Jan. 1834

tution had, of necessity, become a defence. 'It is well to venerate the institutions of that best of Governments,' thought the *Niagara Gleaner,* 'but we should be able to render a reason why we esteem and wish to retain our constitutional privileges according to the principles of the British constitution.'[61] Of course, its admirers had always believed that they had *reasons* to celebrate it. Simcoe told the first colonial legislators that they were 'blessed' with 'the very image and transcript' of the British constitution, not because it was British, but because it had 'stood the test of experience' and had 'secured to her subjects as much freedom and happiness as it is possible to be enjoyed under the subordination necessary to civilized Society.' By the 1830s, others needed to be convinced of the continued relevance of his understanding of that constitution.

Simcoe's two reasons – that it had proved itself by surviving longer than other constitutions, republican or monarchical; and that it had created the most powerful, free, and enlightened nation – remained key arguments in Upper Canada. Of course, considerable cultural chauvinism went into assessing the relative value of other nations and their forms of government. Even so, the argument that mixed monarchy was the best was subject to evidence, argument, and refutation in ways that appeals to the *de facto* power of the empire or national origin were not. Moreover, even the best might be improved.

The radical *Reformer* grew impatient with the analogy to Britain. Advocating the secret ballot, the editor noted that its opponents saw it as 'un-English. If it were what then? If it is superior in many respects to open voting, though it be un-English, ought it not to be adopted?'[62] The question remained even if the *Reformer* undermined it by proceeding to deny that the secret ballot was, in fact, 'un-English.' The politics of analogy was difficult to escape.

Supporters of the British constitution never admitted that it was anything but the best: 'In advocating the cause of British connexion, and the ascendancy of British institutions and principles in this province,' the editor of the *Toronto Courier* firmly believed 'we are promoting the true interests of the country of our adoption.' He divided opponents into two groups, those 'decidedly republican' and those loyal to the empire though 'ignorant of the nature and advantages of the British Constitution.' The latter's allegiance, though preferable to outright republicanism, was insufficient. It was purely prudential, existing only

---

61 *Niagara Gleaner,* 10 Mar. 1832
62 *Reformer,* 30 June 1835

'because they know and feel the advantages which, in common with us all, they enjoy from the connexion.' Unlike the *Courier*, they were not loyal 'from the principle of attachment arising out of a conviction of its great superiority over every other form of government in the world.'[63] The history of the British nation, especially when compared to the alternating tyranny and anarchy suffered elsewhere, offered conclusive proof to the *Courier* and others. Was not the British constitution 'justly the admiration of the most wise and enlightened statesmen and legislators of civilized Europe?'[64]

Even during the polarizing election of 1836, William Hamilton Merritt, promoter of the Welland Canal, rejected calls for radical reforms, yet told his constituents that if the economic prosperity of New York state was due to 'being administered by a Democracy ... it would not only be our duty, but our individual interest, as well as in the interest of our posterity, to use every peaceable and legitimate means to bring about that form of Government, which produced such beneficial effects.'[65] Isaac Buchanan, another politically moderate entrepreneur, was equally emphatic in 1844. 'It is under British monarchical institutions alone that liberty is protected at once from tyranny and licentiousness. If that vital object could be better attained by other than British systems, we, on British principles, must be willing gladly to change them; for *it is not the name, but the realities of liberty*, (of which the British systems are but the instruments, not the embodyment,) that we are enamoured of.'[66] Ultimately, the British constitution claimed the support of many Upper Canadians not because it was British, but because they thought it was the best.

They knew it was the best – that it was worth emulating – from their study of the 'science of politics.' The understanding of this science had originally been limited to the colony's privileged few, but as education and political information became more accessible, reformers and radicals insisted that a broader audience could discuss and heed its lessons. Such ability grounded that audience's claims to greater political participation and proved the undoing of the theory of mixed monarchy.

---

63 *Courier* copied in *Cobourg Star*, 29 Oct. 1834
64 A British Subject, *Patriot*, 21 Feb. 1832
65 Merritt, *Patriot*, 25 Oct. 1836. On Merritt and reform see Craig, 'The American Impact,' 339.
66 [Buchanan], *First Series of Five Letters*, 11

For Hugh Scobie, editor of the *British Colonist*, 'A nobler study than politics ... cannot be conceived, – to investigate the history of the past, and compare it with the experience of present times, – to ascertain and expound the principles of government, under which man in our circumstances, can enjoy the greatest happiness and peace. In this sense, the greatest philosopher is the greatest politician. Every improvement in science or art; every development of mind; every moral benefit conferred on humanity; and every *progress* made in the advancement and spread of Divine truth, may be called *political movements*.'[67] The noble science of politics was inductive, historical and comparative. It was the study of the formation, operation, and effects of historical and contemporary forms of government. The principles of good government could be distilled from comparative constitutional history.

In 1836 the conservative *Royal Standard* deplored the state of the parliamentary library for 'what light might have been thrown on the Executive Council Question, had a copy of Pownall's Administration of the Colonies, or Chief Justice Stokes's Work, or even the Federalist, stood upon the shelves of the Library.'[68] The insights of a governor of prerevolutionary Massachusetts or the architects of the republican constitution of 1787 were relevant to Upper Canada's recent constitutional dispute because, ultimately, all politics was about achieving good government and the advantages thought to flow from it.

In the colony's first decades, only the few could fully appreciate such a science. John Strachan, then rector of Cornwall, insisted in his *Discourse on the Character of King George the Third* (1810) that the foundations of the British constitution were 'the more durable, because visionary empiricks have not been allowed to touch them. No fine spun theories of metaphysicians, which promise much and end in misery, have shared in its formation; such men may destroy, but they can never build.' Repudiating attempts to deduce constitutional structures from abstract first principles is often identified with conservatism and pragmatism, but it was shared by nineteenth-century Whigs, especially in their quarrel with the utilitarian calculus of the Philosophical Radicals.[69] Strachan took part in a dispute about methods, not about the existence of a science of politics.

---

67 *British Colonist*, 4 June 1844
68 *Royal Standard*, 19 Nov. 1836
69 Stefan Collins, Donald Winch, and John Burrow, *That Noble Science of Politics: A Study of Nineteenth-Century Intellectual History* (Cambridge: Cambridge University Press 1983), chap. 3

He preferred the writings of the ancients and 'Lock's [*sic*] treatises on government, [the Swiss jurist John Louis] De Lolme on the British constitution, Blackstone, [and] Montesquieu' to the works of more abstract theory written since the American Revolution. From these authorities on balanced government, Strachan concluded that 'those who understand it best must love it the best ... In maintaining its purity, they will oppose any encroachment tending to arbitrary power on the one hand, or popular authority on the other. Preserving the balance with steady care, they will admit no changes on either side without the greatest deliberation.' The inductive, historical, and comparative science of politics demonstrated the value of the British constitution and enabled its students to recognize threats to its equilibrium from one of its branches or from those who, blinded by abstract theories, championed alternative forms of government. Strachan was 'not however so blind an admirer of the British constitution as not to be aware of several imperfections.' It was simply 'the best practical form of government that ever existed.' Further, Strachan also conceded that 'a man may be a firm friend to the constitution and hostile to the minister's measures.' It was, after all, a limited or free form of government designed to maximize civil liberty. Only the few versed in the science of politics could, however, be entrusted with the delicate task of criticizing ministers without endangering the constitution.[70]

If an extensive understanding of the science of politics was crucial, then the number of Upper Canadians able to claim a leading part in public life was limited. Cato, writing in support of 'an eminent candidate' in 1800, told fellow electors that 'something more than plebian honesty, than rugged uprightness is necessary, to qualify an individual for the dignified station' of elected representative. Indeed, it was 'a field on which volumes might be written.' Any potential representative's 'knowledge of governments and the constitutions of empires should be general.' Along with the requisite character, this knowledge translated into candidates of particular social standing. Thus, when the elector 'shall find these combined with eminence of station such an one should

---

70 Strachan, *Discourse on the Character of King George*, 39, 53–4. For a somewhat contrary interpretation, see Mills, *Idea of Loyalty*, 18–19. Strachan's sermons also endorsed a political division of labour. S.F. Wise, 'Sermon Literature and Canadian Intellectual History,' in A.B. McKillop and Paul Romney, eds., *God's Peculiar Peoples: Essays on Political Culture in Nineteenth Century Canada* (Ottawa: Carleton University Press 1988), esp. 16

be the object of general choice. His station will give weight to his coun-
sels – currency to his opinions and strengthen his desire and endeavors
of serving his king and his country.'[71]

Political leadership belonged to gentlemen, that tiny fraction of the
population who alone had the leisure, refinement, cosmopolitan outlook, finances, and skills to study and apply the science of politics – to
perceive and advance the common, rather than a partial, good. Social
standing was a necessary condition for political and intellectual leadership, not the consequence of them. As Gordon S. Wood says of the
American context, gentlemen 'were civic minded by necessity: they
thought they ought to lead society both politically and intellectually –
indeed, they could not help but lead the society – by sheer force of their
position and character. Ordinary men would respect and follow them
precisely because the members of the elite possessed what ordinary men
by definition could not have.'[72]

Cato demanded that York electors *recognize* the pre-existing social
standing and consequent political and intellectual superiority of 'an
eminent candidate.' Their vote would add nothing to that standing or
ability. Moreover, Cato expressed no interest in educating his readers in
the science of politics to empower them to make more informed electoral choices. Only gentlemen, not the electorate, were capable of such
discrimination. The relative scarcity in early Upper Canada of the great
books of the science of politics identified by Strachan heightened their
authority and the authority of those who had access to them.[73]

Conservatives continued to use access to the science of politics to
measure the intellectual and social worthiness of their opponents. In
1819, one editor ridiculed what he took to be the American doctrine
that neither social standing nor learning was required for political
understanding. Even 'the common street beggar thinks himself qualified to give gratuitous opinions on the science of legislation, though his
abilities and judgement have been totally inadequate to the task of

---

71 Cato, 'To the Free Electors of the County of York,' *Upper Canada Gazette*, 15 Mar. 1800
   and *Town of York*, 157–8
72 Gordon S. Wood, 'The Democratization of Mind in the American Revolution,' in *Leadership in the American Revolution*, Library of Congress Symposia (Washington: Library of
   Congress 1974), 66–7
73 For parallels see Rhys Isaac, 'Books and the Social Authority of Learning: The Case of
   Mid-Eighteenth-Century Virginia,' in William L. Joyce, David D. Hall, Richard D.
   Brown, and John B. Hench, eds., *Printing and Society in Early America* (Worcester, Mass.:
   American Antiquarian Society 1983), 228–49.

devising "ways and means" for keeping himself from rags and starvation.' The Upper Canadian assembly needed those who had studied the British constitution and its laws. It had no room for 'an ignorant artisan' who 'presumed to step over the threshold to give his opinion upon momentous subjects about which he knows nothing.'[74] The presumption was as much social as intellectual.

In 1831, Americans were again disparaged for supposedly believing that 'knowledge obtained by chopping, plowing, tinkering and tailoring, is all that is necessary even for the Presidential chair.' Was it not better to be governed 'by men of talent than by ignorant blackhearts? – Which are most likely to understand human nature, and the science of government, those who devote their time to study and observation in general literature, and an acquaintance with the world, or those who stand from day to day at the Work Bench?' If politics was truly a difficult science, contrasting the few who studied it with the many who did not was an easy way to restrict the capacity to judge.[75]

Such attempts did not go unchallenged. 'A Farmer in Support of an Honest Candidate' thought Cato's 1800 address 'pompous.' While his preferred candidate 'has not had the advantage of a refined education, he is nevertheless possessed of a large share of mother wit and good sense; and it can justly be said of him, that he is, "that noblest work of God, an honest, upright, and just man."' Confident that 'A Farmer' did not merit genteel politeness, Cato characterized his challenge as 'the idle, the nefarious belchings of an assuming ignoramus.'[76] From his perspective, both 'A Farmer' and his candidate were assuming positions to which they had no claim. 'A Farmer' considered identity of interests with the electorate, independence from the executive, and good sense more valuable than social standing or a familiarity with the science of politics. He did not, however, claim that the general electorate was versed in that science. By the mid-1830s, some made precisely this claim – and, by so doing, demanded equal political participation for the many.

In the most developed exposition of this claim, the editor of the

---

74 *Kingston Chronicle*, 4 June 1819
75 One of the People, *Kingston Chronicle*, 26 Mar. 1831 and also 'Points in History: English Constitution,' *Chronicle*, 25 Dec. 1830, Phospher, *Brockville Gazette*, 26 Apr. 1832, A Simple Tory, *Patriot*, 2 Feb. 1836, and *Dundas Weekly Post*, 16 Feb. and 22 April 1836.
76 A Farmer and Cato, *Upper Canada Gazette*, 22 Mar. and 26 Apr. 1800 and *Town of York*, 159–61

Reformer detected 'some slight movements among the people' by 1835. 'Politics may be now than formerly a more general and more serious subject of enquiry.' The 'interested adherents of our corrupt government' resisted the 'diffusion of useful knowledge, especially political knowledge, among the operative classes of society,' but, aided by cheap and accessible newspapers, 'men are beginning to discover that unless they understand their own affairs and show themselves determined by their union and intelligence to exercise a check on their government, they must expect that their rulers will look to their own interests and not make the interests of the governed the paramount object of their care.' Whatever their claims, the few were not the disinterested students of political science.

To channel this discovery, 'reading should be more generally encouraged, useful knowledge should be more widely diffused and politics, instead of being a mere topic of desultory conversation, should be made a much more general as well as a much more serious subject of enquiry.' Such diffusion was crucial because, the science of politics

> presents a field of observation worthy of employing the noblest faculties of man. It unfolds to him a vast picture of the human family, exhibiting its character and condition in all their interesting diversity and under those endless modifications, in whose production the institutions of government are uniformly found to exercise a predominant influence. It leads him through the various stages of civilization, tracing the progress and marking the workings of the great variety of institutions which human sagacity and experience have framed to exalt the character and ameliorate the social condition of the species. It teaches him to apply the principles which he acquires in these investigations to the laudable purpose of advancing the knowledge of good government in his fellow men; thus arousing them to exertion for the salutary renovation of the old and corrupt institutions, and for the adoption of others that are manifestly conducive to the happiness and prosperity of the community.

Politics was indeed a noble science, here decoupled from gentility. No longer the preserve of the socially privileged, political science would empower the general reading public 'to exercise a check on their government.' Studying it, Upper Canadians 'must become thoroughly convinced that it is the advance of the popular mind and the expression of enlightened public opinion alone that can originate important and beneficial changes in our hitherto corrupt, expensive, and irresponsible government.'[77] Popular participation, if based on an understanding of politics, was positive and inevitable. Government would become responsible to such a public. The science of politics would become 'enlightened public opinion.'

Charles Clarke, a radical, thought that the *Reformer*'s goal had been achieved by the close of the 1840s. There had indeed been a time 'when wealth was necessary to and almost synonymous with intelligence ... when the popular voice was the mere echo of the will of the privileged few,' but that time had passed. The expanding newspaper press, greater educational opportunities, improved internal communications, and a general spirit of inquiry meant that 'every laborer has become a thinker.' Indeed, 'the pages of De Tocqueville and Montesquieu are seen as often in the hands of the "proscribed" as in those of their more fortunate brethren.' Finally, 'the poor may remain poor still; but they are not necessarily ignorant.'[78] Social and economic inequalities could no longer justify intellectual, and thus political, inequalities. To the extent that this assessment was accepted, much had changed since Cato and John Strachan had invoked the science of politics to dismiss the opinions of most Upper Canadians. The science of politics was democraticized.

Strachan had been confident that the gentlemen who studied constitutional history would become the most able defenders of mixed monarchy, whereas the *Reformer* advocated such study to empower ordinary Upper Canadians to renovate their constitution. The *Correspondent & Advocate*, in a passage already quoted, equated the British constitution itself with 'successive improvements advancing with the intelligence of the people.' Was there a point at which 'improvements' in the popular knowledge and intelligence were incompatible with mixed monarchy? Or, to put the question another way, did *Reformer*'s 'enlightened public opinion' signal the demise of mixed monarchy?

In a public letter to the 'agitator' Robert Gourlay in 1818, John Simpson thought so. Gourlay called on 'every man resident in Canada' to help organize township meetings, elect delegates to a provincial convention, and petition the Prince Regent. By such means they could 'lay a simple foundation for public prosperity.' He worried, however, that colonists

---

77 *Reformer*, 22 Sept. 1835
78 Reformator [Clarke], *Mirror*, 10 Aug. 1848, 17 Aug. 1849, and 22 Feb., 29 Mar. and 7 June 1850

might shy away from such bold action as 'it has been the cant of time immemorial to make mystery of the art of Government. The folly of the million, and the cunning of the few in power, have equally strengthened the reigning belief; but it is false, deceitful, and ruinous.' This was all too much for Simpson. Pointing to these very lines, Simpson declared: 'Here sir, you have passed the Rubicon ... Here is the renewal of the old cry of Revolutionary France, Egalite.' Gourlay's agitation – his 'appeal to the ignorant' – reflected his belief that the science of politics could be widely understood. Such conviction 'reduce[d] the arcana of Political ethics to the capacity of a school boy, and the forms of Government to the routine of a Counting House occupation.' Its egalitarianism was revolutionary.

In part, this was yet another example of one of the self-professed enlightened few equating the many with ignorance, but Simpson explicitly linked the British constitution to this intellectual inequality and the political division of labour that flowed from it. As a complex balance of ancient institutions, social classes, and political conventions, the British constitution was anything but 'simple.' Only when the people were 'all virtuous' could they be 'omnipotent.' Only then could democracy – a simple rather than a mixed form – result in good government.[79]

Another John Simpson, this one in his first appearance as editor of the *Niagara Chronicle* in 1837, conceded that 'we would advocate the Republican form of Government, if we were all educated to the same standard, and possessed the same natural faculty of judging rightly, but as this unhappily is not the case, we must be permitted to adhere to our natural and national predilection for the British Constitution in *its* purity, as the best mode of ruling yet constituted, viewing it in reference to the present nature of mankind.'[80] Both Simpsons reformulated the old adage that republics were fit only for angels, or, in more current parlance, only for where the 'faculty of judging rightly' was widely shared.

In the absence of such a society, mixed monarchy justified two legislative branches, the King and Lords, that lacked direct links to non-legislators. They existed precisely because they offered the needed 'independent and controlling power in the government of a free people.' Republicanism or popular self-government resulted in the tyranny of the

79 Gourlay, 2 Apr. 1818, *Statistical Account*, v. 2, 582–3, 585, and Simpson, *Essay on Modern Reformers*, 13–14
80 *Niagara Chronicle & Advertiser* copied in *Chronicle & Gazette*, 9 Sept. 1837

majority, lack of protection for minorities, intellectual conformity, and general turmoil.[81] In short, the theory of mixed monarchy rested on the belief in the basic incapacity of 'the people' to govern alone. Good government required either a corporate society of nobles and monarch or at least one unequal enough to reflect the basic intellectual inadequacy of most of its members. In any society conceived as an organic whole, claims of equal insight into the science of politics, like Gourlay's, could only be read as attempts to subvert providential hierarchy and disrupt the reciprocal duties among its functionally distinct components.[82]

The theory of mixed monarchy was obsessed with relations among three legislative branches. Issues as diverse as whether executive officeholders should be elected to the assembly or whether land policy should be used to promote inequality were debated in terms of their impact on those relations. As J.A.W. Gunn has argued, 'The major consequence of such a parsimony with categories was that the perceived constitutional framework excluded a number of significant political units, both governmental and social.'[83] If the balance of governor, legislative council, and assembly was at the heart of the constitution, what formal role was left to those who weren't members of these institutions? What status did their opinions have?

Emphasizing the sociological aspect of the theory of mixed monarchy offered a facile answer. The 'people' were one social category. The monarch and aristocracy, each with its own legislative branch, formed the other two. This solution could hardly be compelling in Upper Canada. Appointed by the Crown, what social entity did legislative councillors represent? Simplistic uses of this approach implied that every Upper Canadian except the handful of legislative and executive councillors could identify with only one of the law-making bodies. The other two

81 An Englishman, 'To the Reformers of Upper Canada,' *Patriot,* 26 Dec. 1837
82 Eckhart Hellmuth, '"The palladium of all other English liberties": Reflections on the Liberty of the Press in England during the 1760s and 1770s,' in Hellmuth, ed., *The Transformation of Political Culture in England and Germany in the Late Eighteenth Century* (Oxford: Oxford University Press 1990), 473–4. Despite its emphasis on social estates and hierarchy, mixed monarchy did not preclude all notions of secular equality. The British aristocracy was seen as open rather than closed; the legislative council obviously more so. Every subject was equal under the Crown. All adults had the right to petition. All had the right to the equal protection of the law and to the same liberties derived from them.
83 Gunn, 'The Fourth Estate: The Language of Political Innovation,' in *Beyond Liberty and Property,* 43

were left to represent little more than their members' self-interest or the imperial government. This solution also said nothing about the nature of the 'people's' relationship to the assembly. Of course, supporters of the theory of mixed monarchy argued that when King, Lords, and Commons acted together they embodied the national will and arrived at the best possible outcome.[84] Despite the electoral process and the right to petition, actual individuals and their opinions remained only tenuously connected to the theory of mixed monarchy.[85]

Focused on three branches, mixed monarchy bred suspicion of any 'fourth estate' likely to conflict with or impinge upon its balance. As many worried, if the 'people' or their opinions became powerful, King and Lords combined would not be able to check the Commons as the only elected estate. If the power of the people's opinions and the press continued to grow, they could effectively censure all three estates, including the Commons, and thus stand above them. The tripartite constitution had evolved as a response to the potential tyranny of an absolute monarch, but it was equally hostile to other unitary sovereigns, including 'the people.' Thus, extreme popular pressure on the three estates had to be avoided and popular deliberations judging all three estates constrained.[86]

The rise of the concept of public opinion and the development of its principal mechanisms, the subject of the next three chapters, destroyed the utility of the theory of mixed monarchy. Many Upper Canadians came to accept that rational decisions about the common good could be arrived at through open deliberation. Those decisions were preferable to any reached by individuals, groups, or institutions – including the balance of monarchy, aristocracy, and democracy. Legislative bodies would have to be redesigned to ensure that their decisions reflected, rather than checked, public opinion. The increasing belief in the capacity and

---

84 Thus the conservative *Patriot,* 19 Nov. 1833, argued that by expanding the definition of the 'people' to include 'the King and the Peers, and the Clergy, and the Middle Class,' the three estates truly gave 'the unequivocal expression of the people's will, – and Vox Populi Vox Dei, say we. IT IS THE BASIS OF THE BRITISH CONSTITUTION.'

85 Gunn, 'The Fourth Estate,' 73–88 discusses 'the people's' role in eighteenth-century constitutional debate in Britain. See also Edmund S. Morgan, *Inventing the People: The Rise of Popular Sovereignty in England and America* (New York: W.W. Norton 1988).

86 Besides Gunn, *Beyond Liberty and Property,* see Hellmuth, '"The palladium of all other English liberties,"' 484–6, 494, 498 and Keith Michael Baker, 'Fixing the French Constitution,' in *Inventing the French Revolution: Essays on French Political Culture in the Eighteenth Century* (Cambridge: Cambridge University Press 1990), 286–7.

right of the public to judge replaced the balance of King, Lords, and Commons at the heart of constitutional theory.

The process, however, was arduous. In some of the greatest studies of British government of the late eighteenth century, the concept of public opinion was given a variety of roles and attributes but coexisted in variable degrees of tension with older constitutional principles. For example, the jurist praised by John Strachan, John Louis De Lolme, spent considerable time in his *The Constitution of England* describing 'the resources allotted to the different parts of the English government for balancing each other, and how their reciprocal actions and re-actions produce the freedom of the constitution, which is no more than an equilibrium between the ruling powers of the state.' De Lolme, like most observers, was also struck by the number, freedom, and importance of British periodicals compared to their continental counterparts, but floundered when trying to integrate this observation into his discussion of the constitution. The press, according to De Lolme, enabled every man 'to communicate his sentiments to the public ... and it is this public notoriety of all things that constitutes the supplemental power, or check ... [to] keep within their respective bounds all those persons who enjoy any share of public authority.' Government officers acted in the knowledge that any incompetence or corruption would be exposed.

De Lolme rejected the equation of knowledge and leadership with gentility. A free press made political information and argument more widely available, thereby offering a more positive and active role to those outside legislative institutions. 'Every individual may, at his leisure and in retirement, inform himself of every thing that relates to the question on which he is to take a resolution ... a whole nation as it were holds a council, and deliberates ... all matters of fact are at length made clear; and, through the conflict of the different answers and replies, nothing at last remains but the sound part of the arguments.' When the public 'perseveres in opinions which have for a long time been discussed in public writing ... then it is, though only then, that we may with safety say, – "the voice of the people is the voice of God."' De Lolme ably described an idealized public sphere, but how did it relate to the three 'ruling powers in the state' he had just expounded?

His answer, that public opinion acted 'by means of the right they have of electing their representatives,' was surely inadequate – an obvious come-down from the equation of public opinion with the voice of God. The check of public opinion remained 'supplemental' and, except at elections, largely external to the British constitution as understood by

De Lolme.[87] The next three chapters examine the decades during which Upper Canada came to the point marked by De Lolme: the free and extensive discussion of politics in the press and a growing tension between 'public opinion' and still widely accepted constitutional principles. If public opinion was as De Lolme and a growing number of Upper Canadians believed – if the whole nation deliberated – it deserved a more secure and substantial place in constitutional theory than De Lolme, or anyone else trapped in the paradigm of mixed monarchy, could make for it.

---

87 De Lolme, *Constitution of England*, 52, 141, 199–213. For a somewhat different interpretation see Francis with Morrow, 'After the Ancient Constitution,' 288–93.

CHAPTER II

Experiments in Democratic Sociability: The Political Significance of Voluntary Associations

In 1797 the *Upper Canada Gazette* reprinted an American article, 'Differences in opinion are an advantage to Society.' Its author expressed surprise that 'even in this enlightened age' many sought uniformity from a prejudice 'against those who happened to differ from them in opinion.' Here was cause for alarm. Differences of opinion, far from being dangerous, 'rouse the attentions, give exercise to the understanding, and sharpen the reasoning faculty.' Literary societies should be founded 'to suppress such illiberal sentiments' and 'to see knowledge and rational principles diffused.' 'By such means,' he concluded, 'reason will resume her sovereign authority, and speedily banish the remains of bigotry and illiberality of sentiment from civil Society.'[1] Literary societies promoted liberalism.

There was more here than an attempt to dress up a local pet project in grand cultural argument. In similar voluntary associations Upper Canadians grew accustomed to coming together to further common goals; to working with others of different social, occupational, religious, or national backgrounds; to devising and abiding by mutually agreed-upon rules; to discussing topics of common concern; to speaking in front of others; to listening to others with opposing views; and to disagreeing without attacking the speaker, offending others, or trying to mandate uniformity. In voluntary associations people learned and practised the norms of reasoned discussion and mutual respect vital to sustained public deliberation.

---

1 *Princeton Packet* copied in *Upper Canada Gazette*, 4 Oct. 1797

Appeals to an informed and rational public opinion imagined an ideal decision-making process. That process made demanding assumptions about individuals and how they could relate to each other – about possible forms of sociability. It assumed that individuals were aware of and interested in issues beyond their immediate family, work, or locality; that they were knowledgeable about and capable of judging among competing arguments; that they were willing to discuss or at least pay attention to the discussion of others; and that they were willing to abide by the outcome of such discussions. The public sphere was defined by the institutions and practices that made such discussion possible. Membership was to be based on the capacity and willingness to participate, not on prescription or law, birth or revelation. Members had to deliberate with others of different experiences and points of view. They had to try to understand and persuade; they had to be open to being persuaded. They had to try to transcend a number of differences to relate to others, at least temporarily, as fellow participants in a deliberative process.

At its best, politics itself could bring Upper Canadians together in ways that approximated the assumptions of the public sphere. A gentlewoman recently from England was struck by the patrons of an inn at York: 'Some had the appearance of gentlemen, others of young farmers. They were strangely mingled together, as it seemed by politics, which they were discussing freely before us.'[2] Politics brought men together for discussions who might not otherwise have 'mingled.'

Public meetings, petitioning, and voting provided additional opportunities for such sociability. William Lyon Mackenzie painted a colourful portrait of a frontier election for his British audience: 'There were Christians and Heathens, Menonists and Tunkards, Quakers and Universalists, Presbyterians and Baptists, Roman Catholics and American Methodists; there were Frenchmen and Yankees, Irishmen and Mulattoes, Scotchmen and Indians, Englishmen, Canadians, Americans and Negroes, Dutchmen and Germans, Welshmen and Swedes, Highlanders and Lowlanders, poetical as well as most prosaical phizes, horsemen and footmen, fiddlers and dancers, honourables and reverends, captains and colonels, beaux and belles, waggons and tilburies, coaches and chaises, gigs and carts; in short, Europe, Asia, Africa, and America had each its representative among the loyal subjects and servants of our

2 O'Brien, *Journals*, 21 Feb. 1829, 40

good King George ...' At open-air hustings, this collection of religions, nationalities, races, sexes, financial means, and social stations – all British subjects – assembled as 'spectators' or 'actors' in the great drama of nominating and electing Niagara's parliamentary representative.[3]

As Mackenzie well knew, colonial elections were often far less picturesque. Verbal and physical intimidation, ignorance and prejudice, fraud and riot drew more attention than peaceful gatherings to enact community rituals. Given the localized and fractured nature of frontier society and the extent of fierce, not infrequently violent, conflict, it seems surprising that those who appealed to public opinion with its assumptions of a rational, informed public weren't laughed at. Moreover, competing beliefs about how people should relate to each other retained their currency. As S.F. Wise and others have shown, intellectual traditions that emphasized individuals' corporate identities over their commonalities, providential hierarchy over equality, and natural depravity over rational capacity remained prevalent in the colony.[4] Finally, membership in the groups singled out by Mackenzie may have shaped political opinions as much as deliberation with members of other groups. Paul Romney has shown that voting at Toronto in 1836 was strongly correlated with nationality, religious denomination, occupation, and date of arrival in Upper Canada.[5] Public debate may have persuaded Toronto voters that they had different interests based upon such categories, but other factors probably contributed to these voting patterns as well.

Against the stark realities of colonial politics, the claims of the public sphere appear Olympian. To some extent they were. They defined an ideal polity sustained by reason and discussion rather than habit, prejudice, or force – a standard against which reality could never quite measure up. It was, however, an ideal that Upper Canadians came to believe could and should be approximated. Such approximation was possible, not only because a few political leaders appealed to 'public opinion,' but because the experience of a sufficient number of Upper Canadians confirmed that some people some of the time could deliberate in public using arguments that others understood and could find persuasive.

---

3 Mackenzie, *Sketches of Canada*, 89

4 S.F. Wise, *God's Peculiar Peoples: Essays on Political Culture in Nineteenth Century Canada*, ed. A.B. McKillop and Paul Romney (Ottawa: Carleton University Press 1988)

5 Paul Romney, 'On the Eve of the Rebellion: Nationality, Religion and Class in the Toronto Election of 1836,' in David Keane and Colin Read, eds., *Old Ontario: Essays in Honour of J.M.S. Careless* (Toronto: Dundurn Press 1990), 192–216

Such experience made rhetorical appeals to 'public opinion' credible. Voluntary associations, as key sites for these experiences, were among the colony's most important political institutions.

Some of the discussions from which public opinion emerged occurred in and around the increasing number of voluntary associations, yet these associations were more than potential sites for political conversation. They helped to create and maintain a social space that was relatively autonomous from family, economic production, and the state for private individuals to coordinate common projects. This space developed its own norms about how people should relate to each other and how and by whom power should be exercised. Within it, the hierarchy and fractures of the broader society might be set aside temporarily to allow for a free association of equal members discussing topics of mutual concern, choosing leaders, and joining province-wide networks of the like-minded. Participants in any given association came to see themselves as only part of a larger universe of potential members and discussants – the public.[6]

By the 1830s, pioneering conditions had abated in significant parts of the province. Discretionary income, leisure time, the ability to travel with relative ease to the increasing number of secondary population centres, and further integration into local and regional markets were part of the experience of a growing number of colonists. The province's population almost quadrupled between 1820 and 1838 and included many who had experienced a rich associational life elsewhere. A cursory comparison of the sense of isolation depicted by Susanna Moodie in *Roughing It in the Bush* with her later *Life in the Clearings* reveals the cumulative impact of these factors. The Belleville of the latter hosted parades, balls given by the Odd Fellows, Freemasons, and fire company, travelling theatre, public lectures at the Mechanics' Institute, and a market where 'politics, commercial speculations, and the little floating gossip of the village are freely talked over and discussed.'[7]

Galt was another small community rapidly developing an impressive

---

6 Jürgen Habermas, *The Structural Transformation of the Public Sphere: An Inquiry into a Category of Bourgeois Society*, trans. Thomas Burger (Cambridge, Mass.: MIT Press 1989), 27, 37–8 and Geoff Eley, 'Nations, Publics, and Political Cultures: Placing Habermas in the Nineteenth Century,' in Craig Calhoun, ed., *Habermas and the Public Sphere* (Cambridge, Mass.: MIT Press 1993), esp. 290–1
7 Moodie, *Life in the Clearings*, 17–76, 88–114

public life. A debating society was formed in 1834, when the population had just reached 250. Seventeen men met regularly to debate topics in political economy, aesthetics, and ethics. In January 1836 a public meeting established the Galt Subscription and Circulating Library. Ninety-nine subscribers secured access to its books and newspapers. Over the next few years, membership climbed by half. The number of public spaces also increased. The first tavern opened in 1821 and was soon joined by a schoolhouse, churches, the King's Arms Hotel, and, in 1838, a Township Hall. A curling club was formed in the same year. An amateur theatre group and a Harmonic Society already existed. The following summer, an agricultural society was established and efforts were soon under way to launch a local newspaper. Annual township meetings had been held at Galt since 1819. On his 1833 tour of the province, William Lyon Mackenzie stopped at Galt to address a crowd of two to three hundred. The village also held the first public meeting to endorse Lord Durham's *Report*.[8]

This level of activity was not unique to Galt. Alexis de Tocqueville marvelled at the propensity of Americans to form associations for every conceivable purpose.[9] The same was true of British Americans. The *York Commercial Directory* for 1833–4 listed twenty-two voluntary associations in a city of 9254. Some were denominational, such as the Missionary Society of the St Andrew's Scotch Church, the Missionary Society of the Methodist Episcopal Church, the York Branch of the Canada Auxiliary Wesleyan Missionary Society, or the Missionary Society of the Upper Canada Primitive Methodists. Non-denominational religious societies included the York Auxiliary Bible Society, the Society for Promoting Christian Knowledge, the Upper Canada Religious Tract and Book Society, and the Society for Converting and Civilizing the Indians and Propagating the Gospel among the Destitute Settlers in Upper Canada. Benevolent associations included the Society for the General Relief and Benefit of Strangers and the Distressed Poor of York, the Institution for the Relief of the Orphan, the Fatherless, and the Widow, the York Annual Bazaar, and the Lying in Charity. There were two temperance societies. Civic groups included the Fire Engine Company and the Hook and Ladder Company for the Extinguishing of Fires. Economic self-help was institutionalized in the Home District Saving Bank. Fraternity was

8 James Young, *Reminiscences of the Early History of Galt and the Settlement of Dumfries, in the Province of Ontario* (Toronto: Hunter, Rose 1880)
9 Tocqueville, *Democracy in America*, 513

represented by the Freemasons. The provision and exchange of knowledge were organized by the Young Men's Society, Commercial News Room, York Mechanics' Institute, Home District Agricultural Society, and the Literary & Philosophical Society of Upper Canada.

By 1837, there were notable additions. The capital boasted two literary clubs, while economic interests were represented by the Board of Trade and the Mechanics' Association. The St George's Society had been founded in 1835 and was followed a year later by the St Andrew's and St Patrick's Societies. Two associations primarily aimed at elite sociability were also listed: the Upper Canada College Cricket Club and the City of Toronto Horticultural Society.[10]

The prominence of voluntary associations in city directories is telling. They provided the principal means to address problems beyond the competence of family, work, congregation, or government – to combat irreligion, ignorance, vice, poverty, and disease; to protect property and promote harmony; to integrate newcomers, make friends, and have fun; to coordinate civic projects and boost the community; and to improve and refashion oneself. Men and women of different ages, backgrounds, and social standings grouped and regrouped to work towards these ends in ways that, as historian Mary Ryan puts it, 'seemed to wreak havoc with the orderly gradations of the social hierarchy.'[11]

Most of these groups had no formal connection to politics, although gatherings of the like-minded undoubtedly occasioned casual political discussion. Voluntary associations were, however, political in a number of senses. The exponential growth of their number and range between 1820 and 1840 created and maintained a social space for the development of public opinion. Some associations were also political because they sought to influence government policy or officials. Some were political in that they were vehicles for the ideas and ambitions of those who felt slighted by existing political structures. Conversely, the same association might be used by the already powerful to try to contain popular mobilization or to direct it along 'safer' lines. Some associations were significant politically because they acted as forums for the exchange and diffusion of information and ideas, teaching their members to debate and think critically.

Nearly all voluntary associations were also mini-republics. Typically,

10 *York Commercial Directory*, 126–56 and *City of Toronto ... Commercial Directory*, 41–8
11 Mary P. Ryan, *Cradle of the Middle Class: The Family in Oneida County, New York, 1790–1865* (Cambridge: Cambridge University Press 1981), 106

each was a self-governing body composed of members of equal standing who had freely consented to join. Members created the association, devised its rules and policies, and elected officers from among their ranks to carry out their wishes. Obligations were limited and self-imposed. Members grew accustomed to expressing ideas in front of others and abiding by collective decisions. They came to expect a voice in the organizations to which they belonged. By generalizing these skills and expectations, voluntary associations encouraged participants to reproduce them elsewhere. In the assembly, one of the arguments made in favour of voting by secret ballot was simply that 'in societies the ballot was used.'[12] Voluntary associations gave particular meaning and concrete expression to the concepts of consent and participation.

Finally, the contested lines of inclusion and exclusion of voluntary associations were largely those of the public sphere. Some individuals, because of their sex, race, or social standing, were less visible in associational life than others. Just as voluntary associations *diffused* the norms and mechanisms of the public sphere, in part, by *differentiating* them from alternatives (such as social deference or violence), they differentiated those deemed capable of participating from those who weren't.

Few associations were simultaneously political in all these senses, while almost all had other, non-political, consequences beyond the scope of this chapter. Nonetheless, collectively, voluntary associations can be seen as experiments in democratic sociability: experiments because they represented something new in Upper Canada and something that was not always successful; democratic because they fostered relations that were typically horizontal and among individuals, rather than vertical and among groups.[13]

The earliest voluntary association in the colony, Freemasonry, was also the best example of this sociability. According to Gordon S. Wood, 'for thousands of Americans it was a major means by which they participated directly in the Enlightenment.'[14] Freemasonry offered a heady combina-

---

12 Charles Duncombe, *Brockville Recorder*, 7 Feb. 1834
13 See Roger Chartier, *The Cultural Origins of the French Revolution*, trans. Lydia G. Cochrane (Durham: Duke University Press 1991), 161 and, more broadly, Daniel Gordon, *Citizens without Sovereignty: Equality and Sociability in French Thought, 1670–1789* (Princeton: Princeton University Press 1994), 30–42.
14 Gordon S. Wood, *Radicalism of the American Revolution* (New York: Alfred A. Knopf 1992), 223–4. I have been particularly influenced by Margaret C. Jacob, *Living the Enlightenment: Freemasonry and Politics in Eighteenth-Century Europe* (New York: Oxford

tion of modern Newtonian science mixed with a historical mythology traced back to the builders of Solomon's Temple; the rational and useful with the esoteric and occult. It offered membership in a worldwide fraternity and cosmopolitan fellowship cemented by ritual, friendship, and benevolence.

Several lodges pre-date the founding of the colony: by 1793 there were ten; about forty were warranted in Upper Canada between 1792 and 1815. During any of Freemasonry's phases of growth and decay, the total number of lodges and members in the colony is unclear. Attendance at meetings ranged from single digits to over fifty.[15] The order's significance lay not in being the colony's first voluntary association or in the number of its members, but in its ideals and practices.

James FitzGibbon, Provincial Deputy Grand Master, expressed those ideals best in his oration to the 1823 meeting of the Provincial Grand Lodge. Twenty-one lodges from nineteen communities were represented. For FitzGibbon, the relative absence of poverty in the colony and the mixed nature of its population called for a broader understanding of Masonic benevolence than simple charity. 'Our population being made up of persons of many nations, languages and religions,' FitzGibbon, himself born an Irish Roman Catholic, was not surprised 'at sometimes hearing the offensive terms of insolent Englishman! selfish Scot! savage Irishman! cunning Yankee!' Such prejudices resulted in 'national calamities ... family feuds, in heart burning between neighbours, in religious differences and dislikes between sects, and though last, not least, in political dissentions.' By teaching its members to 'love one another, and to serve one another,' Freemasonry could have the 'most harmonising effect upon the minds of the People of this Province.'

As a force for collective enlightenment, Masonry reached beyond its membership. FitzGibbon anticipated a time when the order would be prosperous enough to promote education by establishing new schools, subsidizing existing ones, and endowing local libraries; 'proceeding in

---

University Press 1991), but see also Stephen Conrad Bullock, *Revolutionary Brotherhood: Freemasonry and the Transformation of the American Social Order, 1730–1849* (Chapel Hill: University of North Carolina Press 1996), Chartier, *Cultural Origins,* 162–8, and Anthony J. La Vopa, 'Conceiving a Public: Ideas and Society in Eighteenth-Century Europe,' *Journal of Modern History* 64, no. 4 (March 1992), 82–98.

15 J. Ross Robertson, *The History of Freemasonry in Canada from Its Introduction in 1749 ... Compiled and Written from official records and from MSS ...* (Toronto: Hunter Rose Co. 1899), v. 1, 177–8, 592. Most citations of this work refer to the primary sources Robertson copies, not his commentary.

short, to make war upon Ignorance, which is of all the evils the greatest enemy of Man.' Masons could serve as models for their neighbours and teachers for their families. They could prove that reason and knowledge promoted self-discipline and harmony. Working to end ignorance and prejudice and 'towards subjecting the passions of men to the government of religion and of reason,' Freemasonry 'shall contribute to the building up of a social edifice, in our Province, worthy of the principles of our Order.'[16] This was not the program of a mere social club.

The assembled brethren also heard their Grand Chaplain, the Rev. William Smart, a secessionist Presbyterian, emphasize the international aspects of this missionary program. Perhaps responding to those of his Kingston congregation who disapproved of his lodge activities, Smart insisted 'from the principles that form the basis of the Masonic institution, the spirit that ought to animate its members, and from the duties inseparably connected with it, that it has not only been the means of preserving and diffusing the light of science and truth, and disseminating the blessings of order, and subordination in society,' but it could also 'spread through the world, the light of Divine revelation.' Enlightenment and the Christian gospels – Masonry and evangelicalism – were one. Further, not only Freemasonry's ideals, but also the 'spirit that ought to animate its members' – its sociability – promised international harmony.[17]

Similar ideals were expressed at regular lodge meetings and when Masons laid the cornerstones of numerous churches, public buildings, and monuments, or gathered at local churches for Masonic festivals and funerals. For instance, when Masons laid the cornerstone of St George's Church, St Catharines, in 1835, the Anglican rector, James Clarke, although not himself a Mason, addressed the assembled lodges using texts they had provided. Clarke began by deploring excessive divisions within Christianity and society. Uniformity, however, was unlikely since no one should interfere with another's divine right of private judgment 'in the management either of his spiritual or temporal concerns.' Caught between the sanctity of private judgment and its potentially harmful social consequences, Clarke praised Freemasonry for seeking

---

16 *Weekly Register*, 24 July 1823

17 Smart, *An Address*, 3–7. His 1820 decision to join the order almost split his congregation. Ruth McKenzie, 'Smart, William,' *Dictionary of Canadian Biography*, 10 (Toronto: University of Toronto Press 1972), 659–60.

'to harmonize the jarring passions of men – to bring all denominations
of Christians to love one another, to love as brethren, to be at peace.'
Masons were also to be congratulated for practising their ideals –
because 'you exclude none ... from your society, but the selfish, the
uncharitable, the contentious, blasphemers of God's name and word,
and traitors of the King, or the Government under which they live: all
others, no matter of what sect, religion or country, you receive as brethren, and treat them as such.' Clarke was convinced that 'no association
seems to have contributed more in allaying differences, and healing
divisions.' In the politically charged Upper Canada of the 1830s, this was
high praise indeed.

Clarke concluded by enjoining Masons to remain true to their four
cardinal virtues: temperance, fortitude, prudence, and justice; each with
a predominantly civic meaning. 'Temperance, you say, is that due
restraint upon our affections and passions which renders the body tame
and governable ... Fortitude, you say, enables us to undergo every priva-
tion, pain or danger, in support of truth ... Prudence teaches you to regulate your lives and actions agreeably to the dictates of reason, and the
law of God; whilst Justice is that standard or boundary of right which,
without distinction or particularity, gives to every one his due.'[18] In
other words, Masonic rituals and rules created self-governing individuals
capable of moderating their passions and 'affections' for kin, nation,
sect, or language. Despite everything that divided them, all men shared
a common core as rational beings capable of self-government. They
sought truth and lived by its precepts. Here was the essence of a liberal
individualism that, far from creating alienated atoms, allowed those able
to transcend ignorance and particularities to create and sustain fraternal bonds. The concept of a public sphere would have been easily
understood by all who took such orations to heart.

Similar ideals also found expression in less formal texts such as these
stanzas from a banquet toast: 'The Masons' social brotherhood, around
the festive board./ Reveals a wealth more precious far than selfish
miner's [miser's?] hoard;/ They fairly share the priceless stores that
generous hearts contain .../ Amidst our mirth we drink "To all poor
Masons o'er the world:"/ On every shore our flag of love is gloriously
unfurled;/ We prize each brother, fair or dark, who bears no moral

---

18 Clarke, *An Address*, 3–12. For a contrary interpretation see Curtis Fahey, *In His Name:
The Anglican Experience in Upper Canada, 1791–1854* (Ottawa: Carleton University Press
1991), 250, 280n.

stain –/ The Mason feels the noble truth the Scottish peasant told,/ That rank is but the guinea's stamp; the man himself the gold/ With us the rich and poor unite, and equal rights maintain.'[19] Masonry was a fraternal organization of men who valued associational life and strove for a sociability that transcended divisions within society at home and abroad. It equated harmony with reason, dissension with ignorance. It judged by behaviour, not birth or material wealth.

The *Constitutions* of English Freemasonry, reprinted in Upper Canada in 1823, not only reiterated these ideals, but also stipulated the rules by which they could be pursued. For instance, the first charge read, 'Let a man's religion or mode of worship be what it may, he is not excluded from the order, provided he believe in the glorious architect of heaven and earth, and practise the sacred duties of morality.'[20] The order was 'the happy means of conciliating friendship amongst those who must otherwise have remained at a perpetual distance.' Once admitted to the order, a member's meritorious behaviour was his sole means to advance through its degrees and elective offices: 'All masons are, as brethren, upon the same level.'

Among the rules required to realize these ideals, brothers were to 'avoid all ill language, and to call each other by no disobliging name, but brother or fellow.' Masons were also enjoined neither 'to talk of any thing impertinently or unseemly, nor interrupt ... nor behave yourself ludicrously or jestingly ... nor use any unbecoming language ... but to pay due reverence to your master, wardens, and fellows.' They were prohibited from 'doing or saying any thing offensive, or that may forbid an easy and free conversation; for that would blast our harmony, and defeat our laudable purposes.' Thus, 'private piques or quarrels' could not be admitted into the lodge, 'far less any quarrels about religion, or nations, or state policy, we being only, as masons, of the universal reli-

---

19 Humphreys, *Junior Warden's Toast*
20 Such latitudinarian, almost deist, language represented a remarkable degree of toleration. The relationship between Masonry, Newtonian science, natural religion, and particular denominations is beyond the scope of this chapter. Caution should also be used before generalizing from elsewhere. For the U.S. see Wood, *Radicalism of the American Revolution*, 223, Bullock, *Revolutionary Brotherhood*, 163–84, and Wayne A. Huss, 'Pennsylvania Freemasonry: An Intellectual and Social Analysis, 1727–1829,' PhD thesis, Temple University 1984, 68–76. For England see John Money, 'Freemasonry and the Fabric of Loyalism in Hanoverian England,' in Eckhart Hellmuth, ed., *The Transformation of Political Culture in England and Germany in the Late Eighteenth Century* (Oxford: Oxford University Press 1990), esp. 258–60, 265.

gion above-mentioned; we are also of all nations, tongues, kindred, and languages, and are resolved against all politics.'[21]

The exclusion of private business, personal interests, and politics was necessary to ensure harmony and 'easy conversation' within a mixed and voluntary association. According to the chaplain of a Kingston lodge, 'no angry passions are allowed to rise; no violent discussions to provoke dissension; no political sentiments to disturb unanimity.'[22] The ideals, structure, and sociability of its meetings, not the content of its conversations, gave Freemasonry its political significance. As Margaret Jacob argues with reference to European lodges, 'these were political societies, not in a party or faction sense of the term but in a larger connotation. Within the framework of civility and in the service of an imagined social cohesion, the lodges practised a civil administration.' Masons 'met out of mutual interest and not as a result of confessional affiliation, birth, or rank in society per se. And they always met separately from their families ... they met as individuals.'[23]

They also consented to general rules and agreed to abide by the decisions of their peers. Dues and fines were a form of self-imposed taxation disbursed by those who paid them. Non-financial obligations included attendance at meetings and conformity to a code of behaviour. Each Mason was bound by this code because he had consented to it. It was enforced by the majority, usually after committee investigation, discussion in the lodge, and attempts at mediation. Members also participated in formal deliberations concerning lodge activities and their constitutional relationship to the Provincial Grand Lodge and the English Grand Lodge. Such discussions were structured by norms of equality of voice and access, deference to the chair, civility, and majority rule.

Freemasonry was hierarchical with three basic degrees, (apprentice, fellow, and master), and a hierarchical executive (including eleven or more officers). This hierarchy, like the order's rules and morality, was explicitly man-made, not revealed by God or nature. Preferment was by merit judged by fellow Masons. All officers were elected semi-annually or annually by ballot from the membership. Officers represented the lodge at provincial conventions, but the *Constitutions* stipulated that 'the majority of the members of a lodge duly assembled have the privilege of giving instructions ... because these officers are their representatives,

---

21 *Constitutions*, 3–11
22 Herchmer, *Love, The Spirit of Masonry*, 9
23 Jacob, *Living the Enlightenment*, 20, 50

and are supposed to speak their sentiments.'[24] Collectively, these rules, and the sociability they fostered, created what Margaret Jacob calls a 'civic consciousness.'[25] The concepts of liberal equality and individualism, social contract, consent, rule of law, constitutionalism, and representative government found their ideal expression not in Upper Canada's constitution, but in its Masonic lodges.

It is not surprising, then, that there were parallels between debates about the structure of provincial Freemasonry and the colony's constitution. In 1836, Charles Duncombe's lodge attempted to create a schismatic Grand Lodge independent of England and led by an elective Grand Master (Duncombe himself) rather than one appointed from London. It can hardly be coincidental that Duncombe soon led the western phase of the rebellion against British colonial rule. The secret organization of those rebels, the Hunters, was closely modelled on Masonic lodges.[26]

Likewise, after fruitless appeals to England to exercise the leadership necessary to rejuvenate the Provincial Grand Lodge, a prominent local Mason assumed the title of Grand High Priest and called a convention at Smith's Falls. Forty-six Masons, mostly from eastern counties, declared that 'master Masons are invested with inherent Rights to adopt any measures for the benefit of the Craft' before proceeding to establish a new executive and legislature. To justify this assumption of constituent power, the resolutions rehearsed a series of grievances against the English Grand Lodge. Here was a convention adopting the form and rhetoric of a declaration of independence to create a government for Upper Canadians without imperial sanction.[27] Meeting in February 1844 these Masons must have been aware of the resonance that issues of

---

24 *Constitutions*, 59–60. The extent to which Upper Canada shared the American experience of multiplying degrees, more elaborate titles and rituals, and greater bureaucracy warrants further study. See Bullock, *Revolutionary Brotherhood*, 239–73.

25 Jacob, *Living the Enlightenment*, 32

26 Duncombe, among others, had questioned the superiority of the English Grand Lodge over Upper Canadian Masonry as early as 1822. The prolonged conflict between Provincial Grand Master William Jarvis at York and a rival Grand Lodge formed at Niagara in 1802 was also driven, in part, by American-born Masons who favoured autonomy for Upper Canadian Masonry from Britain and the retention of ties to American lodges. Robertson, *History of Freemasonry*, v. 1, 339, 390–410; v. 2, 21–3, 187, 191. On the Hunters see Colin Read, *The Rising in Western Upper Canada, 1837–8* (Toronto: University of Toronto Press 1982), 140.

27 Robertson, *History of Freemasonry*, v. 2, 207–9, 251. The degree to which the resulting organization remained under even the nominal control of the English Grand Lodge is unclear.

rights, grievances, government structure, and colonial status had with the constitutional dispute then raging between Governor Metcalfe and his former advisers (the subject of chapter 5).

Despite these examples and the order's reputation on the European continent, Freemasonry was not inherently radical; it was not necessarily a breeding ground for dissatisfaction with the colonial constitution. Some of the staunchest supporters and most rewarded officers of that constitution were prominent Freemasons. Government officials and gentlemen dominated the executive of the Provincial Grand Lodge. They probably relished the idea of being freely chosen as enlightened leaders of an association devoid of partisan politics. The regular aspects of Masonic constitutionalism were probably more important than its controversies. Charges from the *Constitutions* were read aloud, supplementing regular lectures as a form of instruction. Lodges held elections and most members probably served in some local office. Norms of speaking, deference to the chair, respect for procedure and precedent, acceptance of majority rule, and socializing with diverse but equal fellows were also inculcated.

Not everyone was deemed capable of participating in this constitutional and convivial order. The *Constitutions* stipulated that Masons 'must be good and true men, free born, and of mature and discreet age and sound judgement, no bondmen, no women, no immoral or scandalous men, but of good report.'[28] Women and slaves were lumped together with those free men lacking sufficient maturity or moral rectitude. All lacked independence; subject to fathers, husbands, owners, or their own ignorance and passions. None was an autonomous moral agent. Certain standards, such as age and character, could discriminate among free men, but all women, like slaves, were deemed incapable of meeting the threshold.

The ideals and rules of Freemasonry gain much of their significance from the extent to which its members tried to live by them.[29] Minutes frequently concluded on the same note: 'The lodge was closed in due form, and in harmony.' Masons celebrated the fulfilment of their ideals after their festivals, banquets, and processions. As one secretary recorded, 'It appeared to be every brother's desire to do honor to the day with conviviality accompanied by the true decorum, after many Masonic toasts were drunk, the Brethren retired with the utmost har-

---

28 *Constitutions*, 4–5
29 This is the central point of Jacob, *Living the Enlightenment.*

mony and felicity.' Formal rituals followed by drinking toasts, dining, and easy conversation were hallmarks of Freemasonry and several other associations in Upper Canada, contributing to a 'vision of masculine camaraderie.'[30]

Masons also practised the benevolence they preached. Philanthropy Lodge No. 4, Newark, was not alone in establishing a fund 'for the benefit of Free Mason's widows, the education of orphans, and indigent brethren's children.' Lodges responded to petitions for aid from fellow Masons and occasionally from the broader community. St John's, Kingston, donated money to the Female Benevolent Society in 1826, and various lodges investigated the possibility of creating a Masonic asylum, purchasing public libraries, or assisting in other educational projects.[31] The emphasis on education, also evident in FitzGibbon's oration, reflected the belief that reason could transcend parochial interests and prejudices; that meritorious behaviour, not monarchical hierarchy or patronage, was the ultimate standard of worth. As one historian of American Freemasonry puts it, the emphasis on education 'recognized natural equality, not by fixing a person's status, but by allowing all the opportunity to rise to their merit position without hindrance from unnatural barriers.'[32]

The extent of social and cultural diversity within each lodge varied. Some were fairly homogeneous. The nine men who met at William Campbell's home in 1822 to form St Andrew's, York, were already connected by status and office. Campbell was puisne judge of the King's Bench. The receiver-general, lieutenant-governor's aide-de-camp, adjutant-general of the colonial militia, Usher of the Black Rod, and a legislative councillor were founding members. The following year, when two members of the assembly joined, the lodge resolved that 'any mem-

---

30 Robertson, *History of Freemasonry*, v. 1, 319 and Mary Ann Clawson, *Constructing Brotherhood: Class, Gender and Fraternalism* (Princeton: Princeton University Press 1989), 14. Masonry makes a good case study for examining gender identities. See Leonore Davidoff and Catherine Hall, *Family Fortunes: Men and Women of the English Middle Class, 1780–1850* (Chicago: University of Chicago Press 1987), 426–7.

31 Robertson, *History of Freemasonry*, v. 1, 291, 532, 653; v. 2, 81–2, 107, 291, 297, 317 and *Kingston Chronicle*, 20 Jan. 1826

32 S.C. Bullock, 'The Ancient and Honorable Society: Freemasonry in America, 1730–1830,' PhD thesis, Brown University 1986, 287. The emphasis upon merit and education has led American historians to see Freemasonry as quintessentially republican. See Wood, *Radicalism of the American Revolution*, 233 and esp. Bullock, *Revolutionary Brotherhood*, 138–62, 235–6, 297–8.

ber of the Branches of the Legislature wishing to celebrate that Festival [of St John the Evangelist] with the members of this lodge on that day, may be at liberty to do so.' Their initiation fee was twice that of most lodges, but, as Mary Ann Clawson notes, 'since the rite creates a fraternal bond predicated upon the formal equality of members, even the most socially restrictive lodges engaged in a symbolic repudiation of distinctions of rank and class.'[33] In other lodges, men of more varied occupations, religious denominations, nationalities, and political persuasions participated in collective rituals, adhered to a common set of rules, and celebrated their equality.

The hierarchy created within the lodge, celebrated in Masonic rituals, and displayed at Masonic processions did not always correspond to the social standing of its members. In his study of voluntary associations in mid-century Halifax, David A. Sutherland finds that 44 per cent of Masons were artisans or pursued other 'low status' occupations, 42 per cent were merchants, professionals, or from other 'high status' occupations, with the remaining 14 per cent in retail trade. The 'higher status' category was over-represented among lodge officers at 56 per cent, but almost a quarter of those elected in this period were artisans (only 3 per cent lower than their proportion of the entire membership) and a further 7 per cent came from other 'low status' occupations.[34] Thus, to gain admission to a lodge and to be elevated through its degrees and elected to its leadership, those from 'higher status' occupations required the votes of those from 'lower status' occupations. Many agreed to treat as brothers, obey, be instructed by, and have their behaviour monitored by lodge leaders of lower occupational status.

Scattered evidence from lodge registers suggests a similar occupational range in Upper Canada. The by-laws of one lodge stipulated that members be 'endowed with an Estate, Office, Trade, Occupation, or some Visible way of acquiring an honest and reputable Livelihood.'[35] The ability to pay dues was an unwritten requirement of most associations, but this

33 Robertson, *History of Freemasonry*, v. 1, 41, v. 2, 255–65, 304–5, and Clawson, *Constructing Brotherhood*, 16, 76, 78

34 David A. Sutherland, 'Voluntary Societies and the Process of Middle-Class Formation in Early-Victorian Halifax, Nova Scotia,' *Journal of the Canadian Historical Association* 5 (1994), 258–9. These figures roughly correspond to those Bryan Palmer found in a Hamilton lodge for 1855 to 1905: 36% were from skilled trades, 6% from unskilled. *A Culture in Conflict: Skilled Workers and Industrial Capitalism in Hamilton, Ontario, 1860–1914* (Montreal: McGill-Queen's University Press 1979), 41–2

35 Robertson, *History of Freemasonry*, v. 1, 549

lodge was explicit that members not be dependent upon others or upon disreputable means to pay them. Reputable here implied no distinction between landed and non-landed forms of wealth or between manual and non-manual labour. Of the thirteen members present at Hiram Lodge No. 20, Cornwall, in 1804, there were three farmers, two clothiers, as well as a tinsmith, innkeeper, schoolmaster, weaver, joiner, artist, merchant, and blacksmith. Only 38 of 105 names in the registry of Lodge No. 12, Stamford, 1806–22, included occupations: twenty-five farmers, three blacksmiths, two members of the military, two wheelwrights, two teachers, and a physician, joiner, and surveyor and carpenter. Twenty of the 139 men subscribing to the bylaws of St John's Lodge No. 16, York, during the first quarter of the nineteenth century, listed their occupation: three farmers, two tailors, two innkeepers, two carpenters, and a blacksmith, clergyman, barracks master, saddler, surveyor, tinsmith, merchant, mason, mariner, goldsmith, and cabinetmaker. Between 1820 and 1822, nine self-described 'gentlemen' associated in fraternal equality with two carpenter-joiners, a tanner-currier, and a plasterer in Unity Lodge, Township of Murray, Northumberland County.[36]

The same range was probably true of religious denomination as well as occupation, although proportions within each lodge are unknown and varied. In various jurisdictions, Roman Catholic and Methodist officials condemned Freemasonry, but members from both remained Masons.[37] The order laid the cornerstones of numerous Anglican churches, several lodges had Anglican chaplains, divine service for Masonic festivals was often held in the local Anglican church, and Rev. A.N. Bethune, Bishop John Strachan's lieutenant, served as Provincial Grand Chaplain.[38] Nonetheless, as already noted, one of Bethune's predecessors was a secessionist Presbyterian and the chaplain of one of the largest and most active lodges in the 1840s, St Andrew's, Toronto, was a Kirk Presbyterian.

Perhaps a new frame church at Ancaster best symbolizes the relationship between religious denomination and colonial Masonry. The cornerstone was dedicated in 1824 according to Masonic rituals, followed

---

36 Ibid., v. 1, 716–8, 796–8, 875, 1135

37 For reference to Roman Catholic Masons see ibid. v. 2, 298–9 and for the complexities of papal injunctions, see W. McLead, 'Freemasonry, As a Matter of Fact,' *Canadian Historical Review* 79, no. 1 (March 1988), 53n.

38 Robertson, *History of Freemasonry*, v. 2, 300, 327. Robertson at 439 claims that 'the large proportion of the members of the Craft in the early years of York were members of the Anglican church.' Anglicans were also the largest denomination of Pennsylvania Masons; Huss, 'Pennsylvania Freemasonry,' 209–10.

by a 'very appropriate oration ... in which the progress of masonry was traced from the earliest ages to the present period, and its benefits to the society depicted in a manner that evidently delighted the fraternity, inspired the uninitiated with a high opinion of the Masonic Institutions and pleased every one.' The church, financed by subscription, was dedicated 'indiscriminately to the worshippers of God, of every Christian Profession, without distinction of sect or party – with this reservation, viz. that the resident minister of the Episcopal Church is at all times to have the right of preaching in it once a day.'[39] A tolerance of Christian diversity with a nod towards the special status of the Anglican church would not have satisfied everyone, but it represented an externalization of Masonic ideals into the wider society on one of the most divisive issues in the colony. Masons even revelled in the fact that their cosmopolitanism crossed racial boundaries, prizing 'each brother fair or dark.' The possible inclusion of blacks with other races in the same lodge, however, was far more contentious.[40]

Lodges did, however, transcend political boundaries. Barton Lodge, composed almost entirely of Loyalists, including many who had served in Butler's Rangers, purchased black crepe and went into official mourning in 1800 to mark the death of America's most prominent Mason – George Washington.[41] J.K. Johnson found at least 57 known Masons among the 283 men elected to the colonial assembly before 1841.[42] For example, Hugh C. Thomson was initiated into St John's,

---

39 George Gurnett to Charles Fothergill, 13 July 1824 in Robertson, *History of Freemasonry*, v. 1, 972–4

40 Humphreys, *Junior Warden's Toast*. Among subscribers to Barton Lodge in 1796 was Thayendanegea (Joseph Brant). His youngest son was also a Mason and there may have been a lodge at Mohawk Village (Robertson, *History of Freemasonry*, v. 1, 632, 643, 688–9). In 1842 a number of blacks applied for affiliation to Barton Lodge as members of the African Grand Lodge of Masons in the U.S. Some officers of Barton Lodge suggested that they communicate directly with the 'Grand Lodge of Canada.' Not only was such action unnecessary for affiliation, but no such body existed. While the intent of some was clearly to frustrate the applicants' affiliation, the senior warden argued that 'our obligation obliged us to admit even colored men.' After debate the lodge resolved to communicate directly with the African Grand Lodge to ensure that the petitioners were indeed Masons. Robertson, *History of Freemasonry*, v. 2, 460–1 and Norman Macdonald, *The Barton Lodge, A.F. and A.M. No. 6, G.R.C. 1795–1945* (Toronto: Ryerson Press 1945), 32–41. It appears the stalling tactics worked.

41 Macdonald, *Barton Lodge*, 58

42 J.K. Johnson, *Becoming Prominent: Regional Leadership in Upper Canada, 1791–1841* (Kingston and Montreal: McGill-Queen's University Press 1989), 89, 84–95, 249–50

Kingston, in 1818. The following year he established *The Upper Canada Herald*, an important reform organ. He was elected junior warden in 1823, senior warden in 1824, and master in 1827 and 1828. He had also been elected to the assembly in 1824. The following April, Christopher Hagerman, a fellow member of the assembly but a frequent target of Thomson's editorial pen, was initiated into the lodge. The next year, Marshall Spring Bidwell, who had replaced his father as the member for Lennox and Addington, was also initiated. Given their starkly different politics and Hagerman's leading role in ousting the elder Bidwell from the legislature, one wishes for more evidence of the degree of conviviality between them within the order. In January 1827, Donald Bethune became a member of the same lodge. The following year he too was elected to the assembly. His strident conservatism was ridiculed in the *Upper Canada Herald*, but in 1828 he was elected junior warden to serve under Master Thomson.[43]

Upper Canadian lodges took the qualifications for admission and the preservation of their sociability seriously. They investigated prospective members, denied admission to some, and expelled those who later proved unworthy or threatened to bring the order into disrepute by flagrantly violating wider community norms, especially regarding intemperance or the treatment of women and dependents. More frequently, members were expelled for failure to pay dues, dishonesty (especially in business contracts), or incivility towards fellow Masons.[44] Lodge rules, rituals, fellowship, and quasi-judicial proceedings enforced broader community norms and taught discipline and civility to protect a social space within which members, divided by personal interest, occupation, religion, and politics, could still be brothers. The order could diffuse its sociability to this large and diverse group only by regulating members' behaviour, differentiating between those capable and incapable of such discipline, and repeatedly contrasting its definitions of civility, reason, and knowledge with rudeness, prejudice, and ignorance.

Freemasonry thus embodied the liberalism of the period. It believed that individual men were capable of reasoning and self-government and

---

43 Robertson, *History of Freemasonry*, v. 1, 327–30, 344. Perhaps the distance between such prominent political opponents was too great. Bidwell withdrew from St John's in June 1828, although his affiliation with Masonry continued. Yet as Bidwell was fleeing the colony after the rebellion suspected of disloyalty, Hagerman wrote to express his continued personal respect.

44 Ibid., v. 1, 298–9, 579–84, 590, 592, 599, 601–2

thus shared a common identity despite differences of race, nationality, religion, and social status. Its sociability was not designed to do away with these differences, but to bring to light, develop, and operate from its members' commonality. Self-interested individuals could enter into social contracts, create and abide by self-imposed rules, govern an association, achieve harmony, and accept communal responsibilities through the use of their reason and by practising the appropriate sociability. Participants were equal, while all positions of authority were to be earned by merit. Inequality of result was thereby legitimized, but its older justifications, such as birth, legal privilege, or corporate identity, were rejected.[45] Masons believed in their own enlightened status and their ability to act as a model for society. Finally, in keeping with the liberalism of their time, they did not believe that everyone was capable of such status. The dependent position of women, the young, the poor, and the morally weak excluded them from enlightenment.

Freemasonry's contribution to collective social and political perceptions was ambiguous. The equality achieved within the lodge was never intended to displace broader social hierarchies. As the *Constitutions* put it, 'though all masons are, as brethren, upon the same level, masonry takes no honour from a man that he had before.'[46] They accepted existing social structures, but posed a subtle challenge. Even given social inequalities, a space could be created where they could be held in temporary abeyance – where those structures did not matter and where equality and advancement by merit could operate. The ability to conceive of distinct social spaces (familial, economic, associational, congregational, political) that were sufficiently isolated from each other to develop their own norms and organization was precisely the key conceptual demand of the public sphere: people could be equal, rational participants in public debate while organized by different principles for other purposes.

The contribution of Masonry to political self-perception was also complex. The order upheld the status quo by valuing loyalty to existing authorities and prohibiting partisan discussions. By deeming politics to be destructive of fellowship, even among the enlightened, Masonry also bolstered the idea that only a few were fit for political leadership.

---

45 Clawson, *Constructing Brotherhood*, 14

46 *Constitution*, 9. Masonic ideals could be used to bolster conservative social imagery. For one Masonic chaplain, the injunction to love as brothers 'teaches man to be content with the lot assigned him by Providence.' Herchmer, *Love, Spirit of Masonry*, 8–9

Finally, the Newtonian imagery of Masonic rhetoric and symbols complemented interpretations of the colony's constitution as a highly developed machine of checks and balances.[47] Yet the experience of Upper Canadian Masons offered a glimpse at another world: a world where men could be equal, rational, and benevolent, transcend social divisions, and cooperate in the governing of their order. Protected by rules and rituals, such a world could exist even in a fractured and hierarchical society. But could individuals in society at large create a self-directed space for rational discursive practices or would selfishness, anarchy, and prejudice reign?

Like Freemasonry, literary and debating societies contributed to the possibility of harmony among diverse individuals. They also taught the skills and sociability of public deliberation. The first example was probably the Literary Society of York, established in June 1820 by ten young men with such prominent surnames as Baldwin, Cartwright, Ridout, and Sherwood.[48] Despite their shared background and small number, they adopted an elaborate code of seven articles and twenty-eight bylaws: twenty for internal government and eight for conducting debates. Coming together 'for the purpose of mental improvement,' they promised to meet twice monthly to discuss any question unconnected with 'particular policy or religious controversy.' Even in an association devoted to debate and limited to a select few, harmony required a prohibition on the most contentious topics. The ban may also have sheltered the group from the concerns of the powerful in church and state, who might fear the critical potential of unsupervised debate among young men.[49] Other bylaws were intended to manage conflict during debate: a president 'moderated'; questions were to be framed in a particular fashion; and the opportunity to be heard was widely dispersed by limiting the number of times a member could speak.

Participants were prevented from interrupting or attacking each other or from raising a certain class of questions. Something of the immediacy, focus, and excitement of a passionate two-way fight may

---

47 For the potentially loyalist/conservative nature of English Masonry, see Money, 'Freemasonry and the Fabric of Loyalism,' esp. 243, 251, 257, 266–7.

48 Archives of Ontario, Ridout Papers, 'Rules and Regulations, "Literary Society of York,"' 20 June 1820

49 David S. Shields, *Civil Tongues: Polite Letters in British America* (Chapel Hill: University of North Carolina Press 1997), 214

have been lost. But, as Don Herzog points out, much more was gained by such limits – the very ability to meet as equals, solicit a variety of views, challenge each other's arguments, hone their skills, and reinforce mutual respect. Enacted by the York and subsequent literary and debating societies, these constraints – the rules of civility – opened more and better doors than they shut.[50]

It is unclear how active this first society was. Several of its instigators were soon involved in the Juvenile Advocate Society established the following year. According to the eight founding students-at-law, it was to be a 'little Seminary of Law and Eloquence,' designed 'for the increase and cultivation particularly of Legal and Constitutional but generally of all useful knowledge.' It met weekly to debate a variety of topics, including the nature of civil liberty, the limits of just laws, primogeniture, annual parliaments, republican versus monarchical government, case studies of international law, the jury system, and taxation without representation. Elaborate rules were developed to maintain civility and decorum. Conduct deemed 'indecent and improper' was met with admonitions, fines, or even incarceration by the 'sergeant-in-waiting.' G. Blaine Baker sees these as the means to instil professionalism and gentility, but they were also attempts to foster a sociability whereby individuals could challenge each other's opinions without causing offence or discord. Frequent injunctions in the society's journals to maintain 'decorum and a gentlemanly and forbearing conduct,' or to 'smooth away the acrimony that will always arise upon a difference of opinion,' or to preserve 'coolness and presence of mind,' marked the boundaries of a space where reason could overcome passion and personality. Members learned from both the exchange of argument and the rules and norms that made such exchange possible. Controversy could be made safe and enlightening in a rule-governed environment where participation was limited to an educated few bound together by social background and professional interest.[51]

The number of such environments multiplied. During the 1830s, literary, philosophical, scientific, and debating societies were founded at

50 Don Herzog, *Poisoning the Minds of the Lower Orders* (Princeton: Princeton University Press 1998), 165–8 and, for the concept of enabling constraints, see Stephen Holmes, *Passions & Constraint: On the Theory of Liberal Democracy* (Chicago: University of Chicago Press 1995).

51 G. Blaine Baker, 'The Juvenile Advocate Society, 1821–1826: Self-Proclaimed Schoolroom for Upper Canada's Governing Class,' Canadian Historical Association *Historical Papers*, 1985, esp. 77–9, 86, 90–3

York/Toronto (in 1830, 1831, 1833, 1835, 1836, 1838), Hallowell (1833, 1834), Kingston (1833, 1836, 1837), Galt (1834), Niagara (1835), Perth (1835), Hamilton (1836), St Catharines (1836), Cobourg (1831, 1837?), Bytown (1838), Ancaster (1839?), and Chatham (1839). There were undoubtedly others. Most could have echoed the City of Toronto Ethical and Literary Society, whose object was 'the reading of Essays on Ethical and Literary subjects, and also debating on questions given out for discussion.'[52] The rules of Niagara Literary and Debating Society were followed by the signatures of sixty who were 'deeply impressed with a sense of benefit and general utility likely to result, from the organization of a Debating Society.'[53]

During the spring and fall of 1837, the Kingston Young Men's Society debated fifteen subjects, discussed eleven original essays, and attended sermons delivered by the clergy of four denominations. Weekly attendance ranged from twenty to thirty-five. Within a year, its library contained ninety volumes.[54] It provided instructional or improving uses for leisure and furthered both personal and public ends. It trained public leaders (John A. Macdonald was elected president; Oliver Mowat recording secretary) and citizens. On the eve of the rebellion, a promoter remained confident that debating societies prevented demagogues from 'enclosing in their ruinous embrace the unwary and unsuspecting.'[55] Those trained in the public use of reason would not be deluded by false prophets.

While none of these associations was limited, like the Juvenile Advocate Society, to a single profession, a few were relatively patrician. Established in 1831, the York Literary and Philosophical Society was forced to advertise its openness, but still survived only about a year.[56] Another literary society was reportedly 'formed by the mercantile young men' of Toronto.[57] Their counterparts in Kingston and Brockville had successfully petitioned their employers to curtail evening business hours to allow them to join associations for 'improving our education, clearing our judgement, and enlarging our knowledge upon all subjects.'[58] The

---

52 *City of Toronto ... Commercial Directory*, 45
53 In Janet Carochan, *History of Niagara, (In Part)* (Toronto: William Briggs 1914), 269–70
54 *Chronicle & Gazette*, 11 Nov. 1837
55 A.N., *Cobourg Star*, 11 Oct. 1837
56 *Courier of Upper Canada* copied in *Colonial Advocate*, 4 Oct. 1832
57 *Royal Standard*, 9 Nov. 1836
58 Y.S. to the Young Men of Bytown, *Bytown Gazette*, 20 Apr. 1837

officers of the Kingston Young Men's Society included a law student, a bookseller and a bank teller.[59] In sum, most of these societies were probably dominated by young clerks and professionals and others of middling ranks with the requisite skills and an inclination to make contacts, acquire knowledge, and practise their public speaking.[60]

Bringing this group together, debating societies refused to recognize distinctions of religion, politics, nationality, or occupation. Article 4 of the Literary Society of York of 1820 expressed relative openness by declaring that 'any Gentleman is eligible to a seat.' The demise of Toronto's Shakespeare Club, catering mostly to professionals and businessmen, reveals the potential conflict between such declarations and balloting for members. In February 1836, sufficient black balls were cast to exclude John Godfrey Spragge, a former pupil of John Strachan who had articled with prominent members of the bar before establishing his own practice.[61] The majority of members immediately agreed to dissolve the club. According to one, 'no gentleman would allow himself to be proposed as a Member, when he found that the respectability and talents of Mr. Spragge were insufficient to secure him from the insult of being rejected.' Election was not a barometer of popularity, but recognition of 'respectability and talents.' Failure to recognize was an insult. A week later the disbanded Shakespeare Club reconstituted itself as the Toronto Literary Club.[62]

Harmony was not, however, so easily purchased. Another 'stormy discussion' over membership erupted the following April, and when the relevant minutes were re-examined, a second 'very stormy discussion and rather a personal one in some instances' ensued, although 'it all terminated peaceably.' A new constitution bore the scars, stipulating that

---

59 Bryan D. Palmer, 'Kingston Mechanics and the Rise of the Penitentiary, 1833–1836,' *Histoire sociale – Social History* 13, no. 25 (May 1980), 29–32

60 For similar American societies, see Richard D. Brown, *The Strength of a People: The Idea of an Informed Citizenry in America, 1650–1826* (Chapel Hill: University of North Carolina Press 1996), 105, 122, 127–8 and Ryan, *Cradle of the Middle Class,* 128–30. See Cecilia Morgan, *Public Men and Virtuous Women: The Gendered Languages of Religion and Politics in Upper Canada, 1791–1850* (Toronto: University of Toronto Press 1996), 153–6, 215–7, for discussions of the perils facing young bachelors and the role of voluntary associations in protecting them.

61 Brian H. Morrison, 'Spragge, John Godfrey,' *Dictionary of Canadian Biography,* 11 (Toronto: University of Toronto Press 1982), 845–6

62 Toronto Reference Library, Baldwin Room, Henry Rowsell's Toronto Journal, 1, 8, and 9 Feb. 1836

minutes not record the name of a proposed member who had been black-balled and that any discussion of such a rejection be ruled out of order.[63] Even in a controlled environment among the genteel, damaging breeches in decorum and civility occurred. Separating positive intellectual controversy from destructive social discord – a central task of voluntary associations – was never complete although, in this case, the difficulty appears to have been limited to questions of membership, rather than those for formal debate.

Most other debating societies of the 1830s had even more imprecise rules of eligibility and broader membership than the Shakespeare Club. For the Western District Literary, Philosophical and Agricultural Association, 'the only qualification necessary in a candidate is a love of knowledge.'[64] 'Good moral character' was the only qualification for the Kingston Young Men's Society.[65] Its York counterpart had no subscription fee, accepting anonymous donations from members instead. (Without a monetary barrier to entry, it placed the severest limits on debate. Encouraging the reading and writing of essays on moral and religious topics, the York society gave 'free scope for every member to make remarks on the subject,' but prohibited 'all criticism and controversy' to avoid silencing its most diffident members.[66]) More typical, with a annual fee of 10s, disposition and self-confidence were probably greater hurdles to joining the Hamilton Literary Society than money for those above the means of the propertyless or labourers.[67]

Sex was another barrier. The constitution of the York Young Men's Society limited membership to 'young men under the age of thirty-five.'[68] At least one woman submitted work to the Quebec Literary and Historical Society, but when its proceedings were published, a commentator focused more on her ability to influence the morals of male members than on her contribution to knowledge: 'The labours of Mrs. Sheppard we very much admire; and who would not admire those of a

---

63 Ibid., 11 and 18 Apr. 1836 and Archives of Ontario, MU2107, Miscellaneous Collection, 1837, #2, 'Laws of the Toronto Literary Club, Oct. 2, 1837'
64 *By-Laws of the Western District Literary*, 6. Did this mean that women could be full members?
65 *Upper Canada Herald*, 20 Nov. 1833
66 *Christian Guardian*, 11 Jan. 1832
67 *Constitution and Laws of the Hamilton Literary Society*
68 *Canadian Freeman*, 3 Nov. 1831. By the end of the year it had raised the age limit to 40; *Christian Guardian*, 11 Jan. 1832. For this society's other activities, see Morgan, *Public Men and Virtuous Women*, 155–6.

lady in the cause of science. – It is principally to female virtue and benevolence that general society owes its main and best support.'[69] No women made the published list of officers of Upper Canada's debating societies. Most often, they were probably excluded from equal membership, but were occasionally invited to lectures and similar activities. The constitution of the York Literary and Philosophical Society created two categories of affiliation: 'members' who governed the society and could read papers or give lectures and 'subscribers' who could watch. 'Ladies' could either subscribe or attend lectures and readings as guests of male members. This may have represented the pinnacle of formal recognition by these debating societies, but women were still not equal members.[70] The British 'pattern of active membership for men combined with passive consumption for women' held in Upper Canada.[71] Excluded from professions like the law and not full participants in politics, women were thought in less need of what debating societies had to offer. No matter how educated, informed, accomplished as authors, or versed in the art of conversation individual women were acknowledged to be, their reading, writing, and conversing were not to extend equally to these new manifestations of associational life. Women may have been ideally suited to influence male behaviour, but men sought non-domestic spaces to practise behaviour conforming to the norms of the public sphere.

Whatever their precise composition, most debating societies were explicitly designed to export those norms beyond the already prominent. They were also collective vehicles for enlightenment through discussion. In the preamble to their constitution, members of the Kingston Literary Society declared that, 'being aware of the advantages which result from the interchange of thought,' they associated for 'mutual information.'[72] Knowledge was to be diffused through associations of '*mutual instruction*' or 'mutual improvement,'[73] not by passively taking in received wisdom or revealed truth from social superiors. This emphasis on mutuality and the cooperative nature of enlightenment incorporated a further dimension of equality. Knowledge and education were the great social equalizers: 'A person of cultivated mind to a very great

69 Communicated, *Kingston Chronicle,* 5 Dec. 1829
70 *Laws for … the York Literary and Philosophical Society,* 5–8
71 Davidoff and Hall, *Family Fortunes,* 292 and quotation at 444
72 *The British Whig,* 10 Feb. 1836
73 *By-laws of the Western District Literary,* 3, 5, 14 and *The Canadian Casket,* 12 Nov. 1831

degree, is rendered independent of circumstances.'[74] The ability to reason in public was a standard independent of money and occupation that
no adverse financial fortune could obliterate.

Like other advocates, the *Christian Guardian* saw the benefits of
'young men, associated for intellectual criticism and improvement'
extending beyond personal growth and career advancement to encompass politics. Debating societies 'are very important, especially in a free
country. They are schools of reason, where the human mind is cultivated and expounded, and men taught to arrange their ideas, and to
speak in public ... and, above all, where men are learned [*sic*] to govern
their passions – without which no man can reason. One may *passionate*
or *opinionate*, but without cool and deliberate reflection, men seldom
compare things correctly; and reasoning is simply a comparison of
proved, self-evident or acknowledged facts.' 'Common people' would
learn to formulate and express their own ideas, not only on 'private concerns' but on public issues. 'We should then see, after a while respectable farmers and mechanics, qualified to fill every station in the
Country.' With the help of debating societies, they would acquire the
information and self-confidence necessary to participate effectively in
public debate with merchants and professionals.

Debating societies were so important because only in the company of
others could reasoning, the construction of an argument, public speaking, and disciplining the passions be taught and practised. Debating
societies countered the temptation to resort to ridicule, abuse, or personality because 'to trifle or jest, in reply to serious or just argument,
evinces want of decency, and a lack of sense, as well as a deficiency of
argument.' Likewise, the members of the Toronto Literary Club were
told to avoid 'declamation and personal sarcasm or invective ... On the
other hand, a display of legal knowledge, or of sound political opinion,
made in a frank, high-toned and benevolent temper, with courtesy and
good will towards an opponent, is sure to win the approbation of all
who[se] approbation is worth possession.' Debating societies maintained 'urbanity and good feeling' and fostered 'a noble spirit of emulation' while pursuing knowledge through the conflict of arguments.[75] By

---

74 A Friend, *Upper Canada Herald*, 12 June 1838
75 'Philosophical and Debating Societies,' *Christian Guardian*, 13 Mar. 1833, 'Address to
   the Members of the Toronto Literary Club delivered at the opening of the Institution
   by a Gentleman of that City,' *Cobourg Star*, 7 Feb. 1838, and A.N., *Cobourg Star*, 20 Sept.
   1837

internalizing these norms, participants learned the self-control necessary to participate effectively in public debate. Politeness was repeatedly
distinguished from vulgarity, but by diffusing competence in the
former, debating societies contributed to the process whereby the once
clear 'sociological resonance' of such terms 'became vaguer allusions to
cultural styles.'[76] The ability to reason effectively in public no longer distinguished the few from the many.

'A Friend' of the Kingston Young Men's Society reiterated many of
these themes. Only in formal debate – only when 'opposed by argument' – did the mind develop. Furthermore, 'controversy is the very life
of the intellectual world. It is often [by] the most vigorous controversial
struggles, after conflicting efforts, that Truth now takes such a formidable, and victorious position.' This epistemological point was crucial to
the notion that rational discussion was the best form of decision-
making. The process of debate educated its participants, but, more
important, it advanced the cause of truth. The outcome of that process
'has been the powerful and successful instrument of banishing many
debasing and superstitious practices, in every region enlightened by its
diffusion.' Participation in this noble project 'excludes neither sect nor
party, it regards not strength of intellect or poverty of genius, nor yet
worldly circumstances.' The only requirement was the moral character
and discipline to pursue its objects. 'The sociabilities created and cultivated by the exercise of such institutions' were an additional benefit.
Members made friends and came together as equal seekers of the public
good. 'Here party is annihilated, bigotry receives a deadly wound, distinctions are forgotten, selfishness is crushed in the bud of life, and the
heart is taught to expand in the most liberal exercises.'[77] Here was the
idealized public sphere.

The political significance of debating societies thus lay more in their
guiding principles and in the skills and sociability they fostered than in
the content of their meetings. Since most brought together men from
various religious and partisan affiliations, denominational and political
controversy was shunned and, in most cases, prohibited. Societies provided a haven from the less-controlled debate of public politics, but as
training grounds their political role was undiminished.

Yet overtly political topics were, on occasion, debated. On Christmas

---

76 Kenneth Cmiel, *Democratic Eloquence: The Fight over Popular Speech in Nineteenth-Century
    America* (New York: William Morrow 1990), 15
77 A Friend, *Upper Canada Herald*, 12 June 1838

Eve, 1833, the Hallowell Lyceum tackled a question frequently before the assembly: 'Ought the present system of imprisonment for debt to be abolished?' The Perth Debating Society devoted one of its weekly meetings in November 1835 to 'whether the Union of the upper and lower Provinces would be beneficial or injurious to the former.'[78] More frequently, debating questions concerned comparative history, ethics, philosophy, political economy, and literature. While the content of these debates is unknown, participants likely exchanged opinions and information of broad political relevance. In 1837, the Kingston Young Men's Society debated 'Whether is Commerce or Agriculture to be most highly prized in the present state of the Provinces.' The debate was probably not immune to the partisan explanations prevalent outside the Society for the colony's economic distress or without reference to several prominent reform grievances, including the government's land policies and support for the Welland canal. Likewise, the society's debate, 'Whether has the Science of Navigation or the Art of Printing been more beneficial to mankind,' was undoubtedly informed by participants' experience with printing in Upper Canada, dominated as it was by fiercely partisan newspapers. Even an innocuous-looking question like 'Was Wellington or Bonaparte the greater Man' probably strayed from personal character and military strategy to their political, legal, and constitutional contribution to Britain and France.[79] Political discussion might also erupt on seemingly unrelated topics. A lecture to the Toronto Literary Society in 1843 on the thought of the Greek orator and statesman Demosthenes sparked a heated debate on the merits of church establishment in Upper Canada.[80]

Debating societies were microcosms of the public sphere and as such they met with sporadic opposition. While their advocates were clear that the diffusion of the information, skills, and norms of public debate to the hitherto silenced required discipline and regulation, a few remained uncomfortable with the idea of unsupervised non-specialists, mostly young men, discussing broad issues. They feared that there was more diffusion than discipline. Rev. John Barry, for instance, worried that the Young Men's Societies 'were nothing but nurseries of infidelity

---

78 *Hallowell Free Press*, 23 Dec. 1833 and *Bathurst Courier*, 20 Nov. 1835

79 Another question, 'Are the works of Nature sufficient, without the assistance of Revelation, to prove the existence of a Supreme Being,' must have raised a few clerical eyebrows. For the questions see *Chronicle & Gazette*, 15, 29 Apr., 5 May, and 2, 12 Aug. 1837.

80 Oliver to John Mowat, 7 Mar. 1843, in '"Neither Radical Nor Tory Nor Whig,"' 125

and Atheism,' while the *British Whig* ridiculed the notion that young men could compare Bonaparte and Wellington with profit.[81] These were isolated voices. In how they were organized, in the skills they fostered, and in the information they exchanged, debating societies made an important contribution to the credibility of the public sphere. With explicit and implicit qualifications for membership and rules of behaviour, debating societies attempted to control controversy and thereby demonstrate its utility and extend its social reach.

Mechanics' institutes and agricultural societies were also designed to instruct and inform. Despite catering to different needs, debating societies, mechanics' institutes, and agricultural societies were part of the same culture of improvement, drawing from what contemporaries saw as a unified body of knowledge.[82] Membership in the young men's societies and mechanics' institutes probably overlapped, although one contemporary thought the latter better suited to 'those who are more in need of instruction than to think of debating the parallels of latitude, [the relationship] one vice or one virtue bears to another, or one event or another, &c.'[83] Rather than promoting debate among equals, most mechanics' institutes and agricultural societies sought to transmit knowledge and values from those who claimed to possess them to those they claimed were in need of them. Individuals were to come together for mutual benefit and to acquire knowledge, but information was to flow vertically rather than horizontally. Thus, these organizations were often fostered by the locally prominent, who were eager to bolster their claims to enlightened, benevolent leadership. Their superior status would be acknowledged in their roles as patron, association official, and instructor. They were the ones to be emulated.

Most local elites, however, were divided and many such associations were caught in that division. More conservative elements, in particular, were torn between their support for such improving associations and their fear of thereby empowering too broad a segment of the popula-

---

81 Barry, *Colonial Advocate*, 11 Apr. 1833 and *British Whig*, 17 May and 16 June 1837. The latter smells of sour grapes, as its author had supported the Kingston Literary Society, which had been unable to compete with the Young Men's Society. Unexplained opposition also met its Hallowell counterpart. It relocated its meetings after disruptions caused by someone beating a drum outside. *Hallowell Free Press*, 5 May 1834

82 Patrick Joyce, *Democratic Subjects: The Self and the Social in Nineteenth-Century England* (Cambridge: Cambridge University Press 1994), 166–8

83 Some Body, *Chronicle & Gazette*, 1 Mar. 1834

tion. On the one hand, they saw their own privileged positions as having been earned by merit. Others were thought rational enough to emulate them, thereby reaffirming existing social and political hierarchies. On the other hand, if farmers and mechanics were rational enough to recognize merit and act in their own self-interest, perhaps they were also capable of organizing voluntary associations and the flow of knowledge along more democratic lines. Conservatives wanted to spread 'useful' knowledge and a belief in rational, disciplined behaviour, but often feared the political implications of popular organizations, widespread and unregulated reading, and the habit of enquiry – especially when encouraged by reformers.

The colony's first agricultural society was established by 1793 at Newark under the patronage of Lieutenant-Governor Simcoe.[84] 'It is not to be supposed,' conceded a traveller, 'that in such a settlement, many essays would be produced on the theory of good farming, or that much time would be taken up with deep deliberation,' but monthly meetings at the Masonic Hall afforded valuable occasions for 'chatting in parties after dinner on the state of crops, tillage, etc.'[85] These sociable gatherings were followed in 1806 by meetings of the Upper Canada Agricultural and Commercial Society, acting largely as a cover for opposition to Lieutenant-Governor Francis Gore.[86] The original, somewhat obscure, Agricultural Society of Niagara stood by authority; it offered Gore honourary membership and resolved to purchase and circulate a hundred copies of a pamphlet defending his administration.[87]

Enmeshed in colonial politics from the beginning, it is not surprising that agricultural societies reappeared with renewed political opposition.

---

84 The following account is indebted to E.A. Heaman, *The Inglorious Arts of Peace: Exhibitions in Canadian Society during the Nineteenth Century* (Toronto: University of Toronto Press 1999), 35, 44–51, but see also Foster Vernon, 'The Development of Adult Education in Ontario, 1790–1900,' D.Ed. thesis, University of Toronto 1969, chap. 3 and J.J. Talman, 'Agricultural Societies in Upper Canada,' Ontario Historical Society *Papers and Records* 27 (1931), 545–52.

85 In Vernon, 'Adult Education,' 28

86 One of these critics, John Thorpe, was thanked 'for his laudable zeal in establishing this society' at its February 1806 meeting. See also the pamphlet of another critic, Jackson, *View of the Political Situation*, app. 20 and *Upper Canada Gazette*, 15 Feb. 1806 and 6 Jan. 1808.

87 Falkland, *Kingston Gazette*, 18 Dec. 1810 and, on these two societies, Ross D. Fair, 'Gentlemen, Farmers, and Gentlemen-Half-Farmers: The Development of Agricultural Societies in Upper Canada, 1792–1808,' unpublished paper, Canadian Historical Association 1998

A meeting of 'several Magistrates and other gentlemen' in December 1818 established the Agricultural Society of Upper Canada, with Lieutenant-Governor Maitland as patron. The society and its affiliates across the province would instruct farmers in the best and latest techniques, not by reading essays or debating questions, but by awarding prizes and premiums – marks of honour from social superiors that would 'create competition and emulation' among farmers. The society's constitution was similar to that of most voluntary associations, except that potential members had to be approved by its officers. This vetting process and the active support of such prominent officials as Rev. John Strachan reflected Robert Gourlay's anti-government campaigning. The *Kingston Chronicle* was explicit about the political intent: 'These Societies, while they tend to diffuse general information on agricultural subjects, must naturally excite a spirit of emulation and enterprise among the farmers and [demonstrate] how much depends upon them for promoting the general prosperity of this new country and their own advantage at the same time. Thus discontent would soon cease – imaginary grievances would no longer be heard of.' Economic rationality, promoted by competition for prizes, would underwrite political stability. By the following year, there were similar, mostly short-lived, societies in several districts.[88]

The formation of agricultural societies received considerable impetus from the offer of a public subsidy in 1830. Sponsoring the idea in the assembly, Charles Fothergill argued that agricultural societies furthered public ends – 'they bring together people from different parts; and the various means of promoting the grand objects of the whole are made known to all.' Some wanted to stipulate rules for their internal government, but James Lyons, the member for Northumberland, prevailed, arguing that 'the prosperity of all societies and institutions depended on their being established on liberal principles, and if we wished the agricultural societies to be successful, they must be untrammelled.'[89] In this context, 'liberal' meant self-governing organizations of open and voluntary membership electing their own officers 'untrammelled' by state control.

Liberal or otherwise, the political implications of such associations were self-evident to Brockville's newspapers. To take advantage of the

---

88 For the constitution see *Kingston Chronicle*, 1 Jan. 1819, for its justification, 8 Jan., for the existence of other societies, 28 May 1819 and for their failure, 11 Oct. 1822.

89 *Colonial Advocate*, 21 Jan. 1830. According to Heaman, *Inglorious Arts of Peace*, 45, ten societies applied for grant within a year.

public subsidy, the sheriff had called a public meeting to establish a district agricultural society. According to the reform *Brockville Recorder*, 'various gentlemen and *two farmers* attended, and formed resolutions, entered into a subscription, appointed officers, &c. It now only remains for the Farmers to enter and humbly compete for the prizes under these great men and all will be complete.' To reformers, such proceedings reflected all that was wrong with the colony: 'A certain set of men must manage all public matters their own way or they will withdraw their support ... while a no less respectable and worthy class ... [who] see that they can have no chance of enjoying equal privileges, quietly attend their private occupations.' Denied equality, farmers withdrew.

The conservative *Brockville Gazette* did not dispute its rival's account of the public meeting. Rather, it accused the *Recorder* of 'attempting to create a popular excitement' by suggesting that agricultural societies should be 'under the management of such persons as least understand the subject.' The *Recorder* had a higher opinion of farmers, but the *Gazette* countered that, given the nature of the colony's economy, all Upper Canadians had a vital interest in agriculture. It followed that the *Recorder*'s concern for 'the rank of farmers in society' was 'as remote from the possibility of rational definition as the revolutionary cant of "the Sovereignty of the people."' Both slogans rejected hierarchy. In an agricultural society, as in society as a whole, egalitarianism 'has a tendency to crush that noble emulation by which in countries where honours are not hereditary[,] individuals ever do acquire rank. – Rank among us means distinction, either conferred by authority, or admitted by common consent, where there is either positive or implied merit, and it is but a bad compliment to the profession in general, and such as none other would be proud of, to suppose that the best and the worst are on the same footing in society.'[90] More was at stake here than who coordinated the local fair. According to the *Gazette*, voluntary associations were safe only insofar as they reflected and thus reinforced broader hierarchies. Of course, it assumed that the gentlemen and government officers attempting to dominate the agricultural society were, by definition, the most able to organize community life and the most worthy of emulation. It was an assumption the *Recorder* was sure to reject.

The formation of an agricultural society for the Home District was

90 *Brockville Recorder*, 18 and 25 May, *Brockville Gazette*, 14 May and 4 June 1830

also contentious, but elsewhere the process was supported by conservatives and reformers alike.[91] Contests over structure and control were not simply bitter personal or political feuds spilling over into voluntary associations. First, as gathering places for individuals to discuss issues of rural economy and to pursue common interests in improved farming and better roads, agricultural societies were widely acknowledged as political entities. Second, even where the already prominent were in control, they mingled with farmers of various backgrounds and operated according to formal constitutions that stipulated equality of members, election of officers, and majority rule. For instance, the Western District Agricultural and Horticultural Society, billed as a patriotic, cooperative venture, was open to 'all Landholders and other residents in the District.' The contribution of women and children to the farm economy was at least partially acknowledged by awarding prizes for kitchen gardens and domestic manufactures and by explicitly welcoming female competitors in horticultural exhibitions.[92]

Several societies also included provisions for libraries and planned to award prizes for essays, reports, and meteorological diaries. Major Lachlan, president of the Western District Society, insisted that these prizes were intended for 'practical Farmers.' Although their grammar might need correcting, farmers were 'far more correct and able observers' than 'mere writers.' The widespread acceptance of the inductive and experimental method meant that significant contributions to knowledge could be made by humble, autodidactic farmers and artisans. Two of the many benefits of agricultural societies enumerated by Lachlan further underlined their potential as schools for the political public. First, they led 'to more frequent discussions and interchange of opinions ... and the consequent unavoidable acquisition of additional information and experience.' Second, 'the increased and expanded congenial feelings' produced by such associations 'naturally tend to

---

91 Heaman, *Inglorious Arts of Peace*, 20, 46–8, 81. William Lyon Mackenzie tried to form the Home District society but his detractors called a rival meeting. Their provisional list of officers was dominated by government officials. Finding farmers to attend proved more difficult. When Mackenzie objected to the society's constitution, he was thrown out of the meeting for not being a subscriber. For conflicting accounts, see *Courier of Upper Canada*, June 1830 [date torn], *Colonial Advocate*, 8 July 1830, and O'Brien, *Journals*, 98–9, 122–4, 135, 141–2.

92 [Lachlan], *Address of the Directing President*, 6, 13. On exhibitions both reinforcing and subverting gender stereotypes see Heaman, *Inglorious Arts of Peace*, chap. 9 and, for an earlier example of prizes for domestic manufactures, 265.

draw closer the bonds of *social intercourse* among the inhabitants,' irrespective of petty interests or jealousies.[93]

York's mechanics' institute was founded in 1830, the same year as its district agricultural society. Kingston (1834), Cobourg (1834–5?), London (1835), Woodstock (1835), Brantford (1836), Hamilton (1839) and Niagara (1839) followed. By 1850 there were at least twenty-four mechanics' institutes in the province offering lectures, evening classes, libraries, and reading rooms.[94] As with agricultural societies, the emphasis was on 'exciting to mental cultivation by the pursuit of useful knowledge ... in a manner becoming rational beings.'[95]

A year before the founding of the colony's first institute, William Lyon Mackenzie waxed nostalgic about the democratic sociability he had experienced in a Scottish one: 'Imagine a society of 70 or 80 persons of all ages from 15 to 75, of all ranks, from the apprentice mechanic with his leather apron, up to the city bailie or parish minister with his powdered toupee, met together on an entire equality in a large hall full of books and papers, scientific apparatus, chemical tests, models of machinery, etc., etc., to give and receive valuable information.' It was an image Mackenzie thought frightened the prominent. 'Despising the great body of the Canadian people,' they preferred 'governing an ignorant and bigotted mob' to promoting voluntary associations that would 'delight, instruct and elevate' and thereby encourage social mobility based on merit.[96] Heather Murray concludes that 'Mackenzie was driven as much by faith in the power of the Word as a belief in popular government.'[97] One might go further; Mackenzie thought the two inseparable. Popular self-government flowed naturally from an informed, rational public. Like newspapers, voluntary associations diffused the knowledge and sociability required by that public. Without them, popular government would be anarchy. With them, it was as safe as it was inevitable.

Promoters of a mechanics' institute at Kingston shared the goal of dif-

93 [Lachlan], *Address of the Directing President*, 20–1. For other planned libraries and prizes for essays or reports, see *Constitution of the Midland District Agricultural Society*, 5–7 and Tallam, 'Agricultural Societies,' 548–9.

94 Vernon, 'Adult Education,' 259–61

95 Archives of Ontario, York Mechanics' Institute Papers, report of the Secretaries, 5 Mar. 1832

96 *Colonial Advocate*, 1 Oct. 1829 and 12 July 1827. See also Heather Murray, 'Frozen Pen, Fiery Print, and Fothergill's Folly: Cultural Organization in Toronto, Winter 1836–37,' *Essays in Canadian Writing* no. 61 (Spring 1997), 53.

97 Murray, 'Frozen Pen,' 55

fusing knowledge and democratic sociability. Aware that 'some persons were apprehensive that the Mechanics' Institute would become an arena of political strife,' the *Upper Canadian Herald* assured its readers that it would 'form a neutral ground where all parties may peaceably meet to hold high converse with the mighty dead or the illustrious living' (oddly ignoring conversations they might have with each other). A letter to another Kingston newspaper had already called on mechanics to form an affordable institute, 'embracing the society of every individual' interested in mental culture. There 'he shall hear or be heard ... he shall hear all communications received from other members read, and any he shall have to produce received with pleasure.' A journal might also be published 'embracing instruction in way of their occupation, to every class, from the statesman to the farmer and mechanic; and that unsoured by the thread-bare jargon of politics, and the invectives of contentious sectarians, which so much mar the harmony of society in general.'[98] There was a unity and harmony in knowledge and its pursuit that had yet to manifest itself in Upper Canada.

Mechanics' institutes would change all that. In his 1832 address to the York institute, William Dunlop asked, 'Why do nations and empire fall?' His answer seemed tailor-made for the audience. Ancient polities had fallen 'because though great in the Arts and Sciences, their knowledge was not diffused through the body of society, but confined rigorously to a part of it.' England's continued greatness rested on the reinforcing motors of commerce, the mechanical arts, and knowledge, each priming the other two. Maintaining greatness, diffusing knowledge and creating a heathy social structure were all of a piece. Commerce and manufacturing 'establish a middle order in society, which forms a communicating link between the highest and the lowest: and one rank, shading imperceptibly into another, permits a common sympathy to pervade the whole ... Every man must have an interest in the common good; for though only a part of the community can possess property and be men of rank and of influence, yet, every man sees that the door is open to him to possess these distinctions, and every man feels anxious to promote the good of the community.'[99] The old class structure of the educated few arrayed against the ignorant many had been destroyed. It was replaced less by a new class structure than by an open meritocracy.

98 *Upper Canada Herald*, 9 Apr. and Some Body, *Chronicle & Gazette,* 1 Mar. 1834
99 Dunlop, *Address Delivered to the York Mechanics' Institution*, 3, 6–7 and *Christian Guardian,* 21 Mar. 1832

Little wonder that reformers and merchants, shopkeepers and small manufacturers, professionals and clerks, and aspiring mechanics and the self-made were drawn to the institute. The diffusion of knowledge and commerce blasted social and political barriers, replacing exclusionary castes with equality of opportunity. Society, like mechanics' institutes, was to be divided by merit but united in the pursuit of knowledge and the collective good.

Lectures, like Dunlop's, were the primary tool of instruction.[100] Although scientific and practical subjects predominated, 'On the Improvement of the Mind' was another favoured theme.[101] By 1834, the York institute claimed 140 members, held regular lectures (16 during the winter of 1833–4), planned an evening reading room to increase access to its library (containing 46 volumes in 1832; 370 in 1836), and organized drawing and conversation classes. The last were a sort of study group. As one annual report put it, 'Intricate or difficult problems may be solved, and the important truths of the arts and sciences rendered intelligible to all, with less danger of error than in private study or even public lectures.'[102] The pursuit of knowledge was a social enterprise as well as a social good, but, unsupervised, it was fraught with 'danger.' As well, not all lecture topics were deemed safe, and, if the Halifax Mechanics' Institute is any indication, considerable energy was expended in trying (often without success) to maintain decorum, limit discussion to points of information, and treat the audience more as passive consumers than active participants.[103]

Aspirations frequently outpaced finances. Many classes were under-subscribed or short-lived. Of the 140 members of the York institute in 1834, how many regularly attended its events? Their social profile is also

---

100 The number of public lectures organized by voluntary associations or subscription increased noticeably in leading towns during the 1830s. For later American developments, see Donald M. Scott, 'The Popular Lecture and the Creation of a Public in Mid-Nineteenth-Century America,' *Journal of American History* 66, no. 4 (March 1980), 791–809.

101 *Chronicle & Gazette*, 22 Nov. 1834 and Vernon, 'Adult Education,' 245

102 3rd Annual Report, *Chronicle & Gazette*, 8 Mar. 1834, Vernon, 'Adult Education,' 267–9, 282, 296–8, and James Lesslie's diary, in *Town of York ... Further Collection*, 335–7

103 In 1848 A.A. Riddel was not allowed to lecture to the Toronto institute on 'The Rights of Labour,' although in 1842–3, Rev. D. Rintoul had given a series on political economy. Heaman, *Inglorious Arts of Peace*, 330n and Patrick Keane, 'A Study in Early Problems and Policies of Adult Education: The Halifax Mechanics' Institute,' *Histoire sociale – Social History* 8, no. 16 (November 1975), 263–7

unclear. Prominent and influential figures dominated the institute's elective offices, although several of the fifty-six charter members were tailors and carpenters. Both trades were also represented on the first Committee of Management. Few proprietors or petty producers would have found its five shillings annual subscription prohibitive.[104] A local editor claimed that members of Cobourg's institute were 'nearly all operative Mechanics,' while a Kingston promoter appealed to 'Journeymen Mechanics' on the grounds that 'boarding houses are generally too crowded for allowing the freedom required in stocking the mind.' The constitution of the Kingston institute stipulated that mechanics had to constitute two-thirds of the managing committee, lending credence to reports that the founding meeting of three to four hundred was made up of a 'most high respectable body of mechanics, interspersed with some few of the inhabitants of Kingston.'[105]

As instructional and improving associations reaching beyond the genteel, mechanics' institutes were caught in many of the same political tensions as agricultural societies. James Lesslie, a founder of the York institute, echoed William Lyon Mackenzie when he recorded in his diary that the institute 'is viewed with suspicion by some of our Gentry & some of its professed & warmest friends seem to be influenced by them. – The intelligence of the lower Classes they and their system would if possible keep under – their *Lord and Slave System* is not to be grafted upon the people of U.C. and their favorite maxim "Ignorance is Bliss" ... shows clearly from which their opposition to the dissemination of knowledge arises.'[106] Some of that suspicion reflected reformers' prominence in the institute and support for a more genteel alternative, the York Literary and Philosophical Society. The level of suspicion should not, however, be exaggerated. Both the receiver-general, John H. Dunn, and Lieutenant-Governor Colbourne served as patrons of the York institute and 'establishment figures' like Dr Dunlop and James FitzGibbon were among its earliest enthusiasts.[107]

It was common reform rhetoric that conservatives opposed popular

---

104 Names are provided by Vernon, 'Adult Education,' 182–3, although his analysis is somewhat misleading. For the subscription fee, see Swift, *A New Almanack*, 11.

105 On the Cobourg Mechanics' Institute see *Reformer*, 13 Oct. 1835, for the appeal to journeymen, Some Body, *Chronicle & Gazette*, 1 Mar. 1834, for the constitution and attendance at Kingston, *Chronicle & Gazette*, 15 Mar. and 19 Apr. 1834, and for a report of the preliminary meeting, *British Whig*, 11 Mar. 1834.

106 Lesslie, in *Town of York ... Further Collection*, 335

107 Murray, 'Frozen Pen,' 54. At Kingston and Cobourg, conservatives and reformers

education because the constitutional and social status quo required an ignorant populace. This caricatured the tension conservatives felt between their desire to instruct and their fear that, without proper controls, instruction might consist of pernicious doctrines or lead people to value their abilities and opinions too highly. One worried that 'the facilities which the present day affords of disseminating any set of opinions,' especially mechanics' institutes, lectures, and libraries, 'place the great body of the people open to the attacks of mistaken zeal, ill directed talent and ambitious policy.' Referring to the 'universal diffusion of knowledge,' this conservative insisted that 'without proper checks we believe it a dangerous principle as it leads to serious consequences, both to the individual and the state.'[108] Reformers, like Mackenzie and Lesslie, were more optimistic since they welcomed such consequences, but they too saw the need for 'proper checks.' Disseminating information and democratic sociability was impossible without self-discipline and the internalized norms to distinguish knowledge from ignorance and 'improving' from 'vicious' uses of scarce money and leisure. The choice between conservatives and reformers was not between control and dissemination. It was already about who would control that dissemination and for what ends. Pointing to the new mechanics' institutes as evidence, the staunchly conservative *Cobourg Star* observed 'that there is a thirst for knowledge among the people, and it should be encouraged by their rulers.'[109] What had been a reform claim was fast becoming a platitude.

Over the next few decades conservatives, as well as reformers, discovered just how essential the existence of individuals capable of rational deliberation was to good government. In 1866, the *Toronto Leader* underlined the connection between mechanics' institutes and the status of public opinion: 'Class education was a very excusable thing when the work of government and the guidance of public opinion were supposed to be the privileges of a class; but the inevitable tendency of social and political power to the masses, the confusion and intermixture of ranks ... warns us that if we would preserve the State in its integrity, we must as liberally and as fast as we can educate to the highest point every member of the state.'[110] Previously, conservatives had been wary of the claims of

---

jointly supported mechanics' institutes, although control of the former appears to have been contested. See Palmer, 'Kingston Mechanics,' 26–7.

108 W.C., 'On a Taste for Reading,' *Cobourg Star*, 30 June 1841
109 *Cobourg Star*, 14 Dec. 1836
110 *Leader*, 9 Oct. 1866 in Heaman, *Inglorious Arts of Peace*, 19

public opinion and of voluntary associations that had lent credence to them by confusing social ranks and by diffusing information and the ability to reason in public. Once such claims could no longer be denied, the task at hand was to ensure that public opinion was as informed and rational as possible.

Not all voluntary associations had such obvious ties to democratic sociability as Freemasonry, literary and debating clubs, agricultural societies, libraries, mechanics' institutes, and newsrooms (discussed in the next chapter). Some have even been seen to work in contrary directions. For instance, Orange lodges seem to have reinforced divisions between Protestants and Roman Catholics, especially with the violent confrontations that could accompany Orange parades commemorating the Battle of the Boyne. Yet the lodges, originally modelled on Freemasonry, exhibited many of the characteristics of other associations. Like their counterparts in New Brunswick, they drew members from across occupational, ethnic, and denominational lines. Moreover, they were mini-republics where, as Gregory Kealey points out, they 'trained their members in parliamentary procedure and taught them how to conduct and lead meetings.' Moreover, the extent to which sectarian divisions were reinforced during the 1830s, before there was a sizeable Catholic 'threat,' requires further study. Relations with Upper Canadian Catholics (as opposed to Catholicism or the papacy) were far from straightforward, especially when Orange lodges and prominent Catholics found themselves on the same political side before the rebellion.[111]

National societies might also appear divisive. Contemporaries made

111 Scott W. See, *Riots in New Brunswick: Orange Nativism and Social Violence in the 1840s* (Toronto: University of Toronto Press 1993), 10, 84, 89–105 and Gregory S. Kealey, *Toronto Workers Respond to Industrial Capitalism, 1867–1892* (Toronto: University of Toronto Press 1980), 121. For social composition, see Gregory S. Kealey, 'The Orange Order in Toronto: Religious Riot and the Working Class,' in Kealey and Peter Warrian, eds., *Essays in Canadian Working Class History* (Toronto: McClelland and Stewart 1976), 18–19. For occupational, religious, and ethnic diversity, see Cecil J. Houston and William J. Smyth, *The Sash Canada Wore: A Historical Geography of the Orange Order in Canada* (Toronto: University of Toronto Press 1980), 35, 84, 95–6, 101 and Hereward Senior, 'The Genesis of Canadian Orangeism,' *Ontario History* 60, no. 2 (June 1968), 26. For Orange politics, see W.B. Kerr, 'When Orange and Green United, 1832–9: The Alliance of Macdonell and Gowan,' Ontario Historical Society *Papers and Proceedings* 34 (1942), 34–42. Lord Durham thought a few Irish Catholics had actually joined the order and noted, correctly, that it both claimed to be tolerant of Catholics and praised the loyalty of Bishop Macdonell. *Lord Durham's Report*, 98

the accusation, but, just as Orangemen and Catholics could coexist, so members of different national societies often manifested goodwill towards each other. Scotsman John Rolph thanked his Irish and English friends for helping celebrate St Andrew's Day at Ancaster in 1833, swelling with 'national pride' that this 'interchange of social sentiment gives birth to a buoyancy of spirit and an expansion of manly and liberal intercourse.' When London mechanics felt slighted by organizers of the local St Andrew's Day dinner in 1840, they called a public meeting to investigate and express their indignation. Given that the meeting was called to resist a challenge to their respectability, it was fitting that they proceeded to elect officers to re-establish the London Mechanics' Institute.[112]

Similarly, many of the benevolent and religious associations that flourished during this period actively tried to bridge denominational boundaries. The Baptist James Lesslie noted in his diary that 'much unanimity & good feeling [was] manifested by the Speakers of all denominations' at a meeting of the Bible society; 'such institutions tend to make Christians more of "one heart & one mind."'[113] In Upper Canada, divided into diverse groups but with a relatively small and dispersed population, most organizations had to reach beyond a single social category or occupation in order to attract sufficient members. The extent to which these Bible, denominational, missionary, Sunday school, and benevolent associations promoted or hindered aspects of democratic sociability deserves study. Only the most politically significant can be examined here.

Temperance societies were among the largest, most controversial, and most socially and geographically diffused associations in Upper Canada. The first was established in 1828 by a Baptist minister in Bastard Township. Within four years there were roughly 100 societies and 10,000 members. Evangelical Protestants, especially Methodists, and reformers were noticeably over-represented. Jesse Ketchum helped establish the Toronto Temperance Society in 1830. Other prominent reformers holding office included Marshall Spring Bidwell, John Rolph, T.C. Morrison,

---

112 *Western Mercury*, 12 Dec. 1833 and *London Examiner* copied in *Canada Inquirer*, 8 Dec. 1840

113 Lesslie, 9 Jan. 1832, in *Town of York ... Further Collection*, 208–10. The York Bible Society's rules read that it 'shall consist of all who are disposed to promote the object of the Institution without regard to differences of religious sentiment.' As well as denominational lines, it also crossed political ones to incorporate office-holders, conservatives, and both moderate and radical reformers. *Loyalist*, 15 Nov. 1828

and James Lesslie. Within a year, the society attracted 252 members with a constitution that declared simply that 'any person may become a member of this society, by subscribing his name to the constitution.'

Jan Noel argues that early temperance was a 'mass movement' although leaders were drawn primarily from 'the broad middle class of preachers and journalists, and doctors, druggists, wholesalers, grocers, shopkeepers, and booksellers.' Incorporating large numbers of women and the young, it 'moved hitherto silent souls to speak.' After its first year, the Young Men's Temperance Society at Toronto claimed 201 members, including 80 women. Only leading Compact figures, those who profited from liquor, and those 'who saw little opportunity for self-advancement whether or not they stayed sober,' were noticeably absent.[114] The movement incorporated both rural and urban areas into an international network of shared aspirations, common tracts, newspapers (including Ketchum's *Temperance Record*), and travelling lecturers.

This network attempted to reorder Upper Canadian society into supporters and opponents of temperance irrespective of several pre-existing fault lines. As the *Canadian Watchman* put it, 'the interest felt in opposing the grand enemy – intemperance – in every form ... banished all invidious distinctions and created a real enjoyment in the exercise of those social and kindly feelings which soothe and allure the mind of men to make common cause in promoting a good object.'[115] Individual responsibility and downplaying social distinctions were also evident in its ideals. As Noel argues, 'The hallmark of the early movement was its insistence that *everyone* take the pledge and cease to deal in the stuff.' It 'blasted immoral profits and comfortable tippling clergy-

---

114 For the constitution of the Toronto Temperance Society, *Christian Guardian*, 27 Feb. 1830, for the membership of the Young Men's Temperance Society, *Guardian*, 12 Mar. 1834, and *Town of York ... Further Collection*, 342n–3n, 347. Jan Noel, *Canada Dry: Temperance Crusades before Confederation* (Toronto: University of Toronto Press 1995), 7–9, 11. See also Ryan, *Cradle of the Middle Class*, 135.

115 *Canadian Watchman*, 7 Jan. 1831, in F.L. Barron, 'The American Origins of the Temperance Movement in Ontario, 1828–1850,' *Canadian Review of American Studies* 11, no. 2 (Fall 1980), 142. Blacks and natives were also incorporated, but without subverting their perceived inferior status. Blacks joined temperance organizations but few were interracial. Where they were, they probably adopted the system at Coldwater – one multiracial society but segregated 'branches' with the leadership generally confined to non-blacks. Natives were also admitted to mission temperance societies, though they were not seen as adults voluntarily banding together, but as 'children' in need of special protection from missionaries and the state. F.L. Barron, 'The Genesis of Temperance in Ontario, 1828–1850,' PhD thesis, University of Guelph 1976, 4, 10–12

men ... In this they attacked the existing social order.' Moreover, temperance sought to motivate and educate individuals to join societies, take the pledge, and work in the collective struggle to remake society. The prime enemies of temperance included ignorance, fashion, and prejudice as well as the misuse of alcohol. More practically, since temperance societies were trying to build a new consensus on a divisive issue, they had to educate their members through the extensive use of printed tracts, newspapers, lectures, and debates.[116]

Many of these themes were brought together at a meeting of the Young Men's Temperance Society in August 1833. Chaired by its president, a carriagemaker, the meeting 'was filled to over flowing by our fellow-citizens of all grades and persuasions, in eager and anxious expectation of hearing our talented and distinguished fellow-citizen (Dr. Rolph) lecture on Intemperance.' His lecture was worthy of remembrance, said the society, 'not only by the friends of Temperance, but by every person who was capable of being delighted by sound reason, founded on facts.'[117] British subjects, divided by social status and religious and other persuasions, could be 'fellow citizens' open to reason and capable of working together.

Heavily influenced by their American counterparts,[118] dominated by Protestant and political dissenters, drawing individuals of diverse status into formal organizations; and attacking the leisure and economic activities of social superiors, temperance societies inevitably drew fire. Col. John Talbot blamed unrest around London on meetings of 'Damned Cold water drinking Societies where they ["rebels"] met at night to communicate their poisonous and seditious schemes to each other.' The conservative *Patriot* referred to temperance societies as 'ingenious inventions of the crafty, for lifting themselves into political power.'[119] Sir Richard Henry Bonnycastle, a military engineer resident in the colony since 1826, made much the same point. 'Obscure individuals ... without the previous acquirement of education, observation and research' achieved a 'pseudo celebrity' in temperance societies. 'Thus you will

---

116 See Noel, *Canada Dry*, 7–11, 59, 62, 84–5, 104–7 and Barron, 'The Genesis of Temperance,' 101–2, 166–8, which notes that a military society at Amhertsburg had its own reading room.

117 *Canadian Correspondent*, August 1833, and annual report, *Christian Guardian*, 12 Mar. 1834, in *Town of York ... Further Collection*, 342–3, 347

118 Barron, 'The American Origins,' 133

119 Talbot, draft speech, 23 Apr. 1832 and *Patriot*, 15 Nov. 1833, in Barron, 'The American Origins,' 141. See also *Kingston Spectator*, 2 July 1835.

find, that political quacks, whose whole dependence and livelihood depend on keeping up a scurrilous, agitating, unprincipled newspaper, are generally the firmest and most untiring temperance advocates.'[120]

Bonnycastle analysed as well as complained. These unworthy agitators

read these pestiferous productions to the wholly uneducated, and make as great merit of politically converting from the habitual dram, as they do from the Catholic, the Scotch, the English, or the Methodist Church; and upon the same reasoning too, because their situation and limited education, assure them they can rise no higher; and they are willing therefore to have a drink and a religion of their own, where neither science nor reason shall sway, any more than birth, the customs of good society, nor education.

By-and-by, comes the re-action; – the drunkard who never read before, reads now a little, and he finds he is just as good a reasoner as his teacher, and quite equal to him as a man; and why should he, forsooth, be controlled?

Bonnycastle's condescension is obvious and his prose difficult, but neither defeat his insight. Those 'whose previous career has convinced the thinking' that they should be excluded from political and social leadership turned to voluntary associations, creating a social space organized on different principles from those of existing hierarchies – a space where, according to Bonnycastle, 'neither science nor reason shall sway, any more than birth, the customs of good society, nor education.' Using this space and armed with newspapers, tracts, and lectures, they threatened to become the primary influence on popular mores and attitudes.

As Bonnycastle saw, the process generated its own dynamic. Once the 'half-educated' 'political quacks' undermined respect for the existing order, their audience felt empowered to go further. Thus 'the drunkard ... reads now ... and he finds he is just as good a reasoner as his teacher, and quite equal to him as a man.' The 'half-educated' attempted to replace existing elites, but their means, voluntary associations and printed texts, could undermine the potential for hierarchy altogether. Bonnycastle did not condemn temperance societies outright, but they ought to avoid politics and religion. Popular drinking habits could be altered by persuading someone that 'his superiors in society can never admit him to a confidence, or a level, if you please,' if he was not tem-

---

120 Bonnycastle, *The Canadas*, v.1, 127–30, 171–2

perate. Preying on the desire for respect from social superiors, such associations would bolster, rather than undermine, hierarchy.

As an active Freemason and having been promoted through the ranks of the British army, Bonnycastle was emphatic that only hierarchies based on merit should be reinforced. He attacked the Family Compact at York as exclusive. Social progress was possible only if 'honours are alike open to all classes of the British people in it, as they are in England, where the poorest man from Upper Canada, if he be a man of high talent, may become lord-chancellor.' Even the least fortunate could be reasoned with and admitted to 'a level' by those who, like Bonnycastle, had earned their superior stations. One might query his analysis of British society, but the principle was clear enough. Bonnycastle articulated an insightful, if exaggerated and prejudiced, view of the process many conservatives feared would result from unregulated agricultural societies or mechanics' institutes. Reformers supported such associations to organize and instruct precisely because they did not believe that existing hierarchies reflected merit.

The establishment of the British Constitutional Society, Political Unions, and the Canadian Alliance Society in the 1830s brought the model of voluntary associations into the political realm. Committees to promote particular causes, nominate parliamentary candidates, or garner signatures for a petition were already common, but more formal associations, especially on a province-wide basis, remained something of a novelty.[121] These political societies resembled contemporary voluntary associations far more than later political parties. They reflected the perceived need for collective over individual action and the inadequacy of both informal mechanisms and existing institutions. 'Party,' like faction, remained a label for one's opponents.

Political associations were formed at public meetings. Constitutions were adopted, subscribers sought, and officers elected. The fifth resolution of the York Constitutional Society could have been taken from

---

121 Hartwell Bowsfield, 'Upper Canada in the 1820's: The Development of Political Consciousness,' PhD thesis, University of Toronto 1976, esp. chaps. 7–8. The following paragraphs are informed by Kathleen Wilson, *The Sense of the People: Politics, Culture and Imperialism in England, 1715–1785* (Cambridge: Cambridge University Press 1995), 65, 69, 336, Morgan, *Public Men and Virtuous Women*, 66, 85–6, and James Vernon, *Politics and the People: A Study in English Political Culture, c. 1815–1867* (Cambridge: Cambridge University Press 1993), 173, 183–4, 205.

numerous other voluntary associations: 'Every male inhabitant of this town of good character, over 21 years of age, without distinction of rank, religion or country, shall be eligible to become a member of this Society, provided he subscribes his assent to the principles and objects on, and for which it is organized.' Women, not full political beings, were excluded, but respectable adult men were to be divided by political principles, not 'rank, religion or country.'[122] Political associations gathered the like-minded together, overriding other divisions.

Partly in response to the Constitutional Society, radicals formed Political Unions modelled on British associations of the same name. One advocate pointed out that while they were political, the Unions remained distinct from the state. They were 'neither more nor less, than a voluntary association of freemen, united for the purpose of mutual intelligence and natural protection.'[123] The constitution of the radical Canadian Alliance Society spelled out twenty-three objectives. As its corresponding secretary, William Lyon Mackenzie, told the editor of the *Brockville Recorder*, 'there is no test reqd than an approbation of the views of the society.' Nineteen rules were also adopted to regulate elections, committees, and speaking at meetings. Inclusion, participation, local self-government, and the election of accountable officers were more easily implemented in political associations than in the state they were meant to influence. Sounding much like a fraternity, the Alliance Society's sixteenth rule stipulated that 'any member of a Branch Society shall be admitted as a brother into every other branch ... by producing a certificate of fellowship.' While political parties were condemned as disruptive, fraternal organizations could bring men together in a community of political interest.[124]

These organizations consciously adopted the model of voluntary associations for overtly political ends. As such, they bore an ambiguous relationship to the theory of mixed monarchy, fixated as it was on legislative institutions and social estates. They helped build extra-parliamentary alliances and implied that political principles could be understood and advanced by every 'inhabitant' or 'freeman' invited to join them. Politics was now within the grasp of members of voluntary associations. It

---

122 *Courier of Upper Canada*, 4 Apr. and *Western Mercury*, 12 Apr. 1832. The provision that social rank was irrelevant carried particular force since there was no subscription fee.
123 *Cobourg Reformer* copied in *St Thomas Liberal*, 27 Dec. 1832. For the York Political Union see *Colonial Advocate*, 13 Dec. 1832.
124 *Bathurst Courier*, 9 Jan. 1835 and Archives of Ontario, Mackenzie-Lindsey Papers, Mackenzie to A.N. Buell, 15 Dec. 1834

was no longer the preserve of gentlemen students of the science of politics. Yet the tension between voluntary associations and constitutional theory went much further.

By developing distinctive norms and sociability, voluntary associations carved out a social space with a degree of autonomy from family, economic production, and the state. They introduced more and more Upper Canadians to a space where they could develop the requisite skills, expectations, and sociability for political deliberation. Colonial elites could no longer claim a monopoly on the ability to organize or to reason effectively in public. Opportunities to participate in this space were not, however, equal. If associations were too inclusive, members could not imagine themselves as equals with common objectives and compatible interests. Those who could not be equal for the purposes of the association were confined to inferior stations or ignored altogether. Yet if associations were too exclusive, they fuelled external demands for inclusion and forfeited any claim to represent a broader, potentially universal, public. By diffusing democratic sociability to once-excluded groups, the voluntary associations of this period seemed to point towards the eventual inclusion of everyone. Yet, by simultaneously judging some as still incapable, they also seemed to render their exclusion particularly problematic.[125]

Informal constraints and formal prohibitions minimized the opportunities of the most economically marginal to participate in associational life. They were thought to lack two prerequisites: the independence to exercise their reason in public and the time, skills, and resources to contribute to common projects. They therefore lacked the right to claim a full stake in them. By using printed material extensively, voluntary associations also risked deepening the gulf between the literate and illiterate.

Opportunities for women to participate in this social space were ambiguous.[126] Some voluntary associations were primarily seen as exten-

---

125 Mary Ryan, *Civic Wars: Democracy and Public Life in the American City during the Nineteenth Century* (Berkeley: University of California Press 1997), 91–2 and David D. Bien, 'Old Regime Origins of Democratic Liberty,' in Dale Van Kley, ed., *The French Idea of Freedom: The Old Regime and the Declaration of Rights of 1789* (Stanford: Stanford University Press 1994), 71

126 Morgan, *Public Men and Virtuous Women*, 125–6, 180–2, 202–11, 222. Compare Joan B. Landes, *Women and the Public Sphere in the Age of the French Revolution* (Ithaca: Cornell University Press 1988) with Dena Goodman, *The Republic of Letters: A Cultural History of the French Enlightenment* (Ithaca: Cornell University Press 1994). See also chapter 4 below.

sions of the roles of mother, wife, moral exemplar, and caregiver. Women donated time and money to religious and benevolent organizations. By the 1820s, the more prominent were establishing independent, female-only societies. The Female Benevolent Society of Kingston, for instance, dispensed relief to over 100 persons in 1825. To do so, its female members organized, ran meetings, elected directresses, visited the needy, and raised and managed funds.[127] While those involved had organized themselves independent of their fathers and husbands, and gained skills and public attention, most female philanthropic societies were not formed at public meetings; their members met in each other's homes, were limited in the range of their concerns by ideas of appropriate female behaviour, and included only prominent women – a prominence that was usually a function of the status of their fathers or husbands. Elizabeth Jane Errington has argued that this restricted, self-selected, membership, combined with an emphasis on giving charity to those they deemed needy and deserving, may have reinforced, rather than blurred, socio-economic distinctions.[128]

Less-prominent women gained visibility and many of the same skills in temperance societies. Some, however, were only 'visiting ladies' who took the pledge but paid no dues and could hold no office. By the 1840s exclusive female temperance societies were increasingly common. It is difficult to judge whether this reflected the growing number and importance of women in the movement or a desire, perhaps on the part of both men and women, to remain separate.[129] In 1846, female temperance supporters petitioned local officials to more effectively regulate taverns. Gradually, women began to speak to mixed audiences, but when a Miss Maria Lamas lectured at Hamilton in 1851 it was still 'rather a novel thing.' A public role, albeit a confined one, was possible on those issues, like temperance or help for the destitute, that either affected women directly or could be seen as extensions of their primary domestic responsibilities. These were necessary steps towards greater public participation and many women took advantage of them, but they also risked reinforcing notions of what responsibilities best suited each

---

127 *Kingston Chronicle*, 20 Jan. 1826
128 Elizabeth Jane Errington, *Wives and Mothers, School Mistresses and Scullery Maids: Working Women in Upper Canada, 1790–1840* (Kingston and Montreal: McGill-Queen's University Press 1995), 161, 170–82, 236–9 and Ryan, *Cradle of the Middle Class*, 53–4, 84–5, 110
129 Racial segregation appears less ambiguous. See notes 40 and 115 above.

sex. In fact, Jan Noel suggests that the increasing presence of women in the temperance movement after 1837 helped erode its reputation as an adjunct of reform politics. It could still be inferred from the presence of women that a cause or meeting was, in the narrow sense of the term, apolitical.[130]

Those associations and activities most closely associated with democratic sociability and the public use of reason offered fewer opportunities to women. They did not overtly challenge reigning gender ideologies. If more men were learning about democratic sociability from these voluntary associations, it was largely, as Catherine Hall notes, 'an education which women were excluded from.'[131]

Freemasonry, renowned for its inclusiveness, explicitly denied membership to women. As already noted, the crucial factor was their perceived lack of moral and intellectual independence. Other, more gender-specific, factors became evident in 1859 and 1864 when the Canadian assembly considered petitions for incorporation from a temperance fraternity, the Good Templars. Supporters argued that, despite being a secret society, the fraternity deserved incorporation because, by admitting women, it could not be political. Opponents cracked jokes about wanting to become members to meet women. Female presence threatened to replace male friendship and harmonious conviviality with heterosexual attractions and competition for female attention. Legislators also worried that wives might subscribe against the wishes of their husbands, thus threatening the entrenched doctrine of marital unity. Further, one member sparked considerable laughter when he reminded his colleagues that 'ladies were admitted and there was very little fear of secrets being kept.' Gossip and indiscretion were not hallmarks of fraternity.[132] Women might be seen as ideally suited to influence their male relations, even outside the home, but their presence was also seen as potentially destructive to the democratic sociability of fraternities.

The notice for the founding meeting of the York Mechanics' Institute promised that 'suitable accommodations will be provided for the

---

130 Noel, *Canada Dry*, 96–102 and Barron, 'The Genesis of Temperance,' 196–7

131 Catherine Hall, 'Private Persons versus Public Someones: Class, Gender and Politics in England, 1780–1850,' in Carolyn Steedman, Cathy Urwin, and Valerie Walkerdine, eds., *Language, Gender and Childhood* (London: Routledge & Kegan Paul 1985), 20

132 Scrapbook debates, 2 Apr. 1859 and 15 Mar. 1864

ladies.'[133] With such assurances, women were encouraged to attend, but were placed in a sort of gallery to observe the proceedings from a safe distance. The institute's constitution provided that 'junior members shall be under 18 years of age, and shall not be eligible to office, or to vote at elections, or on any other question: but shall enjoy all the other privileges of ordinary members. Females shall be junior members in every case.'[134] Regardless of age, occupation, or degree of economic independence, women were excluded from the management of the association. They could attend lectures and classes and use the library and reading room (although the extent to which they did so is unclear). The same norm – possible participation, usually as a spectator, without the full rights and responsibilities of membership – marked public or subscription lectures and some of the colony's debating and literary societies.

Yet even in the political realm, tentative steps were under way. The radical Canadian Alliance Society, founded at Toronto in December 1834, adopted the provision that 'the wives and daughters and sisters of members may be admitted as spectators – and members are earnestly invited to bring their female relations to the lectures as a means of interesting them in the success of the association and the promotion of its measures.' Women could not attend in their own right but only as the kin of male members. This was one more consequence of the notion that women should have no interest independent of their male protectors. Yet, as William Lyon Mackenzie put it, the society 'may be distinguished from most meetings by the mark that women *may* be present.'[135] In fact, the constitution encouraged their presence, publicly acknowledging their political influence. While offering only a subordinate role and conforming to the doctrine of marital unity, it used familial ties to bring women into, not exclude them from, public politics.[136] This was an unprecedented and necessary step towards full participation. Whether women were, in fact, only 'spectators' is unknown. In what purported to be a letter to a conservative editor, 'Stephan Randall'

---

133 *Colonial Advocate*, 25 Nov. 1830
134 York Mechanics' Institute Papers, Constitutions, 1839 and 1855. Women were invited to the institute's first lecture; *Christian Guardian*, 28 Mar. 1832.
135 *Bathurst Courier*, 9 Jan. 1835 and Mackenzie-Lindsey Papers, Mackenzie to Buell, 15 Dec. 1834.
136 Anna Clark, 'The Rhetoric of Chartist Domesticity: Gender, Language, and Class in the 1830s and 1840s,' *Journal of British Studies* 31 (January 1992), 65

claimed to have found women attending radical meetings, voicing their own opinions, and contradicting their husbands by disapproving of reform agitation.[137]

In the Alliance Society and York Mechanics' Institute, women's public status was subordinate, but they were considered capable of using their reason with profit on philosophical, literary, scientific, and even political questions. Voluntary associations and the rise of the public sphere in Upper Canada did not invent the principles by which women's opportunities were limited. The common-law doctrine of marital unity and notions about the essentially moral and nurturing role of women predated both. Growing up in their midst, voluntary associations could simultaneously reflect, reinforce, and challenge them. The standards of inclusion, however, now centred on the ability to use reason in public and to act independently. Once women could claim these attributes, they could claim admittance to this public space on the same grounds and using many of the same tools as men. (After all, the Canadian Woman's Suffrage Association grew out of the Toronto Women's Literary Club.) Women, like other marginalized groups, did not wish to pull down everything their predecessors had built; they wanted in.

For those more fully incorporated, the political significance of voluntary associations was reinforced by their belonging to several at once. One might become an officer in one association, socialize with people of different social status in another, learn to debate in a third, and be introduced to matters of state in a fourth. Some of this overlap is captured by two little-known residents of Kingston, both active in establishing the local mechanics' institute. William Lesslie, a bookseller, was also secretary of a temperance society, librarian of the Young Men's Society, and later president of the Canadian Alliance Society. Thomas Smith, a merchant hatter, joined Lesslie in promoting the mechanics' institute, subscribed to the Kingston Auxiliary Bible and Common Prayer Book Society and the Kingston Compassionate Society, was a steward of the St George's Society, captain of the Volunteer Fire Company, a founder of

---

137 'Stephan Randall,' 'Huzza for the Women!!' *Patriot*, 7 July 1837. This may have been Stephen Randal who had edited the radical *Hamilton Free Press*. The letter's authenticity cannot be determined, but its findings are in line with the stance of most of the Lower Canadian women for whom evidence has survived. Allan Greer, *The Patriots and the People: The Rebellion of 1837 in Rural Lower Canada* (Toronto: University of Toronto Press 1993), 215

the British Constitutional Society, and a member of the Frontenac County Agricultural Society.[138] A sense of efficacy, awareness of general issues, ability to organize and be heard, and the holding of local offices were all highly correlated with membership in voluntary associations.

Such associations were part of an increasingly complex social world – a world no longer sufficiently captured by family, church, neighbourhood, occupation, or fine distinctions of rank. A new social space – potentially political but independent of the state – developed with its own norms and sociability. By creating, maintaining, and defining that space, voluntary associations were among the colony's most important political institutions. They offered the possibility of alternative leadership, the extension of the public use of reason, and a sociability capable of transforming those principles into lived experience. They provided a haven for social intercourse and the pursuit of enlightenment when political divisions were inflamed. In turn, their sociability held out the promise of a more rational, less divisive, politics. Voluntary associations incorporated far more people and reflected different principles of political and social coordination than did pre-democratic governments or corporatist models of society: the rational and progressive capacity of individuals rather than their natural depravity; formal equality rather than ranked orders; active debate and deliberation rather than habit, force, arbitrary will, or revelation. They reinforced the belief that the best answers and the greatest results could be achieved only by active citizens working together, not by solitary individuals or a self-selected few.

In 1840, an anonymous resident of Perth, 'Amicus Mentis,' reiterated the platitude that ignorance lay at the root of all vice. Government should be 'anxious to enlighten the public mind; both that the people may be more easily governed, and that they may be enabled to understand and appreciate the advantages of good government, which the ignorant never can do.' The diffusion of enlightenment and self-discipline were inseparable. Both would empower the people 'to judge correctly of them and their measures.' Community leaders also had a duty to eliminate ignorance, 'to use their exertions to disseminate knowledge and to encourage the cultivation of the mental and moral faculties.' In practice, extending the capacity 'to judge correctly' meant supporting 'an Agricultural Society, a Mechanic's [*sic*] Institute, a Public Library ... [and] a debating Club.'[139] The political history of voluntary

138 Palmer, 'Kingston Mechanics,' 29–30
139 Amicus Mentis, *Bathurst Courier*, 11 Dec. 1840

associations was not over in 1840 and, as heightened religious and ethnic tensions over the next decade attest, it was not a linear story of progress. Yet Amicus Mentis and others already understood the connection between voluntary associations and politics; between the activities and sociability of local societies and the public sphere; between an agricultural society and governance. Ultimately, the state itself became little more than a voluntary association.

CHAPTER III

'The most powerful engine of the human mind': The Press and Its Readers

In his *Essay on the History of the English Government and Constitution* (1823), Lord John Russell was confident that 'there can be no doubt that public opinion acquired prodigious force during the late reign [of George III, 1760–1820].' He attributed this amplified power to 'the publication of the debates in parliament, and the general diffusion of political knowledge.' Both were products of an expanded periodical press. William Lyon Mackenzie agreed that the 'great increase of the production of the press will account for the influence of public opinion in Great Britain ... Where the press is free, *mind*, and not wealth or high family honours, will govern.'[1]

Whatever sociability or skills voluntary associations fostered, appeals to public opinion could not be credible if the deliberations upon which it was based were ill informed. Little is yet known about what Upper Canadians read, how they understood it, and its impact, but most of their political information ultimately came from colonial newspapers. From the 1820s, their nature, number, distribution, and regular reports of parliamentary intelligence reflected their centrality to the emergent public sphere. Physically, their readers met most obviously in newsrooms and taverns, but collectively they formed the colony's largest and most important voluntary association.

The author of 'Domestic Recreations,' a series of essays published in 1819 by the *Kingston Chronicle*, described his move to the area as being 'transplanted from the midst of a lively circle into the woods.' He 'first

---

1 Russell, *Essay on the History of English Government*, 429 and *Colonial Advocate*, 31 May 1827

felt like one who is suddenly struck dead and dumb.' Relieved only by the arrival of the newly established *Chronicle*, he announced his intention 'through its medium to talk to the public by *proxy*.' Such talk would lessen his sense of isolation. More important, it would allow him to participate in a cornerstone of polite sociability.

The man living in a city was 'blessed with the means of daily communicating his opinion to his fellow-mortals,' making him feel that he 'has a vote in the general concerns of the world.' This 'reciprocal communication of sentiments and ideas' was 'one great subordinate principle upon which the existence of society depends.' It induced men to congregate and develop 'sympathy, friendship, or cordiality.' It broadened horizons, tempered selfishness, and 'the desire of exhibiting himself to advantage, and communicating importance to his opinions, induces him to cultivate his mind, and enlarge his ideas, by the acquisition of knowledge.'[2]

These claims on behalf of polite conversation echoed those of such eighteenth-century British commentators as the Third Earl of Shaftesbury. In the wake of the civil and religious strife of the previous century, polite conversation was thought capable of taming partisanship and bigotry. The principles of a new political order could be found in the measured exchange of opinion among gentlemen and in the cultural institutions and practices that promoted that exchange, rather than in a monarchical court or established church.[3] The British coffeehouse epitomized these principles. Similar associations, such as the Upper Canada Club or its short-lived predecessor, the Toronto Club House, devoted to 'kindly intercourse, and intellectual conversation,' began to appear at the provincial capital by the end of the 1830s.[4] In 1819, however, the author of 'Domestic Recreations' was surely right to insist that other means were required in a colonial setting.

He found them in newspapers as 'organs of sentiment, and theatres for discussion.' Four positive consequences were to flow from an ex-

---

2 'Domestic Recreations,' *Kingston Chronicle*, 5 Feb., 5 and 19 Mar. 1819
3 Lawrence E. Klein, *Shaftesbury and the Culture of Politeness: Moral Discourse and Cultural Politics in Early Eighteenth-Century England* (Cambridge: Cambridge University Press 1994), 96–101, Marvin B. Becker, *The Emergence of Civil Society in the Eighteenth-Century: A Privileged Moment in the History of England, Scotland, and France* (Bloomington: Indiana University Press 1994), 43–4, 55–6, 69, and Dena Goodman, *The Republic of Letters: A Cultural History of the French Enlightenment* (Ithaca: Cornell University Press 1994), 5, 114, 120–2
4 *Royal Standard*, 9 and 11 Nov. 1836

panded colonial press. First, by diffusing knowledge, more newspapers
would spark readers' curiosity and awaken 'that intelligent spirit, which
will urge men to seek deeper sources of information.' Second, they
would reduce apathy by calling attention to topics of common concern.
Newspapers helped define those issues, furnished the necessary
information, and encouraged readers to act. Third, newspapers, much
like agricultural societies, held up models worthy of emulation. They
'celebrate the bravery of the hero – they display the eloquences
and genius of the orator – they communicate to mankind all over the
world a mutual knowledge of the local and general concerns of each
other, and encourage an emulation in arts, sciences, elegances and
accomplishments.'

Finally, a flourishing press had important political implications. If
free, newspapers became 'the organs through which the public feelings
are manifested.' From the number of newspapers on each side of a public question 'a pretty correct estimate of the state of public opinion may
generally be formed.' By disseminating information and argument,
newspapers helped to create, not just reflect, public opinion. By exposing misdeeds, newspapers were also able 'to check the abuses which are
often exercised by those who hold office.' Moreover, 'when a government encourages political discussion, the people are inspired with a
confidence in their rulers,' who thereby appeared to have nothing to
hide, but 'when public discussion is fettered ... the people begin to be
suspicious.'[5]

Writing in 1819, this essayist stood at a threshold in the history of the
colonial press. Previously, most of the colony's handful of newspapers
had provided their limited readership with commercial and foreign
intelligence mixed with 'the opportunity to participate imaginatively in'
what David Shields characterizes as 'a discursive analogue of genteel
company.'[6] Frequent essays, letters, and copied articles on morals and
manners, history and literature, and the arts and sciences mimicked the
form and content of polite conversation. A reader of the *Chronicle*'s predecessor complained of the frequent use of Greek and Latin, revealing
much about the content and assumed readership of the early colonial
press.[7] The essayist's first three goals – sparking curiosity, defining issues

---

5 'Domestic Recreations,' *Kingston Chronicle,* 5 Feb., 5 and 19 Mar. 1819
6 David S. Shields, *Civil Tongues: Polite Letters in British America* (Chapel Hill: University of
    North Carolina Press 1997), 12
7 Timothy Peaseblossom (?), *Kingston Gazette,* 23 Mar. 1816

of common concern, and encouraging emulation – were evident in the earliest colonial newspapers.

Writing in the wake of Robert Gourlay's agitation against the government and its officials (greatly amplified by his use of the press), the author of the 'Domestic Recreations' added a fourth, explicitly political, role for newspapers. With a couple of notable exceptions, earlier newspapers had been wary of commenting on provincial politics. With the expansion of the periodical press called for by these essays soon under way, the political role threatened to engulf the other three. By the 1820s, diffusing the norms and content of polite sociability was nearly eclipsed as most newspapers became political weapons to create and reflect public opinion. Concurrently, most became less genteel in readership, tone, and intent. Democratic sociability was replacing its polite precursor.

Even if this essayist was right to think that newspapers could substitute for polite conversation, there were still significant differences between publication and verbal transmission or private correspondence.[8] Oral conversation reached only those in range of the speaker. The identity of the speaker influenced how his or her words were received. Conversation also demanded an immediate response, which might come from passion or insufficient reflection. In print, opinions could be abstracted from the person of their original author and could reach countless others. Authors might be unknown and could thus exercise influence only by their words, not their identities. The resulting conversation could appear as general in location and universal in applicability.

Not only did publication differ from oral communication, but publication predominantly in newspapers or pamphlets, rather than books, was also significant. The periodic and more ephemeral nature of newspapers, their increasing number, often clearer biases and errors, and fierce attacks on each other, fostered critical distance between reader and text. For some readers, surrounded by abundant publications, active choice was possible, even required. Other forms of public communication, such as sermons or charges to grand juries, were autho-

---

8 See Roger Chartier, *The Cultural Origins of the French Revolution*, trans. Lydia G. Cochrane (Durham: Duke University Press 1991), 26, 31–2, 65–6, Michael Warner, *The Letters of the Republic: Publication and the Public Sphere in Eighteenth Century America* (Cambridge, Mass.: Harvard University Press 1990), and Richard D. Brown, *Knowledge Is Power: The Diffusion of Information in Early America, 1700–1865* (New York: Oxford University Press 1989).

rized by social superiors for consumers who were to be largely passive. They spoke to their audience. Colonial readers were increasingly faced with competing and combative newspapers, divorced from formal state or devotional practices. Few originated from obvious social superiors. They conversed with their audience. Readers were thus encouraged to adopt a more casual and sceptical attitude towards printed texts.[9] Finally, newspapers integrated their readers into a common political community. They participated in public debate by talking with each other and their readers. As Michael Warner argues, 'The reader does not simply imagine him- or herself receiving a direct communication or hearing the voice of the author. He or she now also incorporates ... an awareness of the potentially limitless others who may also be reading. For that reason, it becomes possible to imagine oneself, in the act of reading, becoming part of an arena of the national people that cannot be realized except through such mediating imaginings.'[10]

The growth of the provincial press is the single best indicator of the size of that arena.[11] The first newspaper printed in Upper Canada, the *Upper Canada Gazette*, appeared in April 1793 as the official, subsidized organ of government. The first privately owned paper, the *Canada Constellation*, appeared five years later at Newark, after the *Gazette* had followed the government to York. By 1819, papers had been published in six towns, but only three (Niagara, Kingston, and York) could sustain a paper for any length of time. Thirty years later, thirty-nine communities had supported at least one local newspaper. Some supported several; others saw repeated failures.

Ten of these communities boasted at least one newspaper between 1820 and 1829. Nine (excluding the capital) accounted for nineteen different titles in this decade. Five (Brockville, Kingston, Markham, Niagara, and York) sustained at least two newspapers simultaneously at

---

9 David Jaffee, 'The Village Enlightenment in New England, 1760–1820,' *William and Mary Quarterly*, 3rd Ser., 47, no. 3 (July 1990), 342–3. For contrasting evaluations of the theory of an eighteenth-century 'reading revolution,' see Chartier, *Cultural Origins of the French Revolution*, 89–90 and David D. Hall, 'The Uses of Literacy in New England, 1600–1850,' in William L. Joyce, D.D. Hall, Richard D. Brown, and John B. Hench, eds., *Printing and Society in Early America* (Worcester: American Antiquarian Society 1983), esp. 21–34.

10 Warner, *Letters of the Republic*, xiii

11 Statistics in the following paragraphs were calculated from Brian J. Gilchrist, *Inventory of Ontario Newspapers, 1793–1986* (Toronto: Micromedia 1987).

some point during the 1820s. The number of communities with a local press more than doubled during the next decade (from 10 to 23) while the number sustaining two or more simultaneously doubled (from 5 to 10). Competitive local markets could be found in both the eastern (Cobourg, Prescott, Belleville, and Kingston) and western (Hamilton, St Catharines, St Thomas, London, and Niagara) sections of the colony as well as at the capital. Five of these ten supported more than two newspapers simultaneously at some point during the 1830s. In all, 73 newspapers were published in Upper Canada outside the capital between 1830 and 1839; 51 lasted at least a year. At the capital, 20 newspapers survived from the 1820s or were established during the following 10 years. Of these 20, at least 14 appeared regularly for a year or more during the 1830s. Of course, not all 65 papers (51 plus 14) lasting at least one year during the decade were published at the same time.

Comparing two specific years, 1828 and 1836, reveals more (see map, p. xii). In 1828, the colony faced a heated election after prolonged conflict over the rights of former American citizens then resident in Upper Canada. In July, at the time of the election, eight communities had at least one paper and accounted for at least fourteen titles (and perhaps as many as sixteen). Competition existed in at least four local markets (Brockville, Kingston, Niagara, and York). By 1836, these figures more than doubled: from eight communities with at least one newspaper to eighteen; from approximately eighteen different titles by the end of 1828 to forty-six published some time in 1836; and from four competitive markets to nine or ten. In the same period, the colony's population barely doubled. By the election in July 1836, the radical *Constitution* had been founded by William Lyon Mackenzie, joining thirty-four newspapers already in existence. It was the seventh in Toronto alone. In November, the *Statesman* appeared at Brockville and, with the addition of the daily *Royal Standard*, eight newspapers were published at Toronto. The capital's population had yet to reach 10,000.

Impressive as they are, such figures can mislead. As we shall see, readers were not restricted to the place of publication. The number of titles also says little about the number of readers – except that, given the remarkable stability of printing technology across these decades, successful expansion was largely driven by demand. Such demand fueled competition, which in turn further broadened the market.[12] Living at or

---

12 David Vincent, *Literacy and Popular Culture: England, 1750–1914* (Cambridge: Cambridge University Press 1989), 11, 210

near a competitive market could be important. Alternative interpretations of local issues and events were more likely from newspapers published in the region. The expansion and decentralization of the newspaper press to non-metropolitan centres provided not only local sources of information and a sense of connectedness to the larger community, but also the potential to produce pamphlets, broadsheets, and books locally. Editors frequently doubled as local booksellers and agents for other newspapers or bookstores. The nature and ideals of their profession also made them prominent promoters of libraries, newsrooms, schools, literary and agricultural societies, and mechanics' institutes. A disproportionate number also appear to have been Freemasons. Cultural production in the hinterlands was a key component of what David Jaffee aptly calls the 'village enlightenment.'[13]

The amount of purely local material in any colonial newspaper was, however, relatively small. Notices or minutes from local associations and coverage of local officials or local candidates for the assembly were fairly common, but most communities were still small enough that any community-based news was already known before it could appear in the local weekly. Newspaper editors usually found out about local events at the same time and in much the same way as fellow residents. To be sustainable, newspapers had to provide what was not otherwise readily available. That meant non-local material. In the days before the telegraph transformed them into vehicles for the rapid transmission of 'news,' newspapers were especially suited to reproducing lengthy documents and commentary. Subscribers might bind their copies to form reference works.[14] Thus, much of what was printed at one location was relevant to readers elsewhere. This was particularly true of newspapers at the capital, where editors had easier and more timely access to political news and documents. The number of presses at the capital underlines the importance of politics to readers throughout the colony. Shortly after founding the *Globe*, George Brown solicited 'communications' from an acquaintance at Brockville – 'anything spicy – accounts of

---

13 Jaffee, 'The Village Enlightenment,' 333 and Richard D. Brown, 'The Emergence of Urban Society in Rural Massachusetts, 1760–1820,' *Journal of American History* 61, no. 1 (June 1974), 43–4

14 Peter G. Goheen, 'The Changing Bias of Inter-urban Communications in Nineteenth-Century Canada,' *Journal of Historical Geography* 16, no. 2 (1990), 183 and Brown, *Knowledge Is Power*, 36–8. The *Western Herald*, 10 Feb. 1838, encouraged more of its readers to preserve their copies in bound volumes.

meetings – interesting trials – but especially political news.'[15] Nonetheless, a rigid division of labour had yet to develop between metropolitan and local papers or between papers serving sizeable market segments and those aimed at the public as a whole. By the 1830s, community papers were dominated by provincial politics, including reports of parliamentary debates, not local matters. There was no paper of record in Upper Canada like the *Times* of London. None approached such dominance during these decades.

Geographic diffusion was not just a matter of more communities sustaining a local newspaper. It also involved agents, private carriers, and the post office.[16] The *Weekly Post* was printed at York, but had agents in nineteen other communities. Brockville's small conservative paper, the *Gazette*, was primarily intended to counter the moderate reform *Brockville Recorder*. Its agents were concentrated in eastern Upper Canada, but they could also be found at York, Hamilton, and Niagara, communities with one or more conservative organs of their own. In 1835, *The Reformer*, a radical Cobourg paper, had agents in at least forty-two communities in Upper Canada. With the exception of the largest and most prestigious newspapers, most concentrated on their immediate hinterland, but still sought subscribers further afield.[17]

Newspaper agents fulfilled a variety of roles.[18] Some were largely passive, merely forwarding subscriptions to the editor. Others were energetic salesmen. William Lyon Mackenzie mailed out the *Colonial Advocate* to people he hoped would subscribe. He then depended upon his agents to keep track of the individuals who took, refused, or returned these early issues. A few agents, including Marshall Spring Bidwell, distributed copies themselves. Charles Duncombe forwarded the names of forty-five subscribers to Mackenzie and ordered eight copies of each issue for himself. The acting agent at Ancaster tried to arrange for

15 National Archives of Canada, George Brown Papers, Brown to W.B. Richards, 8 Mar. 1844
16 The role of pedlars in the transmission of texts has not been studied, but see Brian S. Osborne, 'Trading on a Frontier: The Function of Peddlers, Markets, and Fairs in Nineteenth-Century Ontario,' in Donald H. Akenson, ed., *Canadian Papers in Rural History*, 2 (Gananoque, Ont.: Langdale Press 1980), 61–8. Critics charged that itinerant preachers increased the speed of delivery and geographic reach of the *Christian Guardian*.
17 *Weekly Post*, 1 Mar. 1821, *Brockville Gazette*, 22 Aug. 1828, and *The Reformer*, 24 Feb. 1835
18 Information on agents is from Archives of Ontario, Mackenzie-Lindsey Papers, especially the letters to Mackenzie from M.S. Bidwell, 19 June 1824, G. Tiffany, 6 Jan. 1825, Henry Lasher, 11 Dec. 1825, Charles McDonell, 20 Feb. 1826, Jacob Keefer, 25 Feb. 1825, Matthew Crooks, 9 June 1826, and Charles Duncombe, 15 Apr. 1831.

a prominent London merchant with a branch store in Ancaster to 'take at your office 150 or 200 Advocates weekly' for the Thames region, thus saving Mackenzie the postage.

Agents also had the daunting task of trying to collect payment from subscribers. Some forwarded advertisements, reported on local opinion and reaction to the newspaper, discussed editorials with Mackenzie, or relayed concerns about the ease and regularity of delivery. Agents also helped to distribute pamphlets and books published by newspaper editors, an especially valuable service for those readers without easy access to a bookseller.[19]

In return, agents might get a free subscription. A few, like Charles Duncombe, advanced their own political careers by distributing supportive newspapers, but this was far from typical. Most were motivated by confidence in the paper. Charles McDonell, Mackenzie's agent at Cornwall, told his fellow Scotsman, 'I feel really proud of a countryman conducting such an independent paper as the Advocate.' In 1825 Henry Lasher, agent at Bath, congratulated Mackenzie on the appearance of a new series of the *Advocate*. It could not 'be denied to be superior in every respect to any circulating newspaper ever yet published within this Province and which has therefore enabled me to procure the names annexed as subscribers.' In the same year, Jacob Keefer of Beaverdam was less fawning: 'If your political statements had not been such as I admired and approved I should not have taken that interest in the circulation of the Advocate for which you are pleased to express your satisfaction.'[20] Active agents believed in the newspaper they represented to their neighbours. By helping to construct a network of readers beyond its place of publication, they were vital to its survival.

Several newspaper agents and a few editors doubled as postmasters. The connection made considerable sense since many papers flowed through the mails. Despite frequent, not always unjustified, complaints about slow or irregular delivery, the expansion of the postal system remains impressive. There were seven postmasters in Upper Canada in

---

19 E.g., *The Reformer*, 29 Dec. 1835.
20 Relationships based on political affinity were fragile. In 1826, Matthew Crooks, Mackenzie's agent for two years, refused to continue and cancelled his own subscription. He, like the youths who vandalized Mackenzie's shop, now believed that the *Advocate* was 'degrading itself by becoming the vehicle of the most low and contemptible scurrility.' Reversing the usual relationship, a Brockville agent was accused of sabotaging the *Banner*'s circulation owing to its stand in the Metcalfe crisis. George Brown Papers, Brown to W.B. Richardson, 8 Mar. 1844

1791. By 1817 there were still only about a dozen but, by the end of 1831, more than a hundred post offices had been established in the province. A further 127 were added by 1841, roughly mirroring population growth. By then, there was a post office for about every 1800 Upper Canadians.[21] About ten communities had a post office for every one that had a newspaper.

Until 1841, the standard postal rate, set by British statute, failed to distinguish inland letters from newspapers or pamphlets. Determined on the basis of distance and the number of sheets, the rate would have effectively prohibited the dissemination of newspapers by post. It never appears to have been enforced. Instead, a highly preferential rate was arranged whereby the sender of a weekly newspaper was charged four shillings currency a year per copy or one pence per issue to mail it anywhere in the colony. The postage for an average letter was estimated to be eight or nine times higher. While critics charged that any postage was a 'tax on knowledge,' editors from smaller centres had no interest in free postage. It would only allow papers from larger centres to swamp their smaller, local market. Thus, the preferential rate was low enough to encourage the distribution of colonial newspapers outside of their place of publication, but high enough to offer some protection to local markets.[22]

Editors could also send a copy free of charge to their colleagues. The resulting exchange of newspapers was the primary method of newsgathering. It created a free pool of material from which to copy and increased the number of potential readers for a copied item. As Anna Jameson noted, 'Paragraphs printed from English or American papers, on subjects of general interest, the summary of political events, extracts from books or magazines, are copied from one paper into another, til they have travelled round the country.'[23] If some editors copied only to

21 *Report of the Commissioners*, app. F, no. 16. For a list of post offices, see F.H. Armstrong, *Handbook of Upper Canadian Chronology*, rev. ed. (Toronto: Dundurn Press 1985), 229–37.

22 *Report of the Commissioners*, esp. app. D and O. The Province of Canada experimented with free transmission but reverted to a preferential rate. American newspapers mailed to Canadians were charged a fairly nominal rate of one penny per issue, while, after 1834, British newspapers arriving by the Halifax Packets travelled to their Canadian destination free of charge.

23 Jameson, *Winter Studies and Summer Rambles*, 153. Peter G. Goheen, 'Canadian Communications circa 1845,' *Geographical Review* 77 (1987), 48 notes that two small newspapers at Prescott and Dundas received six and seven free exchange copies per week respectively in 1841. For the U.S., see Richard B. Kielbowicz, *News in the Mail: The Press, Post Office, and Public Information, 1700–1860s* (New York: Greenwood Press 1989), 141–51.

criticize, they still informed their readers that other opinions were being expressed, what some of those opposing arguments were, where to find such analysis, and, finally, that readers of other newspapers were part of the same discursive community. Editors could also compare reports of the same event or issue in several papers and often commented on discrepancies.

Apparently editors often failed to pay all the postage they owed. They declared the number of issues being mailed and were 'seldom afterward questioned.' Postmasters had little incentive to count through bundles of newspapers. An official report concluded that the sums collected 'fall considerably short' of what the regulations suggested. 'In many cases, indeed, it appears that a fixed sum is paid under an old agreement, without any reference to the number of papers now mailed.'[24]

Thus in three ways – with a preferential rate, by supporting the exchange system, and through lax enforcement – the postal system subsidized the diffusion of newspapers. In the two Canadas, the system generated a gross revenue of £62,400 for the fiscal year ending July 1840. Only about £3,000 or less than 5 per cent came from distributing newspapers. For the same period, Deputy Provincial Post Master General Thomas Stayner estimated that the number of newspapers and pamphlets circulated was slightly higher than the number of chargeable letters. Since newspapers were bulkier and heavier than most letters and often constituted about half of the items handled by post masters, the preferential rate combined with its lax enforcement meant that the post office's other business heavily subsidized the transmission of newspapers.[25]

The existence of a network of agents and post offices meant that a colonial newspaper was potentially available to any Upper Canadian living close to one of these conduits. But to what extent did newspapers actually circulate beyond their own locality? How many Upper Canadians could afford to subscribe to a colonial newspaper even if its diffusion was subsidized by the post office? Of those who could afford to, how many actually subscribed?

Several contemporaries tried to use postal records to answer these questions. According to Anna Jameson, 427,567 papers circulated through the mails in 1836 among a population of about 370,000. Almost a quarter were transmitted free of charge, and, of those with postage

---

24 *Report of the Commissioners*
25 Ibid.

paid, almost half originated in the United States or elsewhere.[26] This suggested a newspaper per week for as few as one family in seven. The proportion receiving a provincial paper and paying postage comes out as low as one in fifteen or sixteen. Jameson herself was impressed, but did so few families have direct access to a provincial newspaper? The *Christian Guardian* was rightly sceptical. In its review of *Winter Studies and Summer Rambles*, it asserted that 'in Upper Canada there is twice the number of newspapers read, in proportion to the population than there is in any county, city, town or village, in England.'[27]

If Jameson had read William Lyon Mackenzie's *Sketches of Canada* before leaving Britain, she missed the footnote in which he noted that, to avoid paying postage, colonial newspapers sent as many copies as possible by other means.[28] Yet Mackenzie had himself used the amount of postage paid by nineteen colonial papers in 1831 to compare their circulation to his claimed printing of 1000 to 1250 *Colonial Advocates*. There is no way of knowing how many actually went to paying subscribers or if his claim was inflated, and, if so, by how much.[29] In 1831, the *Advocate* paid the second highest amount of postage, £57, or enough for about 265 yearly subscriptions. Mackenzie probably mailed more copies than he paid for; others were sent free of charge or by other means. Nonetheless, if we can give any credence to his figures, the post office transmitted as little as a third of his print run.

Many of Mackenzie's competitors paid remarkably little postage, which suggests that they focused on their own regions or relied on private means to transport their publications. For instance, Kingston's two leading papers, both highly respected and widely copied, either did not pay postage to reach their customers outside the Kingston area or had few such subscribers. For 1831, the *Chronicle* and *Upper Canada Herald* combined did not pay enough postage to reach one hundred yearly subscribers. This figure undoubtedly underestimates their diffusion outside Kingston, but it still represents a small proportion of their total output.

---

26 Jameson, *Winter Studies and Summer Rambles*, 153. For the *Report of the Commissioners* Stayner estimated that postage was paid on 600,000 sheets (newspapers and pamphlets) by their printers in both Canadas and a further 50,000 were sent by someone else. Non-printers also paid to import 210,000 sheets from the U.S. He estimated that a further 596,000 sheets were posted free of charge, including 320,000 sheets from Britain via the Halifax Packets.

27 *Christian Guardian*, 20 Feb. 1839. See also *Colonial Advocate*, 1 Nov. 1832.

28 Mackenzie, *Sketches of Canada*, 451n

29 *Colonial Advocate*, 19 Sept. 1833

Denominational papers paid considerably more postage. In particular, the Methodist *Christian Guardian* paid enough to post a yearly subscription to over a thousand families. Besides the *Advocate*, the conservative *Courier* also paid a noticeable sum to the post office, £45. These figures undoubtedly underestimate transmission through the post, but they still suggest that many newspapers were read primarily at or near their place of publication. In the village or town, people could call at the printing office themselves. In larger markets, a crude delivery system was possible. By the late 1820s, Francis Collins of York's *Canadian Freeman* hired 'a boy, who usually carried the papers through town.'[30] Nonetheless, at least three Toronto papers, the *Guardian*, *Advocate*, and *Courier*, made considerable use of the post office to reach Upper Canadians outside the capital.

Postal records still give little sense of the overall number of readers. Guesses ranged wildly from one in ten in the Niagara area to one copy for almost every family in Hamilton.[31] In 1824, Mackenzie tried to be more systematic. He listed the print runs of his six competitors as follows: *Gazette* 300, *Observer* 290, *Chronicle* 350, *Upper Canada Herald* 420, *Brockville Recorder* 300, and *Gleaner* 190, for a total of 1850. Mackenzie boasted a rapidly expanding readership 'and will now print upwards of 1000 copies of the Advocate, weekly, being more than one third of all the papers printed in the Province.' Again, these figures cannot be verified. Marshall Spring Bidwell wrote from Kingston to add one hundred copies to Mackenzie's total for the *Upper Canada Herald*. The *Niagara Gleaner* accused Mackenzie of attempting to steal advertisers by pegging its circulation at only 190, claiming to have printed an average of 300 copies a week for the past seven years.[32]

While Mackenzie's individual numbers were disputed, the average, just over 300, seems reasonable. If the seven papers in 1824 printed no more than 2500 copies a week, only about one family in ten had direct access to a newspaper each week. The proportion in Toronto (where

---

30 Levius P. Sherwood, charge to the jury, Collins libel case, Fifth report of the committee on Francis Collins's petition to the Assembly, *Journals*, 1829
31 *Niagara Gleaner*, 16 Mar. and A Subscriber, *Western Mercury*, 11 Apr. 1833. I have adopted an average household size of six. For the household size of 5.8 in Hamilton and 6.4 in Peel in 1851, see Michael B. Katz, *The People of Hamilton, Canada West: Family and Class in a Mid-Nineteenth-Century City* (Cambridge, Mass.: Harvard University Press 1975), 221 and David Gagan, *Hopeful Travellers: Families, Land, and Social Change in Mid-Victorian Peel County, Canada West* (Toronto: University of Toronto Press 1981), 69.
32 *Colonial Advocate*, 5 Aug. 1824, Mackenzie-Lindsey Papers, Bidwell to Mackenzie, 24 Aug. 1824 and *Gleaner*, 21 Aug. 1824

the *Gazette*, the *Observer*, and shortly the *Advocate* were published) and Kingston (home to the *Chronicle* and the *Herald*) was probably higher. Others had indirect access, but totals remained small.

Five years later, in 1829, when Thomas Dalton established the *Patriot* at Kingston (the fourth local paper), Mackenzie forecast that 6000 issues would soon be printed by eighteen colonial papers, which would 'average a number a week among every five families.'[33] In the five years from 1824 to 1829 the population had increased by only a quarter, but the number of families receiving a weekly paper had probably doubled. During the next decade, the newspaper press continued to grow faster than the population, although far less dramatically. Mackenzie was not alone in noticing the sudden expansion at the close of the 1820s. The St Catharines *Farmers' Journal* fretted that many of the new publications could not be sustained 'and yet all seem to prosper ... Should these, together with the older Journals ... receive as liberal support as present appearances indicate, it will auger well for the moral and intellectual improvement of their patrons, and the rising generation.'[34] The *Journal* thought it saw the dawning of a new era for the colony. It saw the beginnings of the public sphere.

During the 1830s, several papers, especially those at the capital, printed considerably more than the average of 300 to 350 copies per week used here for the previous decade. By 1831, the *Christian Guardian* was paying to mail at least 1000 copies per week and claimed 1900 subscribers, up almost 300 from the year before.[35] The *Correspondent & Advocate* claimed 1400 subscribers in 1834, and two years later Mackenzie claimed that 1250 subscribed to the *Constitution*. Given that these were among the leading papers, such figures are not incredible. Newspapers outside the capital may still have averaged around 350 copies, although several claimed substantially higher print runs: in 1832 the *Brockville Antidote* and the *St Thomas Liberal* claimed 645 and 600 subscribers respectively.[36]

---

33 *Colonial Advocate*, 8 Oct. 1829. Mackenzie was using the reasonable averages of about 330 issues per newspaper and 6.7 people per household. When considering relaunching the *Western Herald* at Sandwich, the publisher refused to 'incur the risk of another publication, till we are possessed of at least three hundred and fifty subscribers.' *Western Herald*, 3 Jan. 1838

34 *Farmers' Journal*, 23 Dec. 1829

35 *Christian Guardian*, 16 Nov. 1831 and 11 Dec. 1830

36 J.J. Talman, 'The Newspapers of Upper Canada a Century Ago,' *Canadian Historical Review* 19, no. 1 (March 1938), 12 and Mary Lucinda MacDonald, 'Literature and Society in the Canadas, 1830–1850,' PhD thesis, Carleton University 1984, 68–9

There is no entirely satisfactory way to compare the proportion of families receiving their own weekly newspaper in 1829 (about one in five) with the proportion in 1836. To be cautious, if we assume that four of the newspapers at the capital had a circulation of three times our base average of 350 (or 1050 – still well below each of their claims), and that three other papers had twice that average, almost 16,000 newspapers would have been printed each week.[37] While a conservative estimate, this is still well over four times Anna Jameson's conclusion from postal records and translates into a weekly paper for about one in four families. The press continued to expand. According to the *Christian Guardian*, by 1841 the more than fifty newspapers and journals printed in Upper Canada had a combined weekly circulation of at least 40,000. This was the equivalent of one copy for every two families. Some families subscribed to several journals, but any over-counting this may represent is compensated for by using all families as our universe rather than only those families who *could* have subscribed (that is, minus those that were too isolated or in which none could read). Regardless, the community of newspaper subscribers had outgrown the electorate.[38]

The ability to join this community was partially set by income, although for many geography and family priorities were probably greater determinants. Who could afford the fifteen or twenty shillings a year that most weekly newspapers charged in the 1830s?[39] The lowest advertised wage rate for craftsmen Douglas McCalla found in that decade was about five shillings per day; it could reach almost twice as much. Thus, artisans and some journeymen could subscribe to a colonial newspaper for about three days' wages. Again relying on McCalla, with a bushel of wheat selling for 5s in 1831, a year's subscription was the

---

37 Thus, only about one-quarter to one-third of newspapers were transmitted by the post. Richard B. Kielbowicz, 'The Press, Post Office, and Flow of News in the Early Republic,' *Journal of the Early Republic* 3, no. 3 (Fall 1983), 270, estimates that the post carried only about one in six American newspapers in 1810. Talman, 'Newspapers of Upper Canada,' 15, reasonably suggests 20,000 copies for 1835 but gives none of his calculations.

38 *Christian Guardian*, 27 Oct. 1841. Elwood Jones has estimated that about 40% of adult males had the right to vote. For his unpublished study, see Carol Wilton, '"Lawless Law": Conservative Political Violence in Upper Canada, 1818–1841,' *Law and History Review* 13, no. 1 (Spring 1995), 115.

39 Macdonald, 'Literature and Society,' table 1, 62. Most early papers charged a similar amount; Carl Benn, 'The Upper Canadian Press, 1793–1815,' *Ontario History* 70, no. 2 (June 1978), 100. Thus, absolute cost remained stable despite economic fluctuations.

equivalent of three or four bushels. The conversion rate was important since subscribers often paid in kind.[40]

Newspaper subscriptions still represented a considerable investment or unattainable luxury for many. For male farm labourers earning fifty to sixty shillings a month or for shantymen in the Ottawa Valley timber trade earning as little as forty shillings a month, the price of a subscription was measured by the week rather than by the day.[41] Many subscribers were constantly in arrears. They paid only what and when they could – to the constant complaint of proprietors. It was not uncommon for papers to threaten to stop sending copies to subscribers only when they were more than a year behind in payment – a standard feature of the colony's credit system and one that created opportunities to receive numerous copies without incurring the expense.[42]

A profile of potential subscribers emerges. Merchants and professionals, clerks and shopkeepers, skilled artisans and journeymen, and most relatively established farm families could afford a newspaper subscription. Within this disparate group, inclination was probably crucial in determining whether or not to subscribe for any given year. Few women probably subscribed independent of their fathers or husbands.[43] William Lyon Mackenzie counted Mississauga natives at Credit River among his subscribers[44] and a paper was established for unilingual Germans at Berlin in 1835. Only the most isolated or transient, unskilled wage labourers and others with highly unstable employment, marginal farmers, and families in which no one could read were largely absent from the community of newspaper *subscribers*.

Neither members of these groups nor those who chose not to sub-

---

40 Douglas McCalla, *Planting the Province: The Economic History of Upper Canada, 1784–1870* (Toronto: University of Toronto Press 1993), 114–15, 336–7. As late as 12 Dec. 1838, the *Chronicle & Gazette* advertised its need for firewood for the benefit of those who paid their subscription in that commodity.

41 McCalla, *Planting the Province*, 55 and Terry Crowley, 'Rural Labour,' in Paul Craven, ed., *Labouring Lives: Work & Workers in Nineteenth-Century Ontario* (Toronto: University of Toronto Press 1995), 24. If female wage labour or male seasonal wages supplemented other income or a form of agriculture, some of these families might have had the economic means to subscribe. Thus, one of Mackenzie's agents could not remit payment from a subscriber, since he 'is at the canals working for money.' Mackenzie-Lindsey Papers, Thomas Fyfe to Mackenzie, 23 May 1827

42 McCalla, *Planting the Province*, 144 and *Gleaner*, 24 Apr. 1830

43 Of the original 33 subscribers to the *Colonial Advocate* at York, only one, a tavern owner, was a woman. Mackenzie-Lindsey Papers, W. Beggin to Mackenzie, 31 Aug. 1824

44 Mackenzie, *Sketches of Canada*, 133

scribe were thereby excluded from the community of newspaper *readers*. Each copy probably had multiple readers. Mackenzie was informed that non-subscribers were reading copies of the *Advocate* 'for by their appearance they must have made the tour of Brockville half a dozen times.'[45] Such indirect access was possible through family and friends, at local stores, inns and taverns, and through voluntary associations, especially libraries, newsrooms, and mechanics' institutes.[46] Some may also have found newspapers at their place of work or where they boarded. Anne Hales of Kingston insisted that '*they* only take the *Christian Guardian* for the servants to read.'[47] While the Hales family may have enlisted the Methodist organ to provide moral instruction for their domestic help, they also provided them with some of the most extensive reports of parliamentary debates. Finally, Michael Katz found boarders in mid-century Hamilton predominantly in the homes of the relatively affluent – those most able to subscribe to newspapers – not in the homes of the poor.[48]

Joseph Howe claimed that everyone who desired it had access to his *Novascotian*. 'The merchant reads it to his customers round the counter; the smith drops his hammer for a reference to its pages; and it passes from hand to hand, around each farmer's fire all over the broad bosom of the country whose name it bears.' A subscriber to one of Howe's competitors found himself at the centre of a micro-public. 'Generally on the evening after the paper comes to hand, a few of the neighbours assemble in my house ... a reader is appointed, who after drawing his chair up to the head of the table, trimming the candle, coughing, and clearing his throat, unceremoniously bawls out "*Silence*" – and immediately all are attention. After the reading is over, then come the remarks.'[49] Reading aloud and otherwise sharing newspapers encouraged critical discussion.

Patterns of community and family reading in Upper Canada await their historian. John Howison, one of the more caustic travellers to the colony,

45 Mackenzie-Lindsey Papers, Thomas S. Maitland to Mackenzie, 8 Mar. 1825

46 On the passing of newspapers by family and friends, recall that Stayner estimated that 50,000 sheets travelled in the Canadas through the post office in 1840 with the postage paid by someone other than the printer. See note 26 above. More undoubtedly reached non-subscribers by other means.

47 Egerton Ryerson to Samuel Junkin, 30 Mar. 1838, in C.B. Sissions, *Egerton Ryerson: His Life and Letters*, 1 (Toronto: Clarke, Irwin 1937), 438

48 Katz, *People of Hamilton*, 36–8, 77, 231–2

49 *Nova Scotian*, 1 Mar. 1832 and *Colonial Patriot*, 28 Mar. 1828 in J.S. Martell, 'The Press of the Maritime Provinces in the 1830s,' *Canadian Historical Review* 19, no. 1 (March 1938), 47

recorded the scene when the landlord entered the parlour of his tavern 'and having seated himself among the seamstresses [including his wife], began to read articles of foreign intelligence. His female auditors listened with undivided attention until he had got through a paragraph and then they all broke silence at once and commented with much prolixity upon what it contained.'[50] If Howison, like everyone else, thought some were less suited to the effective use of their reason in public than others (French seamstresses in this case), the reading aloud and discussion of newspapers in mixed audiences did not itself strike him as unusual.

The *Artisan*, founded in 1848, may have been the colony's first non-religious paper to appeal explicitly to women as well as men in its prospectus. Some classes of women may also have had fewer points of direct access to newspapers than did their male relations with greater recourse to certain types of taverns and voluntary associations. Yet women had long read and commented on the colonial press. While political commentary was usually written as if its readers were male, the goods and services advertised on the same page acknowledged women as readers as well as consumers. Wives might also manage newspapers during the absence of their editor-husbands and retain ownership as widows.[51]

If women were not systematically excluded from the community of readers, neither were the illiterate. The best estimates suggest that, by 1840, about 80 per cent of Upper Canadian adults could read and write, compared to only about two-thirds of British men and half of British women. (Earlier colonial patterns probably varied considerably and are far less clear.)[52] The high rate by 1840 was partly the product of individ-

---

50 Howison, *Sketches of Upper Canada*, 207–8
51 *Artisan*, 12 Oct. 1848, Kathleen Wilson, *The Sense of the People: Politics, Culture and Imperialism in England, 1715–1785* (Cambridge: Cambridge University Press 1995), 41n, and H.P. Gundy, 'Publishing and Bookselling in Kingston since 1810,' *Historical Kingston* 10 (January 1962), 26 on Hugh Thomson's wife managing their Kingston newspaper while he attended the assembly at York. She assumed ownership after his death. Thomas Dalton's widow retained the *Patriot*. See also the discussion of the Child family in the next chapter. Mary O'Brien, Anna Jameson, Susanna Moodie, and Anne Murray Powell commented on public issues in their writings. For the last's frequent letters to her American brother on political and constitutional issues, see Katherine M.J. McKenna, *A Life of Propriety: Anne Murray Powell and Her Family, 1755–1849* (Montreal and Kingston: McGill-Queen's University Press 1994), 253–5. For family reading in the U.S., see Brown, *Knowledge Is Power*, 160–96.
52 Gordon Darroch and Lee Soltow, *Property and Inequality in Victorian Ontario: Structural Patterns and Cultural Communities in the 1871 Census* (Toronto: University of Toronto Press 1994), 119. For a summary, see Susan E. Houston and Alison Prentice, *Schooling*

ual and family initiative combined with private academies and an increasingly state-directed system of elementary schools. Considerable work had, however, also been done by hundreds of free Sunday schools devoted to basic literacy. Almost all were products of local, interdenominational, voluntary associations – yet another contribution of voluntary associations to the public sphere.[53] Reflecting its appreciation of the impact of these efforts to school the young, the *Brockville Recorder* urged the illiterate to put newspapers 'into the hands of your children, direct them to read their contents aloud.'[54] Reading aloud in non-familial settings further mitigated against inadequate literacy.

Despite its impressive reach, the community of newspaper readers was not universal. Access was easier for some groups than others. Subscribers formed an even smaller, if partly self-selected, association. Editors exaggerated and assumed a community of interest when they spoke of 'the people' rather than the public of newspaper readers. Yet for those who had lived through the exponential growth of the press over less than two decades, it must have been easy to extrapolate from that recent past to a future possibility that already seemed visible on the horizon.

It is no coincidence that potential newspaper subscribers and the membership of most voluntary associations had similar social profiles. Indeed, subscribing to a newspaper was much like joining a voluntary association. Since newspapers often covered the same events, commented on the same issues, copied extensively from each other, and were widely distributed, their readers formed the only truly province-wide association.

Reading brought the individual into an impersonal public arena of other readers. Beyond access to newspapers and the ability to assimilate their content, no further rules or norms existed to exclude potential participants as they did in most other voluntary associations. Since members of this association met only as anonymous readers, the social standing or wealth of any particular reader was irrelevant. Readers were not passive consumers. As subscribers, potential contributors, and discus-

and Scholars in Nineteenth-Century Ontario (Toronto: University of Toronto Press 1991), 84–5. For Britain, see James Vernon, *Politics and the People: A Study in English Political Culture, c. 1815–1867* (Cambridge: Cambridge University Press 1993), 106.

53 Allan Greer, 'The Sunday Schools of Upper Canada,' *Ontario History* 67, no. 3 (September 1975), 173

54 *Brockville Recorder*, 17 Jan. 1834. How were the illiterate to read such advice? See also Bird, *English Woman in America*, 317.

sants with other real or imagined readers, they were active participants. Subscribing to a newspaper was not merely a monetary transaction between consumer and producer. It was a conscious decision to participate in the public sphere and to support a particular vehicle for that participation. Thus, as Dena Goodman argues, 'to subscribe also meant to join a community of subscribers.' Subscribing, even to a newspaper whose editorial viewpoint the reader did not share, kept members of the public 'connected with one another and engaged in the intellectual activity that united them. Subscriptions to periodicals made members out of readers, citizens out of subscribers.'[55]

Subscribers' choice of newspaper was influenced by numerous factors. Among them was their degree of support for its principles. A subscriber to the *Advocate* told one of Mackenzie's agents that he had 'resolved not to support you any longer, from a belief that you were wavering in your political sentiments; but, from the tenor of your late address ... he has determined to contribute to the support of a useful Journal so long as it perseveres in its avowed sentiments to the general interests of this province.'[56] The decentralized and competitive nature of the press increased the proportion of readers who were able to choose among alternative sources. The choice, often conditional, was influenced by more than the timely delivery of paper and ink.

The analogy between newspaper readers and voluntary associations also exposes important differences. Voluntary associations, especially those most closely associated with the public sphere, were rule-governed. Most debating and literary societies, for instance, had rules to instil norms of civility and to exclude religious and partisan discussions. They elected presiding officers to 'moderate' their proceedings. Their membership was smaller and more homogeneous than the general population. Controversy was to be contained within strict limits. Little of this applied to the association of newspaper readers. Membership was more open, incorporating a broader range of interests, backgrounds, and abilities. Politics, far from being excluded, preoccupied most newspapers from the 1820s. Finally, no governing force or presiding officer effectively disciplined the discussants. Such differences explain why some were enthusiastic about literary or debating societies while wary of, if not hostile to, a public of newspaper readers.

It would be misleading, however, to conclude that the community of

55 Goodman, *Republic of Letters*, 175–7
56 Mackenzie-Lindsey Papers, Henry Lasher to Mackenzie, 11 Dec. 1825

newspaper readers lacked structure and rules. With the rise of the independent press, editors became the gatekeepers of the public sphere.
They could not, like the chair of a meeting, control discussion, but they
determined what was published. They decided which issues to address
and how, what to copy and from where, and which letters or contributions deserved a wider audience. Editors often announced their decisions. Some submissions were not of general interest or were simply
'inadmissible.'[57] Gatekeeping also involved inclusion, as when the editor
of the *Kingston Gazette* offered to 'give room to a reply' to a letter he had
printed but whose accuracy he was unable to judge.[58] The editor of the
reform *Brockville Recorder* called for publishing 'as much substantial matter as possible, and often on both sides of a question. It is wholesome for
the people to hear occasionally what their opponents have to say, and
not depend alone on the writings of their friends.'[59] Such principles
were often breached, but by copying from each other and publishing
reports of parliamentary debates, most newspapers offered a wider
range of opinion than was expressed in their editorials.

In 1836 the *Patriot*, frequently among the government's most rabid
supporters, provided material on both sides of the quarrel between Sir
Francis Bond Head and his former executive council. There was no
doubt about its editorial position. The *Patriot* provided reasoned arguments, but also attacked the intelligence, integrity, and loyalty of Head's
opponents. Readers who did not share the paper's viewpoint were not,
however, left in the dark. The *Patriot* broke the news of the executive
council's resignation by publishing its lengthy letter of justification. A
week later, it printed a letter by Robert Baldwin, one of the former
councillors, further outlining their constitutional position and criticism
of the lieutenant-governor. The same issue copied the address of the
Toronto City Council from the radical *Correspondent & Advocate* expressing its lack of confidence in Head's new advisers. The next issue broadcast the resolutions of a Toronto public meeting reiterating the
constitutional position of the governor's opponents. The *Patriot* also
provided readers with reports of the assembly's debate on the dispute
and a letter of support from the Speaker of the Lower Canadian assembly to his Upper Canadian counterpart.[60] In sum, those whose access to

---

57 *Kingston Gazette*, 24 Mar. 1812 and *Niagara Spectator*, 21 Mar. 1817
58 *Kingston Gazette*, 1 Apr. 1815
59 *Brockville Recorder*, 26 Dec. 1839
60 *Patriot*, 18, 25, and 29 Mar. and 8, 12, 19 and 26 Apr. 1836

the community of newspaper readers was limited to the *Patriot* were bombarded with documents and commentary favourable to its editorial position, but they were not thereby deprived of the essential arguments of Head's opponents, often in their own words. Newspapers were fiercely partisan, but they participated in public debate with their opponents and thus exposed their readers, however imperfectly, to that debate.

To take one more example, in 1832, the conservative *Kingston Chronicle* published a letter from 'A British Subject' that referred to the lieutenant-governor's advisers as a faction and called for reforms to the legislative council. The editorial rejected the letter's arguments, but the decision to publish it still angered some readers. In the next issue, the editor responded that 'the columns of a public journal should at all times be open to a fair and candid discussion of the events that are hourly passing before our view.' To serve that ideal, a second letter from 'A British Subject,' shorn of its references to private character, and a submission from 'John Bull' responding to the first letter, appeared. 'A British Subject' returned in the following issue with further constitutional arguments that provoke yet more editorial comment. 'A British Subject' replied again. The editorial called him a disloyal democrat, but undeterred, he submitted a fifth letter that the editor chose not to publish; 'we must decline continuing a correspondent so manifestly opposed to our public principles.' No new arguments were being made and '"The Subject" is no longer edifying to either side.'[61]

The *Chronicle*'s editor defended hearing both sides. He debated, printed letters from opposing viewpoints, edited a submission to meet his sense of propriety, and cut off discussion when he deemed it no longer instructive. Others might have acted differently. Readers frequently complained that particular editors failed to exercise their gatekeeping function properly; that their newspapers were too partisan and scurrilous. The degree of scurrility points to several things: the contested nature of politics; the rejection of deference and genteel norms of politeness; how much participants thought was at stake; and editors' attempts to mobilize those who had been politically inactive by making politics exciting and comprehensible to all.[62] Its presence suggested that

---

61 *Chronicle*, 31 Mar. and 7, 14, 21 and 28 Apr. 1832
62 Gordon S. Wood, 'The Democratization of Mind in the American Revolution,' in *Leadership in the American Revolution*, Library of Congress Symposia (Washington: Library of Congress 1974), 71

cold reason was not enough to excite and motivate an ever-expanding audience, but did not too great an appeal to the senses or passions threaten to jettison 'calm' reason altogether? If effective public discussion required accurate information and balanced analysis, who disciplined those editors who failed to offer either? Violence, as in the so-called 'Type Riots' of 1826, when several youths with prominent government and social connections vandalized William Lyon Mackenzie's print shop, proved counter-productive at best.[63] Perhaps the law could impose accuracy and decorum.

Even those most anxious to police public commentary claimed to be champions of the freedom of the press, by which, following Blackstone, they largely meant that the press faced no *prior* restraint.[64] There were no state censors; no licence was required to write, publish, or distribute comments on affairs of state or anything else. (Further, the law took no notice of individual thought or inquiry and petitioning for redress of grievances had special status.) Such freedom was compatible with imposing legal sanctions after publication for disturbing the peace, undermining the state or its officers, or maliciously attacking individuals' reputations. Such sanctions were required to discriminate between liberty of the press and its licentiousness; between what one Upper Canadian judge called 'fair and candid opinions,' or 'just and useful criticism' that should be encouraged, and 'public calumny and open abuse' that should be punished for the harm they caused.[65] Echoing Blackstone, Attorney-General John Beverley Robinson insisted that its 'licentiousness MAY, but no other cause, or power, or combination ever can destroy or abridge the rational liberty of the Press.'[66] Far from abridging it, the law protected freedom of the press.

---

63 Mackenzie was awarded sufficient damages to purchase a new press and the reputation of ruling circles was severely tarnished. Other extra-legal means to influence editors included withholding money for reporting parliamentary debates or transferring government advertising to a competing paper. In 1825 Charles Fothergill was dismissed as King's Printer for failing to support the government as a member of the assembly.

64 Eckhart Hellmuth, '"The palladium of all other English liberties": Reflections on the Liberty of the Press in England during the 1760s and 1770s,' in Hellmuth, ed., *The Transformation of Political Culture in England and Germany in the Late Eighteenth Century* (Oxford: Oxford University Press 1990), 478–80

65 Levius P. Sherwood to Z. Mudge, 2 Dec. 1828, in Murray Greenwood and Barry Wright, eds., *Canadian State Trials: Law, Politics, and Security Measures, 1608–1837* (Toronto: University of Toronto Press 1996), app. 3, 709–10

66 Robinson, evidence before assembly select committee, 1829, in ibid., 713

Thus, Upper Canadian editors faced potential prosecution in the assembly (for breach of its privileges) or in the courts at the behest of either the government (for seditious libel) or private individuals (for libel). There were several examples of each.[67] Our modern notion of the liberty of the press combines absence of prior restraint with the severest limits on post-publication sanction. Essentially, this expansive notion grew out of the opposition aroused by the use of these policing mechanisms – an opposition that had also undermined their effectiveness.

Not surprisingly, the three principal uses of the law against opposition newspapers coincided with periods of government insecurity: in 1808 against Joseph Willcocks's *Upper Canadian Guardian*; in 1819 against Bartimus Ferguson's *Niagara Spectator;* and in 1828 against William Lyon Mackenzie's *Colonial Advocate*, Hugh C. Thomson's *Upper Canadian Herald*, and Francis Collins's *Canadian Freeman*. The assembly's privileges, used to jail Willcocks, will be discussed later. Ferguson continued to publish Robert Gourlay's addresses despite warnings that such conduct risked legal sanction. He was successfully prosecuted for seditious libel, his harsh sentence effectively killing the *Spectator*. Despite this success and the growing number and boldness of opposition newspapers, officials rightly feared that resort to similar tactics might backfire.

The next – and last – prosecution of editors for seditious libel was brought against Francis Collins in 1828 for criticizing the colonial administration of justice. Charges against Mackenzie and Thomson were dropped, but the indictment of three opposition editors in the same year; demands that they post substantial sureties for future good behaviour (i.e., for refraining from publishing other libels) *prior* to their trial for the first, alleged, libel; judicial proceedings too easily characterized as irregular and partial; and the extreme sentence meted out to Collins aroused strong opposition. The legal mechanisms regulating the press were brought into irreparable disrepute. The apparently selective, partisan use of the law did more to undermine its credibility than its basic principles. Newspapers critical of the government and its officers

---

67 This and subsequent paragraphs provide only the barest summary. For individual cases and the legal and political complexities of the issues, see H. Pearson Gundy, 'Liberty and Licence of the Press in Upper Canada,' in W.H. Heick and Roger Graham, eds., *His Own Man: Essays in Honour of Arthur Reginald Mansden Lower* (Montreal: McGill-Queen's University Press 1974), 71–92, Barry Wright, 'Sedition in Upper Canada: Contested Legality,' *Labour / Le Travail* 29 (Spring 1992), 7–57, and essays 12, 14, and 15 in Greenwood and Wright, eds., *Canadian State Trials*.

were warned or prosecuted on the grounds that excessive criticism threatened to disturb the peace or undermine the state, while government-friendly editors appeared to have free reign to abuse the assembly and its opposition members.[68]

In the period after the War of 1812, individual editors were intimidated or punished, two severely, but the executive, judiciary, and assembly failed to end criticism or to narrow the range of published opinion significantly. Several juries refused to convict. Far from silence or contrition, legal proceedings often brought increased notoriety and martyrdom for the editors and even greater abuse aimed at government and the courts. Moreover, the opposition press continued to grow. For its supporters, the inappropriateness of the law as a policing mechanism for public commentary was confirmed. In their defence, they developed a more expansive notion of press freedom. For those who remained content with a more limited notion of that freedom, the law's inability to impose standards of accuracy and civility was all too apparent.

Collins was the last editor prosecuted for seditious libel. Private actions brought by public figures for libel also appeared to be waning. When a jury refused to convict George Gurnett, editor of the conservative *Courier*, in such a case in 1834, editors of various politics were nearly unanimous in their support of the verdict. It seemed to mark the end of vexatious libel cases. According to one editor, Upper Canadians could be proud of living in a country 'where the freedom of discussion is protected by the force of publick [*sic*] opinion.'[69]

Two years earlier, after Mackenzie complained about government harassment of the press, Colonial Secretary Lord Goderich wryly noted, 'It is needless to look beyond Mr. Mackenzie's journal to be convinced that there is no latitude which the most ardent lover of free discussion ever claimed for such writers, which is not enjoyed with perfect impunity in Upper Canada.' Mackenzie seems to have reached the same conclusion. While in London to present grievance petitions to Goderich, he flatly told Britons that 'the press is free.' The issue was also noticeably absent from his otherwise exhaustive catalogue of complaints in 1835, the Seventh Report of the Grievance Committee.[70]

The theory of the liberty of the press as it evolved during the various

---

68 Partiality was central to John Rolph's defence of Collins; *Canadian Freeman*, 6 Nov. 1828.
69 *British American Journal*, 15 Apr. 1834
70 Goderich in Gundy, 'Liberty and Licence,' 88 and Mackenzie, *Sketches of Canada*, 346

attempts to restrain editors cannot be traced here, but the grounds upon which at least one such attempt was resisted are worth noting. In 1829, Robert Baldwin represented John Carey, editor of the *Observer*, in a private libel action brought by a government office-holder. Baldwin warned the York Assizes that the physical attack on the *Colonial Advocate* in 1826, the criminal indictment and disproportionate punishment of Francis Collins in 1828, and the private libel action against Carey were much more than isolated strikes at radical newspapers. They were part of a concerted attack 'directed against yourselves, your children and your country.' Baldwin did not defend Carey's right to publish his own opinions. At issue was the public's right to discuss, not the individual's right to speak.

For Baldwin, the liberty of the press was a social rather than an individual right. Both government and the people profited from the free circulation of ideas. Government learned the wishes of its citizens. The people learned the intentions of their government. Baldwin implored the jury to ignore the law of libel as expounded by Justice Macaulay: 'I deny it is law – because I deny the morality of it – I deny the common sense of it – I assert that that cannot be an immoral crime which so greatly benefits the public at large, as the freedom of discussion for which I contend.' Liberty of the press was grounded in a basic social good: freedom of discussion.[71]

Few resisted any such opportunity to exalt press freedom as the 'palladium' of British liberties. It is hard to recapture the earnest wonder with which contemporaries celebrated print culture from their courtrooms to their toasts at the annual dinner of the York Typographical Society.[72] In his defence of Francis Collins, John Rolph rehearsed all the usual claims for the press – 'the most powerful engine of the human mind.' It diffused knowledge, enlightened the people, protected liberty, and threw light on those who, from shame at their misdeeds, hid in the darkness of royal courts and cabinets. Far more than by the mechanics of mixed monarchy, public officials were restrained by fear of public scorn following exposure in the press. Its presence was a measure of civilization, its absence of tyranny. Colonial editors boasted of increased circulation or the launching of a new paper as much to proclaim their

---

71 Baldwin, *Canadian Freeman* copied in *Patriot*, 19 Nov. 1829. For the liberty to publish as a social right, see Samuel H. Beer, *To Make a Nation: The Rediscovery of American Federalism* (Cambridge, Mass.: Harvard University Press 1993), 74–7.

72 This paragraph is indebted to Hellmuth, '"The palladium of all other English liberties,"' 486–94. For the Typographical Society, see *Colonial Advocate*, 17 Oct. 1833.

community's membership in the free, progressive world as to attract subscribers and advertisers. Great advances in liberty, especially the Protestant Reformation and the Glorious Revolution, were presented as chapters in the history of the printed word. Conveniently, the common law of libel could be associated with the infamous Stuarts and Star Chamber. Unenlightened absolutism betrayed its reliance on arbitrary power, corruption, superstition, and ignorance by attempting to muzzle the press, the most formidable enemy of each.[73]

The pervasiveness of this celebration of print democracy helps explain the optimistic founding of so many new titles even where insufficient subscribers were to be found – one reason for the frequency of newspaper failures.[74] Such grandiloquent claims also highlighted the dangers of using the law to restrain the press, but said little about what to do when individual editors undermined the very possibility of rational discussion by systematically spreading invective or falsehood. If not the law, what would combat malicious attempts to stir up trouble or limit what John Beverley Robinson called the 'mere unmeaning ribaldry, and vulgar abuse, which so much disfigure political discussions in this Province?'[75] The answer was evident by 1831 when the assembly first considered expelling one of its members, William Lyon Mackenzie, for denigrating the House as editor of the *Advocate*.

William Morris, for one, failed to see how the expulsion could be opposed as a violation of the liberty of the press. 'How is it possible that the people of the country can be rightly informed,' he asked, 'when the public journals of this town disseminate such falsehoods?' When the press 'fairly comments upon our public acts, I consider it entitled to our most unbounded protection; but when it is wholly employed in the propagation of falsehood – foul, malicious and slanderous – I think it should be arrested in its unholy career, and taught to pay some respect to the opinions and feelings of mankind.' Morris presented the privileges of the assembly and the laws of libel as defenders of the public sphere.[76] In principle, he was right. In practice, there

73 Rolph, *Canadian Freeman*, 6 Nov. 1828
74 John C. Nerone, 'A Local History of the Early U.S. Press: Cincinnati, 1793–1848,' in William S. Solomon and Robert W. McChesney, eds., *Ruthless Criticism: New Perspectives in U.S. Communication History* (Minneapolis: University of Minnesota Press 1993), 42
75 Robinson to John Colborne, 4 Apr. 1829, in Greenwood and Wright, eds., *Canadian State Trials*, app. 3, 722
76 Morris, *Cobourg Star*, 27 Dec. 1831. See also H.J. Boulton, *Canadian Freeman*, 8 Dec. 1831.

was no way to distinguish between the uses and abuses of the press or
to enforce those privileges and laws against the latter that would be
widely seen as safe and fair.

More wary of the enormous potential for abuse of parliamentary privileges and the law, Marshall Spring Bidwell responded that 'if that press
transcended its legitimate privileges, he would leave the press itself to
correct the evil. If one newspaper published falsehoods, and misrepresentations, other papers would expose the falsehoods, and correct the
misrepresentation – the public would be undeceived, and the libeller
would soon meet with public scorn, as the just reward of his dishonest
conduct.'[77] Several editors had already come to this conclusion in the
wake of the 'Type Riots.' The *Upper Canada Herald* argued that 'public
opinion inflicts a punishment, in consequence of which real abuse generally operates more against its authors and publishers, than against the
persons abused. This is the natural and salutary corrective of an evil
which seems to be inseparable from a full enjoyment of the benefit of a
Free Press.'[78] Decency and fairness were to be enforced by public opinion and subscribers, not by legislative and judicial institutions. Other
papers would correct inaccurate information; subscribers would abandon any paper that repeatedly violated community norms. It was a reas-
suring conclusion for advocates of an expansive definition of press
freedom.

By the early 1830s, readers had become the principal check on newspapers. Given the financial precariousness of newspapers and their
dependence on subscribers, the potential for control by readers was
probably greater than it would become once advertisers contributed the
bulk of newspapers' revenue. In the meantime, public opinion was to
control the individual organs of public opinion. This self-referential
quality pointed to the growing belief in the autonomy and ultimate
authority of the public sphere.

Even the staunchly conservative *Patriot* conceded that, while much
poison had been spread by the press, 'the only way of averting the
intended ill, is by applying more force to the same engine in counter-

---

77 Bidwell, *Cobourg Star*, 27 Dec. 1831. Also commenting on Mackenzie's expulsion, the
    Christian Guardian, 7 Dec. 1831, argued that 'public opinion is the true supporter of
    the press – and public opinion is the proper and only effectual corrector of its licen-
    tiousness.'
78 *Upper Canada Herald*, 30 June 1826 and also the conservative *Courier* copied in *Farmers'
    Journal*, 5 July 1826.

action, which is always successful in repressing arrogant presumption and maintaining truth.'[79] These two contentions, that only argument could counter argument and that the right answer always emerged from the resulting clash, marked the *Patriot's* acceptance of the voluntary, self-regulating, association of newspaper readers.

The most tangible manifestations of this association were news or reading rooms. Most were probably quite utilitarian: a room with chairs, lamps, a table for the most recent newspapers and journals, and shelves for earlier issues. Here men (there is no evidence that women frequented them) congregated to read newspapers and journals.

Since membership involved annual fees, reading rooms did not extend the social reach of periodicals. Rather, they offered numerous papers and more specialized, expensive, or distant publications for roughly the cost of subscribing to a single title. Their members were thus exposed to a greater range of editorial opinion, as when an Irish Catholic reformer read the conservative Orange organ the *Brockville Statesmen*, 'a paper I had never before seen, and was indeed prejudiced against.'[80] Reading rooms could also 'increase society'[81] by providing occasion for readers, away from family or business, to exchange information, discuss topics of mutual interest and develop critical skills through conversation with fellow readers. One newsroom formally prohibited discussion and reading aloud since they might disturb other members or endanger their harmony, but it is unlikely that silence always prevailed even where it was mandated.[82] Finally, by storing periodicals over time, reading rooms acted as a sort of reference library.

Many such rooms were organized by a local newspaper editor/publisher. They might be housed in the same building as the print shop and stocked with exchange copies of periodicals. Thus, the full benefits of the exchange system were extended to members of the community. Others were established by public meeting and subscription. Given their intimate connection with newspapers and the likely overlap in patronage, newsrooms were probably attempted in every community able to sustain a newspaper or debating society.[83]

---

79 *Patriot,* 7 Feb. 1834

80 'An Irish Roman Catholic and Constitutional Reformer,' *Examiner,* 29 Aug. 1838

81 *Brockville Gazette,* 23 Aug. 1830

82 *St Catharines Journal,* 23 Mar. 1839

83 Some of the attempts to establish independent newsrooms mentioned in the press

Bartemus Ferguson, editor of the *Niagara Spectator*, may have made the first such attempt in 1817. His notice is worth quoting in full since the advertised features remained typical.

> Having obtained a more central situation for our office, we are induced, from the voluntary encouragement of several Gentlemen, to establish a Newspaper Reading Room. A very convenient room, directly over the Printing Office, will shortly be in readiness, and appropriated exclusively to that purpose. The terms will be one dollar for three months, or four dollars per year, payable at the end of every quarter. The room will be furnished with necessary accommodations for reading, and will be open for readers from nine in the morning until nine in the evening.
>
> Our terms, we conceive, can afford no objection to the undertaking, particularly when it is considered that an individual publication would cost an equal, if not a larger sum. Here the reader will have at his leisure, the perusal of from thirty to forty publications weekly, besides a few choice Magazines and Monthly Reviews.[84]

Such concrete manifestations of the community of newspaper readers were increasingly common by the 1830s.

In 1829, the editor of the *Farmers' Journal* attempted to found 'a respectable Reading Room' at St Catharines by calling a meeting 'of the gentlemen of this village and its vicinity.'[85] Labels like 'respectable' and 'gentlemen' often referred to various social ranks in Upper Canada, but several newsrooms do appear to have been designed, in part, to offer a more refined atmosphere than was possible in many taverns.

The name of the colony's most famous example, the Commercial News Room, opened at the capital in 1833, speaks of its mercantile founders and purpose. In 1846, the membership rate was £1 5s, probably sufficient to exclude most artisans. The room, located upstairs in the Market Buildings, was open twelve hours a day and provided space for meetings, including those of the Toronto Board of Trade. In 1850, sixty-two period-

---

include Niagara (1817), St Catharines (1829, 1834, 1839, 1840), York/Toronto (1824, 1827, 1833, 1838), Kingston (1827 for religious works?, 1832), Cobourg (1849), Perth (1853), Brockville (1830, 1852), Hallowell (by 1833), Hamilton (1832), and Bytown (1838 or 1839).

84 *Spectator*, 16 Oct. 1817 and Jennifer Ruth Johnson, 'The Availability of Reading Material for the Pioneer in Upper Canada: Niagara District, 1792–1841,' MA thesis, University of Western Ontario 1982, 98

85 *Farmers' Journal*, 6 May 1829 and also *British Colonial Argus*, 11 Jan. 1834

icals were on hand: forty-nine newspapers (all ten from Toronto, an equal number from elsewhere in the Canadas, ten from London, five from elsewhere in Britain, seven from New York City, and seven from elsewhere in the United States), ten reviews from Britain and the United States, and three specialized periodicals published in the province.[86]

Two newsrooms established by reform editors were intended to be more accessible. In 1827, William Lyon Mackenzie assailed attempts to establish a York newsroom with a $10 subscription fee. Mackenzie thought 'so absurd a sum is named ... to keep out all except a few individuals of a certain class.' The founding of a polite newsroom was, for Mackenzie, yet another example of the elite's penchant for exclusive cultural, not to mention political, institutions. Three years before, Mackenzie had established the 'York Reading Room.' At $4, its yearly subscription was significantly lower, if hardly negligible, but it was open to *Advocate* subscribers at half price.[87] Francis Hincks opened a newsroom soon after founding the *Examiner* in 1838. Local subscribers gained access, free of charge, to the newspapers with which the *Examiner* exchanged.[88]

At Kingston, the *Chronicle* praised the editor of its major competitor, the *Upper Canada Herald,* for opening a newsroom in 1832, 'supplied with nearly 60 newspapers and periodicals of the best description. The list of subscribers is increasing, and this desideratum so long required in Kingston, is likely to become the resort of "all the talents," a valuable acquisition to the daily increasing advantages of the town, and a repository of useful and improving information.'[89] For the *Chronicle*, those with the money and inclination to join constituted 'all the talents.' Informed opinion in Kingston was to be found in its newsroom. If so, one wants even more to eavesdrop on Henry Jones, a clerk in the Crown Lands Office, when, in 1843, he 'had a confab in the [Kingston] Newsroom with Hawke and Patton on the rights of women.'[90] Readers came

86 *Examiner,* 30 Jan. 1839 claimed that it owed its continued existence to the city's mercantile interest. For its founders and other details see, *York Commercial Directory*, 133, *Brown's Toronto City ... Directory*, 29, and *Rowsell's City of Toronto ... Directory*, xlix–l.

87 *Colonial Advocate*, 2 Dec. 1824 and 22 Mar. 1827

88 *Examiner,* 30 Jan. 1839

89 *Chronicle*, 19 May 1832. For an earlier call to establish a local newsroom, see *Patriot*, 8 June 1830. For similar estimates of the number of periodicals in other newsrooms, see *Western Mercury*, 29 Dec. 1831 and *St Catharines Journal*, 16 Mar. 1839.

90 Lambton County Archives, Henry John Jones Diary, 3 Apr. 1843. I owe this reference to H. Julia Roberts. For further evidence of newsroom discussion and one patron's resentment see Marcus to Lydia Child, 2 Nov. 1843, *Child Letters*, 92.

together as a community in a public, albeit respectable, setting to collectively purchase, read, and discuss printed material.

Other voluntary associations, especially libraries, offered reading
rooms to their members. One reader of the *Advocate* cancelled his subscription upon becoming a founding member of the Ancaster Library
Society, reportedly 'supported by most of the inhabitants here,' and the
Dalhousie Library at Perth asked editors in both Canadas to forward
their papers 'to be filed in the Library room.'[91] Associations for elite
sociability, such as the United Services Club and the Upper Canada
Club, also incorporated reading rooms. Besides various colonial and
American newspapers, the latter subscribed to Britain's leading conservative, Whig, and radical reviews.[92] Mechanics' institutes extended the
social reach of such periodicals. In January 1835, the Kingston Institute
began ordering 'reprints of the principal European periodical Literary
Reviews,' and by April claimed 'there are 20 or 30 Reviews and newspapers regularly taken in for the Reading Room table.' At Toronto,
successive annual reports noted that reading-room attendance was
'unprecedentedly great,' that the executive was 'gratified' by the large
number of readers, and that the room 'has now [in 1854] become the
favorite resort of a large number, who but for it might find it impossible
to gain access to the periodical literature of the day.' The following year,
its catalogue listed forty-eight reviews, magazines, and newspapers.[93]
Their number and range mirrored that of the Commercial News Room,
but the institute, with annual fees a fraction of the newsroom's, offered
them to a broader social range. Different social groups may have frequented different venues, but they accessed the same periodicals.

91 Mackenzie-Lindsey Papers, Matthew Crooks to William Lyon Mackenzie, 11 Jan. 1825
    and *Perth Examiner* copied in *Kingston Chronicle*, 11 July 1829. When Francis Collins
    accused the Ancaster library of not subscribing to his reform *Freeman*, its treasurer,
    George Gurnett, assured him in his conservative *Gore Gazette*, 21 Dec. 1827, that the
    library did indeed take the *Freeman*.

92 On the United Services Club (for the military and navy at York), see *Courier* copied in
    Upper Canada Herald, 23 Oct. 1833. J.K. Johnson, 'The U.C. Club and the Upper Cana-
    dian Elite, 1837–1840,' *Ontario History* 69, no. 3 (September 1977), 154. The Free &
    Easy Club established at Chatham in 1839 also appears to have had a reading room.
    Foster Vernon, 'The Development of Adult Education in Ontario, 1790–1900,' D.Ed.
    thesis, University of Toronto 1969, 52

93 *Chronicle & Gazette*, 14 Jan. and 14 Apr. 1835. For Toronto see the catalogues in
    Archives of Ontario, MU2020 and annual reports for 1846, 1851, 1852, and 1854. For
    the reading room of the Cobourg Mechanics' Institute, see *Cobourg Reformer*, 3 Mar.
    1835.

Commercial ventures such as hotels and Toronto's Floating Baths incorporated reading rooms.[94] Catering to that city's prominent and hoping to board out-of-town members of parliament during the upcoming session, the owner of the British Coffee House advertised that 'among the attractions which he intends to add to the establishment will be a reading room which will be furnished with the principal English and provincial papers.'[95] The founding of independent newsrooms and their prevalence elsewhere attests to the importance of print culture in this period. As physical spaces created by readers, newsrooms embodied the larger public sphere.

Even without designated reading rooms, newspapers were probably available in leading inns and hotels. Oliver Mowat, a young Presbyterian lawyer boarding in Toronto, subscribed to the Commercial News Room, but had read the latest issue of *The Church*, the organ of the Anglican hierarchy, 'in MacDonald's barroom the other day while waiting for the glad sound of the dinner Bell.'[96] Left alone in Cobourg, Susanna Moodie 'had to get through the long day at the inn in the best manner I could. The local papers were soon exhausted.' She mentions only the *Reformer* by name, but her plural reference suggests that the conservative *Star* was available as well.[97]

Did the thousand or so taverns scattered across the province in the early 1830s and frequented by a socially and politically mixed clientele contain newspapers as well? J.J. Talman was probably right to argue that taverns, 'where the contents of one newspaper, probably much distorted by repetition and discussion, could influence several score of non-readers,' multiplied the power of the press.[98] Taverns certainly acted as community bulletin-boards. The proprietors of the *Royal Standard* asked tavern keepers to post 'this Prospectus in some conspicuous place.'[99] Copies of newspapers were also widely available. When a traveller found

---

94 Heather Murray, 'Frozen Pen, Fiery Print, and Fothergill's Folly: Cultural Organization in Toronto, Winter 1836–37,' *Essays in Canadian Writing* 61 (Spring 1997), 48
95 *Upper Canada Gazette*, 17 Dec. 1829
96 Oliver Mowat to John Mowat, 29 July 1844 and 20 Nov. 1845, in '"Neither Radical Nor Tory Nor Whig,"' 106, 121, 131
97 Moodie, *Roughing It in the Bush*, 83
98 Talman, 'Newspapers of Upper Canada,' 15. The following discussion is much indebted to H. Julia Roberts and her 'Taverns and Tavern-goers in Upper Canada: The 1790s to the 1850s,' PhD thesis, University of Toronto 1999, esp. 8, 28–31, 75–6, 105–21.
99 Prospectus, *Royal Standard*, Oct. 1836 and also *Niagara Herald*, 7 Feb. 1801

himself in a Chatham tavern in 1840, a local Justice of the Peace introduced himself 'by lending me a well-thumbed newspaper.' Continuing on to Detroit, he noted that 'the bar-room of the American was the only place in which a newspaper could be seen for five minutes.'[100]

Innkeepers subscribed to newspapers, probably in disproportionate numbers. In 1826, when the *Advocate*'s Cornwall agent sent Mackenzie the names of ten new subscribers, five were listed as innkeepers: three at Cornwall and one each at nearby MilleRoche and Williamsburg. Taverns could also serve as distribution centres for other subscribers. All four *Advocates* destined for MilleRoche were to be sent care of a local innkeeper.[101] Mackenzie had already been accused (with considerable truth) of sending the *Advocate* 'unbidden to Taverns and other places, to meet the eyes of the people in the Country in every quarter.'[102] In 1808, the *Upper Canada Gazette* announced that 'the Gazette for Subscribers living out of Town, will hereafter be left at the tavern of Messr. Deary & Campbell.'[103]

Except for places of worship, taverns were often the only spaces outside the home where large numbers of Upper Canadians regularly congregated and conversed. As such, they served as information clearing houses, places to learn or have confirmed the latest news and gossip. Travellers and pedlars stopping at the local tavern extended the geographic range of its face-to-face communications.[104] Moreover, unlike sermons, charges to juries, or other examples of early information diffusion, information in taverns was not exchanged in a controlled or hierarchical fashion by elites intent on providing instruction. Taverns were places where people could mingle, hold a variety of meetings, and exchange gossip and news. Some of that talk concerned newspapers and politics.

When Joseph Willcocks was tried by the House of Assembly for libel in 1808, his only defence witness had overheard one of Willcocks's accusers 'assert at a tavern in York, that he did not think Willcocks would be

---

100 Morleigh, *Life in the West*, 203, 227. Note that the newspaper was 'well-thumbed,' indicating either intensive reading or extensive circulation.

101 Mackenzie-Lindsey Papers, Charles McDonell to Mackenzie, 20 Feb. 1826

102 Jarvis, *Statement of Facts*, 10 and Cecilia Morgan, *Public Men and Virtuous Women: The Gendered Languages of Religion and Politics in Upper Canada, 1791–1850* (Toronto: University of Toronto Press 1996), 169

103 *Gazette*, 27 Aug. 1808

104 David Conroy, *In Public Houses: Drink & the Revolution of Authority in Colonial Massachusetts* (Chapel Hill: University of North Carolina Press 1995), 45, 48

brought to trial.' A reader of the *Kingston Gazette* at Gananoque in 1812 informed its editor that a recent article on medical doctors had sparked discussion: 'Three of them were disputing in a small Tavern where I happened to be last evening, on the propriety of the prescriptions of your correspondent.' Four years later, the *Niagara Spectator* complained about the lack of parliamentary intelligence from York, but 'it is true we hear in Bar-Rooms and in the public Streets, that the District is divided and about County Towns &c.' It was also in a tavern where an illiterate Upper Canadian heard an election handbill read aloud the night before the poll.[105]

Taverns worried the privileged less because of popular drinking habits than because of the potential for unguarded expression and behaviour in quasi-public, if relatively unregulated, spaces. One critic of bar rooms in inns argued that 'the glorious rendezvous of true liberalism is the bar room ... Their only use is to encourage loafers and idlers to congregate together to talk, spit and smoke, to run down the good fame of their neighbors, traduce the character of their betters, and abuse the government under which they live. They are nests of filth, and arenas for political and other useless discussions ... A man may drop in for a few minutes, free from all restraint, talk to Tom, Dick and Jerry about what concerns them not.'[106] Without the restraints of family, work, or social superiors, bar rooms provided liberal democratic 'arenas for political and other useless discussions.'

As part of a general condemnation of Mackenzie, another commentator asserted that 'he may ape the man of talents in a low tavern, – a place he seems particularly fond of, – to circulate his opinion; but even here his want of principle is condemned and his follies are discussed and derided.'[107] After the rebellion, there were renewed calls to ensure the loyalty of tavern keepers. Those owned by Americans were singled out as

---

105 *Upper Canada Gazette*, 17 Sept. 1808, Candidus to Reckoner, *Kingston Gazette*, 6 May 1812, *Spectator*, 15 Mar. 1816, and Roberts, 'Taverns and Tavern-goers,' 121. See also Howison, *Sketches of Upper Canada*, 180.

106 Roger North, *Cobourg Star*, 19 June 1839. See also *Patriot*, 9 Aug. 1833.

107 Scrutator, *Patriot*, 29 Sept. 1835. Note the similarity between the concern that Mackenzie could 'ape the man of talents' in taverns and Richard Bonnycastle's concerns about temperance societies discussed in the previous chapter. The equation of government opponents with taverns was also not new. Anon., *Spectator*, 6 Aug. 1818, referring to Robert Gourlay's supporters, complained that 'men who have hitherto confined their efforts to the forests, and often made them ring with the stroke of their axes, now assume the title of patriots, and awaken the echoes of the bar-room.'

'dens of sedition' and platforms for 'speechifying' on the virtues of republicanism. Why did authorities care about the allegiance of tavern keepers if they were not thought to provide important political spaces and potentially influence their patrons?[108]

The growth of newspapers did not replace face-to-face communication in inns and taverns. Some read their newspapers there, talked about what they had read, or heard others talk about their reading. Writing about colonial Massachusetts, David Conroy notes that 'non-subscribers, even the illiterate, could hear the news read and interpreted at taverns.' The concept of the public sphere demanded that people be informed. Newspapers and pamphlets were primary vehicles for information, but as Conroy points out, 'public readings and discussions' in taverns that catered to all segments of the population 'provided a physical representation symbolic' of the new critical public. The sight of others reading or discussing in newsrooms, voluntary associations, and taverns, across the counter of the local store, or around a neighbour's fireplace offered tangible evidence of the broader public sphere.[109]

We know little of the content of these discussions, but, after 1821, the most striking feature of colonial newspapers was the mass of close type devoted to third-person summaries of the debates of the assembly. Here readers found much of the raw material from which to make informed political judgments. The move from scarcity to abundance of parliamentary intelligence redefined the roles and political status of newspaper readers, elected representatives, and non-elective institutions. It contributed to the belief that a 'public' existed that could safely monopolize political power.

In Britain, the House of Commons jealously guarded its privacy as part of its epic struggle with the Crown and later with the people 'out-of-doors.' From 1770, magazines, followed by newspapers, began to offer relatively full reports of important debates, but not until the construction of new Houses of Parliament after the fire of 1834 was an official

---

108 *Niagara Chronicle,* 17 Jan. 1839. On the politics of licensing in Toronto see Gregory Kealey, 'Orangemen and the Corporation: The Politics of Class during the Union of the Canadas,' in Victor L. Russell, ed., *Forging a Consensus: Historical Essays on Toronto* (Toronto: University of Toronto Press 1984), 47–50.

109 Conroy, *In Public Houses,* 234, 180n, 189, 219, 232–5, 237n, 298, 304–5 and Brown, *Knowledge Is Power,* 18, 129

Reporters' Gallery designated. Jürgen Habermas emphasizes the coincidence of this designation with the Reform Act of 1832. The alteration of the franchise marked the end of the Commons' long road from privileged estate of the realm to national assembly. Its legitimacy now rested on its claim to represent the interests and opinions of 'the people.' The availability of its deliberations was integral to that change. As Habermas concludes, 'In the role of a permanent critical commentator,' the British public 'had definitively broken the exclusiveness of Parliament and evolved into the officially designated discussion partner of the delegate.' Those who read newspapers 'were no longer treated as people whom, like "strangers," one could exclude from the deliberations.' Indeed, the great social and moral critic of the age, Thomas Carlyle, elevated the parliamentary reporter to his pantheon of heroes, since 'does not, though the name Parliament subsists, the parliamentary debate go on now, everywhere and at all times in a far more comprehensive way, *out* of Parliament altogether?'[110]

The same would come to be said in Upper Canada. Its first parliament assembled at Newark in September 1792, but knowledge of this and other early parliaments was scarce. The inaugural issue of the first colonial newspaper, the official *Upper Canada Gazette*, appeared the following April. When the second session opened at the end of May 1793, it printed Lieutenant-Governor Simcoe's opening speech and both houses' replies. Just before the end of the session, the *Gazette* provided highly abbreviated journals of the assembly from one week of the session and a list of acts receiving royal assent. Addresses from both houses to the king on affairs in France were also published. The *Gazette* later printed at least two of the colony's new statutes.[111] Rumour and private correspondence from members or visitors to the public gallery broadcast some knowledge of early sessions, but the number reached and amount of information conveyed must have been quite limited.

---

110 Jürgen Habermas, *The Structural Transformation of the Public Sphere: An Inquiry into a Category of Bourgeois Society,* trans. Thomas Burger (Cambridge, Mass.: MIT Press 1989), 60–6 and Carlyle, 'The Hero as Man of Letters,' 141. See J.R. Pole, *The Gift of Government: Political Responsibility from the English Restoration to American Independence* (Athens: University of Georgia Press 1983), chap. 4 and 104–38, Peter D.G. Thomas, 'The Beginning of Parliamentary Reporting in the Newspaper, 1768–1774,' *English Historical Review* 74 (October 1959), 623–36, and A. Aspinall, 'The Reporting and Publishing of the House of Commons' Debates, 1771–1834,' in Richard Pares and A.J.P. Taylor, eds., *Essays Presented to Sir Lewis Namier* (London: Macmillan 1956), 227–57.

111 *Upper Canada Gazette,* 6 June and 4, 11, 18, and 25 July 1793

The incomplete survival of many early newspapers makes it difficult to ascertain precisely what was or was not published, but the pattern is clear. The government's official organ usually published the vice-regal speech opening the session, the replies of both houses, a list of the bills receiving royal assent, and the vice-regal speech closing the session. Important new statutes were then published. From December 1794, the *Gazette* was published by Gideon Tiffany, later with the help of his brother, Silvester. As American printers, they were suspected of republican sympathies. Once removed from the *Gazette* in 1797, they intended, according to Chief Justice Elmsley, to establish an independent paper 'for the purposes of *disseminating political knowledge.*'[112] For Elmsley, this was cause for alarm.

Their first, short-lived, attempt, the *Canada* (later *Canadian*) *Constellation*, printed a draft bill from the assembly, but Silvester Tiffany's only slightly less precarious *Niagara Herald* published important parliamentary intelligence from the 1801 session. Despite ambitious intentions, time and space constrained it to offering 'the journalizing and arguments in as dense form as possible' – some day's proceedings were condensed to a single sentence. Yet the *Herald* provided unprecedented access to the legislature, including basic lines of argument and votes on a number of issues – some of the latter at the request of readers.[113] Well aware of the hostility of York administrators and the power of the assembly and the courts, Tiffany tread carefully. A rather cryptic editorial referred to parliamentary debate on two contentious issues, but noted that 'it is not always prudent to repeat what has been said by those who are privileged to say.'[114] Newspaper readers were not so privileged. While a fascinating first instance of parliamentary reporting, the *Herald* failed to establish a precedent. Officials had not made it notorious by prosecuting it for letting ordinary Upper Canadians read a little of what the privileged had said and, the next year, it collapsed. Not until the establishment of the *Guardian* at Niagara in 1807 and the *Kingston*

---

112 Douglas G. Lockhead, 'Tiffany, Silvester,' *Dictionary of Canadian Biography*, 5 (Toronto: University of Toronto Press 1983), 814–16
113 *Canadian Constellation*, 14 Dec. 1799 and *Niagara Herald*, 6 June, 4 July, and 1 Aug. 1801
114 *Niagara Herald*, 18 July 1801. Tiffany may have feared prosecution for repeating words outside the assembly that had been protected by members' privileges inside. Such a case arose in Prince Edward Island, but none has come to light for Upper Canada. J.M. Bumsted, 'Liberty of the Press in Early Prince Edward Island,' in Greenwood and Wright, eds., *Canadian State Trials*, 539–40

Gazette in 1810 did the official *Gazette* face more serious, long-standing, rivals.[115]

Even those with access to the *Gazette* still learned little: when parliament was in session, the issues singled out by the lieutenant-governor, the titles of new statutes, and the contents of some of them. In 1793, the *Gazette* published abbreviated journals for one week of the session. While it contained no division lists, it revealed such parliamentary details as the resolutions and motions proposed, who had moved and seconded them, and their fate. Even such minimal publicity was the exception. Selected journals appeared in the *Gazette* only three more times before 1817: from about three weeks of the second session of the third parliament (1802), a little more than one week of the fourth session of the fourth parliament (1808), and part of one day of the second session of the fifth parliament (1810). No journals were printed for the remainder of the fifth parliament and, with the American invasion of York, the *Gazette* ceased to function during part of the sixth parliament.

The *Kingston Gazette* was the only colonial newspaper operating throughout the war, but it published little more than the speeches opening the first four sessions of the sixth parliament. For the fifth session (1816), it printed what had generally appeared in the official paper, including a list of the new statutes copied from the recently established *Spectator* at Niagara. In its inaugural issue, the *Spectator*'s editor regretted 'the want of opportunity of laying before the public, the proceedings of the present Session.' No member had sent him the information. He called on electors to 'choose men who will pay some attention to your business ... it is proper that you should from time to time be informed of what the parliament is doing ... we are all in the dark.'[116] Parliament's business was the public's business.

---

115 The prospectus of the *Kingston Gazette* copied in *York Gazette*, 16 July 1810, promised that it would 'exhibit, from time to time, a statement of Parliamentary proceedings,' but during the third and fourth sessions of the fifth parliament (1811 and 1812), it published nothing more than what usually appeared in the official *Gazette*.

116 *Spectator*, 15 Mar. 1816. This may have elicited the desired response, since the *Spectator* soon published an 'extract of a letter from a gentleman at York to his friend lately returned to Niagara.' The letter was a highly favourable (and cursory) review of the sentiments, legislation, and members of the sixth parliament (1812–16 and recently dissolved). It sought to fill the gap in published information created by the war (and to influence the elections of 1816?). See the *Kingston Gazette*, 11 and 18 May 1816, which attributed the letter to the *Spectator*. The *Kingston Gazette*, 7 Apr. 1818, relied on a traveller from York for news that the House had been prorogued and for a list of bills passed.

The extent to which Upper Canadians were 'in the dark' soon changed. With a new editor, Robert C. Horne, the *Upper Canada Gazette* was re-established in 1817. Besides the usual official speeches, addresses, and list of new statutes, he published the names of the members of both houses, the journals of the assembly for a substantial portion of the first session of the seventh parliament, a list of acts reserved as well as those assented to, a brief summary of arguments from one day, and the results of a division from the same day (but without names). He continued to print fairly extensive reports of the journals for the second and third sessions (1818), at least some of which were copied by the *Kingston Gazette* and the *Spectator*.

The first session of the seventh parliament also saw the third reporting of actual debates in the House. A member of the House, James Durand, was charged with contempt for his 'Address to the Independent Electors of Wentworth,' in the *Spectator*. In March 1817, the *Upper Canada Gazette* published a fairly extensive summary of actual speeches made regarding the alleged libel, which were copied by the *Kingston Gazette* and the *Spectator*.[117] Further information about this session came in a letter from 'A Canadian Commoner' to the *Kingston Gazette*, complaining, among other things, that the session had been prorogued before the House could consider resolutions the lieutenant-governor disapproved of. In fact, he had acted in large measure to prevent the resolutions from appearing in the colonial press, a goal defeated by the 'Commoner.'[118] In 1817, fear of publicity was already long-standing, but responses to it were about to be transformed by a new information environment.

After the close of the following session, four issues of the *Spectator* included columns entitled 'Resolutions, Addresses &c., &c., &c., of the Commons House of Assembly, and the Legislative Council, and the minutes of a By-Stander, at the bar of the House of Commons during the last session of Parliament.'[119] Despite their grandiose title, the reports

---

117 *Kingston Gazette*, 22 Mar. 1817, attributing the report to the official *Gazette*, and
     Spectator, 21 Mar. 1817, without attribution. The *Spectator* noted that 'we have received
     the York Gazette up to the 13th instant, but can obtain nothing later from the Provin-
     cial Parliament, than what will be found in our preceding columns' which covered
     26 February to 3 March. The official *Gazette* continued its coverage of the journals on
     20 March.
118 A Canadian Commoner, *Kingston Gazette*, 12 Apr. 1817 and Hartwell Bowsfield,
     'Upper Canada in the 1820's: The Development of Political Consciousness,' PhD the-
     sis, University of Toronto 1976, 121
119 *Spectator*, 28 May, 11 and 18 June 1818. The first is marked 'continued' but the previ-
     ous issue is not extant.

were dominated by editorializing and official resolutions concerning a dispute between the two chambers. There was little attempt to report members' arguments or speeches. Nonetheless, through the publicity they gave to the dispute, to the regular journals of the assembly for the first three sessions of the seventh parliament, and especially to the trial of James Durand, these three newspapers did much to lift the veil on the legislative process.[120]

Once the journals began to appear regularly in 1817 and 1818, reporting actual debates seemed logical. The first public call for such reporting was probably a letter to the editor of the *Kingston Gazette* from a Niagara reader in 1811. He subscribed 'to two American papers, from which I receive the earliest foreign information.' A colonial newspaper was of little use for foreign intelligence or the local news of Niagara, but 'our parliament is now in session, and I wish you could procure and publish their debates; as I am now too aged and infirm to attend as an auditor.'[121] Glimpses of the debates of the assembly had been directly accessible to those who could not 'attend as an auditor' only twice before, in 1801 and 1808.[122] They appeared again briefly on a single issue in 1817 and would only be available to most newspaper readers from 1821.

In 1808, the government faced opposition in the House from Joseph Willcocks, who had established the colony's first fully opposition newspaper, the *Upper Canadian Guardian and Freeman's Journal*, in July 1807, shortly after his dismissal as Home District sheriff.[123] The official *Gazette* printed journals for the beginning of the session and summarized the speeches and positions of several identified members of the House. For

---

120 Reports of the assembly's journals for the fourth session do not appear to have been published. They reappeared for the fifth. For material reported from the first two sessions see *Upper Canada Gazette* and *Kingston Gazette*, February, March, and April 1817 and 1818 and *Spectator*, 28 Feb. 1817 and 9 Apr. 1818. For the third session see *Kingston Gazette*, 20 Oct., 10 and 24 Nov., and 8 Dec. 1818, attributed to the official *Gazette*. For the lack of journals for the fourth session and for their reappearance in the fifth, see *Kingston Chronicle*, 2 July 1819 and 3 Mar. 1820.

121 R.A. [Randy Absalom?], *Kingston Gazette*, 19 Feb. 1811

122 Upper Canadians could visit the assembly in open session. When the House tried Joseph Willcocks for libel in 1808, 'the bar and gallery were crowded with a concourse of spectators'; *Gazette*, 17 Sept. 1808.

123 See Elwood H. Jones, 'Willcocks (Wilcox), Joseph,' *Dictionary of Canadian Biography*, v. 5, 854–9. For an unsympathetic treatment of government critics in this period see Harry H. Guest, 'Upper Canada's First Political Party,' *Ontario History* 54, no. 4 (December 1962), 275–96.

the first time, *Gazette* readers were invited inside the House of Assembly. This was not, however, a precedent for the later publication of the debates. On the contrary, it revealed the widespread fear of words.

Three days after taking his seat, Willcocks moved that 'every member should have access to the journals and be permitted to take extracts from them.' As Solicitor-General D'Arcy Boulton pointed out, 'Every member had unquestionably a right to see the journals.' Taking extracts was another matter. Boulton feared that, as a printer, Willcocks 'might make such extracts as suit his own private purposes, and the journals would appear to the public in an imperfect state.' Boulton, as well as Willcocks, knew that printed parliamentary intelligence, imperfect or not, was a powerful weapon in the hands of any group claiming to enlighten 'the people.' In fact, the opposition group to which Willcocks belonged had already printed at least part of the journals of an earlier session in the United States. According to another opposition figure, it 'exposes a great deal' and would further agitate the 'public mind.' The *Guardian* 'will soon blow up the flame.'[124] Exposing the legislature to scrutiny, especially when the printing press was controlled by government critics, was precisely what Boulton feared and others hoped from the Willcocks motion two years later. To allay such fears, Willcocks pledged 'to give the whole of them to the public as far as he was able,' but the issue was as much the very publication of the journals as their accuracy. Samuel Sherwood, the member for Grenville, doubted the right of any member to publish them, although they, and summaries of selected speeches, were then appearing in the official *Gazette*. Willcocks's motion was defeated.

The House, however, was not finished trying to silence Willcocks. Captain David Cowan, the member for Essex, 'begged to call the attention of the House to a Newspaper ... published by Mr. Joseph Willcocks. He alleged that a paragraph of that paper, would to the common sense of any person, amount to an accusation that the present House of Assembly had been bribed by the Governor, with lands, to vote against the interests of their constituents.' Since Willcocks was already being prosecuting in the courts by the government for the same paragraph, the House postponed its own consideration of the alleged libel. The

---

124 Justice Robert Thorpe to Edward Cooke, 1 Apr. 1806, in Public Archives of Canada, 'Political State of Upper Canada,' 46–7. Printing in the U.S. points to both the dangers of breaching the assembly's privileges and to the then monopoly of the official *Gazette*.

Gazette continued to report selected journals and printed the usual parliamentary items: a list of new statutes, Gore's speech proroguing the session, and recently enacted statutes.[125]

During the elections of May 1808, Willcocks was returned without opposition for the first riding of Lincoln and Haldimand. In September, the *Gazette* announced that 'the publication of the proceedings of the last House of Assembly has been for some time forborne. We now, temporarily resume it, to discharge our duties to the enlightened and robust Constituents of J. Wilcocks, Esq.' The *Gazette* printed summaries of the proceedings of the House for the 20th of February, when it had decided to try Willcocks for libel upon learning that he had boasted publicly that the House did not dare proceed against him. The *Gazette*'s account of the trial was heavily slanted against Willcocks, dismissing his defence as 'virulent.' Little was printed to allow readers to make an independent assessment. Selective newspaper exposure could work both ways.

Employing a recurring analogy, Samuel Sherwood compared the *Guardian* to 'a pestilence in the land, that disseminated poison from one end of the colony to the other.'[126] In trying to prevent Willcocks from publishing the journals of the assembly and in jailing him for libel, elected representatives demonstrated a pervasive fear of words – and, by extension, a fear of those 'out-of-doors' who might listen. The antidote to Willcocks's poison was silence.

For the first time, the *Gazette* had reported words spoken in assembly debates, but it would not do so again for more than a decade. Moreover, it disavowed 'the unjustifiable intention, of leaving an impression upon his [Willcocks's] present judges.' After all, it resumed printing the debates long after voters had judged. Rather, the *Gazette* appealed to a judge 'independent of mankind, a high Power, who metes his own vengeance upon wilful depravation.'[127] This was hardly a precedent for the regular publication of parliamentary debates. This brief and partial

---

125 *Gazette*, 27 Jan., 4 and 26 Feb., 2, 9, and 16 Mar., and 1 and 7 Apr. 1808. So few copies of the *Guardian* are extant that it is unclear what he was publishing from the House. He later printed summarized journals; see A.J. Clark, 'Extracts from a Niagara Newspaper of 1810,' Ontario Historical Society *Papers and Records* 23 (1926), 28–32.

126 *Gazette*, 17 Sept. 1808. For Willcocks's version of the trial see his address to his constituents, *Guardian*, 18 Mar. 1808, repr. in Gourlay, *Statistical Account*, v. 2, 656–62. See also William Renwick Riddell, 'The Legislature of Upper Canada and Contempt: Drastic Methods of Early Provincial Parliaments with Critics,' Ontario Historical Society *Papers and Records* 22 (1925), 193.

127 *Gazette*, 17 Sept. 1808

unveiling of the legislative process was not an exercise in transparency or an appeal to public reason. Instead, it was symptomatic of an abiding fear of words.

The fear was also evident when the *Gazette* again printed from the journals of the House for one day in 1810. Another government critic, John Mills Jackson, had published a pamphlet the House unanimously resolved was 'a false, scandalous and seditious LIBEL; comprising expressions of the most unexampled insolence ... and most manifestly tending to alienate the affections of the People from his Majesty's Government of this Province; to withdraw them from their obedience to the Laws of the Country, and to excite them to insurrection.'[128] Criticism was insolence. Words could transform the relationship between ruler and ruled. They could incite revolution. They had to be controlled.

Once published, such control was impossible. Publication broadcast speech beyond its original social context and the control of institution within which it was uttered. Under conditions of greater publicity, government and social leaders could not decide what was to be made known, to whom, and how it was to be received. As American historian Richard Brown notes, 'Such a phenomenon of information moving freely, without the exercise of personal discretion and out of context, was a new phenomenon with important ramifications for the redistribution of cultural and political power.'[129]

Government control over what appeared in the *Gazette*, its willingness to prosecute critics for seditious libel, and the assembly's repeated efforts 'to maintain its dignity,' demonstrate that Upper Canadians understood the consequences of this phenomenon.[130] What appeared in the official newspaper in 1808 and 1810 was not intended to initiate debate. It was intended to condemn and silence. Unveiling government before readers was a weapon too easily turned against the status quo. Only with the rise of an independent press in the 1820s and a growing acceptance of the need for those 'out-of-doors' to be informed about politics would greater transparency be attempted. In the meantime,

---

128 *York Gazette*, 21 Mar. 1810. The address of the assembly to Lieutenant-Governor Gore condemning the publication was also printed. Willcocks voted for the sweeping indictment. The extracts were also published as an appendix in [Cartwright], *Letters from an American Loyalist*, 105–8.

129 Brown, *Knowledge Is Power*, 41

130 On the relationship between government and the *Gazette*, see Benn, 'The Upper Canadian Press,' 102–6.

silence and upholding the privileges of the House – not incorporating the reading public into the deliberations of government – was the norm.

As already noted, it was not until 1817, when another member, James Durand, was accused of libelling the House, that reports of the debates were again published. Some of the debates during the fifth session of the seventh parliament (1820) may also have been published.[131] From a position of relative scarcity, parliamentary news soon became abundant – and with considerable consequences. The fear of words remained, but silence was no longer an option.

Who was thought to need such information was also changing. In July 1819, the *Kingston Chronicle*, generally supportive of the government, regretted being unable to 'gratify the reasonable curiosity of our readers with the proceedings of our Provincial Parliament,' since they had not been published in the *Upper Canada Gazette*: 'It would certainly be desirable that every subject which is introduced into Parliament, and discussed with open doors, should be made still more public, through the medium of the different periodical Journals of the Province. In this way the community at large would not only be made acquainted with the manner in which every Bill is brought into the House, but by whom introduced and supported; by whom opposed, and the grounds upon which opposed.' The reference to actual arguments in the House meant the *Chronicle* was calling for the publication of debates as well as journals. Discussion in an open assembly was no longer sufficiently public. Only newspaper publication could 'gratify the reasonable curiosity' of 'the community at large.'

The *Chronicle* was clear as to why such curiosity was reasonable. 'A full and correct report of the proceedings of the Legislature ... would not, we think, fail to be a powerful antidote against corruption in its members. Their principles and conduct are in that way more immediately brought before the eyes of their constituents.' Members would be made more accountable. On another occasion, the paper added that reporting the

---

131 *Canadian Argus and Niagara Spectator*, 2 Mar. 1820. It is unclear whether the *Gazette* began reporting in 1820 (during the last session of the seventh parliament) or in 1821 (during the first session of the eighth parliament). This *Spectator* editorial does not say where it got the report, no relevant copies of the *Gazette* are extant, and no reports from it were copied in the *Chronicle*. Talbot, *Five Years' Residence in the Canadas*, 410, put the date for the first reports at 1820. This is accepted by Mary McLean, 'Early Parliamentary Reporting in Upper Canada,' *Canadian Historical Review* 20, no. 4 (December 1939), 380, and by Edith G. Firth, 'Carey, John,' *Dictionary of Canadian Biography*, 8 (Toronto: University of Toronto Press 1985), 124–6.

debates would also 'prove the surest and safest protection of members against private misrepresentation of their parliamentary conduct.' Information would flow in both directions. Increased transparency would bind reading public to legislature, elector to representative, governed to governors. For the *Chronicle*, the judge of these bonds was the people, who 'would thereby be furnished with the only correct means of judging with what diligence, ability, and integrity their representatives were discharging the high trust committed to them, and their confidence and support would be given or withheld accordingly.' Increased knowledge was now required to perform electoral duties properly.

The *Chronicle*'s York correspondent refused to take this crucial step. Instead, he explained the nature of two new laws so that the people could 'now see clearly that the object of the Government is exactly the same with their own ... nor will it ever be possible for any incendiary to induce them to withdraw their confidence from an administration so anxious to promote their prosperity.'[132] The correspondent was attempting to fight critics, especially Robert Gourlay, with brief explanations of two new statutes. Since newspapers already printed the titles of new measures and the contents of important ones, no additional access to the legislature was being offered. On the other hand, the *Chronicle* insisted that only a more substantial flow of information – only an invitation to listen in on the assembly – would guard against the machinations of the disaffected. Silence no longer offered sufficient protection.

Agreeing with the *Chronicle*, American historian J.R. Pole emphasizes the difference between making legislative outcomes known and informing non-legislators about how those decisions were reached, the nature of the arguments for and against those decisions, and the degree of consensus or conflict they represented.[133] Announcing results was different from inviting broader deliberation. The latter entailed new attitudes towards the elected assembly and the rights and capacities of those beyond its walls.

By the first session of the eighth parliament (1821), Upper Canadians could read the debates in the growing number of colonial newspapers. John Carey, recently from Ireland, did much of the early reporting and founded York's first unofficial paper, the *Observer*, in May 1820. Richard Horne, still editor of the *Gazette*, hired another recent Irish immigrant, Francis Collins, to report the debates. The reports of both York papers

---

132 *Chronicle*, 2, 16, and 30 July 1819
133 Pole, *Gift of Government*, 88–9

were copied by the two Kingston papers, the *Chronicle* and the *Upper Canada Herald*. The assembly refrained from using its formidable powers to prevent regular publication of its debates.

On 8 February 1821, the *Gazette* announced the start of its parliamentary reporting: 'From the great accession of talent as well as of number to the House of Assembly, the proceedings have acquired an interest much beyond what they ever before possessed ... We have commenced this week and shall endeavour to continue to give as full and impartial an outline of the Debates, as it is in our power to do so.'[134] On the same day, the House voted that the *Gazette* 'contains a gross misrepresentation of the proceedings of this House and is a breach of its privileges.' Horne was summoned to the bar. He escaped with a reprimand from the Speaker, in part because he expressed his 'extreme mortification,' but also because Collins had taken the offending notes. The House was not interested in pursuing the reporter. Rather, it wished to impress upon the editor the risks he ran if members were dissatisfied with how their words were reported.[135] It was not an auspicious inauguration for regular parliamentary reporting.

The conviction for breach of privilege convinced Lieutenant-Governor Maitland that parliamentary reports of questionable accuracy should not appear in the *Gazette* under the imprint of the King's Printer. As George Hillier, his civil secretary, put it, 'It has been judged expedient to divide Horne's publication and to separate what is official from what is not so.'[136] The distinction was crucial. The proclamations, notices, and advertisements from administrative officials that dominated the *Gazette* were 'official.' They appeared 'by authority.' Driving home the point, 'By Authority' began to appear immediately under the masthead of the *Gazette*, while Horne's new *York Weekly Post* was largely devoted to parliamentary reporting.[137] The government's official organ

---

134 *Gazette*, 8 Feb. 1821. Representation had increased from 25 to 40 in 1820.
135 *Journals*, 8 and 9 Feb. 1821. Other papers copying from the *Gazette* or the *Observer* were also at risk. John Macaulay, co-editor of the *Kingston Chronicle*, had hired his own reporter but he had proved so incompetent that the *Chronicle* copied from the York papers. The scarcity of stenographers in the colony continued to plague parliamentary reporting.
136 Archives of Ontario, Macaulay Family Papers, Hillier to John Macaulay, 23 Feb. 1821
137 *Gazette*, 19 Feb. 1821. The phrase 'by authority' had been used before the term 'King's Printer' became common after 1805. It occasionally reappeared on the masthead after 1805 to clearly differentiate the *Gazette* from independent papers that might use it to mark columns devoted to printing provincial statutes.

was to be received by readers in a particular way based on its origins, not its content. It could be accepted without independent judgment because of the speaker's identity. The etymological connection between an 'authority' or expert and 'authority' as legitimate power remained strong. Neither was to be questioned.

None of this applied to reports of parliamentary debates. They required a different relationship between reader and text. They might be inaccurate or partial. More important, the content was of a different order than 'official' texts. Legislative speeches made arguments that others contested. They made questionable assertions or were selective with the 'facts.' They were meant to cajole, ridicule, motivate, or persuade. They did not announce outcomes. Like a listener in the legislature, the newspaper reader had to ascertain the relevant facts and issues and weigh competing arguments. In contrast, the *Gazette's* official notices were to be received by passive consumers. There was to be no need to inquire 'behind' the announced decision into the process by which it had been reached. The debates of the assembly, however, invited, even compelled, Upper Canadians to investigate how legislative outcomes were reached. The publication of parliamentary debates transformed newspaper readers into participants in the legislative process.

Despite efforts to lessen the likelihood of again running afoul of the House,[138] Horne continued to anger some of its members. John Beverley Robinson and Christopher Hagerman felt slighted (and not without reason) by reports in the *Gazette* from Collins and in the *Observer* from Carey. Horne requested and received the substance of their remarks against repeal of the colony's controversial sedition law. They expected to see their views in the *Gazette* to counter the arguments in favour of repeal emphasized by the *Observer*. The *Gazette*, however, failed to report the debate at all. Hagerman's letter to the co-editor of the *Kingston Chronicle* reveals his awareness of the implications of parliamentary reporting. Horne 'gives as an excuse that he does not like to ... [copy the arguments in favour of repeal from Carey] ... and thinks it improper to give only one side of the question, what [?] delicacy! had we known this before[,] you [would] have received our remarks by the first post by which means the ... antidote would accompany the poison contained in Mr Carey's paper and furnished him by persons who appear there to have taken the lead in the debate, as however, it is important that our real sentiments should be known to our constituents, I hope you will ...

138 *York Weekly Post,* 1 Mar. and 26 Apr. 1821

give them a place in the next Chronicle.'[139] However fierce his commitment to monarchical government, Hagerman was caught in a dynamic whereby newspapers readers were provided with more, and competing, arguments. Inescapably, readers were being asked to judge among them – even by those who remained convinced that most of them were incapable of judging wisely. A new political world was being created.

Countering published criticism of the government meant ensuring the publication of pro-government speeches, a tactical retreat from attempts to impose silence. Multiplying the arguments and opinions before newspaper readers – broadcasting more, not fewer, words – was now the best response to criticism – the antidote to poison. A decade later, Allan MacNab thought another member's words 'were given out for the purpose of their being taken down by the reporters and published to the world, and not as words intended for that house.'[140] A new, more important arena for political debate had been created.

Allegations of unfairness and inaccuracy in published reports remained frequent, if often unsubstantiated.[141] Editors cautioned readers to treat early reports with appropriate scepticism. At least one called for competing sources of parliamentary intelligence. Readers had to judge among information providers, not just among arguments. Competing parliamentary reports to 'enable the public to get near the truth' were available by the early 1830s.[142] Earlier, in 1808, the House had attempted to impose silence and punish inappropriate talk. In February 1821, it

---

139 Macaulay Family Papers, Hagerman to Macaulay, 28 Feb. 1821. See also John Beverley Robinson and John Strachan to Macaulay, 4, 11, and 15 Mar. 1821. George Hillier was also anxious to enlist friendly editors. He was particularly troubled by the fact that for 'the Speeches on one side his [Carey's] report is full, ample and (I doubt not, by the after aid of the Speakers themselves) laboured – on the other, general and cursory.' Macaulay Family Papers, Hillier to Macaulay, 15 Jan. and 12 Feb. 1822. With the second letter, he enclosed notes on a Robinson speech he had ordered taken by an official attending the House.

140 MacNab, *Hallowell Free Press*, 27 Nov. 1832. The letters of Marcus Child, a member of the Canadian assembly from the Eastern Townships, and his family attest to the importance of the extra-parliamentary audience. *Child Letters*, esp. 59–60, 65, 77–8, 82, 88, 93, 95, 97, 102. Some, like James Small, also thought that extensive reporting 'would tend to lengthen discussion,' since more members spoke for longer to appear active before their constituents. *Christian Guardian*, 11 Dec. 1839

141 For an evaluation of these complaints, see Talman, 'Newspapers of Upper Canada,' 17–18.

142 *Niagara Gleaner*, 29 Jan. 1825. Collins and Carey, both government critics, were joined by reporters from the *Christian Guardian* and the conservative *Courier*.

had used its privileges in an attempt to impose accuracy. This proved a clumsy and contested weapon that soon fell into disuse.[143] From 1823 to 1850,[144] the assembly refrained from using its privileges to try to prevent or influence parliamentary reporting. Rather, it turned to actively encouraging dissemination. Once the idea gained currency that the people *needed* to know what transpired in the assembly, it was a short step to the idea that they had the *right* to know. The right to know was inseparable from the right to discuss and thereby to criticize. The right to judge undercut the legitimacy of ancient parliamentary privileges.

In November 1821, less than a week into the session following Horne's conviction for contempt, Charles Jones, Brockville's leading conservative, moved that 'it is expedient that the debates of this House during the present Session be taken, and that a shorthand writer be employed [by the House] for that purpose.' The motion passed 20 to 11. Attorney-General Robinson called it 'the most undignified and disgusting motion that ever came before the House.' If employed by the House, how could a reporter be punished for breaching its privileges? Robinson 'was sure no gentleman would object to the Reports being taken, but the idea of the members of that house paying persons for giving their speeches to the Public, was contrary to every parliamentary usage.' It was certainly unprecedented.

Supporters of the motion argued that without financial assistance newspapers could not hire competent reporters or publish more than a fraction of the debates. Encouraging reporting meant more accurate and complete reports. For Jones, such reports were 'to give his constituents the power of judging of his conduct ... to give their constituents an opportunity of viewing their proceedings. That it was not parliamentary he did not care about it, if it did a public good.' If the publication of

---

143 From the assembly's initial use of its privileges in 1821 until the end of the eleventh parliament (March 1834), only four other motions were made against editors for what had appeared in their newspapers; three in the eighth parliament. A motion during the third session to declare a paragraph of the *Observer* a libel was dismissed 3 to 21. Another, against Thomson of the *Upper Canada Herald*, concerned aspersions on the House, not the paper's parliamentary reporting. On the final day of the second session, a paragraph in the *Chronicle* was voted a breach of privilege by 23 to 1. At the beginning of the following session, a motion to adjourn debate on the matter passed 18 to 10. Only one such motion, against Carey and the *Observer* in February 1830, occurred outside the eighteen parliament. A motion to put the question was lost 13 to 15.

144 For the 1850 affray between the House and reporters see Elizabeth Nish, 'Canadian Parliamentary Reporting,' in *Debates*, v. 1, xxxvi–xxxvii.

parliamentary debates altered the nature of newspaper readers, it also altered that of their representatives. The need, even the right, to know what arguments they made and how they voted meant that representatives were to be chosen for what they said and did, not in recognition of their social standing.[145]

Employing reporters remained contentious. Most subsequent sessions debated the principles and mechanisms (financial or otherwise) of encouraging the publication of reports. The House experimented with several options, none of which proved satisfactory.[146] No member, however, argued that speeches should not be published, and they continued to appear regardless of the action of the House. The arguments for encouraging reporting, however, highlight the importance attached to the widespread dissemination of parliamentary intelligence.

John Willson of Wentworth consistently supported hiring a reporter. He prided himself on speaking for ordinary farmers and desired widespread education and a reformed judicial system. Increasingly seen as an independent conservative,[147] Willson seconded the first motion in 1821 by arguing that 'the house was liable to sink into a degree of despotism, more dangerous than that of a monarchical despotism, without a proper check being placed upon their conduct.'[148] Reporting debates brought newspaper readers into common deliberation with their representatives and transformed them into the foremost check on the assem-

---

145 Pole, *Gift of Government*, 122
146 While critics of the executive tended to support employing reporters more consistently, the divisions were not entirely partisan. Charles Jones was a friend of Robinson and a leader of the Brockville family compact. Allan MacNab favoured paying reporters in 1833 and 1834. Robert Nichol, sometime government critic, was a vocal opponent of employing reporters. Reporting was encouraged by allowing reporters to sit inside the bar of the House. Motions to employ a reporter or to pay those employed by local editors also passed in several sessions. In others, the House purchased large quantities of newspapers that reported the debates, or awarded its printing contracts to printers whose newspapers reported the debates rather than to the lowest bidder, or responded favourably to petitions for payment for reporting a previous session. Thus, with few exceptions and much inconsistency, the majority of the House regularly provided some financial support to the press. The politics of editors applying for financial assistance affected some votes. Many of these editors were also members of the House. Predictably, once the assembly used its own printing business to reward selected printers or responded favourably to ad hoc petitions, the situation degenerated into a confused and partisan mess. See McLean, 'Early Parliamentary Reporting,' 382–9.
147 Robert L. Fraser, 'Willson, John,' *Dictionary of Canadian Biography*, v. 8, 945–7
148 *Observer* copied in *Chronicle*, 14 Dec. 1821

bly. The theory of mixed monarchy had given that role to the lieutenant-governor and legislative council – not to a reading public.

Willson supported the second attempt to employ reporters in January 1823 on sweeping grounds. It would provide Upper Canadians with knowledge of 'what was passing within these walls,' empowering them 'to decide upon the justice or injustice of their decisions.' Moreover, 'without free discussion, and the liberty of the press, there could be no security for the person or property of any individual. In a free country every subject had a share in the Government, and therefore every subject not only has a right, but was in duty bound to enquire into the manner justice was administered, and into the public measures pursued.'[149]

Willson referred to 'every subject' – not every voter. The need to inform voters had been an early argument for publishing the debates. Willson's more inclusive language reflected the broader function he envisaged for published debates. They would allow 'every subject' 'to decide upon the justice or injustice' of legislative decisions. Properly informed, the anonymous reading public could assume a critical position vis-à-vis the state. It would rule the state via public opinion. This was a larger role than voting in periodic elections and was not necessarily limited, like the effective franchise, to property-owning men.

During yet another debate on encouraging reporters, Willson argued that 'when a reporter gives a general statement from both sides, and that his report is laid before the public, it is easy to take a fair view of the proceedings, to judge the propriety of measures, and to draw proper conclusions ... The publication of the debates in this Province for the last few years has been of infinite service – it has given the people of a remote part a disposition to read, and drew their attention to seek after other information.'[150] By exporting their deliberations, the House, aided by the press, ensured that Upper Canadians, regardless of geographical location, could 'hear' arguments from both sides of public questions and judge between them. The more they did so, the more information they demanded.

---

149 Willson, *Observer* copied in *Chronicle*, 31 Jan. 1823. Mackenzie expressed similar sentiments in his usual over-wrought style: 'I will, through the medium of a free and unshackled press, make known the sentiments of your loyal, honest, and independent breasts ... I will sit in the gallery of your house; and ... record and promulgate the language of truth, as it is elicited by your body in argument and debate, until the most distant boundary of our land shall echo back the tidings.' *Colonial Advocate*, 28 Oct. 1824
150 Willson, *Weekly Register*, 4 Dec. 1823

Marshall Spring Bidwell, the leading reformer, made much the same point in 1827. 'Public opinion called for such information ... – the debates when given [generate] great interest and excite attention – they become the subject of conversation, and an opportunity is afforded for enabling the public to express their sentiments on various subjects which are discussed, and by this means at the next Session the opinion of the public was better known.'[151] Readers were developing the necessary skills and appetite for political information. They were drawn into public deliberations further by competing political leaders. They grew self-confident in their capacity, and thus right, to judge. This process took time and could only succeed if the debates were actively read. We cannot know precisely what was read or how individuals reacted to it, but parliamentary debates were widely published after 1821 in large measure because newspaper readers demanded it.

Parliamentary reports were copied in almost every newspaper. Different versions might appear, but a significant amount of parliamentary debate, including at least a sketch of competing arguments, reached almost all newspaper readers. Many editors, rather than hire their own reporter, copied from those who did. They often reported and copied to the point where they had little room for much else. The assembly struck a select committee to investigate the petition of the editor of the *Courier* praying for remuneration for reporting earlier debates. The committee examined 'a file of his paper, containing about one hundred and thirty columns (chiefly small brevier type) of printed reports of Debates between the 31st of October 1832 and the 20th February 1833.'[152] Applying for public money, editors made two claims: that printing the debates brought no new subscribers and that their subscribers demanded the debates. A newspaper with its own reporter failed to gain subscribers because other papers, in order to retain their readership, simply copied from them, meeting the demand without incurring the expense.

Such arguments were convenient when petitioning for public funds. Did subscribers really demand extensive coverage of parliamentary deliberations? If not, why did editors bother? Most pursued a political agenda and had an elevated sense of their own importance, but most were also small entrepreneurs dependent on subscribers in a volatile

---

151 Bidwell, *Upper Canada Herald*, 9 Jan. 1827, adding that since the majority's opinion was expressed in the actions of the House, published debates protected the minority. *Cobourg Star*, 29 Nov. 1831
152 *Journals*, 11th Parliament, 4th Session, adopted by the House, 10 Feb. 1834

market. They had no trouble filling their columns with other material when the House was not in session.

In December 1825, Henry Lasher, agent for the *Colonial Advocate* at Bath, wrote to William Lyon Mackenzie with the names of six local residents wishing to continue their subscriptions. Lasher informed Mackenzie that 'as the above persons do not get any newspapers from York, they will expect you to give them the debates and principle [*sic*] proceedings of the Assembly during their present sitting.' Earlier the same year, Mackenzie had noted that 'our chief reason for coming to York [from Queenston], was, that we might be enabled to give an early and faithful account of the proceedings in parliament.'[153]

Other newspapers also made special arrangements to carry the debates. Some hired their own reporter(s) at considerable expense or changed their format to accommodate the increased material. At the beginning of one session, the *Courier* advertised in other papers that it had hired a reporter and that 'to furnish our readers with as prompt and detailed a report of the debates as possible, we shall issue Two Papers per Week from the commencement of the Session.' The *Courier* was conservative, but 'as it is our determination to give a fair, impartial, condensed report of all that occurs in the House, without the least regard to persons or parties, we may venture to Solicit the patronage of the public at large, who take an interest in the Parliamentary proceedings.'[154] To take only one more example, the *Patriot* announced two years later that it had purchased another printing press, hired a reporter, and would move to a semi-weekly format, in order to carry the debates of the upcoming session.'[155] Such advertising reveals editors' expectation that readers made decisions about when to subscribe and about which newspaper to subscribe to based, in part, on the parliamentary calendar and a paper's ability to furnish the debates.[156]

Whatever arrangements editors might make, parliamentary reports

---

153 Mackenzie-Lindsey Papers, Henry Lasher to Mackenzie, 11 Dec. 1825 and *Colonial Advocate*, 27 Jan. 1825

154 Ad., *Western Mercury*, 17 Nov. 1831

155 *Patriot*, 1 Nov. 1833. The *Royal Standard* intended to print daily during the session, but only thrice weekly otherwise.

156 In 1826, Mackenzie worried that his unpopularity accounted for the paucity of *Advocate* subscribers in the London area. According to his local agent, 'some persons' had approached him 'before the commencement of the Session,' but when the *Advocate* appeared irregularly and slowly, they 'sent for the Freeman' instead. Mackenzie-Lindsey Papers, Law Lawrason to Mackenzie, 18 Feb. 1826

frequently crowded out other material. In February 1831, the *Christian Guardian*, which had only recently begun to report the debates, noted that 'we have left out all the articles of temperance intelligence with which correspondents have favored us, and postponed our principal editorial articles, in order to present, undivided, Mr. Bidwell's masterly speech [on primogeniture] ... and to bring down our parliamentary sketches to the latest date. Indeed, our parliamentary intelligence has thus far given such very general satisfaction, and is so loudly and anxiously called for in every part of the Province, as we learn from our correspondents, that we allow it a larger space than we at first intended.'[157] Years later the paper noted that it had 'devoted a large portion of our columns to the proceedings and debates of the Assembly, in compliance with the expressed wishes of many of our readers ... although it may occasion a paucity of Editorial matter.'[158] Readers demanded 'news' in the form of legislative debates before editorial comment.

The prospectus of the *Western Mercury*, published at Hamilton in January 1831, promised to provide the earliest European news and to copy literary pieces from foreign periodicals, as well as 'to give an account of the proceedings of our Provincial Parliament as early as they may be obtained from any other quarter.' Two weeks later it apologized that 'the debates in the House of Assembly have been so lengthy and so important, we have not had space for that general variety of news which we were desirous of giving.' A little over a month later, it stopped apologizing: 'As the majority of our readers seem to find a deeper interest in the debates of the House of Assembly, than any other description of news we could give them, our columns afford less variety than we should wish and such must continue to be the case until those debates are disposed of.' For the next session, the *Mercury* hired its own reporter at York. Two years later, it noted that 'to make room for the parliamentary debates we have again abridged every other description of matter, conceiving they would be more acceptable to our readers than any thing else we could offer.'[159] In an increasingly crowded market, editors could

---

157 *Christian Guardian*, 5 Feb. 1831. The *Guardian*, 16 Nov. 1831, claimed that upwards of 300 names had been added to its subscription list in the year it began to report the debates. Of course, the increase could have had other causes.

158 *Christian Guardian*, 7 Dec. 1836

159 *Western Mercury*, 20 Jan., 3 Feb., 17 Mar., 10 and 21 Nov. 1831 and 21 and 26 Nov. 1833. See also the *Patriot*, 6 Dec. 1833 and, even earlier, *Niagara Gleaner*, 12 and 19 Feb. 1825.

not afford to lose subscribers because they failed to carry a sufficient quantity of the debates in as timely a manner as possible.[160] Editors devoted so much space to the debates to meet the public's appetite for them. The conclusion is as inescapable as its three main consequences.

First, as already discussed, regular reports changed the nature of newspaper readers and elected representatives. The information and skills needed to participate in public debate were exported beyond the assembly. Readers were invited to sift through reports for the relevant 'facts' and arguments and come to their own conclusions. By so doing, they could evaluate the performance of their local representatives and the assembly as a whole. The invitation could be explicit: 'How far the house was justifiable in this transaction,' concluded one editorial, 'we shall leave our readers to judge from the debates, part of which will be found in this day's paper.'[161] Anonymous readers of indeterminate social standing had been elevated to ultimate judge.

By helping to channel political participation into literate and discursive forms, regular reporting further marginalized the illiterate and others largely absent from the community of newspaper readers. Likewise, non-discursive or violent forms of political behaviour became increasingly suspect. In the aftermath of post-election rioting at Toronto in 1841, both government supporters and opponents condemned political violence. The following year, electoral law reform tried to limit the likelihood of such violence: bribery in money or alcohol was prohibited; the nomination of candidates was to take place several days before polling; weapons were banned from polling places; to disperse crowds, such polls were now to be held throughout the constituency; and voting itself was to be limited to two days and conducted in the absence of flags and banners. Ideal political participation and conflict resolution were being redefined as the rational, measured exchange of argument and information.[162] The ubiquity of printed parliamentary debates rein-

---

160 This was one reason why John Macaulay was so angered when the assembly voted the *Chronicle* in breach of its privileges. When he learned of the inaccuracy of Carey's reports, 'we consequently discontinued the reports, though by this course we diminished the sale of our papers.' Macaulay Family Papers, Macaulay to Levius P. Sherwood, 8 Jan. 1823. The interruption, however, was brief.

161 *Hallowell Free Press*, 20 Dec. 1831. See also *Niagara Gleaner*, 26 Feb. 1825.

162 Peter Way, 'Street Politics: Orangemen, Tories and the 1841 Election Riot in Toronto,' *British Journal of Canadian Studies* 6, no. 2 (1991), 276, 283, 286, 291–4 and John Garner, *The Franchise and Politics in British North America, 1775–1867* (Toronto: University of Toronto Press 1969), 101–2. For an (over)emphasis on print's disabling features and

forced the notion that politics *was* a dialogue – the public exchange of information and argument. Other forms of participation were judged according to whether or not they contributed to that dialogue. Just as the diffusion of democratic sociability by voluntary associations was inseparable from its differentiation from other forms of interaction, so too the democratic empowerment promised by the dissemination of parliamentary intelligence was incoherent without its own regulations.

Second, the mere fact of publication told Upper Canadians that the arguments made in parliament were relevant to them. Editors (by publishing the debates) and the House (by encouraging reporting) told newspaper readers that they ought to be informed about the colony's public business. It was *their* business and *their* assembly. Discussion of the public good could no longer be limited to legislators. Once the debates were reported, the proportion of colonial to foreign content in newspapers increased considerably. In 1822 the *Kingston Chronicle* thought that Upper Canada had 'not yet acquired so large a reading public.' With relative tranquillity, newspapers 'have almost altogether been looked at for gleanings of foreign news.' 'The prospect however begins to brighten ... A taste for reading is beginning to manifest itself ... Far greater interest is given to our internal affairs, and to the proceedings of our Legislature. This interest has been much heightened by the publication of the debates of the House of Assembly.'[163] This interest, and especially the end of political tranquillity, created a large reading public preoccupied with domestic politics. By reading similar parliamentary reports, members of this public, regardless of social rank or location, were invited to see themselves as members of the same discursive community.

Third, the publication of parliamentary debates changed the constitution, even if its formal institutions remained unaltered.[164] Advocates for the wide dissemination of parliamentary intelligence insisted that voting only reflected real choice if the electorate was informed. The publication of the debates ensured that representatives and public were bound together in a two-way flow of information. Representatives were to be accountable to the public. Thus power flowed more obviously up from the latter to the former. Publication of the debates, however, did much

---

the tendency of reforms aimed at violence to limit and discipline participation, see Vernon, *Politics and the People*, 99–103, 106, 131–60, 336–7. While such reforms constrained some forms of 'participation,' they enabled others.

163 *Chronicle*, 4 Jan. 1822
164 Aspinall, 'Reporting and Publishing,' 227

more. Newspaper readers, whether or not they could vote, were invited to participate in public deliberations – to be members of the public sphere. If, as many began to argue, they were capable of holding representatives accountable, if they could come to decisions about the common good, and if they could act as a check on the assembly, a key rationale for the governor and legislative council provided by the theory of mixed monarchy was obsolete.

The publication of the debates of the House undercut the legislative council in a second way. Debates in the upper house were rarely reported. When available, they were usually brief and copied by fewer papers. In 1833, George Gurnett of the *Courier* planned to publish the council's debates, but his reporter could not hear the speakers. Gurnett expressed his regret 'because we think it would be alike interesting to the country, and advantageous to that Hon. body, in the public estimation, that their proceedings should go forth to the country.'[165]

At the end of a session, all that most colonists knew of the legislative council was conveyed in the list of bills passed by the assembly but lost in the upper house. A few years of reading the assembly debates accustomed Upper Canadians to greater institutional transparency. The public needed reasons, not just decisions. In 1825 the *Upper Canada Herald* attacked the actions of the upper house, but 'as the debates in the Council, if they have any, are not in the presence of the public, we do not know their reasons, but only the results of them, the rejection of many measures adopted by the House of Assembly.'[166] The council stood outside the discursive community that bound assembly to public. Gurnett was probably not the only conservative to recognize the risks to the council's status. 'If the Legislative Council wishes to be regarded with the admiration and respect that are paid to the House of Lords, it must, in homely phraseology, show its face.' Once the council did so, 'the public, being enabled to know what passes within the Chamber, will begin to take an interest in its proceedings, and no longer bestow an undivided attention on the Lower House.'[167] If, however, as fellow conservative John Kent argued, the council's proceedings 'may be fairly likened to a stagnant pool' in which John Beverley Robinson acted as 'Speaker, the Government party, the opposition party, the Judge, the

---

165 *Courier* copied in *Western Mercury*, 7 Feb. 1833
166 *Upper Canada Herald*, 26 Apr. 1825. See also *British American Journal*, 20 May and *St Thomas Liberal*, 18 Dec. 1834.
167 *Courier*, 7 Dec. 1836

Jury, the Court, the Plaintiff [and] the Defendant,' perhaps 'showing its face' would have had far different consequences.[168] Regardless, only by engaging in the deliberations of newspaper readers could a legislative institution retain its legitimacy.

Newspaper readers listened to and participated in the assembly's deliberations. They watched as it came to a decision, only to have it nullified by a body that did not appear to deliberate and whose reasons for acting were often unknown. This could only confirm suspicions that the legislative council was influenced more by private interest and appointed position than by arguments about the common good. A similar process helped undermine the legitimacy of the Colonial Office, since its opaque process of reviewing colonial legislation and the behaviour of imperial officers could also pre-empt decisions of the local assembly. In short, it, like the council, stood outside the process of public deliberation. As that process took on more real and symbolic weight, secrecy and silence carried ever higher costs.

Colonial newspapers – their number, distribution, readership, the associations they spawned, and their reports of parliamentary debates – were at the centre of the emergent public sphere. Imperial officials and provincial legislators could no longer claim a monopoly on political information or the public use of reason. Private citizens with access to colonial newspapers were informed. On this basis, they were invited to participate in public deliberations that increasing numbers thought capable of generating authoritative decisions about the common good, but that stood outside traditional institutions and theories. Once Upper Canadians believed that public deliberation could be rational and informed – something to be encouraged, influenced, and heeded rather than shunned or silenced – constitutional change was all but inevitable.

When, precisely, did most Upper Canadians come to this belief? When did the concept of public opinion become widely credible? What constituted adequate information, sufficient rationality, or widespread participation? No quantitative measure can answer such questions since their key terms are partially subjective.[169] The conditions for the public

---

168 Alan Fairford [Kent], 'A Sketch of the Chief Justice,' *Courier*, 24 Mar. 1835 with editorial defending the council.

169 I am heavily indebted here to Keith Michael Baker, 'Public Opinion as Political Invention,' in *Inventing the French Revolution: Essays on French Political Culture in the Eighteenth Century* (Cambridge: Cambridge University Press 1990), 167–99.

sphere were largely in place by the mid-1830s. There was a large, decentralized, and independent press that relied on subscribers, voiced a range of editorial opinions, and printed substantial political information relatively free of legal harassment. Various voluntary associations diffused the principles of democratic sociability beyond the ranks of the most privileged. Without such developments, appeals to concrete problem-solving by public deliberation would have been incomprehensible or ridiculous.

Yet the uneven success of many voluntary associations and the gap between their tangled practices and lofty ideals, the continued role of bribery, patronage, force, and ignorance in politics, persisting barriers to the community of readers, and the prevalence of lies, misinformation, and scurrility in its newspapers could generate descriptions of colonial politics largely divorced from rational deliberation. Most Upper Canadians accepted public opinion, in part, because the concept was increasingly employed to legitimate competing claims. Appealing to public opinion while making strenuous efforts to influence its verdict acknowledged its existence and augmented its power. Government, as well as its critics, began to appeal to it. By doing so, they legitimized it. The concept of public opinion was a credible description of practices because of broad social, economic, and cultural developments. Politics made it a functioning reality.

CHAPTER IV

'A united public opinion that must be obeyed': The Politics of Public Opinion

Public opinion was increasingly invoked in Upper Canada. In fact, in the early 1840s, it was accepted as the final tribunal or court of appeal – a source of authority and legitimacy outside of and eventually above political institutions. Part of the explanation lies in the developments before 1840 explored in the two previous chapters. They lent credibility to the ideal, but, as Keith Michael Baker says of the French experience, public opinion was also a 'political invention.'[1] Belief in its existence was one interpretation of those developments forged during particular political contests to meet particular needs. Political actors grappled with and attempted to appropriate the power of debate circulating widely in print. Appeals to public opinion began as a rhetorical device – a device deeply rooted in changing experiences of social communication – but faith in 'public opinion' was not the inevitable outcome of those experiences. Rather, it was one interpretation of their consequences. By the early 1840s, competing political actors sought legitimacy and power by actively participating in the public sphere. They appealed to and tried to manipulate public opinion – thereby helping to create it and invest it with authority.

Although various meanings persisted, from the eighteenth century

---

1 Besides Keith Michael Baker, 'Public Opinion as Political Invention,' in *Inventing the French Revolution: Essays on French Political Culture in the Eighteenth Century* (Cambridge: Cambridge University Press 1990), 167–99, see also Mona Ozouf, '"Public Opinion" at the End of the Old Regime,' *Journal of Modern History* 60, suppl. (September 1988), 1–21 and Dror Wahrman, 'Public Opinion, Violence and the Limits of Constitutional Politics,' in James Vernon, ed., *Re-reading the Constitution: New Narratives in the Political History of England's Long Nineteenth Century* (Cambridge: Cambridge University Press 1996), 89, 96, 109–10.

'public opinion' was routinely distinguished from 'opinion.' The latter was usually contrasted with reason and allied with the passions. It required neither information nor reflection and was thus subject to erratic fluctuation.[2] According to one Upper Canadian commentator, 'the fickle variations of popular will are proverbial.' Taste in clothing provided a good example, since 'fashion is under the tyrant-sway of fancy, and that is almost synonymous with folly and nearly allied to frenzy.' This was portrayed as a female domain. Wives squandered their husbands' money according to the whims of fashion: 'But when this capricious tyrant whose only reason is to be always unreasonable, is allowed to usurp the rule over higher matters than the fantasies of dress, and sway the public mind in things which mightily affect the public welfare, we may justly pause, and ask the people if they are willing to be ruled by the moon – if they are willing to become in fact lunatics.'[3] Good government could not rely on such a force. While comparable usages persisted, 'public opinion' more commonly referred to the very opposite of 'opinion.' The modifier 'public' did not convey that 'opinions' concerned the state (as in public questions) or were an aggregate of the opinions of several individuals (as in a public). Rather, 'public opinion,' in the enlightenment sense, was the outcome of a collective process of informed deliberation. It bore no analogy to fashion or the feminine. It became the only basis for good government.

During Upper Canada's first half-century, appeals to the collective judgment of a public were most conspicuous at times of acute political conflict – or, to be more precise, when such conflict could not be contained within existing institutions or private channels of communication. Those who felt slighted by or excluded from those institutions and channels sought an alternative source of legitimacy – another way to bolster their claims – thus underlining their own marginality. They appealed to the court of public opinion to challenge those who drew their authority from social standing, monarchical institutions, or the imperial state, and who often denied the efficacy, if not the existence, of public opinion. Only later, when political contests were framed as competing claims to express public opinion and when all combatants tried

2 For various meanings, see J.A.W. Gunn, 'Public Opinion,' in Terrence Ball, James Farr, and Russell L. Hanson, eds., *Political Innovation and Conceptual Change* (Cambridge: Cambridge University Press 1989), 247–65.

3 *Upper Canada Herald*, 30 May 1837

to inform or manipulate that opinion, was its ultimate authority acknowledged.

In 1799, the *Upper Canada Gazette* suspected the *Constellation* of trying 'to draw us into a paper war,' but it 'passed them over in silence' rather than participate in 'childish combat ... A war of ink we despise.'[4] Such yearning for silence and the haughty refusal to engage in public discussion it often prompted were also evident in the response of the government and assembly to Joseph Willcocks in 1807–8 discussed in the previous chapter. Robert Thorpe, judge of the Court of King's Bench, led Willcocks's faction after quickly falling out with York's narrow administrative circles. To justify suspending Thorpe from office, Lieutenant-Governor Sir Francis Gore made more of his having gone public with his complaints than of the complaints themselves.

Gore accused Thorpe of using his charges to the jury 'to make the Courts of Justice the theatres for Political harangues' and, by helping his allies engineer addresses in reply, 'to encourage strictures on the Government from every description of persons, however incompetent they might be to form any correct opinion upon the subject, or however foreign such a subject might be, from the occasion for which they were convened.' Having grievances wasn't the point. Voicing them to the wrong audience – to 'every description of persons' – was. Gore insisted that he, representing the monarch as the font of justice and virtue, was the only appropriate audience. 'However absurd and malevolent some part of Mr. Thorpe's assertions may be, and however it may betray Ignorance' and indecent warmth of that Gentleman, these circumstances might be overlooked and forgiven, had his observations been reserved for my ear alone, but it is notorious that Mr. Thorpe, upon all occasions, is anxious to introduce and enforce those Topics, and ... made them the constant subject of conversation in all Companies where he is admitted.'[5] As an informed, reasonable gentleman with a paternal regard for his monarch's subjects, Gore would judge complaints brought to his attention privately or in petitions by respectful supplicants. Both avenues acknowledged his competence and superior position. On behalf of an absent monarch, he represented the unity of the state, standing above the partiality of particular interests. He alone could judge accord-

---

4 *Upper Canada Gazette*, 5 Oct. 1799
5 Gore to Mr Windham, 13 Mar. 1807, Public Archives of Canada, 'Political State of Upper Canada,' 61, 64 and Daniel Gordon, *Citizens without Sovereignty: Equality and Sociability in French Thought, 1670–1789* (Princeton: Princeton University Press), 202

ing to the common good. Making grievances public, as Thorpe had done, threatened disorder by implying both that the Crown and its representative might themselves be partial and that there was another, rhetorically superior, audience.

The gist of Gore's charge was that Thorpe was an agitator; a self-interested and malevolent demagogue who was attempting to use his 'indecent warmth' in the spoken and written word to incite the populace against their government by inventing or amplifying grievances to gratify his own ambitions. While intentionally pejorative, 'agitation' was not a bad description of what Thorpe and others did; more than exercise their private reasoning, they tried to incite – to inform, inflame, and empower – others.[6] Painting Thorpe in this way, however, cast his audience as dupes. According to Gore, they were 'incompetent,' 'plain, uneducated men ... induced to subscribe their names to it [an address], without being fully aware of its dangerous tendency.'[7] The educated few could see through attempts to arouse the ill-informed and undiscerning many. Without such base efforts, the many would remain as they were thought by nature to be – docile and appreciative subjects; that is, silent about general matters of state. This unflattering, rather unidimensional explanation of agitation would reappear frequently and with little variation in subsequent decades.[8]

Thorpe retaliated by writing anonymously for Willcocks's *Upper Canadian Guardian.* Just as 'the people of this Province are too enlightened and too loyal to suffer themselves to become the dupes of unprincipled discontented demagogues,' they were 'too well acquainted with the full extent of their rights' and 'too independent to remain silent under real grievances.' The constitution actually required them to speak out in defence of their rights. Those who surrounded Gore 'arrogate to themselves the exclusive right of deciding upon the policy and justice of every public measure, and who with no little effrontery continually assert that the people are stupid, ignorant, and rebellious, not competent to judge between right and wrong, and that they are utterly incapable of knowing

---

6 David Vincent, *Literacy and Popular Culture: England, 1750–1914* (Cambridge: Cambridge University Press 1989), 263

7 Gore to Mr Windham, 13 Mar. 1807, Public Archives of Canada, 'Political State of Upper Canada,' 61–2. For the psychology of agitators, see also Simpson, *Essay on Modern Reformers*, 3–11.

8 S.F. Wise, 'Sermon Literature and Canadian Intellectual History,' in A.B. McKillop and Paul Romney, eds., *God's Peculiar Peoples: Essays on Political Culture in Nineteenth Century Canada* (Ottawa: Carleton University Press 1988), 10–11

what is calculated for their good, or the extent of their rights and privileges.'⁹ Reversing Gore's typology, courtiers were self-interested; agitators defended the constitution. As early as 1807, political conflict was
framed as much around who was able to judge as around the merits of
the case.

Such commentary, appearing as it did in the first fully oppositional
newspaper, terrified York administrators. The *Gazette* refused to engage
the *Guardian* in debate. According to a government supporter, disaffection had been spread 'by circulation with the aid of this Press, through a
wider range.' One of its patrons put the point more positively: the
Guardian had 'produced a great exposure, and has exhibited such transactions as we lament.'¹⁰ The connection between opposition and the
press, the medium and the nature or 'range' of the audience, and
exposing and reforming was already clear.

Criticism of Gore's administration was also made public in John Mills
Jackson's *A View of the Political Situation of the Province.* Published in
Britain after Jackson had left the colony, it does not appear to have circulated openly in Upper Canada. It was addressed to the Colonial Secretary and dedicated to the British Parliament. Two supporters of the local
government responded, but their pamphlets were neither extensively
circulated in Upper Canada nor addressed to its residents. One,
addressed to the Colonial Secretary and published at Quebec, claimed
to have entered the fray only because Jackson and others 'have had the
effrontery to bring their complaints before the public.' The second,
published at Halifax, was addressed to a 'friend in England.' It was, however, available for purchase at York, Queenston, and Kingston, and the
Agricultural Society of Niagara resolved to purchase and distribute one
hundred copies.¹¹ By publishing their defence of colonial governance,
these two pamphleteers appealed indirectly to a colonial reading public
but by addressing their arguments to distant others they simultaneously
denied it political standing.¹²

The *Guardian* dismissed the second pamphlet as 'the last speech of

---

9 A Loyalist, *Guardian*, 3 Sept. 1807, transcribed, National Archives of Canada, MG 11
   CO42, 350. Gore claimed to have proof that Thorpe was the author.
10 [Cartwright], *Letters, from an American Loyalist*, 61–2 and Jackson, *View of the Political
   Situation*, 16
11 Anon., *To the Right Honorable Lord Castlereagh*, 1, [Cartwright], *Letters, from an American
   Loyalist*, 4, *York Gazette*, 21 Nov. 1810, and Falkland, *Kingston Gazette*, 18 Dec. 1810
12 Keith Michael Baker, 'Memory and Practice: Politics and the Representation of the
   Past in Eighteenth-Century France,' in *Inventing the French Revolution*, 51

despotism,' objecting further that it had appeared anonymously. 'Falkland' reminded the *Guardian* that 'it is with the truth and tendency of a work that the public is concerned, and not with the name of the author; and its merits will generally be estimated with greater impartiality when the writer is unknown.'[13] The *Guardian* had to be lectured in the norms of public discussion. To engage it in serious debate would be to admit it to a status it had not earned. It spread falsehoods and behaved in a manner that could only prevail upon those who were likewise unschooled in rational conversation. From such a perspective, it made considerable sense to use the laws of libel and the privileges of the assembly to silence it. Gentlemen with the education, experience, information, and leisure to profit from reading such pamphlets thought of themselves as part of a transatlantic public. Outside such narrow circles, public contention – a powerful social solvent – was to be shunned.

Government supporters were not, however, unconcerned with the general disposition of Upper Canadians. Recent experience in America and France graphically illustrated the revolutionary potential of a mobilized populace. In 1810, John Strachan addressed his *Discourse on the Character of King George the Third* 'to the inhabitants of British America.' Strachan worried that 'even the bulk of our own population in these colonies, are but very imperfectly acquainted with his true character.' Strachan hoped his pamphlet would 'assist in quieting the minds of my fellow subjects, and dissipate murmurs and discontent by proving them totally unfounded.'[14] Strachan's fellow subjects were to be informed enough to quiet their minds. Strachan addressed them, but he did not intend to engage them in critical dialogue. They were to 'know' the British monarch and constitution so they could 'love' them and thus abandon any doubts they may have had. Such doubts were not forthright, reasoned arguments, but 'murmurs.' The populace was to be inoculated against falsehood. Their loyalty and deference, not their active participation or critical assessment, were sought.[15]

Strachan's *Discourse* rested on a notion of 'opinion' developed in the seventeenth century. Blaise Pascal declared it 'Queen of the World.'

13 Falkland, *Kingston Gazette*, 18 Dec. 1810, quoting from the *Guardian*. Falkland may have been Richard Cartwright, author of the pamphlet in question.

14 Strachan, *Discourse on the Character of King George*, advertisement

15 On informing people in non-democratic systems, see Richard D. Brown, *The Strength of a People: The Idea of an Informed Citizenry in America, 1650–1826* (Chapel Hill: University of North Carolina Press 1996), 43–4.

The rule of such a monarch was preferable to the rule of the tyrant of force. Later, David Hume made much of the same dichotomy: 'As force is always on the side of the governed, the governors have nothing to support them but opinion.' Government rested on opinion, but such opinion was not typically conceptualized as the outcome of active, rational discussion. Rather, popular opinion, in this sense, was part of a family of ambiguous terms that were largely passive and not necessarily rational, including national sentiment, public spirit, the public mind, and popular prejudice or disposition. Such terms had less to do with public debate than with customs, character traits, or some sort of innate common sense.[16] Since they did not actively govern, such entities were compatible with a constitutional theory focused on legislative institutions embodying discreet social estates or interests. Strachan sought to thwart demagogues' efforts because misled popular opinion could topple even the best regime. It was not, however, capable of positive, sustained participation in government.

Although Strachan's *Discourse* probably reached few of the 'populace,' it managed to reach some who felt qualified to judge. 'A Friend to Peace' objected to its strictures on the American constitution and people, but was confident that although 'the writer of them may be under the influence of prejudice ... an unprejudiced Public, to whom they are addressed, will judge of them with impartiality.'[17] The tables were turned. Prejudice came from one of the enlightened few, but the wider public would judge best. Strachan had not intended to provoke such public commentary, but it was a potential consequence of all but the most anodyne publication.

In 1818, the legislative council and assembly came to a standstill when the former claimed the right to amend money bills – a claim the assembly rejected unanimously. The council bypassed the elected lower house, taking its case directly to Upper Canadians. It ordered its resolutions and the assembly's reply printed. Members of an assembly committee felt compelled 'to express their indignant feelings on this most

---

16 For Pascal see Paul A. Palmer, 'The Concept of Public Opinion in Political Theory,' in Carl Witke, ed., *Essays in History and Political Theory in Honor of Charles Howard McIlwain* (Cambridge, Mass.: Harvard University Press 1936), 234 and for Hume, see Daniel Gordon, 'Philosophy, Sociology, and Gender in the Enlightenment Conception of Public Opinion,' *French Historical Studies* 17, no. 4 (Fall 1992), 886–9.
17 'A Friend to Peace' [Barnabus Bidwell], *Kingston Gazette*, 9 Oct. 1810

important occasion; and particularly as the Legislative Council by ordering their resolutions, together with those of your House (to which they are purposely annexed as an intended refutation) to be printed, submit to the public the justice and propriety of their proceedings.' The assembly was not alone in responding in kind to the legislative council. 'A Commoner' informed readers of the *Kingston Gazette* that 'the Council having ordered the Resolutions to be printed, the subject is now fairly before the public, at whose tribunal any inhabitant of the Province is, of course, at liberty to discuss the constitutional question.'[18] Within a few years, correspondents felt no need to justify their participation in public discussions or to wonder whether a subject was 'fairly' before them or not.

Parliament was quickly dissolved, cutting off such appeals for public judgment. Their practical force had been limited anyway by the small amount of information published in the colony's few newspapers. The degree to which the legislative council had been playing with fire was, however, made abundantly clear by the steep increase in political commentary by or in response to Robert Gourlay. Public meetings to answer his questionnaire, garner signatures for various petitions, or by the 'Upper Canadian Convention of the Friends to Enquiry' occasioned comment.[19] The mutually reinforcing relationships among newspapers, public meetings, and petitions that came to dominate later reform politics was already in place. Limits, however, remained. Gourlay praised the zeal of the inhabitants of the Midland and parts of the Newcastle Districts, but noted that 'this spirit was manifested as near as might be to the limit of the circulation of the Kingston Gazette. Toward the middle of the Newcastle District few of the farmers are in the habit of reading and thence feel little interest in public concerns.'[20] The expansion and decentralization of the press described in the previous chapter were preconditions for political participation. Reading aroused interest, precipitating both further reading and other forms of political participation.

Gourlay's opponents organized counter–public meetings and published various addresses of their own. Their efforts were fewer in number and most avoided explicit appeals to public opinion. The 'Clergy, Magistrates, Officers of Militia and other inhabitants' of Glengarry were

---

18 *Niagara Spectator*, 11 June and 'A Commoner,' *Kingston Gazette*, 5 May 1818
19 Hartwell Bowsfield, 'Upper Canada in the 1820's: The Development of Political Consciousness,' PhD thesis, University of Toronto 1976, 6, 120–2, 150
20 Gourlay, *Niagara Spectator*, 10 Dec. 1818

indignant 'at the attempts of desperate demagogues, to disturb the public mind' and 'create confusion.' A Cornwall meeting assured the lieutenant-governor that 'the good sense of His Majesty's subjects will ultimately prevail' over such agitation.[21] In the summer of 1818, an anonymous opponent of Gourlay anxiously awaited the approaching harvest. Farmers, too ignorant of politics and the English language to say anything of value at public meetings or in newspapers, would soon be preoccupied with something they were better suited to.[22] Using the law of seditious libel against Gourlay and the editor of the *Niagara Spectator*, banishing Gourlay from the province, and prohibiting province-wide meetings showed an awareness of the implications of politicizing non-legislators and an unwillingness to rely solely on the 'good sense' of the people.

During the 1820s a number of political issues helped to create a broader public beyond formal institutions. Early deference to parliament in the form of apologies for raising issues or pledges to respect its autonomy[23] were soon eclipsed by a sense of entitlement reinforced by the regular publication of parliamentary intelligence. Public meetings and newspaper commentary in the summer and fall of 1822 considered the merits of the proposed reunion of Upper and Lower Canada.[24] The following year, however, the *Weekly Register* reminded its readers that criticism was 'a dangerous weapon in the hands of the ignorant and an illiterate person' – a point reinforced in this case by having ignorance and illiteracy personified by a woman.[25] Throughout the decade, petitions were organized against the Naturalization Act (respecting the rights of former American citizens resident in the colony), the pretensions of the Anglican hierarchy, and other perceived grievances. The scale of these efforts could not be ignored. To counter what it considered misrepresentations, the *Loyalist* printed the Naturalization Bill: 'Now we only ask those who are interested in the matter, to read the Bill which is before them, carefully and attentively, and setting aside any representations which may have been made to them, to exercise their

21 *Kingston Chronicle*, 8 and 15 Jan. 1819
22 Anon., *Niagara Spectator*, 6 Aug. 1818
23 Camden and Amicus Curle, *Kingston Gazette*, 21 Sept. 1816 and 18 Nov. 1817
24 *Weekly Register*, 29 Aug., 5 Sept., and 3 Oct. 1822, and *Kingston Chronicle*, 1 and 22 Nov. and 20 Dec. 1822
25 *Weekly Register*, 25 Jan. 1823 in Cecilia Morgan, *Public Men and Virtuous Women: The Gendered Languages of Religion and Politics in Upper Canada, 1791–1850* (Toronto: University of Toronto Press 1996), 69–70

own unbiased judgements.'[26] Aware of significant opposition but convinced of the merits of its case, the *Loyalist* was willing to test the proposition that truth was discoverable by all who sincerely sought after it. Others were less sanguine. Moreover, there was little sense of what to do with the test results.

Surveying recent political history in 1827, the moderate reform *Upper Canada Herald* concluded that 'public opinion is acquiring strength in every Government, in proportion to its freedom. In Great Britain its influence is more and more manifest.' The same could not be said of her colonies. 'Instead of being controlled by a junta of bigoted advisers, the administrator of every Province should listen to the voice of the Public. By the public voice, we do not mean the clamour of interested partisans, but the general sense of the People at large, to which the measures of Government ought to be conformed.'[27] Specific institutional mechanisms were secondary to the underlying principle: free government was government by public opinion. If judgment was dispersed to the 'people at large,' how was its 'general sense' to be distinguished from 'clamour?'

Elections were one way. On the basis of the 1828 results, Francis Collins of the *Canadian Freeman* concluded that the people had succeeded in electing an assembly committed to ending the abuse of power. 'Now that public opinion has taken a stand from which it cannot be driven during the present generation,' the only question left was 'how will our ministerialists and officials act? ... Instead of setting public opinion at defiance, as heretofore, and forcing upon the country unjust and unpopular measures, will they consult the feelings of the people ...? We fear not.'[28] Collins overestimated both the constancy of the electorate and the stubbornness of ministerialists. Subsequent elections sent conflicting messages, returning 'ministerialist' majorities in 1830 and 1836. Conservatives were often sceptical about the ability, moderation, and knowledge of 'the people,' but many of them began to adopt elements of reform rhetoric and methods. Faced with continued opposition and reformers' potential control of the assembly, they could no longer guarantee the success of their measures by relying solely on traditional institutions. They too began to appeal to the judgment of a wider segment of the population and to make a more concerted effort to influence that judgment.

---

26 *U. E. Loyalist,* 24 Feb. 1827
27 *Upper Canada Herald,* 31 July 1827
28 *Canadian Freeman,* 14 Aug. 1828, but Collins, soon harshly critical of this assembly, also welcomed the 1830 results as the verdict of public opinion; 28 Oct. 1830.

Public meeting, like elections, could distil the public's 'general sense.' William Warren Baldwin called for more meetings, since 'this course of expressing public opinion ... has not been so frequently pursued as it ought.'[29] The same could not be said for the 1830s. William Lyon Mackenzie was an energetic instigator of public meetings to legitimate his claim that he, not the government or its supporters in the assembly and press, spoke for public opinion. The dozens of public meetings organized by, for, or against Mackenzie and his colleagues between the fall of 1831 and the spring of 1833 gave greater prominence to the public use of reason by Upper Canadians outside the electoral process and thus to the concept of public opinion.

In the first year of the *Colonial Advocate*, Mackenzie was confident that 'the difference between passive obedience and non-resistance, to a tyrannical government, as compared with free discussion of the public measures of a represented [representative?] and responsible one, is known by our meanest peasants.'[30] His *Catechism of Education* (1830) argued that society's judgment was the ultimate motivation for human action and the standard by which it should be judged. Proper systems of education and government would ensure that such collective judgments rewarded virtue and merit rather than 'servility and meanness to those above, and tyranny to those below.'[31] For Mackenzie, Upper Canada's government failed the test. Only servility to its pretentious officers ensconced in the legislative and executive councils promised advancement in Upper Canada, while 'the road to honour, power, and preferment in the United States is "public opinion."'[32] Promotion should flow up from the people's verdict, not down from the Crown – a power from which Mackenzie had received far less favour. Likewise, by 1834, Marshall Spring Bidwell concluded that 'public opinion does not have that influence here as it does in England ... The government of England is a government of public opinion.' Recurring policy conflicts, such as the one over primogeniture discussed in the final chapter, taught Bidwell and others that the people's judgment could be frustrated by the Crown and legislative council, no matter how rational, informed, or persistent it was.[33]

29 Baldwin, *Canadian Freeman*, 11 July 1828
30 *Colonial Advocate*, 10 June 1824
31 *Catechism of Education: Part First*, esp. 22, 39–42
32 Mackenzie, *Sketches of Canada*, 171
33 Bidwell, *Christian Guardian*, 18 Dec. 1834

In 1831–2, Mackenzie toured the province distributing pamphlets, calling public meetings, gathering signatures for grievance petitions, and helping to organize Political Unions. In December 1831, the assembly expelled him for libelling it in the *Advocate*. He was re-elected, expelled again in January 1832, and, although declared ineligible to sit again, re-elected at the end of the month. The assembly having been prorogued, Mackenzie could not attempt to retake his seat. Instead, he went from public meeting to public meeting presenting grievance resolutions before travelling to Britain to present them to the Colonial Office with as many as ten thousand signatures. Local reformers organized additional public meetings and more followed in 1833 when the Colonial Secretary's response to Mackenzie's mission became known in the colony.[34]

After his second expulsion from the House, Mackenzie called on 'all the independent inhabitants ... young and old, whether they be landowners or not landowners' to assemble at York: 'Public opinion, clearly expressed, is set at defiance ... Up then and be doing!'[35] It was not, however, only Mackenzie supporters who were up and doing. The unprecedented level of opposition activity, the stridency of Mackenzie's demands, and his direct appeal to Britain galvanized his opponents. The *Kingston Chronicle* ended its self-imposed silence on Mackenzie to attack his principles and tactics.[36] Others organized counter-meetings to adopt loyal addresses, attempted to disrupt opposition meetings (sometimes with force), and formed their own association, the British Constitutional Society.

In order to refute Mackenzie's claim to speak for colonial public opinion, his detractors had to speak out themselves. Thus, according to their address, 'the intelligent and loyal inhabitants' of the Newcastle District had 'hitherto abstained from any public expression of their sentiments' against the unintelligent and disloyal from utter contempt. Now, seeing them grow so bold as to try to mislead the Crown, 'we feel ourselves called upon by our duty to our Sovereign, to ourselves and posterity, to counteract these malevolent and mischievous designs, by

34 Gerald M. Craig, *Upper Canada: The Formative Years, 1784–1841* (Toronto: McClelland and Stewart 1963), 212–15 and Carol Wilton, '"Lawless Law": Conservative Political Violence in Upper Canada, 1818–1841,' *Law and History Review* 13, no. 1 (Spring 1995), 121–2

35 Mackenzie, 'An Appeal to the People,' *Brockville Recorder*, 19 Jan. 1832

36 *Kingston Chronicle*, 22 Oct. 1831

representations of truth, at the foot of your Majesty's throne.' Of course, by meeting, speaking, and publishing, their 'representations' came before other Upper Canadians as well as the king and, in such a competitive arena, could hardly be received as unmediated 'truth.' Despite some initial hesitancy about the democratizing potential of participation in this arena, most conservative newspapers welcomed the counter-publicity it generated.[37]

Public meetings, by their very nature, were meant to form and express collective decisions or, as Mackenzie put it, were called 'that due force may be given to public opinion.'[38] They were physical, face-to-face gatherings of the community in a public space. They were opportunities for collective political action: to adopt addresses or petitions, nominate candidates for office, or establish corporate entities for the provision of public services. Norms regulated how they were convened, how notice of their location and purpose was given, how a chair and secretary were elected, and how the business of speeches and resolutions was conducted. They expressed the ideal of an engaged, active citizenry able to act as a unit by narrowing some of the distance among their number. Even when the meetings were orchestrated by a self-selected few, participation took the form of attending, listening, speaking, heckling, disrupting, voting, and signing or refusing to sign the resolutions, petition, or address. As Allan Greer notes, open elections to colonial assemblies can be seen as a specialized subset of public meetings.

As large, often tumultuous, and hotly contested gatherings, public meetings were especially difficult sites in which to police distinctions between residents and outsiders, voters and non-voters, property-owners and the propertyless. They posed the question of who 'the people' were

---

37 Newcastle address, *Niagara Gleaner*, 10 Mar. and also *Western Mercury*, 8 Mar. and 3 May 1832
38 'An Appeal to the People,' *Brockville Recorder*, 19 Jan. 1832. The following paragraphs are indebted to Mary Ryan, *Civic Wars: Democracy and Public Life in the American City during the Nineteenth Century* (Berkeley: University of California Press 1997), 94–131 as well as to James Vernon, *Politics and the People: A Study of English Political Culture, c. 1815– 1867* (Cambridge: Cambridge University Press 1993), 16–17, 66, 121, 125–6. For a good Upper Canadian example, see H.V. Nelles, 'Loyalism and Local Power: The District of Niagara, 1792–1837,' *Ontario History* 58, no. 2 (June 1966), 107–10. The importance of public meetings to popular oppositional politics is also explored by Wilton, '"Lawless Law"' and '"A Firebrand amongst the People": The Durham Meetings and Popular Politics in Upper Canada,' *Canadian Historical Review* 75, no. 3 (September 1994), 346– 75 and for Lower Canada, see Allan Greer, *Patriots and the People: The Rebellion of 1837 in Rural Lower Canada* (Toronto: University of Toronto Press 1993), 115–16.

in its most acute form. According to one observer at a 'Meeting of the Electors of Toronto' in 1836, 'Not a third of those present were Electors.'[39] The widespread acceptance that, 'properly' conducted, public meetings provided one of the most authoritative expressions of local opinion often ensured that whichever side lost control of a particular meeting would challenge its legitimacy by attacking how it had been conducted, the number and status of those who had attended, or the accuracy of later reports. As well, they might organize another gathering limited to their own supporters and then try to claim that it alone was truly a public, as opposed to merely a partisan, meeting. Much newspaper space was devoted to disseminating requisitions for meetings and their proceedings, addresses, resolutions, and petitions, thus underlying the close relationship between the oral and print. Newspapers also participated in the almost inevitable, often bitter post-mortems. Conservatives were wary of the effects of this further dissemination and the potential to empower the disenfranchised and propertyless or to spark social disorder. They remained convinced that large, mass meetings were more conducive to mob enthusiasm than to calm deliberation. In short, public meetings epitomized many of the promises and limits of the public sphere.

At York, conservatives organized a committee to prepare a loyal address in response to Mackenzie. They did not, however, call a public meeting. As the *Courier* explained, 'We do not think that a large body of people collected together, and subjected to the various excitements which exist upon such occasions, affords the best means of ascertaining the real and unbiased sentiments of the people upon any question. We think that a calm appeal to the deliberate judgement of each individual of a community, upon any public question, is calculated to elicit by far the most accurate and certain evidence of the opinions of that community.' Convinced that many would be more amenable if approached individually by prominent local conservatives, the committee planned to present its address 'to each individual of this town for signatures.'[40] Like Mackenzie's call to both landowners and non-landowners, this reference to 'every individual' suggests non-voters were not excluded, but by trying to largely privatize the process, the committee also hoped to deny radicals the space to organize, express opposition, and otherwise mar the adoption of

39 Toronto Reference Library, Baldwin Room, Henry Rowsell's Toronto Journal, 20 May 1836
40 *Courier of Upper Canada,* 17 Mar. 1832

their address. The ploy to divorce much of the democratic potential of a public meeting from the legitimacy and support it conferred was thwarted when Mackenzie called a public meeting to counter the address. Its supporters organized to ensure that they had a majority at the meeting. Outnumbered, Mackenzie and his sympathizers withdrew to hold a separate meeting, which was broken up by the first of three riots.[41]

This was not the only use of force connected to the round of public meetings in the early 1830s. Mackenzie had just been assaulted at Hamilton. Violence also broke out at Amherst and Farmersville.[42] The *Hamilton Free Press* argued that violence was being used to destroy the people's 'right of meeting and expressing their sentiments ... or to deprive such meetings of the character of order and quiet deliberation.' The *Christian Guardian* agreed that those could be the only motives and worried that 'scarcely a question appears to be calmly considered & decided by an orderly vote, – all is carried by acclamation, so that the several motions are not decided by reason, judgement, sense of numbers, but by noise and violence.'[43] Both the *Guardian* and the conservative *Courier* with its preference for door-to-door canvassing thought that calm deliberation was often absent at public meetings; that public opinion had to be distinguished from 'noise and violence.' They disagreed about whom to blame, government's supporters or its critics.

For his part during the Newcastle District meeting, G.M. Boswell was labelled an 'advocate of Mr. Mackenzie's principles' by the *Cobourg Star*. Boswell countered that, by stigmatizing all critics as radicals, the *Star* was attempting to silence differences of opinion, undermining his 'liberty as a reasonable being ... of evincing my sentiments.' At the meeting, the first to come forward in support of the grievance resolutions was shouted down. All those who, like Boswell, 'attended with the expectation of hearing the resolutions submitted for their approval temperately and fairly discussed' had been insulted. Refusal to hear both sides betrayed a will to tyrannize, for 'every Government unless its measures are subject to the controlling ordeal of public opinion has a tendency to despotism.' Boswell concluded with a list of the reforms he had been unable to bring to the attention of the meeting, conceding, 'I may be in error, and many wiser than I am may possess opinions very different

41 F.H. Armstrong, 'The York Riots of March 23, 1832,' *Ontario History* 55, no. 2 (June 1963), 61–72
42 Wilton, '"Lawless Law,"' 118
43 *Hamilton Free Press* copied in *Colonial Advocate* and *Christian Guardian*, 28 Mar. 1832

from mine. – If however I be wrong, a yelling mob, or an opprobrious epithet can never convince me of my error – and an attempt to stifle temperate discussion can have no other tendency, than to confirm me in my opinion.'[44] Only those unsure of the justice of their case hid from public opinion. Continued refusal to engage critics constructively was fast becoming a liability.

The radical *St Thomas Liberal* also accused government supporters of attempting to silence criticism by falsely equating it with Mackenzie. Reformers were 'the men who take the liberty to think for themselves – they do not receive opinions from others without careful examination.' This should have protected them from charges of being Mackenzie's dupes, but 'this is indeed their crime, – for arrogantly exercising this prerogative, they have incurred the displeasure of the self-styled patricians of British America. They have dared to investigate the public conduct of public men.'[45] Moreover, these investigations had become paramount. In response to Mackenzie's mission, the Colonial Secretary removed H.J. Boulton from office. The *Canadian Correspondent's* appreciation was grudging at best. Boulton 'has been long since tried at the bar of public opinion.'[46] Rhetorically, the right of judgment had shifted from the Crown to public opinion. Legally, no such transfer had taken place. Rhetoric and law – claims to authority and actual power – were increasingly dissonant.

It would be a mistake, however, to suggest that government supporters limited their public reaction to critics to violence, shouting them down, or branding them with epithets. Many remained wary of the potential for disorder and empowerment at public meetings,[47] but faced with unprecedented public opposition, conservatives began to adopt their opponents' tactics and rhetoric selectively. They moved to organize and marshal public support, redirecting their efforts from calls for political quietude to promoting calm deliberation – from denying public opinion to distinguishing it from public clamour.

The committee that had prepared York's loyal address became the British Constitutional Society. 'Every male inhabitant of this town of

---

44 Boswell, *Cobourg Star*, 7 Mar. 1832. George Morss Boswell was elected as a moderate supporter of Lord Sydenham in 1841.
45 *St Thomas Liberal*, 13 Oct. 1832
46 *Correspondent* copied in *Cobourg Star*, 22 May 1833
47 E.g., *Niagara Gleaner*, 18 Feb. and 24 Mar. 1832, and *Western Mercury*, 3 May, 14 June, and 12 July 1832, and *Cobourg Star*, 27 Feb. 1833

good character, over 21 years of age, without distinction of rank, religion, or country' was invited to join a voluntary association to administer 'an antidote to that poison which has been so industriously disseminated by the unprincipled inventors of grievances.'[48] Such efforts reflected the belief that the rational and unprejudiced could be brought to see through Mackenzie's rhetoric. By actively countering Mackenzie in this way, these 'constitutionalists' were attempting to mould public opinion. By doing so, they paid homage to its power.

Speaking at Scarborough, Robert Douglas Hamilton told his audience that public meetings preserved their liberty 'against the encroachments of the government, as well as against the despotic roar of our fellow subjects.' To counter that roar, Hamilton warned his audience not to 'trust either my propositions or conclusions, examine for yourselves, read fully and think freely ... Let me admonish you never to place implicit confidence in any man, however commanding his talents may be, for authority is not proof, and assertions are not arguments.' Confident that those who examined for themselves would spurn Mackenzie, Hamilton invited the public to judge his own arguments, the government, and the constitution. Reacting to the York meetings, another supporter of the existing constitution advised 'men of common sense' to boycott radical gatherings and to 'think for yourselves. Do not yield up your understandings and believe what any man says to you without trying every question by the test of your own judgements.'[49] Of course, 'any man' encompassed government supporters as well as critics.

In August 1832, Henry Ruttan, sheriff of the Newcastle District, 'in order to afford my fellow subjects in this district some opportunity of forming a clear judgement' amidst 'an effervescence of the public mind, entirely unparalleled in its history,' felt 'a duty to step forward and state my views on the great questions at issue.' In particular, he addressed himself to 'the honest, sober, thinking part; those who do not make up their minds hastily and without consideration, but who are willing to set aside for a few moments, every impression which may militate against a dispassionate consideration of the subject under discussion.' This increasingly common attempt to distinguish between the 'dispas-

---

48 Society resolutions and commentary, *Western Mercury*, 12 Apr. 1832. Note again the appeal to 'inhabitants,' not voters. See also F.H. Armstrong, 'The Carfrae Family: A Study in Early Toronto Toryism,' *Ontario History* 54, no. 3 (1962), 161–81.
49 Guy Pollock, *Courier* copied in *Western Mercury*, 22 Mar. and Simcoe, *Upper Canada Herald*, 4 Apr. 1832

sionate' who contributed to public opinion and the passionate who only fomented the 'effervescence' of the public mind was immediately diluted by Ruttan's claim that the former 'form a vast majority of the people of this District.' Citing an unnamed authority that 'public opinion is seldom erroneous when founded on just information,' Ruttan set out to provide that information in an address serialized over eight issues of the *Cobourg Star*. He returned repeatedly to the same point: the people should 'test everything by their own judgement and experience,' 'a vast majority of our farmers and mechanics are now ... generally men of reading and intelligence' able to assess his arguments, and 'we should take nothing for granted, until it is proved to us ... I say proved by the touchstone of our own deliberate judgement, formed from *the evidence of our own senses*.' Ruttan had come to believe that the developments surveyed in the two previous chapters had opened the possibility of intelligent, public reasoning. His task was to ensure that it was used responsibly, and thus he was willing to criticize government supporters when their behaviour at public meetings failed to measure up.[50]

No longer able to silence or ignore their opponents, many conservatives turned to calling for the reasonable, moderate exercise of public reason. Hamilton and Ruttan were confident that such reasoning would lead to the conclusions they expounded. Calling on the people to judge the claims of Mackenzie and other radicals, they also invited their audiences to assess their own arguments and the nature of government itself. By appealing to public opinion and calling for a more vigorous exercise of public reason, they helped create a public capable of judging the state. The implications were not, as yet, fully explored. The explicit aim remained limited – to defeat the radicals. Once its dispassionate deliberation stifled the fury of radical agitation, the public could safely retreat from politics. But would it?

Political conflict ebbed and flowed between 1833 and 1836. For the concept of public opinion, these were years of elaboration, rather than significant departures. With their election victory in 1834, radicals and reformers remained the concept's foremost, though not its sole, champions.

---

50 Ruttan, 'Address to the People of the Newcastle District,' *Cobourg Star*, 1, 8, 15, 22, and 29 Aug. and 5, 12, and 19 Sept. 1832. For his criticism of government supporters see Carol Wilton-Siegel, 'The Transformation of Upper Canadian Politics in the 1840s,' PhD thesis, University of Toronto 1984, 34.

From its survey of western history to 1833, the *St Thomas Liberal* proved to its own satisfaction that the power of the people had not only increased but had changed in nature. It no longer exploded in episodic food riots, attacks on tax-collectors, or other 'outbreakings of a sudden indignation; the result of some peculiar evil, and expiring almost at its birth.' Popular power was now 'the off-spring of knowledge, not of passion ... founded on increased information, a discontent aided as well as produced by reason. This is the new and formidable power to which the last few years have given birth.' It would continue to grow until it became 'the sole existing power in the state – all others will yield to, or be merged into it.' Several months later, the *Liberal* named this power in an editorial entitled 'Public Opinion.' While it was 'a powerful check upon the malevolent action of man,' the editor worried that 'there is some danger of individuals rising to such a degree of wealth and independence; of official power and influence; and of forming family compacts for interested purposes, as to set public opinion almost at defiance.' To forestall such troubling developments, public opinion had to be better informed and more united. In the meantime, identifying the enemy was easy. 'Many plans are formed to elude the force of public opinion or to stifle its expression. But there is not a more sure criterion by which to judge that something is wrong, than when such attempts are made.'

A year later, the *Liberal* made the connection to Upper Canada explicit. Colonial government operated according to 'exclusive principles ... whereby the few rule the many without regard to their opinion.' This 'stoical insensibility of our rulers to the voice of public opinion' was unjust and, by risking revolution, foolish. 'Opposition may retard the claims of the people for a time, but it will whet their desires, and render them irresistible in the end.' Constitutional reforms, especially those that would augment the powers of the elective assembly, would redirect this restless force into more peaceful channels.[51]

Other radicals used the concept of public opinion to various ends. The *Cobourg Reformer* called for a greater study of the science of politics to enlighten public opinion and promote constitutional change. It also noted that while 'Englishmen boast of their liberal institutions and their government by the enlightened opinion of the nation,' open voting and an irresponsible legislative council rendered this boast empty in Upper

---

51 *St Thomas Liberal*, 1 Aug. and 19 Dec. 1833 and 18 Dec. 1834. The editorial 'Public Opinion' was also copied by the moderate *Brockville Recorder*, 3 Jan. 1834.

Canada.[52] In August 1834, the *Canadian Correspondent* laid down the principle that 'public feeling and public opinion are the life and the aliment of social institutions.' Bitter partisanship would end only 'by discussing fairly and argumentatively before the high tribunal of public opinion, the existence and the extent of the oppressions complained of, and the judgement of that tribunal, uninfluenced by men scrambling for power, would be heard and heeded by His Majesty's [British] Government.'[53] Not all radicals retained their faith in the ultimate responsiveness of the imperial government, but buoyed by their election victory in 1834 and seemingly thwarted only by the irresponsibility of the legislative and executive councils, their belief in the reality and rhetorical value of that voice grew apace.

Conversely, they agreed that the government and its supporters feared, ignored, or tried to pervert public opinion. Discontinuing the *Reformer*, James Radcliffe was comforted by evidence of the 'ultimate success' of his cause in 'the growing symptoms of weakness and desperation, in the style resorted to by the advocates of misrule.' 'The field of reason and of fair argument, has been abandoned ... He who cannot reason may rail; and though he cannot refute, he can slander and call names.'[54] Almost simultaneously, one such 'advocate of misrule' affirmed 'the soundness of the doctrine which ascribes the healthful vitality of the British Constitution to the free discussion of public measures.' He was also 'perfectly aware of the lesson taught by all history and experience – the difference namely between rational freedom and a wild and desperate licentiousness ... that political discussions, besides being free, must also be temperate and well-regulated.'[55] Likewise, when the *Brockville Recorder* berated the *Patriot* for failing to met reform arguments, the *Patriot* responded with ridicule: 'Combat ignorance and prejudice with argument! hew blocks of

---

52 *Reformer*, 30 June and 22 Sept. 1835 and also *Colonial Advocate*, 13 Feb. 1834, and
   Mathew Howard on the debate to incorporate York, *Brockville Recorder*, 14 Feb. 1834.
   See also the *Reformer*, 1 Dec. 1835, on the perversion of public opinion during elections
   due to rotten boroughs. Likewise, the *Reformer* copied in *Correspondent & Advocate*,
   22 Oct. 1835, dismissed the analogy between Britain and Upper Canada because 'the
   Privy Council [it should have said the cabinet] changes with the current of public opinion, the Executive Council is permanent.'
53 *Canadian Correspondent*, 9 Aug. 1834 and also *Correspondent & Advocate*, 29 Jan. and
   22 Oct. 1835
54 Radcliffe, copied in *Patriot*, 19 Aug. 1834
55 Vale to William Lyon Mackenzie, *Patriot*, 19 Aug. 1834

granite with a razor!!'[56] One side's temperate debate was another's
ignorant appeal to emotion.

Much had transpired since Gore's response to Thorpe in 1807.
The value of free and enlightened public reason was an increasingly
shared rhetorical space, but who decided what was 'temperate' or
'well-regulated'? Many conservatives and some moderates remained
suspicious of radicals' appeals to public opinion. They could mask recourse to numbers over wisdom, popular prejudices over reason, and
ignorance over information.[57] To government critics, the distinction
between public opinion and popular clamour seemed to be applied
more rigorously to their activities than to those of government supporters. It appeared to be used to deny the status of public opinion
only to unpleasant verdicts.

Early in 1835, public conflict was again on the increase. The political
potential of voluntary associations was re-harnessed when radicals organized the Canadian Alliance Society. One branch began by resolving
that 'government and the choice of those who administer it, should
depend entirely on the preponderance of free unbiased opinion.'
Another called for the periodic publication of a 'political Tract' to help
'concentrate public opinion' and, indeed, the society raised money by
selling copies of Mackenzie's Seventh Report on Grievances. The first
resolution of a third branch declared that 'the political condition of the
inhabitants of this Province will never be ameliorated, nor their grievances redressed, except by a steady, firm and unanimous expression of
public opinion.'[58] These branches were meant to form and express just
such an opinion. In April, conservatives revived the British Constitutional Society, convinced that 'we have only to make the electors of the
Province understand the real state of the case, to induce one simultaneous and effectual demonstration of public feeling' and rid the assembly of radicals. To this end, they resolved that 'the inhabitants of the
country in general, should be made thoroughly acquainted with the real

---

56 *Patriot,* 8 May 1835
57 For conservatives, see Solon, *Patriot,* 6 Feb. 1835, and for moderates, see *Upper Canada
    Herald,* 21 July and 1 Dec. 1835. For moderate reformers making much the same point
    against radicals' demand for a directly elective legislative council, see Anon., *Cobourg
    Star,* 21 Jan. and *St Catharines Journal,* 22 Oct. 1835.
58 North of King and South of Techumseth, Fourth Riding of Lincoln, Whitchurch, and
    King, *Correspondent & Advocate,* 2 and 26 Feb., 12 Mar., 30 Apr., 7 May, and 30 July 1835.
    By March, the society claimed 654 members.

situation of affairs, and the true state of the parties.'[59] Ignorance, not conviction, lay behind the reform victory of 1834. No effort was to be spared to avoid a repeat in 1836. The result accelerated the ascent of the concept of public opinion.

Privately, Sir Francis Bond Head, the new lieutenant-governor, had little use for the concept. He lectured the Colonial Secretary on the 'fatal error' of conciliating 'party public opinion,' since 'every man in office should make public opinion follow *him*, and never attempt to follow *it*.'[60] Ironically, Head's strenuous efforts to lead public opinion helped ensure that his successors had little choice but to follow it. His appointment of two reformers and a neutral administrator to the executive council as an attempt to conciliate opposition was followed by the resignation of the entire council three weeks later. Conflicting interpretations of the constitution were aired when the ex-councillors' reasons for resigning and Head's response were published. Appearing in most newspapers, both were but the first instalment of an explosion of printed commentary in the spring of 1836.[61] Privately, John Beverley Robinson opposed Head's decision to allow publication of both sides of the conflict 'for every body knows every thing – and all the shoemakers and tailors in town are discussing the ____ of the "Cabinet pudding."'[62] To some, it remained unseemly for the highest matters of state to be discussed irrespective of social status.

Publicly, both sides welcomed the exposure. According to the radical *Correspondent & Advocate*, 'the public mind is becoming more and more informed on several subjects connected with the political constitution of this province.' The conservative *Patriot* conceded that 'all this may be heedlessly swallowed by the ignorant, the idle and the dissolute, whose show of hands may gladden the heart of a renegade Priest [the *Correspondent*'s editor], or a worthless Mayor of Toronto [Mackenzie] ... but small is the chance, that such mendacity can operate upon an intelligent people, who have grown and prospered ... Let the people reflect.'[63] Public opinion, divorced from 'the ignorant, the idle and the dissolute'

59 Resolutions and commentary, *Courier* copied in *Cobourg Star*, 29 Apr. 1835
60 Head to the Colonial Office, 1 June 1836 copied in Head, *A Narrative*, 56
61 Some of the constitutional issues were discussed in chapter 1 and the publication of material in the *Patriot* was discussed in chapter 3.
62 Robinson to Sir John Colborne, 20 Mar. 1836 in Robert L. Fraser, 'Like Eden in Her Summer Dress: Gentry, Economy, and Society: Upper Canada, 1812–1840,' PhD thesis, University of Toronto 1979, 221
63 *Correspondent & Advocate*, 21 Mar. and *Patriot*, 22 Mar. 1836

would reflect correctly. Similarly, the *Chronicle & Gazette* was confident that if the 'unprejudiced reader' would 'deliberately review this discussion, and weigh well the opinions and arguments which have been adduced in support of the different positions ... we venture to affirm that he must come to the conclusion that His Excellency is perfectly justifiable in pursuing the course he has adopted.' But how many of these idealized readers were there in the colony? A recent convert to Head's cause thought there were enough: 'Our readers are as fully capable of forming an opinion of the propriety of Sir Francis Head's conduct as we are: the facts are before them.'[64]

When the assembly endorsed the constitutional arguments of the ex-councillors, Head called new elections. Confidence in the 'unprejudiced reader' was about to be tested. Head's unusually vigorous campaigning[65] had significant consequences. The representative of royalty appealed directly to the local electorate, not simply to choose representatives he could work with, but to settle constitutional questions: the relative functions of the governor and executive council and, at least in Head's mind, continued membership in the British Empire. By asking the electorate to accept his paternal leadership, Head asked them to choose his interpretation of the constitution over that of the ex-councillors and the majority of their representatives.

Consciously adopting reform and radical tactics, Head set out 'to excite and agitate the public Mind' in his replies to addresses and by speaking in a direct and incisive manner.[66] Some found his tone undignified and overly partisan, but the *British Whig* considered it 'admirably suited to the comprehension and information of every yeoman in the Province.'[67] Appropriateness of style and rhetoric, combined with the extensive use of print, engaged an increasingly diverse and active public. Head led a campaign whereby individuals across the province were to be informed, rallied, and, ultimately, relied upon. As the governor

---

64 *Chronicle* and *British Whig* copied in *Patriot*, 8 Apr. 1836. The *Whig* had formerly supported the reform cause.

65 Craig, *Upper Canada*, 232–41, Bruce Walton, 'The 1836 Election in Lennox and Addington,' *Ontario History* 67, no. 3 (September 1975), 153–67, and Quentin Brown, 'Swinging with the Governors: Newcastle District Elections, 1836 and 1841,' *Ontario History* 86, no. 4 (December 1994), 319–36

66 Head to Glenelg, 8 July 1836 in Walton, 'The 1836 Election,' 159

67 *British Whig*, 26 Aug. 1836 in Sean T. Cadigan, 'Paternalism and Politics: Sir Francis Bond Head, the Orange Order, and the Election of 1836,' *Canadian Historical Review* 72, no. 3 (September 1991), 332, although he makes a different point.

told the inhabitants of the Johnstown District, 'It affords me consolation ... that the yeomanry and farmers of Upper Canada, instead of allowing other people to think for them have at last been driven to the necessity of judging for themselves.'[68]

Head's supporters echoed the theme that 'the people,' if better-informed and reasoned with, would throw off the doctrines of the ex-councillors and those, like William Lyon Mackenzie, Peter Perry, and Marshall Spring Bidwell, who espoused them. Conservative contempt for reform arguments had long been coupled with vague expressions of faith in the innate good sense of Upper Canadians. The more educated and informed could see through reform rhetoric. Others were better tending to their respective occupations than interfering in politics.[69] Such complacency had been punctured in 1831–2 and again in 1835, but during the election of 1836 it was replaced with a concerted, province-wide campaign to enlist the minds, as well as the votes, of the province. Lanark residents admitted that they had 'hitherto refrained from intermeddling in the political strife of the Province,' but 'the present crisis seems to this meeting to demand an unequivocal expression of public opinion' in support of constitution and empire.[70]

The British Constitutional Society was rejuvenated in the spring of 1836 'to disseminate throughout the country the most true and correct political information.'[71] Robert Stanton, King's Printer, noted that 'the *Gazette* office has been regularly converted into a printing room.' A door-to-door canvass in each ward garnered signatures for an address of the Electors of the City of Toronto. After it appeared in the *Patriot* alongside Head's reply, 10,000 additional copies of the address were printed with an additional 5000 copies of Head's speeches. Penetrating even 'into the homes of the Radicals,' print was to reach everyone. In all, the society published and distributed over 100,000 documents, some in German and Gaelic. Its committee met nightly for three weeks before the Toronto poll.

---

68 Head's reply, *Brockville Recorder*, 3 June 1836 and also Head, *A Narrative*, 201. The *Patriot*, 6 May 1836, listed 20 addresses to Head with 8746 signatures. By 27 June, it claimed that the number of signatures totalled 15,847.

69 E.g., Scrutator, *Patriot*, 29 Sept. 1835, *Patriot*, 22 Mar. 1836, Address of the Grand Jury of the Home District, *Patriot*, 12 Apr. 1836, and *Cobourg Star*, 17 June 1835

70 *Bathurst Courier*, 6 May 1836, Inhabitants of the River Trent, *Patriot*, 3 May 1836, and Freeholders and Respectable Inhabitants on Younge Street, *Cobourg Star*, 30 Mar. 1836

71 *Patriot*, 3 May 1836, Stanton to John Macaulay, 20 May and 6 June 1836 in Walton, 'The 1836 Election,' 160–1, Wilton-Siegel, 'The Transformation of Upper Canadian Politics,' 206, and Rowsell's Toronto Journal, 31 May–20 June 1836

Encouraging this unprecedented level of electoral activity, Solicitor-General Christopher Hagerman exhorted the society to emulate the industry of their opponents. He believed that 'all men who exercise their reasoning faculties' could be won over by 'a few plain, dispassionate, well-written papers, containing an exposition of facts, as they really were.' The essentials of colonial politics, far from being the province of the gentlemanly few, were within the grasp of all reasoning men. Individual society members also had to be active – 'We should reason and expostulate with such of the opposite party as we thought at all open to conviction.' They were even to invite opponents to attend society meetings. The constitution and its supporters had nothing to fear from the searching enquiries of others – 'We court publicity for our deeds, for they are not of darkness.'[72]

Commenting on the society's widely distributed Declaration, the *Cobourg Star* also insisted that 'ours is a cause, that will be ever invincible to the malice of its enemies, while it relies, not upon appeals to the passions, but to the honest judgement of the people.' Conservatives should 'strive to reason with those who may differ from us ... Let the people consider this: let them judge for themselves ... By the exercise of their reason, they cannot fail to be convinced.'[73] Conservatives naturally assumed the superior rationality of their own case, but their increasing faith that 'the people,' or at least the electorate, could be brought to appreciate this and act accordingly had distinctly non-conservative implications.

The *Bathurst Courier*, for one, might rejoice that 'the people are now aroused ... They will no longer allow themselves to be deceived ... and will now think and judge for themselves,' but why should such a tribunal be limited to silencing demagogues? Similarly, 'A British Reformer' told the *Patriot* that 'the time has now arrived when they [the yeomen] must assert the birthright of freeborn men, by judging of government for themselves, and by laughing to scorn those mendacious and wily partisans who would fain lead them by the nose to serve their own paltry ends.'[74] Yeomen capable of 'judging of government' and rejecting false prophets of either partisan stripe were surely capable of active participa-

---

72 Hagerman, *Courier of Upper Canada*, 5 May 1836
73 *Cobourg Star*, 25 May 1836. See also *Chronicle & Gazette*, 30 Mar. and 9 and 13 Apr. 1836. The editor printed 1000 extra copies of the issue of his *Patriot* containing the declaration as his subscription to the Constitutional Society, *Patriot*, 17 and 20 May 1836.
74 *Bathurst Courier*, 13 May and A British Reformer, *Patriot*, 6 May 1836

tion in government; capable of moving beyond the largely negative and electoral function most conservatives continued to assign to them. The implications of publicity, once courted, were not easily contained. Pandora's box lay wide open.

The results of the 1836 election surpassed conservatives' most sanguine hopes with a constitutionalist majority and the defeat of Mackenzie, Perry, and Bidwell. When the executive council had resigned, the *Chronicle & Gazette* thought its proposals for responsible government 'absurd and visionary.' Although 'public opinion when fairly settled should be consulted ... the sudden and transient fits of feeling often visible in the public mind could never be met with and complied with, without producing infinite confusion and disorder.' Government had to be relatively autonomous from something so unanchored. Nonetheless, the paper was confident that its readers could judge between the protagonists during the ensuing crisis. The *Gazette* was relieved when loyal addresses materialized; 'the people may be safely relied on.' They formed a 'tribunal' exhibiting all the qualities usually reserved for British governors; they were 'too intelligent to be deceived – too honest to be partial, and too generous to be unjust.'[75]

Confidence in this tribunal peaked with the favourable election results. 'The difference of opinion that prevailed between Sir Francis Head and the late Executive Council, and the subsequent proceedings of the House of Assembly have been discussed – fully, freely, generally discussed among the people, and commented upon from the Hustings ... The people have become too deliberate to be misled, and too reflecting to be deceived ... Arguments upon either side of the late questions at issue were candidly received ... They have of late evinced a determination to think, reason and judge for themselves.' The 'people' had decided fundamental questions arising from competing interpretations of their constitution.

To avoid misunderstanding and charges of naiveté, the editorial silenced the 'wavering fickle multitude, that act not from reason, but from impulse' in favour of the 'intelligent portion of the people whose voice is now heard.' The distinction was banal. More telling, this conservative editor was now convinced that a decisive portion of the electorate was capable of successful action based on its own deliberations. The

---

75 *Chronicle & Gazette,* 2 and 16 Apr. 1836

Chronicle had found a new source of legitimacy for the British constitution. Opponents no longer had to be silenced by violence or the laws of
sedition or met only with contempt. The efforts of the British Constitutional Society showed that they could be countered effectively by full-
scale participation in the public sphere. Dependence on a deliberative
public rendered violence and derision counter-productive. The constitution was safe in the hands of the reasoned judgment of the electorate.
Small wonder the *Chronicle* imagined 'a new era is dawning.'[76]

Military metaphors aptly summarized the election. As the chair of a
celebratory dinner at Guelph saw it, 'the Governor had flung himself
on the loyalty, good sense and magnanimity of the people, and they
had most gloriously responded to his call.' Another of the seventy din-
ers spoke fondly of the 'great battle' when 'the nest of plunderers,
after a frothy struggle, yielded before the irresistible force of public
opinion, the outer work of republicanism has been successfully
stormed, and the vanquished have submitted to the victors.'[77] The vanquished, however, read the battle differently. For the *Correspondent &
Advocate*, Head had gained only 'the apparent sanction of public opinion ... But he cannot lay the flattering unction to his soul, that the
result of the Elections is the fair, impartial, unbiased expression of
public opinion. His conscience tells him, that it is merely a sinister
opinion propagated by himself and an unprincipled faction.'[78] The
more questionable tactics of the victors meant that their opponents
could continue to champion public opinion since they could continue
to portray it as being on their side – as something denied, not
revealed, by the election. Ironically, the 1836 election permitted both
sides to advance the claims of public opinion as informed and rational
because both thought it supported them. Distinguishing public opinion from the clamour of mobs or machinations of faction had become
common rhetorical practice – a means to celebrate the majesty of public opinion while denying its existence in those particular instances
when it appeared to be on the other side.

---

76 *Chronicle & Gazette*, 6 July 1836. Wilton, '"Lawless Law,"' 132–4 argues that lack of effec-
    tive means to deal with dissent had led some to violence. See also D.P.S., *The Royal Stan-
    dard*, 19 Nov. and *Niagara Telegraph*, 16 Nov. 1836: Head chose 'rather to appeal to the
    good sense of the People, in the sober language of rationation than to have recourse
    to any physical power.'
77 John Poole and Adam Fergusson, *Dundas Weekly Post*, 19 and 26 July 1836
78 *Correspondent & Advocate*, 6 and 13 July 1836 and 11 Jan. 1837

Despite the now common use of the language of public opinion, the concept had yet to be fully integrated into constitutional theory. First, its institutional role between elections went largely unexplored. Second, many conservatives were less confident than the *Chronicle* in this new source of legitimacy. The editor of the *Courier*, an officer in the British Constitutional Society, hoped that once the election was over most Upper Canadians would again retire from politics. The election had been an emergency requiring unprecedented reliance on ordinary Upper Canadians. The success of those appeals in routing the disaffected did not, for this editor, alter the basic 'fact' that most people were not fully capable of positive, sustained political participation. With the emergency seemingly passed, widespread political participation should again be discouraged.[79]

The post-election revival of radicalism humbled such logic. Mackenzie was soon promoting his new organ, *The Constitution*. 'Let but an adequate opinion of their [the people's] wrongs be diffused and they burst their bonds asunder, and crush the oppressor. Revolutions do not arise from what men suffer, but from what they think.'[80] From the summer of 1837, radicals again held public meetings, including one at Lloydtown that confidently declared that 'the array of public opinion, if properly brought into operation may be opposed, but cannot be controlled.' For another, 'the price of liberty and free government is continual watchfulness and discussion on the part of the people.'[81] The 'vanquished' refused to be quiet and so shattered the fragile hopes of those who interpreted the election of 1836 as an extraordinary, one-time response to extraordinary circumstances. The outbreak of armed rebellion the following December made the hopes of those who had seen the 1836 election as proof of public rationality appear woefully premature.

Yet Lieutenant-Governor Head, among others, interpreted the outcome of that rebellion as evidence of Upper Canadians' overwhelming loyalty. The people, without the aid of British regulars, had quashed rebellion. Since they had freely chosen to defend their constitution and empire, Head concluded that 'there has never been a question more fairly submitted to the judgement of a free people, than that which, in Upper Canada has just ended, in the total defeat, moral as well as physical, of

---

79 *Courier*, 8 Oct. 1836
80 *Constitution*, 28 June 1837
81 *Constitution*, 9 Aug. and *Hamilton Express* copied in *Constitution*, 6 Dec. 1837

the opponents of the British Constitution.'[82] In short, the rebellion was the ultimate test of public opinion.

Interpreting the rebellion in this light offered little explanation as to why a minority had resorted to arms. Moreover, if the colony was so overwhelmingly loyal, the post-rebellion crack-down and the siege mentality lurking in much ultra-conservative rhetoric were unwarranted and counter-productive. To prevent a reoccurrence and to heal its ill effects, the rebellion had to be placed within some broader historical narrative. Further reflection on the nature of citizenship and political obligation in a free country was the result.[83]

Almost everyone fell back on the hackneyed explanation of agitation. The leaders of the rebellion, especially Mackenzie, were ambitious, self-serving, hypocritical, and evil demagogues who were cunning enough to mislead, seduce, and flatter the ignorant, unthinking portion of the population in an attempt to secure undeserved political power and social recognition.[84] In one of the more colourful formulations, order was said to have broken down from 'a dabbling, meddling, scribbling, resolving, addressing, speechifying, pamphleteering, petitioning, book-making spirit, some for place and all for favour.'[85] All these verbs involve participation in a public sphere that had offered Mackenzie far greater scope for mischief than had been available to previous 'agitators.'

Religious services gave the explanation further currency. The prayer appointed for the day of 'Public Fasting and Humiliation' implored God to 'defeat the counsel of the wicked; open the eyes of the deluded.' The Rev. A.N. Bethune, Anglican rector of Cobourg, singled out 'sour and malicious spirits' as a principal cause of rebellion. By making so-called grievances 'the engrossing topic of the domestic firesides or the social meeting,' such spirits had tried to persuade people that their 'free and untrammelled limbs were really in bondage.' The Methodist Eger-

82 Head's Speech from the Throne, *Patriot*, 2 Jan. 1838. See also the addresses of the legislative council and the assembly, *Report, from the Select Committee of the Legislative Council*, 9–10, and *Upper Canada Herald*, 19 Dec. 1837.

83 See Constant's grappling with the French Revolution; Biancamaria Fontana, *Benjamin Constant and The Post-Revolutionary Mind* (New Haven: Yale University Press 1991), 31.

84 As well as the sources in note 82 above see M.N., *Upper Canada Herald*, 26 Dec. 1837, *Upper Canada Herald*, 19 Mar. 1837 and 20 Mar. 1838, *Christian Guardian*, 13 Dec. 1837, *Bathurst Courier*, 20 Sept. 1839, *The Church*, 5 May 1838, *Niagara Reporter* copied in *St Catharines Journal*, 31 May 1838, Darvy Cognovit, *Mirror*, 21 Apr. 1838, Sir George Arthur to Lord Glenelg, 5 June 1838, *Arthur Papers*, 1, 191, and J.K., *Plain Reasons for Loyalty*, 4–5.

85 Aristides, *Patriot*, 1 May 1838

ton Ryerson found little to agree with in Bethune's ultra-conservative sermon, but he took as his text Psalm 64: 'Hide me from the secret counsel of the wicked; from the insurrection of the workers of iniquity:/ Who whet their tongue like a sword, and bend their bows to shoot their arrows, even bitter words: .../ They search out iniquities; they accomplish a diligent search.'[86] Agitators and their tactics stood condemned by divine authority.

Likewise, Niagara's Anglican rector painted a vivid picture of God delivering peaceful, quiet-loving colonists out of the hands of 'vipers' who had spread their 'deadly poison' through a 'system of falsehood' in the press, infesting 'their ignorant and credulous dupes.' His Presbyterian counterpart also attributed the rebellion to an overexposure to all that was supposedly faulty, corrupt, or selfish in government, albeit in more measured tones. These alleged faults had become 'the subject of a constant newspaper reading, and the theme of endless talk in the family, and of exciting harangues when we assemble with village groups.'[87] The political potential of newspapers and voluntary associations had been harnessed to the wrong ends. Rebellion, in short, had resulted from the abuse of the public sphere.

Such an explanation was convenient. Those implicated in rebellion could plead ignorance as a mitigating factor – one that the forces of order were willing to accept. It placed no explanatory weight on legitimate grievances and reinforced the association between their political dominance and reason. Such agreement, however, masked multiple meanings of 'ignorance.' Those implicated referred to being misled about the size of the rebel force and its likelihood of success. Those from whom they sought mercy called them ignorant, not because they had misjudged the balance of force in the province or even because they were devoid of all principles and information, but because they lacked the right political principles and information – principles and information that would have foreclosed the very possibility of radical sympathies.[88] *Plain Reasons for Loyalty: Addressed to Plain People* was an aptly

86 *A Form of Prayer*, 6. For Bethune's *National Judgements Provoked by National Sins*, see the extensive review in *Christian Guardian*, 30 Jan. 1839. Ryerson, *Civil Government – the Late Conspiracy*

87 Creen, *Two Discourses*, 5–6 and MacGill, *Love of Country*

88 E.g., the petition to Col. MacNab by the Rebels in the London District, *Report, from the Select Committee of the Legislative Council*, 47, appendix, Colin Read, *The Rising in Western Upper Canada, 1837–8* (Toronto: University of Toronto Press 1982), 206, 210, and Vincent, *Literacy and Popular Culture*, 233.

titled, if condescending, response to such 'ignorance.' This explanation of rebellion was also convenient for moderates and chastened reformers, allowing them to contrast their own respectability and constitutional approach with the social status, motives, and methods of the rebels.

However self-serving, the explanation was important because it was acted upon. Plans for coping with the aftermath of rebellion and preventing a reoccurrence rested on this interpretation of its causes. If rebellion resulted from an overheated public sphere, most conservatives advocated not its destruction through silence, censorship, or violence, but a redoubling of efforts made during the election of 1836 to strengthen and redirect public deliberations. The colonial state and its supporters had to be enlisted to make Upper Canadians more governable. The result was to make more people more capable of governing the state.

Given the centrality of newspapers to the reform cause, Mackenzie again serving as the principal example, it is not surprising that the radical press was singled out for particular condemnation. While not publicly condoning the physical violence against several radical editors,[89] conservatives welcomed the demise of such radical organs as the *Constitution, Correspondent & Advocate,* and *Liberal.* Their relief, however, was short-lived. The *Brockville Recorder, Hamilton Express,* and *Toronto Mirror* survived while, in 1838, Francis Hincks established the *Examiner* to afford reformers 'a channel of reciprocal communication' with the new governor.[90]

Even more so, the renewal of large-scale public agitation to advocate Lord Durham's recommendations at sixteen 'Durham Meetings' ended conservatives' hopes for 'peace.' The widespread dissemination of Durham's *Report on the Affairs of British North America* drew more fire than its content, for which they had little but scorn. Coming so soon after the rebellion and with continued tension along the United States border, such agitation was seen as ill timed at best. After driving Durhamites from the field, a gathering north of Toronto resolved that attempts 'to renew political discussions on questions that have heretofore produced

---

89 E.g., R.T., 'A few reasons for Radicalism,' *Bathurst Courier,* 22 Dec. 1837. On the violence, see Douglas Fetherling, *The Rise of the Canadian Newspaper* (Toronto: Oxford University Press 1990), 24.

90 Prospectus, *Examiner,* 11 July 1838. Durham solicited local views for his famous *Report.* He was the last governor to play the rhetorical role of impartial but informed arbitrator soon assumed by public opinion.

the most disastrous results ... must ... eventually lead to dissensions that can be followed by no other consequences than the revival of past disagreements' best forgotten.[91] Too many were agitating questions that were too divisive too soon after the breakdown of order.[92] Nonetheless, and despite reform charges to the contrary, even the staunchest government supporters were unwilling to openly deny the right of public discussion.[93] It was easier to return to pre-rebellion themes – to insist that the 'Durham Meetings' were more 'agitation' than 'reflection.'[94] Supporters countered by portraying them as vehicles for re-establishing the rights of public assembly and discussion, increasing the spirit of inquiry, and expressing public opinion.[95]

Whatever their disappointment, conservatives had once again to adopt the tools and strategies of their opponents. If Durham's *Report* was 'poison,' the 'antidote' was circulating thousands of copies of conservative rejoinders such as Christopher Hagerman's *Report of the Select Committee of the Assembly*, Sir Francis Bond Head's *Narrative*, and the *London Quarterly Review*'s favourable comparison of Head's policies with those of Durham. Rebellion had exposed the risk of letting criticism go unanswered. It had to be 'promptly exposed and refuted.'[96]

Similarly, the lesson drawn by the organ of the Anglican hierarchy to mark the 190th anniversary of the beheading of Charles I in 1839, was 'not to despise or neglect the power of the press.' Betraying more about Upper Canada in the wake of rebellion than about the role of sedition in seventeenth-century England, *The Church* concluded that the time had

---

91 *Bytown Gazette*, 7 Nov. 1839. See also Arthur to Colborne and Bond Head, 19, 21, and 26 Aug. 1839, *Arthur Papers*, v. 2, 211, 214, 219–20, *The Church*, 24 Aug. 1839, and *Bytown Gazette*, 20 Sept. and 25 Oct. 1839.

92 *Cobourg Star*, 21 Aug. 1839, Fidelis, *Cobourg Star*, 16 Oct. 1839, and *British Whig* copied in *Western Herald*, 14 Oct. 1839

93 For those charges, see *Mirror*, 8 Feb. and *Hamilton Express* copied in *Mirror*, 26 July 1839. Conservatives did counsel that less time be devoted to politics. J.K., *Plain Reasons*, 5 and *British Whig* copied in *Western Herald*, 14 Oct. 1839

94 *The Church*, 23 Nov. 1839, *Niagara Chronicle* copied in *Cobourg Star*, 11 Sept. 1839

95 Canadian Oak, *Brockville Recorder*, 15 Aug. 1839, *Backwoodsman* [Peterborough] copied in *Brockville Recorder*, 29 Aug. 1839, A Correspondent, *British Colonist*, 28 Aug. 1839, and Ryerson, 'The Story of My Life,' 259. See also Wilton, '"A Firebrand amongst the People."'

96 *Chronicle & Gazette*, 20 Aug. 1838. The *Patriot* printed 2000 copies of Hagerman's report and 5000 cheap copies of the *London Quarterly Review*'s critique, hoping they would be purchased by 'the friends of good order' for gratuitous distribution. Only 2000 had been disposed of a month later. *Patriot*, 10 May, and 5 and 30 July, and *Bytown Gazette*, 17 July 1839

come when 'politics, civil and ecclesiastical, when assailed by the Press, must be defended by the Press. It may not be dignified, it may be attended with some inconvenience, for a government to descend into the arena of daily discussion, and to defend its actions, as if it were on trial before a jury of the country, – it may be all this, and more – but it is nevertheless necessary for the preservation of the state.'[97] Whatever the loss of dignity or convenience, the public sphere could no longer be ignored. The government had to act 'as if it were on trial' before the court of public opinion – a court conducted daily through the circulation of print and as potentially deadly to the state as the executioner's axe.

A couple of months later, Henry Ruttan, whose address as Newcastle sheriff four years earlier has already been discussed, presented the report of the select committee of the assembly 'appointed to enquire into the present mode of publishing the Statutes and other public documents and papers.' Ignoring its mandate, the committee had investigated the press as a cause of the rebellion and recommended the establishment of an official government newspaper to disseminate political information as widely as possible. According to the report, radical newspapers had gone largely unopposed, particularly in 'remote agricultural parts' where it thought support for rebellion had been the strongest.

To allay fears of government misinformation, the report endorsed the reform article of faith that free states had nothing to fear from public scrutiny: 'A Government Press therefore is not to be regarded as an instrument for arbitrary power, but as a firm ally of popular liberty – as a correspondence addressed by the Governor to the Governed, with a view of arriving at the true state of their feelings, opinions and wishes, – as a means of shedding truth and light, and clearing away the mist of error and falsehood – not of enwrapping the public in mystery and darkness.' Reformers rejected the comforting notion that only 'imaginary wrongs' arising from misinformation had existed before the rebellion. Any suggestion that public money should be spent on what they were sure would be a partisan, rather than state, publication and thus a subsidized competitor for their own organs was also dismissed.[98]

---

97 *The Church*, 2 Feb. 1839. The founding of *The Church* to garner lay support for the hierarchy was itself an example of this development.

98 Report, 29 Apr. 1839 copied in *Cobourg Star*, 3 July 1839. It was strongly endorsed by the *Star* and *Bytown Gazette*, 24 July 1839. For reformers' reaction see *British Colonist*, 1 May and 24 July copied in *Christian Guardian*, 8 May and 31 July 1839, *Examiner*, 8 May 1839, and *Brockville Recorder*, 18 July 1839.

Probably as a result of his experience as secretary of the British Constitutional Society during the 1836 election, John Kent became another advocate of a government newspaper. Hannah More's efforts to instil loyalism in Britain during the French Revolution provided a model more effective than 'rural police.' The comparison with armed government forces highlights the emphasis some conservatives still placed upon the negative functions of maintaining order and defeating demagogues rather than the more positive function of empowering informed discussion. Nonetheless, printing a government newspaper assumed that readers could evaluate competing sources of information and come to appropriate conclusions. Kent maintained that 'it is not because the agricultural population[s] either of England or of Canada are inaccessible to reason, that they are often led into a belief in the most palpable falsehoods'; but because their 'craving for political information' had been met solely 'by men hostile to every existing institution.'[99] Reluctantly and not unanimously, conservatives recognized the basic capacity of newspaper readers and the ideals of the public sphere. People craved political information. It was only prudent to oblige.

In reviewing Ruttan's report, the *Quebec Gazette*, a leading opponent of responsible government, pointed out the inconsistency in such arguments. 'However much it may be desirable to stand well with the inhabitants of the colony, its [the government's] responsibility is not to them, but to the Imperial Government.'[100] Undeniably perceptive, the observation was supremely unhelpful. A *Niagara Reporter* editorial began with a disclaimer: 'We do not like discussions respecting theories of government in the public prints as the majority of the readers must be totally unqualified for forming decisive opinions.' Such reluctance had to be overcome. 'So much error has however already been imbibed by this channel, that through the same medium, endeavours must be made to counteract it.' The editorial was a lengthy critique of responsible government.[101] Whatever the motive, countering argument with argument to inform popular deliberation was the essence of the public sphere.

Second only to the press, education also drew conservative attention in the wake of the rebellion. The grand jury of the Gore District attributed the breakdown of order to the 'want of a more general and better

---

99 Alan Fairford [Kent], 'The Press,' *The Church* copied in *Patriot*, 3 July 1838. See also *Chronicle & Gazette*, 29 Feb. 1839.
100 Copied in *Brockville Recorder*, 25 July 1839
101 *Niagara Reporter*, 18 Jan. 1839

system of public instruction.' Others simply invoked 'ignorance.'[102] Radicals could not have incited rebellion if more people had been able to evaluate motives, challenge arguments, and grasp their duties as subjects. Convinced that the rebellion had resulted from a lack of understanding of mixed monarchy, John George Bridges, self-appointed government spy and doctor, toured Upper Canada in 1839 delivering his lecture 'A Digest of the British Constitution.'[103] The purpose of such individual efforts, a government newspaper, and improved schooling was the same. While there was the usual scapegoating of American teachers and textbooks,[104] education, in its broadest sense, would 'fortify the minds of our people against the wiles of the demagogue and the devices of the traitor.'[105] For conservatives, every 'proper' school was 'a pillar of support to the fabric of social order and constitutional law,' since 'tyrants dare not oppress, and demagogues cannot delude, an intelligent people.'[106] Reformers and radicals had been saying the same thing for years.

If appropriate education and the conservative press could bring people to see through demagogues and weigh competing arguments, the collective judgment of such a public deserved a positive role in government. For some, education might be intended to make subjects more governable,[107] but it would also make them more capable of governing. Increasingly, conservatives were participating in public debate and relying on the potential capacity of the people in much the same way as their opponents.

Throughout the 1830s, most conservatives believed that their opponents, with an explosive combination of newspapers, voluntary associations, and public meetings, had politicized more Upper Canadians than were capable of judging the questions brought before them. In the wake

---

102 *Patriot*, 13 Apr., 1 May, and 8 May 1838, *Niagara Chronicle* copied in *Christian Guardian*, 15 Aug. 1838, *Niagara Chronicle* copied in *Western Herald*, 11 Sept. 1838, David Walker, *Bathurst Courier*, 28 Sept. 1838, and Amicus Mentis, *Bathurst Courier*, 11 Dec. 1840

103 On Bridges, see Colin Read, 'The London District Oligarchy in the Rebellion Era,' *Ontario History* 72, no. 4 (December 1980), 204 and the next chapter.

104 *Patriot*, 13 Apr., 1 and 8 May 1838, David Walker and Dugald C. McNab, *Bathurst Courier*, 28 Sept. 1838 and 18 Jan. 1839, and *St Catharines Journal* copied in *Western Herald*, 13 June 1839

105 *The Church*, 5 May and 23 June 1838

106 *Niagara Reporter* copied in *Western Herald*, 31 July 1838

107 On the creation of political subjects, see Bruce Curtis, *Building the Educational State: Canada West, 1836–1871* (London, Ont.: Althouse Press 1988).

of the rebellion, widely blamed on this asymmetry, most concluded that there was no going back – that there was no alternative but to make the already politicized capable. Some conservatives continued to worry that too many Upper Canadians thought too highly of their own abilities;[108] the more abstract the question or the more popular the audience, the more anxious these conservatives became. It was now, however, largely a matter of degree – a question of empirical observation and the standard used. Both were easily challenged by reformers. More important, and whatever the partisan observations or the standard used, a public was seen to exist by 1840 that mocked any easy distinction between the few and the many.

Although conscious of these developments, conservatives had yet to integrate public opinion into their constitutional outlook. The ideals of the public sphere that they participated in and increasingly tried to harness remained in tension with some of their constitutional sympathies. After the rebellion, self-styled moderates worked hard to assimilate public opinion and constitutional theory. The *Upper Canada Herald*, in a cardinal example, agreed with conservatives that armed revolt had resulted from abuses of the public sphere,[109] but worried that their attacks on 'agitation' flirted with repression. The rebellion proved that oppositional politics *could* lead to the breakdown of order, but rather than contemplating retreat, moderates forged ahead to make it a constitutive part of maintaining order.

First, any lingering reluctance to participate in public political debate had to be abandoned. Second, the exchange of conflicting arguments should be welcomed and placed on a regular, constructive basis before it again became so polarizing and belligerent as to spill over into other, far less desirable forms of political behaviour:

> In every free state there will and must be opposition. Competition is the life of trade, and there must be opposition for the honours, power and emoluments of government as much as for the profits of trade. And the party competing with the possessors of government places and authority, must, of course, do so by proposing other plans professedly better than those of their opponents. The discussions thus raised may degenerate into

---

108 E.g., *Niagara Chronicle* copied in *Western Herald*, 11 Sept. 1838 and *Niagara Reporter*, 18 Jan. 1839
109 *Upper Canada Herald*, 20 Mar. and 10 Apr. 1838

personal contests, either verbal or written, but that is no good reason for wishing to suppress them altogether, in order to reduce civil society to the state of a stagnant pool. The contest[s] of party though bitter and pro-longed, are not only a thousand times better than the quietude of despo-tism, but are also productive of good by eliciting truth and talent, sharpening wit and wisdom, enforcing frugality, and compelling the use-less drone to give place to the working bee ... Bad must be the state of that government which is not made better by the conflict of opinions in politi-cal warfare.[110]

Whatever its negative side-effects, political competition, like commerce, resulted in 'truth and talent,' not anarchy. Competition in the public sphere was a vital sign of health, not an unavoidable evil.

For the *Herald*, the lesson of the rebellion was 'moderation,' defined as the desire to use rational arguments to persuade rather than 'mutual abuse' to berate.[111] Modern governments, in order to act wisely and with strength, required active popular support, not loyal acquiescence. To secure the people's backing, the state 'should govern itself by their opin-ions when deliberately formed and expressed.' Government based on public opinion was a prerequisite for state formation. Officials could try to shape opinion on questions not yet 'fully discussed and determined by the people,' but after such discussion 'for the government to attempt to carry any measure in opposition to that deliberate judgement, is at once both foolish and criminal; – foolish because utterly useless; – crim-inal because it is an attempt to violate the conditions on which govern-ment exists ... the welfare of the people, and they are the only final judges of what is adapted to promote their welfare.'[112] In a few editorials in the spring and summer of 1838, the *Herald* mapped out a theory of government based on public opinion for the post-rebellion world.

Others newspapers, especially the *British Colonist, Palladium of British America*, and *St Catharines Journal*, also rejected the political extremes of radical change or a return to pre-rebellion politics and thus became the natural proponents of moderation, calm deliberation, and tempered partisanship.[113] The *Christian Guardian* insisted upon the utility of con-

---

110 Ibid., 22 May 1838. For instructive parallels see Wahrman, 'Public Opinion,' esp. 115.
111 *Upper Canada Herald*, 24 July 1838
112 Ibid., 18 Sept. and also 23 Oct. 1838
113 *The Scotchman / British Colonist*, 1 Feb. 1838 and 28 August 1839, *Palladium of British America*, 28 Mar. 1838, and *St Catharines Journal*, 26 Jan., 2 Mar. 1839, and 3 Dec. 1840

stitutional opposition, since 'discussion is favourable to truth of every kind,' but denounced extremism.[114] In 1839 one of its essayists concluded that while 'not every hasty or transient ebullition of public feeling ... public opinion, temperately, legally, steadily, and with sufficient frequency expressed, is to be regarded by rulers as a rule of legislation ... If public opinion, thus expressed, is to be utterly disregarded or but slightly heeded, then the principles and end of civil government are essentially changed and are perfectly inexplicable.'[115]

Little wonder, then, that the new governor, Charles Poulett Thomson (later Lord Sydenham), called on Egerton Ryerson and John Wauby, editors of the *Christian Guardian* and the *Upper Canada Herald* respectively, to help him mould colonial opinion.[116] Ryerson urged the establishment of a government organ to promote the liberal-utilitarianism of the governor and his supporters. For Ryerson, such an organ was crucial because 'now is the time – perhaps the only time – to establish our institutions and relations upon the cheapest, the surest, and the only permanent foundation of any system or form of Government – the sentiments and feelings of the population.'[117] He wrote the prospectus for the new *Monthly Review*, but declined to serve as its editor in favour of John Wauby. The *Review*'s discussion of public opinion was taken almost verbatim from the editorials of the *Upper Canada Herald* just discussed.[118]

The vexed question of responsible government was now largely about how, not if, public opinion was to be integrated into existing institutions. Robert Baldwin and Francis Hincks's *Examiner* demanded that executive powers be vested in a colonial cabinet of department heads collectively responsible to the elective assembly. This alone would ensure the primacy of public opinion. Instead, Colonial Secretary Lord John Russell, Governor Thomson, and their local supporters insisted that the appointed governor had to remain the effective head of the

114 *Christian Guardian*, 7 Jan. and 18 Mar. 1835, 30 Nov. 1836, and 9 May and 19 Dec. 1838. For the debate within Methodism see Goldwin French, *Parsons & Politics: The Role of the Wesleyan Methodists in Upper Canada and the Maritimes from 1780–1855* (Toronto: Ryerson Press 1962), 161.
115 M.N., 'The Necessity, the Origin, the End, and Principles of Civil Government,' *Christian Guardian*, 3 Apr. 1839 and French, *Parsons & Politics*, 175
116 Government advertising was transferred to the *Guardian* and the governor asked Ryerson to use the Methodist organ to correct what he saw as errors in other newspapers. *Patriot*, 21 and 25 Feb. 1840 and Ryerson, 'The Story of My Life,' 264
117 Ryerson, 'The Story of My Life,' 264–6
118 *The Monthly Review* 1, no. 2 (February 1841), 82–7

executive. The *Christian Guardian* assured its readers that Russell's famous despatch on responsible government made 'the House of Assembly the constitutional medium of Public Opinion without any intervention of heads of departments. Responsibility is connected with both systems; both systems contemplate a Government accordant with public opinion.'[119]

From this perspective, a colonial cabinet was not only incompatible with the imperial connection, it might interfere with the assembly's expression of public opinion. Further, ministerial government might give too much power to elected representatives. Canadian representatives should not be entrusted with as much power as their British counterparts, in part because public opinion was not yet as readily deferred to in Canada as in Britain. As Thomson put it, 'You must keep power in the Executive, to govern Colonies where the M.P.P.s [Members of Provincial Parliament] have not the same discretion, or are under the same control of public opinion, as in older Countries.'[120] The need for an executive independent of elected representatives became the fault-line between those moderates and reformers who supported Governor Metcalfe and those who supported Baldwin and Hincks during the Metcalfe crisis of 1843–4.

In outline, the Metcalfe crisis resembled the events that had precipitated the 1836 election. Both began as disputes between a British governor and his resigning advisers led by Robert Baldwin. It was the Metcalfe crisis, however, that secured public opinion's place in the political imagination of Upper Canadians. It was the first full example, and perhaps the best in English Canadian history, of the public sphere in action. The unprecedented scale of the debate incorporated more people into the public,[121] intensified its discussions, and brought more information to bear on an increasing number of questions. The structure of the debate – its length, diverse participants, and accessibility – fostered explicit statements about the ideals of the public sphere and the role of public opinion.

---

119 *Christian Guardian*, 15 Apr. 1840 and also *St Catharines Journal*, 26 Jan. 1839
120 Thomson to Arthur, 15 May 1840, *Arthur Papers*, v. 3, 67–8. In general, see Ian Radforth, 'Sydenham and Utilitarian Reform,' in Allan Greer and Radforth, eds., *Colonial Leviathan: State Formation in Mid-Nineteenth Century Canada* (Toronto: University of Toronto Press 1992), 64–102.
121 Voting turnout was about 40% higher in 1844 than in 1841, but the increase was facilitated by Baldwin's electoral reforms of 1842. John Garner, *The Franchise and Politics in British North America, 1775–1867* (Toronto: University of Toronto Press 1969), 106

From his seat in the assembly, Robert Baldwin, late attorney-general for Upper Canada, announced the resignation of all but one member of the first reform executive council, confirming repeated rumours of friction between it and the governor-general. The council's majority in the House remained, but according to Baldwin 'a state of avowed antagonism' existed between the leaders of that majority and Metcalfe, especially over the right of the executive council to advise on all appointments to office. Speaking on behalf of the governor, the sole remaining councillor, Dominick Daly, charged that reform leaders had demanded the 'surrender' of the prerogatives of the Crown 'for the purchase of Parliamentary support.' They had tried to make partisanship, rather than public service, the criterion for holding office. Metcalfe adhered to responsible government, but if, by that system, 'the late Council mean that the Council is to be supreme, and the authority of the Crown a nullity, then he cannot agree with them, and must declare his dissent from that perversion of the acknowledged principle.'[122]

From this opening volley, most of the points of contention were in play: the meaning of responsible government, its applicability to a colony, the exercise of royal prerogatives, the uses of patronage, and the legitimacy of political parties. The debate soon raised more abstract questions about the nature of good government. The length of the debate added to its complexity and range. For some it began in 1842 when reform leaders Baldwin and Louis-Hippolyte LaFontaine were appointed to the executive council by Governor Bagot. Some conservatives attempted to resuscitate, yet again, the British Constitutional Society to protest against the elevation of those too closely associated with rebellion. Reorganized in the spring of 1843, the Brock Constitutional Society of 1836 was the means to 'exhibit' the preponderance of the loyal population and to 'express' their opinions through 'public meetings, addresses ... [and] the Conservative press.'[123] Rumours of a rift with Metcalfe began soon after his arrival, and while the councillors resigned in November 1843, a new ministry was not formed until the autumn of 1844. Unlike Head, Metcalfe did not turn immediately to conservatives to form a new council. Had he been able to complete an executive council soon after the resignations or to avoid a general election, a more limited discussion might have ensued. The need to explain the year-long delay and to mobilize the electorate created both the

---

122 Baldwin and Daly, 29 Nov. 1843, *Debates*, 1034–41
123 J.R. Yielding, *Woodstock Monarch* copied in *London Herald*, 18 Mar. 1843

space and the need for full-scale public debate. 'Normal politics' was suspended for almost a year. The lines of opposition were also unclear. Metcalfe's supporters ranged from the *Cobourg Star* with its flat rejection of any form of responsible government to those whose constitutional positions were almost indistinguishable from Robert Baldwin's. They were often as preoccupied with distinguishing themselves from their unlikely allies as from their common opponents.

With the assembly adjourned, the ex-ministers established the Reform Association at Toronto with at least ten branches elsewhere in Upper Canada. From exile in New York, William Lyon Mackenzie concluded that 'these reform associations ... wont do much. But they keep people talking.'[124] Using meetings and print to keep people talking was precisely what they were supposed to do. The association published the verbatim proceedings of its first general meeting, its constitution, 'several thousand copies' of a lengthy *Address to the People of Canada*, and an *Address to the Electors of Frontenac*. It planned a series of *Tracts for the People*, although only the first, *The Resignation*, materialized. The *Banner*, boasting the largest circulation in the province at 1700, printed four times as many copies of its issue reporting the speeches at a dinner for the late administration. Upwards of three thousand people attended a Reform Association meeting at Sharon.[125]

What the association portrayed as the 'means of which correct and most important information is being diffused among the people,' Metcalfe's supporters thought were designed 'to flood the country with addresses and harangues.'[126] The resemblance to pre-rebellion agitation was uncomfortably close. The *Woodstock Monarch* and the *Patriot* reprinted Henry Ruttan's 1839 report recommending the establishment of a government newspaper to counter radicals' use of print.[127] Also hinting at the recent past, an anonymous republican lectured the gover-

124 National Archives of Canada, William Lyon Mackenzie Papers, Mackenzie to John Stewart, 6 June 1844, v. 2, 122–5. For the branches outside Toronto see Wilton-Siegel, 'Transformation of Upper Canadian Politics,' 217–18.

125 *Mirror*, 24 May and 7 June 1844 and *Banner*, 1, 5, and 19 Jan. 1844. In February 1844, James Lesslie, editor of the *Examiner*, told Robert Baldwin that the *Banner* had 1700 subscribers to his 700. See J.M.S. Careless, *Brown of the Globe*, Vol. One: *The Voice of Upper Canada, 1818–1857* (Toronto: Macmillan 1959), 40.

126 *Mirror*, 24 May 1844, *Cobourg Star*, 5 June 1844, *Patriot*, 15 and 22 Mar. 1844, A U.E. Loyalist, *Cobourg Star*, 27 Mar. 1844, *Church*, 26 Apr. and 24 May 1844, and 'Letters of 1844 and 1846 from Scobie to Ryerson,' 407

127 *Monarch*, 9 Jan. and *Patriot*, 16 Feb. 1844

nor that 'Canada is not at present about to battle for her rights with a sword, she will do this with the tongue, and with the pen.'[128] The governor's supporters were indeed afraid that the Reform Association would achieve with the tongue and the pen – in the public sphere – what only six years before Mackenzie had failed to accomplish with the sword. They responded in kind.

Older attitudes towards such large-scale participation in public debate persisted among the more extreme and intellectually rigid conservatives. The *Monarch* wanted knowledge of the constitution more widely disseminated 'by the free circulation of sound, loyal, and ably conducted newspapers,' but revealed its total incomprehension of reformers when it argued that 'as little, or even less, objection could lie against this employment of a portion of public money as against the payment of an efficient police.'[129] A broad consensus had emerged on the power of print, although immoderate conservatives were especially alert to its ability to preserve order, while others, on both sides of the Metcalfe crisis, emphasized its ability to enlighten and empower.[130] Another 'Tory' organ thought the establishment of a counter-organization to the Reform Association inconsistent with its ends: 'The opinions of the people are governed really by the few, and if the few were really the best men, all would go well. But this is not the case, generally, either at public meetings, or in political associations.'[131] However credible as amateur psychology, such reservations were simply too late.

If only because their opponents were already in the field, participation in the debate was unavoidable. Most of their conservative colleagues were too busy founding constitutional societies, participating in the public sphere, and holding others to its ideals to pay much attention. Those who fought by the pen would have to live by it. Moreover, the governor was increasingly dependent, not on conservatives, but on moderate reformers such as Egerton Ryerson and the *British Colonist* – precisely those most emphatic about the primacy of public opinion.

---

128 'An Observer' to Metcalfe, *Woodstock Herald*, 2 Mar. 1844
129 *Monarch*, 9 Jan. 1844
130 For the distinction see J.A.W. Gunn, 'Public Spirit to Public Opinion,' in *Beyond Liberty and Property: The Process of Self-Recognition in Eighteenth-Century Political Thought* (Kingston and Montreal: McGill-Queen's University Press 1983). For further examples of distaste for full-scale debate see *Church*, 24 May 1844, *Cobourg Star*, 27 Mar. and 3 Apr. 1844, *The News*, 9 May 1844, and *Patriot*, 15 Mar. 1844.
131 *St Thomas Standard*, 30 May 1844, referring to attempts to establish an United Empire Loyalist Association.

Thus, while the ex-ministers could count on the support of two new papers, Francis Hincks's *Pilot* in Montreal and George Brown's *Globe* in Toronto,[132] their opponents were also active. In November 1842, Major John Richardson issued the prospectus for the *Canadian Loyalist & Spirit of 1812*, since 'it becomes the imperative duty of every Canadian, who has the power of wielding a pen in the field of politics, to throw himself into the breach' created by the appointment of Baldwin and LaFontaine to executive office.[133] In May 1843 the 'leading Conservative gentlemen' of the Brock District relieved the *Monarch*'s editor of pecuniary difficulties. Four months later, they placed the paper under a 'Committee of Direction' to ensure its survival.[134] That a few men of self-proclaimed social standing felt compelled to replace subscribers as the primary patron of the paper says much about the importance they attached to the press and the declining resonance of their ideas. Likewise, as the election approached, Edward Ermatinger, a 'Tory' candidate, had to purchase the reform *St Thomas Chronicle*, renamed the *St Thomas Standard*, 'to rescue this fine District from the power of a rampant radical majority'; that is, to secure his own return.[135] The *London Herald*, recently of Sandwich, noticed the re-emergence of uncompromising conservative papers of which it was one. By copying extensively from each other, they created a network to disseminate a strictly conservative point of view with renewed vigour.[136] It had the air of a desperate last stand. Other papers established during the crisis, including the *Niagara Argus*, *Cornwall Freeholder*, and *Prescott Packet*, had to begin by declaring support for one side or the other.[137]

Metcalfe also received more than ninety supportive addresses; over two-thirds originated in Upper Canada. Aware of the opportunity they offered to explain his constitutional position directly to Upper Canadians, Metcalfe replied individually. The more noteworthy replies were widely copied in the colonial press and a few found their way into sympathetic newspapers before arriving in the locality to which they were

---

132 Underlining the connection between printed communication and politics, the *Globe* was the first paper in the province to adopt the latest, and much faster, printing technology – the rotary press. Careless, *Brown of the Globe*, 41–6

133 Prospectus, *Canadian Loyalist & Spirit of 1812*, 29 June 1843

134 *Monarch*, 23 May and 12 Sept. 1843

135 *St Thomas Standard*, 16 May 1844 and 23 May 1846

136 *London Herald*, 14 Jan. 1843

137 E.g., prospectus, *Packett* copied in *British Whig*, 24 May 1844

addressed.[138] The address of the District of Newcastle arrived with 4810 signatures, Victoria District's with 1596, and Talbot District's with 1418. Even those of smaller localities such as the Township of Whitby and the Village of Carleton Place garnered 620 and 178 signatures respectively. When compiled, the addresses and replies constituted one of the fifteen English-language pamphlets published during the crisis.[139]

Three of the Upper Canadian addresses came from natives: the Mohawk of the Bay of Quinte, 'the sachems and chief warriors of the Chippawas, Munsees, Onedias and Delewares of the river Thames,' and thirteen chiefs from the Western District. These addresses signalled both native awareness of colonial political debate and the different stances assumed by observers of that debate and its full participants.

While the Mohawk of the Bay of Quinte regretted the move of the capital from nearby Kingston to Montreal, all three native addresses were preoccupied with the imperial connection and monarchy. Their silence on the mechanics of the local constitution at issue is not surprising given their historic connection to the Crown and the continued imperial responsibility for native policy. Even when they entered public debate, natives could not always share its preoccupations. More important, and whatever their views of British authority, they adopted a paternal language that had long since been abandoned by most non-native males. As his 'red children,' natives asked the governor, their 'Great Father,' for his protection on the basis of their past services and present loyalty to the Queen, their 'gracious Mother.' Symbolically, they approached an external and more powerful authority as dependent supplicants. Fulfilling his paternal role, Metcalfe recognized the past deeds of 'my children' and assured them that their continued loyalty to the Queen would 'be fondly estimated in her maternal bosom.'

Making the point impossible to miss, the Mohawks, 'as helpless children of the soil,' sprinkled their address with apologies: they were aware that 'it is not our business to meddle in politics,' prayed they would 'not

138 *Woodstock Herald*, 23 Mar. 1844, reported that the reply to the Brock District Council was printed in a Montreal paper before it arrived in Woodstock. A similar claim was made by the *Hamilton Journal & Express*, copied in *Mirror*, 16 Feb. 1844 regarding the reply to the Gore address.

139 *Addresses Presented to His Excellency*. According to the *Canadian Loyalist & Spirit of 1812*, 18 Jan. 1844, the Niagara address was signed by 149 men out of an electorate of 194. H.J. Boulton, chair of the Reform Association, was Niagara's elected representative. John William Kayle, *The Life and Correspondence of Charles, Lord Metcalfe ...* (London: Richard Bently 1854), 505, 531n., notes that draft replies were in Metcalfe's own hand.

be considered officious in addressing you on this subject,' and would comment only 'if we may be allowed to speak on the subject.' By 1843–4, non-native males spoke far more confidently to authority. They did not claim helplessness to invoke a paternal response.[140] They assumed their right to interrogate government and its officers – even the representative of royalty. Those external to the public sphere could make no such assumption. Hierarchical and paternal connections invoked by these natives (for their own reasons, in conformity with their own speaking conventions, or perhaps by Indian agents) and accepted by Metcalfe were incompatible with an informed, reasoned exchange among equal discussants to which most of the other addresses contributed.

Finally, the form of participation on offer exposed the gulf separating native from non-native. All three native groups pledged their support, but the Western District chiefs were more explicit. In what was probably a reference to their role in suppressing the rebellion, as much as to their better-known services to the Crown during the American Revolution and War of 1812, they promised Metcalfe that 'so shall we leave the plough to strike one strong blow in her behalf whenever the dark hour come ... Call upon us and we shall come.' While 'sensible to your bravery and devotion,' Metcalfe was quick to assure them (and one suspects their neighbours as well) that 'you will never again have occasion to manifest your known bravery and zeal.' British governors had no further need for either the stereotyped image or the reality of the native warrior to settle political disputes. Metcalfe needed electoral and legislative votes and assent, or at least acquiescence, to his views of colonial governance. Most natives were barred from offering the first two. Their views on the colonial constitution were neither offered nor sought.[141]

More than the many addresses and the extensive circulation of his replies, Metcalfe's greatest coup was to convince Egerton Ryerson to enter the debate. Ryerson told the governor's civil secretary that he was confident of victory over the Reform Association, 'not, to be sure, before a jury of twelve men ... but before the jury of the whole country, and upon principles sanctioned by the Constitution and history of England, which, I believe ... will result in a triumphant acquittal and

---

140 Petitions from female Loyalists had similar features. Janice Potter-MacKinnon, *While the Women Only Wept: Loyalist Refugee Women* (Montreal and Kingston: McGill-Queen's University Press 1993), 98–9, 103

141 *Addresses Presented to His Excellency*, 76–8, 110–12. For native participation in suppressing the rebellion, see Read, *Rising in Western Upper Canada*, 99, 105, 138–9, 147, 155.

Freemasons adopted architectural and geometric images to emphasize their mythical founding by the builders of Solomon's temple and their commitment to harmony, reason, and man-made order.

The standard lodge interior, like this one at Bath in 1820, had an elevated seat for the presiding master and benches around the perimeter. Members faced each other and a chest that probably held their lodge warrant, seal, minute-book, gavel, and ballot box.

Beneath the motto 'Knowledge is power,' allegorial figures celebrated Science, Art, Skill, and Industry in Sandford Fleming's 1850 design for the Toronto Mechanics' Institute diploma. The pictures along the bottom represented his own interests in engineering and surveying more than the independent-artisan tradition with which early institutes were often associated.

Debates of the provincial assembly occupied four of the five front-page columns of this issue of William Lyon Mackenzie's *Advocate*. With such access to political information and opinion, anonymous newspaper readers participated in common deliberations with law-makers and other readers.

LIBERTY OF THE
PRESS!

A deadly attack having been made upon the rights and liberties of the people of this Province, by the *fining* and *imprisonment* of the *Editor* of

The CANADIAN FREEMAN.

The friends of public liberty are requested to meet in the *Market Square*, at **12** o'clock noon, on **Monday** next, in order to devise means to repel the attack that has been so unexpectedly made upon this great bulwark of our liberties, and to shield a free **PRESS** from annihilation.

York, 30th Oct., 1828.

Public meetings were intended as physical representations of the ideal of an informed and active citizenry capable of collective judgment. This one was called in a public place to discuss freedom of the press and was announced and then reported on in the press, thus underlining the importance attached to print culture and the interdependence of that culture and oral communication.

THE

EVERY BOY'S BOOK,

OR

A DIGEST OF THE

BRITISH CONSTITUTION.

COMPILED AND ARRANGED

FOR THE USE OF SCHOOLS AND PRIVATE FAMILIES

BY

JOHN GEORGE BRIDGES.

" It is the duty of every expounder of our laws to lay this Constitution before the Student, in its true and genuine light ; it is the duty of every good subject to understand, to revere, and to defend it."

HALE.

PRINTED AND PUBLISHED,

BY THE PROPRIETOR AT THE OTTAWA ADVOCATE OFFICE, DISTRICT OF SYDENHAM, PROVINCE OF CANADA,

1842.

Convinced that disaffection was the product of 'ignorance' rather than substantive grievances, conservatives launched a didactic offensive to inform Upper Canadians about the existing constitution – as they understood it. Subjects would then 'revere' and 'defend' it. Print also circulated competing conceptions of that constitution and the duties of citizenship.

On election day, here depicted at Perth in 1828, great crowds gathered to hear nomination and campaign speeches delivered from the hustings or platform. Those who claimed the right to vote then ascended to declare their choice openly. Note the presence of several 'ladies' on the platform.

The colony's first elaborate masthead captured the renewed vigour of ultra-conservatism during the Metcalfe crisis. According to a sympathetic observer, 'on one side stands a soldier ... with his left foot on the neck of a queer looking animal of the quadruped race ... From the *morale* of the design we should take it to be a member of the canine species.' Thus, American invaders in 1812 and Metcalfe's reform opponents were 'dogs.'

YOUNG CANADA
DELIGHTED WITH RESPONSIBLE GOVERNMENT.

Not mature enough to know better, Canada is dazzled by responsible government. The system was depicted by *Punch* as leaving the country at the mercy of
devious politicians who have so corrupted her by reading from 'La Fontaine's
Fables' that they can use Governor General Lord Elgin as their puppet. Lord
Metcalfe, Elgin's predecessor, looks on in disgust.

A PROBABLE CONTINGENCY!

Tim.—Yath'n Teddy avic hwhare are you goan hwhy?
Teddy.—Faix an' its just goan to imigrate sthraight back home I am — bekase if I stop in
Kenada they'll be for makin' a Legislaytive Counciller of me — and I was brought up among
dacent people, sure!

The previous *Punch* cartoon showed elected reformers emasculating the vice-regal governor. This one focused on how their theory of government also degraded the 'aristocratic' legislative council. Even a stereotypical Irish 'Paddy' would be ashamed to associate with those they had elevated to Canada's upper house.

justification of the Vice-Regal defendant.'[142] The governor and constitution were on trial before public opinion. Ryerson would act as chief counsel.

In his own words: 'The ablest and most meritorious public men in the province were arrayed on the opposite side; but I felt that truth and justice did not rest on numbers – that there was a public, as well as an individual, conscience, and to that conscience I appealed, supporting my appeal by reference to the past professions of Reformers, the best illustrations from Greek, Roman, and English history, and the authority of the best writers on constitutional government, and moral and political philosophy, and the highest interests, civil and social, of all classes of society in Upper Canada.'[143] Ryerson's *Sir Charles Metcalfe Defended* began as letters to the *British Colonist*. Despite its 182 pages it ended modestly: 'The independent and impartial judgment which I myself endeavour to exercise, I desire to see exercised by every man in Canada.'[144] After citing so many authorities in support of his own judgment, it was a remarkably egalitarian conclusion.

Critics were quick to dismiss the work as too long, too labourious, and too technical – a 'farrago of historical names culled from a classical dictionary' one called it.[145] Yet Robert Baldwin Sullivan, assuming the name Legion, felt it necessary to respond point by point in letters to the *Examiner*, republished as the 215-page *Letters on Responsible Government*. The efforts of the governor and Hugh Scobie, editor of the *British Colonist*, to circulate Ryerson's work suggest that they too were unwilling to discount its power. Scobie printed 2000 extra copies of the *Colonist* to disseminate individual letters further. An issue of the *Colonist* containing one of them was sent to every subscriber of the *Christian Guardian*. Scobie also distributed 10,000 free copies of Ryerson's less noticed 63-page *Reply to Legion* to friendly editors throughout Upper Canada.

---

142 '*The Story of My Life,*' 318
143 Ibid., 329
144 Ryerson, *Sir Charles Metcalfe Defended*, 164. Besides the *Colonist*, Ryerson's letters were copied in the *Chronicle & Gazette*, and less fully in the *Chatham Journal*, *Bytown Gazette*, and *Niagara Chronicle*. The announcement and preface could be found in any number of papers including the *Banner*, *Brockville Recorder*, *Cobourg Star*, and *Examiner*. There were many other papers, such as *The Church*, that refused to copy them but advertised their existence by frequent criticism.
145 *Globe*, 6 Aug., 11 June, and 9 July 1844, *The Church*, 7 June and 11 Oct. 1844, *Mirror*, 12 July 1844, *Woodstock Herald*, 20 July 1844, and, for the quotation, *Monarch*, 25 June and 23 July 1844.

Newspaper extras containing an earlier pro-Metcalfe pamphlet by Isaac Buchanan were made available to twice that number.[146]

Given the scale of this debate, it is not surprising that commentators were explicit about its ideals. As the *Chronicle & Gazette* put it, 'The free circulation of political sentiment, like the free circulation of the air we breathe ... is essential for the political health of the community.'[147] 'Tories,' moderates, and reformers all joined in contrasting 'reason,' 'argument,' 'judgment,' and 'calm discussion' with 'abuse,' 'effusions,' 'assertions,' and 'passion,' although rarely in reference to the same statement.[148] Much of this commentary appeared anonymously. If reason and the merits of an argument were the sole standard, then it did not matter who advanced the argument. As an unnamed pamphleteer put it, 'For the purposes of an argument that is strictly political, and neither assails private character nor deals in other than notorious facts, there is no occasion for the writer's name to be made public. On the contrary, if he be a well known man, his name will be likely to prevent his argument from being read dispassionately.' Likewise, Robert Baldwin Sullivan, appearing as Legion, thought it 'a piece of misjudged egoism' on Ryerson's part 'to mix the name of a public writer up with his arguments: it always is calculated to mislead.'[149] One editor censured attempts to connect the person of the editor with the contents of editorials. They threatened to turn newspapers into a 'vehicle for abuse and personalities' rather than 'rational gentlemanly debate.'[150] Given their past history, some probably thought it was a little late.

By copying Ryerson's letters despite disagreeing with them, the *St Catharines Journal* came closer to these ideals than many: 'There is something to be learned from them: "There's music everywhere." Mr. R.'s character is no consideration with the reflecting – it is with argument that they have to deal. The authority of names is the argument of the

146 'Letters of 1844 and 1846 from Scobie to Ryerson,' 397, 407, 410. These figures do not include regular newspaper circulation or copies in pamphlet form. Apparently, anyone who purchased a copy of the *Colonist* could receive four copies of Buchanan's pamphlet. *British Colonist*, 5 Jan. 1844. According to the *Mirror*, 26 Jan. 1844, two copies were also sent to the *Toronto Herald*'s subscribers.

147 *Chronicle & Gazette*, 27 Aug., 23 Nov., and 21 Dec. and *Mirror*, 30 Dec. 1842

148 E.g., *Cobourg Star*, 23 Mar., *Monarch*, 8 Sept. 1842, *Woodstock Herald*, 13 July, *Banner*, 12 Jan., and *The News*, 20 Sept. 1844.

149 Anon., *Responsible Government for Canada*, notice and Legion, *Letters on Responsible Government*, 16

150 *Cobourg Star*, 23 Mar. 1842

weak, and little regarded by all who have claims for unbiased judgement and freedom of thought.'[151] It is easy to be cynical about colonial political practice. In part, there were so many affirmations of the ideal of rational-critical discussion because reality fell short. According to the *Bathurst Courier*, 'Fair and legitimate discussion is the proper course to follow ... But the question is not being fairly discussed – quite the reverse.'[152] It was, however, being widely and fully, if not always fairly, discussed. Conduct was now measured against the ideals of the public sphere. The Metcalfe crisis did not live up to them, but it established their primacy and came closer than many political contests.

The prominence given to its ideals not only solidified the status of public opinion, but also helped to undermine the usefulness of the theory of mixed monarchy. Formally, the Metcalfe crisis was a dispute between the representative of the British sovereign and leaders of the majority of the local assembly. Who should judge?

Ryerson thought it was the imperial government, but 'Mr. Baldwin practically renounces the Imperial authority by refusing to appeal to it, and by appealing through the Toronto [Reform] Association to the people of Canada. If the people of Canada are the tribunal of judgement on one question of constitutional prerogative, they are so on every question of constitutional prerogative. Then the Governor is no longer responsible to the Imperial authority, and Canada is an independent country.' There was nothing illogical in appealing to the local public to convince it that it was not the appropriate judge. But by having to publicly debate the point, Ryerson conceded that they had the power, if not the right, to decide. They would judge who should judge. If they were capable of such discernment were they not also capable of governing themselves? Perhaps they had outgrown the need for a governor and the monarchical system he represented. If they weren't capable, then why all the debate and appeals to their collective wisdom? Was it not, as Robert Baldwin Sullivan insisted, a 'slavish doctrine' to look elsewhere for judges?[153]

---

151 *St Catharines Journal*, 14 June and also *Mirror*, 12 July 1844

152 *Bathurst Courier*, 27 Feb. 1844

153 Ryerson, *Sir Charles Metcalfe Defended*, 11, 34–5, 80, 83, 130 and Legion, *Letters on Responsible Government*, 19, 56–60, 135. The *Chronicle & Gazette*, 24 Jan., *Canadian Loyalist & Spirit of 1812*, 8 Feb., *The News*, 23 May, and *Niagara Chronicle*, 10 July 1844 agreed with Ryerson. The point was hotly disputed by the *Examiner*, 3 July, and *Montreal Times* and *St Catharines Journal*, 29 March 1844.

Mixed monarchy incorporated the checks of royal governor and appointive upper house, in part, because of the presumed incapacity of the people to govern alone. As discussed in the next chapter, the governor and his conservative supporters accused the ex-councillors of trying to subvert mixed monarchy by advocating a form of responsible government that would extinguish those checks. Metcalfe's moderate supporters also charged that the constitutional position of the Reform Association would monopolize power in the assembly, but their emphasis was different. The *British Colonist* concluded that Metcalfe's opponents 'would extend the direct power of the assembly beyond its legislative limits, under a mixed monarchical government, overlooking the stubborn fact of its being a united public opinion that must be obeyed, and not the furious dictum of the individual, petty though for the time, popular tyrant.'[154] In other words, the people's representatives should not be the sole interpreters of public opinion. Nonetheless, local public opinion, not a mixture of three social estates or three forms of government, grounded good government.

The preference, expressed here by the *Colonist*, for more than one directly elected assembly, was compatible with the American system of two legislative chambers and an elective chief magistrate. Different mechanisms for transmitting public opinion from society to government – not for balancing monarchy, aristocracy, and democracy – became the central problem. In August 1844, William Hamilton Merritt urged William Henry Draper, Metcalfe's leading executive councillor from Upper Canada, to stop obsessing about who had been right or wrong at the time of the resignations. Too much had happened. 'In reviewing the situation of Canada – a Statesman will in the first place, endeavour to ascertain the true state of the existing public feelings. Secondly, whether he has a reasonable prospect of changing that feeling by any measure he can propose, in time to conduct his Government in accordance with the principles [of ministerial responsibility] now fully admitted.'[155] In a free country, statesmen discerned public opinion and attempted to guide it towards their own sense of the public good. Failing that, they acquiesced.

Public opinion had become the only safe basis for modern government.

---

154 *British Colonist*, 20 Sept. and 12 Nov. 1844
155 National Archives of Canada, William Hamilton Merritt Papers, Merritt to Draper, 12 Aug. 1844, v. 18, 2916–19

It was the entity to which governments were to be responsible. For Ogle Gowan, responsible government would 'place the Executive government of the province, at the *head* of public opinion, instead of leaving it at the *tail*.'[156] Public opinion, no longer the rhetorical preserve of those alienated from existing political institutions, had to be incorporated into the very structure and meaning of those institutions. Government by public opinion meant democratic participation, but it was participation of a particular type: calm deliberation rather than violent action; submission to collective decisions rather than continued resistance. It seemed to offer a middle way between the potential despotism of monarchy and the tyranny of pure democracy; between the irresponsibility of pre-1840 government in Upper Canada and the anarchy of Jacksonian democracy in the United States. By the 1830s, Upper Canadian observers agreed with de Tocqueville that American government was driven more by the passions of the mob than by public opinion.[157] Government by the latter promised a politics where authority derived from the people but remained firmly tied to reason; where people were formally equal but officials and the privileged could try to influence and interpret collective judgments; where universality of access was promised but effective participation remained limited to those deemed capable of sound judgment; and where the conflict inherent in debate and agitation was healthy but government rested upon the peaceful and stable outcome of those divisions.[158]

Of course, what counted as 'sound,' 'intelligent,' 'reasonable,' or 'informed' was not always self-evident. The knowledge and consistency of the 'public' could always be contrasted with the ignorance and fickleness of the 'mob.' Certain groups and opinions remained marginal. The criteria for legitimate exclusion had, however, shifted. They no longer

---

156 Gowan, *Important Letter on Responsible Government*, 7

157 *Western Herald*, 5 June 1838: 'The inestimable privilege of expressing our opinions – of freely discussing matters of church and state ... can no longer be enjoyed in the "great[est] republic in the world." The very temples of liberty are razed to the ground, to gratify the demonic vengeance of an irresponsible mob.' R.B. Sullivan was also adamant that 'public opinion does not practically prevail in the United States'; 'Report on the State of the Province, 1838,' *Arthur Papers*, v. 1, 161–2.

158 Baker, 'Public Opinion as Political Invention,' esp. 190–7, argues that the concept of popular opinion occupied a middle ground in France between *ancien régime* absolutism and the perceived anarchy of British politics. Belying its more populist origins, public opinion in Upper Canada never took on the Rousseauan collectivism Baker ascribes to it in France.

included social standing, law, prescription, or accidents of birth. Exclusion was now to be justified only on the grounds that a group or individual was irrational or ill informed – standards that could be contested and were, in principle, capable of generic application; that is, that could be applied fairly across groups and classes.

The universality proclaimed for the public was not to be taken literally. It was the universality of those thought able and willing to participate, not of everyone. Voluntary associations diffused democratic sociability while differentiating it from other forms of social interaction. They continued to deny full membership to those thought incapable of learning or exercising it. Likewise, as more Upper Canadians claimed the ability to reason in public, such reasoning was increasingly marked off from other forms of activity and those thought most likely to engage in them. In the short term, this did little to alter the status of those pushed to the margins. In the longer term, it opened up possibilities and suggested strategies for smashing persistent barriers to equality.

In its many forms, dependence was the mark of a political outsider. One could not assume that the opinions expressed by those without a minimal degree of independence really belonged to them (rather than to their passions or a demagogue, creditor, employer, landlord, spouse, or parent). Nor could one assume that they were free to revise those opinions in the face of convincing counter-evidence. Dependence was a short form for this lack of discursive liberty – for others' lack of confidence in a speaker's authenticity and sincerity. They were, therefore, unable to treat him or her as an equal discussant. The more collective solutions were to be sought through public deliberation, the more the participation of identifiable groups whose discursive liberty was suspect had to be discounted.

Public meetings, for instance, did more than form and voice decisions. They were to manifest the worthiness of that public. Speakers flattered the 'manliness' or 'independence' of their audience – its capacity to act as a micro-public. Otherwise, the judgment expressed in its resolutions was worthless. Insulting the 'incapable' was an easy way to achieve this end. Charles Fothergill, speaking in favour of a loyal address to the king, 'never had the pleasure of meeting so numerous and respectable an assemblage.' By contrast, Mackenzie's grievance petitions were circulated 'for the signatures of women and children, (for surely no man of sense would sign such a farrago.)' Here, certain 'men' were juxtaposed to children and others weaker in 'sense'; that is, those more easily intimidated or more willing to accept paternalism rather than earn, demand, and exercise equality of judgment.[159]

An important gender component remained – boys, not girls, could grow up to be such men. The inclusion of adult women with certain classes of adult men as dependents was not, however, the result of the use of language by those who did not share our current sensibilities. Although intermittent jeers like Fothergill's may have unintentionally reinforced this inclusion, his aim was to denigrate the participation of certain adult men – Mackenzie's supporters. As late as 1871, as many as 95 per cent of adult women in Ontario owned no real property in their own right.[160] The overwhelming majority of colonial women married or lived with male relatives. This was a society in which longstanding ideas of women's dependence on male kin were still powerful and in which newer ideas of women as social and moral exemplars best suited to domestic endeavours found strong support. Both ideas made it difficult to see women, as a group, qualified for equal participation in the political public sphere.

Deeply embedded in the common law, for instance, was the 'doctrine of marital unity' whereby, as Lori Chambers puts it, 'marriage, for women, represented civil death.'[161] By definition, well-ordered families had only a single interest, usually represented at law and voiced in public by the head of that family. In a society dominated by family farms and artisanal production, the family was also a single economic unit. The particular forms of individualism, equality, and fraternity offered by the political public sphere applied first to relations among actual or potential male heads of households, not to relations within what were seen to be single units of interest.

Seven female property-owners, at least six of whom were widows, did vote in 1844, but their participation failed to suggest political independence to observers. Rather, the women appear to have been brought forward to vote for only one of the candidates in front (and perhaps at

159 Fothergill, District of Newcastle meeting, *Niagara Gleaner*, 10 Mar. 1832 and Anna Clark, 'The Rhetoric of Chartist Domesticity: Gender, Language, and Class in the 1830s and 1840s,' *Journal of British Studies* 31 (January 1992), 70

160 Gordon Darroch and Lee Soltow, *Property and Inequality in Victorian Ontario: Structural Patterns and Cultural Communities in the 1871 Census* (Toronto: University of Toronto Press 1994), 205

161 Lori Chambers, *Married Women and Property Law in Victorian Ontario* (Toronto: University of Toronto Press 1997), 3 and, for several useful ideas, Patrick Joyce, *Democratic Subjects: The Self and the Social in Nineteenth-Century England* (Cambridge: Cambridge University Press 1994), 88, 122–4, 196–7, 206

the behest) of their male kin and neighbours by a conservative deputy returning officer in desperate need of their 'votes' to defeat the reform candidate at an extremely close poll. This was yet another form of the 'corruption,' 'interference,' and 'intimidation' by which officials were accused of trying to overturn electoral outcomes. (Of course, not all male voters exhibited the independence at the hustings the status presupposed, but it was much harder and more contentious to define them as an identifiable group.) The events of 1844 prompted reformers to limit the Upper Canadian franchise explicitly to males for the first time in 1849 as part of a broader consolidation of electoral laws designed to close loopholes and otherwise limit various forms of 'fraud.' The 'reform' occasioned little comment at the time.[162]

Many women were aware of the political debates around them, read and occasionally owned newspapers, frequented public spaces, sat in the gallery of the assembly, and perhaps attended political meetings. Mary O'Brien's journals record her numerous discussions of colonial politics with male kin, friends, neighbours, and relative strangers.[163] In theory, the anonymity of most published commentary did not preclude women from discussing politics in print as well since their sex could be hidden from readers. This was undoubtedly rare and, more important, it was not participation by women as such but by anonymous writers generally assumed to be male.

By their very nature, political discussions within a household are often lost to historians, but the exceptions are revealing. Our understanding of Confederation, for instance, would be much diminished if not for what George Brown wrote to his wife, Anne. The letters of Marcus Child to his wife, Lydia, and unmarried daughter, Elizabeth, both at home in Stanstead, Lower Canada, while he was in Kingston to attend the Canadian assembly in the early 1840s, offer another glimpse. Political information was conveyed by almost every letter: the principles and details of legislation, their progress through parliament, party political news, and the constitutional principles of the Metcalfe crisis. Many were accompanied by newspapers, especially reports of the proceedings of the House

---

162 Garner, *Franchise and Politics*, 159 and Kim Klein, 'A "Petticoat Polity"? Women Voters in New Brunswick before Confederation,' *Acadiensis* 26, no. 1 (Autumn 1996), 71–5.

163 O'Brien, *Journals*, 25 Jan. 1829, 8 and 10 Feb. and 20 Sept. 1830, and 19 Jan. 1831, 32–3, 91, 133, 149. A toast to the 'ladies' was drunk at the end of a meeting of the Reform Association, although the public record is almost always silent about their presence; *Globe*, 25 Sept. 1844

that were read by both wife and daughter. Still, Lydia Child regretted that her husband could not provide a more regular paper with a day-by-day parliamentary report, for 'then I could have known how you were getting on, and could have satisfied some others perhaps.'

To follow a single strand of their correspondence, Lydia Child relayed local newspaper commentary on the duties to be levied on foreign produce by an agricultural bill before the assembly. She volunteered her own opinion on the bill and solicited her husband's. Anticipating his wife's interest, Marcus had already forwarded the relevant newspaper reports to her. Once he received her letter, he responded to her questions in detail. Subsequently, Lydia conveyed local opinion on both the bill and his legislative performance. After speculating about the government's motives for particular clauses, she confessed to not understanding the complex issues, a claim her husband ignored. As well as providing a continuing stream of newspapers and political news, he was careful to keep her abreast of his own position on the bill, the forces shaping it, and speculation about its future. A week later, Lydia alerted him to the discrepancy between his prediction that a particular clause would be repealed and a report in the local press that it was soon due to expire, a discrepancy that prompted her to reiterate her desire for a more complete and accurate source of political news. At the start of the Metcalfe crisis, Marcus wrote almost daily, further acknowledging his wife's political role. She was to use her own discretion in relaying information from his letters to political friends who might call on her (clearly with the expectation that she would be better informed about events at the capital than they). Besides overseeing home and business during his absence and notwithstanding a couple of faint protests of diminished capacity, Lydia Child emerges from these letters as her husband's most cherished political confidante.[164]

While it was increasingly accepted that women were rational creatures who should be educated, informed, and exercise influence (if not power) over their male kin – even on political questions – open conflict between husband and wife, according to Upper Canadian newspapers, 'ought to be considered the greatest calamity.' A wife's primary respon-

---

164 See esp. Marcus to Lydia Child, 24, 25, and 26 Oct. and 10, 12, 28, and 29 Nov. 1843, Lydia to Marcus, 15 Oct. and 5, 7 and 19 Nov. 1843, and Elizabeth to Marcus, 12 Nov. 1843, *Child Letters*, 68–9, 77–83, 93–6, 102–6, 112–14, 122–3, 126–7. See also Françoise Noël, '"My Dear Eliza": The Letters of Robert Hoyle (1831–1844),' *Histoire sociale – Social History* 26, no. 51 (May 1993), 119, 130.

sibility was 'to soothe the troubles of others' by being 'amiable' – to the point of denying herself 'the trifling satisfaction of having your will or gaining the better of an argument.'[165]

Despite the substantial political role of his wife, Marcus Child probably endorsed such prescriptions. He concurred with the wife of a fellow parliamentarian who told him that 'ladies ought not to espouse the political animosities of their Husbands.' Women of this class were not thereby excluded from politics. Besides her role as an informed confidante, Marcus praised his wife for pouring 'oil on the troubled waters of political strife' and saving him 'a good deal of toil, if not from going to pieces on a lee shore.' She pointed her husband towards charity and forgiveness, offering a model of manners and etiquette as valuable in politics as in domestic relations. In fact, Marcus Child frequently noted the large number of women observing the assembly from its gallery. He only wished there were more (including his wife and daughter, who wanted to hear the proceedings), for 'their presence modifies the rancour of party feeling in debate, and disposes to public decency & pleasantry from debaters.'[166] With their family unit already 'represented' by their fathers or husbands and lacking sufficient legal and economic independence, women could not participate in the public sphere as certain classes of men could. They were generally not the 'debaters.' They were, however, often crucial sources of support, political information, and advice and, in this case at least, underwrote the ideals of the public sphere itself by helping men avoid revenge, insults, and passion.

The public sphere was deeply implicated in its time and place, developing alongside such prescriptive norms. Naturally, its membership and metaphors reflected them. Joan Landes, however, goes further, arguing that the rise of the public sphere was predicated upon such norms and the relative absence of women they entailed; that is, that 'the bourgeois public is essentially, not just contingently, masculinist.'[167] The Upper Canadian experience does not support this further claim. The norms of female 'propriety,' well understood by certain classes of women from

165 In Elizabeth Jane Errington, *Wives and Mothers, School Mistresses and Scullery Maids: Working Women in Upper Canada, 1790–1840* (Montreal and Kingston: McGill-Queen's University Press 1991), 34–5
166 Marcus to Lydia Child, 4, 23, and 31 Oct. and 13 Nov. 1843, Marcus to Elizabeth, 7 Nov. 1843, and Elizabeth to Marcus, 12 Nov. 1843, *Child Letters*, 60–2, 75–7, 88–9, 98–9, 104–8
167 Joan B. Landes, *Women and the Public Sphere in the Age of the French Revolution* (Ithaca: Cornell University Press 1988), 7. To pursue the issue further, see Johanna Meehan, ed., *Feminists Read Habermas: Gendering the Subject of Discourse* (New York: Routledge 1995).

the founding of the colony,[168] were not invented or required by the rise of its political public sphere. Women were not excluded from some previously acknowledged role in Upper Canada to make way for the expanding public. It developed without their equal participation, not against them. While the public sphere did not defeat the norms and practices whereby adult women were denied full and immediate participation in its deliberations, neither was it responsible for them. In fact, its logic pointed in the other direction. Economic and legal circumstances seen through the lenses of pre-existing gender stereotypes deprived women of that participation in the political public sphere gained by those classes of men who could claim independence – not the ideals of the public sphere itself, much less the metaphors and adjectives occasionally used to express them. In sum, the public sphere promised equality of voice to all who were capable but, for reasons external to that sphere, women, as a group, were not seen as capable.[169]

Full political agents were independent men in (often only implicit) contrast to all who were thought to share some disqualifying dependence, whether women and children or the morally unfit, the impoverished, the unreasoning, and the ill-informed, regardless of age or sex. It is hardly surprising, then, that those adult males who felt excluded from full political citizenship exploited the most agreed-upon examples of 'dependency' to bolster their demands for inclusion and to paper over fractures within their own ranks. They insisted on their own 'manly' independence. They were not to be treated like those thought in need of protection. Occasionally, they also tried to portray officeholders as 'courtiers' who, dependent upon royal favour and government pensions or salaries, were forced to express the views of the governor rather than their own. Such dependence placed them outside the range of gender roles demanded by the public sphere.[170] Similarly, attempting to deny the political competence

---

168 Katherine M.J. McKenna, *A Life of Propriety: Anne Murray Powell and Her Family, 1755–1849* (Montreal and Kingston: McGill-Queen's University Press 1994) shows the subject's preoccupation with propriety long before mixed monarchy was under attack.

169 For a comparable construction regarding suffrage, see E.A. Heaman, *The Inglorious Arts of Peace: Exhibitions in Canadian Society during the Nineteenth Century* (Toronto: University of Toronto Press 1999), 260.

170 Mackenzie, 'A Courtier,' in *Sketches of Canada*, glossary. For more invective drawing on notions of masculinity, see Cecilia Morgan, '"When Bad Men Conspire, Good Men Must Unite!": Gender and Political Discourses in Upper Canada, 1820s–1830s,' in Kathryn McPherson, Cecilia Morgan, and Nancy M. Forestell, eds., *Gendered Pasts: Historical Essays in Femininity and Masculinity in Canada* (Toronto: Oxford University Press 1999), 12–28.

of men who advocated radical reform, Fothergill turned to the least contested examples of dependence, women and children, to mock these men's claims to independence and thus to belittle their resolutions.

'Manly' came to mean those qualities and behaviour required by the public sphere. Contemporaries fought over which categories of men were 'manly'; that is, capable of full political citizenship. Those qualities and behaviour could be, and in most cases were, expressed in gender-neutral terms: candid, forceful, firm, reasonable, and public-spirited. Even when they weren't, they could still apply to women. Thus, Mary Wollstonecraft set out to persuade her female readers 'to become more masculine.' Since biological men could be either 'manly' or 'effeminate,' a non-biological and non-essentialist definition of these qualities was being crafted, opening up possibilities for the still marginal.[171] Ordinary Upper Canadian reformers and radicals in the 1820s and 1830s demanded the right to participate fully in public debate by claiming to be informed, rational political actors willing and able to work towards the collective good. Others would come to demand full citizenship in the same way. They challenged their association with those still accepted as dependent by attempting to redraw, yet again, the boundary between the capable and the incapable.

According to Cecilia Morgan, the use of gender-specific language such as 'manly independence' declined as early as the 1840s, increasingly replaced by 'public man' as a universal, impartial figure without connection to (and thus partiality for) private or familial interests.[172] Hierarchies of family, economy, religion, and ethnicity were not thereby forgotten. Contemporaries lived them daily, but in order to extend the right of political participation, they came to deny their relevance as absolute boundary markers of the public sphere.

The revolution represented by the new status of public opinion and its belief in the possibility of such impartiality should not be underestimated because its universalist language and potential were not

---

171 Wollstonecraft, 'A Vindication of the Rights of Woman,' in *Vindication*, 78: I am heavily indebted in this section to Kathleen Wilson, *The Sense of the People: Politics, Culture and Imperialism in England, 1715–1785* (Cambridge: Cambridge University Press 1995), 51–3, 83, 219, 225–7, 350, 438–9.

172 Morgan, *Public Men and Virtuous Women*, 197. More speculatively, if as Potter-MacKinnon (*While the Women Only Wept*, xv, 7, 9–10, 29, 143) and Errington (*Wives and Mothers*, 22), have argued, the analogy between king and father reinforced the patriarchy of the family, then the replacement of monarchical government by a conception of politics as public discussion undercut one of the props of the patriarchal family.

immediately realized. Rational 'independence' was, in practice, inscribed on a subset of the adult population in this period, but the potential universality of the principles themselves was not thereby tarnished. Government by discussion required the voice and active participation of far more Upper Canadians than the theory of mixed monarchy did. Public opinion promised a government based on reason and participation rather than unquestioning obedience, domination, violence, birth, revelation, sacred text, tradition, or social deference. It would be perverse (not to mention historically inaccurate), to deny either the revolutionary impact or promise of the principles because they had yet to be actualized in all their grandeur.

Charting the fortunes of the concept of public opinion in detail makes its use as a rhetorical strategy obvious. Its meaning and prominence were dependent upon the specific context of its use. It provided an alternative source of legitimacy for those who felt slighted by traditional institutions. The resulting public contests for power drove supporters of those institutions to participate in public debate, to make their own appeals to public opinion, and to attempt to influence it. Voluntary associations and newspapers provided the sites, expectations, and mechanisms for this social communication. By the conclusion of the Metcalfe crisis, it was generally recognized that those who won the war of opinion had the right to govern. Commentators continued to debate the relative merits of institutional mechanisms to achieve government by discussion. The goal, however, was no longer in dispute.

Looking back from the Metcalfe crisis, Robert Baldwin Sullivan pointed out that 'when a representation was given to the Canadas, there was no popular opinion, properly so called,' but 'as the population became numerous, and as education became more generally diffused; and as the people became more accustomed to a representation, popular opinion grew with the growth of the country.' Public opinion, rather than some alternative such as bargaining among class- or corporate-based interests, was the favoured interpretation of these developments. Sullivan was also aware of the role of politics in the salience of this interpretation. Those whose power rested on social status or the institutions of mixed monarchy had refused to defer to it, creating what, for Sullivan, was a straightforward struggle between the voice of public opinion and its detractors.[173] This too was common rhetorical practice.

---

173 Legion, *Letters on Responsible Government*, 86

In its stead, this chapter offers a more confused tangle of actors and positions. Even the staunchest government supporters did more than resist. Many tactically retreated from outright hostility to an acknowledgment of the power and legitimacy of public opinion while attempting to direct it along lines they approved of. They emphasized its distinctiveness from ignorance, partiality, passion, and non-discursive forms of political actions. Tactical considerations were no less central to the use of 'public opinion' by radicals, reformers, and moderates. They emphasized its distinctiveness from passivity, deference, paternalism, and the use of violence and crowd behaviour in support of the status quo. Political actors of all stripes struggled with and attempted to appropriate the emergent power of public reason. In the end, consciously or not and with different goals and levels of sincerity, they recognized, participated in, and attempted to manipulate that power. Each helped invent 'a united public opinion that must be obeyed.'

PART TWO

Debating the Alternatives

Which is best for us? Under whatever name a government may exist –
whether democracy, republic, or monarchy – one grand principle is
acknowledged, and that is the right of the people to govern themselves.

Charles Clarke, 1849

CHAPTER V

'We are become in every thing but name, a Republic': The Metcalfe Crisis and the Demise of Mixed Monarchy

Periods of crisis usually occasion robust articulations of political idioms and accelerate transformations within them. To take one of the most studied examples, the debate and mobilization required by the American Revolution destroyed or gave new meaning to familiar concepts.[1] The Metcalfe crisis was the final signpost on Upper Canada's conceptional road to democracy. Lacking the scale of the American Revolution, it nonetheless forced a comparable articulation and rethinking of the basics of political dialogue in the province. As the previous chapter concluded, the Metcalfe crisis cemented the primacy of the ideals of the public sphere. It was not, then, coincidental that it also revealed the inability of the theory of mixed monarchy to capture sufficiently either the ideal or reality of Upper Canada's evolving constitution and highlighted the marginality of the language of social estates. Debates about good government and a healthy social structure were hardly new, but the Metcalfe crisis was a kind of crucible – a great political and intellectual trial that found long-standing principles and assumptions wanting.

From the end of November 1843, when all but one member of the first reform executive council resigned, to the elections of November 1844, Upper Canadians debated the meaning of responsible government, the value and scope of royal prerogatives, the safest way to dispense patronage, the legitimacy of political parties, and the nature of empire. Only by incorporating various themes into ever more encompassing arguments

---

1 Gordon S. Wood, *The Creation of the American Republic, 1776–1787* (New York: Norton 1972) and Terence Ball and J.G.A. Pocock, eds., *Conceptual Change and the Constitution* (Lawrence: University Press of Kansas 1988)

could participants impose something resembling order and clarity. Moreover, their need to mobilize the electorate almost a year after the resignations created the space and necessity for full-scale public debate. A variety of positions also received serious scrutiny, in part because Metcalfe's supporters ranged from near-antediluvian 'Tories' to moderates and prominent reformers. The natural response to ever more elaborate criticism from a diversity of perspectives was to further refine one's own position, to reach for principles that had hitherto remained implicit, to experiment with new rhetorical weapons, and to try to fashion these developments into a coherent whole. The Metcalfe crisis both intensified and clarified an on-going process of conceptual innovation.

Some bemoaned the proliferation of issues. The 'real' point of contention was being clouded with 'spurious' cries of 'loyalty to empire' or 'responsible government in danger.'[2] The *Niagara Chronicle* thought the central question straightforward, but it was 'getting mixed up (intentionally, of course) with long tirades about liberty ... It is getting so complicated, as to be in danger of being forgotten.'[3] Others protested that Upper Canadians generally agreed upon the basics of good government. The only question remaining was how to apply these essentials to a case where the facts were in dispute. Such attempts at containment failed. Trying to demonstrate just how the ex-ministers had falsely applied agreed-upon principles still made Egerton Ryerson one of the most prolific and wide-ranging participants in the debate.[4] The crisis distributed an impressive amount of print, but it was more than a matter of quantity. It also generated one of the richest bodies of constitutional theorizing in English Canadian history. While much might be learned from continuing to chart the shifting fortunes of voluntary associations, the press, and the concept of public opinion, it is time to turn to their impact on the province's constitutional and social self-image.

The *Patriot*, a leading conservative organ, summarized the meaning of the ministerial resignations in a single question, 'Which will Canada have, a Monarchy or a Republic?'[5] This sounds melodramatic – a transparent attempt to paint the ex-ministers as revolutionary and disloyal.

---

2 Anon., *Responsible Government for Canada,* 8
3 *Niagara Chronicle* copied in *Monarch,* 18 May 1844
4 *Chronicle & Gazette,* 26 June, *Woodstock Herald,* 6 July and 19 Oct. 1844, and Ryerson, *Sir Charles Metcalfe Defended,* 12, 32, 162
5 *Patriot,* 5 Dec. and *Monarch,* 12 Dec. 1843

The question's tactical intent should not disguise its basis in the theory of mixed monarchy. For the *Patriot*, a republic or a democracy (the terms were interchangeable) was a system of government where all power came from the people. Democracy was not defined by the frequency of elections, the number of elective offices, or the qualifications for the franchise. These were the issues of mere mechanics. Democracy was a rejection of King, Lords, and Commons as a mixture of monarchy, aristocracy, and democracy in favour of one of its elements.

When discussing the British constitution in abstract terms, the more doctrinaire conservatives continued to rely on a theory of mixed monarchy little changed since the eighteenth century. A correspondent of the *Woodstock Monarch* enlisted Plato, Cicero, and Polybius in support of his contention that the British constitution had achieved that mixture praised by the wisest of antiquity.[6] It was also the mixed constitution that John George Bridges, now editor of the *Ottawa Advocate*, sought to popularize. Convinced that rebellion had stemmed from an insufficient appreciation of the constitution's principles, Bridges toured the province in 1839 to deliver his lecture 'A Digest of the British Constitution.' After publishing it, he petitioned the legislative council (a revealing, though unsuccessful, choice) to undertake its mass distribution. Not easily put off, when Baldwin and other reformers were appointed to the executive council in 1842, Bridges repackaged his lecture as eighteen lessons in *Every Boy's Book, or a Digest of the British Constitution Compiled and Arranged for the Use of Schools and Private Families*. Amid rumours of an impending rift between Metcalfe and his advisers, he offered 1500 copies gratis to renew his as yet underappreciated didactic offensive.

Lecture and book expounded the British constitution solely in terms of three estates, the 'regal,' 'aristocratical,' and 'democratical.' Neither mentioned the existence of a cabinet of ministers, an organized opposition in the Commons, or other developments in British constitutional practice over the previous half-century. Indeed, by insisting that Parliament controlled the King's Privy Council only through the judicial power of impeachment, Bridges foreclosed the very possibility of a cabinet of ministers politically accountable to elected representatives as envisaged by the Reform Association and many of Metcalfe's own supporters.[7] For political ends, the ability to describe the British constitu-

---

6 JRY, *Monarch*, 5 Jan. 1843
7 Bridges, *Digest of the British Constitution, Every Boy's Book*, and adv. in *Monarch*, 28 Nov. 1843

tion as it actually functioned was sacrificed to the elegance of an outdated theory.

From the vantage point of that theory, calling the ex-ministers 'democrats' or 'republicans' was not entirely inaccurate. The governor-general's supporters were united by the belief that the ex-councillors' demands to act as a unified cabinet of ministers, able to meet without even the presence of the governor, responsible to the assembly, and advising the Crown on every appointment to office would deprive Upper Canada of a mixed constitution. It was, however, Metcalfe's more conservative supporters who made the most use of the theory of mixed monarchy. The *Kingston News* told its readers that acceding to the demands of the late ministers would amount to a 'surrender of the most valuable safeguards' of their constitution located in 'the monarchical and aristocratical powers.' Since institutional forms might persist, 'strictly speaking, we may possess three estates; but they will consist no longer of the monarch, the aristocracy and the democracy; we shall have a *pure democracy*, assuming perhaps, three different forms, but remaining of one substance.'[8] Whatever the form, real power would flow from only 'one substance' – the people. Likewise, the Orillia Constitutional Society condemned 'the principle of the present system of Responsible Government so generally democratic as to divest the Governor General of adequate powers for Colonial purposes, and to deprive us of every benefit of the British Constitution.'[9] As the history of that constitution demonstrated, while democratic input was essential to good government, pure democracy was incompatible with it. More was not always better.

The basic charge was developed in two directions: critics contended that, under the constitutional program of the ex-ministers, the executive council would dominate all three branches of the legislature or the assembly would dominate the other two estates and the executive. Governor and legislative council would be rendered powerless against either the cabinet or the assembly. The ex-ministers' demands would result in 'oligarchical despotism on the one hand, and democratic despotism on the other.'[10]

During the assembly's debate on the resignations, Sir Allan MacNab emphasized the dictatorial powers that would accrue to the executive

---

8 *News* copied in *Banner*, 12 Jan. and also *News*, 15 Aug. 1844
9 *Chronicle & Gazette*, 11 Mar. and *Patriot*, 24 Feb. 1843. See also *Monarch*, 12 Dec. 1843, Canadian, *Monarch*, 16 Jan., and *Church*, 6 Sept. 1844.
10 *Montreal Gazette* copied in *British Colonist*, 22 Dec. 1843

council from the ex-ministers' terms.[11] This line of argument was bolstered by the contention that any responsibility of the executive council to the assembly would be chimerical since the assembly was dominated by office-holders and others dependent upon the executive. Ogle Gowan's *Statesman* estimated that thirty-seven members favourable to the Baldwin-LaFontaine government were influenced by office-holding, 'the majority in the popular branch being actually and bona fide responsible to the Government instead of vice versa.'[12] The executive council would control the representatives of the people as well as the Crown.

The theory of mixed monarchy made a particularly prominent appearance in the conservative reaction against the recent appointment of six new legislative councillors. These reform appointees were widely thought to have pledged themselves to vote for the ministers' choice of provincial capital, Montreal, as a condition of their appointment. With the addition of these new members, the council reversed an earlier resolution in favour of Kingston. The parliamentary principle that a question once decided cannot be reintroduced in the same session was violated. Thirteen councillors, all from Upper Canada and including the Speaker, withdrew in protest for the remainder of the 1843–4 session. In his last speech before leaving the chamber, William Henry Draper declared it was 'far better that the country should possess no Legislative Council than that its honor should be sacrificed, and that it should stand as a weathercock to yield to every passing wind.'[13] As the *News* was quick to point out, 'If the Executive Council can control the organization of the Upper House for particular purposes, the three estates of Parliament are a mere sham.' The *Patriot* also lamented that the executive council seemed determined 'to trample into the dust the independence of one branch of the Legislature – to dash aside every constitutional barrier.'[14] Once they broke with the governor over demands for executive powers he was unwilling to confer upon them, reformers were charged with disrespect for both the legislative council and the Crown – for two of the three estates.

---

11 MacNab, *Debates*, 1 Dec. 1843, 1095
12 *Statesman* copied in *Patriot*, 24 Feb. 1843. See also Nemo, *London Herald*, 21 Jan. 1843 and *Cobourg Star*, 6 Mar. 1844.
13 Draper, *News* and *Cobourg Star*, 29 Nov. 1843
14 *News* copied in *Patriot*, 7 Nov. and *Patriot*, 10 and 21 Nov. 1843. See also *Chronicle & Gazette*, 4 and 8 Nov. and *Cobourg Star*, 29 Nov. 1843.

The argumentative thread 'mixed monarchy in danger' received influential support from the governor himself. In his replies to the addresses of the Districts of Ottawa and Brock and the County of Russell, Metcalfe accused his former executive councillors of trying to subvert mixed monarchy. Although careful to frame their demands with reference to British ministerial government, essentially they had demanded that the governor should be their 'subservient tool,' 'that the Legislative Council should be elected by the Executive Council,' and that the assembly should 'nominate the Executive Council.' Such demands violated the basic norms of free government. 'The authority of the Crown and the Legislative Council being thus annihilated, and every balance in the constitution destroyed, the whole power of the state would be usurped by either the Executive Council exercising undue interference over the House of Assembly, or by the House of Assembly exercising unlimited interference in the Executive Administration. It would be either a despotic and exclusive oligarchy, or an absolute unqualified democracy.' Such concentration of authority defined tyranny and was not, therefore, 'the constitution of any state in existence; for even in the most republican constitutions the powers of government are more carefully distributed among different authorities.' Metcalfe, one of the three 'authorities,' was attempting to preserve constitutional balance and liberty by resisting 'the tyranny of an oligarchy which would trample' both Crown and people.[15] Metcalfe and his supporters, not Baldwin and the Reform Association, were the champions of limited, liberal government.

Similar charges were levelled by those reformers and moderates who came to Metcalfe's defence. The emphasis, however, was different. Like Metcalfe and conservatives, the *Bytown Gazette* worried that ministerial control of patronage might concentrate power in the executive council. Its primary aim, however, was preserving ministerial responsibility, not mixed monarchy. Ministers might be tempted to sustain themselves in office by abusing their control of executive patronage. In fact, the ex-ministers had tried to free themselves from their responsibility to the people by bribing the people's elected representatives. An anonymous pamphlet conceded the central axiom of the Reform Association, that ministerial responsibility had become 'the essential feature of British monarchy.' Without it, the British constitution was 'either an unbal-

---

15 Replies to the County of Russell and to District of Ottawa, *Addresses Presented to His Excellency*, 138, 134. See also reply to the District of Brock, 141.

anced Monarchy of the older time of civil wars and dethronements, or else a Republic.' Canada had to choose between the British constitution and the 'Absolute Democracy' sought by the Reform Association. Thus, the Sydenham reformer Isaac Buchanan charged Robert Baldwin with abandoning 'the principle of Responsibility to the People *under Monarchical institutions.*'[16] Metcalfe and his supporters, not Baldwin and the Reform Association, were the champions of responsible government.

Egerton Ryerson, another Sydenham ally, repeatedly described the British and Canadian constitutions as King, Lords, and Commons or simply as mixed. The ex-councillors' demands, by stripping the governor of independent authority, would make Canada 'an oligarchy, instead of a mixed monarchy' or would 'convert our monarchical government into the worst kind of democracy.' The form of tyranny, whether oligarchy or democracy, was unclear, but the object of the attack, British constitutional monarchy, was not. Ryerson insisted on the seemingly obvious point that 'unless the whole notion of a fixed [mixed?] monarchy, and a balance of three powers is a mere fiction and a dream, the royal portion of the composition must be allowed to have some power to produce some effect upon the quality of the whole.' Unlike John George Bridges, he did not contend that this balance had no room for a body of advisers to the Crown pledged to resign whenever they could not take responsibility for an executive act: 'Responsible Government is the *practice* of that mixed form of government after a certain mode.'[17] Mixed monarchy persisted, although its mode of operation evolved. As one such mode, responsible government was a set of complex conventions and unwritten understandings about how each of the three estates was to exercise its formal powers and informal influence in harmony with the other two. The ex-councillors threatened to undermine mixed monarchy by pressuring the governor to promise to make no appointment without their advice, by their disrespect for his office, by attempting to stipulate rigid and precise definitions of ministerial responsibility, and especially by their determination to act as a disciplined political party, thus severely curtailing the flexibility of all three legislative estates.

Ryerson was also distressed by the ex-councillors' cavalier attitude

---

16 *Bytown Gazette,* 14 Dec. 1843, 11 Jan. and 4 July 1844, Anon., *Responsible Government for Canada,* esp. 2, 7, 9, 11–12, 20, and [Buchanan], *First Series of Five Letters,* 18. See also *Belleville Intelligencer* copied in *Canadian Loyalist,* 28 Dec. 1843.

17 Ryerson, *Sir Charles Metcalfe Defended,* 19, 72, 82, 99, 102, 148–9, 169 and *Sullivan's Attacks upon Sir Charles Metcalfe Refuted,* 60

towards the legislative council. They demanded that the Speaker of the upper house be appointed solely on the executive council's advice, seemingly making members of that house 'mere nominees' of the leaders of the assembly rather than 'a third estate of the Canadian realm.'[18] This was also one of the grounds Thomas Parke, a reformer and surveyor-general, cited for breaking with his long-time colleagues. In a widely published letter, Parke reasoned that the legislative council could only maintain its position as 'one of the three independent Legislative bodies' if appointments to it were made without reference to the people's representatives or cabinet ministers.[19]

In July 1844, the moderate *British Colonist* joined those accusing the ex-ministers of attempting to subvert mixed monarchy. They 'recklessly throw aside the acknowledged constitutional checks' and had a 'grasping desire to concentrate all power in their own hands,' thus threatening the harmony essential to a system of 'various branches, possessing co-ordinate powers.'[20] For those reformers and moderates supporting Metcalfe, responsible government was a 'method,' 'mode,' or 'practice' for ensuring harmony among branches that might otherwise produce endless conflict and even deadlock. They worried about the concentration of power in the hands of ministers, but mostly because it might undermine their accountability or because governor and legislative council would be unable to check hasty, ill-considered legislation. For Metcalfe's more conservative supporters, the need for 'sober second thought' was only one part of the case for mixed monarchy. They focused less on the perversion of responsible government by the ex-ministers and more on the danger that any form of ministerial responsibility posed to the existence of three independent estates – and to the constitutional place that two of them secured for the privileged in society.

Thus, when the *Colonist* renewed these charges before the election, it contended that mixed monarchy should be preserved because it best reflected public opinion, not because it represented three social estates or because the clash of three independent branches of government

---

18 Ryerson, *Sir Charles Metcalfe Defended*, 97
19 Parke to Adam Hope, originally *St Thomas Chronicle* copied in *Patriot*, 17 May, *Chronicle & Gazette*, 11 May, *British Colonist*, 10 May, and *Examiner*, 29 May 1844. For related commentary see also *Monarch*, 21 May, *Journal & Express* copied in *St Catharines Journal*, 17 May, *Cobourg Star*, 22 May, *Mirror*, 10 May, and *Niagara Chronicle* copied in *British Colonist*, 21 May 1844.
20 *British Colonist*, 2 July 1844

would itself result in the best legislative outcome.[21] A single body of the people's representatives could not be trusted as the sole interpreter of public opinion. A system of institutional checks, some sort of 'balance,' would safeguard minorities from the short-sightedness or animus of a temporary majority and would ensure that a ministry, though supported by the majority of the people's representatives, reflected public opinion rather than popular clamour. Such principles may have led the *Colonist* and others into the governor-general's camp, but they did not constitute an endorsement of mixed monarchy. Conservative champions of that theory had found strange bedfellows.

The ex-ministers and their supporters in the Reform Association experimented with four responses to accusations that their constitutional demands spelt the end of mixed monarchy: first, they contended that the governor and his allies posed the greater threat to that system; second, they ignored the charge; third, they tried to redefine mixed monarchy as consistent with their constitutional position; and fourth, they argued that the British constitution itself was no longer mixed or balanced. Taken together, these responses demonstrated that the theory of mixed monarchy no longer provided an agreed-upon framework for constitutional debate in Upper Canada. What had once been common wisdom was, by 1844, a party nostrum.

As the opening chapter noted, the first strategy of turning the charge of subverting mixed monarchy against the governor had deep roots in the colony. There was nothing specific to the Metcalfe crisis that lessened the utility of this strategy. Indeed, once the assembly expressed its continued confidence in the ex-ministers, it would have been easy to rehearse well-worn arguments that by disregarding the wishes of the people's representatives the governor threatened the balance of the constitution. George Brown's new *Globe* offered one avenue for developing this theme. The charge that the late ministry had attempted to concentrate authority in its own hands was, for Brown, ridiculous: 'The Governor ... representing the Sovereign, holds one-third of the power of the whole Estates, and appoints another third, viz., the Legislative Council, leaving only one-third for the popular voice.' The governor was more likely to become a despot than a nullity.[22] He, not the executive council or assembly, posed the greatest danger to balance.

21 *British Colonist*, 20 Sept. and also 12 Nov. 1844
22 *Globe*, 15 Oct. 1844

Given the structure of most previous constitutional debates, this type of argument might have been pervasive. In fact, it was noticeably rare.

Supporters of the late ministry still talked about three branches and were more than willing to emphasize the formal similarities between British and Canadian institutions,[23] but, with a few notable exceptions, they preferred to discuss the motives of their opponents, the inevitability of party government, the rights of British subjects, the need for popular control of patronage, and the primacy of ministerial responsibility. In fact, the second strategy, simply ignoring the charge of subverting mixed monarchy, was pursued by Toronto's Irish Catholic *Mirror*. It copied none of the leading texts that made the charge. It commented on none of them and refrained from using the theory of mixed monarchy in its own editorials. It was as if claims based on it were no longer relevant.

Henry John Boulton, chairman of the Reform Association, adopted the third strategy – attempting to redefine mixed monarchy. (Perhaps having been a prominent conservative before the rebellion, he was particularly attached to the idiom as a way to suggest a degree of consistency in his own political trajectory.) In a speech to the association, Boulton described the British constitution as 'a mild, free, and popular form of mixed monarchy,' since 'the Sovereign has a large share of power, although by the admixture of popular controul, no arbitrary authority.' Thus, he frequently employed the term 'mixed' to refer to a 'Government in which the voice of the people is to mingle with the command of the Sovereign,' or to a government in which there was no despotic power because there was no 'power acting independently of [i.e., not mixed with] the people.'

Arriving at the core of his linguistic strategy, Boulton asked: 'How can a monarchy be regarded as a mixed or popular Government, if the Monarch can act independently of the people? ... The very principle of mixed monarchy imports that the Sovereign can do no official act alone ... Herein consists the distinction between a mixed Monarchy and an absolute Sovereignty.' Mixed monarchy now meant that the monarch acted only through advisers responsible to the people. It was a popular form of government because it contained a mixture – not a mixture of three estates or of three coordinate legislatures – but of the people and the monarch in the exercise of executive power. Boulton proved what no one disputed, that Canada's monarchy was not absolute. Boulton

23 E.g., William Hume Blake in Reform Association, *'The Globe' Extra*, 17, *Examiner*, 13 Mar. and 2 Oct. 1844, and Zeno, *The 'Crise' Metcalfe*, 30, 39, 43

tried to make Baldwinite responsible government compatible with mixed monarchy by making it 'the very principle' of the mixture itself. Thus, he was able to conclude that 'in theory we now, thanks to the Reform party, have a sound system of mixed government.'[24] Responsible government and mixed monarchy weren't just compatible – they were the same thing.

The theory of mixed monarchy was too familiar for such blatant manipulation. Further, the Reform Association could assert the primacy of ministerial responsibility more easily by adopting a fourth strategy: contending that Britain itself no longer clung to its ancient, balanced constitution. Boulton's mixture of monarch and people occurred not among governor, legislative council, and assembly, not in an assembly that already represented the interests of all three estates, and certainly not among ranks in society as a whole, but in the cabinet. Of all the ex-ministers' supporters, George Brown made the most extensive use of the terminology of mixed monarchy and balance. He could do so because he had fully integrated the cabinet into his constitutional program. Ministerial responsibility, not mixed monarchy, defined the British constitution.

Brown, speaking at another meeting of the Reform Association, praised the 'checks on unjust or hasty legislation' in the British system of government that ensured 'the just balance of power.' This balance occurred in the cabinet. An elected representative who proved himself worthy of his colleagues' confidence became, with their support, an adviser to the Crown, 'the life, the moving power of every wheel in the whole machine of Government – he is the very government itself.' Thus, 'the Sovereign and the cabinet together form one power in the State – Royalty as practically embodied in the British Constitution.'[25] Egerton Ryerson countered that this made the monarch 'a mere name' – a symbol rather than head of the executive. 'It appears, then,' Ryerson concluded with not a little exasperation, 'that the British world has been sadly astray in saying, "King, Lords and Commons." Mr. George Brown will teach them better.'[26]

---

24 Boulton, *Globe*, 25 Sept. 1844
25 Brown in Reform Association, *'The Globe' Extra*, 30–1. See also *Globe*, 11 June, 1 and 15 Oct. 1844 and *Banner*, 8 Dec. copied in *Chronicle & Gazette*, 20 Dec. 1843.
26 Ryerson, *Sir Charles Metcalfe Defended*, 72. Ryerson insisted that 'the power of the Cabinet Council, as distinct from that of the Sovereign is unknown in the British constitution, which consists of King, Lords and Commons only.' Relying on De Lolme, he argued that ministers were formally only '*voluntary* instruments or advisers.' Ibid., 19

Responding in the *Globe*, Brown allowed that 'a Cabinet Council is unknown to the British Constitution. Such is the ancient theory of the constitution certainly, but the practice is entirely opposed to it.'[27] The *Bathurst Courier* was equally blunt: 'The British Government is nothing more or less than Responsible Government.'[28] Symptomatic of this narrowing of the meaning of the British constitution, the assembly's resolutions of September 1841 affirming broad principles of executive responsibility (virtually ignored by the Upper Canadian press at the time), were now resurrected as 'Canada's Magna Carta.' Ambiguous enough to permit nearly everyone, including the governor, to claim adherence to them, the resolutions were, the Reform Association insisted, a full recognition of ministerial responsibility, now the sole defining element of the British constitution.[29] George Brown may have been hostile to American republicanism, but the alternative for Canada was parliamentary government with a limited franchise, not mixed monarchy. The 'ancient theory of the constitution' had been replaced by a modern one.

Metcalfe's critics had abandoned the traditional theory of mixed monarchy. The moderates and reformers whose support he desperately needed had significantly diluted, if not forsaken, it as well. In any robust form, the theory had become the property of a single group unable to muster adequate support for the governor in the assembly or the country. This marginalization was mirrored in a parallel decline in the currency of corporatist and hierarchical depictions of society.

Upper Canada became a democracy not because Upper Canadians exercised equal political power or were socially or economically equal, but because, by the time of the Metcalfe crisis, they saw themselves as political actors whose formal equality of citizenship translated into an equality of opportunity to define the collective good. Further, they convinced themselves that their society lacked those extremes of wealth and status that might render such political equality meaningless or a cruel hoax. Upper Canadians, even at their most sanguine, did not seriously contend that conditions were equal for all. Rather, the *range* of inequalities in their society was thought sufficiently narrow to sustain political

---

27 *Globe*, 11 June 1844
28 *Bathurst Courier*, 23 Jan. 1844
29 J.M.S. Careless, *The Union of the Canadas: The Growth of Canadian Institutions, 1841–1857* (Toronto: McClelland and Stewart 1967), 55, 58, 68, 83, 88

equality. According to their self-description, the top and bottom of the European social pyramid were, thankfully, absent in Upper Canada. They came to celebrate what Gordon S. Wood has called 'a truncated society.'[30]

Without a definable aristocracy based on blood, political or corporate privilege, or economic clout, there were no lords capable of poisoning the political system. Nor was there a sizeable, entrenched, and menacing underclass or 'mob' threatening disorder and irrational tumult from 'below.' The acceptance of the public sphere was part of this process of social redefinition – away from monarch, nobles, and subjects or the few and the many; towards an imagined and socially cohesive entity, 'the people,' as the principal collective political subject. As 'the people' became a positive term, the public, as its most capable members, either represented it or, in some accounts, was nearly synonymous with it. The eclipse of the theory of mixed monarchy ensured that this entity became the foundation and ultimate source of authority in a new constitutional order.

The intimate relationship between constitutional theory and social vision was evident in disputes about the evolution of the British constitution. As the *Globe*'s distinction between ancient theory and modern practice suggests, different aspects of British constitutional history were mined for precedents.[31] Most conservatives were not oblivious to changes in British constitutional theory and practice since the eighteenth century. The *Montreal Herald* conceded that ministerial responsibility now defined British government, but this had been the result of centuries of evolution. According to the *Herald*, Canada was no more ready for ministerial responsibility in 1844 than England would have been ready for the constitution of 1688 (the Glorious Revolution) in 1215 (Magna Charta). Such historicism drew the *Examiner*'s fury: 'Talk then of the constitution of 1215, or 1688 or 1828. We know what we require ... The example of England is before us; not the rebellious England of 1688; when she drove out her own anointed King, and

---

30 Gordon S. Wood, *The Radicalism of the American Revolution* (New York: Alfred A. Knopf 1992), chap. 7
31 Ryerson was prone to choose examples from George III's reign, but for Sullivan 'the question is not what George III did – for he did many things that were wrong.' He drew instead from the nineteenth century, particularly the ministerial changes associated with Catholic Emancipation and the Reform Act. Ryerson, *Sir Charles Metcalfe Defended*, 19–20, 56, 73, 148–9, *Sullivan's Attacks upon Sir Charles Metcalfe Refuted*, 21, and Legion, *Letters on Responsible Government*, 30–1, 39–42, 164, 202

placed an usurper on his throne; but of the England, when in 1831, she wrenched from the hands of her entrenched Aristocracy the boon of Parliamentary Reform ... Let no "men in their senses," then, talk to us of the various phases of the British constitution. We do not want any of its phases but the present one.' This almost unprecedented denigration of the Glorious Revolution was likely provoked by the implications the *Herald* drew from its evolutionary reading of British history. As in Britain, Canada's constitution could only evolve 'gradually, and according to the progressive wealth, intelligence, and social independence' of its own society.[32] As discussed in the first chapter, Sir Francis Bond Head had made the same point in 1836. Different social structures required different constitutions. For local, largely social reasons, British ministerial responsibility was not applicable to Canada – an inference supporters of the Reform Association angrily rejected.

Robert Baldwin, for instance, was convinced that the case against responsible government was so weak that opponents were reduced to the 'old worn out ditty of its incompatibility with Colonial dependence.' To lay this ditty to rest once and for all (it wasn't worthy of being called an argument), Baldwin asserted that British subjects, whether in Britain or British North America, had the same 'inalienable' and 'absolute constitutional rights' to free and representative government. The British constitution was merely a 'model' of how those rights might be exercised. On British principles, therefore, Canadians had the right to choose any model of self-government. As members of an empire, their self-government did not extend to international trade and foreign relations since these two 'matters of common interest' – and there were only two – required coordination in London. For Baldwin, 'this arose not from any principle involving the superiority of the people of one part of the Empire over those of another, but from the *necessity* arising out of local position.' The British government coordinated the trade and foreign policy of the empire, not from right or superior ability, but from practical necessity. Otherwise, the governments of Britain and Canada were equal, reflecting the basic equality of their citizens. Canada's government and social structure were complete and self-sufficient. As the *Examiner* had insisted, 'Canadians are to be governed upon the principles of democratic and not trans-atlantic, policy.'[33]

---

32 *Examiner*, 24 Jan. 1844
33 Baldwin to the Reform Association, *Examiner*, 3 Jan. and *Globe*, 25 Sept. 1844 and *Examiner* 24 May and 6 Dec. 1843

While offering an important formulation of the empire as a federation of equal parts free to choose their own models of self-government, Baldwin ignored the degree to which critics of the model he championed saw Canada's colonial status as sociological rather than juridical. Conservatives continued to advocate the theory of mixed monarchy bequeathed to the Canadas in 1791 not because it conformed to current British practice, but because they contended that it still held out the greatest hope for good government.

Like the *Montreal Herald*, the *Patriot* argued that the Reform Association 'need not have had to resort to [such authorities on the British constitution as] Hallam, De Lolme or Mackintosh' to prove the existence of ministerial responsibility in Britain. 'They might with equal reason have quoted the veracious history of "Jack and the Beanstalk," to prove that fairy tales are popular among children.'[34] The question was not what kind of constitution Britain had but what kind of constitution Canada should have. The *Canadian Loyalist & Spirit of 1812* made the same point by quoting reformers' own textbook, Lord Durham's *Report*: 'When we transplant the Institutions of England into our Colonies we ought, at least to take care before hand that the Social State of the Colony should possess those peculiar materials on which alone the excellence of those Institutions depends in the Mother Country.'[35]

For such critics, the British social structure that had sustained mixed monarchy now prevented parliamentary government from degenerating into pure democracy. Lacking such a society, Canadian parliamentary government could not avoid such a fate: 'Disguise it as you will, an amount of responsibility to the people, (of one class only in this colony) equal to the amount of responsibility to all the many classes in England, is republicanism neither more nor less.'[36] This social argument – that for political purposes Canada had only one class – was developed in two directions: one emphasized the quality of the men elected to the assembly or appointed to office; the other emphasized the need to reinforce the institutions of mixed monarchy to compensate for Canada's lack of resident monarch and nobility.

For the *Patriot*, full-scale ministerial responsibility as practised in Britain was inapplicable to Canada because of 'the poverty of the Colony, and the absence of a large class of educated men of independent for-

34 *Patriot*, 5 Apr. 1844, 29 Aug. 1843, and 23 Dec. 1842
35 Durham, *Canadian Loyalist*, 28 Dec. 1843
36 A Canadian, *Monarch*, 16 Jan. 1844

tunes who might aptly form the Representative body.'[37] Without such a class, responsible government would result in corruption. Rather than holding ministers accountable, elected members would be beholden to them for offices and emoluments. The problem was exacerbated by holding elections in such a society. 'Where an aristocracy is unknown – where large bodies of tenantry look not with trust and reverence on the landlord they hold under, votes can only be canvassed and gained by personal knowledge of, and local contact with the holders of these votes.' Ironically, an egalitarian and non-deferential electorate encouraged legislators to 'lie, fawn, wheedle, pimp [and] cajole' and, needing to earn their living from politics, they were forced to do the bidding of the executive at the same time they told the people whatever it took to get re-elected. 'From such it would be childish to look for any heroic devotion to the maintenance of constitutional truth, or any sublime resistance to either the advances of arrogant prerogative or democratic assumption.' Only further social evolution offered responsible government 'a fair chance of success in a colony.' Constitutional balance was under threat in 1843–4 because the ex-ministers had tried to use executive patronage to take advantage of Canada's social imbalance.[38]

Given its opinion of the electorate and their representatives, it is not surprising that the *Patriot* took a jaundiced view of the ex-councillors and those they had appointed to office. Popularity had eclipsed merit. 'A familiarity with the use of the adze and the handsaw will constitute strong claims on the office of Surveyor-General,' whereas, in Britain, people like Francis Hincks 'would sink to their proper level,' under the salutary weight of rank, hereditary privilege, wealth, and education.[39] Returning to once common notions of the science of politics, the *Monarch* insisted that statesmen were the product of years of study and experience. Even the colony's naturally gifted were too preoccupied with subsistence and too little exposed to the refinements of civilization.[40] Twice, exhorting fellow conservatives to greater effort, the *Patriot* screeched, 'The Philistines are upon us.'[41] It didn't pause long enough to explain how its long-standing contribution to the public sphere or its call for greater participation by fellow conservatives was compatible with

---

37 *Patriot*, 23 Dec. 1842
38 Ibid., 30 and 16 Aug. 1844. See also 23 Aug. and 23 Dec. 1842.
39 Ibid., 30 Aug. and 19 Mar. 1844
40 Review of Isaac Buchanan's letters, *Monarch*, 12 Mar. 1844 and C.B., *Monarch*, 2 Mar. 1843
41 *Patriot*, 20 Sept. and 1 Oct. 1844. See also *Monarch*, 13 Oct. 1842.

its shrill denunciation of elected reformers and increasing doubts about the capacity of the electorate.

Before the resignations, the Baldwin-LaFontaine ministry had come under considerable fire for the poor quality, low social status, and excessive partisanship of their appointments, especially to the local magistracy. The *Patriot* thought that popularity should be irrelevant for the post. A knowledge of the law and honesty were certainly qualifications, but even these were insufficient: 'England is an essentially monarchical country – and if Canada desires to retain her institutions, she must conform as far as possible to British practice. The most respectable of the gentry of every section of the Country ought to form, without any reference to politics or elections, the local Magistracy. We must not drop too eagerly into the bathos of republicanism and democratic equality. Even the most ignorant of the population will know and appreciate the presence of a respectable magistrate seated on the bench, and regard with very different feelings his administration and exposition of the law, and the ridiculous exhibition of authority from one from their own ranks.'[42] The appointment of reformers to office had brought an increasingly conservative and harsh tone to the *Patriot*, but here it merely repeated one of the platitudes of contemporary political theory: monarchy rested on deference to social superiors; democracy was ground in social equality. In a monarchy, appointment recognized existing social standing; it did not create it. Authority exercised by one's peers was simply 'ridiculous.' Thus, after the resignations, the *Patriot* claimed that the appointment of the 'illiterate and disaffected' resulted in more than bad officials. It was 'gradually sapping and undermining the venerable fabric of the British constitution,' putting the 'whole super-structure' at risk.[43]

But surely it was dangerous to emphasize the social distance between Britain and Canada. If Canada's social structure could not prevent ministerial responsibility from degenerating into democracy, it also lacked the aristocracy essential to mixed monarchy. Some, like the *Montreal Gazette*, were consistent enough to deny that Canada could ever have a transcript of the British constitution in any of its forms. Even if Metcalfe prevailed, 'without a Monarchy and a House of Peers' Canada would

---

42 *Patriot*, 13 June 1843. For other complaints about new JPs, see *London Herald*, 3 June, *Cobourg Star*, 2 Aug., and *Church*, 3 Nov. 1843. Reformers courted some of this opposition to score political points. See Carol Wilton-Siegel, 'The Transformation of Upper Canadian Politics in the 1840s,' PhD thesis, University of Toronto 1984, 295–6.

43 *Patriot*, 14 Feb. and 12 Dec. 1843

still risk 'the crudest and worst form of democracy, that of One Absolute Chamber.'[44]

Most attempts by the more doctrinaire conservatives to relate mixed monarchy to the colony's social structure were not so clear-headed. Instead, they urged extra vigilance and further bulwarks to protect mixed monarchy from its hostile social setting. The *Monarch* and the organ of the Anglican hierarchy advocated an established Church to augment the monarchical principle.[45] The empire itself could also act as a prop. If Canada lacked the social materials for good government, Britain did not. Forgetting their denunciation of Whig colonial policy in the 1830s for giving succour to Canadian reformers, at least one conservative now thought it better to trust the balance of interests and classes in Britain than the undifferentiated mass of Canadians represented in the local assembly.[46] Third, and more immediately connected to the issues at hand, it was necessary to preserve the Crown's independent control of patronage. Impartiality and merit, not popularity, had to guide appointments – discrimination that was unlikely from an executive council of fierce partisans.[47] The ambitious should look up to the Crown rather than down to the multitude. Fourth, if Canada lacked an aristocracy, perhaps it was not too late to create one. The *Canadian Loyalist & Spirit of 1812*, for instance, rehearsed the argument that a Canadian assembly of 'adventurers and speculators' required more supervision than the existing legislative council could provide. Councillors were socially too similar to those elected to the lower house and bore little resemblance to hereditary peers of Britain. A Canadian order of knighthood was needed to 'ripen' into a hereditary aristocracy seated in the legislative council.[48] The idea was endorsed by the *Church, Cobourg Star*, and *Monarch*. As the first acknowledged, only a return to the ambitious policy of Simcoe could reinvigorate mixed monarchy.[49]

44　*Montreal Gazette* copied in *British Colonist*, 22 Dec. 1843, correspondent, *Montreal Gazette* copied in *Church*, 16 Feb. 1844, and *Montreal Courier* copied in *Church*, 5 July 1844
45　*Monarch*, 15 Dec. 1842
46　Ibid., 12 Mar. 1844
47　The centrality of impartiality to sovereignty is emphasized by Mark Francis, *Governors and Settlers: Images of Authority in British Colonies, 1820–1860* (London: Macmillan 1992), 86–212.
48　*Canadian Loyalist*, 28 Dec. 1843 and 4 Jan. 1844. See also *Church*, 6 Feb. 1841 and 5 July 1844.
49　*Cobourg Star*, 17 Jan. 1844, *Church* copied in *Monarch*, 12 Sept. 1843, and *Church*, 3 Nov. 1843

Many conservatives recognized that such a policy was anachronistic, undesirable, or both, but they shared a belief in the need for social hierarchy to be reflected in constitutional theory and practice, especially in the selection of leaders and administrators. This was merely a further episode in the ongoing transatlantic debate about whether aristocracy or equality formed the basis of good government.[50] One conservative identified education, religion, honour, morality, courage, and patriotism as the 'heroic virtues' a political system should reward. Responsible government, by contrast, seemed to value only numbers and rewarded anyone able to gain a temporary majority with little regard to the means.[51] Responsibility to mere numbers or to the majority of a community composed of only one class had to be avoided. Instead, a political system should recognize and make room for the best in society (among whom conservatives naturally felt over-represented), and the best in each individual.

The reinvigoration of these older social arguments during the Metcalfe crisis by more doctrinaire conservatives did little but expose their political vulnerability. Such arguments seemed defensive and strangely divorced from the public sphere in which they were made. It was difficult to argue that the undifferentiated masses were incapable of self-government when they were the audience to which such arguments were addressed, when their reason was being appealed to, and when it was their votes that were needed. Those who made the social arguments were well aware that many would 'sneer' at the mere mention of a colonial aristocracy. 'Aristocracy' and 'hierarchy' had become terms of abuse.[52] Moderates and those reformers who supported the governor advanced none of these social arguments and even many conservatives shied away from the extremes of the *Patriot* or *Monarch*. The unpopularity of these social arguments was also manifest from the obvious relish with which supporters of the ex-ministry trashed them.

The Reform Association's assault on aristocratic principles proceeded along three fronts: first, they denied that Canada had an aristocracy; second, they rejected the notion that this prevented Canada from enjoying

---

50 See David Paul Crook, *American Democracy in English Politics, 1815–1850* (Oxford: Oxford University Press 1965).

51 C.B. [Captain Beales?], *Monarch*, 13 Oct. 1842

52 *Canadian Loyalist*, 4 Jan. 1844, Beales to the Brock Constitutional Society, *Monarch*, 2 Feb. 1843, and *Church* copied in *Cobourg Star*, 17 Jan. 1844

parliamentary government; and third, they insisted that the lack of an aristocracy and political hierarchy, far from being a problem, was to be praised. In essence, conservatives maintained that the British constitution, even after the introduction of ministerial responsibility, was essentially aristocratic *because* of the British social structure, while supporters of the Reform Association thought that the British constitution was essentially democratic *despite* the British social structure.[53]

Tory government, according to the *Globe*, held 'that there is a certain class, on whose brows is stampt *Legislator*, or *Ruler* of the mass, without regard to their qualification for such an office.' The *Examiner* also ridiculed the notion that there was a class which ought to monopolize government office. There was only 'an assumed caste' of ambitious men who cloaked 'their selfishness and the haughty superciliousness' of their demands in talk of a virtuous gentry. 'Canada, we contend knows no *aristocracy* beyond that which is based upon the industry and intelligence of those who are the sinews of her strength. Here are not ducal coronets, no proud and princely domains, no jewelled splendour to contrast with fags and hunger ... the happiness of the many, in preference to the aggrandisement, the pride, the insolence and the haughty bearing of the few.'[54] The many might still confront the few, but without accepted and institutionalized inequality, the few were undeserving. After years of struggle, they were now, finally, to be driven from political influence.

Sir Charles Metcalfe, Colonial Secretary Lord Stanley, and many conservatives wondered aloud how such a truncated social structure could support mixed monarchy or prevent parliamentary government from sliding into unchecked democracy. In his reply to the Ottawa District, Metcalfe stressed the differences between Britain and Canada; 'between one in which a wealthy aristocracy possesses great influence, and another in which no such influence exists.' Canada was younger, poorer, and less civilized than Britain. It simply lacked the means of producing 'a nice balance of counterpoising influence.'[55]

Francis Hincks's *Montreal Pilot* thought Metcalfe's reply rendered valuable service to the Reform Association: 'We are told that here there is no wealthy aristocracy possessing great influence, and powerful enough to resist the wishes of the people. The Prerogative of the Crown

---

53 See J.R. Jennings, 'Conceptions of England and Its Constitution in Nineteenth-Century French Political Thought,' *Historical Journal* 29, no. 1 (1986), 65–85
54 *Globe*, 22 Oct. 1844 and *Examiner*, 25 Jan. 1843
55 Metcalfe to the Ottawa District, *Addresses Presented to His Excellency*, 134

is here to be the instrument by which public opinion is to be kept in check ... There is not ... any danger of the people being gulled by an alarming picture held up before them of the consequences of their getting too much power into their own hands.'[56] Canada needed no institutional checks to counteract its relatively egalitarian social structure. The 'people' needed no such supervision. Their judgment, not a 'nice balance of counter-posing influence,' grounded good government. The term aristocracy appeared frequently during the Metcalfe crisis because it referred to any self-interested minority, not just to a hereditary nobility. Such minorities tried to stand aloof from 'the people' and thwart public opinion, especially by seeking unearned and exclusive privileges, monopolies, or other forms of unfair influence from the state.[57] The supremacy of public opinion entailed the destruction of all such influence.

The Reform Association's *Address to the People of Canada* followed Robert Baldwin in asserting that the only relevant difference between Britain and Canada was that the former coordinated matters of war and international commerce. The association could not see 'upon what constitutional principles the want of a spiritual and temporal aristocracy should deprive you of constitutional government.' The sheer confidence of the statement must have left mixed monarchy's defenders breathless. According to the association, since property was represented in the assembly, there was 'no other interest ... whose protection requires the existence of an aristocracy.'[58] No social entity, no interest, and no judgment existed independent of the people. Thus, no political institution ought to be independent of them.

Two letters to the *Globe* echoed these themes. 'A Friend' knew Canada had no aristocracy, but it hardly followed that Canadians should be denied the power over the executive 'which the Commons of England with such *disadvantages*, were yet enabled to wrest from the Crown.' 'Common Sense' also thought it an 'unnatural doctrine' that 'the want of an aristocracy should deprive us of the free enjoyment of the British Constitution.' That many Britons were tenants influenced by their land-

---

56 *Pilot* copied in *St Catharines Journal*, 5 Apr. 1844
57 Stephen Conrad Bullock, *Revolutionary Brotherhood: Freemasonry and the Transformation of the American Social Order, 1730–1849* (Chapel Hill: University of North Carolina Press 1996), 297 and, more broadly, Judith N. Shklar, 'The American Idea of Aristocracy' in Stanley Hoffman and Dennis F. Thompson, eds., *Redeeming American Political Thought* (Chicago: University of Chicago Press 1998), 146–57
58 Reform Association of Canada, *Address to the People of Canada*, 10–12

lords was an absurd reason why the Commons should be trusted with greater political weight than a Canadian assembly. It simply meant that the British electorate was 'more oppressed' than the Canadian. The British constitution operated better, that is, more democratically, in Canada than it did in Britain precisely because the former lacked such social 'disadvantages.'[59]

If there was only one estate in Canada, and if that estate was equally or even more capable of operating the British constitution than the British themselves, then the denial of Baldwinite ministerial responsibility was an insult. Metcalfe was not protecting the constitution from the encroachment of another coordinate branch. He was 'spurning a free people.' Canadians had no time for the long lectures on the British constitution that Metcalfe, Ryerson, and the British government seemed intent on patronizing 'ignorant colonists' with. Canadians risked being treated as 'serfs' or 'slaves' or the Jamaicans Metcalfe had previously governed rather than the capable, worthy, intelligent, and patriotic freemen they claimed to be.[60] Robert Baldwin Sullivan thought only 'the newness of the feeling of love of country as applied to Canada' explained why there was not even more indignation at the suggestion that there was 'some essential difference between Colonists and the British people, – some humiliating distinction ... something which makes the Provincial Parliament untrustworthy.'[61] (Among its many achievements, the Metcalfe crisis cemented the relationship between the independence of individual Canadians and the juridical independence of Canada from Britain.) Supporters of the ex-ministry insisted on (mis)interpreting conservative social rhetoric as the claim that individual Canadians were inferior to individual Britons. It was more that the proportions of social classes found in Canada (or, more often, the absence of all but one) worked against mixed monarchy and favoured democracy. Essentially, supporters of the ex-ministry agreed.

Frequent invocations of Upper Canada's yeomanry at meetings of the

---

59 A Friend to British Interests to Charles Metcalfe, *Globe*, 9 July 1844 (emphasis added) and Common Sense, 'Want of an Aristocracy Considered,' *Globe*, 10 Sept. 1844. See also *Banner*, 29 Mar. 1844.

60 *Globe*, 11 June, 9 July, and 15 Oct. 1844, *Examiner*, 6 Dec. 1843 and 28 Feb., 2 Oct., and 6 Nov. 1844

61 Legion, *Letters on Responsible Government*, 151 and 71, ridiculing the British debate on colonial incapacities.

Reform Association and elsewhere served the dual purpose of underlining the virtuous independence of most Upper Canadian heads of household and contrasting this happy social state with the more hierarchical one of Britain.[62] Just after the elections of 1844, the *Globe* responded to charges in the *London Times* that British America was 'a pauper colony, without capital, without intelligence, without dignity,' destined to become a 'vulgar republic.' Given the recent election of 'so many servile Tories,' the *Globe* conceded that there was as yet insufficient intelligence, but Canada already compared favourably with 'any agricultural district of England.' Once even more books and newspapers disseminated 'sound information, ... the population of Upper Canada will exercise an independence of which the yeomen of England, from their relation to their landlord, can have no conception.' Ever greater access to the means of social communication would guarantee a strength to public opinion unknown in England.

While the *Globe* admitted that there were few of 'high rank and station' in Canada, it reminded the *Times* that there was also little destitution: 'That is the best state of society which gives competence to the greatest number – that competence standing between poverty and riches, we have high authority for believing to be the most satisfactory state. There is doubtless a dignity and grace in high rank, and when accompanied by becoming virtues, society derives polish and improvement from such a class, which arises in all civilized countries in the course of time. Universality of education, which is the great refiner, renders a high class less necessary in the meantime.'[63] As we shall see in the final chapter, this social ideal had already been articulated as part of the reform critique of the common law of primogeniture. By the time of the Metcalfe crisis, the ideal was widely accepted, its constitutional implications more clearly drawn. Stung by metropolitan condescension, reformers renewed their insistence that democracy and public opinion were strongest where relatively equal households were not threatened by lords or peasants. 'Competence' in economic well-being translated into competence in government.

---

62 *Globe* 6 Aug. and 10 Sept. 1844, Peter Perry to the Reform Association, *Examiner*, 10 Jan. and 23 Oct. 1844, and Adam Fergusson to the Reform Association, *Chronicle & Gazette*, 25 May 1844

63 *Globe*, 10 Dec. 1844. On the broader implications of 'competence,' see Daniel Vickers, 'Competency and Competition: Economic Culture in Early America,' *William and Mary Quarterly*, 3rd ser., 47 (January 1990), 3–29.

The *Times* and like-minded colonists were, however, talking about more than 'polish.' The truncated nature of colonial society meant that the great mass of adult male property-owners formed the social basis of colonial politics. In governor and legislative council, Canada had political institutions to counteract this social imbalance, but it lacked the social elements to give them life. Reformers, whether or not they supported the ex-ministers, boasted about Canada's social structure. 'Equality of civil and religious rights' or 'equal justice to all' were pervasive slogans. Supporters of the governor used them to attack the notion that appointments to office should be made on the basis of party. The Reform Association used them to insist on the political equality of members of the public with each other and with Britons. Even the *Christian Guardian*, circumspect throughout the crisis, extended the notion of equality beyond the religious sphere to encompass an outright rejection of hereditary aristocracy.[64]

'Tories' saw such claims to equality as precisely the sort of self-serving flattery that made colonial politics dangerously democratic. They charged the Reform Association with limiting its definition of the 'people' to those who supported the temporary majority in the assembly (leaving unsaid the role of those factors such as race, gender, and economic circumstance that also coloured who could effectively speak for the 'people' but that were not subjects of contention among the various factions). A minority should be able to look to an impartial Sovereign for protection against proscription by an executive council bolstered by its majority in the assembly.[65] There were also frequent charges of hypocrisy. As Captain Beales told the Brock Constitutional Society: 'The republicans [reformers] were themselves aristocrats in every thing but politics. Of two mechanics, a carpenter or shoemaker, one a botcher and the other a good workman, they would chose the best ... In all affairs of life, except politics, they were aristocrats, and they always looked for the best, but in politics, they preferred such a one provided he would praise and flatter some imaginary thing called the people ... They preferred him to the best statesman in the world ... who would not flatter them by telling them what all history refutes – that they were the fountain of all power.'[66] Beales had a point. Leaders of the Reform Association advocated equality of condition or leadership no more than he

---

64 *Christian Guardian*, 30 Oct. 1844
65 UEL, *Cobourg Star*, 27 Mar. 1844
66 Beales to the Brock Constitutional Society, *Monarch*, 2 Feb. 1843

did.[67] They did, however, believe in the people's capacity to participate in the public sphere. Qualified leaders were to guide and execute, not to thwart, their will. Upper Canada's collective judgment, not the governor or a social class, would recognize and reward 'the best.'

Reformers drew the very line between the social and the political that Beales denied. Just as their appeal to public opinion assumed equal and rational discussants and readers, so too their rejection of mixed monarchy posited equal, rational, and independent voters. Such citizens knew and could act upon their own interests and those of their community better than any minority or institution and certainly better than anyone in Britain. Reinforced by voluntary associations, the concept of the public sphere insisted that a space could be carved out where the inequalities and hierarchies of other realms of social experience were held in temporary abeyance. Drawing this line between the political and the social to shelter the former from the inequalities of the latter was made easier by portraying society as truncated; that is, lacking those extremes of wealth and poverty that could pervert the process of political deliberation. The *relevance*, not the *existence*, of socio-economic and other distinctions was denied.

The portrayal of colonial society as truncated was widely praised and occupied an important place in constitutional theorizing. So, in an important sense, Beales was right to see 'the people' as 'some imaginary thing.' It, like public opinion, was a political invention. Invoking 'the people' wrote out other categories of political actors, especially those like 'mob' or 'aristocracy' that threatened the primacy of public opinion. Instead, a common political community was offered in which no category of political actors was, in principle, beyond the reach of public opinion. Such a society also contained a narrower range of interests among which fruitful dialogue was more likely. It was not perceived as riddled by hostile, starkly defined classes with incompatible interests that would render such dialogue difficult. The social ambiguity of a term like 'the people' was among its greatest political assets.

Considerable support for contemporaries' image of their society as truncated can be found in Gordon Darroch and Lee Soltow's statistical analysis of property distribution during the three decades before

---

67 Before the crisis, the *Banner*, 18 Aug. 1843, praised the British constitution for balancing popular rights with 'the influence of property, rank, and station.' During the crisis, the moderate *Woodstock Herald*, 27 July and 3 and 10 Aug. 1844, felt called upon to defend ranks based on ability and merit.

the census of 1871. Sharp inequalities in the ownership of rural property persisted – about 20 per cent of farmers controlled almost 60 per
cent of the land – but the wide base of the land-distribution pyramid
was probably more visible than its steep incline. Almost two-thirds of
adult male farmers owned land, while the propertyless third included
many of their sons who could reasonably expect to inherit land or to
otherwise acquire it with family assistance. Crucial to such expectations and broader social perceptions, Darroch and Soltow find, was
that 'about 3 per cent of all landless adult farmers could expect to
become owners in every year.' This annual movement into the ranks of
the propertied provided concrete local evidence of opportunity. The
substantial tracts of yet-to-be-cleared land on most farms held out further promise of future prosperity. Tenancy and agricultural wage-
labour were more likely to reflect stages of the life cycle than social
class. In an urban context, David Burley finds that over a third of adult
men in Brantford had been, were, or would become self-employed in
at least one of his six sample years to 1881. Such movement in and out
of the ranks of the self-employed not only offered additional local
examples of visible social mobility but also inhibited stable class identi-
fications.[68]

There was also more to the comparisons to Britain than smug self-
congratulations. For instance, Darroch and Soltow estimate that in 1851
about two-thirds of adult males working in British agriculture were
labourers, four times the proportion in Ontario two decades later.
While most of the remaining third in Britain were farm operators or
tenants, the majority of the remaining five-sixths in Ontario were owners.[69] The starkness of the contrast only encouraged speculation about
its political consequences. Mid-century Upper Canada appeared to

---

68 Gordon Darroch and Lee Soltow, *Property and Inequality in Victorian Ontario: Structural
Patterns and Cultural Communities in the 1871 Census* (Toronto: University of Toronto
Press 1994), 24, 29, 32, 37–9, 41–3, 62–4, 201–7. Much of this remained true even in
areas of more marginal agricultural land. See Chad Gaffield, *Language, Schooling, and
Cultural Conflict: The Origins of the French-Language Controversy in Ontario* (Kingston and
Montreal: McGill-Queen's University Press 1987), 63–4. David G. Burley, *A Particular
Condition in Life: Self-Employment and Social Mobility in Mid-Victorian Brantford, Ontario*
(Kingston and Montreal: McGill-Queen's University Press 1994), 7, 14, 20, and 170–97.
On the importance of uncleared land see Peter A. Russell, *Attitudes to Social Structure
and Mobility in Upper Canada* (Lewiston: E. Mellen Press 1990), 22. Chapter 8 returns to
many of these issues.
69 Darroch and Soltow, *Property and Inequality*, 194–8

observers as a land of opportunity, not for everyone and certainly not for equal wealth or without risk, hardship, gruelling labour, and social conflict, but for a socially recognized family competency beyond the reach of many in almost every other society of the period. During the Metcalfe crisis commentators exaggerated and drew their own lessons, but they did not falsify.

For political and cultural reasons, contemporaries now glorified their society's lack of an aristocracy, earlier bemoaned as conclusive evidence of colonial immaturity and frontier rudeness. The inappropriateness of the institutions of mixed monarchy to this society could no longer be denied. Far from being a rationale for constitutional dependence, it became a mark of provincial superiority over metropolitan Britain. Here, in reformers' social vision, was a kind of *North* American exceptionalism. The continent lacked Europe's social past and class structure. It would not share the same political future. Here the notion that peripheries take on the character of their metropolitan centre was repudiated.

Such a social structure made it easier to image actual and potential heads of household as political equals. Yet wasn't the social commentary of the Metcalfe crisis fictitious in another sense? Weren't 'the people' simply a disguise for an emerging 'middle class' that generalized its own particular interests as universal or classless? Shouldn't we read all these claims about competence, respectability, and the vitality of a society not polarized between rich and poor as codes for incipient middle-class hegemony?

Probably not. Upper Canada was not an egalitarian or classless society. It encompassed numerous divisions based on shared material circumstance, economic experience, or group consciousness, but contemporaries had no clear sense of the term 'middle class' and historians of Upper Canada have been unable to locate anything that might meaningfully be called a middle class, especially as a hegemonic historical agent. The relative absence of polarizing extremes was not the same as the preponderance of a 'middle' class. It only made spatial metaphors more problematic; the middle of what? Appealing to 'public opinion' further mitigated against the systematic use of social categories. Precision in social references risked implying that one's political program was supported by or would benefit only a single group within the more inclusive tribunal to which one appealed. The claims of public opinion to represent a broader, collective judgment could be used against a 'middle class' as easily as they were against any other partial or class interest.[70] Simply equating the 'people' or 'public' with a middle class, however defined, is probably no more helpful or precise than retaining contemporaries' terms. Given the ideological baggage that 'middle class' often carries, it may be less so. As Dror Wahrman argues, references to the 'middle class' in Britain pointed to diverse, often purposively ambiguous, social and political groupings, often to blur important divisions. Its use and meaning were linked to the shifting languages of constitutional, political, religious, and cultural conflict. Its boundaries and definition were no less contested than were those of other terms used to describe British society. In short, the British 'middle class' was no less an idea, ideological construct, or political invention (and therefore no more an objective or sociological 'thing') than were the 'public' or 'people.'[71]

Regardless, the previous discussions of voluntary associations, the press, and public meetings make it clear that while Upper Canada's public sphere was not open to everyone on the same terms, its membership was too numerous and varied to be shoehorned into a single sociological category.[72] The characteristics of any term broad enough to encompass the office-holders, gentry, farmers, villagers, mechanics, journeymen, shopkeepers, clerks, merchants, professionals, and others who joined voluntary associations, attended public meetings, signed petitions, and read newspapers would be vague indeed. It would efface some of the diverse and potentially conflicting interests and perspectives within the public sphere itself and risk incorporating the vast majority of colonial families into a single category. We should not, therefore, be surprised that Upper Canadians, unlike some of their British counterparts, rarely spoke of a 'middle class.'

Thus, the Irish gentleman Edward Allen Talbot, writing in 1824,

---

70 Dror Wahrman, 'Public Opinion, Violence and the Limits of Constitutional Politics,' in James Vernon, ed., *Re-reading the Constitution: New Narratives in the Political History of England's Long Nineteenth Century* (Cambridge: Cambridge University Press 1996), 113 and *Imaging the Middle Class: The Political Representation of Class in Britain, c. 1780–1840* (Cambridge: Cambridge University Press 1995), 192, 195–6

71 Wahrman, *Imaging the Middle Class*, but on the need to include religious and cultural conflict, as well as politics, see Patrick Joyce, *Democratic Subject: The Self and the Social in Nineteenth-Century England* (Cambridge: Cambridge University Press 1994), 161–3. I am much indebted to Wahrman's general approach.

72 J.I. Little, *State and Society in Transition: The Politics of Institutional Reform in the Eastern Townships, 1838–1852* (Montreal and Kingston: McGill-Queen's University Press 1997), 12, 240 and Jan Noel, *Canada Dry: Temperance Crusades before Confederation* (Toronto: University of Toronto Press 1995), 8, 241 come to a similar conclusion.

found only two classes in Upper Canada: 'professional men, merchants, civil and military officers, and the members of the Provincial Parliament' in the first and 'farmers, mechanics, and labourers, who associate together on all occasions without any distinction' in the second. For British readers more accustomed to a three-class model, Talbot noted that the second 'would in more civilized regions, be called the MIDDLE CLASS.'[73] Failing to find a tripartite class structure, Talbot had done little more than put an occupational gloss on the traditional division between the few and the many and, translating for his British audience, had equated the many, not the few, with the 'middle class.'

His particular categorization, especially placing labourers among a colonial middle class that excluded professionals, raises a number of intriguing questions. In the absence of a thorough investigation of the vocabulary used by settlers and observers to describe Upper Canada's social structure, it may be tempting to dismiss Talbot's account as that of a single, perhaps idiosyncratic, European traveller writing a couple of decades too early to observe a more nuanced social structure. Yet it is important to emphasize that there are any number of plausible ways to describe a given social structure or to capture long-term and ongoing socio-economic change. Colonists singled out various markers, especially education and manners, as well as material circumstances, occupation, and property ownership. They adopted a variety of terms and analogies, although the spatial metaphor of upper, middle, and lower was rarely among them. Each choice served particular ends, highlighting some aspects of their society while clouding others. The fluctuating popularity and social referents of these terms need to be studied.[74]

In the meantime, to take a few examples, the *Canada Inquirer* developed a four-class model during the Metcalfe crisis: first, the 'manual' labour of farmers and mechanics; second, the 'mental' labour of doctors and lawyers; third, clergy and teachers; and fourth, the military. 'Merchants, Bankers, and Storekeepers' were to 'be classed promiscuously, according to circumstances.' Those who improved communications or extended 'trade and manufactures' were placed in the manual class, thereby ensuring that one category came close to incorporating all but a fraction of the colonial population. Four years later, when the *Artisan* talked of 'the three great classes which constitute the foundation of our

---

73 Talbot, *Five Years' Residence in the Canadas*, v. 2, 20, 29
74 Again, I am heavily indebted to Wahrman, *Imagining the Middle Class*, esp. 4–6. An equivalent study for British North America is desperately needed.

social fabric,' it was referring to 'the Canadian Mechanic, Farmer, and Merchant,' not the upper, middle and lower. Indeed, class itself referred to any group united by a characteristic, identity, or interest not shared by everyone. Thus, leading blacks in the province formed a newspaper, the *Provincial Freeman*, to debate questions 'affecting us as a class.'[75]

Each of these and the many other social schemas involved plausible generalizations about Upper Canadian society. Each was pressed to serve political, religious, or cultural ends. Thus, the *Canada Inquirer* was advocating an educational system geared more to the needs of the 'manual' class than to doctors and lawyers. It bolstered this agenda by defining the former as the most productive class and by incorporating the vast majority of colonists into it. The issue could then be presented in essentially political terms as democracy versus privilege. The political dimension was also uppermost in the second example. As its name implied, the *Artisan* sought to present mechanics as an informed, interested, and numerous 'class' deserving an equal role with merchants and farmers in determining economic policy. 'Class' distinctions need not imply hierarchy. In this case, they advanced claims to political equality. Finally, the *Freeman* justified its existence and solicited subscriptions by positing the existence of a class of colonists whose separate interests needed articulation.

The terms of analysis in these three newspapers were not tools of the social sciences. They were the contested weapons of competing claims in the public sphere. Even a widely used, seemingly transparent term like 'yeoman' had various meanings that could be more political than occupational. Each of those captured during the western phase of the rebellion was officially listed as 'yeoman' even though the group included artisans, merchants, innkeepers, labourers, and professionals.[76]

In Britain, however, the link between public opinion and the 'middle class' was often explicit, not a hidden contradiction exposed later by scholars. Thus, William MacKinnon's *On the Rise, Progress and Present State of Public Opinion* (1828) was perfectly clear that the power of public opinion in a society 'resolves itself into the question whether such a community is possessed of an extensive middle class of society, when compared to the lower class.' Only an urban middle class combined sufficient numeric weight with the 'requisites for the formation of public

---

75 *Canada Inquirer*, 20 Sept. 1844, *Artisan*, 7 Dec. 1848, and *Provincial Freeman*, 25 Mar. 1854
76 Colin Read, *The Rising in Western Upper Canada, 1837–8* (Toronto: University of Toronto Press 1982), 172

opinion,' especially education, cosmopolitan experience, and access to information. MacKinnon, however, recognized how little sense this made 'in newly-colonised countries, where the settlers obtain land at will.' There, agriculture, rather than commerce and manufacturing, sustained the public sphere. Where land was cultivated by owner-occupiers, 'an extensive middle class rises up in a short time.'[77] Public opinion, established without a traditional urban middle class, was actually more powerful in such a society. MacKinnon retained the relationship between the middle class and public opinion, but if that class included actual and potential farmers as well as those involved in commerce, manufacturing, and the professions, much of the specificity of the term, and thus the utility of the class analysis, was lost.

By charting the rise of the *bourgeois* public sphere, Jürgen Habermas also appears to equate public opinion with a middle class. It is important, however, to distinguish between bourgeois as referring to a distinct social group or class and a post-feudal society (or post-frontier, in the case of Upper Canada) in which the mechanisms of the public sphere became possible.[78] Roads, canals, post offices, and other improvements in internal communications were often spearheaded by merchants and traders. Newspapers were, in part, supported by commercial advertising, many were one product of a larger printing enterprise, and most sold 'news' and opinion in a crowded market. The development of villages, towns, and cities helped to support a greater array of occupations, cultural endeavours, clubs, associations, and public spaces. Those with above-average financial means enjoyed greater access to some of these mechanisms and promoted their development, but they were not alone and neither defined themselves nor acted as a single, identifiable social class. The acknowledgment of public opinion also entailed a repudiation of the absolutism, cringing deference, and rigid hierarchy associated with 'feudal' society. It is tempting to refer to this political outlook – like a social and economic order capable of supporting the mechanisms of the public sphere – as 'bourgeois,' but this says little about the existence of a 'middle class' that invented, controlled, or disproportionately benefited from the public sphere.[79]

---

77 MacKinnon, *On the Rise, Progress and Present State of Public Opinion*, 1, 5, 15, 17–18, 22, 29–30n., 43n., 300, 329

78 Wahrman, *Imaging the Middle Class*, 193n.

79 Lynn Hunt, *Politics, Culture and Class in the French Revolution* (Berkeley: University of California Press 1984), 177

Finally, as the introduction pointed out, there was a certain symmetry between highly idealized forms of trade and public deliberation. Commerce was widely seen as a type of communication, a socially beneficial form of interaction based on reason and mutual interest. It broke through isolation, ignorance, and prejudice, substituting interdependence and an expanding community of interest for war, force, or fraud.[80] Commerce and the public sphere shared a belief that certain forms of competition could produce mutual advantage, that exchange rather than isolation was the motor of improvement, and that individuals, under certain conditions, could be equal, rational agents. Yet the terms by which such commercial exchange were celebrated were not necessarily extended to other forms of 'middle class' economic activity by bankers, professionals, or industrialists. Thus, as Terry Eagleton emphasizes, the public sphere can be seen as a kind of idealization of economic exchange among petty producers. Each was autonomous and could generate his own information and argument, allowing for 'exchange without domination.' The object was to persuade, not to control. The currency was rationality, not property. The outcome was mutually beneficial.[81] To repeat, this is not to say that only petty producers fully participated in the public sphere or that, by definition, their interests were favoured. Yet, to the extent that its resemblance to exchange among petty producers lent strength and plausibility to the public sphere, it was potentially stronger and certainly more plausible in Upper Canada than in much of Europe.

None of this, of course, denies that occupation, wealth, or social status (among numerous other things) influenced admission to the public sphere or the arguments and viewpoints pressed in it. The bookseller Henry Rowsell attended a 'Meeting of the Merchants of Toronto' at the Commercial News Room in December 1835 called 'for the purpose of ascertaining the general opinion' of a proposed American law removing the duty on British goods carried through the United States into Canada. The meeting concluded that it would be beneficial if the British government allowed British goods to enter Canada via New York duty-free, charging only the prevailing colony duty. Further, it 'resolved to call a general Meeting of the whole District ... to hear the matter more

---

80 See esp. Duncombe, 'Report on Education,' 292 and, more broadly, Daniel Gordon, *Citizens without Sovereignty: Equality and Sociability in French Thought, 1670–1789* (Princeton: Princeton University Press 1994), 71, 131, 155.
81 Terry Eagleton, *The Function of Criticism: From* The Spectator *to Post-Structuralism* (London: Verso 1984), 15, 26

fully discussed' and, if agreeable, to adopt and sign a petition to the British Parliament. The subsequent public meeting failed to proceed as the merchants had planned. According to Rowsell, the meeting was well attended, 'but the greater number were Mechanics and Labouring Men and they were in some way prejudiced against the measure and from their number were able to considerably out vote us and the Petition.' Unwilling to abandon their proposal, the minority determined to circulate a petition for signatures anyway.[82]

Toronto's 'merchants' advocated a response to proposed American legislation that they claimed would benefit the entire district. Since it was to advance the common interest and required parliamentary sanction, they had to submit their judgment to the ordeal of a public meeting, even though they had already spent an evening debating it amongst themselves. They proved unable to control the subsequent meeting and could not claim to speak for public opinion without its sanction. 'Mechanics and Laboring Men' were aware of the meeting, had an opinion on the issue, and felt entitled to attend the meeting, debate its resolutions, and determine their fate. Rowsell did not challenge their right to participate in the meeting and thus to help determine public opinion. For him, this was not an irreconcilable clash of economic interests in a zero-sum game. Rather, the majority, 'in some way prejudiced against the measure,' had failed to fully appreciate the proposals' merits. That majority undoubtedly saw things differently. Moreover, what precisely were the interests of merchants, mechanics, labouring men, or Toronto as a whole? How did any of those attending the meetings know? The merchants had not determined what was best until they had considered and debated the options. The mechanics and labouring men disagreed, having determined otherwise.

Interest is not some sort of brute social reality naturally adhering to occupation or economic circumstance, but, on public issues of any complexity, is itself constructed in the process of public debate (and is thus subject to error and modification).[83] Given the ambiguity of precisely

---

82 Toronto Reference Library, Baldwin Room, Henry Rowsell's Toronto Journal, 17 and 29 Dec. 1835

83 Keith Michael Baker, 'Introduction,' in *Inventing the French Revolution: Essays on French Political Culture in the Eighteenth Century* (Cambridge: Cambridge University Press 1990), 5–6. Thus it has proved extremely difficult to link political decisions such as participation in the rebellion to economic interests. See Douglas McCalla, *Planting the Province: The Economic History of Upper Canada, 1784–1870* (Toronto: University of Toronto Press 1993), 187–93.

who counted as a merchant, mechanic, or labouring man; relations among them based on other factors such as political persuasion, religion, or nationality; and the likelihood that at least some had been or expected to become members of other economic groups, the role of public debate in defining 'interests' was inescapable. Given a world of imperfect information and potentially competing ends, couldn't the well-meaning, even when they appear to us to have similar 'interests,' honestly disagree about the appropriate response to proposed changes in American trade legislation? Interests were being defined as well as advanced. How had each considered the issues? In light of what information, experience, and argument? Who had judged for the common good as best they could? Which side was right? Calling either the merchants alone or all who participated in the public meeting 'middle class' does little to help us answer these questions. The final chapter, a detailed case study of another policy question, returns to the thorny problem of the relationship between social process and the terms used to describe it; between interest and argument.

In the public sphere, numbers were to proceed from the strength of an argument, not the other way around. A position's status as public opinion rested on the concurrence of the relevant public in its merits. Thus, the merchant minority, unwilling to admit it was in error and thus unwilling to abandon its proposal, turned to another mechanism for testing public opinion, the circulation of a petition for signatures. The public debate would continue in the hopes of overcoming the 'prejudice' of others. In the meantime, only the merchant proposal and, in Rowsell's terms, the prejudice of mechanics and labourers existed. As yet, there was no public opinion. By the Metcalfe crisis (and in part because of it), there was no legitimate alternative to the mechanisms of public opinion for defining the common good. As part of that development, 'the people' – not some corporate estate or social class – had become the ultimate collective subject of a new constitutional order.

The Metcalfe crisis was a political and intellectual trial of the first order. Into the 1880s, Metcalfe served as a useful bogeyman for reformers.[84] With his disparate allies, he won the electoral battle in Upper Canada, but lost the conceptual war. Supporters of the Reform Association con-

---

84 Paul Romney, 'From Constitutionalism to Legalism: Trial by Jury, Responsible Government, and the Rule of Law in the Canadian Political Culture,' *Law and History Review* 7, no. 1 (Spring 1989), 157

soled themselves that many elected to support the governor were none-theless pledged to uphold the resolutions of 1841 on ministerial responsibility. Their election appeared to have been purchased at the price of prior principle.[85] The crisis demonstrated the inadequacy of the theory of mixed monarchy and corporatist social ideals. Neither offered an agreed-upon basis for constitutionalism in Upper Canada. The province retained its governor, legislative council, and assembly, but these institutions were disengaged from both the social imagery that gave them meaning and the constitutional theory that knit them into a coherent whole. Without a new constitutional paradigm, constitutional self-understanding would remain elusive.

Not surprisingly, it was the Metcalfe crisis that prompted Robert Baldwin to articulate a clear, federal view of the empire, Robert Baldwin Sullivan to make important strides towards a theory of political parties rooted in public opinion (discussed in chapter 7), and George Brown to bring the cabinet to the centre of institutional analysis. Each was developing and marketing the theory of parliamentary government. Some of their fellow-travellers from 1843–4 came to advocate an alternative grounded in a more robust reading of the power of public opinion and the equality promised by the Metcalfe crisis. Conservatives were left without a constitutional program. They had criticized the Reform Association's without offering much of an alternative beyond support for the current, already dying, governor. After the Metcalfe crisis, only three options remained: parliamentary government, populist democracy, and the checks and balances of American republicanism. Upper Canada's constitutional task for the next two decades was to choose. Mixed monarchy, or any other form of government that failed to assume political equality and the primacy of public opinion, had been knocked out of contention. The *Canadian Loyalist & Spirit of 1812* was surely right to conclude that 'we are become in every thing but name, a Republic.'[86]

---

85 E.g., *Victoria Chronicle* copied in *Niagara Argus*, 20 Nov. 1844
86 *Canadian Loyalist*, 30 Nov. 1843

CHAPTER VI

Publius of the North:
Tory Republicanism and
the American Constitution

In the second edition of his classic *The English Constitution* (1872), Walter Bagehot justified his preoccupation with comparisons of the British and American constitutions: 'The practical choice of first-rate nations is between the Presidential government and the Parliamentary; no State can be first-rate which is not a government by discussion, and those are the only two existing species of that government. It is between them that a nation which has to choose its government must choose.'[1] Bagehot had aptly, though unwittingly, described Upper Canada's constitutional position a quarter of a century earlier. The Metcalfe crisis had demonstrated the obsolescence of mixed monarchy and the necessity that its replacement be a form of government by discussion.

How to realize such a government was the overarching problem of Canadian constitutionalism from the election of a reform majority in 1848 to the Liberal-Conservative coalition of 1854. The Metcalfe crisis erased the older understanding of the provincial constitution, but produced no corresponding change in institutional form. Could government by discussion be achieved by infusing its principles into existing institutions or would new ones be required? Lord Metcalfe predicted that the subversion of mixed monarchy would result in 'either the Executive Council exercising undue interference over the House of Assembly,' or 'the House of Assembly exercising unlimited interference in the Executive Administration. It would be either a despotic and exclusive oligarchy, or an absolute unqualified democracy.'[2] His dire warning haunted the more perceptive colonial commentators, many of whom, both conserva-

---

1 Bagehot, 'Introduction to the Second Edition,' *The English Constitution*, 310
2 Metcalfe, reply to County of Russell, *Addresses Presented to His Excellency*, 138

tive and reform, struggled to fashion a constitutional order capable of escaping both fates. Ultimately, none was entirely successful.

The loss of the mixed-monarchy paradigm posed the greater challenge to conservatives. They had been its most vocal champions, the most hesitant about government by discussion. They had criticized responsible government as understood by the Reform Association without offering much of an alternative. Between 1849 and 1854, a significant minority met the challenge by advocating a package of substantial constitutional change that bears striking resemblance to the American Federalist project. Analogous circumstances propelled them along a path similar to that of the Federalists, but these conservatives were also well aware of and drew strength from their American forerunners.[3]

Often told, the history of conservatives in this period has been the story of their belated acceptance of responsible government.[4] Tory ideals went up in smoke with the parliament buildings in 1849. The passage of the Rebellion Losses Bill with the consent of the governor and the British parliament was the final, inescapable recognition of local self-government. It has been the story of Sir Allan MacNab's transformation from High Church Toryism to the politics of railroads and the emergence of John A. Macdonald as the undisputed leader of moderate conservatives in Upper Canada.

In fact, MacNab and Macdonald were among the least articulate conservative notables of the period. For others, such as John W. Gamble, William H. Boulton, Ogle Gowan, and Henry Sherwood, the period was not marked by a painful transition to responsible government but by the advocacy of an alternative – American republicanism. In essence, conservatives after the Metcalfe crisis faced the same questions as did the Federalists after the American Revolution. What were the social sources of conservatism in the 'new' world? Could stability be maintained in the absence of monarchy and aristocracy? If all power came from the people, how were

---

3 'Federalist' here refers to those who drafted and advocated the ratification of the constitution of 1787, not to the party that formed in opposition to Jeffersonian Republicans. Robert Vipond, 'Confederation and the Federal Principle,' in *Liberty & Community: Canadian Federalism and the Failure of the Constitution* (Albany: State University of New York Press 1991), chap. 2, argues that Upper Canadian reformers, during the Confederation debates, developed a view of federalism parallel to that of the Federalists, although they may have been unaware of the similarities.

4 E.g., Donald Creighton, *John A. Macdonald: The Young Politician* (Toronto: University of Toronto Press 1952) and Donald R. Beer, 'Toryism in Transition: Upper Canadian Conservative Leaders, 1836–1854,' *Ontario History* 80, no. 3 (September 1988), 207–25

property and authority to be protected from the passions and short-sight-edness of the mob? The Federalists contended that a new constitution ratified by the people, a strong federal union, an upper house elected on different principles from the lower, and an elective chief magistrate with extensive executive powers could meet these challenges. Democracy was unavoidable, but elective institutions could be fashioned to avoid its worst defects. Many of Upper Canada's most thoughtful and dynamic conservatives agreed. They considered a series of proposals: a written constitution ratified by the people, an elective legislative council and governor, British North American union, and imperial representation. Two generations of conservatives faced similar problems and offered similar solutions. Both implicitly and explicitly, Upper Canadian conservatives drew on the earlier Federalist experience and the constitution of 1787.

After independence, American state constitutions appeared as radically democratic because of the supremacy they gave to directly elected assemblies. Executive power was severely curtailed. Two states dispensed with a single chief magistrate altogether. In eight the governor was chosen by the legislature. While all states except Pennsylvania retained an upper house, they were directly elected by the people and proved ineffective. For the Federalists, the result was what Alexander Hamilton called 'impending anarchy.' Instability, international ridicule, interstate conflict, paper-money schemes, debtor legislation, interference with the judiciary, and a general concentration of powers ensued. 'An elective despotism,' Thomas Jefferson insisted, 'was not the government fought for.' The American Revolution rendered any thought of limited government in the form of the British mixture of monarchy, aristocracy, and democracy unthinkable. At its most basic, the Federalists' greatest achievement was to devise a system of democratic institutions that, while resting squaring on popular sovereignty, still encapsulated the benefits of the three classical forms of government. Sovereignty remained in one unified entity – the people – who, through a written constitution, delegated limited power to two levels of government and to separate institutions charged with executive, legislative, and judicial functions.[5]

---

5 My debt to Gordon S. Wood, *The Creation of the American Republic, 1776–1787* (New York: Norton 1972) is considerable. Samuel H. Beer, *To Make a Nation: The Rediscovery of American Federalism* (Cambridge, Mass.: Harvard University Press 1993) was also influential. For background see 'Introduction,' in Kramnick, ed., *Federalist Papers*. For Hamilton see *Federalist Papers*, XV, 146 and for Jefferson see *Notes on the State of Virginia*, in Kramnick, 'Introduction,' 25.

For Upper Canada's conservatives, the details were different but the problem was comparable. The Metcalfe crisis had marked the eclipse of the theory of mixed monarchy, while the formation of the Baldwin-LaFontaine Reform ministry in 1848 signalled an experiment with parliamentary government. As Lord Elgin warned the colonial secretary, Earl Grey, 'the working of the system of Government established in these Colonies is about to be subjected to a trial.'[6] According to Grey, parliamentary government, or what was more commonly referred to in Canada as responsible government, had come to require that 'the powers belonging to the Crown to be exercised through Ministers, who are held responsible for the manner in which they are used, who are expected to be members of the two Houses of Parliament, the proceedings of which they must be able generally to guide, and who are considered entitled to hold their offices only while they possess the confidence of Parliament, and more especially of the House of Commons.'[7] For colonial conservatives, this system was both too democratic and too tyrannical. It was too democratic because all power was assumed by the elected assembly. Governor and legislative council were unable to check the people's representatives effectively. It was tyrannical because ministers holding the confidence of the assembly could direct not only the governor and the upper house but the assembly itself.

As the *Toronto Independent* saw it, parliamentary government in Canada 'is at best a grand sham – a mock monarchy – a one-sided democracy. That it enables some half dozen men by patronage, fear, and corruption, to control the majority of the Lower House; to pack the Upper House, and humbug the Governor.'[8] Various forms of this critique were voiced by every conservative newspaper in Upper Canada.[9] The rise of the cabi-

---

6 Lord Elgin to Earl Grey, 5 Feb. and Grey to Elgin, 22 Mar. 1848, *Elgin-Grey Papers*, v. 1, 122–3, 125–7

7 Grey, *Parliamentary Government*, 4. Much of the conservative case against parliamentary government in Canada can also be found in Grey's final chapter, 'Parliamentary Government in the British Colonies,' 198–219.

8 *Independent*, 3 Apr. 1850

9 E.g., *British Colonist*, 30 Oct. 1849, *Amherstburg Courier* copied in *British Colonist*, 10 Sept. 1850, *Hamilton Spectator*, 21 June 1848 and 7 Feb. 1849, *Independent*, 27 Feb. 1850, Lincoln to W.H. Merritt, *Niagara Chronicle*, 19 Oct. 1848, *Patriot*, 5 Sept. 1851, and *Cobourg Star*, 2 Feb. 1848. There were also frequent complaints about corruption due to abuses of patronage and power, the expense of such corruption and the trappings of monarchy, the difficulties in applying the general precepts of responsible government to concrete cases, and the instability caused by doubts about the system's permanence. Given the loss of protection in British markets and the refusal of the British parliament to

net meant, as many had predicted, a new 'democratic oligarchy' dictating to governor, legislative council, and other members of the assembly.[10] Far from being responsible to public opinion, once a cabinet gained control of a parliamentary majority through its extensive patronage, it could ignore the people with impunity. As the *Hamilton Spectator* put it, 'The days of the Stuarts have returned upon us in a different shape. The Divine right of Kings has given place to the uncontrolled privileges of the People, with this simple difference, that the opinions of the people can only be expressed by the gentlemen who find their way to Parliament.'[11]

The critique was particularly prominent at the passage of the Rebellion Losses Bill. Conservatives' basic case against ministerial responsibility had changed little since the Metcalfe crisis, but dire predictions were confirmed by their reading of recent experience. As Allan MacNab put it, the cabinet 'had now however got possession of King, Lords and Commons.'[12] On the advice of his ministers, Elgin had created sufficient new legislative councillors to ensure the passage of the measure and had himself given it royal assent. The swamping of the upper house, the agreement of Elgin to a bill conservatives argued compensated, and thus legitimized, rebels, and the refusal of the British parliament to intervene meant that a Canadian ministry supported by a majority in the assembly was without limits.[13] Even worse, the elected assembly 'is pure despotism in the hands of Oligarchy, the worst of all Governments.'[14] Just how powerful and irresponsible that oligarchy had become was brought home when petitions for the disallowance of the 'Indemnity Bill' and for Elgin's recall – which, 'as an expression of public opinion cannot be mistaken' – were, nonetheless, without effect.[15] The legisla-

---

intervene against the Rebellion Losses Bill, one of the oldest conservative arguments against responsible government – that it was incompatible with empire – had virtually disappeared. Only an ultra-'Tory' commentator for the *Hamilton Spectator*, 25 Aug. 1849, bothered to mention it.

10 Address of the Central Committee of the British American League, *British Colonist*, 7 May 1850

11 *Hamilton Spectator*, 24 July 1850 and also *Niagara Chronicle*, 23 Aug. 1849

12 MacNab, *Debates*, 16 Feb. 1849, 764, 14 May 1849, 2294, and also *Hamilton Spectator*, 17 Mar. 1849.

13 See Phillip A. Buckner, *The Transition to Responsible Government: British Policy in British North America, 1815–1850* (Westport, Conn.: Greenwood Press 1985), 316 and Ged Martin, 'The Canadian Rebellion Losses Bill of 1849 in British Politics,' *Journal of Imperial and Commonwealth History* 6, no. 1 (October 1977), 3–22.

14 *Cobourg Star*, 6 June and 5 Sept. 1849

15 National Archives of Canada, Sir Allan MacNab Papers, Robert R. to MacNab, 31 May 1849

tive council and the governor had become 'mere *pageants* to make up a show.' 'They may still be ornamental; they have lost their use.'[16]

Parliamentary government operated differently in Canada than in Britain. Canada lacked an aristocracy, resident monarch, large landowners, and a dependent tenantry. Britain had a more restricted franchise and legislators with the wealth and independence to resist the blandishments of executive patronage. Such a social structure ensured a role for conservative-hierarchical principles even with the responsibility of the Queen's ministers to the House of Commons. In Canada, as in the United States, a relatively egalitarian social structure had resulted in unchecked democracy.

Upon his arrival in the colony, Lord Elgin was greeted by a pamphlet subtitled *On Responsible Government, as applied simply to the Province of Canada*. According to its author, the system in Britain was noted for 'its harmonious working,' but 'in Canada, all the evils that can spring from the system are to be met with, while few of its benefits are anywhere manifest.' Regardless of the party in office, Canada possessed 'none of the proper germs from which can spring the requisites necessary to the perfection of Responsible Government.'[17] The *Cobourg Star* admitted that England was a democracy, but it was one 'duly coerced by an adequate weight of aristocratic power, – constituting a government founded on the stability of the patrician, but invigorated by the activity of the plebian race.'[18] Conservatives repeatedly referred to Canada as a young country, lacking an upper class for leadership and to populate a Canadian House of Lords.[19] Perhaps recalling the debate during the Metcalfe crisis, 'A British Canadian' reminded readers of the *Hamilton Spectator* that 'there is in North America a very general feeling of repugnance to the growth and spread of Aristocracy, and this feeling is not confined to the people of the United States – it extends to Canada.' Another Hamilton paper judged responsible government a failure

---

16 *Hamilton Gazette*, 3 June 1850 and *British Colonist*, 3 Aug. 1849
17 Fuimus, *Letter to His Excellency*, 6–7, 10. For Fuimus the crucial social difference was Canada's lack of independent legislators – a lack also stressed by VOX, *British Whig*, 24 Feb. 1849, A British Canadian, *Hamilton Spectator*, 16 Feb. 1848, and Yorkshire, *Patriot*, 9 Jan. 1850.
18 *Cobourg Star*, 1 Mar. 1848. See also A British Canadian, *Hamilton Spectator*, 25 Aug. 1849 and *British Colonist*, 26 Aug. 1853.
19 E.g., A British Canadian, *Hamilton Spectator*, 4 Nov. 1848, *Quebec Mercury* copied in *British Colonist*, 8 Dec. 1848, P. Vankoughnet, *Minutes of ... the Second Convention*, 5 Nov. 1849, xxxvi, *Independent*, 27 Feb. 1850, and *Patriot*, 23 Jan. 1850

because of the 'present transitional state' of Canadian society.[20] Facing a social structure that worked against their ideals, conservatives became the institutional innovators of the 'new' world.

Many conservatives concluded that whatever the institutional similarity, Canada did not possess a transcript of the British constitution.[21] As one letter to the editor concluded, 'The elective principle seems indigenous to the American soil.'[22] This central axiom of Tocquevillian political science was echoed by the *British Colonist* when it concluded that 'political institutions will not bear transplanting.'[23] In a single phrase, the *Colonist* abandoned the fulcrum of Upper Canadian constitutional debate: that Upper Canada was to have 'the very image and transcript' of the British constitution as promised by its first lieutenant-governor.

Accepting reformers' reading of the political implications of a truncated society, another conservative concluded that he 'did not know that there was any part of the world in which there was more equality as to the position in life and circumstances of our existence than in this Colony. He contended that the tendencies of this community are as democratic as they can be.'[24] This social argument, originally the preserve of radicals, formed the basis of much conservative thinking after 1848. For some, it led to two related conclusions: first, that Upper Canada was and would remain a democracy, and, second, that the American system of government was a more relevant model than the British.

Not all conservatives accepted such a bold formulation of their thought, but most agreed that voting reformers out of office was no solution.[25]

---

20 A British Canadian, *Hamilton Spectator*, 24 Nov. 1849 and *Hamilton Gazette*, 19 and 23 Aug. and 13 Sept. 1852
21 E.g., A British Canadian, *Hamilton Spectator*, 4 Nov. 1848, *Independent*, 27 Feb. 1850, *British American*, 7 May 1852, Alpha, *Hamilton Spectator*, 28 Mar. 1849, and J.W. Gamble to the Yorkmills branch of the British American League, *British Colonist*, 29 Jan. 1850
22 VOX, *British Colonist*, 28 June 1850. See also A British Canadian, *Hamilton Spectator*, 24 Nov. 1848, *Independent*, 1 Nov. 1849, and Wilson (Quebec), *Minutes of the ... Second Convention*, 3 Nov. 1849, xxiv.
23 *British Colonist*, 16 Jan. and 26 Mar. 1852
24 McKenzie, *Minutes of the ... Second Convention*, 5 Nov. 1849, xxxviii
25 Except Miller and D'Arcy Boulton, *Minutes of the ... Second Convention*, 2 and 5 Nov. 1849, x and xxxvii–xxxviii. Conservative papers frequently charged reformers with perverting the constitution, but this rarely led to calls for measures to ensure electoral success under the existing constitution. Of course, those who resisted significant constitutional change implied that electoral means were adequate. See *Hamilton Spectator*, 9 Nov. 1850.

With the passage of the Rebellion Losses Bill and cries of 'French domination,' repeal of the union with Lower Canada was a common starting point.[26] Since it implied that responsible government would function effectively in a separate Upper Canada, repeal of the union was also inadequate.[27] A sense of crisis brought on by the cumulative impact of Britain's move to free trade, commercial depression, the European revolutions of 1848, political defeat, the swamping of the legislative council, the Rebellion Losses Bill, the burning of the parliament buildings, the annexation movement, and the rise of Grit radicalism forced something of a return to first principles. Thus, the *British Colonist* demanded 'a thorough *theoretical* investigation of our existing constitution ... [to] occasion the ultimate adoption of those wise checks and safeguards by which not only the present incumbents in office, but all their future successors should be deprived for ever of power to tyrannise.'[28] Political frustration combined with the logic of their arguments to drive many conservatives to a more ambitious and theoretically sophisticated constitutional agenda. Other conservatives might continue to criticize responsible government, but they offered little in its place.

Canvassing a number of options in the aftermath of the Rebellion Losses Bill, the *British American* thought 'one thing is certain, the country cannot remain as it is.'[29] Numerous conservatives began to cast about for some alternative political existence, including annexation to the United States, British North American union, imperial federation, and myriad changes to how laws were made and administered in Canada. Conservatives such as Henry Sherwood, John Strachan (son of the bishop of Toronto), J.W. Gamble, and William H. Boulton drafted new constitutions for Upper Canada. Criticizing reformers or responsible government was not enough.

The reform *Guelph Advertiser* divided its opponents into two camps: 'Liberal Conservatives' advocating constitutional change and 'old croakers' destined to drop 'into oblivion.' While the 'Liberal Conservatives'

---

26 RC, *Patriot*, 26 Feb., *Cobourg Star*, 4 Apr., *British Whig*, 21, 24, and 27 Mar. and 5 Apr., *Niagara Chronicle*, 23 Aug. 1849, and W.H. Boulton, *Debates*, 10 May 1849, 2238–9

27 This point was made explicitly by RC, *Patriot*, 26 Feb. and *British Whig*, 5 Apr. 1849. It also underpinned the *Patriot*'s support for the principle of double majority, 27 Jan. 1852.

28 *British Colonist*, 14 Aug. 1849. For the concept of a 'resort to first principles,' see Gerald Stourzh, *Alexander Hamilton and the Idea of Republican Government* (Stanford: Stanford University Press 1970), chap. 1.

29 *British American*, 7 and 14 July and also *Niagara Chronicle*, 23 Aug. 1849

included several legislators, they were more prominent in the conservative press than in the parliamentary party. In an article entitled 'Republican Tories,' George Brown's *Globe*, itself fending off constitutional
demands from fellow partisans, expressed sympathy for Sir Allan Mac-
Nab's organ, the *Hamilton Spectator*, as it tried to stem the tide of republicanism among fellow conservatives.[30] Upper Canada's political world had
fractured along new and interesting lines. The emergence of 'Republican Tories' was one result. Despite public antagonism among some of
their spokesmen, and the incidental or fragmented nature of many of
their writings and speeches, what emerged was remarkably coherent.[31]

Conservative proposals for constitutional change assumed Canadians'
right to frame their own constitution. Retroactively, the Act of Union
became an (unsuccessful) imperial imposition. The vague conventions
of an unwritten constitution could be replaced. Canada's relationship
with Britain was as much a matter for local self-determination as its constitution.[32] The various proposals were part of public debate in Upper
Canada, not attempts to persuade the Colonial Office. Constituent
power – sovereignty – lay with Upper Canadians, not in London.

While even annexationists acknowledged the formal requirement of
imperial sanction, politically, morally, and constitutionally these conservatives had accepted the existence of what the *Patriot* called the 'sovereign people.'[33] Thus, most conservative proposals included provisions

---

30 *Guelph Advertiser*, 24 Apr. 1851 and *Globe*, 21 Nov. 1850. Moderate reform papers (like
the *Brockville Recorder*, 10 May and 2 and 9 Aug. 1849) tended to question the sincerity
of conservative constitutional reformers. More radical reform organs (like the *North
American*, 21 May and 8 Nov. 1850) welcomed them as potential allies who demonstrated the inevitability of democratic progress. For the failure of these conservatives to
create an effective alliance with radical reformers, see Thompson, *Reminiscences*, 181.
The legislative focus of Paul G. Cornell, *The Alignment of Political Groups in Canada,
1841–1867* (Toronto: University of Toronto Press 1962), 29, 102–5, leaves conservatives,
other than W.H. Boulton, as an undifferentiated and rather shadowy category after
1848.

31 Beer, *To Make a Nation*, 219 makes a similar point about the Federalists.

32 *Independent*, 14 Nov. 1849 and 30 Jan. 1850, *British Whig*, 20 Jan. 1849, *Cobourg Star*,
21 Nov. 1849, Alpha, *Hamilton Spectator*, 28 Mar. 1849, H. Sherwood, *Debates*, 16 Mar.
1849, 1391–2, W.H. Boulton, *Debates*, 17, 24, and 28 June 1850, 606, 765, 881–2, and
resolutions for a convention, Sherwood and Boulton, *Debates*, 28 July 1851, 1068–70,
and O. Gowan, *Minutes of the ... Second Convention*, 3 Nov. 1849, xxiii: 'Let us not be
under the constitution which she [Britain] has dictated to us, but under the constitution which we approve of.'

33 *Patriot*, 12 Oct. 1853

for constituent assemblies or conventions to frame a new constitution. It was a radical mode of proceeding indeed. Previously, Robert Gourlay and William Lyon Mackenzie had been among the few to advocate some sort of convention. In response to Gourlay's efforts, province-wide meetings were prohibited, while Mackenzie's call for a convention was treated as tantamount to treason. The reaction could have been predicted. The creation of new popular bodies to assume legislative or constituent functions was a direct attack on the legitimacy of existing institutions. It questioned their ability to govern and their exclusive claims to represent 'the people.' The American invention of constitutional conventions assumed popular sovereignty. It asserted the primacy of a constitution over legislation and of citizens over legislators. It was a complete rejection of parliamentary sovereignty whereby institutions could be limited only by internal mechanisms, not higher man-made law. A few conservative proposals for a convention went on to incorporate ratification by direct popular vote following the precedent set by the 1780 Massachusetts state constitution.[34]

While most of these proposals called for either provincial or imperial legislation to authorize such a convention, in 1849 the British American League held two of its own.[35] Since the conventions were composed of elected delegates from supposedly non-partisan local associations, some implied that they could themselves frame a new constitution to be ratified by the electorate or the British parliament. Thus, during the first

34 Calls for a constituent convention were made by Sherwood, W.H. Boulton, and O. Gowan, *Debates*, 28 July 1851, 1068–70 and 13 May 1853, 3058–62 and by Alpha, *Hamilton Spectator*, 28 Mar. 1849. The *Independent*, 14 Nov. 1849 and J.W. Gamble, *Minutes of the ... Second Convention*, 1 Nov. 1849, 5 called for direct popular ratification. The *Independent* also adopted Jefferson's notion of constituent authority being exercised by each generation. For the importance of the idea of a convention in the American context see Beer, *To Make a Nation*, 346 and Stourzh, *Alexander Hamilton*, 60.

35 The League was formed in 1849 with local branches throughout Upper Canada and at Montreal and Quebec. The branches elected 150 delegates to the Kingston convention in July. The second convention, at Toronto in November, attracted significantly fewer delegates but was more radical in its agenda. To avoid open revolt over an elective legislative council, the question was referred back to local associations. See Chepas D. Allin, 'The British North American League, 1849,' Ontario Historical Society *Papers and Records* 13 (1915), 74–115, Gerald A. Hallowell, 'The Reaction of the Upper Canadian Tories to the Adversity of 1849: Annexation and the British American League,' *Ontario History* 63 (1971), 41–56, and W.N.T. Wylie, 'Toronto and the Montreal Annexation Crisis of 1849–1850: Ideologies and Considerations of Personal Gain,' MA thesis, Queen's University 1971.

convention at Kingston, Hugh Ruttan, editor of the *Cobourg Star*, boldly declared that 'the constitution under which Canada is living just now is a very bad one, and therefore, they had a perfect right to alter it, and they were met there for the express purpose of altering it.'[36] The *British Whig* denied the legitimacy of this meeting, but nonetheless called for a broader gathering of popular delegates, since 'a Convention might almost be considered as the Government ... Attention must be paid to the wishes and desires of a people, when constitutionally assembled.'[37] That such wishes could be authoritatively expressed outside legislative institutions was an American invention incompatible with British theory and practice. Reporting on the British American League, the reform *Mirror* concluded that, 'the right of the people to meet in solemn convention, and calmly, and unopposed by government, to discuss great fundamental questions of state, and national policy, has been confirmed.'[38] Disillusioned conservatives, not Gourlay or Mackenzie, smashed the prohibition on such extra-parliamentary bodies.

While continued membership in a monarchical empire limited explicit avowals, after 1848 there were few public denials of popular sovereignty from conservative organs except the *Hamilton Spectator*.[39] Conservatives opposed to constitutional change might still employ the language of mixed monarchy,[40] but as a viable alternative to responsible government it had few supporters. In advocating a hereditary peerage

---

36 Ruttan, *Globe*, 2 Aug. 1849. At the second convention Gamble made his plea for a convention and written constitution, while another delegate asserted 'the Constitutional right to alter the fundamental principles of the Constitution when circumstances required it.' Hamilton, *Minutes of the ... Second Convention*, 6 Nov. 1849, lix and Gamble, ibid., 3 Nov. 1849, 5, xix–xx

37 *British Whig*, 8 May 1849

38 *Mirror*, 9 Nov. 1849. For Britain, see T.M. Parssiren, 'Association, Convention, and Anti-Parliament in British Radical Politics, 1771–1848,' *English Historical Review* 88 (July 1973), 504–33.

39 For explicit rejections of popular sovereignty see A British Canadian, *Hamilton Spectator*, 15 Dec. 1849 and *Hamilton Spectator*, 9 Feb. 1850, and against conventions, ibid., 11 May 1850. A British Canadian also fought the ideas that democracy was inevitable in North America, that Canadians were capable of self-government, and that public opinion was absolute, 12 June 1850, 19 Feb., and 5 Mar. 1851. The *Patriot*, 6 Feb. 1850, also attacked Gamble's contention that monarchy itself rested on popular sovereignty.

40 See esp. the successful amendment at the first convention of the League against an elective legislative council, *Globe*, 31 July 1849: 'Devoted in their attachment to the principles of Monarchical Government, and revering the mixed form of Government established by the British Constitution ...' See also *Hamilton Gazette*, 10 May 1852 and A British Canadian, *Hamilton Spectator*, 25 Aug. and 17 Nov. 1849.

and a royal court for Canada, the *Hamilton Gazette* and *Spectator* mixed logical consistency with practical absurdity.[41] An older generation of conservative leaders, largely withdrawn from political life, might sound a similar note. In 1851 John Beverley Robinson predicted privately that although 'we shall have some years of coarse, vulgar democracy, enough to worry us in our time, our sons, or at least our grandsons will see the beginnings of a reconstruction of the social edifice ... after men have seen one fallacy after another in the democratic system exposed and have suffered enough from this mistake.'[42] Such patrician hopes were worse than useless in the rough-and-tumble world of Upper Canada's public sphere. Conservatives still engaged in electoral politics could not wait for nostalgia for old 'Tory' principles to appear. Instead, many began to cast about for an alternative. Ironically, Robinson himself had shown the way in 1839, pointing out that, compared to Lord Durham's recommendation of ministerial responsibility for the Canadas, 'the republican government of the United States would be strongly conservative.'[43]

Within a decade, rhetorical effect had become practical program. Most conservatives came to accept, like the Federalists before them, that their job was to manage a democratic society, not to create a monarchical one. Canada was self-governing; the task was to fashion institutions to make self-government safe. Many might have quoted John Dickenson at the Philadelphia Convention of 1787: 'A limited Monarchy he considered as one of the best Governments in the world. It was certain that equal blessings had never yet been derived from any of the republican form. A limited monarchy however was out of the question.' Time had passed it by.[44] Conservatives could choose between a grudging, scarcely articulated acceptance of parliamentary government and the advocacy of another form of democracy. The *British Colonist* plumped for the latter, for 'when you have made a step in the direction of democracy, the

---

41 *Hamilton Gazette*, 3 June 1852 and A British Canadian, *Hamilton Spectator*, 24 Nov. 1849. A colonial peerage was also advocated by the Bathurst District Branch of the British American League, *Patriot*, 19 Jan. 1850.

42 Robinson to Strachan, 8 Apr. 1851 in Patrick Brode, *Sir John Beverley Robinson: Bone and Sinew of the Compact* (Toronto: University of Toronto Press 1984), 273

43 National Archives of Canada, Grey Papers, v. 20, Robinson, confidential memo to Lord Normanby, 23 Feb. 1839, 9

44 *Records of the Federal Convention*, v. 1, 2 June 1787, 86–7. Even those who doubted the applicability of mixed monarchy to Canada praised its operation in Britain or retained it as an abstract ideal. E.g., *British American*, 7 May 1852 and *British Colonist*, 26 Aug. 1853

next best thing to do, is to find a suitable check, not to try to reverse the action taken.'[45]

The *Toronto Independent* found that check in the American constitution. As it told the monarchical *Hamilton Spectator*, 'If he be a true conservative, he should join with us and assist in introducing the more conservative principles of the American Government with as little delay as possible.'[46] As an annexationist, the *Independent* extolled the advantages of American republicanism over Canadian parliamentary government. Its editor, Hugh Willson, described himself as a 'moderate conservative'[47] and emphasized constitutional, rather than economic, reasons for annexation.[48] Canada had a democratic oligarchy rather than the British constitution. 'Canadians have waited long enough for the revelation of this new principle in politics, which is to produce a King and Lords.' The Federalists had already come to terms with the problem. 'We believe,' declared Willson, 'that a Republican form of government, surrounded and guarded by checks like those of the American States, is better than a badly regulated Colonial Democracy, divested of every Conservative principle.'

The American federal constitution was little more than the British constitution modified to the social circumstances of North America. Canada had the 'forms and resemblances' of the British constitution. The United States had the 'reality' and 'consequently have more of the conservative principles, essential to the vitality of all good governments: – that their systems, whilst they are eminently popular being based wholly on the people, afford such ample checks upon the Democracy, as effectually to prevent those demoralizing and disorganizing tendencies which unhappily for Canada, threaten to overturn the whole fabric of society.' That an 'eminently popular' government could check democratic excess, that it could be conservative, was the essence of the Federalist achievement.[49]

45 *British Colonist*, 28 Oct. 1853
46 *Independent*, 12 Dec. 1849
47 *Independent*, 25 Oct. 1849. Willson was also the secretary of the Toronto Annexation Society. The *Hamilton Spectator*, 5 Sept. 1849, noted Willson's conservative credentials with regret. Willson had frequently contributed to the *Spectator*.
48 *Independent*, 25 Oct., 21 Nov. 1849, and 2 Jan. 1850. For a reassessment of the annexation movement see Michael S. McCulloch, 'English Speaking Liberals in Canada East, 1840–1854,' PhD thesis, University of Ottawa 1985, 411–71.
49 *Independent*, 25 Oct. 1849, 27 Feb., 27 Mar., and 3 Apr. 1850

As another annexationist told the Literary Society of Dundas, annexation offered Canada something closer to the British constitution than it had managed within the empire. 'The sovereign people ... divests itself ... of its sovereignty, – and confers it upon chosen agents divided into three estates ... The people require that at certain intervals the power shall all revert to itself ... This system might not unaptly be called an elective limited monarchy.'[50] Annexation meant that Upper Canadians could frame their own state constitution while joining federal institutions designed to preserve conservative elements despite the democratic social structure of the 'new' world.[51]

The number of vocal conservative annexationists in Upper Canada was small, but the reaction of fellow conservatives is revealing. Even the *Hamilton Spectator* published a series of letters from 'Alpha' promoting a constitutional convention, pointing out the benefits of annexation, and praising American independence as an application of British principles.[52] Other conservative organs, such as the *Patriot, Cobourg Star,* and *British Colonist,* saw annexation as an understandable, if not preferred, response to just and widely shared complaints. The *British Colonist* concluded that the annexationists 'thought every remedy hopeless, which was consistent with allegiance, and in that we differ from them.'[53] Conservative annexationists wanted to replace parliamentary government with American republicanism by joining the union. A significantly larger number of conservatives wanted to do the same thing without joining the union.

One of the most prominent and thoughtful of these was John William Gamble, a local magistrate, 'Constitutionalist' member of the assembly elected in 1838, successful businessman, Loyalist descendant,

---

50 Dr Wraith, 'Address to the Literary Society of Dundas,' *Independent,* 2 Jan. 1850
51 *Independent,* 25 Oct. 1849 and 27 Mar. 1850. Willson rightly noted that in their state constitution, Canadians did not have to adopt universal suffrage or the election of officials and judges. An acceptance of popular sovereignty and an elective legislature and executive were all that were required by the guarantee in the 1787 constitution that each state of the union have a republican constitution.
52 Alpha, *Hamilton Spectator,* 28 Mar. and 4, 11, and 18 Apr. 1849. The *British Whig,* 16 Dec. 1848, 13 and 15 Oct. 1849, and 5 Feb. 1850, supported annexation for economic reasons but retreated when Earl Grey's despatch declaring Britain's intention to maintain the empire arrived in the province.
53 *British Colonist,* 30 Oct. and 4 Sept. 1849, Anglo-Canadian, *British Colonist,* 11 May 1849, *Cobourg Star,* 17 Oct. 1849, and *Patriot,* 5 July 1849

and High Church Anglican.[54] His constitutional program included neither annexation nor complete independence, but otherwise differed
little from that of conservative annexationists. Seeking election for the
First Riding of York, Gamble made his debt to the Federalists explicit:
'It was necessary to follow the same course which had been pursued by
the wise men who drew up the American Constitution.'[55] While unsuc-
cessfully opposed by a second conservative candidate who argued that
fully democratic institutions were incompatible with conservatism,
Gamble claimed to hold the same political principles as Allan Mac-
Nab.[56] He argued that only new institutions reflecting the progressive
and democratic nature of Upper Canada could implement them. British forms in Canada had resulted in cabinet dictatorship, tyranny of
the majority, instability, and party government. 'Compared with this,
are not the elective institutions, associated with those checks common
to the free republics of the United States, conservatism itself?' Thus,
the Federalists had 'preserved more of the spirit of the British constitution than we have in Canada.' Employing a distinction crucial to the
Federalists, Gamble advocated a federal union based on the 'concen-

---

54 *Examiner,* 8 Sept. 1852, referred to Gamble as 'the High Church republican.' See Barrie
    Dyster, 'Gamble, John William,' *Dictionary of Canadian Biography,* 10 (Toronto: Univer-
    sity of Toronto Press 1972), 299–300.
55 Gamble, *Patriot,* 9 Dec. 1851. Thus the *Examiner*'s attempt, 7 Nov. 1849, at ridicule fell a
    bit flat when it referred to Gamble as 'the Washington of a "peaceful revolution."' The
    following synthesis of Gamble's constitutionalism is from *Minutes of the ... Second Con-
    vention,* 1, 3, and 5 Nov. 1849, 4–6, xiv–xx, xlii–xliii, Gamble to the Yorkmills branch of
    the British American League, *British Colonist,* 29 Jan. 1850, his nomination speech to
    the First Riding of York, *Patriot,* 9 Dec. 1851, and his speeches on A.N. Morin's resolu-
    tions in favour of an elective legislative council, *Debates,* 13 and 28 May 1853, 3058–62
    and 3159–63. That Gamble repeated his program in 1853 counters interpretations that
    see such arguments as a temporary loss of faith in British forms from the shocks of
    1848–9.
56 Gamble won the 1851 election against the incumbent and prominent reformer James
    Hervey Price, a Clear Grit, and a second conservative candidate. 'A Friend to Conserva-
    tism,' *Patriot,* 21 Nov. 1851, also accused Gamble of being a democrat, but 'A Weston-
    ian' had already written to the *Patriot,* 2 Dec. 1850, that 'with regard to the charge
    brought against Mr. Gamble, as to a change in that gentleman's political creed, it may
    simply be remarked, that he is not alone among the Conservatives in that particular.'
    Interestingly, Gamble deserted the conservatives in 1856 when MacNab was manoeu-
    vred out of the premiership, repeating his critique of responsible government and call-
    ing for an elective, written constitution such that 'power would be placed in the hands
    of the three branches of the legislature, which at present was held by one.' *Debates,*
    29 May 1856, 2284–90

tration' of power in the people without its 'centralization' in any one institution. He would abandon the division of sovereignty in King, Lords, and Commons for the separation of legislative, executive, and judicial powers.

Thus, Gamble advocated a directly elected governor to protect minorities and check 'sudden ebullitions of popular feeling' with a legislative veto. 'Instead of prerogatives that cannot be exercised, I propose substituting defined powers.' A Canadian governor, like his American counterpart, would be willing to use the veto since it was directly delegated to him by the people. Gamble advocated an elective upper house on the same principle; the people were the sole source of authority. While Gamble actively supported the reform government's proposals for a directly elective legislative council in 1853, he was true to the American model by preferring indirect election by municipal councils.[57] Serving the same purpose as American states, these electoral bodies would mediate between the people and the upper house. They would 'filter' and 'refine' popular choices. Indirect election, a smaller number of members, and rotation would ensure the conservative character of an upper house. Again following the Federalists, the separation of powers would be preserved by barring office-holders from legislative bodies, by giving the upper house the power to ratify executive appointments, and by empowering two-thirds of the legislators to override the governor's veto. All of this required a written constitution, drafted by a specially elected convention and ratified by direct popular vote. Further checks could be achieved in a federal union of British North America. In short, a similar social structure made the United States the appropriate constitutional model for Upper Canada from within a common Anglo-Saxon heritage of 'civic freedom.'[58]

The argument was clever; perhaps too clever. Gamble's own Yorkmills branch of the British American League resolved that 'how Mr. Gamble can suppose that this evil [dominance by a democratic assembly] can be

---

57 For the 1852 Hincks-Morin resolutions regarding the legislative council, see the next chapter. As part of the deal with Hincksite reformers, a revised plan was implemented in 1856 by a government headed by Sir Allan MacNab and led in the assembly by John A. Macdonald.

58 Gamble argued that such a program would allow the conservative party to regain popular support. He favoured increased powers for local government and representation by population, and was willing to entertain the possibility of universal manhood suffrage. See *British Colonist*, 4 Aug. 1852 and *Debates*, 22 Feb. 1853, 1668, and 2 Mar. 1853, 1839. He is, however, best remembered for his advocacy of protective tariffs.

counteracted by making the Constitution more democratic we are at a loss to conceive.'[59] Other conservatives, like William Henry Boulton, the member for Toronto, were at no such loss. Gregory Kealey has rightly emphasized the role of leaders of the Orange Lodge, especially Boulton and Ogle Gowan, in pushing conservatives towards a more populist position.[60] Not only did leading Orangemen decide that British mixed monarchy was irrelevant, but, ironically (given the Lodge's association with British imperialism), they turned to American republicanism for an alternative to Britain's parliamentary system. In supporting a constitutional convention and elective legislative council, Boulton compared the constitutions of New York state and Canada, concluding that 'the one was a government of checks, the other a rampant democracy.'[61] He repeated these sentiments to Toronto voters during his successful bid for re-election in 1851.[62] Given its different social environment, Boulton announced that 'there was nothing in the English system that was applicable to our state.' Facing the same problem, Americans had adopted a constitution of checks and balances, proving the 'wisdom and sagacity of those who framed it.'[63]

Speaking to the House two years later, Boulton quoted James Madison from the *Federalist Papers*, Montesquieu, and Thomas Jefferson on the need for a separation of powers to prevent tyranny. After surveying the experience of several American states, Boulton concluded that good government required a second legislative chamber and that only popular election could give legitimacy to such a body in North America. A smaller number in the upper house would mean larger constituencies that could be won only by prominent men transcending parochial interests and perspectives. With longer tenure, these men would act as a conservative check upon the lower house. At the same time, Boulton

---

59 *Patriot,* 6 Feb. 1850
60 Gregory Kealey, 'Orangemen and the Corporation: The Politics of Class during the Union of the Canadas,' in Victor L. Russell, ed., *Forging a Consensus: Historical Essays on Toronto* (Toronto: University of Toronto Press 1984), 62. Leading conservative republicans appear to have shared little in terms of religious denomination, nationality, or economic experience to account for their constitutional theorizing or to differentiate them from other conservatives.
61 Boulton, *Debates,* 3 June 1850, 377
62 Boulton's nomination speech, *Patriot,* 2 Dec. 1851. Boulton was re-elected with thirty more votes than fellow conservative Henry Sherwood, who criticized the extent of Boulton's proposals.
63 Boulton, *Debates,* 21 May, 3 and 17 June 1850, 77, 376–7, 606, 765–6, 769–70

advanced the case for an 'independent Governor' capable of taking responsibility for his own actions.[64]

Boulton presented the House with a draft constitution in June 1850: a mixture of the American federal and New York state constitutions. The legislative council was to be elective and given the power to approve executive and judicial appointments. Office-holders were barred from the legislature. The governor and his lieutenant were to be appointed for life or elected by the people. The governor was entrusted with executive powers and could veto legislation within ten days. His veto could be overridden by two-thirds majorities in both houses. Other provisions, such as the office of lieutenant-governor, impeachment, and fixed elections, were modelled on the American federal constitution, while provisions on legal reform and retrenchment were copied from New York state.[65]

Since they were 'republican in nature,' the *Hamilton Spectator* refused to analyse Boulton's proposals, but its Toronto correspondent conceded that 'sooner or later the elective principle which they embody will be carried out.'[66] The *Patriot*, the leading conservative organ in Toronto, took them more seriously. In the course of devoting most of its commentary to those aspects it rejected, it laid down two general principles: '1st. That the whole of the Judiciary and Executive must be more or less *independent* of the People *directly*. 2nd. – That all other officers, responsible to, and paid by the people, through their various councils, &c., must be removable by, or in other words, dependent upon those bodies.'[67] These principles emphasized the separation of executive and legislative functions (rather than three separate legislative estates), underpinned the *Patriot*'s support for an elective upper house, and left open the possibility of indirect election for other powers by subordinate bodies or electoral colleges.

The *Cobourg Star*, one of the more ultra-conservative voices during the Metcalfe crisis, had gone further. 'Where the source of political power is vested in the people at large, the institutions of government, both Executive and Legislative must originate from, and rest upon the same

---

64 Ibid., 8 Oct. 1852, 930–4. Boulton was not present for the remainder of the session, having been unseated for failing to meet the property qualification. Earlier, he had advocated the abolition of property qualifications as unsuited to a democracy.

65 The resolution is printed in *Debates*, 24 June 1850, 789–95.

66 *Hamilton Spectator*, 29 June and 3 July 1850

67 *Patriot*, 16 July and also 27 Mar. 1850

source, in order to act as checks, real efficient checks, the one on the other.'[68] Checks and balances, not British forms, were key. In September 1849 the *Star* advocated an upper house elected by provincial assemblies in a federal union of British North America, but by early November was calling for a directly elected Canadian upper house. An editorial near the end of the month concluded that Canada was a 'purely democratic community' where stability and the public good could only be achieved by a directly elected governor and legislative council and a suffrage extended to 'the whole permanent taxpaying community.'[69]

Much of the debate about elective institutions occurred in connection with the British American League. At its first convention a minority favoured an elective legislative council, but were defeated by an ambiguous motion endorsing monarchical government. The majority, including John A. Macdonald, adopted a platform of retrenchment, British North American union, and tariff protection.[70] At the second convention of the League, about half the delegates were in favour of at least an elective legislative council, with two of its leaders, John Gamble and Ogle Gowan, pushing further. Gowan demanded a settled constitution, an elective legislative council, and any other reform 'to leave nothing in the neighbouring Republic for us to envy.'[71] After his report, the Elizabethtown branch resolved in favour of household suffrage and an elective governor, legislative council, and local officers. Nearby, the Brockville branch endorsed an elective governor and legislative council. Gowan's organ, the *Brockville Statesman*, continued to advocate elective institutions, while he made his constitutional agenda an integral part of his 1851 election campaign in Leeds.[72]

Confronted by the Elizabethtown and Brockville resolutions, conser-

---

68 *Cobourg Star*, 20 Mar. 1850
69 *Cobourg Star*, 5 Sept., 7 and 21 Nov., and 19 Dec. 1849, and 20 Mar. 1850
70 For the majority and their resolution on an elective legislative council see notes 35 and
    40 above. Macdonald was an enthusiastic supporter of the first convention as a means
    to create 'an economic movement' that would avoid constitutional matters. Mac-
    donald to David Barker Stevenson, *Papers of the Prime Ministers*, 5 July 1849, 155
71 Gowan, *Minutes of the ... Second Convention*, 2, 3, and 5 Nov. 1849, ix, xxiii, xxxi
72 On the *Statesman*, see copied articles in *Patriot*, 5 Jan. 1850, and *Guelph Advertiser*,
    24 Apr. 1851, and for Gowan's election speech at Coleman's Corners, see *Brockville
    Recorder*, 20 Nov. 1851. His support for elective officials was rare among conservatives
    but, like the Grits, he saw it as a way to reduce the ability of the cabinet to build a
    majority by patronage. By mid-1852, Gowan was exercising editorial control over the
    Patriot, Toronto's leading conservative organ.

vatives opposed to constitutional change abandoned the League. Ironically, the *Hamilton Spectator* thought that, compared to such resolutions, 'the well balanced constitution of the United States is Conservative and practically Monarchical.'[73] The League's first historian concludes that a majority of the branches resolved in favour of the elective principle, but newspaper accounts suggest otherwise.[74] The question was, however, debated by conservatives throughout Upper Canada, with a significant minority advocating a variety of constitutional reforms. In a public letter, Stuart Easton Mackechnie, leading industrialist and future mayor of Cobourg, declared that 'in a community so purely democratic as ourselves, we will never obey any authority in the Province not of our own choosing.'[75] The Haldimand branch of the League proceeded to elect Mackechnie as its representative.

A federal union of British North America was, like the separation of powers, an attempt to check democratic excess without denying democracy itself. From 1849, union had widespread conservative support. It was a central plank of the British American League and was advocated by such party organs as the *Cobourg Star, Patriot, British Colonist, British American,* and *St Catharines Constitutional.* Henry Sherwood, former attorney-general and contender for party leader, published a detailed draft constitution.[76]

Arguments in favour of union touched on themes of commerce and

---

73 *Hamilton Spectator,* 15 Dec. 1849. The *Patriot,* 12 Dec. 1849, thought an elective governor was too radical a proposal. Its endorsement would not only end any broader support for the League, but would encourage annexation as well.

74 Allin, 'The British North American League,' 111. *Examiner,* 16 Jan. 1850, also argued that the majority of the branches had declared in favour of the elective principle. There is direct evidence that besides the Elizabethtown and Brockville branches, the Montreal, Peterborough, Lloydtown, Oakland, and Haldimand branches resolved in favour of at least an elective legislative council. The Hamilton, Richmond Hill, Wolford, Dereham, East Flamboro, Trafalgar, and Bathurst District branches resolved against introducing the elective principle with varying degrees of vehemence. The *Patriot* claimed that all nine branches in the Gore District, all but one in the Brock District, and most in the London and Niagara Districts opposed the elective principle. For resolutions see *Hamilton Gazette,* 27 Dec. 1849, *Hamilton Spectator,* 8 Dec. 1849, *Patriot,* 5, 9, 19, 23, and 30 Jan. and 9, 13, and 20 Feb. 1850, and *Cobourg Star,* 9 Jan. 1850.

75 Mackechnie to the Haldimand branch, *Patriot,* 20 Feb. 1850

76 The *Patriot* initially supported a legislative union, but most schemes were for a federal union. Federalism was central to the idea rather than merely a pragmatic accommodation of regional diversity.

defence as well as illusions of transcontinental grandeur and international stature, but constitutional concerns dominated. Inter-colonial union would solve constitutional problems within *Upper* Canada itself. Sherwood's proposed constitution was preoccupied with institutional structures at both levels. Scant attention was paid to the federal division of powers.[77] Federalism would submerge Lower Canada in a larger English polity and recreate a distinct Upper Canada, but it would also provide another check, create a larger scope for the ambitious, break down local particularism, and destroy existing factions.

Checking the excesses of elective assemblies and providing greater stages for the ambitious were among the aims of proposals for inter-colonial union developed earlier by American Loyalists and Upper Canadian conservatives, and studied by Peter J. Smith.[78] By supporting union, 'Tory republicans' could draw on long-standing aspects of colonial conservatism and gain the support of colleagues hostile to further constitutional change. Continuity should not, however, be overemphasized. Earlier conservative proposals were intended to resist democratic tendencies by creating a more monarchical government and a more hierarchical social structure. Conservative republicans looked to the American model and advocated inter-colonial union because they accepted popular sovereignty and believed that a relatively egalitarian social structure was irreversible. Their republicanism was almost exclusively institutional (that is, concerned mechanisms for structuring democracy without ministerial responsibility) and was born of specific political circumstances and concerns. It was not a re-articulation of strands of civic humanism surviving from the eighteenth century.

In 1849, Hugh Ruttan argued that federal union would promote a number of ends: 'justice,' 'domestic tranquility,' and 'defence.' While he made no mention of the United States, Ruttan's list was almost identical to that of the preamble to the American federal constitution.[79]

---

77 Sherwood wanted to give the new British North American level the powers necessary to create and manage a national economy while, following the American constitution, reserving all other powers 'for peace, welfare, and good government' to the provinces.

78 Peter J. Smith, 'The Ideological Origins of Canadian Confederation,' *Canadian Journal of Political Science* 20, no. 1 (March 1987), 3–29 and 'The Dream of Political Union: Loyalism, Toryism and the Federal Idea in Pre-Confederation Canada,' in Ged Martin, ed., *The Causes of Canadian Confederation* (Fredericton: Acadiensis Press 1990), 148–71

79 'We the people of the United States, in Order to form a more perfect Union, establish justice, insure domestic tranquility, provide for the common defence, promote the general Welfare, and secure the Blessings of Liberty ...'

Likewise, his description of justice as 'the great end of all Governments' is a close paraphrase of the formulation in *The Federalist Papers*, no. 51, where Madison discussed the relationship between the separation of powers and federalism – Ruttan's topic as well. For both, justice would be served because federalism and checks and balances would prevent the exercise of arbitrary power by any single individual or institution. Further regarding justice, the Sherwood draft copied the American constitution's protection for the rule of law in the form of special status for *habeas corpus* and prohibitions on bills of attainder and *ex post facto* legislation. While Sherwood suggested an appointed viceroy as the independent head of the executive, much of his draft was an exact replica of the American separation of powers, including a Supreme Court, elective provincial upper houses, and a federal upper house elected in equal numbers by provincial assemblies.[80]

Ruttan's second end, 'domestic tranquility,' was to be achieved by destroying local factions. Smaller units of government were more concentrated; representatives were closer to the people and were preoccupied with local or parochial interests; demagogues could operate more effectively; and the legislature was dominated by factions. In short, smaller units of government were more democratic. Larger units contained more potential representatives to choose from, 'lessen[ing],' as the *Patriot* put it, 'the proportion of representation' to people,[81] and created forums for the discussion of more general, or 'higher,' issues. As a reader told the *British Colonist*, union offered 'the prospect of a termination to the present system of cliques ... The narrow strides of our present political arena would be merged in the wider field.'[82] Sherwood spoke for many conservatives when he argued that 'hitherto the exertions of public men have been confined within the limits of contracted localities ... A more extended stage for action should be afforded to them.'[83] Seats at the higher level would attract the right sort of candidate and mould them into statesmen, rather than local politicians or demagogues who appealed to divisive passions and interests.

As Ruttan himself put it, 'Factions are more violent in small than in

---

80 Sherwood, *Federative Union*
81 *Patriot*, 29 Mar. 1849
82 Cleander, *British Colonist*, 13 May 1851
83 Sherwood, *Federative Union* (1851), 8. See also Cleander, *British Colonist*, 13 May 1851, Fuimus, *Letter to His Excellency*, 12, H. Sherwood, *Debates*, 3 June 1850, 370, and Strachan, *Minutes of the ... Second Convention*, 6 Nov. 1849, xlviii–xlix.

large communities,' and were there 'even more dangerous and enfee-
bling ... A Federal Government is calculated to disarm the violence of
domestic faction by its superior influence, and to diminish the exciting
causes and leave fewer chances of success to their operations.' After discussing the contribution of union to defence and commerce, Ruttan
concluded that 'a Federal Constitution aims at these ends by the
arrangements and distributions of its powers, by the introduction of
checks and balances in all its departments; by making the existence of
the Provincial Government an essential part of its own organization; by
leaving them the management of all local affairs, and at the same time
by drawing to itself those powers only which concern the common good
of all ... The blessings of liberty secured by the federal government are
far more certain, more various and most extensive than they would be
under their own distinct independent sovereignties.'[84] While a few conservatives might support union simply to swamp French Canada,[85]
many, including John Strachan, son of the bishop of Toronto, supported elective institutions for a federal union they rejected for Canada
alone.[86] Such a union would also allow the adoption of the American
model of a senate indirectly elected by provincial or state assemblies.
The senate would protect the people from a concentration of power in
the executive and the provinces from concentration at the centre.[87]
Many of these arguments were the same for conservative annexationists,
since annexation was little more than federal union with American
states rather than with other British colonies.[88]

George Duggan, a major proponent of federal union in the British
American League, talked of creating a 'great nation' and 'a united

---

84 *Cobourg Star*, 1 Aug. 1849 copied in *Hamilton Spectator*, 4 Aug. 1849. Aspects of the argu-
    ment were repeated in the *Star*, 15 Aug., 5 Sept., and 17 Oct. 1849. Notice again how
    similar Ruttan's phrasing 'the blessings of liberty secured' is to the preamble to the
    American constitution. Upper Canadians appear here closer to the arguments of Alex-
    ander Hamilton than to those of James Madison. Both thought that union would destroy
    local factions but Madison relied on creating a greater plurality of interests and thus
    making the formation of majorities on anything but the public interest more difficult.
85 Col. Playfair, *Minutes of the ... Second Convention*, 5 Nov. 1849, xliv. The Dereham branch
    of the League also supported union without elective institutions, *Patriot*, 19 Jan. 1850.
86 Rolland MacDonald, VanKoughnet, and D'Arcy Boulton, *Minutes of the ... Second Con-
    vention*, 5 Nov. 1849, xxxii, xxv–xxvi, xxxvii and Strachan, 6 Nov. 1849, 20, xlviii–xlix
87 Support for an elective federal senate included *British Colonist*, 20 Nov. 1849 and
    Patriot, 27 Mar. 1850 and 8 Aug. 1851.
88 E.g., *Independent*, 27 Mar. 1850 and Col. Prince's widely copied letter to Arthur Rankin
    supporting Canadian independence, *Independent*, 6 Mar. 1850.

people.'[89] The political assimilation of French Canadians was only one aspect. Ending party, local, ethnic, and regional divisions were others. Through political and commercial interchange, union would help create a 'common interest' and give concrete expression to a politically homogenous nation – a people capable of self-government.

Conservative proposals that assumed popular sovereignty and advocated elective institutions had inescapable implications for the British Empire. The overwhelming majority of conservatives supported neither annexation nor immediate independence, but, as William Boulton put it, 'it was absurd to expect to maintain the connection by crying loyalty, and shouting hurra[h] for the Queen.'[90] Indeed, for those supporting substantial constitutional change, the major stumbling block to electing the governor was his position as the only formal link to empire, not as some sort of surrogate Canadian monarch.[91] Monarchy had once stood at the centre of conservative thought. Through the exercise of power by British governors and the imperial state, monarchy had presented itself as a vital force in the local government of the colony. Monarchy had also stood at the pinnacle of a providential and hierarchical society, serving as a means of conceptualizing authority and sovereignty within the colony itself. After 1848, most conservatives retained a cultural commitment to a member of the British royal family as the hereditary head of the empire, but monarchy no longer served as a primary means of organizing either the image or reality of Upper Canada's political and social structure.

---

89 Duggan to the British American League, *Globe*, 2 Aug. 1849. Similar phrases reoccurred in the address of the Central Committee of the British American League, *British Colonist*, 7 May 1850.

90 Boulton, *Debates*, 3 June 1850, 377

91 E.g., when discussing the possibility of a governor popularly elected or appointed for life, the only criticism the *Patriot* offered of the former was that 'the unity of the Empire could hardly be preserved.' It said nothing about monarchy or even about the dangers of an elective chief magistrate it perceived after the 1848 American presidential elections; *Patriot*, 16 July 1850 and 7 Jan. 1848. The constant complaint that Elgin had proved powerless and useless was an implicit rejection of symbolic monarchy. Little wonder several found the American model more congenial. The *British Whig*, 2 May 1849, called for the abolition of the office: 'What is Royal authority in this province but a mere pageant ...?' Agricola, *British Colonist*, 6 Apr. 1850, had doubts about the American model, but thought that talk of an elective governor was a waste of time since Britain would refuse out of 'national pride.' None of this amounted to a defence of monarchy.

While this was also true for Upper Canadian reformers and conservatives who accepted parliamentary government, those conservatives who wanted to create checks, particularly along American lines, needed to disentangle the governor's role of imperial officer from that of head of the local executive in ways that were compatible with both local sovereignty and empire. Sherwood's option of a viceroy was his alone.[92] Imperial federation was the only logical solution. Indeed, Hugh Willson advocated independence followed by annexation only after his motion that imperial representation was a necessary part of inter-colonial union was defeated at the first convention of the British American League.[93]

The concept of the empire as a federation had been developed by North American colonists during the 1760s and 1770s in response to metropolitan attempts to strength the role of the British parliament in the colonies. Robert Baldwin used the concept effectively during the Metcalfe crisis to advocate unfettered local self-government without total independence from Britain. Reformers, however, were generally wary of the related idea of colonial representation at Westminster, since it might consolidate the empire and undermine the case for an Upper Canadian constitution responsible to local opinion. Upper Canadian conservatives had occasionally considered colonial representation to strengthen jurisdictional and cultural ties to Britain.[94]

Such proposals were revived after 1848, but were now shaped by an acceptance of Canada as a self-governing entity where sovereignty resided in its own population. Representation in the British parliament would perpetuate the empire on the increasingly narrow range of 'imperial' issues. It was not intended to extend Britain's residual constitutional role in Upper Canada. Sherwood's plan for federal union gave the empire exclusive jurisdiction over defence and foreign affairs, but explicitly denied it any role in all other matters. Imperial representation

---

92 But see also P.S. Hamilton of Nova Scotia, who, in 1864, advocated a hereditary viceroy for British North America since, without a stable executive, 'our political institutions are essentially republican.' In Smith, 'Ideological Origins,' 21–2

93 Willson, *Globe*, 2 Aug. 1849. See also the first issue of the *Independent*, 25 Oct. 1849. For context see Ged Martin, 'Empire, Federation and Imperial Parliamentary Union, 1820–1870,' *Historical Journal* 16, no. 1 (1973), 65–92.

94 Jack P. Greene, *Peripheries and Center: Constitutional Development in the Extended Polities of the British Empire and the United States, 1607–1788* (Athens: University of Georgia Press 1986), 91 and 103. For Baldwin, see *Globe*, 25 Sept. 1844 and the previous chapter. For an earlier discussion of colonial representation in the conservative press, see the essays in the *Kingston Chronicle* beginning 3 Sept. 1831.

would retain the connection in a manner consistent with Canadian popular sovereignty. Even with its greatly diminished jurisdiction, the empire could be a real force in North America only if it was democratic.

Thus, once the governor was hamstrung by local advisers, a range of conservative commentators agreed on the desirability of imperial federation, but the connection of this constitutional reform to others was evident.[95] As Stuart Easton Mackechnie put it, 'With Imperial Representation we would be much better off were we to elect our own Governor.' Likewise, the *Cobourg Star*, while advancing Canadians' right to frame their own democratic constitution, argued that only elective representation at Westminster could maintain the imperial tie.[96]

The most comprehensive and theoretical exposition of the case for colonial representation appeared in thirteen lengthy and widely copied essays in Ogle Gowan's *Patriot*. Drawing lessons from Greek, Roman, British, and American history and from French, Swiss, American, Scottish, and English philosophers, the essays argued that Canadians had 'the *natural* and *inherent right* to be heard' in the councils of the empire. Sounding much like American Whigs before the Revolution, the essays asked, 'What principle of the British Constitution dictates obedience to those laws, by Britons who have no voice in their imposition?' Advanced colonies were 'Independent Sovereignties' demanding representation in London on the same principle that gave American states representation in Washington. As the last essay concluded, 'We do not ask Separation, but we demand Equality.'[97]

From 1791, Canadian constitutional discourse had been clouded by a confusion of the three constitutions at issue: the British, the Canadian, and the imperial. Conservative constitutional reformers did much to clear away the conceptual tangle. The British constitution as expressed

---

95 *Niagara Chronicle*, 25 Oct. 1849, *Hamilton Gazette*, 26 Apr. and 19 Aug. 1852, and the Bathurst District of the British American League (*Patriot*, 19 Jan. 1850), advocated elected colonial representation without further constitutional changes.

96 Mackechnie, *Patriot*, 20 Feb. 1850 and *Cobourg Star*, 12 Dec. 1849. Other supporters of elected imperial representation as part of a broader package included Strachan, *Minutes of the ... Second Convention*, 5 Nov. 1849, 20, Cleander, *British Colonist*, 13 May 1851, and *British Whig*, 12 Feb. 1850.

97 The essays, 'Colonial Representation,' appeared in the *Weekly Patriot* from 30 June to 22 September 1852. Like British North American Union, colonial representation would also create higher positions for the ambitious to aspire to and help to create a community of interest transcending local divisions.

in the institutions and procedures at Westminster could not be replicated in Canada. Canada's constitution had to be an application of the principles of good government to its own circumstances. Likewise, the imperial constitution was distinct from the constitutions of its constituent (and now equal) parts. The British constitution was a model praised throughout the world but it was not the only one. In the tradition of the comparative science of politics, conservative constitutional reformers searched for the best form of good government based on their experience in Canada.[98] What these conservatives (and the more radical reformers discussed in the next chapter) offered was a fully made-in-Canada constitution that, like its American counterpart, could have become a potent symbol of national purpose. The price of their failure is still being paid.

With their party in disarray, a significant and vocal minority of conservatives found the best model in American republicanism. They stressed the degree to which its institutions were derived from Britain and were a better approximation of British principles than was Canadian responsible government. They also pointed to the elective colonial constitutions of seventeenth-century Rhode Island and Connecticut. Their emphasis on the 'British-ness' of their proposals is hardly surprising. More striking is their willingness to be explicit about their debt to the American Federalists in the face of charges of disloyalty, closet annexationism, and opportunism.

Yet these conservatives did not delude themselves. What they advocated may have been the closest approximation to mixed monarchy possible in North America, but it was profoundly different; not a mixture of the three classical forms of government or the balancing of social estates, but an institutional structure for democracy and 'the people.' With nothing to mix with the latter, mixed government was irrelevant. As the first chapter pointed out, the separation of powers and checks and balances among them had often found a subordinate place in the theory of mixed or balanced government, but they now emerged as independent principles able to define limited government on their own. Thus, the American Federalist project as advocated in Upper Canada rested on the basic assumption that the people were capable of governing themselves. Conservative institutional engineers hoped to attract

---

98 As noted in chapter 1, the conservative *Royal Standard*, 19 Nov. 1836, listed the *Federalist Papers* as one of three works on the science of politics that might have shed light on the controversy between Sir Francis Bond Head and his former advisers.

the ablest to political institutions that, in turn, were designed to promote statesmanship, but these institutions did not embody the virtues
and vices of separate social estates or classes. In their plans for an effective upper house, for example, they did not seek to create a new social
class or the rule of the virtuous few, but a chamber of sober second
thought.[99] Mixed monarchy's corporatist vision had been jettisoned.

Rather than corporate social bodies, incompatible interests, or political principles that required special representation, these conservatives
had adopted 'government by discussion' as the premise of good government. American republicanism was more capable of achieving good
government based on public opinion than was ministerial responsibility.
Thus, the *Patriot* framed its demands for elective imperial representation in terms of being 'heard' and having 'voice.' Such constitutional
changes, if they were to be permanent and effective, had to be 'well considered, to approve themselves to the judgement of the community at
large, and to be pursued with a general feeling in their favor.' The British American League sought a constitutional convention precisely
because it would be 'an arena where the advocates of every shade of
conflicting opinion can assemble and contend for their particular views
... Then when the arguments have been duly weighed, the vote taken,
the decision had, each must submit to the thus expressed opinion of the
whole, and adopt it as the voice of his country.'[100]

Institutional reform was driven by the same principle. Appointed by
the cabinet, the legislative council was a rubber stamp. It was useless, not
because it lacked power but because it did not deliberate – it did not
debate proposed legislation and act accordingly. Even the assembly was
not a true deliberative chamber. The power and patronage of the ministry ensured its compliance rather than an independent assessment of
the merits of ministerial proposals. Removing office-holders, giving
the power of appointment to a separate executive, and destroying local
factions would transform the lower house into a deliberative chamber. Finally, the governor, as the puppet of his ministers, voiced their
opinions rather than acting upon his own. Checks and balances would

---

99 See M.J.C. Vile, *Constitutionalism and the Separation of Powers* (Oxford: Oxford Univer-
    sity Press 1967), 98, Jack N. Rakove, *Original Meanings: Politics and Ideas in the Making of
    the Constitution* (New York: Vintage Books 1997), 276–7, and Beer, *To Make a Nation*,
    285.
100 *Niagara Chronicle*, 23 Aug. 1849 and Address of the Central Committee of the British
    American League, *British Colonist*, 7 May 1850

prevent the concentration of power and ensure that any decision arising from such a process of deliberation approximated the common good. A single representative body might get swept along by 'popular clamour,' but multiple institutions or centres of power could be designed to act collectively as a barometer of the public's more settled convictions.

Even the desire to assimilate French Canada politically must be seen in these terms. Repeal of the union, annexation to the United States, and British North American union all offered Upper Canadians escape from 'French domination' – a prerequisite for government by discussion. French Canadians were not ready for such a government; they 'never progress' and were preoccupied with 'bitter prejudices and silly dreams of Nationality,' 'bigoted,' and held in a 'species of vassalage' to their church, a feudal land system, and political demagogues.[101] As the *St Catharines Constitutional* put it, they were 'too ignorant to judge for themselves, and slavishly submissive to their leaders.' Although different in tone and intent, *rouge* commentators in Lower Canada made similar points about the constraints on French Canadian public opinion as part of their own program for political and constitutional reform.[102] Upper Canadian conservatives agreed that such fetters worked against the best interests of French Canadians, but were far more concerned about their tendency to create a solid bloc of votes in the united assembly based on the claims of nationality rather than political principle, 'whilst the British inhabitants, following the example of all really free governments, are divided into parties entertaining quite distinct and opposite opinions upon important public questions.' With the addition of only a minority from Upper Canada, such a bloc ensured a subservient majority in the assembly and 'by this means public opinion is disregarded.'[103] French Canadian nationalism, as understood in Upper Canada, was incompatible with government by discussion in either its parliamentary or republican form.

---

101 Anglo-Canadian, *British Colonist*, 11 May, *British American*, 14 July, *Cobourg Star*, 4 Apr., A British Canadian, *Hamilton Spectator*, 16 Feb. 1849, *Cornwall Constitutional*, 20 Mar. 1851, *Address of the Hamilton Branch of the British American League*, 4, and P.B. DeBlaquiere to Henry Sherwood, *British Colonist*, 31 Dec. 1850. This political critique of French Canada was the diffusion of one made during the Metcalfe crisis by Nemo, *London Herald*, 21 and 28 Jan. 1843.

102 *St Catharines Constitutional*, 25 June 1851 and Jacques Monet, *The Last Cannon Shot: A Study of French-Canadian Nationalism, 1837–1850* (Toronto: University of Toronto Press 1969), 366–74

103 *Address of the Hamilton Branch*, 4

While conservatives borrowed freely from the American model, they were not slavish. Different circumstances meant that they were much less concerned than the Federalists had been about 'interests,' the militia, foreign influence, and property. Moreover, they did not propose transplanting mechanisms, such as the electoral college, that had failed to function as anticipated. As well, they did not propose importing the first ten amendments to the American federal constitution, the Bill of Rights. More important, they focused on the institutional forms advocated by the Federalists. Conservatives had traditionally singled out universal suffrage, the ballot, and frequent elections as the roots of the republic's problems. In the debates surveyed here, the ballot was a peripheral issue, the legislative terms suggested were substantially longer than those found in much of the United States, and most conservatives either favoured the existing franchise or supported only gradual and partial extensions. Just as these conservatives thought that the British model was not entirely appropriate, neither was the American.

After 1848, many conservatives advocated a form of the well-balanced republic of Washington and Adams, with which the Loyalists had been familiar, and not the later mobocracy of Jackson and Van Buren.[104] By the mid-1850s, John Strachan, bishop of Toronto, once one of mixed monarchy's greatest champions, preferred British ministerial government to American republicanism because the latter 'has deteriorated since Washington's time.' Far from the system of checks portrayed by conservative republicans, it now 'has no safety valves.' An American administration, regardless of its merits or behaviour, could not be politically removed from office except at fixed quadrennial elections. Furthermore, the likelihood of electing an administration worthy of such secure tenure had diminished since America now had 'no public opinion of a sedate & conservative character.' By comparison, a British cabinet could be changed without an election and elections, if needed, could be held whenever the Crown or the people's representatives thought expedient.[105] For Strachan, those, like his son, who sought institutional safety valves in the 1850s should look to the British, not the

---

104 The earlier connection is well documented by Jane Errington and George Rawlyk, 'The Loyalist-Federalist Alliance of Upper Canada,' *American Journal of Canadian Studies* 14, no. 2 (1984), 157–76. The constitutional distinction between the presidencies of Washington and Jackson is also central to Vipond, *Liberty & Community*, chap. 2.

105 National Archives of Canada, William Hamilton Merritt Papers, Strachan to Merritt, 16 May 1856, v. 26, 4599

American, constitution. Those enamoured with the eighteenth-century republic of Washington ignored its subsequent history at their peril.

Conservative republicans never fully confronted the question of why, once Canada had adopted many of the institutions of the Federalist period, it too would not degenerate into the widely reviled mobocracy inaugurated by Andrew Jackson's presidency. Would a more restricted franchise, longer terms of office, and open voting be sufficient to sustain the Federalist project in Canada? Could conservatives successfully defend such mechanisms after the adoption of republican institutions? Such questions were never really asked. Perhaps part of an answer can be found in the reaction of one Upper Canadian newspaper to *Rule and Misrule of the English in America* (1851) by Thomas Haliburton, Nova Scotia's most prominent, though not its only, conservative admirer of the American separation of powers. Haliburton argued that responsible government had destroyed governors and legislative councils in British America and, with similar social structures, only American Federalists offered a viable conservative alternative.[106] At the conclusion of its laudatory review, the *British Colonist* mused that 'the trouble is to establish monarchical institutions, without a king or aristocracy, among a people who have predilections that way.'[107] Canadians were not Americans and had learnt from the history of the republic. Ironically, the Federalist dream of a well-balanced compound republic would succeed in Canada, albeit in modified form, where it had failed in the United States. When, during the *Confederation Debates*, none other than John A. Macdonald declared that the American constitution was 'one of the most skillful works which human intelligence ever created; is one of the most perfect organizations that ever governed a free people,' he was, as we have seen, expressing a degree of discrimination about the principles and forms of good government that had marked Upper Canadian conservatism from the beginning.[108]

After the Metcalfe crisis, constitutional questions in Upper Canada revolved around the appropriateness of competing institutions to realize government by discussion. A vocal minority of Upper Canadian conservatives turned to the American Federalists to help formulate an

106 For other Nova Scotian conservatives see note 92 above and Kenneth G. Pryke, *Nova Scotia and Confederation, 1864–74* (Toronto: University of Toronto Press 1979), x, 12.
107 *British Colonist*, 16 Jan. 1852
108 *Confederation Debates*, Macdonald, 6 Feb. 1865, 43

alternative to responsible government. Balance among potentially con-flicting institutions was still valued, even if that meant forsaking the Brit-ish model. By accepting the reformers' premise of popular government resting on a relatively egalitarian social structure, conservative constitu-tional reformers helped to narrow ideological divisions. They were also an important part of the coalition that passed legislation in 1854 to cre-ate an elective legislative council. Their adoption of American forms may have prompted other conservatives to accept parliamentary govern-ment as the lesser of two evils. The return of conservatives to office, something that had appeared almost unthinkable in 1848–9, removed the political pressure behind critical self-examination. The parliamen-tary leadership of MacNab and Macdonald further obscured the ideas and contribution of their colleagues.

American republicanism was an alternative not taken. The sense of crisis that prompted it faded. The opportunity, seized by conservative republicans and by the radical reformers discussed in the next chapter, was lost. Nonetheless, Upper Canadians, both conservatives and reform-ers, settled on parliamentary government not from lack of an alternative or serious reflection, or from some sort of innate conservatism or blind devotion to all things British, but because most came to accept it as the best institutional means to reflect political equality, popular sovereignty, and government by discussion. Although not ultimately successful, 'Tory republicans' proved to be conservatives first and monarchists second; Canadians first and Britons second; and more thoughtful and discerning than they have been given credit for.

CHAPTER VII

Mistaking 'the shadow for the substance': Laying the Foundations of Parliamentary Government

The aftermath of the Metcalfe crisis appeared more promising for Upper Canada's reformers than for its conservatives. The theory of mixed monarchy was abandoned, but reformers were already working on alternatives. They came up short during the 1844 election battle in Upper Canada, but won the conceptual war. Electoral victory followed four years later, offering reformers the opportunity to implement their constitutional principles. They were thus forced to define, articulate, and defend those principles – a process that revealed major fault lines and helped shatter their unity at the moment of their greatest triumph.

As we have just seen, the need to replace mixed monarchy led some conservatives to favour the checks and balances of republicanism. Simultaneously, reformers advocated the other two options: parliamentary government (which eventually most conservatives also came to endorse) and a more directly elective or delegate-style democracy. Reformers were a larger and more diverse group than conservative republicans. They lacked some of the coherence the latter gained as an oppositional minority developing its constitutional program along the lines of a shared historical source – the Federalists. Reformers had to implement, not just formulate, new constitutional principles. Specific issues provided the occasions and context for the articulation and defence of those principles: the future of the legislative council, the power of the cabinet, the relationship between partisan patronage and public service, the cohesiveness of political parties, and the appropriate basis for representation and the franchise. As each is surveyed in turn, two important themes emerge. First, all were framed by the concept of public opinion. Time and again, constitutional arguments turned on the promise and limits of government by discussion. Second, while

Upper Canadians came to accept parliamentary government, its reform advocates failed to articulate fully or defend successfully some of its foundational principles. The victory of responsible government remained partial, the shadow mistaken for the substance.

For reformers, electoral victory in 1848 was the culmination of 'the long, the arduous, and the sometimes almost hopeless struggle for establishing Responsible Government in its integrity.' Lord Metcalfe's constitutional principles were swept aside with his narrow majority in the assembly. Non-interference in the 1848 election by his successor, Lord Elgin, ensured that 'the voice of the people was truly expressed' – and that expression was an unequivocal verdict in favour of responsible government.[1] Those who had clung tenaciously to their faith in the power of public reason had been rewarded. Those who had refused to retreat from the oppositional politics of 'public opinion,' even when faced with the violence of rebellion or the electoral setback of 1844, had been vindicated. The outcome of the subsequent election, as Dror Wahrman says of parallel developments in Britain, provided 'the necessary proof that this longed-for constitutional arbitration mechanism actually *worked.*'[2]

Self-congratulation lasted longer than unanimity. The meaning of responsible government proved harder to read than the election returns. Some of the fellow travellers from the Metcalfe crisis quickly grew disillusioned. The promises of a government responsible to public opinion proved easier to make than fulfil. Lord Elgin's appointment of a reform-party administration concluded a chapter of 'the struggle for responsible government,' but the story was far from over.

Nonetheless, the meaning of key terms in which that story was narrated shifted. The story was still structured around two antagonists, but rather than monarchy and democracy they were parliamentary government and republicanism. Earlier, republicanism had often been synonymous with democracy: a system of government where all power came from 'the people' directly or indirectly. A narrower definition now eclipsed this usage. Republicanism, as evident from the previous chap-

---

1 *Guelph & Galt Advertiser*, 28 Jan. 1848 and *Examiner*, 9 Feb. 1848. See also *Globe*, 5 Jan. 1848, *Provincialist*, 18 Jan. 1848, and Robert Baldwin, *Debates*, 3 Mar. 1848, 185.
2 Dror Wahrman, 'Public Opinion, Violence and the Limits of Constitutional Politics,' in James Vernon, ed., *Re-reading the Constitution: New Narratives in the Political History of England's Long Nineteenth Century* (Cambridge: Cambridge University Press 1996), 119

ter, now referred to a particular form of democracy where the executive and legislative branches of government were elective and separate. Parliamentary government was a competing form of democracy where, at its crudest, the executive was a committee of those (mostly elected) legislators supported by the majority of their colleagues.

The definition of monarchical government also shifted. It no longer referred to three separate legislative branches or to a mixture of three forms of government. Occasionally the British constitution might still be referred to as 'well-balanced,' but references to 'King, Lords, and Commons,' once ubiquitous, were now noticeably rare.[3] Monarchy no longer meant that there was something unelected or undemocratic about lawmaking. Its meaning shrunk to little more than a cultural commitment to a hereditary and symbolic head of state from the British royal family. As the *Whitby Reporter* explained, 'Monarchy ... is separable from all the forms of accidents with which we have been accustomed to see it associated.' The *St Catharines Journal* was equally confident that governing for the Crown rather than the people had dwindled into 'a constitutional and legal fiction.'[4] An appointed judiciary or a property qualification for holding public office were tagged 'monarchical' to distinguish them from 'republican' or American alternatives. They could just as easily have been called 'parliamentary.'[5] Britain and the United States continued to represent twin contenders in the constitutional narrative, but they were now competing models of the same form of government – democracy.

The leader of the new government in Upper Canada, Robert Baldwin, still maintained that 'between the two systems – Monarchical and Republican ... there was not a mere formal difference.' Fortunately, the discrepancy was 'altogether in our favour.' Baldwin was contrasting ministerial responsibility with the American separation of powers, not undergoing the late conversion to pre-rebellion conservatism that some suspected. Monarchical meant parliamentary. Baldwin favoured parliamentary government because, unlike with American republicanism, the

---

3 See *Mirror*, 9 Sept. 1853, *Globe*, 6 Sept. 1848, and *Cobourg Courier* copied in *Mirror*, 25 Feb. 1848. For references to King, Lords, and Commons among reformers see *Globe*, 21 Mar. 1849, *Examiner*, 11 Oct. 1848, and 'John Galt,' *Huron Signal*, 21 July 1848.

4 *Whitby Reporter*, 15 June 1850: 'Loyalty is the homage of a nation to a ruler whose acts are the embodiment of the public will; it cares nothing for the name by which he is known'; and *St Catharines Journal*, 11 Sept. 1851.

5 E.g., *Globe*, 23 Aug. 1849 and 23 Mar. 1850.

people's representatives could remove the executive at any time.[6] He preferred what he persisted in calling 'monarchical' because it made the executive more responsive to the people's will. It was more democratic than republicanism.

The constitutional point dividing moderate reformers, like Baldwin, from their more radical colleagues, the so-called Grits, was essentially whether or not parliamentary government was as democratic as Baldwin claimed. He insisted on the distinction between parliamentary and republican government because commentators of all descriptions minimized it. Since both were forms of democracy, constitutional debates now centred on the best institutional means to achieve the same ends as judged by utilitarian standards. The narrative of epic struggle between monarchy and republicanism as two antagonistic world-views had already concluded.

George Brown and his *Globe*, two powerful voices for parliamentary government, held that Canada was 'as free as any country in the world,' and like Baldwin, insisted that Canada was more democratic than the United States.[7] Declarations of popular sovereignty and democratic self-government, once boldly revolutionary, quickly became matter-of-fact platitudes.[8] Moderate reformers stressed the democratic nature of the British constitution to ensure its continued relevance to Canada. Radicals stressed its democratic nature to underscore the point that the question was now a pragmatic one about means and techniques.[9] 'Which is best for us?' asked Reformator, the name under which Charles Clarke wrote numerous essays trying to define a radical reform program. 'Under whatever name a government may exist – whether democracy, republic, or monarchy – one grand principle is acknowledged, and that is the right of the people to govern themselves.' Likewise, the *Bathurst Courier* asserted that '*even* under a limited monarchy such as

6 Baldwin, *Debates*, 3 June 1850, 372–5
7 *Globe*, 25 Sept. 1847, 15 Apr. 1848, 17 Nov. 1849, 7 Nov. 1850, 13 Apr. 1852, and 21 Mar. 1855. See also James Hervey Price, *Globe*, 18 Dec. 1849 and *St Catharines Journal*, 25 Oct. 1849, 21 Mar. 1850, and 25 May 1854.
8 See *Examiner*, 9 May 1849 and 19 Apr. 1854, *Brockville Recorder*, 22 Nov. 1849 and 29 Jan. 1852, *Mirror*, 9 May 1850, *Huron Signal*, 15 Nov. 1849, and Dunbar Ross, *Debates*, 24 June 1850, 787.
9 Francis Hincks, *Debates*, 24 Jan. 1849, 199, *Brockville Recorder*, 1 Aug. 1850, *Bathurst Courier*, 12 Aug. 1851 and 8 Sept. 1854, and *Provincialist*, 29 Mar. 1849. The same end could be pursued by emphasizing the British origins of American republicanism; *Mirror*, 22 Oct. 1852.

ours (whose tendency however is towards Republicanism), the voice of the people is all-powerful.'[10]

For the *Courier*, public opinion – the 'voice of the people' – had become omnipotent. Prior to the rebellion, Upper Canada had suffered under 'irresponsible government' – a case study of 'the effects of power on men who riot in the intoxication of perfect freedom from the controul of public opinion.'[11] Such freedom was no longer possible. First and foremost, then, responsible government was government responsible to public opinion. The concept was no longer contested and rather than being an external force impinging upon government was an integral component of it – what the *Examiner* thought 'the most reliable part of the constitution.'[12] Reform newspapers were replete with repetitious declarations of the power and justice of public opinion. They were certain of its ultimate triumph and its status as the only foundation for free government.[13] One measured the worthiness of a constitution by its responsiveness to public opinion.

Yoking government so closely to the public sphere imposed heavy responsibilities on ordinary Upper Canadians. Greater deliberation of public questions was among 'the natural consequences of the possession of Responsible Government. Hitherto men have fought for the right to be heard – that right has been granted, and now they tell their wants.' Responsible government was the 'right to be heard.' Established in 1848 for 'the youth of both sexes, ... mechanics in general, domestic servants, and such other persons whose circumstances bar them' from more expensive periodicals, the *Artisan* contended that 'the rapid extension of the democratic principle in our form of Government, requires that our people be intelligent and virtuous.' To think and act independently, 'the people must read, reflect upon and discuss among themselves.' Others urged every male 'to acquaint himself,' 'to watch,' 'to observe,'

---

10 Reformator, *Mirror*, 19 Oct. 1849 and *Bathurst Courier* copied in *North American*, 9 Oct. 1850. See Kenneth C. Dewar, 'Charles Clarke's "Reformator": Early Victorian Radicalism in Upper Canada,' *Ontario History* 78, no. 3 (September 1986), 233–52.

11 Publicola to Lord Elgin, *Examiner*, 6 Oct. 1847. Sir Francis Head's contention, cited in chapter 4, that leaders should make public opinion follow them rather than follow it was explicitly dismissed by the *Mirror*, 31 Oct. 1851.

12 *Examiner*, 11 Jan. 1854

13 E.g., *Huron Signal*, 4 Feb. 1848, *Globe*, 23 Feb. 1848, A., *Examiner*, 28 Apr. 1847, *Examiner*, 21 Mar. 1849 and 9 July 1851, *Bathurst Courier*, 17 June 1851 and 19 Nov. 1852, and John Rolph, *Debates*, 27 Aug. 1852, 155.

and to 'point out' desirable measures to his representative. 'Every one should read about these subjects, *think* about them ... *every man should be a politician.*'[14]

Some singled out new political associations or newspapers like the *Artisan*; others called for more public meetings and petitions. Their point was the same – 'with the dawn of Responsible Government in Canada, was commenced the study of its science by the mass of the people ... They are learning that to obtain and keep a good government for the majority, they must apply themselves to a vigorous and constant investigation of all the propositions that come before them.'[15] As noted in the first chapter, the science of politics was democratized. The *Huron Signal*, published at Goderich in the recently developed Huron Tract, worried that the public sphere was not yet sufficiently robust to sustain government by discussion. Sheer distance and being 'removed from towns, from circulating libraries, and even from intelligent society' remained obstacles. The *Signal* consoled itself that newspapers were cheaper and more readily available in Upper Canada than in Britain and that post offices were 'pretty thickly established.' In areas of earlier settlement, commentators were more sanguine. According to a reader of Brockville's reform newspaper, the majority of Upper Canadians 'read and consequently reflect more than in days gone by, and must now have the why's and wherefore's before moving in or approving of any great change.'[16] Sustained extra-parliamentary activity was essential to parliamentary government.

To mark its eighth anniversary, the *Globe* celebrated the recent growth of the provincial press. By its count, there had been only 34 newspapers in Upper Canada in 1844; in 1852 there were 77. Most were larger and published more frequently. Assuming an average subscription list of 800 and multiple readers for each copy, the *Globe* calculated that there were 'about 600,000 users of [domestic] newspapers out of a population of 950,000.' An English visitor in 1854 concluded that 'a workman would as soon think of depriving himself of his breakfast as of his morning journal.'[17] The precise validity of these observations is perhaps less impor-

---

14 *Artisan*, 12 Oct. and 7 Dec. 1848 and *Bathurst Courier*, 16 Apr. 1852
15 *Brockville Recorder*, 8 Nov. 1849. See also O.P., *Brockville Recorder*, 6 Dec. 1849, *Globe*, 19 Apr. 1848, *Canadian Freeman*, 22 Nov. 1848, *Provincialist*, 8 Nov. 1849, and An Elector, *Port Hope Watchman*, 28 Nov. 1851.
16 *Huron Signal*, 4 Feb. 1848 and Leeds, *Brockville Recorder*, 27 Dec. 1849
17 *Globe*, 8 Apr. 1852 and Bird, *English Woman in America*, 317

tant than the conviction that the reading public was so large and inclusive.

The period was also one of expanding library facilities, often explicitly justified by the belief in the necessary connection between reading and the increasing duties and privileges of colonial citizenship. In 1850, municipalities were empowered to levy taxes to supplement a provincial grant in support of local public libraries. The initial response was overwhelming. Between 1853 and 1856, 289 libraries with 1000 branches placed orders for tens of thousands of books. A further 1703 Sunday school and subscription libraries contained well over 300,000 volumes.[18] For contemporaries, the public sphere was now an established fact. With responsible government, it assumed its appropriate function: the authoritative tribunal of public men and measures. Every 'man' could be his own politician because every man was his own reader.

Reformers frequently situated this transformation within a broader progressive narrative – the history of the Western world's struggle for liberty. The *Globe* was specific about the stages by which Upper Canada had joined the ranks of free nations. In the first, the 'hardy pioneer of the forest' was largely isolated from government. The structure of government developed during the second stage, but corrupt and self-interested placemen oppressed a people still too preoccupied with daily survival. Nonetheless, the second stage spawned the very forces that would destroy it. 'A new stage is foreshadowed, by a rising public opinion, a bolder tone in the public press, a deeper interest in public affairs.' The rise of the public sphere ushered in the third stage, where 'all matters affecting the common weal are determined at the bar of public opinion ... and the fact becomes impressed on every mind that there is but one class, THE PEOPLE – who entrust certain authority to men from among themselves to carry out *their* wishes.' The Metcalfe crisis 'thoroughly woke up the people. Constitutional questions were the topics of the day ... Lord Metcalfe's attempts to overturn self-government, advanced the Liberal cause ten years; the people were forced to learn their own power.'[19] Here was the *Globe*'s cheery version of the transformation charted in previous chapters: the development of the concept of public opinion, its impact on constitutional theory, the elim-

---

18 Bruce Curtis, '"Littery Merit," and "Useful Knowledge," and the Organization of Township Libraries in Canada West, 1840–1860,' *Ontario History* 78, no. 4 (December 1986), 286, 288, 293, 296–8
19 *Globe*, 19 Apr. 1848

ination of all social classes from politics except 'the people,' and the
role of the Metcalfe crisis as a crucible for these forces.

Reformers like Robert Baldwin and the *Globe* contended that British parliamentary government best expressed this transformation. By placing
the province in the last of its three stages, the *Globe* tried to close the
province's constitutional narrative. After the climax of the Metcalfe crisis, public opinion was ascendant. The struggle was over. The story had
reached its final, happy, ending. As we shall see, other reformers
insisted on a more open, on-going narrative, convinced that barriers to
the popular will persisted, that the power and mechanisms of public
opinion would continue to evolve, and that other political institutions
and practices might better reflect its assumptions and conclusions.[20]
Reformers were united, however, on the standard by which to judge
such constitutional mechanisms. For its supporters, the parliamentary
system was superior to other forms of representative government
because it better reflected the assumptions of the public sphere; it better embodied government by discussion.

Accordingly, in Earl Grey's *Parliamentary Government* (1858) the system's principal advantages were tied to open deliberation. First, the
executive, as a committee of the legislature, was constantly subjected to
the 'ordeal of free discussion' in the very body that created and could
destroy it. Second, because it selected the executive, parliament was 'the
arena in which the contest [for power] is mainly carried on. Its debates
are the means by which rival parties chiefly seek to recommend themselves to the House itself and to the Public.' Electing the executive by
direct popular vote would only encourage flattery and appeals to popular passions. Third, since the visible contest for power took the form of
the public use of reason, parliamentary government 'has tended to raise
these contests above those of a mere selfish or personal character ... and
though the practice of politicians has fallen lamentably short of their
theory, the habit of Parliamentary debates ... has tended to raise by
degrees the standard to which men are expected to conform in public
life.' Finally, these debates 'instruct the Nation.' 'If men's passions and
feelings were not so much excited by political struggles, it is not likely
they would read, as they do, the debates in parliament in which these
subjects are discussed, and in which, amidst all the trash and sophistry

20 On attempts to conclude constitutional narratives, see James Vernon, 'Notes towards
an Introduction,' in Vernon, ed., *Re-reading the Constitution,* 16.

that disfigure them, the keen encounter of intellects seldom fails in the
end to lead to the discovery of truth and to the triumph of sound reason
over error.'[21]

For Grey and its Canadian supporters, parliamentary government
best infused existing institutions with the principles of the public
sphere. Indeed, they were practically meaningless without those principles. Public deliberation selected legislators and determined society's
wants and wishes. In turn, those legislators formed an electoral college
for the executive, scrutinized that executive in an open forum, and further informed public debate through their published deliberations. Tyranny was avoided by a series of checks, not between multiple branches
of government, but between the cabinet and the assembly and between
the assembly and the people.

The governor and legislative council no longer figured prominently.
'England might to-morrow lapse into Republicanism,' thought the
Toronto Mirror, 'and unless in the neighbourhood of Whitehall, the
change would scarcely be perceptible. Her Lordly Commoners, and her
Common Lords might amalgamate, and nothing but the Herald's office
would be abolished, or a little change of dress be apparent at the opening of Parliament ... As to the Monarchy, nothing would be required but
a little shortening of robes of State, and the substitution of a plain Straw
bonnet for an expensive and very unmeaning *Crown*.'[22] Canada, without
monarch or nobles, was even more obviously republican. The governor's power (as opposed to his moral influence) was often described as
'nominal.'[23] What, asked the *Provincialist*, 'is that high personage any
thing more than an individual, if not formally elected, at least fairly
approved of by the people to personify, represent, or embody the will of
the nation?'[24] He was certainly not a coordinate branch of government.

The legislative council shared his demotion. Robert Baldwin rejected
proposals for restructuring the council, because it was now 'so acted
upon by public opinion, that it would not oppose the popular will.' The
council had a new, if clearly subordinate, function in government by dis-

---

21 Grey, *Parliamentary Government*, 16–35. Bagehot's better known *The English Constitution*
    (1867) should be interpreted in this context as well.
22 *Mirror*, 31 Mar. 1848
23 See *Examiner*, 9 May 1849, *North American*, 28 May 1850, and more generally, *Globe*,
    30 Jan. 1847, 31 Oct. 1850, and 17 Oct. 1854 and *Mirror*, 9 May 1850. As with the 'Tory
    republicans,' the debate between an appointive or elective governor hinged on his role
    as imperial representative, not surrogate Canadian monarch.
24 *Provincialist*, 4 Oct. 1849

cussion: 'it might not be prepared to pass every measure immediately – it might be necessary that the people should discuss some subjects more fully, and express their views more decidedly, before they would move.'[25] Others found the council useless or offensive. Upper Canadians did not have to wait for Walter Bagehot's *The English Constitution* (1867) to distinguish between the 'dignified' and 'efficient' elements of their constitution.

Critics of parliamentary government could be found among reformers as well as conservatives. The latter's critique of parliamentary government focused on the demotion of governor and legislative council. As we have already seen, conservative republicans wanted to reinvigorate these checks by making them elective. Reformers, by contrast, saw public opinion as the principal check on government. While both mixed monarchy and the checks and balances of American republicanism envisaged a balance or equilibrium struck between potentially conflicting forces, parliamentary government envisaged harmony between executive and legislature. In part, the shift reflected the unitary nature of 'the people' and 'public opinion' that had replaced the imagery of hierarchy and social estates.[26] Harmony between executive and legislature was to be achieved only when the former reflected public opinion. Legislators were to withdraw their confidence from, and thus destroy, a wayward executive, but many reformers quickly dismissed this mechanism as inadequate. They began to search for new ways to ensure the responsibility of both the executive and legislature to public opinion.

'Tory republicans' and dissatisfied reformers, or 'Grits,' offered similar criticisms of parliamentary government, but the degree to which the latter also offered a republican solution is unclear. They called for 'elective institutions,' more to reinforce the democratic nature of the constitution as a whole and to limit the power of the cabinet; less to create new checks on the assembly. Like conservative republicans, they praised the American system of government and borrowed freely from it, but, unlike them, they did not distinguish between the republics of Washington and Jackson and drew strength from the British radical tradition as well as from their republican neighbours. Grits demanded an elective governor, legislative council, and local officials, an extended franchise,

25 Baldwin, *Debates*, 3 June 1850, 373–5
26 M.J.C. Vile, *Constitutionalism and the Separation of Powers* (Oxford: Oxford University Press 1967), 212

the ballot, and cheaper or simpler government. Moderate reformers called these demands revolutionary and republican, but were they?[27] In other words, did these Grit demands repudiate or only seek to modify parliamentary government?

Grits certainly challenged the notion that responsible government had been 'achieved' in 1848–9. Canada's constitution should continue to evolve. Responsible government was an experiment that many judged a failure.[28] But what had failed, parliamentary government or the particular version supported by more moderate reformers opposed to further institutional change? Some Grits wanted to import most of American republicanism. Others seemed to prefer a more radical or populist version of parliamentary government. Confusion reigned.

In 1854, the *North American*, the leading Grit organ, tried to tidy up the past by claiming that 'we came to the conclusion some years ago that this undefinable, intangible, elastic system called Responsible Government ... is not suited to a new country like Canada ... The experience of thirty States with populations and interests very similar to our own has proved the advantage of giving small discretionary powers to public officers. Checks and limitations are the only safe-guards against abuse.'[29] This relatively straightforward endorsement of republicanism was not matched by the Grit platform of 1850, published by the same paper, although its first plank was indeed 'elective institutions.'

An elective governor appears the most obviously republican demand, but this was not necessarily the case. The measure was also not a priority. Grits advanced it out of consistency and in the belief that a local would be more familiar with Canada than a British peer. Lord Elgin, the current governor, also believed that Canadians should eventually elect his successors.[30] As he understood, if the functions of the office remained unchanged, an elective head of government was compatible with parliamentary government. Unlike the conservative republicans, Grit advocates of an elective governor said little about the functions of the office.

Besides the demand for an elective legislative council, to be discussed shortly, Grits also proposed a number of measures to limit the power of

---

27 See esp. *Globe*, 23 Mar. 1850.
28 See *Examiner*, 29 May and 26 June 1850 and *North American*, 13 Dec. 1850 and 21 Feb. 1851.
29 *North American*, 16 Feb. 1854
30 *North American*, 30 Oct. and 8 Nov. 1850 and 3 Jan. 1851. Elgin to Earl Grey, 23 Mar. 1850, *Elgin-Grey Papers*, v. 2, 609. See also *Examiner*, 30 Aug. 1848 and 27 Mar. 1850.

the cabinet and to further separate it from the legislature. These included fixing the time of parliamentary sittings, more frequent general elections, and prohibiting the expenditure of public money without the prior consent of the assembly. Grits were either unclear or inconsistent about whether such proposals were meant to modify or to replace parliamentary government. The Grit platform concluded with a slogan: 'We must have Elective Institutions, wholly Elective institutions, and nothing but Elective Institutions.' Such institutions were to be designed by a constitutional convention and codified by a written constitution.[31] None of this, however, clarified the central ambiguity. Implemented together and at once, the Grit platform would probably have spelt the end of parliamentary government. Some intended as much. Some would have had few regrets. Others seemed to support these proposals to improve, not replace, ministerial responsibility. Many Grits wavered between these goals, advocating incremental changes almost regardless of their cumulative impact on the form of government as a whole and perhaps reflecting their fluctuating levels of enthusiasm for the various reform ministries after 1848.

Focusing on the specific planks of their platform, the Grits appear to have failed. Moderate reformers were able to resist most of their specific demands: Canada's governor continued to be appointed by Britain, the cabinet continued to appoint most officers, the parliamentary term was not shortened, and universal suffrage and the ballot lay in the future. The legislative council was made elective, but the innovation was reversed at Confederation.

This picture of failure needs to be modified in two respects. First, as already noted, elective institutions were not necessarily incompatible with parliamentary government. Second, Grit arguments and assumptions gained more acceptance in this period than did specific institutional proposals. Some of those principles were hostile to parliamentary government. Moderate reformers fended off Grit demands for institutional change, but were less successful in countering the assumptions behind them. Poorly grounded, parliamentary government was less resilient in the face of later practices that transformed it into cabinet

---

31 Peter Perry introduced a motion for a convention in the assembly in August 1850. It was debated by several municipal councils. See *Examiner*, 21 Aug., *Bathurst Courier*, 13 Sept. and 11 Oct., *North American*, 16 and 23 Aug. and 9 Oct. and A Looker On, *Whitby Reporter*, 16 Nov. 1850. On the right to frame a written constitution see *Provincialist*, 8 Nov. and *Mirror*, 23 Nov. 1849, and *Examiner*, 1 Jan. 1854.

government. The power of the executive and political parties increased relative to that of the assembly and individual representatives to the point where the supervision of the assembly over cabinet and of the people over individual representatives became the constitutional fictions of this century.[32] Ironically, some of the Grit proposals attacked at the time as incompatible with parliamentary government might have helped contain the power of political parties and the cabinet. They, rather than some of the more successful arguments and assumptions used to justify them, might have helped sustain parliamentary government.

Heading the list of issues around which reformers struggled to define and implement deliberative democracy, the future of the legislative council was also the single major victory of the campaign for elective institutions. The theory of mixed monarchy had provided a secure rationale. The council was a coordinate branch of the legislature representing aristocracy. It prevented despotism on the part of the monarchical governor and anarchy arising from the democratic assembly. Parliamentary government provided no such security. Grey's *Parliamentary Government* barely mentioned the House of Lords. Walter Bagehot's *The English Constitution* was more thorough, but largely relegated it to the 'dignified' part of the constitution. Whatever the theory, the appointed council had never looked much like the House of Lords. Before the rebellion, it had thwarted much of the legislative agenda of reformers, fuelling their demand for an elective upper house. After 1848, the council was even more vulnerable. What justification could there be for a non-elective legislative body in a democracy? No longer a harmful barrier, the council was now a useless, atavistic appendage.

The future of the legislative council reappeared on the public agenda when France abolished its upper house in 1848. Nothing illustrated the council's lack of independence more graphically than when the new reform ministry nominated a sufficient number of sympathetic councillors the following year to secure the passage of the Rebellion Losses Bill. Demands for an elective legislative council came from several conservative newspapers and from within the British American League. Reformers raised the issue in the assembly in 1850 and it appeared in the Grit platform of the same year. The Hincks-Morin government introduced a

32 See esp. Thomas A. Hockin, 'Flexible and Structured Parliamentarism: From 1848 to Contemporary Party Government,' *Journal of Canadian Studies* 17 no. 2 (Summer 1979), 8–17.

series of resolutions endorsing an elective legislative council in 1853. The British parliament passed legislation enabling Canada to amend its own constitution pertaining to the council – surely the ultimate recognition of independence. Numerous proposals were canvassed, but the assembly, now led by Sir Allan MacNab and John A. Macdonald, was nearly unanimous on the principle. The bill to create an elective upper house passed second reading by eighty votes to four.

Such near-unanimity marks the distance travelled since the 1830s, when support for an elective upper house defined radicalism. Everyone now admitted that Canadians controlled their constitution and that any legislative institution, to be effective, had to be elective. The near-unanimity, however, masked several divisions. Some moderate reformers, including Francis Hincks, argued that an elective legislative council was a desirable extension of parliamentary government. Other moderate reformers, including Robert Baldwin and George Brown, opposed an elective council on the grounds that having two elective houses was incompatible with parliamentary government. Radical reformers were also divided. Some wanted to abolish the council. Others thought an elective council would increase the power of 'the people.' Some also saw it as only the first step towards American republicanism, the position of conservative republicans. Nonetheless, neither abolition of the council nor its democratization was necessarily incompatible with parliamentary government.

Few reformers defended the existing legislative council. None did so on the basis of mixed monarchy.[33] After 1848, the council merely echoed the majority in the assembly. In future, each new ministry would make enough appointments to ensure it a workable majority. Whereas many executive councillors had once held seats in the legislative council, most now sat in the assembly. People could feel little but jealousy and contempt for a body whose deliberations were unknown and now unimportant.[34] The council was an 'expensive farce.'[35] Combined with demands for reform, such ridicule ensured declining council atten-

---

33 Besides Baldwin, note 25 above, see *Brockville Recorder*, 22 Nov. 1849, *Globe*, 18 May 1850 and 13 Apr. 1852, and George Brown, *Debates*, 19 Oct. 1852, 1113.

34 For examples from all shades of reformers, see H.J. Boulton, *Debates*, 22 May 1850, 134–5, Reformator, *Mirror*, 19 Oct. 1849, *Dundas Warder* copied *Mirror*, 18 Jan. 1850, *Mirror*, 22 Mar. and 5 July 1850, *Examiner*, 22 May 1850, *Bathurst Courier*, 8 Oct. 1852 and 27 May 1853, *North American*, 19 May 1853, and *Daily Leader*, 11 July and 15 Oct. 1853 and 14 July 1854.

35 Constant, *Bathurst Courier*, 14 June 1850

dance to the point where quorum became difficult to muster.[36] Many reformers were suspicious when conservatives began to contemplate an elective legislative council. Conservatives had generally supported the appointive system as long as it had thwarted reform majorities in the assembly. Now that it no longer did so, some were demanding that the council be restructured. In the 1830s, radicals had advocated making it elective to remove a barrier to public opinion, but the barrier had been removed by other means.[37] If the problem was no longer what the Legislative council did, but how little it did, why not abolish it altogether?

Despite considerable support in the reform press, the assembly did not seriously consider abolition. Commenting on the French constitution of 1848, the *Examiner* argued that, lacking an aristocracy or privileged ranks, democracies had no need for a second legislature. 'If the public will be truly and fully expressed in one House, we cannot see why that will should be counteracted or expressed a second time in another House.' The *Examiner* went on to dismiss 'the fiction about "checks and balances"' that remained a central tenet of Anglo-American constitutionalism. Representative government was meant to express public opinion. Any check on that expression negated representation itself.[38] At various points, abolition was also supported by the *Mirror, Bathurst Courier, Niagara Mail, Dumfries Reformer, Canadian Free Press*, and *Huron Signal*.[39] They simply pointed out that Canada had been governed since 1848 by ministers responsible to the assembly with little or no interference from the legislative council. A second chamber would either be useless because it echoed the assembly or dangerous because it checked it.[40]

---

36 See Duncan McArthur, 'A Canadian Experiment with an Elective Upper Chamber,' *Proceedings and Transactions of the Royal Society of Canada*, 3rd ser., XXIV, sect. II (1930), 79–88 and S.C. Hart, 'The Elective Legislative Council in Canada under the Union,' MA thesis, Queen's University 1960.

37 Publicola to Lord Elgin, *Examiner*, 29 Sept. 1847, *Examiner*, 4 July 1849, *Mirror*, 16 Nov. 1849, Caution, *Brockville Recorder*, 22 April 1852, and George Brown, *Debates*, 19 Oct. 1852, 1107

38 *Examiner*, 13 Dec. 1848 and 26 Feb. 1851

39 *Mirror*, 22 Mar. and 5 and 12 July 1850, Constant, *Bathurst Courier*, 14 June 1850, *Bathurst Courier*, 23 Apr. and 8 Oct. 1852 and 20 May 1853, *Niagara Mail* copied in *Examiner*, 5 May 1852, *Dumfries Reformer* copied in *Globe*, 7 Oct. 1854, *Canadian Free Press*, 3 Apr. 1851 and 14 Oct. 1852, and *Huron Signal*, 18 May 1849 and 21 Feb. 1850. The *Mirror* and *Examiner* changed their position once they supported the Hincks-Morin government.

40 Once the assembly was elected by manhood suffrage, a few reformers thought there might then be merit in having property represented in a reformed council since it would remain the basis of taxation. See *Dundas Warder* copied *North American*, 22 Nov.

The argument for abolition was vulnerable on one key point. Could public opinion be expressed safely by one elective body? History seemed to provide few, if any, examples of a single legislature sustaining good government.[41] Some supported a second chamber on the age-old grounds that concentrating power in a single body or person was tyranny. There was too much risk of 'executive despotism' without the check of a second elected chamber.[42] Given reformers' concern about the cabinet's power, the rarity of this argument is noteworthy. It may have been a secondary justification, but it did not ground the case for an elective legislative council. Instead, this role was performed by the nature of the pubic sphere. 'A U.E. Loyalist' favoured abolition because 'public opinion is a child of slow growth, and when it comes to maturity, and is the opinion of the majority, it ought to be the law of the land.'[43] Other reformers agreed but worried that one body would not always be able to resist the sudden pressure of popular passions to await the more settled conviction of public opinion. A second chamber was warranted by its function in a deliberative democracy, not by representing something or someone.[44]

John Rolph, one of the Grits who joined the Hincks-Morin government in 1851, argued that the popular excitement of the 1830s, in which he had been implicated, had resulted from misrule and a disregard for the legitimate wishes of the people. The new constitution removed both these causes. Popular excitement was now the product of 'those commotions of the public mind springing from freedom itself; from the free and independent expression of opinion upon all great concerns of the country; from the conflict of opposing views in the arena of free discussion; from the battles for party ascendency under a government based

---

1850, *Paris Star* copied in *Canadian Free Press*, 17 Apr. 1851, and *Examiner*, 5 May 1852 and 26 Jan. 1853.

41 *North American*, 19 May 1853

42 E.g., *Mirror*, 22 Oct. 1852 and D. Christie, *Debates*, 28 May 1853, 3166. Citing Montesquieu, John A. Macdonald made a similar argument, but aimed at limiting the assembly, not the cabinet. He supported an elective legislative council on the grounds that there were insufficient safeguards to prevent the assembly from usurping executive and judicial functions. *Debates*, 27 Mar. 1855, 2495

43 A U.E. Loyalist, *North American*, 18 Sept. 1850

44 David E. Smith, *The Republican Option in Canada, Past and Present* (Toronto: University of Toronto Press 1999), 81, which unfortunately came to hand only after this manuscript was written. It nicely illuminates the issue of 'balance' and the degree to which parliamentary government lost touch with the balances and extra-parliamentary elements that had originally defined it.

upon party principles. Knowing that under this un-restricted freedom of mind, of the tongue, and of the press, there will be occasional excesses, it is an act of wisdom for the people, as in other free countries, to guard against them.' With an elective upper house, 'the political safety-valve and the constitutional ballast are adjusted and regulated by the people themselves.' As one editor put it, 'The very fact of the universal freedom of speech and action which found its reflex in the popular branch, called for another House' to act as a 'barrier against the effects of restlessness and precipitation.'[45] An elective upper house would not check public opinion, but would ensure that government was not guided by the ferment that was a necessary by-product of public deliberation itself.

Far from being an attack on parliamentary government, this argument was essential to it. In Britain, respect for the aristocracy and House of Lords, a more limited franchise, and a more patrician class of politicians was thought to enable parliament to differentiate between popular passion and public opinion and to ignore the first. Was the Canadian assembly able or willing to resist outbursts of popular enthusiasm? Lord Elgin was unsure and therefore strongly supported an elective council. While he praised Baldwin's sincerity in opposing an elective upper house out of an attachment to 'what he imagines to be the likest thing to the British Constitution he can obtain, ... in this instance I cannot but think that he mistakes the shadow for the substance.'[46] Earl Grey, Colonial Secretary and soon-to-be-author of an important study of parliamentary government, agreed.

So did a large number of Baldwin's colleagues. Francis Hincks, for one, praised the British constitution and 'to retain to this country its integrity' proposed making the legislative council elective.[47] Britain had two legislative chambers while, in effect, Canada had only one. Nomination by the Crown neither legitimated legislators nor ensured that the best were chosen.[48] The objectives were limited. A 'court of review' or 'revision' – a chamber of sober second thought – was needed, not another body performing the same functions as the assembly. While its

45 Rolph, *Debates*, 28 May 1853, 3157 and *Mirror*, 15 Dec. 1854. See also fellow Grit D. Christie, *Debates*, 28 May 1853, 3166.

46 Lord Elgin to Earl Grey, 23 Mar. 1850, *Elgin-Grey Papers*, v. 2, 613

47 Hincks, *Debates*, 13 May 1853, 3069, A. Morin, 19 Oct. 1852, 1091, J.A. Macdonald, 27 Mar. 1855, 2526, Spence, 28 Mar. 1855, 2526, and *Daily Leader*, 15 Oct. 1853

48 *Mirror*, 23 Mar. 1855 and also *North American*, 1 Apr. 1852, *Brockville Recorder*, 22 Apr. and 6 May 1852, *Mirror*, 22 Oct. 1852, *Elora Backwoodsman*, 20 Jan. 1853, and *Examiner*, 26 Jan. 1853

public standing would be improved, an elective legislative council would gain no additional legislative functions.[49] The right to originate money bills, and therefore 'the practical control over the ministry of the day,' would remain with the assembly. A ministry would not have to resign if one of its measures was defeated in the council.[50] In fact, Hincks insisted that an elective legislative council would remain weaker than the British House of Lords and that precedents developed in the Lords' relationship with the Commons would continue to govern relations between Canada's two chambers.[51] Rejecting the more imposing-sounding 'Senate,' continuity in name was to symbolize continuity in function.

The two houses were to be similar enough to ensure cooperation. They were to be chosen by the same electorate and both were to be responsible to public opinion. At the same time, the upper house had to be different enough to act as a check – 'preventing precipitate decision' and forcing a particular bill to be 'delayed,' 'abandoned,' or 'modified.'[52] Again, John Rolph best framed this dual requirement in terms of government by discussion. Electing the second chamber would 'produce a practical affinity without identity [between the two houses], and admit of that friendly collision which only serves to elicit the truth.'[53] Friendly collision in the service of truth, an apt description of what debating societies had tried to engineer in the 1830s, was now to guide law-making.

After Baldwin's retirement, George Brown became the most tenacious critic of an elective legislative council as both a member of the assembly and editor of the *Globe*. In the end, he stood almost alone.[54]

---

49 William Lyon Mackenzie to the Earl of Aberdeen, *Mackenzie's Weekly Message*, 3 Mar. 1854 and D. Spence and J.A. Macdonald, *Debates*, 16 and 22 March 1855, 2242, 2495. Once the council was made elective it could, like the House of Lords, act as a court of impeachment.

50 The *North American*, 26 May 1853, however, disagreed with fellow reformers and thought that a ministry needed the general confidence of both chambers. The *Daily Leader*, 23 Feb. 1853, rejected this position as rendering ministerial responsibility impossible.

51 Hincks, *Debates*, 8 Oct. 1852, 927, 13 May 1853, 3068, and 27 March 1855, 2501. Indeed, Rolph suggested that the council would never address the Crown on its confidence in a ministry, *Debates*, 28 May 1853, 3157. For the continued relevance of the House of Lords, see *Brockville Recorder*, 26 May 1853 and esp. Ross, *Seat of Government Question*, 20–3.

52 D. Christie, *Debates*, 28 May 1853, 3167 and also J. Langton, 13 May 1853, 3073 and J.A. Macdonald, 16 Mar. 1855, 2247–50

53 Rolph, *Debates*, 28 May 1853, 3157

54 The synthesis of Brown's position is from the *Globe*, 23 Mar. and 19 Oct. 1852 and 14 and 21 May 1853, and *Debates*, 19 Oct. 1852, 1104–15, 13 May 1853, 3071–3, 16 Mar.

Canada already enjoyed 'the ready and entire control over public affairs.' Conservative support for the reform made sense because such a council was designed 'to fetter public opinion.' Reformers should oppose the change for the same reason. The cabinet, by introducing most measures and generally guiding the assembly, already guarded against hasty legislation.

Moreover, Brown repeatedly insisted that no elective legislature would limit itself to revising or delaying particular bills. The House of Lords and the existing legislative council deferred to a determined lower house because they recognized the superior legitimacy conferred by popular suffrage. Once they too were elected, councillors would not yield. They would claim an equal duty to represent the people and an equal ability to interpret public opinion. Even the stipulation that money bills were to originate in the assembly would prove futile. 'Representatives of the people, like ourselves [members of the assembly], why should they not have the same power over all bills that we have?' An elective legislature would not limit itself to 'a Court of Review,' but would become 'an active political engine.'

Two such engines were incompatible with parliamentary government, but integral to American republicanism whereby the tenure of the executive was independent of the legislature and all were subordinate to a written constitution. A Canadian ministry would have to maintain a majority in both houses. If the same party did not win a majority in each, how could a ministry serve two masters? If the government was to remain responsible to public opinion, only one house could claim to embody that opinion.

Further, parliamentary government entrusted the cabinet with vast powers. Such concentration was safe only because the assembly could swiftly remove it from office. 'The omnipotence of the popular will, as expressed through this House, and the prompt, efficient control we, the House of Assembly, exercise over the Executive, is the very mainspring of our constitutional system. How could it continue, if there were another House that might oppose that Assembly?' The assembly's check

1855, 2242–7, and 27 Mar. 1855, 2472–85. The only noticeable shift in Brown's position was an increasing insistence on representation by population between the Canadas. The only other reform member to employ similar arguments was J. Wilson, *Debates*, 28 Mar. 1855, 2519–23, but for signs of second thoughts by supporters of the coalition of 1854 see, *Daily Leader*, 23 Feb. 1855 and Anon., *Arguments Against an Elective Legislative Council*.

would weaken if a ministry could shift blame for measures to another elective legislature or use its majority in one house to thwart the will of the other. What would a governor do if faced with a vote of confidence from one house and a vote of non-confidence from the other? Constant friction, deadlock, and new elections would fuel calls for a written constitution and an executive independent of the legislature. In short, Brown agreed with conservative republicans like John W. Gamble that an elective legislative council was but the first step towards republicanism. There was 'no half-way house' between it and parliamentary government. One system fused executive and the legislative functions. The other separated them. If the status quo could not be maintained, the legislative council should be abolished.

Whether or not an elective upper house would be a court of revision or an equal legislature – whether or not it would destroy parliamentary government – largely depended upon details. What rules would explicitly limit the power of the upper house? Could it be dissolved in the same manner as the assembly? What were the qualifications for potential councillors? Would they be elected as a group or in rotation? For what term? How large would the new council be? What size of constituency would be entailed? Would those appointed under the old system be removed at once or would the elective principle be introduced gradually? The answers to such questions would determine the degree of similarity between the two houses and thus the likelihood of deadlock and what, if anything, could be done to break one. Significant disagreement over these questions existed among reformers and between the reform government that introduced the measure and the Liberal-Conservative coalition that passed it.

Nonetheless, the debate on the broader principles of an elective legislative council was revealing. Legislation had to reflect public opinion. Whether or not this required two chambers hinged on the nature of the public sphere. Further, the debate showed that 'elective institutions' were not necessarily revolutionary. Canada was already a democracy. No alternative to direct popular election was seriously considered. The Grit demand for an elective legislative council was realized, but moderate reformers helped ensure that the reform was compatible with parliamentary government. The desire to give ministerial responsibility a fair trial, fear of further constitutional change, divisions among radicals and conservative republicans, and the desire to retain formal similarities with Britain to help demarcate Canada culturally from the United States all worked in their favour. Supporters of parliamentary government were successful against frontal assaults, but proved less resilient against more subtle threats. They were unable to clearly and forcefully establish some of the essential underpinnings of parliamentary government. The eventual result, as Lord Metcalfe had feared, was not parliamentary government but cabinet government – not government by discussion but government by democratic oligarchy.

As with the future of the legislative council, disagreement among reformers on the nature of the cabinet and its relationship to the assembly revealed both the primacy of public opinion and competing assessments of parliamentary government. For Walter Bagehot, 'the efficient secret' of the British constitution was its fusion of executive and legislature. The cabinet was both the executive and a committee of the legislature that survived only as long as it retained a working majority in the legislature. It could dissolve the legislature, it alone could propose fiscal measures, and, with the majority that sustained it, was able to direct the legislature. As Bagehot saw it, 'The English system, therefore, is not an absorption of the executive power by the legislative power; it is a fusion of the two ... It is an executive which can annihilate the legislature, as well as an executive which is the nominee of the legislature.'[55]

It was certainly no secret, efficient or otherwise, that the power of the cabinet marked the eclipse of the older theory of a balance among coordinate legislatures. At its most formulaic, responsible government transformed the old executive council of the governor's advisers into a committee of departmental ministers collectively responsible to the elected local assembly. There was no surprise that this increased the role of the cabinet as well as that of the assembly.

George Brown's analysis of the cabinet during the Metcalfe crisis has already been sampled. Those who displayed talent and energy in the 'stormy arena' of the assembly rose in the estimation of their colleagues and the public to be chosen as ministers. Thus the people elected the executive indirectly or through their representatives. Since ministers spoke collectively as the advisers to the Crown, 'they appear in no shape as a party.' In 1847, the *Globe* insisted that it was 'in the Councils of the Executive that the popular branch finds its power, and it is through that channel that harmony is preserved between the different estates of Parliament and the mass of the people.' The people's indirect control of the

---

55 Bagehot, *The English Constitution*, 65, 69

executive ensured harmony among the formal institutions of Crown, legislative council, and assembly and between them and public opinion.[56]

For Robert Baldwin, while the cabinet grew out of the legislature, the public had confidence in ministers 'because they deem them capable of exercising a proper influence over the Legislature.' The cabinet promoted certain legislative initiatives; prevented others. 'Ministers of the Crown ought to be representatives of public opinion ... [They] ought to be those who concur with the great masses of the community upon those questions on which public opinion is settled for it was to that end that they are called on to influence the Councils of the Sovereign.' To carry out this function, 'the Ministers of the Crown ought to possess such a majority as will enable them to pass the measures' they deemed in conformity with public opinion. Two years later, approaching the end of his parliamentary career, Baldwin insisted that while 'the deliberative views of the people effectually made themselves felt on the Administration through the Legislature,' cabinet ministers served as 'watchers on the tower.'[57]

For many reformers, perhaps most, the cabinets led in Upper Canada by Baldwin and Francis Hincks did more than watch. Henry John Boulton, former chairman of the Reform Association, soon pronounced responsible government a failure. It centralized power 'into the hands of a few men, who were nominally responsible to the country, but who in reality possessed no responsibility at all.'[58] Responsibility was 'pretended' or a 'delusion' because the cabinet engulfed the powers of the legislature.[59] From the perspective of William McDougall's *North American*, the cabinet initiated most legislation, vetoed measures it disliked, and claimed to speak for public opinion more directly than the people's own representatives. It attempted to reduce parliament 'to say "Yea" or "Nay" to the propositions of the Government.' Presenting the Grit plat-

---

56 Brown in Reform Asociation of Canada, *'The Globe' Extra*, 30–2 and *Globe*, 16 June 1847

57 Baldwin, *Debates*, 3 Mar. 1848, 186–91 and 3 June 1850, 372–4. See also *Globe*, 21 May 1853.

58 Boulton, *Debates*, 22 May 1851, 35. Boulton broke with the Baldwin-LaFontaine ministry at the end of their first legislative session on the grounds that the cabinet was assuming too great a role in the legislature; *Debates*, 20 Mar. 1848, 508–12. Others offered more mercenary explanations.

59 E.g., Reformator, *North American*, 23 Aug. and 13 Sept. 1850, *North American*, 31 Jan. 1851 and 6 and 27 Jan. 1853, *Examiner*, 22 Nov. 1848, 29 May and 21 Aug. 1850, and 3 Jan. 1855, Resolutions of the Municipal Council of Lanark and Renfrew Counties, *Bathurst Courier*, 11 Oct. 1850, *Bathurst Courier*, 13 Sept. and 15 Nov. 1850, *Brockville Recorder*, 12 Sept. 1850, *Mirror*, 29 Mar. 1850, and *Guelph Advertiser*, 3 Nov. 1853.

form, the paper insisted that 'we are actuated solely by a desire to render the Executive and Members of Parliament, as independent of each other as it is compatible with the general interest for them to be.'[60] Was such a degree of independence compatible with parliamentary government or did it require the adoption of a republican constitution?

Contrasting the republican separation of powers with the fusion of powers in 'the English system,' the *Examiner* thought the principle in the latter that the cabinet initiate important legislation sound. It had, however, been carried to extremes in Canada and was 'accompanied by vices unknown in England.' Initiating key legislation and threatening to resign on matters of principle were one thing. It was a 'quite different thing for them to usurp or control the entire functions of the Legislature.' The diagnosis was interesting, but the prescription lame: 'the line between the Executive and Legislative powers ought to be more distinctly drawn.' A year later, the *Examiner* asked, 'Why should a Cabinet minister argue? Who is simple enough to imagine that one in his position is to bend to those rules which guide men who, wielding no official influence or patronage, depend solely on the strength of their arguments, and the goodness of their cause?'[61] An oligarchy that made its decisions in private and was powerful enough to ignore the ordeal of public discussion did not contribute to the formation of public opinion. It courted public cynicism rather than public debate.

The *Examiner* recalled that the independence of the assembly had been a central imperative of mixed monarchy. 'Now, however, all this is changed. The executive cannot disregard the action of the legislative assembly; the vote of that house is the tenure on which the government holds the reigns of power. Various means of tempering the Assembly are therefore resorted to, for the purpose of maintaining a majority; or, in other words, of keeping a particular ministry in power.' The cost of harmony among institutions had been the assembly's independence. The *Examiner* added a touch of historical irony: 'Tyranny assumes a variety of shapes ... In Canada, it was formerly an undisguised oligarchy. But is a masked oligarchy much better?'[62] The paper failed to recall that this had been Lord Metcalfe's objection to ministerial responsibility when it had worked so assiduously against him.

The cabinet's control of patronage was the most widely condemned of

60 *North American*, 14 Feb. 1851 and 30 Dec. 1852
61 *Examiner*, 17 Apr. 1850 and 26 Feb. 1851
62 *Examiner*, 22 May and 21 Aug. 1850

the 'various means of tempering the Assembly.' A ministry could purchase sufficient support in the assembly to nullify any formal responsibility to it. Conservative republicans proposed that an independent governor nominate officers to be confirmed by the legislature. Such officers were also to be barred from sitting in the legislature. Instead, reform critics (and Ogle Gowan) demanded that office-holders be directly elected by the people. The logic was straightforward: if the people retained 'in their own hands and gift the power to bestow office,' the recipients would serve them rather than the executive.[63] The first proposal was incompatible with parliamentary government. The second was not.

Reformers who favoured ministerial appointment failed to mount significant opposition to the idea of direct election, except when the proposal extended to judicial posts.[64] This was partially a function of timing. The Grit demand was a response to discontent with appointments made by the Baldwin-LaFontaine ministry. In 1848–50, the question was not whether officials should be appointed or elected, but whether office-holders should be non-partisan and serve 'during good behaviour' or be supporters of the party in power and be replaced with each change of administration. At first, reformers agreed on the first option. Moderate reformers maintained this position while their more radical colleagues, dissatisfied with the results, moved on by 1850 to demand elective offices.

When he swore in the Baldwin-LaFontaine ministry, Lord Elgin worried that 'there will be an attempt I fear to deal harshly, Yankee fashion, in some instances with subordinate officials – for the twofold purpose of punishing political opponents and providing places for political friends.'[65] The Baldwin-LaFontaine ministry was indeed under considerable pressure from its supporters to make room for more reformers in office after decades of perceived exclusion. None questioned that all new appointments should go to qualified reformers. The prospectus of one reform organ promised to promote the 'equality of man with man, in regard to his rights and privileges, and advocate the leaving of all offices of trust and distinction open to all, but accessible only to the

---

63 *Provincialist*, 13 Dec. 1849. See also *Examiner*, 11 Sept. 1850, *North American*, 14 Feb. and 2 May 1851, *Mackenzie's Weekly Message*, 29 Sept. 1853 and Reformator, *Mirror*, 31 Aug. and 28 Sept. 1849 and 15 Feb. and 22 Mar. 1850, Reformator, *North American*, 23 Aug. 1850, and An Old Reformer, *Journal & Express* and *Provincialist*, 15 Oct. 1849.

64 But see *Brockville Recorder*, 12 Sept. 1850 and 29 May 1851.

65 Elgin to Earl Grey, 22 Jan. 1848, *Elgin-Grey Papers*, v. 1, 119. See also H.J. Boulton, *Debates*, 3 Mar. 1848, 213–14.

meritorious friends of the majority of the people.' The two propositions were not contradictory. Patronage was not the dirty secret of responsible government, but part of its oft-discussed essence.[66]

Robert Baldwin Sullivan had worked out the justification during the Metcalfe crisis. 'For the purposes of government,' the majority party was 'said to be public opinion.' Thus, the argument that the governor should make appointments without reference to party amounted to 'the substitution of one man's opinion for public opinion.' Sullivan concluded that 'it is not merely upon the principle that those who have won the victory have a right to the spoils of war, but upon the more just and necessary supposal, that those who contended successfully for opinions may be most safely entrusted with their practical maintenance and enforcement.'[67] Tories had appointed mostly fellow partisans. Reformers would do likewise, but with a rationale grounded in government by discussion. Office-holders, like cabinet ministers, had to be responsible to public opinion.

The more difficult question was what to do with non-reformers already in office. Even those reformers most wedded to the exclusive appointment of reformers rejected the American 'system of clearing' whereby officials were replaced by each new administration.[68] Only James Lesslie's *Examiner* dissented on the grounds that 'an identity of opinion' among officials could only be ensured if offices were redistributed after each election, thereby giving 'wider scope to the operation of the beautiful principle, which distinguishes our government from oligarchies and despotisms, of allowing public opinion, as expressed at a general election, to influence the administration of affairs and to change the individuals entrusted therewith.'[69]

Reformers agreed that a responsible executive could dismiss any office-holder, that it could not allow avowed enemies to administer its

66 Carol Wilton-Siegel, 'The Transformation of Upper Canadian Politics in the 1840s,' PhD thesis, University of Toronto 1984, 283–4 and prospectus, *Provincialist*, 14 Oct. 1848. See also Price, *Debates*, 3 Mar. 1848, 204, *Examiner*, 19 Apr. 1848, *Bathurst Courier*, 7 Mar. 1851, *Provincialist*, 2 May 1848, and *St Catharines Journal*, 13 May 1852. For an older, still prevalent, view see J.B. Brebner, 'Patronage and Parliamentary Government,' Canadian Historical Association *Report of the Annual Meeting with Historical Papers* (1938), 22–30.
67 Legion, *Letters on Responsible Government*, 24–5, 78, 139, 141–4
68 E.g., *Globe*, 12 Feb. 1848, *Bathurst Courier*, 21 Apr. 1848, *Provincialist*, 22 Feb. and 2 May 1848, and *Guelph Advertiser*, 20 Sept. 1849
69 *Examiner*, 19 Apr. 1848

policies, and that it had to be able to trust administrators with executive secrets. Further, reformers were committed to removing office-holders from the electoral process to prevent them from trying to pervert the 'free expression of the popular mind.' This had, after all, been a frequent complaint against the 'Family Compact.'[70] The *cause célèbre* was the dismissal of James Moir Ferres as a revenue inspector for his campaigning – on the losing side – in the 1848 election. Conservatives defended Ferres's right to participate in the democratic process as a free citizen without fear of revenge from his employer. Reformers disagreed. If officials could be active partisans, electoral purity would be compromised. Further, new ministries would be left with little choice but to replace all administrative officers with their own supporters. Ferres was dismissed to prevent the politicization of administrative officers. Other opponents of the ministry, notably Egerton Ryerson, in charge of education in Upper Canada, were retained.[71] Reformers remained committed to a non-partisan public service in which new appointments were reserved for their friends. The two principles were compatible. Calls for the popular election of local officers were not only unsuccessful, they were largely ignored.

The question of patronage was inextricably linked to that of party. Patronage was more useful in building and maintaining partisan networks than in buying the votes of individual legislators or electors. Reformers endlessly reiterated that responsible government was party government.[72] It was controversial, but it was also true, as the increased electoral organization of reformers for the 1848 election demonstrated.[73] Political groupings may have been nearly as old as representative institutions in the Canadas, but the untempered acceptance of political parties was impossible as long as the theory of mixed monarchy remained the primary way to understand the constitution.[74]

---

70 E.g., *Globe*, 12 Feb. and 15 Apr. 1848 and *Bathurst Courier*, 12 Apr. 1848

71 For able defences of Ferres's dismissal, see Hincks and Baldwin, *Debates*, 8 Feb. and 5 Mar. 1849, 543–6, 550, 1124, 1132. See also Lorne Ste. Croix, 'James Moir Ferres,' *Dictionary of Canadian Biography*, 9 (Toronto: University of Toronto Press 1976), 257–8 and Wilton-Siegel, 'Transformation of Upper Canadian Politics,' 291–4.

72 E.g., Baldwin, *Debates*, 22 Jan. 1849, 96 and Hincks, 13 May 1853, 3069

73 Wilton-Siegel, 'Transformation of Upper Canadian Politics,' 310

74 On mixed monarchy and party, I am heavily indebted to J.A.W. Gunn, 'Influence, Parties and the Constitution: Changing Attitudes, 1783–1832,' *Historical Journal* 17, no. 2 (1974), 301–28.

As noted in the first chapter, the theory provided limited space for legitimate political conflict. Divergent interests were inherent in the notion of balance, but they were to occur between social estates or legislative institutions. A robust concept of political party could be squared with mixed monarchy under four circumstances. First, when a reform-dominated House confronted a 'Tory'-dominated legislative council, but party conflict persisted even when government supporters controlled the assembly. Second, party could be squared with mixed monarchy if 'Tories' were the party of the pseudo-aristocracy, reformers of the yeomanry. This was more reform rhetoric than electoral reality. Conservatives enjoyed too much electoral success to depict them solely as the party of the legislative council or of an exclusive elite.

Third, party and constitutional theory cohered if one party favoured executive prerogative while the other stood for legislative supremacy, again transforming party conflict into conflict among institutions. This too was a prevalent reform motif, but it failed to capture political reality. Both parties were present in the assembly and the supposedly pro-executive party often held a majority. Moreover, the supposedly pro-assembly party sought to control the executive. In short, it stretched credulity to present each conflict as occurring among different social or institutional elements in the balanced constitution, rather than between parties.

Fourth, the theory of mixed monarchy could accommodate temporary combinations designed to destroy a self-interested clique threatening the constitution's equilibrium. Such temporary combinations to restore balance were still some distance from permanent alignments for advancing particular principles and interests. Once good triumphed over bad – once supporters of the constitution vanquished its foes – there would be no need for such a combination. This was the justification for the various manifestations of the British Constitutional Society in the 1830s. Supporters of mixed monarchy organized and rallied Upper Canadians to defeat the enemies of mixed monarchy. Once the constitution was safe, the society, along with the public information and participation it had mobilized, was expendable, perhaps even dangerous.

Finally, as long as royalty or its representative was politically active, organized and sustained opposition could not escape the taint of disloyalty. The inability of mixed monarchy to adequately reflect the reality of partisan conflict in Upper Canada was one of its major weaknesses.

Some forms of 'party' existed before the demise of mixed monarchy, but they were mis-described and often only tangentially related to constitutional theory.[75]

The public sphere offered a new framework for understanding political parties. During the Metcalfe crisis, their legitimacy was a major fault line between Egerton Ryerson and Robert Baldwin Sullivan. Both began with public opinion, but reached opposite conclusions. Ryerson denounced parties, but without dwelling upon longstanding fears of disorder or divisions within an organic community.[76] He also avoided the image of factious, self-interested cabals that had dominated earlier critiques of party. He accepted that conflict was inherent in public debate, but rejected organized parties because of their effect on that debate. In the wake of the rebellion, Ryerson concluded that 'party spirit ... has neither eyes, nor ears, nor principles, nor reason.' One of his most persistent charges against the Reform Association during the Metcalfe crisis was that 'the first article of their creed is *party*; and therefore truth, and reason, and justice succumb to party.' Party loyalty threatened to replace individual reasoning. It produced what another moderate called 'zeal not according to knowledge.'[77]

Yet other champions of the public sphere offered the best defence of parties. To meet Ryerson's critique, they needed to make them compatible with (or preferably essential to) the public sphere. Thus the *Upper Canada Herald* thought party contests elicited truth. Opposition generated debate and such opposition could only be sustained by parties. The *Canada Inquirer* also saw them as useful adjuncts to the public sphere. As well as giving 'substance to political opinions which without them [?] would vanish like shadows,' parties compensated for the weakness of individual intellect and will. They provided the glue or 'affection' that bound political actors to their general principles even if self-interest

75 See Eric Jackson, 'The Organization of Upper Canadian Reformers, 1818–1867,' in J.K. Johnson, ed., *Historical Essays on Upper Canada* (Toronto: McClelland and Stewart 1975), 96–121, David Mills, *The Idea of Loyalty in Upper Canada, 1784–1850* (Kingston and Montreal: McGill-Queen's University Press 1988), esp. chap. 7, and Wilton-Siegel, 'Transformation of Upper Canadian Politics.'

76 Terence Ball, 'Party,' in Ball, James Farr, and Russell L. Hanson, eds., *Political Innovation and Conceptual Change* (Cambridge: Cambridge University Press 1989), 155–76 is helpful here.

77 *Christian Guardian*, 11 July 1838, Ryerson, *Sir Charles Metcalfe Defended*, 87, and *Woodstock Herald*, 13 July 1844

pointed in another direction. They also organized legislators without the rampant patronage and bribery typical of legislatures composed of 'independent' power-brokers.[78]

Robert Baldwin Sullivan also moved political parties to the very centre of the public sphere. Since unanimity of opinion was highly unlikely, majority and minority parties formed. 'For the purpose of government,' the majority party was 'said to be public opinion.' Therefore, 'if we wish to put down party, we must begin by putting down public opinion.' Members of a public could safely disagree during deliberations. Unanimity, not conflict, was suspect. For the *Leader*, political consensus was 'alarming' since it 'would annihilate everything without so much as a reasonable discussion of the merits of anything.' When a 'body goes in a horde' it might reflect 'not the progress of conviction but the wholesale surrender of opinion.'[79] Regular opposition in the form of criticism had become the barometer of political health – a sign of vigorous public debate; unanimity implied stagnation or expediency.

The theory of parliamentary government incorporated Sullivan's defence of political parties.[80] Parties determined its two central relationships: between executive and legislature and between legislature and electorate. In the legislature, parties had to be cohesive enough to prevent individual legislators from interfering with daily administration and to provide stable support for the cabinet, but not so cohesive that they sustained that cabinet irrespective of its behaviour. Parties had to be cohesive enough to organize representatives, electors, and arguments into competing camps, but not so strong as to make individual representatives mere delegates of the popular will rather than semi-autonomous participants in public deliberations. Nowhere were the fragile balances of parliamentary government more evident.

Nonetheless, reformers were agreed that political parties were inherent in the public sphere. In 1854, the *Bathurst Courier* echoed Sullivan. 'The very essence, the very life as it were of popular institutions ... is the fact that the voice of the many constitutes the chief guide in practical

---

78 *Upper Canada Herald*, 22 May 1838 and 22 Sept. 1840 and *Canada Inquirer*, 4 Oct. 1844

79 Legion, *Letters on Responsible Government*, 24–5, 78, 139, 141–4 and *Daily Leader*, 23 Feb. 1855

80 Angus Hawkins, 'Parliamentary Government and Victorian Political Parties, c.1830– c.1880,' *English Historical Review* 104 (July 1989), 638–69 is vital here, but see also Hockin, 'Flexible and Structured Parliamentarism' and Vile, *Constitutionalism and the Separation of Powers*, 223–4.

legislation. Where all are equally entitled to give free expression to their views there must necessarily be a great diversity of opinion; but notwithstanding this, there are always certain great principles of state policy round which all minor diversities generally arrange themselves and go to form one great party.'[81] Reformers also agreed on the roles of majority and minority party. The majority provided the executive's principles and personnel. Under the theory of mixed monarchy, the assembly had guarded against the encroachments of government; its vigilance ensuring that it acted with probity. Now the assembly chose and sustained the government. Its defensive role was assumed by the minority party within it. The *Canadian Free Press* welcomed party division because it 'secures integrity to the party in power, and as the strength of the latter increases beyond a fair working majority, and that of the former decreases, so will also diminish the care and caution shown by an administration.'[82] The clash of parties had replaced the balance of legislative institutions.

Reformers, however, found less common ground on the appropriate degree of party cohesion. An administration's supporters typically demanded sufficient party unity to sustain it and pass its measures. Reform critics of the same administration typically demanded looser party discipline, often accusing the government of placing party above both principle and public opinion.

Radical reformers were more often hostile to party discipline, especially when it sustained a ministry dominated by moderates. Representatives should reflect the views of their constituents before those of their party. The radical essayist Reformator sought representatives 'able to cast off the trammels of party, and vote from principles instead of expediency.' Ideologues in opposition were always prone to see the compromises required by party loyalty as barriers to the implementation of their own principles; to characterize 'the machinery of party' as 'a dead-weight upon our public energies.' Once they supported an administration, the benefits of the party unity that sustained it became more obvious.[83]

---

81 *Bathurst Courier*, 8 Sept. 1854. See also *Globe*, 10 Mar. and 18 Sept. 1847 and *North American*, 15 Apr. 1852. William Lyon Mackenzie was one of the few reformers who seemed to offer a general critique of party, underscoring his difficulty in bridging the conceptual gulf between the 1830s and the 1850s and his need to justify his career as a maverick or a loose-fish in the assembly. See esp. *Mackenzie's Weekly Message*, 17 Feb. 1854.

82 *Canadian Free Press*, 1 Aug. 1849 and 20 Mar. 1851. See also *Mirror*, 28 Nov. 1851, *Provincialist*, 2 May 1848, *St Catharines Journal*, 15 Sept. 1852 and 14 July 1853, and *Brockville Recorder*, 6 Apr. 1854.

83 Reformator, *Mirror*, 12 Oct. 1849 and *Elora Backwoodsman*, 3 Nov. 1853. Compare

Commentary on partisanship also shifted among moderate reformers. For instance, the *Globe* called upon the reform party to rally around
its chosen leaders and submerge minor differences while it supported
the Baldwin-LaFontaine ministry. When it opposed the Hincks administration, it complained bitterly about calls for party unity. Such positions
were self-serving, but they were not always inconsistent. The *Globe*
opposed the Hincks administration on the grounds that its primary aim
was to stay in office, not to implement the principles endorsed at the
previous election.[84] Parties should not be so cohesive as to sustain such a
ministry. They should, however, be cohesive enough to sustain a more
principled ministry fulfilling its electoral mandate.

Perhaps the *Guelph Advertiser* offered the best summary. Calling on
reform representatives to give a more consistent support to the administration, the editor insisted that 'we do not mean to be understood
that a slavish blindness should be accorded to them, that the party
should have no views but those put forward by their leaders, or do
nothing but what they bid; but we contend that a liberal construction
ought to be put on their acts and the best motives imputed to them.'[85]
Of course, what was 'a more generous support' to one observer was
'slavish blindness' to another. Parliamentary government had transformed executive-legislative relations into a question of party unity in
the legislature.

Party cohesiveness, however, extended beyond the assembly to determine how closely legislators were tied to their constituents. In the
abstract, reformers agreed on the need for channels of communication
between representatives and their local party supporters. County associations promoted discussion among reformers and between them and
their representative. At a township meeting, one enthusiast reported
that 'the opinions and views of different individuals are there brought
together and expressed. The knowledge of all upon the different topics
discussed is conveyed to each, and the ideas of each are made known to
all, and much information is thus acquired by all who will take the trou-

---

Journal & Express copied in *Mirror*, 12 Apr. 1850, calling for independent members
with its plea, copied in *Mirror*, 6 Feb. 1852, for 'strong party government.' See also
Bathurst Courier, 10 Mar. 1854.

84 See *Globe*, 6 Jan. 1853 and 15 Jan. 1852. Some of the ministerial instability of the Union
period, often portrayed as a major problem as well as a cause of Confederation,
marked the high point of parliamentary government in Canada. Hockin, 'Flexible and
Structured Parliamentarism'

85 *Guelph Advertiser*, 21 Oct. 1852

ble to learn.'[86] Associations fostered unity and offered legislators a clearer sense of the principles upon which they would be judged.

Like public opinion itself, such associations were not limited to elections: 'Let them [reformers] meet, talk over and suggest what measures they consider will be beneficial ... Let the results of these deliberations be forwarded to the Representative.'[87] As the *Examiner* said of the reform associations, 'they would give public opinion a control over the executive.' Reformator also quoted Alexis de Tocqueville on the benefits of associations for procuring and more equally distributing the benefits of 'civilization.'[88] The value of associational life to the public sphere was now fully integrated into politics.

While all reformers encouraged unity and deliberation, those critical of their elected colleagues were more insistent about the need for local party associations. The *Provincialist* summed up their case well: 'Let the press speak out – let associations or clubs be formed at which great political questions and the tendency of our institutions shall be continually discussed, until the entire community thoroughly understand public matters; and then every ministry, instead of assuming to dictate to the people and calling upon them for support "lest their opponents should come to power," would at once take their cue from the people and act accordingly.'[89] Continual discussion empowered. Radical reformers demanded that representatives vote according to the majority view of their constituents. Any autonomy given to the people's representatives merely substituted their will for the people's.

Such a populist argument struck at parliamentary government. If members merely echoed their constituents, parliamentary debate was of little use. Parliament would merely aggregate votes determined elsewhere. The prime battlefield for executive power would shift from parliament to the public, where passionate appeals to prejudice and irresponsible promises might gain influence more easily. At best, parliament would be a convenient place to formulate compromises. Public reason to persuade other members or the nation at large would be expendable. In fact, if there were other ways to aggregate the decisions of local electorates, there would be little need for parliament at all.

---

86 W.H. Blanchard, *Brockville Recorder*, 17 June 1852
87 *Brockville Recorder*, 22 Aug., 12 Sept., and 7 and 28 Nov. 1850, *St Catharines Journal*, 11 Oct. 1849 and 15 Aug. 1850, *Huron Signal*, 24 Oct. 1850, *Guelph Advertiser*, 14 Mar. 1850, 14 Apr. 1853, and 8 June 1854, *Bathurst Courier*, 19 Nov. 1852, and *Globe*, 10 Apr. 1854
88 *Examiner*, 26 Sept. 1849 and Reformator, *Toronto Mirror*, 8 Feb. 1850
89 *Provincialist*, 29 Oct. and also 15 Oct. 1849

Robert Baldwin warned against the contention that 'representatives ought to be the mere indices of their constituents.' During a debate on the ever-controversial clergy-reserves question, Baldwin declared that 'he would never be a mere slave of any constituency.' Reading Edmund Burke's famous speech to the electors of Bristol to remind his fellow legislators of their duty to act as representatives, not delegates, Baldwin concluded that, at least on certain questions, they 'were bound to carry out their own opinions, no matter at what sacrifice.' He wanted them to vote according to what they thought was morally right and in the interests of the entire community. They would then appear before their constituents with their honest opinions. If the electorate disliked those opinions or distrusted their judgment, they would not re-elect them.[90]

It was a tough sell. Baldwin's refutation of the delegate theory of representation drew immediate fire from a fellow reform legislator. If the public had come to an ascertainable conclusion, 'a member was bound by the opinions of his constituents.' In the press, only the little-noticed *Hastings Chronicle* fully endorsed Baldwin's position. Even the moderate and usually sympathetic *Brockville Recorder* was more cautious. It conceded that members might legitimately differ from their constituency on matters of detail or when there had been little public debate, but insisted that 'on all matters which have been discussed and decided by the represented, the member is bound either to support the views of those who have delegated their power to him, or resign his charge.'[91] This, not Baldwin's position, was reform orthodoxy.

For instance, Peter Perry stood humbly before a large Grit meeting at Markham: 'He appeared before them to receive their instructions.' While he could not sacrifice his constitutional principles, instructions could apparently overcome his other beliefs. The *Bathurst Courier* also joined the attack on Baldwin's position. Burke was irrelevant. The public had evolved since the late eighteenth century: 'We set down the liberalism of Burke as the Toryism of the present.' It said much the same thing about Baldwin himself. Likewise, the *North American* asked, 'If the Representative is not bound to carry out the wishes of his constituents, whom does he represent?'[92]

---

90 Baldwin, *Debates*, 19 June 1850, 658–9
91 J. Scott, Bytown, ibid., 702, 705, *Hastings Chronicle* copied in *Mirror*, 20 June 1851 and, *Brockville Recorder*, 18 Sept. 1851. See also *Guelph Advertiser*, 16 Mar. 1854.
92 Perry, *Examiner*, 20 Mar. 1850, *Bathurst Courier*, 5 July 1850, and *North American*, 28 June 1850. See also *Bathurst Courier*, 18 Oct. 1850 and *Journal & Express* copied in *Bathurst Courier*, 12 July 1850.

The issue came into sharp focus when, before the 1851 election, several county conventions attempted to chain representatives to their local party. Local reform conventions to nominate candidates and pass resolutions were not new. The demand in Waterloo, Halton, Oxford, and Perth counties that candidates pledge themselves in writing to a 'platform' or 'party creed' and to resign if local 'Committees of Vigilance' determined that they had abandoned that platform was innovative. The movement was clearly motivated by a sense among some reformers that the previous reform government had abandoned reform principles and that the reform majority in the assembly had failed to hold them to account.

When A.J. Ferguson in Waterloo and John Wright in Halton subscribed to platforms, including a pledge to resign when called upon to do so, the *Guelph Advertiser* rejected claims that they had surrendered their independence. If elected reformers did their duty, vigilance committees would not have to meet. Pledges were 'only a formal recognition of a principle of honor in reality existing between every member of Parliament and his constituents.'[93] Giving an extra-parliamentary body the power to establish party principles, to judge the performance of representatives between elections, and to force their recall was far more than a codification of existing principle. If accepted, it threatened parliamentary government more effectively than extending the elective principle.

Oxford County reformers attempted to exact a similar pledge from Francis Hincks, resolving that 'at any time when two-thirds of this Convention in Committee assembled shall consider that the representative of this County has by his act forfeited the confidence of the said committee representing the reform party of the County of Oxford, he be pledged to resign his seat in Parliament.' Hincks angrily rejected the platform, arguing that his ministerial oath required him to advise the Crown of his own views, not those of a committee of local reformers.

It was a weak rebuttal. As commentators were quick to point out, Oxford was choosing a representative, not a cabinet minister. The *Examiner*, established by Hincks, pronounced his argument 'untenable.' Denying that electors could insist on a guarantee of fidelity from their representative was tantamount to denying 'the right of a tradesman to demand a note from his debtor.' Rarely has the delegate theory of representation been put so succinctly. As 'Constant' informed readers of

---

93 *Guelph Advertiser*, 6 Nov. 1851

the *Bathurst Courier*, for Hincks 'to feel insulted because his employers want to know his qualifications for their services, is as rich a piece of insolence and humbug as ever I heard of.'[94] If representatives could abandon the principles that had secured their election, what guaranteed that the assembly would reflect public opinion?

Reform supporters of parliamentary government advanced three main arguments against pledges. The first came from Hincks's organ, the *Montreal Pilot*. The election of candidates bound to local conventions would transform parliament. 'Instead of being an august and independent deliberative body, [it] would be mentally more dependant than, physically speaking, the slaves of the Southern states.' Parliament's legislative function required 'accommodation, of various interests and opinions ... hence the absurdity of pledges which preclude the possibility of accommodation, and thus defeat the end of Legislation itself.' If government by discussion was to apply to the legislature, its members required sufficient autonomy to sustain 'an independent deliberative body.'[95] Grits valued independence from the executive, but parliamentary government also demanded a degree of independence from the local electorate.

The second argument against pledges concerned the type of men most likely to be elected. The *Mirror* predicted that 'the direct tendency of this tyrannical system of binding down candidates so as to deprive them of all freedom of thought and action, is to fill the Legislature with those unprincipled and incompetent men, who are ever ready to swallow any platform' just to get elected. The *Brockville Recorder* agreed that it was better to have an honest member than one willing to curry favour; 'it may be that his opinions do not, in every particular, square with all whom he addresses, still, his character for honesty is a guarantee that whatever his sentiments may be, they are not advanced from motives of selfish interest, but from a desire to direct public opinion aright.'[96]

Francis Hincks provided the third reason why pledges were incompatible with parliamentary government. On the hustings, he declared, he

---

94 *Examiner*, 12 Nov. 1851 and Constant, *Bathurst Courier*, 14 Nov. 1851. See also *Bathurst Courier*, 12 Sept., 17 Oct., and 21 Nov. 1851, *Guelph Advertiser*, 18 Sept., 16 Oct., 6, 13, and 20 Nov. 1851, *Globe*, 18 Oct. 1851, *St Catharines Journal*, 13 Nov. 1851, and *Canadian Free Press*, 23 Oct. and 20 Nov. 1851.

95 *Montreal Pilot* copied in *Guelph Advertiser*, 13 Nov. 1851

96 *Mirror*, 7 Nov. 1851 and *Brockville Recorder*, 3 and 10 Apr. 1851. See also *Mirror*, 5 and 12 July 1850 and *Huron Signal*, 4 Apr. 1850.

'would not submit to be made the victim of a clique or a faction.'[97] Tying members too closely to local conventions would transfer power from parliament to political parties with their committees of dubious accountability. Extra-parliamentary parties helped articulate competing principles, kept representatives informed, and were increasingly important vehicles for electioneering. If, however, they became too powerful, they would replace the public as the primary locus of a representative's loyalty. Power within a party would become more important than directing 'public opinion aright.'

Some supporters of extra-parliamentary control were well aware of these implications. 'Plain Dealer' wrote to the *Guelph Advertiser* that if the 'Tory dogma that the Parliamentary representative has nothing to do but follow his own opinion' was to be fully exploded, pledges to local conventions were not enough. A province-wide convention 'acting as a watch-guard of reform interests, and embodying the living heart and soul of the Reform,' was required.[98] Pointing to the American experience, the *Globe* warned of the unintended consequences of such democratic populism. Professional politicians and wire-pullers had replaced the statesmen of the early republic. 'Party lines were drawn more closely, until at length parties became huge meshes to encumber and entrap the people.' 'Complicated party machinery' tended 'to limit popular influences within narrow channels,' to disgust 'men of lofty sentiments and enlarged capacity,' and 'enabled cunning, unscrupulous minorities to secure the avenues to posts of honour and emolument, eventually placing the interests and policy of a great people in the hands of men who have proved their readiness to sacrifice everything at the shrine of personal avarice and ambition.' An extensive and dense network of voluntary associations made a significant contribution to the ongoing vitality of public opinion, but the *Globe* had good reason to worry that if political parties resembled mass political machines more than voluntary associations, they could undermine that very vitality.[99]

---

97 Hincks, *Guelph Advertiser*, 4 Dec. 1851. Apparently no one thought it worth repeating an older, monarchical argument against recall – that it interfered with the Crown's prerogative of calling new elections. See Smith, *Republican Option in Canada*, 121.

98 'A Plain Dealer,' *Guelph Advertiser*, 27 Nov. 1851. Most advocated only local conventions, partly to avoid comparisons with the U.S., but also as a reflection of Canada's lack of a province-wide elective office.

99 *Globe*, 16 Jan. 1854. James Vernon, *Politics and the People: A Study in English Political Culture, c.1815–1867* (Cambridge: Cambridge University Press 1993), 182 argues that these disabling features predominated in Britain by the 1880s.

Tying representatives too closely to local party organizations could undermine parliamentary government. It could transfer power from parliament to local parties. Deliberation to persuade fellow participants might be replaced by irresponsible rhetoric and party theatrics for passive spectators. Parliament's educational function would be lost. Supporters of parliamentary government won the battle in the early 1850s. In the face of Francis Hincks's intransigence, the Oxford convention capitulated. Extracting pledges spread neither to most constituencies in 1850–1 nor to subsequent elections. Nonetheless, political parties, both inside and outside of parliament, did became more cohesive, especially after Confederation. The consequences were precisely as supporters of parliamentary government had feared.

Party cohesion was only one aspect of the Grits' populist approach to the assembly. Their proposals for the assembly itself were potentially more threatening to parliamentary government than making the other branches elective might have been. Again, Grits were more successful in framing the debate and marshalling support for their assumptions than in achieving specific institutional reforms.

If the executive was responsive to public opinion by virtue of its responsibility to the assembly, then the assembly had to mirror public opinion. As one editor put it, 'A government is free only in proportion as the Legislature is a faithful reflex of public sentiment.'[100] Parliamentary government, however, made the assembly a vital participant in public deliberation, not merely its 'reflex.' Disgruntled reformers emphasized the assembly's role in expressing public opinion to the exclusion of its role in shaping it. Peter Perry told supporters that 'the people would not forget that their [the assembly's] powers were not given them to act as an independent body, but to represent the wishes of those who sent them there, whose servants they are, and whose privileges they are bound to protect.'[101] The master-servant analogy was common Grit rhetoric.

Pledging individual representatives to local party platforms was one way to ensure that the assembly reflected the opinions of the provincial majority. Limiting cabinet power would also allow the assembly to reflect public opinion without interference. A third set of proposals might achieve the same end. 'Can the true opinion of the community be ascertained,' asked a Hamilton paper, with a limited franchise, unequal

---

100 *Examiner,* 26 Feb. 1851
101 Perry, *North American,* 10 Sept. 1850 and also *Bathurst Courier,* 2 Aug. 1850

constituencies, and intimidation at open polls?[102] Only if a greater proportion of adult men could freely register their deliberate judgment in constituencies of equal size would every voter contribute equally and honestly to the outcome. Without such reforms, 'there is no safety in the present system. If public opinion is truly expressed in the House as now constituted, it is a mere accident.'[103] Such reforms might ensure a more accurate aggregation of individuals' opinions, but would they advance the cause of public opinion and parliamentary government?

Of the three issues – the franchise, representation, and the secret ballot – the last was the least considered. Support was coupled with extensions of the franchise. Without the secret ballot, many feared adding those males to the electorate who were most dependent upon customers, creditors, and landlords. Thus protected, the vote of each elector 'is the expression of his own deliberate choice; and not the mere slavish registering of the will of another.' Nonetheless, the question remained peripheral.[104]

The same cannot be said of the franchise or representation. Indeed, constitutional reform in Britain was almost synonymous with reforming representation in the House of Commons. British debates about representation often turned on the likely consequences for parliamentary government. The full title of Earl Grey's book was *Parliamentary Government Considered with Reference to A Reform of Parliament.* While not opposed to further changes after those of 1832, Grey warned that some proposals to extend the franchise or equalize constituencies risked destroying parliamentary government. Chapter 4, 'Reasons of the Success of Parliamentary Government,' emphasized how the Commons differed from other elective legislatures. A restricted franchise and unequal constituencies ensured the presence of a 'variety of elements.' Those blinded by abstract principles of equality and democracy forgot the lessons of experience; that the so-called impurities and 'irregularities of our Representation ... constituted so important a part of the machine of our Government.' Some members were elected by democratic constituencies; others were returned for smaller constituencies or subject to influence from various sources. This guaranteed that the House contained members with unpopular views and spokesmen for various

---

102 *Express* copied in *Mirror*, 10 May 1850
103 *North American*, 30 Dec. 1852
104 *Examiner*, 13 Mar. 1850, *Provincialist*, 1 Apr. 1850, and *North American*, 24 Jan. 1851. For relative indifference, see *Globe*, 28 Mar. 1850, and *North American*, 8 Nov. 1850, and *Daily Leader*, 18 Oct. 1854.

classes or interests that might otherwise go unrepresented. Equal constituencies and universal suffrage might produce greater homogeneity. Government by discussion required variety – one is tempted to say balance.

According to Grey, if the House merely mirrored the population, there would be nothing to prevent it from invading executive or judicial functions or from attacking all those who failed to conform to the majority. 'There would have existed no appeal against any abuse of power by the House of Commons, to the opinions of a larger public than that by which it was elected.' A purely democratic body might become 'an irresistible engine for carrying into effect any measure, however violent, which the passions of the People might dictate.' The Commons was to respond to public opinion, but it also had to ensure 'due consideration of objections to measures for which there is a popular cry, and to afford means for testing by discussion the soundness or fallacy of conflicting arguments.' A legislature based on universal suffrage and equal constituencies would be less able or willing to do either.[105]

Reform in Upper Canada had never centred on the franchise or representation, but the now dominant place of the assembly gave these topics new urgency. Historians have often equated democracy with universal suffrage.[106] While a few Grits began to make the connection during this period, it was far from axiomatic. The debate about the franchise did not hinge upon whether Canada was a democracy. Neither was it about natural or individual rights. The franchise was something to be earned; its price, the capacity to judge. Equally important, the debate in Upper Canada was conducted without reference to the likely implications for parliamentary government.

Peter Perry championed manhood suffrage because only if every sane adult male had the vote would Canadians not 'deprive ourselves of any portion of the mind.'[107] Even those most adverse to universal suffrage

105 Grey, *Parliamentary Government*, 58–83. Bagehot also attacked the 'ultra-democratic theory' as incompatible with parliamentary government, *The English Constitution*, 161–81.

106 E.g., J.M.S. Careless, 'Mid-Victorian Liberalism in Central Canadian Newspapers, 1850–1859,' *Canadian Historical Review* 31, no. 3 (September 1950), 221–36 and Bruce W. Hodgins, 'Democracy and the Ontario Fathers of Confederation,' in *Profiles of a Province: Studies in the History of Ontario* (Toronto: Ontario Historical Society 1967), 83–91

107 Perry, *Examiner*, 20 Mar. 1850. For Grits and the franchise see *St Catharines Journal*, 15 Feb. 1849, 4 July and 12 Sept. 1850, and 11 Dec. 1851, *Mirror*, 22 Mar. 1850, *Provincialist*, 1 Apr. 1850, and *North American*, 17 Jan. 1851.

agreed that mental capacity was the primary standard. The *Globe* defended a moderate property qualification, having 'often contended that under a limited suffrage the expression of the public mind is more truly obtained than by a system of universal suffrage.' Universal suffrage would generate 'a tumultuous constituency' incapable of participating in the public sphere and thus requiring management by undemocratic party machines. Again, what appeared to be the more fully 'democratic' option would produce, according to the *Globe*, unintended and undemocratic consequences. For the *Globe*, 'the best standard of qualification would certainly be the intelligence and integrity of the voter,' but until phrenology was more reliable, a property qualification was the only practical means to exclude the incapable – the 'worthless and intemperate' – from the electorate.[108]

The *Brockville Recorder* pushed the argument to its logical conclusion by supporting 'a literacy line' to exclude any male incapable 'of forming an enlightened opinion as to the fitness or unfitness of Parliamentary Candidates.' Politics and print were inseparable. On the other side of the issue, the *Huron Signal* championed universal suffrage, 'not because every man is qualified to exercise this privilege with discretion and intelligence but because there never has been, and perhaps never can be, any intellectual standard of qualification agreed on and the property qualification is an insult to the higher qualities of our nature.'[109] The intellectual distance between the *Globe*, *Recorder*, and *Signal* was minimal.

Reformator, the leading Grit ideologue, advocated a householder franchise as a preliminary step towards manhood suffrage. His rationale was rooted in a progressive history of the public sphere. A limited franchise had been appropriate 'when wealth was necessary to and almost synonymous with intelligence; when books were sealed to the majority; when the cloister and the hall held the wisdom of the nation; and when the popular voice was the mere echo of the will of the privileged few.' This was no longer the case. 'A wonder-working press is busily scattering broadcast its truths; a mysterious spirit of knowledge ... is let loose in the land ... every laborer has become a thinker.' 'The pages of De Tocqueville and Montesquieu are seen as often in the hands of the "proscribed" as in those of their more fortunate brethren.' The popular voice now echoed the will of the many. 'The poor may remain poor still;

---

108 *Globe*, 28 Jan. 1851, 22 Mar. and 19 July 1848, and 1 June 1850
109 *Brockville Recorder*, 30 Nov. 1854 and *Huron Signal*, 12 Sept. 1850 and 21 July and 18 Aug. 1848

but they are not necessarily ignorant.' Newspapers, schools, and improved roads were now common; isolation from knowledge and public deliberation increasingly rare.[110]

In sum, the debate was framed in terms of the public sphere. The *Huron Signal* even defined universal suffrage as 'the omnipotence of public opinion.' No reformer doubted the role of education in making extensions of the franchise safe. None doubted that voting was itself educational. The *Globe*, for one, was less sanguine than Reformator or the *Signal* about how universal the capacity to reason in public had become, but the degree of consensus was remarkable. Almost no reformer tried to justify a property qualification as such. Thus, it is not surprising that there was little debate about and even less opposition to the adoption of an assessment or taxpayer franchise and voter registration by the Hincks government in 1853.[111] Given widespread belief in progress, universal suffrage seemed only a matter of time.

The *Huron Signal* acknowledged that the shift from economic independence and property ownership to mental capacity as the threshold for voting did not, in principle, exclude women. As a little-noticed component of a package of changes intended to reduce electoral fraud, the franchise had been explicitly restricted to males only in 1849, but the more universalistic implications of grounding political citizenship in the public sphere were already apparent. After considering 'Should women exercise political rights and discharge political duties in common with men?' in January 1851, the majority of the members of the all-male Brockville Debating Club voted in the affirmative. The following year, a female reader of Whitby's *Ontario Reporter* wrote to demand equal rights, including the franchise, in part, because 'males and females are constituted essentially alike in mind.' Met by the entrenched doctrine of marital unity – that it would be useless to grant women the vote since they would only use it in accordance with their husbands' wishes – Martha

---

110 Reformator, *Mirror*, 10 Aug. 1848, 17 Aug. 1849, and 22 Feb., 29 Mar., and 7 June 1850. See Dewar, 'Charles Clarke's "Reformator,"' 237.

111 *Huron Signal*, 18 Aug. 1848. On education and the vote, see the *Globe*, 4 Mar. 1852, *Examiner*, 27 Mar. 1850, *Brockville Recorder*, 29 May 1851, *North American*, 17 Jan. 1851, and *St Catharines Journal*, 8 Jan. 1852. On the relative consensus see *Guelph Advertiser*, 9 Mar. 1854, which predicted that the 1853 reforms would expand the electorate by half. Hincks's Toronto organ, the *Daily Leader*, 22 Sept. 1853, concluded that the expansion brought the franchise 'as near as the state of general intelligence would justify, to manhood suffrage.' In general, see John Garner, *The Franchise and Politics in British North America, 1775–1867* (Toronto: University of Toronto Press 1969), 105–8.

Thomas wryly asked, 'What use then are reason and conscience to her, if they must be exercised in obedience to her husband[?]'[112]

Thomas's remained a minority voice subject to ridicule;[113] it would take decades for universal suffrage to answer her question. More immediately, married women demanded changes to the laws governing their property. Joined by sympathetic men, they set out in 1852 to change public opinion by petitioning and writing letters to the editor in what Lori Chambers sees as 'the first organized effort of women in Upper Canada to improve their own status.' In 1857 alone, thirteen hundred married women signed a single petition. The first married women's property act, passed two years later, symbolized the law's dawning recognition that married women could have interests that differed legitimately from those of their husbands.[114] The campaign also illustrated the potential openness of the public sphere to participation by women. That this openness remained, in the 1850s, more potential than actual had little to do with the public sphere itself (although this in no way lessens the exclusion or makes it more compatible with the ideals of that sphere).

The province's population of African descent also set out to harness the potential of the public sphere. Unlike women of all origins, however, black men already had the right to vote on the same basis as other men. The *Provincial Freeman* was the second newspaper established to 'allow our fellow subjects to know who we are and what we want' and to 'train ourselves as to fit us for the discharge of the duties of freemen, in full.' Synopses of parliamentary intelligence and commentary on the 1854 Kent County election were part of that training. Mary Ann Shadd, teacher, writer, abolitionist, and public speaker, was the 'driving force' behind the paper, serving officially as business agent and later as editor. Faced with community hostility to female editors, she resigned in June

---

112 *Huron Signal*, 18 Aug. 1848, Archives of Ontario, Brockville Debating Club, Records and Proceedings, and Martha F.H. Thomas, *Ontario Reporter*, 10 Apr. and 18 Sept. 1852

113 Cecilia Morgan, *Public Men and Virtuous Women: The Gendered Languages of Religion and Politics in Upper Canada, 1791–1850* (Toronto: University of Toronto Press 1996), 212–14 and 'Woman's Rights,' *Provincial Freeman*, 12 Aug. 1854. For Egerton Ryerson's defence of the right of female freeholders or household heads to vote in school-board elections in 1851, see Allison Prentice, *The School Promoters: Education and Social Class in Mid-Nineteenth Century Upper Canada* (Toronto: McClelland and Stewart 1977), 11.

114 Lori Chambers, *Married Women and Property Law in Victorian Ontario* (Toronto: University of Toronto Press 1997), 9, 70, 73–5, 91. See also Constance B. Backhouse, 'Married Women's Property Law in Nineteenth-Century Canada,' *Law and History Review* 6, no. 2 (Fall 1988), 223, 248–9.

1855. Despite evident hardships, she was proud to conclude: 'To colored women, we have a word – we have "broken the Editorial ice," ... for your class in America; so go to Editing, as many of you as are willing, and able, and as soon as you may.' Other women should help 'by subscribing to the paper, paying for it, and getting your neighbour to do the same.'[115]

Voluntary associations were also important to this community for self-help and to bolster their demands for equality. The Provincial Union was formed at Toronto in the summer of 1854 to promote racial harmony, support the *Freeman*, campaign against slavery, and 'encourage the rising generation in literary, scientific, and mechanical efforts.' While women formed a separate committee to 'prepare articles for the Annual Fair,' all members, male and female, promised to assemble monthly 'for the purpose of promoting the literary objects, specifically by recitations of original pieces, reading, debates &c.' Shadd was appointed to organize auxiliaries that soon appeared in Chatham, Brantford, and London. Blacks had been forming their own Masonic lodges since 1851 and, according to the *Freeman*, also participated in local mechanics' institutes. Black women in Chatham and Windsor formed what were probably the first women-only literary societies in the province. 'The Colored Citizens' of Cannonsburg had already established the mixed-sex Wilberforce Lyceum Educating Society for Moral and Mental Improvement in 1850. Intent on equality and respect in the public sphere, it was committed to 'education, scientific attainments,' religion, 'politeness, and such other genius in our Society as will entitle us to mix more freely in the great crowd of her Majesty's subjects that is befitting a people who love Belle letters, and other polite literature as will tend to make us a nation suitable to appear before the sons of men without remark or any other hindrance derogatory to the enlightened character of dutiful subjects.'[116] Voluntary associations remained impor-

---

115 *Provincial Freeman*, 24 Mar. 1853, 25 Mar., 6 May, 21 and 28 Oct., and 11 Nov. 1854, and 9 and 30 June 1855. See Jane Rhodes, *Mary Ann Shadd Cary: The Black Press and Protest in the Nineteenth Century* (Bloomington: Indiana University Press 1998), esp. 70–99, on the importance of the public sphere to this remarkable figure. In 1859 her father became the first Upper Canadian of African descent to be elected to local office.

116 *Provincial Freeman*, 19 Aug., 28 Oct. and 9 Dec. 1854, Peggy Bristow, '"Whatever you raise in the ground you can see it in Chatham": Black Women in Buxton and Chatham, 1850–65,' in Bristow, coord., *'We're Rooted Here and They Can't Pull Us Up': Essays in African Canadian Women's History* (Toronto: University of Toronto Press 1994), 120–3, and *Constitution and By Laws of the Wilberforce Lyceum Educating Society*, 1

tant vehicles 'to appear before' others as 'enlightened' and thus worthy of recognition and respect as fellow-citizens.

While women and blacks of both sexes tried to harness the recently accepted public sphere to advance demands for improved status, parliament offered political equality to the province's natives in 1857. An act 'to encourage the gradual civilization of the Indian tribes' defined them as minors in need of 'protection,' but sought to end this 'special' status along with the legal discrimination and segregation it entailed. The act offered equality to those adult males who could prove their literacy in English or French, freedom from debt, and good moral character – tests not all non-native voters would have passed. Each would be granted a freehold allotment from the reserves and, after a year's probation, granted all the rights of property ownership and citizenship. Political equality was a carrot to the stick of assimilation.[117]

The public sphere assumed that individuals were sufficiently alike or assimilated to engage in meaningful dialogue with each other and to arrive at mutually agreed-upon decisions. This did not, however, require sameness. Catholics and Protestants or merchants and artisans, for example, could learn to meet as equals in voluntary associations and public debate without assimilating. Likewise, Martha Thomas demanded equality based on women's intellectual similarity to men without implying that the sexes were or had to be the same in other respects. The 1857 act, however, appeared to offer natives a brutal trade-off between inequality and much of their distinctiveness. The concept of different but equal was not foreign to the pluralism of the public sphere, but the limits of legitimate difference remained contested. As 'uncivilized,' traditional forms of native self-government and landownership were beyond the pale.

---

117 John L. Tobias, 'Protection, Civilization, Assimilation: An Outline History of Canada's Indian Policy,' 127, 130 and John S. Milloy, 'The Early Indian Acts: Development Strategy and Constitutional Change,' 146–8 in J.R. Miller, ed., *Sweet Promises: A Reader on Indian-White Relations in Canada* (Toronto: University of Toronto Press 1991). Technically, adult natives who were property owners in their own right could vote on the same basis as non-natives before 1857. Since natives were not recognized as individual owners of communal lands, most could not meet the property qualification. The 1857 act provided a mechanism for the individual ownership of part of those lands and thus for the right to vote, but added additional requirements that were not legally demanded of non-natives. See Sidney L. Harring, *White Man's Law: Native People in Nineteenth-Century Canadian Jurisprudence* (Toronto: University of Toronto Press 1998), 33, 57–8.

Little of this discussion about extending the franchise to taxpayers, all adult men, women, or natives considered the possible impact upon parliamentary government. The *Globe* warned against the growth of parties and feared that public opinion might be drowned out by the voices of the ignorant, but it failed to mount a direct defence of a restricted franchise as essential to parliamentary government. Moreover, the *Globe* was often isolated on this issue. Silence was also noticeable on the question of representation.

In 1849, 1850, and again in 1851, Louis LaFontaine attempted to increase the number of representatives from each of the Canadas from 42 to 75, creating new constituencies in recently populated areas without abolishing smaller ones.[118] Upper Canadian reformers agreed with their leaders that there were constitutional reasons to increase the number of representatives. A larger house would be more independent of the executive. Cabinets could not retain power by bribing a few members or be toppled by the exorbitant demands of a handful of legislators. Ministers would form a smaller proportion of a larger legislature and the talent pool from which they were drawn would expand. Overall, as Lord Elgin told Earl Grey, there would be 'a better chance for the formation of a sound public opinion if it were enlarged.' Nonetheless, equality of representation, not its size, was the crucial issue.[119]

In the early 1850s, 'representation by population' was a demand for fairness *within* Upper Canada, not between the two Canadas. As early as 1847, the *Examiner* had noted that inequality among constituencies enabled a minority of voters to elect the majority of members – a 'wretched caricature' or 'mock system' of representation. The paper calculated that the 18 largest constituencies in Upper Canada contained 435,893 people, while the remaining 25 [24?] accounted for only 287,194. The *Recorder* noted that Brockville, with a population of 3000, returned one representative while the united counties of Leeds and Grenville, with a population of over 43,000, returned only two.[120] There was a strong partisan element in such analyses, since conservatives were typically more

118 Garner, *Franchise and Politics*, 95–6
119 Elgin to Grey, 11 Oct. 1848, 27 May 1847, and 4 Jan. 1849, *Elgin-Grey Papers*, v. 1, 45–6, 245–6, 279. See also *Globe*, 11 Nov. 1848, *Examiner*, 15 Dec. 1847 and 22 Nov. 1848, *Provincialist*, 21 Nov. 1848, *Canadian Freeman*, 22 Nov. 1848, Reformator, *Mirror*, 19 Apr. 1850, *Freeholder*, 9 July 1850, *North American*, 28 Feb. 1851, H.J. Boulton and Notman, *Debates*, 21 Mar. 1849, 1481, 1488, and Adam Fergusson, LaFontaine, and William Hamilton Merritt, *Debates*, 17 May and 28 June 1850, 51–2, 887, 893.
120 *Examiner*, 17 Nov. 1847 and 27 Nov. 1850 and *Brockville Recorder*, 9 May 1850

successful than reformers in towns and cities. As reformers saw it, 'rotten boroughs' diluted the representation of 'sturdy yeoman.'

'An Elector' told the *Port Hope Watchman* that 'no system of representation can be right, where political power is unequally divided. All men should be equal in this respect. To do otherwise is to constitute a minority into a majority, and this is virtually to annihilate representative government. Representation, should therefore be based on population.'[121] The logic was relentless. It was a reform article of faith that population, not Grey's variety of interests or opinions, was the only legitimate basis for representation.[122] They debated the issue's priority, the details of various proposals, the speed at which they could be achieved, and the necessity of grappling with inequality between the Canadas, but these were largely pragmatic matters of strategy. There was no defence of unequal or irregular constituencies; no argument that they were essential to parliamentary government.

The only reform paper to argue against representation by population within Upper Canada was the exception that proves the rule. The principal organ of Hincksite reformers, the *Daily Leader*, argued that since 'a member of parliament represents those, and only those, who elect him, not those whom the law incapacitates from voting,' constituencies were equal if they contained the same number of electors regardless of their total populations. The *Leader*'s rejection of virtual representation was total. If a representative 'were held to represent the non-voters in his constituency, he must, so far as they are concerned be self-elected. But self-election is usurpation, and usurpation is destructive of all freedom.'[123] The *Leader* rejected representation by population, but not to defend unequal constituencies as useful in a parliamentary system. The grounds on which it made its case only highlighted the shaky conceptual foundations of that system. The *Leader* accepted, on this occasion, that representatives were directly tied to local voters. They were not representatives of the nation or of a broader public opinion. Once this was accepted, the logic of binding them more closely to their local party, of limiting their autonomy, and of reducing the legislature to little more

---

121 *Port Hope Watchman*, 28 Nov. 1851
122 E.g., H.J. Boulton, *Debates*, 21 Mar. 1849, 1481, Richards, *Debates*, 28 June 1850, 899–900, Reformator, *Mirror*, 19 Apr. 1850, *Freeholder*, 9 July 1850, *North American*, 28 Feb. 1851, 2 Dec. 1852, and 31 Mar. and 7 Apr. 1853, and *Canadian Free Press*, 21 Feb. and 3 Apr. 1851.
123 *The Daily Leader*, 22 Sept. 1853

than a convenient place to aggregate votes made considerable sense. But it was not parliamentary government.

In 1848, the *Examiner* advocated a Canadian Reform Bill, setting out from the premise that 'representation is simply the sending of substitutes to deliberate and decide on public affairs; the personal attendance of the whole constituent body being impractical.'[124] This premise underpinned the Grits' populist approach to the franchise, representation, and party cohesion. It denied that representative government was morally or intellectually superior to direct democracy. It minimized or excluded meaningful dialogue within political institutions and between those institutions and the public. It undermined parliamentary government. On the issues of suffrage and representation, moderate reformers failed to challenge the premise. On the question of party cohesion, they mounted the challenge, but it was neither unanimous nor very forceful. Parliamentary government's supporters, preoccupied with its more formal institutions and mechanisms, had failed to solidify its conceptual foundations.

Contemporaries knew well that parliamentary government was far more than the conventions by which a majority of the people's representatives sustained or defeated the Crown's advisers, but why had moderate reformers failed to more clearly articulate and defend some of its important principles? Not from lack of opportunity. Many of the Grits' arguments surveyed here might have provoked such a response. Ignorance also seems an inadequate explanation. The classic expositions by Earl Grey and Walter Bagehot lay in the future, but the basics were already known.

Part of the answer lies in political tactics. Moderate reformers had to defeat the Grit charge that ministerial responsibility was insufficiently democratic. Emphasizing the need for elected representatives to be relatively autonomous from their constituents was bound to be unpopular with large segments of the reform party. Emphasizing how different parliamentary government was from either direct democracy or the simplest representative government (where the people's delegates met in a single body to pass laws and supervise their administration) would only confirm suspicions that parliamentary government was conservative and oligarchic.

---

124 *Examiner*, 22 Nov. 1848

Nonetheless, tactical considerations offer only an incomplete explanation. They reduce the debate to a purely instrumental level. Moreover, reformers like Robert Baldwin and George Brown were willing to take vocal and unpopular stands against arguments they believed to be incompatible with ministerial responsibility. Even so, they often failed to convince fellow partisans. Tactical explanations also beg the central question. Why were such arguments unpopular among Upper Canadian reformers? Why, when they made the attempt, were Baldwin, Brown, and others often unable to gain wider support for some of the premises of parliamentary government while preserving its basic institutional form?

Although other possible explanations could be advanced, contemporaries zeroed in on one of the most enduring themes of reform discourse in the colony – the perceived social differences between Britain and Upper Canada and the profound political divergence thought to flow from them. The tension between the evolving lessons of British constitutionalism and the province's own, very different, circumstances had, of course, been central to the history of mixed monarchy in Upper Canada. In 1853, the *Mirror* concluded that 'the forced analogy between states of society so utterly dissimilar as those of Great Britain and Canada, is entirely untenable.'[125] The tension hadn't evaporated with the eclipse of mixed monarchy.

Reformers who pushed for further constitutional evolution after 1848 were convinced that 'the notion of an "exact transcript" is a superstitious dream, a fanatical delusion.' They continued to debate the political sociology so evident in the literature of the Metcalfe crisis. By contrast, reformers satisfied with the constitutional status quo thought Canadian society and its constitution had, at last, been brought into harmony with the demise of mixed monarchy. For their more radical colleagues, Canadians could respect the great principles of the British constitution, but needed to choose its best features, jettison its faults, and adapt the whole to their own society.[126] Commentators continued to visualize a relatively egalitarian population dominated by actual and potential landowners. According to Henry Boulton, 'There was no country under the sun, in which, from the peculiarly agricultural character of its population, eighty per cent were agricultural, democracy was

---

125 *Mirror*, 20 May 1853
126 *Examiner*, 22 May 1850, A Radical Reformer, *Mirror*, 28 Dec. 1849, and Reformator, *Mirror*, 19 Oct. 1849 and 1 Mar. 1850

more firmly established.'[127] In short, the articulate continued to present their society as dominated by precisely those classes singled out by democratic theory as the most knowledgeable and virtuous.

Their belief that they possessed such a social structure (and that Britain did not) influenced Upper Canadians' understanding of parliamentary government. Could it be transplanted any more easily than mixed monarchy? Might it not, once planted in a different environment, operate in ways that were incompatible with its essence? At first, the prerequisite of parliamentary government – a society capable of sustained public deliberation – appeared far less onerous than that of mixed monarchy with its corporatist assumptions, but the widespread impatience with those who continued to rely upon British precedents after 1848 reveals the persistent belief in the cultural specificity of constitutional forms.

The *Examiner* was one of the more thoughtful analysts of that specificity. The British constitution was a set of living principles that had evolved over centuries, becoming fully adapted to British society, circumstance, and intelligence. Upper Canada was different on all three counts. Regarding social structure, the province was marked by 'our general equality as to wealth – our freedom from the encumbrances of patrician and plebian orders.' Regarding circumstance, Upper Canada was 'contiguous to a country, pre-eminent among the nations for its full enjoyment of representative government,' and regarding intelligence, 'our people are unquestionably better acquainted with the principles of self-government than those of the Parent State.' A more widespread system of schools and elective municipal institutions ensured that it was 'within the power of every one to obtain a political knowledge which renders them more capable of exercising the higher rights of subjects with more discretion than the bulk of the population of England.' With such training grounds, the province had a more robust, democratic public sphere.

The constitutional implications of such differences were inescapable:

We may be anxious to retain an exact transcript of the great theoretical principles of the British Constitution, as to the popular rights of free and just representation, and as to the responsibility of the Advisers of the Crown, yet it must be apparent that even were the workings of that Constitution perfectly adapted to the circumstances and the wants of the Parent State, it would by no means correspond to the circumstances of this coun-

---

127 Boulton, *Debates*, 22 May 1850, 135. See also A., *Examiner*, 28 Apr. 1847, *North American*, 10 Jan. 1851, and *Daily Leader*, 14 July 1854.

try or the genius of its people. We are a different people in our thoughts, our habits, our acquirements and in many of our institutions. If we choose to live in Canada, we cease to be British. While we cherish feelings, preferences, and wishes the most loyal, we are not, we cannot be British. This, by no means makes us American. We do not pretend to say most Canadians sympathize with American institutions. It is sufficient to us, that we know our own circumstances and capabilities for self-government.[128]

Once again, the demand for self-government and a fully made-in-Canada constitution pushed commentators towards a proto-nationalism.

Sir Francis Bond Head and Sir Charles Metcalfe had opposed ministerial responsibility because they feared colonial society might alter it. During the Metcalfe crisis, the *Examiner* agreed that Upper Canadian society would alter responsible government, but welcomed the anticipated differences. After the crisis, conservatives made similar observations, but some found the consequences so problematic that they demanded a new constitution modelled on that of the United States. The *Examiner*, now a Grit organ, agreed that the effects being realized required institutional change.

But what, precisely, were the consequences for parliamentary government of the perceived differences between British and Canadian society? One was probably a greater degree of pragmatism concerning political institutions. Moderate reformers were trying to infuse the old forms of governor, legislative council, and assembly with the principles of ministerial responsibility that had developed slowly and painfully in the social and political context of another country. The principles were new to Upper Canada and had to be tested according to their current, local utility. They lacked the weight of habit or tradition. It was difficult to venerate what was new. Thus, one of the first goals of radicals was to go beyond the tyranny of names, labels, and precedents to design a constitution from the first principle of responsibility to public opinion.[129] Supporters of parliamentary government were left to insist upon the potential for unintended, undesirable consequences flowing from even the most logical principle.

Impatience was also evident in the general disdain for the aristocratic and monarchical remnants of mixed monarchy. Increasingly vocal calls

---

128 *Examiner*, 21 Apr. 1852
129 E.g., C., *Provincialist*, 3 Sept. 1849, *St Catharines Journal*, 29 Nov. 1849, and *Huron Signal*, 20 June 1850

for fiscal retrenchment in the 1850s were about more than saving tax-payers' money. They betrayed a penchant for 'republican simplicity' over the 'appearance of Royal Dignity, without the substance.' Reforma-tor thought it 'futile to expect that the mere boundary of a river will always keep us in love with the pageantry, cumbrousness, and expense of a monarchy.' Since it refused to conform to the political and relative social equality of Upper Canada, 'the pageantry of vice-regal establish-ment' was a positive evil. The remnants of the 'Tory' party survived because 'by its love of pomp, glitter, its tinsel, and its appeal to preju-dice, it secured as its votaries the ignorant on the one hand, and the aristocratic on the other.'[130] Reform would remain ascendant as long as it stood for simple, transparent government and reflected the reasoning of the great bulk of the population. The British constitution included feudal remnants alien and harmful to Canada.

Walter Bagehot agreed. While most often celebrated for his distinc-tion between the 'efficient' and 'dignified' elements of that constitu-tion, Bagehot also insisted that the latter were essential to parliamentary government. Britain was a 'disguised republic,' but the disguise was cru-cial. Most Britons were not members of the public sphere since, accord-ing to Bagehot, 'the working classes contribute almost nothing to our corporate public opinion.' A 'double government' was therefore required: one for the people, another for the public. Those who couldn't contribute to public opinion were entertained, misled, and kept deferential by the dignified, 'theatrical' show of monarchy and aris-tocracy – what Reformator called 'pomp, glitter, ... tinsel, and ... preju-dice' – while the middle classes, understanding that actual power rested in cabinet and Commons, attended to public affairs. In a parliamentary system, legislators and the cabinet were not restrained by formal laws and separate institutions as in a republic, but by conventions and tenu-ous balances. Thus, the system required legislators of the highest calibre insulated from all but the educated, informed minority. Bagehot con-cluded that a 'deferential community, even though its lowest classes are not intelligent, is far more suited to a Cabinet government that any kind of democratic country ... A country of respectful poor, though far less happy than where there are no poor to be respectful, is nevertheless far more fitted for the best government.'[131]

---

130 New Era, *Brockville Recorder*, 8 Nov. 1849 and Reformator, *Mirror*, 2 Nov. 1849, 8 Feb.
      1850, 1 and 22 Mar. and 5 Apr. 1850
131 Bagehot, *The English Constitution*, 176, 238, 247–50

Some Canadian reformers doubted the ability of the propertyless and transient to fully participate in public deliberations, but they never described their society as deferential or thought that the majority needed to be distracted by pageantry while a minority governed. The credible belief that the majority of Upper Canadian males were newspaper readers and actual or potential heads of independent households rendered Bagehot's analysis of the social requirements of parliamentary government irrelevant. The *Globe* might admit that 'British Responsible Government without the prestige of a monarchy and peerage, and without the social restraints of older countries, is yet but an experiment,'[132] but few indeed drew the inference that the 'dignified' elements of monarch and aristocracy should be augmented.

Bagehot called this experiment 'the unroyal form of Parliamentary government.' Perhaps, he conceded, there was one type of society capable of sustaining parliamentary government without Britain's deferential class structure; a nation 'where there is no honest poverty, where education is diffused, and political intelligence is common.' With little analysis, Bagehot asserted that 'the idea is roughly realised in the North American colonies of England.' Dispersed settlement posed the greatest obstacle, since 'where population is sparse, discussion is difficult,' but once distance was overcome, 'a people really intelligent, really educated, really comfortable, would soon form a good opinion.'[133] Parliamentary government might be compatible with social democracy if the public sphere was especially vigorous – if all who judged were capable of judging.

As we have already seen, government by discussion made heavy demands of Upper Canadians. In Britain, Bagehot thought the pageantry of the 'dignified' constitution kept those incapable of judging deferential to the decisions of others. To preserve parliamentary government without most of the 'dignified' show required an almost heroic belief in the capacities of a public nearly coequal with the population. That public had to choose between competing party principles, hold their representatives accountable for what they promised at previous elections, and sustain a public dialogue immune to demagogues, the ignorant, and the fickle. Further, it had to acknowledge its own limitations and those of democratic populism. Parliament had to be allowed to represent public opinion rather than popular clamour, competing

---

132 *Globe*, 13 Apr. 1852
133 Bagehot, *The English Constitution*, 245

local interests, party organizations, or an aggregation of each voter's opinions. Its members had to be given sufficient autonomy to deliberate among themselves and to educate the public. They had to be left free to choose the executive and to hold it accountable between elections. Upper Canadians had to be convinced that this balance of activity and self-restraint defined good government.

In their long campaign for a government responsible to public opinion, reformers stressed only half the equation, the active capacity of 'the people.' By continuing to emphasize it, moderate reformers were able to counter Grit demands for institutional reform, but that emphasis also made it more difficult to counter populist assumptions and to gain sufficient recognition for those principles of parliamentary government that limited what could be achieved safely by the electorate. Since there was no source of legitimate authority but 'the people,' such limits had to be self-imposed. If reformers agreed on 'the people's' capacity for self-government, why should they accept such limits? Why shouldn't they hold the executive directly accountable? Why should representatives have a significant degree of autonomy from those who elected them? If 'the people' created the public opinion, why did parliament need to be insulated from more direct links to the people such as recall or referenda? Proponents of parliamentary government had what they believed to be two good answers to such questions: first, that parliamentary government best embodied the strengths and weakness of the public sphere, and second, that it better reflected concrete historical experience and political reality than the logic of apparently purer democratic principles that risked unintended, often undemocratic, consequences. Yet they were unable to offer either of these answers in a manner that many fellow reformers found convincing before they lost control of the government in 1854.

Moreover, once they had succeeded in establishing the primacy of public opinion and a form of government responsive to it, reformers could no longer dodge some of the nagging questions first posed by those who had sneered at the very idea of public opinion. Focusing on the Olympian promise of the public sphere had helped to rally supporters and browbeat opponents. Public deliberation remained the preferred and ultimate (though not always the immediate) mechanism for arriving at widely accepted solutions to concrete public problems and to finding ways for people of diverse interests and backgrounds to understand and accommodate each other. The degree of conformity to the ideals of the public sphere also remained the yardstick by which institutions and practices were measured. Yet Upper Canada's reformers were practical politicians rudely aware that knowledge of the 'facts' and predictions about the outcome of any decision were always imperfect. To await perfect information was never to act. They also knew that some prejudices could be worn down only by prolonged battle in the public sphere. In the meantime, decisions had to be made and justified. There was also a rush to judgment. Could you always tell when a popular decision was sufficiently 'informed,' 'reasoned,' and 'accepted?' The will to listen carefully to what one didn't want to hear and to put one's most cherished beliefs through the rough and tumble of public criticism was inevitably limited. It was more comforting to demand this will of one's opponents than to muster it oneself. Now in control of the state, reformers could not allow their own stirring invocations of the majesty of 'public opinion' to blind them to the day-to-day pitfalls of popular self-government or to silence the potentially competing claims of justice or minority rights.

Thus the *Leader*, a prominent voice of moderate reform, expressed growing concern about the initial capacity of those newly admitted to local institutions, the potential for a majority to replace the haughty few as the source of tyranny, and the need to protect minorities by limiting the power of temporary parliamentary majorities.[134] Establishing, through the mechanisms of the public sphere, that the many had acquired capacities once limited to the few proved easier than establishing that not everything was best achieved by the many's immediate and direct use of those mechanisms. Were parliamentary government and the Upper Canadian public up to the task?

Earl Grey wasn't sure. A decade before Walter Bagehot and with greater knowledge of Upper Canada, he was considerably more cautious about ministerial responsibility in the colonies. In the final chapter of *Parliamentary Government* Grey worried that corruption was likely to be more prevalent in colonies where there were fewer men who could undertake public business without also having to earn a living. The power of patronage had greater influence in societies that lacked a leisured class. Relative social democracy might entail corruption rather than the near-universal and wise public sphere Bagehot predicted. Furthermore, in smaller societies, 'hostile partisans were there brought more immediately into contact with each other.' They debated matters

---

134 *Daily Leader*, 7 Sept. 1853, 18 Nov. 1854, and 30 Jan., 30 June, and 23 Aug. 1855

of local improvements and taxation, only rarely touching on more national or elevating issues, such as foreign policy, that tempered partisanship in Britain. In colonies, 'members of the local government must often be aware that its acts will have a material influence on the interests of persons well known to them, and who are regarded by them as friends they wish to serve, or as political enemies.' Parliamentary government exacerbated such problems. 'Where this spirit prevails, and where sometimes one faction, sometimes another, is invested with the whole power of the Government, it is obvious that little fairness towards opponents is to be expected.'[135] The institutionalized balance of mixed monarchy or American republicanism had something important to offer in social contexts where the balances of parliamentary government might prove too precarious.

By 1854 much of the local criticism of ministerial responsibility in Upper Canada also came to focus on corruption, the abuse of patronage, and the resulting mismanagement of public monies. Francis Hincks himself was soon embroiled in damaging charges of profiting illegitimately from his public position. Increased government participation in railroad construction created more opportunities for such abuse. Parliamentary government seemed to shield all but the worst offenders behind cabinet solidarity, party discipline, and the concentration of the power of appointment in a single set of hands.[136] Were corruption and the perceived abuses of patronage the unavoidable price of colonial parliamentary government? Was it worth paying? Even such an ardent admirer as George Brown wondered aloud if Canadian parliamentary government was compatible with probity. 'It has to be confessed,' he conceded in 1852, 'that the question whether the immense power given to the Executive, under our system, can be worked out on this democratic continent, with advantage to the public, is still undecided ... We may be forced to place the check of republicanism on the Administration.'[137] Many Grits and conservative republicans had already decided before corruption became the dominant issue. During future scandals or fiscal crises, others would ask whether, in return for security of ten-

---

135 Grey, *Parliamentary Government*, 198–219. See also Peter Burroughs, 'Liberal, Paternalist or Cassandra? Earl Grey as a Critic of Colonial Self-Government,' *Journal of Imperial and Commonwealth History* 18, no. 1 (January 1990), 33–60.

136 E.g., *Examiner*, 12 Apr. 1854 and 3 Jan. 1855 and *North American*, 29 Dec. 1853 and 31 May and 27 Dec. 1854

137 Brown, *Debates*, 19 Oct. 1852, 1112 and 27 Mar. 1855, 2482

ure, the administration's sweeping powers should be confined by a written constitution and checked by independent institutions.

Perhaps supporters of parliamentary government were victims of their own success. They had staked their critique of mixed monarchy and their support for parliamentary government on the claims of the public sphere. To significantly modify the British system, much less to abandon it for republicanism, smelled too much like defeat – like a loss of faith in Upper Canada's public sphere. Balancing the expectations of that sphere with the institutions and practices best suited to local circumstances proved difficult. Fashioning existing institutions into a barometer of public opinion required more than the formula of ministerial responsibility had implied. The complexities were evident as reformers debated the mechanisms of that barometer, whether bicameralism, executive-legislative relations, or the electoral process.

The 'unroyal form of Parliamentary Government' became Canada's new constitutional paradigm, but some of its principles, especially those that distinguished it from democratic populism, were less clearly entrenched. Early supporters had failed to persuade their fellow partisans. Indeed, they gave up. Instead, many sought refuge with moderate conservatives in the Liberal-Conservative coalition of 1854. The questions did not go away and some kept asking them, but the concerted effort to find and test the answers dissipated. Perhaps if its principles had taken stronger root, parliamentary government might have been better able to withstand the pressures that pushed it towards either direct democracy or elective despotism. Or perhaps other institutional reforms, including some of those championed by the Grits, might have helped to preserve more of the substance of parliamentary government than its current shadow. Perhaps. Whatever the merits of such speculation, the oligarchic and institutional profile of parliamentary government came to nearly efface its more democratic and extra-parliamentary features. The great experiment began to atrophy – reduced to little more than the formal requirement that the government of the day command the support of a majority of the people's representatives. It had once meant – and promised – much more.

Chapter VIII

'Its success ... must depend on the force of public opinion': Primogeniture and the Necessity of Debate

In one of his first speeches to the assembly, the new member for Kingston, John A. Macdonald, attacked a motion as 'anti-British and anti-Monarchical; it ought not to be introduced here, for the very reason that it had been introduced into the United States; it was folly to raise a Monarchical structure upon a Republican foundation.' This categorical declaration was prompted by a motion to abolish the common law of primogeniture in Upper Canada. In essence, the law required that the real property of those dying intestate (that is, without a valid will) descended to their eldest son. Macdonald went on to argue that 'the law of primogeniture was the great bulwark between the people and the Crown, and the Crown and the people.' Those who, like Robert Baldwin, supported the motion were 'madmen.'

Defending his sanity, Baldwin claimed to support the principle of the motion because 'nine tenths of the people of Upper Canada was in favour of a change.' Further, 'the United States, that great country whose institutions must exercise a great influence upon those of this colony,' had abolished primogeniture, ensuring that public opinion in Upper Canada would become only more insistent. Primogeniture should be abolished 'for the sooner the great principles of the social system were settled the better.'[1] For Baldwin, public deliberation had decided the question. All signs suggested that further debate would only confirm and strengthen its decision. The time had come for legislative institutions to register the verdict of public opinion.

---

1 Baldwin and Macdonald, *Debates*, 30 Jan. 1845, 1233, 1237

How valuable is Baldwin's professed deference to public opinion as an explanation for changes to inheritance law? Was public deliberation as crucial as he suggested or should historians look elsewhere for answers? Sceptics might concede that there was a great deal of public debate in Upper Canada and that Baldwin and others presented various institutional structures as alternative means to express something they called 'public opinion,' but did the content and nature of public debate matter in other ways? Do we really need to pay close attention to Macdonald's talk of republicanism or Baldwin's discussion of public-opinion formation in order to understand the fate of the law of primogeniture? Can't most political decisions, at either the individual or collective level, be explained by a combination of high politics, economic self-interest, and the nature of the society?

These questions land us in some of the most difficult terrain concerning the merits of intellectual history, the nature of language, and the springs of human action. Rather than a direct foray into it, this chapter offers a detailed case study. Its purpose is twofold. First, as Macdonald's speech typifies, public debate about primogeniture often involved the nature of the British constitution and its relationship to society. Moreover, the process of debate on the issue became increasingly significant. It helped to create the concept of public opinion to which government was to be responsible while, at the same time, demonstrating that Upper Canada lacked such a government. Once deliberative democracy was achieved, primogeniture was abolished. This case study thus elaborates themes from previous chapters. Second, it serves an important methodological function. Inheritance laws were seen to have economic and social as well as constitutional and theoretical implications, and to involve the interests of private individuals and social classes. Thus, primogeniture offers something of a 'hard' case by which to assess the role of ideas and public debate. This chapter contends that, on their own, social, economic, and political explanations are inadequate. The content and nature of the public debate must form part of a sufficient analysis.

Only other case studies can determine the broader applicability of such a conclusion. In the meantime, it casts doubt on blanket programmatic statements rooted in cruder forms of materialism that are too willing to sweep aside what contemporaries actually said or to reduce complex ideas to mere instruments mirroring something else. Such a conclusion should also make us wary of less sophisticated forms of idealism too quick to divorce words entirely from their specific political, economic, and social contexts.

Writing in the 1830s, Alexis de Tocqueville was 'surprised that ancient and modern writers have not attributed greater importance to the laws of inheritance and their effect on the progress of human affairs. They are, it is true, civil law, but they should head the list of all political institutions, for they have an unbelievable influence on the social state of peoples.'[2] Upper Canadians agreed, but while historians of Upper Canada have paid considerable attention to inheritance patterns to investigate strategies of family survival, the status of women and children, the structure of kinship networks, and the distribution of property-ownership, little attention has been paid to the laws regulating those practices.[3] Upper Canadians believed that the laws of inheritance affected the distribution of property and, in turn, the distribution of political power and the potential for economic prosperity. In Upper Canada the law of primogeniture also bore tremendous symbolic weight, serving as a barometer for a broader cultural war between monarchy and democracy and between an essentially British and American national identity.

Defining the monarchical and 'British' side of this contest, the inheritance of land in England was governed largely by the common law as expounded by William Blackstone's *Commentaries*. Two of his eight rules of descent directly pertained to primogeniture: first, 'That the male issue shall be admitted before the female,' and second, 'Where there are two or more males, in equal degree, the eldest only shall inherit; but the females all together.' A third rule was also important: 'The lineal descendants, in infinitum, of any person deceased shall represent their ancestors.'[4] Long before the creation of Upper Canada, testators could

---

2 Tocqueville, *Democracy in America*, 51–3

3 For brief mentions, see Bruce S. Elliott, *Irish Migrants in the Canadas: A New Approach* (Kingston and Montreal: McGill-Queen's University Press 1988), 210, 236. The most important study of inheritance patterns to date makes only one reference to intestacy law by noting, incorrectly, that primogeniture was abolished in 1856; David Gagan, *Hopeful Travellers: Families, Land, and Social Change in Mid-Victorian Peel County, Canada West* (Toronto: University of Toronto Press 1981), 51. But see Gerald M. Craig, 'The American Impact on the Upper Canadian Reform Movement before 1837,' *Canadian Historical Review* 29, no. 4 (December 1948), 341–2 and *Upper Canada: The Formative Years, 1784–1841* (Toronto: McClelland and Stewart 1963), 207–8. For important parallels, see Christopher A. Clarkson, 'Property Law and Family Regulation in Pacific British North America, 1862–1873,' *Histoire sociale/Social History* 30, no. 60 (November 1997), esp. 392, 406–8, 413.

4 Blackstone, *Commentaries*, v. 2, 176–202. The implications of these principles are best seen through a fictitious example. If a father, possessed of 100 acres freehold, died without a valid will and was survived by all his children, say two sons and two daughters,

alter these rules by executing a will, while the personal property of those who failed to do so was divided by statute: one-third to the widow and the remainder to the children equally.[5] The importance attached to retaining land in the bloodline is evident from the different intestacy rules for real and personal property.

These rules of descent were imported wholesale into Upper Canada. The colony's first statute stipulated that 'in all matters of controversy relative to property and civil rights, resort shall be had to the Laws of England.' Lieutenant-Governor John Graves Simcoe's commitment to create a truly British colony, complete with an aristocracy and inequalities in the distribution of land and political power, would almost certainly have guaranteed the adoption of primogeniture, but it does not appear to have been singled out from the other elements of the common law being imported. For the next sixty years, the freehold property of those dying intestate descended to the eldest surviving son or his heirs in accordance with the principles of primogeniture.

When Rhode Island abolished primogeniture in 1798, Upper Canada became the only jurisdiction in North America to retain it. Even before colonial inheritance laws existed, some form of partible inheritance or multigeniture was the norm. A system of dividing realty into equal portions, granting two shares to the eldest son and one share to each of the other children, was standard in Plymouth by 1627 and was codified into law by neighbouring colonies. New York, Virginia, Maryland, and the Carolinas opted for primogeniture. Thus, colonial inheritance laws were largely regional: New England except Rhode Island, and the Middle Colonies except New York, adopted some form of multigeniture while primogeniture prevailed among the southern colonies.

The revolutionary decades brought greater uniformity. In Virginia, Thomas Jefferson led the campaign to abolish primogeniture as incompatible with republicanism. A wide distribution of property ownership

---

the 100 acres descended to the eldest son. If the same father was survived by only one of his sons and his two daughters, the younger son inherited the 100 acres. If this father was survived by only his two daughters each would receive 50 acres. If the eldest son predeceased his father but was survived by sons of his own, the grandfather's 100 acres would descend to the eldest son of his deceased eldest son, thus excluding not only his other grandchildren but also his surviving children and their heirs. If the eldest son predeceased his father but was survived only by daughters, these granddaughters would divide the 100 acres equally to the exclusion of their uncles, aunts, and first cousins.

5 Ibid., 71, 468

would prevent the development of a landed aristocracy and ensure the existence of a sufficient number of independent yeomen to act as virtuous citizens. New York and the southern states abolished primogeniture between 1785 and 1791, followed by Rhode Island in 1798. During the same period, other northern states abolished the eldest son's double portion.[6]

Nova Scotia copied its inheritance law from Massachusetts in 1759, only a year after securing an elective assembly. The Halifax merchants who dominated the early assembly rejected the common law of primogeniture. The influx of New Englanders followed by Loyalists produced no change. The colony joined neither the American Revolution nor the resulting revision of inheritance laws. Prince Edward Island adopted the double portion system in 1781. Despite its predominantly Loyalist origins, New Brunswick also adopted a double portion of realty for the eldest son in 1786, a provision that survived the process of legal codification and consolidation begun in 1848.[7] Thus, while Upper Canadians debated the merits of primogeniture for a British colony in North America, Nova Scotia retained its pre-revolutionary American heritage and Prince Edward Island and New Brunswick rejected primogeniture.

In 1829 Thomas Haliburton used long-familiar arguments to explain Nova Scotia's deviation from English law: 'In a new country, the improvements necessary to be made upon land, and the expense of subduing the soil, constantly absorb the whole of the personal property; and that if the real estate were inherited by the eldest, there would be nothing left to provide for the younger children.' American historians agree that social conditions in the colonies mitigated against the adoption or retention of primogeniture. According to one of the earliest scholars of this question, the rejection of primogeniture in the north 'represented a principle of land-distribution which the experience of the colony had shown to be best adapted to its own prosperity and continued existence ... The law was an organic part of the life of the colony.' A recent synthesis likewise concludes that 'the particular wealth mix in

6 See the charts in Carole Shammas, Marylyn Salmon, and Michel Dahlin, *Inheritance in America: From Colonial Times to the Present* (New Brunswick, NJ: Rutgers University Press 1987), 32–3, 64–5. On Jefferson, see Stanley N. Katz, 'Republicanism and the Law of Inheritance in the American Revolutionary Era,' *Michigan Law Review* 76, no. 1 (November 1977), 1–29 and John V. Orth, 'After the Revolution: "Reform" of the Law of Inheritance,' *Law and History Review* 10, no. 1 (Spring 1992), 33–44.

7 'Of Intestate Estates,' *The Revised Statutes of New Brunswick*, v. 1 and Howard, *Laws of The British Colonies*

the early years of the colonies, with land being abundant and some types of personality including financial assets less available, seems to be the main reason for this divergence' from English law.[8] Socio-economic factors dominate such explanations.

With Lower Canada guaranteed its more egalitarian civil law, Upper Canada was an anomaly. Other British colonies did not adopt primogeniture and the arguments advanced against primogeniture by colonial law-makers since the seventeenth century applied to Upper Canada. Primogeniture was not the law in Upper Canada because it was a British colony or because primogeniture was a principle of the English common law. What colonial law-makers had imported they could abolish. The question is not why Upper Canada adopted primogeniture, but why it retained it for so long.

It was not from lack of trying to abolish it. In 1817, the legislative council passed a bill replacing primogeniture only to see it lost in the assembly by a single vote. Apparently the council had acted, not from a sense of the superiority of a competing rule of descent, but because recent legal decisions suggested that no distinction was to be drawn in the colony between real and personal property for the execution of debts. As a consequence, the legislative council, led by Chief Justice William Dummer Powell, sought to harmonize the rules of descent for the two forms of property. Later judicial decisions on debt recovery removed the impetus. The council's bill, however, prompted the first published attack on the principles of primogeniture.[9] The second coincided with Robert Gourlay's agitation. Primogeniture was not mentioned in connection with his famous questionnaire, but it was the last in a series of 'Grievances as stated by certain inhabitants of Ernest Town,' dated 28 November 1818. It echoed much of the first attack and is worth quoting in its entirety:

> The common law rule of descents, by which the oldest son of an intestate inherits all his land, to the exclusion of the other children, appears to us

---

8 Haliburton, *Historical and Statistical Account of Nova Scotia*, v. 2, 337–9, Charles McLean Andrews, 'The Influence of Colonial Conditions as Illustrated in the Connecticut Intestacy Law,' in *Selected Essays in Anglo-American Legal History*, 1 (Boston: Little, Brown and Co. 1907), 446, 449, and Shammas, Salmon, and Dahlin, *Inheritance in America*, 39, 66

9 Amicus Curle, *Kingston Gazette*, 18 Nov. 1817. On the council's bill see John Beverely Robinson, *Canadian Freeman*, 1 Dec. 1825.

not necessary in this Province, there being no hereditary aristocracy among us, requiring to be supported by the perpetuation of the real estate in one branch of the family; nor is it adapted to the circumstances, education, habits and manners of those who are the subjects of it, but is uncongenial with the general sentiments, there being probably few if any parents, in the Province, having more children than an only son, who would be willing to have their estates descend as the law now called the descent; and yet, from a natural propensity to defer the disagreeable business of making a will, and the requisite legal formalities, in cases of sudden death, in the absence of counsel, and amidst the distress and agitation of dying scenes, many persons die, without devising their estate, as they would wish them to be divided. The principle of the statutes of distribution of personal estate, seems to be equally applicable, in this country, to real estates; and we pray your excellency to consider the propriety of recommending an act, to extend and apply that equitable principle to descent of intestate real estates.[10]

While often reformulated, the petition succinctly covered the basic case against primogeniture: it was an aristocratic device, its justification in Britain did not apply to Upper Canada, the people opposed it, parents wanted to treat their children equally, but because many failed to make a will, their land was distributed against their wishes.

The petition was only the start of a prominent and persistent campaign to abolish the common law's rules of descent. In the early 1820s, the merits of primogeniture were considered by the members of the Juvenile Advocate Society, a debating society for lawyers-in-training.[11] In 1831–2, the demand to abolish primogeniture was made at public meetings to circulate grievance petitions. Four hundred people signed the constitution of the Political Union at St Thomas in January 1833 calling for, among other things, the replacement of primogeniture. It was also a plank in the Canadian Alliance Society's platform of 1834–5, and re-emerged at Grit meetings in 1850.[12] The issue also found its way into

---

10 '13th Grievance as stated by certain inhabitants of Ernest Town,' *Upper Canada Gazette* copied in *Kingston Chronicle*, 12 Feb. 1819

11 G. Blaine Baker, 'The Juvenile Advocate Society, 1821–1826: Self-Proclaimed Schoolroom for Upper Canada's Governing Class,' Canadian Historical Association *Historical Papers* (1985), 93, 95–6

12 E.g., *Christian Guardian*, 16 May 1832, *Brockville Recorder*, 2 Jan. 1835, *Correspondent & Advocate*, 30 Apr. 1835, *Patriot*, 6 Sept. 1836, *St Catharines Journal*, 17 Jan. 1850, *Mirror*, 22 Mar. 1850, *Independent*, 27 Mar. 1850, and Colin Read, *The Rising in Western Upper Canada, 1837–8* (Toronto: University of Toronto Press, 1982), 51

TABLE 1
Bills to abolish primogeniture in Upper Canada

Year	Parliament /Session	Sponsor	Final Action	Vote Y / N
1821	8/2	B. Bidwell	Notice of motion to introduce	10 to 16
1823	8/4	Willson	Committee of the Whole, to sit in three months	16 to 15
1825	9/1	Coleman	Second reading	Not reported
1825	9/2	M.S. Bidwell	Third reading	25 to 4
1826	9/3	Bidwell	First reading (?)	Not reported
1828	9/4	Bidwell	Third reading	21 to 3
1829	10/1	Perry	Third reading	33 to 5
1830	10/2	Perry	Third reading (vote at second reading)	21 to 4
1831	11/1	Bidwell	To receive Report of Committee of the Whole, in three months	21 to 20
1831	11/2	Bidwell	Third reading	25 to 14
1835	12/1	Perry	Third reading	35 to 8
1836	12/2	Perry	Third reading	27 to 3
1836	13/1	Norton	Not reported out of Committee of the Whole	
1841	1/1	Hincks	Notice of motion to introduce	
1843	1/3	Roblin	First reading (?)	
1844	2/1	Roblin	Second reading in six months	29 to 28
1850	3/3	Morrison	Notice of motion to introduce	
1851	3/4	Baldwin	Third Reading	35 to 7

Source: *Journals of the House of Assembly of Upper Canada* and *Debates of the Legislative Assembly of United Canada*

election addresses and petitions to the assembly.[13] In his first appearance as a newspaper editor, William Lyon Mackenzie called primogeniture a 'latent source of evil.' It was explicitly forbidden in his draft constitution for a republican Upper Canada.[14] After Mackenzie's rebellion failed to usher in that republic, Francis Hincks tried to rally reform forces in the pages of his *Examiner* around six 'principal measures desired by Reformers,' one of which was the abolition of primogeniture.[15]

13 See *Cobourg Star*, 8 Oct. 1834, W.B. Wells, *Correspondent & Advocate*, 1 Mar. 1837, the petition of Peter Frank and 239 others of Vaughan, *Journals of the House of Assembly*, 23 Nov. 1831, 12–13, and also *St Thomas Liberal*, 29 Nov. 1832.
14 *Colonial Advocate*, 18 May 1824 and section 16 of Mackenzie's draft constitution in *Canadian Political Thought*, 38–9. Mackenzie, *Sketches of Canada*, 305–14, 423 also dealt with the issue stridently and at length.
15 *Examiner*, 1 Aug. 1838

This level of extra-parliamentary activity was mirrored in the assembly. Table 1 lists the eighteen bills originating in the House to abolish primogeniture in favour of equal partibility. Attempts were made in each of the last five parliaments of Upper Canada and in thirteen of its last twenty sessions.[16] Few representatives elected in or after 1820 could escape the issue. Eight of the bills passed the assembly: in 1825, 1828, 1829, 1830, 1831, 1835, 1836, and 1851. The first seven were lost in the legislative council. The *Journals of the Legislative Council* suggest that these bills never reached third reading. A report supporting primogeniture was issued by a select committee of the council in 1830. Its conclusions were endorsed again in 1836. With these two exceptions, the assembly's bills disappeared in the upper house without trace or explanation, a good example of the divergent levels of institutional transparency.[17] Without Upper Canada's appointed legislative council, primogeniture might have disappeared from North America as early as 1825.

The eight bills that passed the assembly often did so by impressive margins; as few as three or four members dissented. The most vocal members of the minority were the law officers of the Crown, especially Christopher Alexander Hagerman and John Beverley Robinson. While promoted by leading reformers, especially the Bidwells and Peter Perry, and more successful when the House was dominated by reformers, these bills often gained the adherence of a significant number of government supporters. The intransigence of the legislative council may have actually inflated these margins. Representatives could vote to abolish primogeniture against their own judgment, safe in the knowledge that the law would be retained.[18] The hostility of the upper house assured, several attempts to

16 The issue came to the attention of the assembly on other occasions. Thomas Parke attempted to abolish primogeniture by attaching a rider to the bill to create a Court of Chancery; *Christian Guardian*, 15 Feb. 1837. The issue also arose when the legislative council sent an unrelated bill amending inheritance laws to the House in 1849, and was brought into debates on other measures such as Peter Perry's speech on a secret-ballot bill; *Christian Guardian*, 22 Apr. 1835.

17 *Correspondent & Advocate* copied in *Brockville Recorder*, 1 May 1835

18 *Examiner*, 1 Aug. 1838, listed conservatives who consistently supported the measure. R. Macdonald, the member for Cornwall 'declared that the Tories who voted for the bill ... voted against their consciences in hopes that the bill would be tomahawked in the Legislative Council. They were he said anxious to shirk the responsibility of opposing it.' *Debates*, 30 Jan. 1845, 1237–8. More generally, see also Sir Francis Bond Head to Lord Glenelg, 22 Sept. 1837: 'The Legislative Council therefore, though it incurs much odium by apparently opposing the House of Assembly, yet in fact affords material assistance to its individual members who relying on its veto are enabled to vote with impunity.' Enclosure, Glenelg to Sir George Arthur, *Arthur Papers*, 21 Dec. 1837, v. 1, 29–32

abolish primogeniture were made without expectation of success. Bills were often introduced at the start of the session; the process became repetitious and something of a stubborn test of wills. The measure passed second reading in 1830 by a vote of 21 to 4 but apparently 'no discussion took place on it.'[19] The arguments were as well known as the outcome.

Primogeniture thus became an important example in the reform argument that the assembly was powerless, thwarted by an appointive and irresponsible legislative council, which, along with the law officers of the Crown, formed a pernicious oligarchy serving its own interests under the cloak of hyper-loyalty to British precedents. As early as 1828, a public meeting at Markham resolved that 'the rejection, refusal, or neglect to proceed upon these and other necessary Bills ... constitutes a public grievance, destructive of the ends of the constitution of government as by law established.'[20] The issue was already as much the constitution's responsiveness as intestacy law.

It is not surprising, therefore, that primogeniture was finally abolished by the second reform administration. As already described, the first reform government resigned in 1843, soon after Attorney-General Robert Baldwin asked a private member to withdraw his bill abolishing primogeniture to allow the government to sponsor a similar measure.[21] After reformers' victory in the 1848 election, the assembly, with the concurrence of the now chastened council, replaced primogeniture with equal partibility, effective the first of January 1852. Constitutional and political structures had helped to ensure the persistence of primogeniture. Once they were transformed into government by discussion, primogeniture was abolished.

Political analysis can also help explain the votes of some legislators. For instance, Robert Baldwin may have mustered his lukewarm enthusiasm for equal partibility in 1850–1 in an (unsuccessful) attempt to blunt radical reform criticism that his government was too conservative. Undoubtedly others were influenced by political motives, although patronage was not among them. Preferment was not to be sought by voting against Robinson and the legislative council to support a measure closely identified with the Bidwells and Peter Perry. With a few notable exceptions,[22] most representatives were remarkably consistent on the

---

19 *Brockville Recorder*, 2 Feb. 1830
20 *Colonial Advocate*, 31 Jan. 1828
21 *Debates*, 11 Oct., and 20 and 28 Nov. 1843, 234, 884, 1013, and 30 Jan. 1845, 1233
22 One exception was W.W. Baldwin, who may have abandoned the support for primogeniture that had earned high praise from Robinson because such company became

issue, and it is hard to see how any could have had a direct or substantial economic self-interest in the outcome (except in the far-fetched case of being a younger son or son-in-law of a father, still living and owning real property, who refused to make a will). In the days before party discipline, the behaviour of most members opposed to primogeniture can probably be explained in one of two ways: they believed in the measure or they believed that the people desired it. If the latter, they either feared electoral sanction or held that the wishes of their constituents ought to be respected. Why did some members believe in equal partibility? Why did popular attitudes push others to vote against primogeniture? Why was the legislative council so determined to resist the repeated voice of the assembly? Finally, why had intestacy law became so controversial in the first place?

It seems natural to look to actual inheritance patterns for the answer; perhaps the nature of the debate and the position adopted by key players can be explained by individual or class behaviour and interests. The *Upper Canada Herald* probably exaggerated when it concluded that 'almost every family in the province is interested' in 'the distribution of intestate estates,'[23] but few other laws had such immediate and personal effects on the families involved. Susanna Moodie observed that 'it is certain that death is looked upon by many Canadians more as a matter of business, and a change of property into other hands, than as a real domestic calamity.'[24] Whatever the emotions involved, she understood the relationship between family and land and between death and land transference. In Gore Township during the 1850s, almost 73 per cent of sons who became first-time landowners did so with family help; almost 45 per cent of them by inheritance.[25]

The economy of Upper Canada was dominated by agriculture, largely the concern of owner-producers and their families, not plantation masters and slaves, manor lords and tenants, or commercial employers and employees. As Toby Ditz points out in his study of Connecticut, 'In

---

increasingly embarrassing as he tried to enlist Marshall Spring Bidwell, the prime opponent of primogeniture, for his version of responsible government.

23 *Upper Canada Herald*, 29 Nov. 1825
24 Moodie, *Life in the Clearings*, 157
25 Herbert J. Mays, '"A Place to Stand": Families, Land, and Permanence in Toronto Gore Township, 1820–1890,' Canadian Historical Association *Historical Papers* (1980), table 8, 204

regions dominated by owner-producers, inheritance transfers are a primary mechanism for allocating economic decision-making powers.' Inter-generational transfers of land created new households – they passed on the actual means of independent livelihood. More than labour markets, such transfers determined the life-chances of many of the next generation.[26]

The common law of primogeniture affected land transfers only at death, and then only if family or creditors petitioned the courts in the absence of a valid will. The legislative council thought intestacy was common among farmers, who were 'seldom so attentive and provident' as to make a will, were often incapable of meeting the legal formalities, and, even when willing and able, 'were from their pursuits more exposed to casualties leading to sudden death.' Councillors claimed that in one district 'it was some years before the Surrogate Judge had a single Will brought to him,' concluding 'that five proprietors of single lots die Intestate for one that makes a valid will.' Opponents of primogeniture also emphasized how difficult it was to make a valid will. The younger Bidwell thought that 'a great proportion of those who had a legal capacity to divide their property neglected to do so.'[27]

Bruce Elliott provides some of our only figures for intestacy in Upper Canada. In March Township, from 1838 to 1900, thirty-eight wills were probated and twenty-five letters of administration were issued by surrogate and probate courts. A further forty-six wills were deposited at the land registry office. Thus, 40 per cent of estates before the courts and 23 per cent of estates for which there were legal records were subject to the common law. Between 1838 and 1849, of the sixteen deceased male heads of household, ten left legal records: six wills and four letters of administration. In this case, the common law affected a quarter of the deceased heads of household and 40 per cent of those whose estates warranted legal action. Thereafter, the rate of intestacy in the township fell sharply.[28] Calculations for Peel County produced the results displayed in table 2.

26 Toby Ditz, *Property and Kinship: Inheritance in Early Connecticut, 1750–1820* (Princeton: Princeton University Press 1986), 3, 36–7, 105

27 'Report of the Select Committee of the Legislative Council on the Intestate Estate Bill,' *Christian Guardian*, 28 Mar. and 4 Apr. 1832, *Mr Bidwell's Speech*, 5, Ernest Town Grievances, *Kingston Chronicle*, 12 Feb. 1819, and Jesse Ketchum, *Cobourg Star* and *Hallowell Free Press*, 8 Feb. 1831. Two decades later, Col. Prince seems to have been the only one to disagree; *Debates*, 15 July 1851, 835.

28 Bruce S. Elliott, 'Sources of Bias in Nineteenth-Century Ontario Wills,' *Histoire sociale/*

TABLE 2
Estates records for Peel County, Upper Canada, 1812–1867

	Surrogate Court				
	Will	W/C	ADM	A/W	Deed
1813–23	2		1		
1824–33	7	1	5		17
1834–43	46	2	19	1	26
1844–53	89		27	8	84
1854–63	153	6	53	11	173
1864–67	54	1	18	10	37
Total	351	10	123	30	337

Legend: W/C = Will with codicil; ADM = letter of administration; A/W = letter of administration with will annexed.
Source: Brian J. Gilchrist, Estate Records of Peel County, Ontario, 1812–1867 (Toronto, 1994)

A total of 514 estates came before the surrogate court.[29] Of these, 153 or about 30 per cent, required letters of administration, but only 123, or a little less than a quarter, left no will at all. The number of estates represented by the 337 registered deeds cannot be determined, since one estate might involve several deeds and estates probated by the courts might also have registered deeds. Further, Bruce Elliott's figures for March Township suggest that the number of estates involved in all these legal procedures might comprise only about half of all deceased males.

In thirty cases, or about 6 per cent, the surrogate court issued letters of administration with a will annexed. Letters of administration were required if the will failed to name an executor or if those named could not or refused to serve. By annexing the will, courts ensured that the estate would be devised according to the wishes of the deceased rather than the laws of intestacy. The courts appear to have emphasized the wishes of the deceased over the technicalities of the law. The principles of the law, not its administration, were at issue.

Social History 18 (May 1985), 126–7, 129. About 70% of these deceased householders were farmers. In her study of inheritance in Stormont, Dundas, and Glengarry County, Marjorie Griffin Cohen concludes that 'in most cases men did not leave wills,' forcing the courts to intervene. The conclusion that most men died without a will does not mean that the laws of intestacy applied. Cohen, Women's Work, Markets, and Economic Development in Nineteenth-Century Ontario (Toronto: University of Toronto Press 1988), 49

29 The probate court dealt with an additional 56 estates.

Thus, it would appear that contemporaries exaggerated the number of estates affected by the laws of intestacy. The legislative council's estimate that five-sixths of small farmers died without a will was too high. It may have been closer to reality if the entire population had been the point of reference, since most of those who died without a will did not engage the legal system at all. Nonetheless, letters of administration were probably more common in the less developed and younger communities, declining in proportion to wills over time, as they did in Peel. Letters of administration seem to have amounted to somewhere between a quarter and a third of cases where the size or nature of the estate warranted recourse to the courts – hardly an insignificant proportion.

Moreover, the law of intestacy was not irrelevant for those heirs ultimately unaffected by its rules of descent. Heirs remained vulnerable until a will was executed. Since wills were often written only when death was imminent (accounting for the small number of wills amended by codicil – under 3 per cent in Peel), sudden death left an estate subject to intestacy law. For some, hostility to primogeniture may have prompted the writing of a will in the first place. Finally, the contemporary conviction that primogeniture affected an even greater proportion of estates was itself important in shaping behaviour and argument.

What most concerned opponents of primogeniture was not that 'many' died without a valid will but that the law devised land in ways that most wills did not. Such concern suggests that the campaign against the common law might best be explained by what Bruce Elliott calls the 'continual tension between law and practice.' Abolition of primogeniture reflected what one colonial law textbook called 'the requirements of the country and of the age.'[30] From this perspective, law was finally brought into conformity with society in 1851. While the common law may not have reflected social practice, neither did the proposed alternative.

In his study of Peel County, David Gagan argues that as nearby land became scarce and expensive, fathers sought to provide for their wives and children without dividing land, the family's major wealth-generating asset. The result was that one son increasingly inherited the family land but, in return, was obliged to provide for other family members from it. As Gagan notes, this 'was a hybrid, a preferential system which

---

30 Elliott, *Irish Migrants*, 210 and Leith, *Commentaries on the Laws of England*, 174

deliberately attempted to combine the economic conservatism of the impartible system with the social and sentimental egalitarianism of the partible.' Thus between two decades, 1845–55 and 1856–65, the number of impartible divisions fell by almost half – from just over 32 per cent to just over 17 per cent – while the number of partible divisions fell by even more – from 28.6 per cent to 11.5 per cent. By 1856–65, the 'single heir plus burdens' system accounted for 71.2 per cent of the probated estates, up from 39.3 per cent in the previous decade.[31]

Primogeniture combined three principles: impartible inheritance for realty, the postponement of female in favour of male heirs, and the preference for the eldest over other male heirs of the same degree. Gagan's findings for Peel reveal an increasing desire to avoid partitioning family land. Over 71 per cent of testators in 1845–55 and 88.5 per cent in 1856–65 adopted some form of single heirship (impartible plus 'single heir plus burdens'). At the same time, an increasing but smaller percentage of testators were also committed to providing for several heirs (partible plus 'single heir plus burdens' or almost 68 per cent in 1845–55 and 82.7 per cent in 1856–65). The common law accorded with the desire to kept landholdings intact, but not with the desire to provide for several heirs. In fact, partibility replaced primogeniture as the legal norm at precisely the time owner-occupiers in Peel increasingly refused to divide their realty in practice.[32]

The law's privileging of male over female heirs closely mirrored practice. Unmarried daughters were often provided for, but only rarely in real estate. Bruce Elliott concludes that 'the devolution of land was strictly from fathers to sons.' Marjorie Griffin Cohen found that the proportion of daughters in Stormont, Dundas, and Glengarry County receiving even lesser portions of land decreased from 22 per cent in 1800–11 to 3.5 per cent in 1850–8.[33] Inheritance by daughters, in land or personalty, was almost always of lesser cash value than that of their brothers. The common law's preference for male over female heirs was a much closer approximation of social practice than equal partibility.

---

31 Gagan, *Hopeful Travellers*, 51–2
32 Conversely, it is likely that partibility among sons was somewhat more common in earlier and/or less developed regions, where population pressures were less or where more and cheaper land was available nearby. Thus, partibility as the legal rule made more sense for many regions in the 1820s than it did when the common law was replaced. Few historians have systematically studied the earlier period, in part because of the paucity of probated estates.
33 Elliott, *Irish Migrants*, 203, Cohen, *Women's Work*, 55, and Gagan, *Hopeful Travellers*, 55

The dissonance between law and social practice was most pronounced in the former's preference for the eldest son over his brothers. Some estates devised as impartible in Peel probably went to the eldest son, although the proportion is unknown. While Gagan originally suggested that under the 'single heir plus burdens' system the inheriting son was usually the eldest, Bruce Elliott convincingly argues that it was more often the youngest. Ultimogeniture, rather than primogeniture, made sense for owner-occupiers. Frequently the eldest son had already been provided for during the life of his father. The youngest, often still working on the family farm, had the fewest years to wait until their father's death or retirement.[34]

Thus, the social practice revealed by existing research conformed to neither the common law nor its eventual replacement. The law left all descendants but one without a share of the land (although with an equal share of personal property). It gave the bulk of most estates, the land, to the eldest son rather than the youngest or some combination of sons. While the proposed alternative would achieve the more egalitarian division of the estate's value sought by most fathers, it would do so in two ways vigorously avoided by even more of the same fathers: extensive divisions of family land and equal treatment of sons and daughters.

The relationship between law and social practice was further complicated by contemporaries' failure to agree upon either the nature of that practice or the degree to which it should be codified into law for intestate estates. Not surprisingly, primogeniture's opponents emphasized familial commitment to multiple heirs and the likelihood that the eldest son had already been provided for.[35] The common law's supporters countered that farmers avoided excessive partitioning of land and only rarely adopted equal partibility. Moreover, they pointed out that the eldest son could use his inheritance to assume parental responsibilities over his younger siblings, some of whom might still be minors.[36] Within limits, what constituted 'social reality' or practice was itself open to

---

34 David P. Gagan, 'The Indivisibility of Land: A Microanalysis of the System of Inheritance in Nineteenth-Century Ontario,' *Journal of Economic History* 36, no. 1 (March 1976), 136 and Elliott, *Irish Migrants*, 236, 306 n11

35 E.g., Ernest Town Grievances, *Kingston Chronicle*, 12 Dec. 1819, Hamilton, *Kingston Chronicle*, 2 Dec. 1825, Bidwell, *Kingston Chronicle*, 9 Dec. 1825, Perry, *Cobourg Star*, 8 Feb. 1831, and Roblin, *Debates*, 30 Jan. 1845, 1226

36 Robinson, *Kingston Chronicle*, 19 Jan. 1827, *Hallowell Free Press*, 8 Feb. 1831, Gowan, Meyers, and Seymour, *Debates*, 30 Jan. 1845, 1230, 1234, 1236, and H. Smith, William Robinson, and W. Boulton, *Debates*, 15 July 1851, 834, 836, 837

interpretation and dispute. So too was its degree of relevance. To what extent should a particular generalization about individuals' current testamentary decisions determine a law for regulating the future decisions of others? Further, what weight should individual decisions carry in the face of other worthy considerations such as the macro-economic or social implications of these micro-decisions and their effect on national identity and the constitution?

If 'social practice' likely fuelled some of the discontent with primogeniture (although it did not suggest its replacement), perhaps elite behaviour helps account for the resistance of leading conservatives and the legislative council. Bruce Elliott, in his study of Irish migration to Upper Canada, notes that some of the minor Irish gentry brought 'the British gentry's preference for primogeniture' with them. Some, like Captain John Benning Monk, gave farms to several sons but left the homestead to their eldest son. Hamnett Pinhey, a member of the local gentry of English descent appointed to the legislative council in 1847, 'anticipated his testamentary arrangements by naming his Canadian estate Horaceville, after the eldest son who would inherit it.' These examples are drawn from March Township, where a number of half-pay officers settled along the Ottawa River and attempted to dominate local society. Only further research can reveal whether similar inheritance patterns occurred elsewhere. Other Irish gentlemen acquired land in Upper Canada to achieve precisely what primogeniture did not – landed independence for several sons.[37]

The inheritance practices of legislative councillors are of some interest given the nature of their office and the council's role in upholding the common law of descent. From the nine men summoned to parliament by royal commission in July 1792 until the union of the colony with Lower Canada in February 1841, a total of sixty-two men were commissioned, took the oath of office, and served (occasionally only in a nominal sense) until their death or the constitutional death of the colony. The estate papers of thirty-seven or almost 60 per cent have been analysed.[38] Others, such as Augustus Baldwin, died without surviving

---

37 Elliott, *Irish Migrants*, 206–7, Elliott, 'Sources of Bias in Nineteenth-Century Ontario Wills,' 130 and Catharine Anne Wilson, *A New Lease on Life: Landlords, Tenants, & Immigrants in Ireland & Canada* (Montreal and Kingston: McGill-Queen's University Press 1994), 51

38 Sixty-nine commissions were issued but seven men were dropped for non-attendance,

children or, like James Kerby, died without surviving sons. Probably several, like John Willson, had already sold most of their land to their sons during their own lifetime. Of the thirty-seven whose legal records were examined, all but three left valid wills. Peter Robinson failed to appoint an executor and the two named by Aeneas Shaw refused to serve. In both cases, letters of administration were issued with the wills annexed. Thus, intestacy law applied fully to the family and creditors of only one of these councillors.[39] Robert Jarvis Hamilton, eldest surviving of the three sons and five daughters of George Hamilton, petitioned the courts as 'Heir at Law' for letters of administration. (Ironically, as a member of the assembly, George Hamilton had voted four times to abolish primogeniture. His hostility to the common law had not prompted him to write a will.) The noticeably smaller proportion of intestacy among these councillors than the general population probably reflects their higher economic and political status and perhaps greater knowledge of the law or access to the legal profession. Since almost all executed valid wills, any hostility to abolishing primogeniture did not spring from a desire to shape the disposition of the estates of the colony's more prominent members.

Did legislative councillors demonstrate a predisposition towards primogeniture in their own wills? Among those with multiple heirs, none devised all their realty to their eldest son; none mimicked the law of primogeniture. Its spirit, however, clearly informed Alexander Fraser. While partitioning his realty among a brother, granddaughter, second son, widow, and daughters, he left 'Fraserville' to his son, Archibald. Should Archibald die without issue, his brother, Alexander George, was to inherit Fraserville. If this second son also died without issue or declined to accept the family seat, it was to revert to the son of one of his daughters,

---

were never sworn in, or never attended a meeting. F.H. Armstrong, *Handbook of Upper Canadian Chronology*, revised ed. (Toronto: Dundurn Press 1985), 55–7. These estate records can be found at the Archives of Ontario, Records of the Probate Court, Surrogate Court of York, and Surrogate Court of Stormont, Dundas & Glengarry. Provisions for personal property, bequests to more distant relations, and the provision of life estates for widows are largely ignored here.

39 There is one rather complicated exception. Thomas Scott, former chief justice of the colony, died in 1824 and, without children, appears to have left his estate in trust to his brother in Scotland. In 1838 William Morris, the lawyer representing Scott's sole surviving heir, a sister in Scotland, petitioned for letters of administration to transfer the estate from the now-deceased brother to his client. It appears that Scott left a will that later proved incomplete.

selected by Alexander's widow, on condition that the grandson and his heirs adopt the Fraser name. Alexander Fraser divided his realty to provide for multiple heirs, but the dynastic ambitions associated with primogeniture were evident. Although applying the spirit of the common law to his own estate, Fraser had voted with the majority of the assembly to abolish primogeniture in favour of equal partibility in 1829.

William Morris provides an almost mirror-opposite case. All his real and personal property were to be divided equally among his daughter and three surviving sons. Since his will was probated after the abolition of primogeniture, Morris had followed the colony's new intestacy law regarding land. His personal adherence, however, did not reflect the conviction that equal partibility was good for the colony. In 1829, Morris had voted to retain primogeniture against thirty-three of his fellow representatives, including Alexander Fraser. Morris repeated his minority vote in 1830 (one of only four), twice in 1831, and again in 1835. Consistent to the end, Morris was the sole legislative councillor to formally dissent from the new intestacy law in 1851.

These two cases aptly demonstrate that individual testamentary decisions by prominent individuals bore no easy relationship to their decisions as legislators. The wills of other legislative councillors reveal none of the hostility to partitioning land that underpinned primogeniture, but rather a desire to provide for other heirs well beyond the common law of primogeniture and often to a greater degree than had most farmers in Peel. Indeed, this segment of the prominent more closely approximated equal partibility than did the population as a whole.

Alexander Fraser came closest to the spirit of primogeniture, but other councillors likewise favoured their eldest over other sons or all sons over daughters. John Macaulay left almost three town lots to his daughter, but his son was eventually to inherit the family residence, other town lots, and about 1000 acres in Kingston Township. Thomas Fraser left land to his two daughters, the children of a deceased son, and his third son, Hugh, but the substantial family farm was given to his two eldest sons, John and Richard Duncan. Nelles Abraham left his farm, other land, and the residual of his estate to one son, Henry William, but partitioned the remainder of his real estate to provide for other family members. Likewise, Alexander Grant Prescott's estate was to pass eventually to his two sons as 'tenants in common.' Unmarried daughters were to be supported and other land was devised to a widowed daughter, a married daughter, and both sons, but Prescott's business and homestead went exclusively to the sons. He appears to have assumed that the eldest would control both, since he bequeathed money for the younger to enter a learned profession.

Strictly speaking, these were not examples of primogeniture, although sympathy for some of its principles is evident. In other cases, particular sons might also be singled out. Peter Robinson divided his property to support his daughter as well as his son, but hoped that his Loyalist grant could be 'assigned to my son Fredrick, so that it remains in the family and tends to strengthen his feelings of loyalty and attachment to his King.' Similarly, Peter Boyle de Blaquiere left the family plate to his eldest son, but expressed the hope that he would freely offer half to his younger brother.[40] Aeneas Shaw left his entire estate to his wife to support her and their minor children. Should she remarry or die, Shaw's 'Heir at Law' was to assume control over the estate to support his minor siblings. Thus, while one or more sons might be privileged, there was a strong desire to provide for other children – a desire that usually entailed partitioning real estate.

William Morris was not the only legislative councillor to adopt equal partibility. William Dickson left the bulk of his estate equally to his three sons; William Dummer Powell divided his estate equally among his son, son-in-law, and unmarried daughter; Alexander McDonell divided his estate equally among his five sons and one daughter; Archibald McLean, who had twice voted in the assembly to retain primogeniture, also adopted equal partibility for his five sons and three daughters; while Alexander Grant did likewise for his one son and as many as six daughters. William Claus left the Fief of Blainsvile in Lower Canada and 15,000 acres along the Grand River to his two sons and two daughters in equal shares. Perhaps reflecting on the common law, John Munro's last testament told his three sons that 'they are all equally beloved by their old father.' It gave them an equal portion of the residual of his estate after bequeaths of 1200 acres to his wife and each of their daughters and sons. Extensive partitioning was also practised by Robert Hamilton, Thomas Ridout, Charles Jones, and Richard Cartwright.[41]

---

40 Blaquiere's second will left the estate almost entirely to his eldest son but this was not from a belief in primogeniture but from the father's recent pecuniary difficulties that called for a single heir to manage his debts and thus forced the replacement of an earlier will dividing the real estate into fifteen equal shares, nine of which were to go to various daughters.

41 The issue here is the division of ownership. A few of these provisions avoided the actual division of realty for a generation by devising it to multiple heirs together.

As these examples attest, daughters of councillors did considerably better regarding real property by their fathers' wills than they would have under the common law. They also did considerably better than most daughters of farm families and many did as well as they would have under equal partibility.[42] In every case, younger sons also fared better than they would have under primogeniture. Such egalitarianism surpassed that found in the general population and could be accomplished only by extensive partitioning of realty. Such division posed fewer risks for the better off because they held more land to partition and because many were not primarily farmers. For merchants, speculators, and professionals, land resembled other forms of capital and personal property such as bank stocks rather than being the sole means of family production.[43]

Only further research can determine more precise patterns of inheritance among the politically prominent or well off. This sample of legislative councillors suggests that these patterns approximated equal partibility. With a few notable exceptions, councillors did not adopt the principles of primogeniture. Likewise, research on elites in colonial America has found that aristocratic devices, including primogeniture, were rarely used.[44] These patterns were also a dismal predictor of legislative behaviour. Finally, the laws of intestacy were less likely to apply to their estates in the first place. The vast majority of legislative councillors could have further concentrated landed wealth, but chose not to. The economic position of many of them made them able, and most were willing, to practise a relative egalitarianism antithetical to primogeniture.

Law and social practice were in tension, particularly in the early decades

---

42 Widows of legislative councillors also fared relatively well. Few women in Upper Canada were in the position of John Jonas's 'dearly beloved wife Mary Elizabeth' who inherited her husband's entire estate without condition since he was 'perfectly satisfied that she will do therewith as I myself would' respecting their many children.

43 Elliott, *Irish Migrants*, 206

44 See C. Ray Keim, 'Primogeniture and Entail in Colonial Virginia,' *William and Mary Quarterly*, 3rd series, 25, no. 4 (October 1968), 552, Ditz, *Property and Kinship*, 30n, David E. Narrett, *Inheritance and Family Life in Colonial New York City* (Ithaca: Cornell University Press 1992), 8, Shammas, Salmon, and Dahlin, *Inheritance in America*, 56, Philip J. Greven Jr, *Four Generations: Population, Land, and Family in Colonial Andover, Massachusetts* (Ithaca: Cornell University Press 1970), 228, and James W. Deen Jr, 'Patterns of Testation: Four Tidewater Counties in Colonial Virginia,' *American Journal of Legal History* 16, no. 1 (January 1972), 162, 173–4.

of the colony. While this tension likely fuelled some of the opposition to primogeniture, it cannot explain the nature of the legal alternative or the opposition of leading conservatives and the legislative council. Moreover, commentators disagreed about what those social practices were, in part, because they reflected several, potentially incompatible, principles. Even if contemporaries had possessed perfect information about individual testamentary behaviour, which of those principles to enshrine in colonial intestacy law, their long-term consequences, and the value judgment to be placed on them were not matters that could be determined solely by individual behaviour or social observation.

At this point, a nagging question emerges: why was no compromise forthcoming? Sufficient common ground seems evident between the inheritance patterns of the general population and legislative councillors to devise a rule to better reflect that commonality than either primogeniture or equal partibility. Two basic principles seemed common: the desire to provide for all children in some form and a commitment, where land represented livelihood and familial independence, to keep it in viably-sized holdings. Equal partibility was one rule of descent reflecting the first of these commitments; primogeniture was one reflecting the second. Other rules might have better incorporated both.

During debate on Bidwell's bill to abolish primogeniture in 1831, William Morris moved to strike a select committee to consider 'a modification of the law of primogeniture which would entitle the younger branches of children, whose father dies intestate, to claim from the heir at law a certain portion of the value of any real estate which the intestate may die seized of, and that Messrs. Attorney General and Bidwell do compose the said committee.' The most articulate proponents of the different rules were to consider a compromise whereby the eldest son would still inherit the land but without denying support to his siblings. The compromise was a considerable move towards the 'single heirs plus burdens' system that came to dominate inheritance practices in farm communities.

Morris's amendment was lost 14 to 20. Ten of its fourteen supporters went on to vote to retain primogeniture, including John Beverley Robinson. Christopher Hagerman was alone in voting both against the compromise and to retain primogeniture. On the other side, only three members supporting Morris's committee went on to vote for Bidwell's original bill. Leading proponents of equal partibility, including Bidwell and Peter Perry, refused the idea of a committee, guaranteeing the defeat of their measure in the legislative council and thus the retention of primogeniture.[45]

In the previous session, Bidwell had added a provision to his bill empowering three freemen chosen by a surrogate court judge, 'when they should judge it best, on account of the smallness of the property or any local circumstances, instead of dividing it, to appraise it, and then, unless some one or more of the heirs would take it, with the consent of the rest, at that appraisal, and pay the others their proportion, the judge was to have it sold, and the avails divided amongst all.'[46] Here was a mechanism that, while it treated all siblings equally, avoided excessive divisions of land. The clause appears to have been incorporated in subsequent bills to abolish primogeniture.

It provoked surprisingly little comment. The process of public criticism had pushed several champions of both extremes to improve their original suggestion, but the debate continued much as before. The select committee of the legislative council offered a detailed critique of the process by which the three freemen would exercise their powers, but both sides continued to debate the merits of equal partibility as if it entailed the actual division of a single plot of land. This was not necessarily the case.[47] The inclusion of this mechanism in Bidwell's bill offered a second compromise. It leaned more towards equal partibility; Morris's towards primogeniture. Both received inadequate attention. There were no other formal attempts at compromise.

In part, this reflected the nature of the international debate. British legal commentators and travellers, such as James Humphreys and James Paul Cobbett, compared Britain's experience of primogeniture to France's experience of equal partibility under the Code Napoléon. Their observations were read in Upper Canada and occasionally excerpted in local newspapers.[48] The debate about primogeniture is

45 *Journals*, 11th Parliament, 2nd Session
46 Bidwell, *Mr. Bidwell's Speech*, 1 and Bidwell, *Christian Guardian*, 5 Feb. 1831
47 Under a similar provision in Bucks County, Pennsylvania, 27 intestate estates were appraised between 1752 and 1765. Actual partitioning was recommended for only three. Shammas, Salmon, and Dahlin, *Inheritance in America*, 66. Of course, some intestate estates involved more than a single plot of land.
48 E.g., Humphreys, *Observations on the Actual State of the English Laws of Real Property with the outline of a Code*, excerpted in *Quarterly Review* and copied in *U. E. Loyalist*, 13 Jan. 1827. The relevant sections of James Paul Cobbett's *A Ride of Eight Hundred Miles in France, 1824* were copied in the *Royal Standard*, 9 Nov. 1836. On France, see also 'France – Primogeniture Laws,' *Colonial Advocate*, 17 Oct. 1833 and Montesquieu, *Upper*

another example of what G. Blaine Baker calls a 'legal pantheism,' 'cross-pollination,' and 'cosmopolitanism' at odds with the routine picture of Upper Canada as an 'exceedingly unimaginative' and subservient 'intellectual and legal colony of England.' Upper Canadians looked beyond Britain to compare it to American states and civil-law jurisdictions.[49] The failure to examine common ground on intestacy more seriously suggests two further points: first, many continued to believe that equal partibility would typically result in the actual division of real estate and second, some believed they had decisive arguments that had little to do with the size of land holdings or the desire to provide for multiple heirs.

One of those arguments involved the degree to which primogeniture had become part of a larger cultural war over national identity. Nova Scotia might be sanguine about retaining New England's pre-revolution laws, but Upper Canada was very much a post-revolutionary creation. After the War of 1812, diverse issues were bound together in a cultural contest between an essentially British and American identity. Primogeniture was associated with the former, equal partibility with the latter. Such constructions were not conducive to compromise.

John Strachan's response to the Ernest Town grievances appeared anonymously in the *Kingston Chronicle* in 1819. He admitted that 'the education, habits, and manners of some persons among us, [are] uncongenial enough with those of England, to be sure, yet there are also others, who think it their greatest pride, and make it their first boast, that their education, habits, and manners, are congenial with those of the most glorious nation on earth, and who would look with a

---

Canada Herald, 20 June 1826. The sweeping away of primogeniture along with the king's head during the French Revolution did not contribute to a more generous assessment of the motives of Upper Canadian critics of the common law. Robinson quoted extensively from a recent discussion of Irish agriculture in the *Edinburgh Review* in *Canadian Freeman*, 1 Dec. 1825, while Bidwell cited Lord Humphrey's observations from his travels to the Netherlands, *Hallowell Free Press*, 8 Feb. 1831. Common-law authorities, especially Blackstone and Matthew Hale, were also frequently cited.

49 G. Blaine Baker, 'The Reconstruction of Upper Canadian Legal Thought in the Late-Victorian Empire,' *Law and History Review* 3 (1985), 233–62, quotations at 233–4, 239, and 247, and also Lori Chambers, *Married Women and Property Law in Victorian Ontario* (Toronto: University of Toronto Press 1997), 82–5. Leith, *Commentaries on the Laws of England*, 159, 173, stressed the civil-law origins of equal partibility and, like Mackenzie, *Sketches of Canada*, 306–7, expounded a New York state statute of 1786.

most jealous eye on any departure from a system of laws, wisely framed, on a model the most perfect the world has known.' To claim, as the Ernest Town grievances had, that Upper Canadians found a central principle of English common law uncongenial 'slanders the public feeling ... We cannot admit it without degradation; or, if forced to confess it, we must feel, that a nearer resemblance should be the great object we should aspire to; that we should draw closer the chain which binds us, not sever the links.'[50] The colony was to be British – not just in a juridical sense, but in its social and political culture. Fortunately, being 'British' meant applying 'a model the most perfect the world has known.'

Such cultural chauvinism was a transparent attempt to portray opponents as 'foreign,' or at least 'disloyal.' Yet construing opponents of primogeniture as 'Americans' was not without some truth. First, there was the legal history of the former colonies. As already noted, after 1798 Upper Canada was the only jurisdiction in North America to retain primogeniture (until it re-emerged on the Pacific coast). The American Revolution may not have been the principal cause of its disappearance in the former colonies, but it provided the occasion and much of the rhetoric. William Lyon Mackenzie, for one, equated equal partibility with Americans' achievement of independence and primogeniture with 'the restraints which the machinery of colonial government had imposed upon their wishes and judgement.'[51] Thomas Jefferson was only the best-known republican to insist that primogeniture was essentially monarchical. Strachan and Mackenzie agreed.

Second, the charge of American influence was credible given Upper Canada's existing population. While a large portion of Upper Canada's Loyalists came from New York where primogeniture was only abolished in 1787, another significant portion migrated from Pennsylvania where partible inheritance had been law since at least 1706. The much larger post-Loyalist American population came from jurisdictions where primogeniture had never existed or where it had been abolished in favour of equal partibility. Thus, except for a portion of the Loyalists, only immigrants from England arrived accustomed to primogeniture.

Third, the early campaign against primogeniture in Upper Canada was likely dominated by recent American immigrants, most of whom probably lacked a deep constitutional or cultural commitment to Brit-

---

50 *Kingston Chronicle*, 5 Mar. 1819 and Archives of Ontario, Macaulay Family Papers, Strachan to John Macaulay, 25 Jan. 1819
51 Mackenzie, *Sketches of Canada*, 305

ain. The authors of the 'Grievances as stated by certain inhabitants of Ernest Town' are not known, but the agitation surrounding Robert Gourlay that provoked it certainly appealed to recent American immigrants – immigrants from a country that had invaded Upper Canada only few years before. Another two hundred men from Ernest Town addressed the lieutenant-governor in January 1819 to express their loyalty and lack of support for their neighbours' grievances. Among them was Peter Perry, son of a Loyalist veteran of the American War of Independence.[52] Ironically, Perry became a prime advocate of the abolition of primogeniture, introducing the measure in the assembly four times. Only Marshall Spring Bidwell was more closely identified with the cause.

It is likely that his father, Barnabas Bidwell, was among the supporters of the Ernest Town grievances. A prominent Massachusetts politician and Jeffersonian republican, the elder Bidwell fled to Upper Canada under suspicion of financial irregularities while county treasurer. In 1811 he became a schoolmaster in Ernest Town. While the extent of his involvement with Robert Gourlay's supporters is unclear, he clerked with the Gourlayite lawyer Daniel Washburn, and is believed to have written 'Sketches of Upper Canada,' later published by Gourlay. After winning a by-election in November 1821, one of his first acts was to introduce a motion to abolish primogeniture. Leave to introduce the motion was denied, 10 to 16. The majority deemed the very consideration of such a measure inappropriate in a British legislature. With typical overstatement, Christopher Hagerman thought that 'if they passed the present bill, they would be departing from every thing venerable, noble, and honorable.' The following January, the assembly decided that Bidwell himself was unfit to sit in a British legislature.[53]

That the measure to abolish primogeniture was introduced to the Upper Canadian assembly by a former attorney-general of Massachusetts and known republican must have appeared to many as conclusive

---

52 H.E. Turner, 'Peter Perry,' *Dictionary of Canadian Biography*, 8 (Toronto: University of Toronto Press 1985), 694–9

53 Hagerman, *Kingston Chronicle*, 11 Jan. 1822, G.H. Patterson, 'Bidwell, Barnabas,' *Dictionary of Canadian Biography*, 6 (Toronto: University of Toronto Press, 1987), 54–8, and Craig, *Upper Canada*, 115–16. Amicus Curle, *Kingston Gazette*, 18 Nov. 1817, included a draft bill that was quite similar to those later introduced to abolish primogeniture. The wording of the letter is also similar to that of the Ernest Town grievances. This may suggest that Bidwell, then living in Kingston, was involved in both. Cato, *Kingston Chronicle*, 10 Mar. 1826, also implied that a series of letters attacking primogeniture by Justinian in the *Upper Canada Herald* were written by the elder Bidwell.

proof that it was only part of a broader campaign to Americanize Upper Canada by politics where armed force had failed. Attorney-General Robinson made the connection abundantly clear when the issue re-emerged in 1825. He 'could easily understand that that proportion of our population which had come from the neighbouring Republic' desired to see primogeniture abolished. 'Their attachment to the constitution and system of laws to which they had been accustomed from their infancy, was perfectly natural and was neither to be wondered at nor blamed.' Likewise, Robinson insisted that it was only reasonable 'that they who had voluntarily come from a republican country to reside here as subjects of a monarchy, should acquiesce in institutions which they found established here, and which were congenial to our form of government.' Robinson had no doubt that the swelling number of British immigrants would likewise insist on retaining primogeniture as much as monarchy itself.[54]

Some of the resentment and near-hysteria of the decade came through when 'Catharus,' sounding more exasperated than sarcastic, pointed out that if primogeniture were abolished, loyal British subjects could still 'return home again, and leave the country to the aliens, Americans, whose prejudices and feelings alone deserve regard.' Warming to his theme, he insisted that any popular prejudice against primogeniture was a foreign contagion from the United States. Moreover, it was only 'the forerunner of other measures hostile to our connection with the greatest and most magnanimous nation in the world.' Not yet finished, he asked if British subjects were 'to permit a few adventurers ... to change our laws and constitution, and to trample our prejudices, our feelings, and our interests under foot – I trust not. This is a British Province, and every thing in it should be British.'[55]

National identity reappeared in subsequent debates on primogeniture but in far more muted tones.[56] It was a desperate weapon to short-

---

54 Robinson, *Canadian Freeman*, 1 Dec. 1825. George Hamilton responded that 'if the government of this colony induced thousands of these people to come in and settle here, why not consult their wishes, and even their prejudices?' The battle-lines of the 'alien question' were already drawn.

55 Catharus, *Kingston Chronicle*, 16 Dec. 1825

56 Robert Baldwin's reference to the intestacy laws of the neighbouring republic in 1845, quoted at the beginning of this chapter, led A.H. Meyers to deny 'that the institutions of the United States ought to have any influence over those of this Colony; the people of Upper Canada recognised no influence but that of the Mother Country.' Meyers was reportedly met by 'tremendous cheering.' Such a collective expression of national

circuit debate by ruling the arguments against primogeniture out of contention as disloyal, illegitimate, and motivated by the prejudices of an alien, hostile state. Such arguments did not have to be rationally engaged. The legislative council's select committee on a bill to abolish primogeniture did not feel 'it necessary to give much consideration to its details from a conviction, that the proposition for making Real Estate distributable like Goods and Chattels is such a departure from one of the first principles of the Laws of England as is never likely to be sanctioned.'[57]

The committee was wrong. Argument and reason rather than (or at least, in addition to) assertion and prejudgment, were required. Despite repeated usage, national identity proved a poor weapon. Even in 1825, the attorney-general was one of only four members voting to retain primogeniture. The twenty-five representatives or the other side could hardly be dismissed as 'a few adventurers.' Four years later, Donald Bethune claimed that if primogeniture was abolished, 'he would abandon the country ... All that was honourable and virtuous would flee from it, and none but demagogues, and the very dregs of society would be left behind.' The desire to abolish primogeniture 'must lead to anarchy and rebellion, and might, if not checked in the bud, uproot every thing that was British and monarchical.' Not only did the bill pass, but Bethune's outburst was reportedly met by 'long and continued bursts of laughter.' The moderate, reform-oriented *Upper Canada Herald* chastised him for disturbing 'the gravity of the Assembly by a farcical speech.'[58] If primogeniture had been successfully construed as essential to national identity and loyalty to Britain, its repeal would not have repeatedly achieved such levels of legislative support.

It was too easy for opponents of primogeniture to question the degree to which English intestacy laws were responsible for Britain's stature. They could also argue that even if primogeniture suited Britain, circumstances were substantially different in North America. They pointed to other British colonies without primogeniture. More fundamentally, they

---

identity had much to do with the recently concluded and bitter election of 1844. Upper Canadian reformers, accused of forsaking the British constitution, had been only narrowly defeated by the governor's supporters. The immediate aftermath of the Metcalfe crisis was not an auspicious moment for reformers to be making favourable references to American law. *Debates*, 30 Jan. 1845, 1233–4

57 Report of the Select Committee, *Christian Guardian*, 28 Mar. and 4 Apr. 1832
58 Bethune and ed., *Upper Canada Herald*, 25 Feb. 1829

added that primogeniture, like the feudalism of which it was a part, was largely a Norman imposition, rather than indigenous. In short, the very meaning of 'British,' the value to be placed upon it, and the ability to transplant it to Upper Canada were contested. This did not mean that appeals to British identity were insincere or inconsequential, but that, even when making such appeals, supporters of primogeniture were forced to fight argument with argument. In so doing, they repeatedly referred to the experience of France, the Netherlands, Ireland, Scotland, Lower Canada, and China, as well as to England and the United States. All provided relevant historical experience from which to judge various rules of descent. In free public debate, the politics of identity was inadequate.

Most of that debate fell into two classes: constitutional and socio-economic.[59] Many simply asserted a necessary connection between primogeniture and the British constitution,[60] but in 1821 William Warren Baldwin sketched the connecting links. He insisted that 'the subdivision of land had too much of the Agrarian system in it; by it society would be condensed, and Aristocracy, upon which the happy Constitution of Great Britain rested, would be destroyed. He would wish to see the principles of Aristocracy supported in this Colony to preserve the constitution conferred upon us by the British Government, and not run into a scheme of Democracy by establishing new fangled laws.' The elder Baldwin later abandoned his support for primogeniture, but his three arguments persisted: monarchy rested on greater social inequality than democracy, aristocracy was desirable, and the British constitution required such a social estate. According to Solicitor-General Hagerman (and many political theorists of his day), 'a well regulated aristocracy was essential to the happiness and good government of any people.'[61]

For John Beverley Robinson, republics, both ancient and modern, might do away with primogeniture, but 'we were not citizens of a republic, we were the subjects of a monarchy, and wished to continue so; whatever, therefore, was most consistent with our own form of government, was that which we ought to prefer.' With Britain's balanced constitution,

---

59 Other arguments included appeals to equity, simplicity, and the natural rights of all children, but these were secondary and have been largely ignored here. The following discussion also concentrates on the pre-rebellion phase of the debate.

60 E.g., A British Constitutionalist, *Patriot*, 17 June 1836

61 W. Baldwin, *Kingston Chronicle*, 11 Jan. 1822 and Hagerman, *Cobourg Star*, 8 Feb. 1831

aristocracy helped to prevent monarchy from degenerating into despotism and democracy from degenerating into anarchy. As John A. Macdonald put it 1845, 'The law of primogeniture was the great bulwark between the people and the Crown, and the Crown and the people.' An attack on primogeniture was an attack on aristocracy. As long as Britain was thought to have a mixed constitution, attacks on aristocracy were attacks on that constitution. For conservatives, if Upper Canada lacked an aristocracy, its laws should help create one. For Robinson, abolishing primogeniture would 'abolish all hopes of ever attaining to the same state of Society as existed in England, which he thought desirable.'[62] As we have seen in previous chapters, constitutional and social structures were inseparable; any law vital to the second was part of the first.

The argument was at least credible. Primogeniture was an aristocratic device and the theory of mixed monarchy entailed some form of social inequality. Further, a pro-aristocracy interpretation of British history and the celebration of that nation's achievements were hardly unique to Upper Canadian conservatives. Nonetheless, such arguments derived much of their resonance from the broader cultural war of which primogeniture was only a part. To give in, even on the smallest of issues, was but the first step towards repeating the American Revolution.

Outside such a context and applied only to intestacy laws, constitutional arguments were less convincing. First, only the land of those dying intestate was at stake. As Robinson himself noted, the well-off were less likely than others to die without a valid will. The land of those most able to create an aristocracy was the least likely to be subject to the laws of intestacy. These laws were also an inefficient tool of aristocracy-building. Entail or 'strict settlement,' whereby the power of heirs to alienate their inheritance was severely curtailed, was much more effective in concentrating landed wealth within families and across generations.

Thus, one could agree that an aristocracy was beneficial to society and vital to the British constitution without endorsing primogeniture. Quoting the annals of Tacitus, Charles Fothergill thought 'the most perfect system of government [was] where the aristocratic and democratic parts are equal; this system seems to be brought to great perfection in England.' He worried that abolishing primogeniture might 'strike at the very root of aristocracy, that he wishes anxiously to exist, with a view to

---

62 Robinson, *Canadian Freeman*, 1 Dec. 1825, *Kingston Chronicle*, 19 Jan. 1827, and *Upper Canada Herald*, 23 Jan. 1827. See also Strachan's response to the Ernest Town grievances, *Kingston Chronicle*, 5 Mar. 1819.

the establishment of a House of Peers in this Province.' Whatever his views of aristocracy or the inadequacy of the current legislative council, Fothergill voted to abolish primogeniture.[63]

Second, though constitutional arguments never disappeared, they became less prominent. They were conspicuously absent from the 1830 report of the legislative council's select committee – the body most dependent upon the analogy to Britain and the idea that aristocracy contributed to good government. The conservative *Cobourg Star* wanted Bidwell's proposal aired further, since 'it seeks the subversion of a principle that has long been considered a main bulwark of our Constitution.' The *Star* hastily added that 'we by no means wish to be understood that such is our opinion.'[64] Robinson and Hagerman had failed to convince even the sympathetic that primogeniture had to be retained for the same reasons and with the same vehemence as an independent upper house or the imperial connection. After the rebellion, mixed monarchy became an increasingly beleaguered interpretation of the British constitution and thus the force of the association between that constitution and aristocracy weakened further. Like appeals to national identity, the force of arguments deduced from monarchical government dissipated over time.

Finally, opponents of primogeniture had strong counter-arguments. They simply denied that intestacy law had constitutional implications. Britain had not restricted the right of colonial parliaments to legislate in this regard. Other British colonies had not adopted primogeniture. Marshall Spring Bidwell also tried to sever the connection between republicanism and equal partibility by pointing to monarchical countries without primogeniture. China was his only example. Perhaps with more effect, he contended that primogeniture was a feudal remnant imposed by the Normans 'at a time unfavourable to the principles of civil liberty.' Just because it was ancient did not mean it should be venerated alongside other 'Saxon' principles such as trial by jury or political representation. 'It was no part,' concluded Peter Perry, 'of the English constitution.'[65]

---

63 Fothergill, *Canadian Freeman*, 1 Dec. 1825, and *Kingston Chronicle*, 2 Dec. 1825 and *Upper Canada Herald*, 4 Mar. 1829. Fothergill's newspaper had supported the abolition of primogeniture earlier and without reservation; *Weekly Register*, 15 Apr. 1824.

64 *Cobourg Star*, 8 Feb. 1831

65 Bidwell, *Canadian Freeman*, 1 Dec. 1825 and *Kingston Chronicle*, 2 and 9 Dec. 1825, *Mr. Bidwell's Speech*, 2, *Substance of Mr. Bidwell's Speech*, 25–6, 28, and Perry, *Upper Canada Herald*, 25 Feb. 1825

Primogeniture's opponents could have stopped there. Instead, they advanced two further arguments that lent considerable credence to suspicions that they sought greater uniformity with their republican neighbour. They insisted, first, that aristocracy was undesirable and, second, that equal partibility, like primogeniture, was not politically neutral, but had, as Robinson and Hagerman feared, decidedly liberal implications.

'Unquestionably,' at least for Perry, the tendency of primogeniture was 'to produce gradually a landed aristocracy; to throw into the hands of a few all the land, all the wealth of the country, and to leave the majority, without any real estate.' For Bidwell, such a concentration was 'one of the greatest evils' that could befall Upper Canada. It had already befallen England, in part, from the 'aristocratic tendency of the law of primogeniture to aggrandize a few and reduce the multitude to a servile and beggared, and frequently a distressed condition.' By buttressing aristocracy, primogeniture created 'a peasantry reduced to pauperism.' Bidwell mocked Robinson for his supposed desire 'to behold a provincial Lord going forth in a splendid equipage, and with a numerous retinue of proud and lazy and liveried menials, and to see ten or twenty miles square of fine land enclosed with a lofty wall, as his Lordship's park ... It might gratify the aristocratic tendencies of the honorable and learned gentleman to have a snug provincial code of game laws, under which the poor plebeian should be liable to be sent to Botany Bay, if he had the audacity to kill a partridge or a hare.' Upper Canada was fortunate to escape the bane of such an aristocracy. It should amend its laws to prevent one from arising.[66]

Bidwell's stinging denunciation of aristocracy reflected an alternative ideal. Without aristocrats there would be no 'menials,' 'plebeians,' 'peasants,' or 'paupers.' Peter Perry waxed eloquently on the theme that 'a country was most happy and most virtuous where wealth was nearly-equally diffused through the community; when none were very rich or very poor.' Proud and independent yeomen dominated a heathy social structure. Game laws and enclosed parks were its antithesis. The ideal of a truncated society, widely applauded by the time of the Metcalfe crisis, had developed earlier during the campaign against primogeniture. It corresponded to the fear of a society reduced to the extremes of rich and poor, master and servant, or aristocrat and peas-

---

66 Perry, *Upper Canada Herald*, 25 Feb. 1825, Bidwell and Hamilton, *Canadian Freeman*, 1 Dec. 1825, Fothergill, *Upper Canada Herald*, 4 Mar. 1829, *Substance of Mr. Bidwell's Speech*, 14, 16, 23, and *St Thomas Liberal*, 2 Nov. 1832

ant; polarization that was thought to invite political instability, excess, and oppression.[67]

To understand the contest over primogeniture, it is crucial to recognize that Bidwell embraced – or rather celebrated – the political implications of this social ideal. Equal partibility would increase the number of property-holders. 'Instead of a peasantry, let us have a yeomanry; and the country, on the one hand, would be more free, and all its liberal and popular institutions be supported with more spirit; and, on the other, the Government, within the just limits of its constitutional power and influence, would be vastly stronger.' Backed by independent yeomen incapable of being misled or corrupted, the powers of the elective assembly would grow. Kept to its 'just limits' by this invigorated assembly, the administration would no longer be viewed with suspicion and could thus act more forcefully. Overall, 'the country would be more free, more moral, more happy, if there was a pretty equal diffusion of property.' Simcoe would have been appalled.

With a property-based franchise, increasing the number of property-holders increased the size of the electorate. Conversely, the concentration of land promoted by primogeniture restricted the size of the electorate, allowing the assembly to 'degenerate into a sycophantic office for registering the decrees of the Executive.' Bidwell conceded that 'there might be well-founded objections' to extending the franchise beyond property-owners (note the conditional tense), but he would extend the right to vote 'by multiplying the number of freeholders, and increasing them in proportion to the whole population.' Thus the political, as much as the social, effects of equal partibility would be entirely 'salutary and favourable.'

Bidwell's approach echoed Thomas Jefferson's: hostility to a landed aristocracy, belief in the benefits of a wide distribution of property-ownership such as the virtual elimination of poverty, adherence to the myth of the Norman yoke and Saxon democracy, and a reliance, politically and socially, on independent yeomen. The function of intestacy law was also the same. Like Jefferson, Bidwell would not 'forbid the

---

67 This and the following paragraphs draw from Bidwell, *Canadian Freeman*, 1 Dec. 1825, and *Kingston Chronicle*, 9 Dec. 1825, *Mr. Bidwell's Speech*, 3–4, 8, *Substance of Mr. Bidwell's Speech*, 15–16, 19–22, and Perry, *Upper Canada Herald*, 25 Feb. 1829. For the political dangers of social polarization see Dror Wahrman, *Imaging the Middle Class: The Political Representation of Class in Britain, c. 1780–1840* (Cambridge: Cambridge University Press 1995), 26–7, 49, 53.

accumulation of property, but I would adopt such laws as have a gradual tendency, without interfering with the free acquirement or disposal of property, to counteract the approximation which is always produced in society by other causes, towards an unequal division of it.' Equal partibility would promote core values, but not at the expense of property rights or a permissive inheritance system.[68] William Baldwin's reference to agrarian laws was not entirely off the mark. Neither were conservatives' suspicions. Bidwell may not have explicitly attacked the institutional superstructure of the British constitution, but his enthusiasm for a republican social base and its liberal political consequences was evident. Could mixed monarchy thrive in the context of such a social ideal? John A. Macdonald was not alone in thinking 'it was folly to raise a Monarchical structure upon a Republican foundation.'

Further, primogeniture's most articulate supporters did not share Bidwell's social ideal. Generally, they saw a more varied social structure as both inevitable and desirable. Aristocracy was only one of its components. Paradoxically, they argued that primogeniture was in the interest of the same yeomanry eulogized by Bidwell. Self-interest was rarely self-evident.

'Catharus' built his case for primogeniture from a series of factual claims: 'first, that the farms here are, in general, small; that the people are prolific; and that none are willing to go into the forest while they can vegetate upon the land in the neighbourhood of our great waters.' Equal partibility would lead to an excessive subdivision of farms. Heirs would subsist on these smaller plots because remaining near settled areas was preferable to subduing the backwoods. In a single generation, a one hundred acre farm would be divided into five to seven equal parts, each with its own frontage and buildings. As an alternative, having a single heir fully compensate others from the inheritance was also ridiculous. Most farms already carried substantial debt. What farmer could sustain existing mortgages while assuming further debts to siblings amounting to four-fifths or six-sevenths its total value?[69] Neither equal partibility nor enforced compensation for all heirs offered a fast track to sturdy independence.

As supporters of primogeniture pointed out, owners of smaller farms were more likely to die intestate. Equal partibility would disproportionately apply to those farms least capable of being subdivided. Citing the

---

68 See Katz, 'Republicanism and the Law of Inheritance.'

69 Catharus, *Kingston Chronicle*, 16 Dec. 1825

state of agriculture in Lower Canada and Ireland, Christopher Hagerman argued that such division would 'destroy a spirit of enterprise –
many would thereby be induced to settle down on little pieces of land,
like potato gardens, instead of emigrating further into the interior,
clearing away the forests of the country, enlarging its cultivated fields,
and promoting its agricultural interests and public enterprise.'[70] Bidwell
and his supporters feared that by concentrating landownership, primogeniture would create a dependent peasantry. Supporters of primogeniture, including John Beverley Robinson, William Dunlop, and John A.
Macdonald, feared that the farms of yeomen would be divided and
become the plots of just such a subsistence peasantry. As Macdonald put
it, 'That which was a comfortable farm house in one generation, [would
be] a cottage in the second, and a hovel in the third; and under it, agriculture, instead of becoming a science, would be degraded, as it was in
Ireland and France, to a mere means of life.'[71] Primogeniture would
preserve more-efficient farm sizes and force younger sons to seek opportunities other than subsistence peasantry. They would develop 'the spirit
of enterprise.'

Equal partibility, by giving all children land, would also allow them to
marry sooner, thus increasing the population. Opponents of primogeniture generally welcomed the subdivision of land and its upward pressure
on population. Both were precisely what a young colony needed. Further, smaller parcels of land could be better cultivated. Bidwell 'wished
to see the country cleared and cultivated like a garden.' While primogeniture would eventually create 'a dependent population, hanging
loose upon society and without any considerable interest in its prosperity and peace,' equal partibility would place a greater proportion of a
growing population on efficient farms. Finally, Bidwell, citing Adam
Smith, a fellow critic of primogeniture and the possible source for several of his arguments, saw greater social benefits from freehold agriculture than other economic activities.[72] Again, the agrarian ideal was
paramount.

---

70 Hagerman, *Cobourg Star, Hallowell Free Press*, 8 Feb. 1831
71 Robinson, *Canadian Freeman*, 1 Dec. 1825, Dunlop and Macdonald, *Debates*, 30 Jan.
   1845, 1232, 1237, and 15 July 1851, 834, 838
72 Bidwell, *Canadian Freeman*, 1 Dec. 1825, *Mr. Bidwell's Speech*, 5–6, *Substance of Mr. Bidwell's Speech*, 17–18. On Smith see Donald Winch, *Riches and Poverty: An Intellectual History of Political Economy in Britain, 1750–1834* (Cambridge: Cambridge University Press
   1996), 85, 150–1.

In an influential article, Leo A. Johnson argues that land policy in Upper Canada was designed to create a landless class to reduce the costs of labour, make the employment of capital easier, and create a more diversified economy and social structure.[73] Marshall Spring Bidwell suspected that the same intentions underlay support for primogeniture. It was, however, recognized that the large-scale population growth that might be capable of creating such a labour pool was more likely under equal partibility than primogeniture. With primogeniture, all but one child from each intestate family would, by not inheriting land, be pressured to postpone marriage.[74]

While some of Bidwell's opponents feared population increase from subdividing land,[75] most usually looked forward to younger sons moving from settled areas to clear the backwoods, and thus predicted, at least in the medium term, an expanding class of independent farmers – also Bidwell's goal. Nonetheless, they were aware that, unlike the United States with its vast reserves of unsettled western land, Upper Canada could not provide adequate land for efficient farms for its entire population indefinitely. In short, Robinson and others saw primogeniture contributing to the long-term maintenance and extension of a yeoman class combined with the forced migration of others, some of whom would invigorate other economic activities. The alternative was a gradual and wider slide towards subsistence peasantry. They articulated none of Bidwell's concerns about other livelihoods.

The frequent references to primogeniture as 'feudal' by its opponents might suggest that its abolition was part of the transition to capitalism. Yet it was primogeniture's supporters who wished to encourage geographic mobility, develop non-agricultural classes, and promote farm sizes they thought more likely to produce a marketable surplus and implement advances in agronomy. Moreover, by arguing that equal partibility, since it multiplied the number of heirs, would make it more difficult to recover debts or secure clear title, it was Robinson and the legislative council who invoked the needs of a capitalistic land market.

---

73 Leo A. Johnson, 'Land Policy, Population Growth and Social Structure in the Home District, 1793–1851,' *Ontario History* 63, no. 1 (March 1971), esp. 57–8, 60

74 For interesting thoughts on the relationship between intestacy laws and the economy see Lee J. Alston and Morton Owen Scapiro, 'Inheritance Laws across Colonies: Causes and Consequences,' *Journal of Economic History* 44, no. 2 (June 1984), 277–87.

75 E.g., Cato, *Kingston Chronicle*, 13 Jan. 1826 and, less clearly, Robinson, *Kingston Chronicle*, 19 Jan. 1827

Just as the value and definition of a 'yeoman' was as much political and constitutional as it was economic, the opposite of feudalism was not capitalism but a widely shared 'competency' in society and politics.

Social and economic historians have much to consider in these competing claims. Some of the most recognized names in British political economy – Smith, Price, Paine, Burke, Malthus, and Richardo – spent considerable time trying to sort out the implications of various intestacy laws in different social settings.[76] While their names were only rarely invoked, Upper Canadian commentators rehearsed many of their arguments. They were reasonably well aware of the influence of inheritance on geographic mobility and population growth. Supporters of primogeniture rightly insisted that intestacy was more common among average farmers than large landholders. They were also right to insist that most farms were too small to be divided equally among an owner's children. In 1851, 83 per cent of farms in Essex County were one hundred acres or less. Opponents of primogeniture, however, were probably right to insist that a more intensive agriculture was still possible. Only 27 per cent of the land in the Western District (including Essex County) was under cultivation in the same year. Marvin McInnis estimates that 60 per cent of all farms were 'standard sized,' averaging 104 acres, less than half of which was cultivated by 1861. In short, there was still significant room for further settlement and the creation of new, viable farms.[77]

Having enough land to establish more than the eldest son as an independent farmer did not, however, mean having enough to do likewise for every child. Recall that farmers did not practise equal partibility, but tenaciously maintained efficient, even extravagant, farm sizes.[78] Moreover, while some of the consequences emphasized by opponents of primogeniture made more sense where nearby land remained available or was under-cultivated, similar results could not be sustained indefinitely into the future – the period for which they were legislating. Thus, some of the competing predictions were generated by different time frames. Primogeniture was abolished when the socio-economic arguments in its favour were increasingly credible. The counter-arguments had already

76 Winch, *Riches and Poverty*, 150–2, 180–1, 184, 268–9, 356–8
77 Leo A. Johnson, 'The State of Agricultural Development in the Western District to 1851,' in *The Western District* (Windsor: Essex County Historical Society and Western District Council 1983), 121, 127 and Marvin McInnis, 'The Size Structure of Farming, Canada West, 1861,' *Research in Economic History*, suppl. 5 (1989), 322
78 This is a central conclusion of Gagan, 'The Indivisibility of Land,' esp. 127–8.

been developed and continued to find an audience despite a slowly changing context. Who was 'right' is not really the issue. As with most political questions, the answers were complex and not as self-evident as contemporary polemicists and those who insist that political arguments necessarily cohere to the economic system and individual or class interests are wont to suggest. Prolonged public debate was required precisely because the answers were difficult and the interests at stake open to multiple readings.

Examining this debate also reveals the relative absence of two potential factors: the status of women and religion. Since, unlike primogeniture, equal partibility made no distinction between male and female heirs, it is tempting to place it in the context of soon-to-follow changes in the legal status of women: improvements in the custody rights of mothers in 1855 and the first married women's property act in 1859. The debate, however, suggests the limits of such a context.

A few months before the abolition of primogeniture, the *Hamilton Spectator* published the first in a promised series of letters, 'On the Rights of Women.' A future number in the series was to discuss primogeniture.[79] It never appeared. This minor accident in colonial publishing is strangely indicative of the role of gender issues in the debate about intestacy law. Equal partibility entailed an egalitarianism not practised by Upper Canada's farmers, yet this feature elicited little comment.

In 1848, a radical reformer attacked primogeniture, in part, because it was 'common sense ... that girls should receive as much as boys.' Besides the inclusion of inheritance rights in a general list of what 'oppressed' women that appeared the previous year in the *Canadian Christian Advocate*, this may have been the only unambiguous criticism of primogeniture for privileging male over female heirs.[80] Supporters of equal partibility insisted that parental love extended to all children who 'have an equal claim on the father.'[81] Occasionally this love was expressed in gender-specific terms, as when the *Christian Guardian* argued that realty should be 'equally divided among the children, male and female.'[82] Far

---

79 *Hamilton Spectator*, 12 Apr. 1851
80 John Galt, 'Thoughts No. 2,' *Huron Signal*, 16 June 1848 and Cecilia Morgan, *Public Men and Virtuous Women: The Gendered Languages of Religion and Politics in Upper Canada, 1791–1850* (Toronto: University of Toronto Press, 1996), 213–14
81 Bidwell, *Kingston Chronicle*, 2 Dec. 1825
82 *Christian Guardian*, 16 May 1832

more common were gender-neutral terms such as 'children,' 'heirs,' or 'descendants.'

Supporters of equal partibility believed that daughters needed or deserved support, but rarely singled them out. In 1829, Marshall Spring Bidwell argued that the eldest son, far from being the first, was the last sibling the law should privilege. If it had to privilege anyone, it should be 'those who needed it most ... the youngest child and the feeblest sex.' In an agricultural country, support for unmarried daughters often required dividing real estate. Nonetheless, the exclusion of younger sons was a more damning, or at least a more frequent, criticism of primogeniture than the exclusion of daughters. It was primogeniture's disregard for the labour of younger sons on the family farm and for their chances of becoming heads of independent households that seemed crucial.

The next line in Bidwell's speech was telling: 'In this province most men were farmers.'[83] Opponents of primogeniture never envisaged that increased inheritance of land would alter women's social or economic status. This was partially because, once married, any property they inherited would be controlled by their husbands. Occasionally, the reasons offered ignored the provisions of the bill they were meant to advance. For instance, Colonel Prince reportedly voted for equal partibility because 'there should be a fair division among all the sons of the family.'[84] Even when legislators were debating a law altering the legal treatment of women, their farm labour – even their existence – could be overlooked.

Neither opponents nor supporters of primogeniture made much of this dimension of the issue. There was widespread agreement about gender roles. Alternative rules of descent more favourable to younger sons than primogeniture but less so to female heirs than equal partibility were never seriously considered despite being more consistent with contemporary practice.[85] From the start, the debate was conducted

---

83 *Upper Canada Herald,* 25 Feb. and 4 Mar. 1825 and also *Substance of Mr. Bidwell's Speech,* 12–13

84 Prince, *Debates,* 15 July 1851, 835. William Lyon Mackenzie made a similar mistake in *Sketches of Canada,* 312–13.

85 As the legislative council's select committee pointed out, those who adopted the County of Kent's gavelkind as a model for equal partibility were mistaken. Gavelkind divided realty equally among sons but postponed female heirs in the same manner as primogeniture. The committee's point, however, was not to criticize the inclusion of female heirs, but rather to insist that the assembly's bill, by including all children, would involve more partitioning of real estate than did gavelkind. *Christian Guardian,*

around two poles. The substantial improvement in the position of female heirs of those dying intestate was largely an unintended consequence of this construction.

Religion also received little attention. Although research on colonial America has uncovered variations in inheritance practices along religious and ethnic lines, the only mention of denominational differences came from Charles Fothergill. Raised by Quakers, he noted their customary adoption of equal partibility.[86] The almost complete absence of biblical references or religious allusion is striking. Primogeniture was frequently referred to as unjust, unfair, or unnatural, but these terms were not tied to a more specifically Christian framework. William Lyon Mackenzie cited Deuteronomy as an authority against primogeniture. A supporter of the common law used the same and other passages to argue that a preference for the eldest son over his siblings and for male over female heirs had biblical sanction.[87] These two contradictory examples appear to have been only uses of Deuteronomy in the debate and its actual rule of descent, the double portion system, was never seriously considered. Extensive public debate marginalized explicitly religious appeals.

Reaching for another argument in favour of primogeniture, Ogle Gowan appealed to the ultimate authority 'for which Hon. Members must entertain the greatest veneration and respect, an authority no less than that great Being who had created and placed them upon this world, had in his holy writ established the law of primogeniture ... In the Patriarchal ages, the great Being who formed us all, gave the precedence to the eldest son.' Gowan's opponents may have venerated God, but they did not venerate such heavy-handed use of the deity in public debate. Gowan was met by ridicule and laughter.[88] The rhetoric of equality within families and against the aristocratic pretensions of pri-

---

28 Mar. and 4 Apr. 1832. 'Cato' alone came close to supporting primogeniture, in part, because it privileged male over female heirs; *Kingston Chronicle*, 6 Jan. 1826. Thus Zeno, *Upper Canada Courier*, 3 Dec. 1831, appears to be the only commentator to both clearly understand and advocate the adoption of gavelkind.

86 Narrett, *Inheritance and Family Life*, 7–8, 201, Shammas, Salmon, and Dahlin, *Inheritance in America*, 30, 33–4, 39, and Fothergill, *Canadian Freeman*, 1 Dec. 1825, *Kingston Chronicle*, 9 Dec. 1825, and *Weekly Register*, 15 Apr. 1824. Gordon Darroch and Lee Soltow, *Property and Inequality in Victorian Ontario: Structural Patterns and Cultural Communities in the 1871 Census* (Toronto: University of Toronto Press 1994), 46 suggest differences between immigrants and the Canadian-born.

87 Mackenzie, *Cobourg Star*, 8 Feb. 1831 and Cato, *Kingston Chronicle*, 6 Jan. 1826

88 Gowan, *Debates*, 30 Jan. 1845, 1229

mogeniture may have appealed to those of some denominations more than others, but the debate, since it had to cross denominational boundaries, was conducted almost exclusively in secular terms.

The content of the debate is revealing – what was and was not discussed, the range of arguments, what was and was not found credible, and how arguments helped define individual and group interests – but the very process of debating was also important. Marshall Spring Bidwell was certain that 'public opinion' supported the abolition of primogeniture and from the early 1830s the concept played an increasing role in his campaign. Stymied by government officials and legislative councillors who drew their legitimacy from the imperial state and the theory of mixed monarchy, Bidwell had little choice but to seek an alternative source of legitimacy by appealing to a broader public. Primogeniture was one of the first and most significant issues in which appeals to public opinion as a rational consensus arising from informed public debate played a prominent part. The persistent opposition of the law officers of the Crown and the legislative council may have preserved primogeniture, but it also forced a repetitious public debate that helped to develop the concept of public opinion – the very force that undermined the constitutional theory that legitimated their power to oppose.

At the outset of his major speech in favour of equal partibility in 1832, Bidwell conceded that he was unlikely to marshal any new arguments. The continued opposition of government officials made yet another reasoned defence of the measure necessary, but Bidwell did not regret the opportunity to rehearse the arguments in favour of his Intestate Estates bill. 'Its success against such strong and formidable opposition must depend on the force of public opinion, which can only be formed and kept alive and strengthened by such clear explanations and such plain reasons as will remove prejudices and convince the understanding.' Bidwell did not appeal to some sort of national sentiment, cultural trait, or the innate common sense of 'the people'; he appealed to the collective judgment of those outside the legislature who listened to and were 'convinced' by the repeated 'explanations' and 'reasons' offered by public debate. He referred to individuals' capacity to judge the common good, not their private testamentary decisions. Concluding his speech, Bidwell reiterated that opposition to his bill served some good since it 'provoked discussion which will be useful ... It will confirm and strengthen the public opinion.' The process of deliberation was itself important.

Further, that private individuals had reached a collective decision –

that 'public opinion' favoured the abolition of primogeniture – was not just one reason among many. It was the trump argument and the power by which the change would be effected. Bidwell remained confident that 'it is not possible for a few men, however great they may be in their own estimation, long to resist the reasonable, and well ascertained wishes of the community.'[89] The previous year, Bidwell had asserted that 'no man or body of men could long successfully resist public opinion, in any country, much less in a country where there could be a free discussion of public matters. They might, indeed, for a time oppose and obstruct the stream; but it would be continually accumulating and acquiring greater strength, until finally it would sweep away all opposition. When he depended upon the force of public opinion, to carry this measure into a law, he relied upon a principle, as simple, to be sure, but as certain and as powerful, as the law of gravitation.' Primogeniture was preserved 'because a few persons, who happened to be in influential stations, under the influence of prejudices, thought they could judge what the people wanted better than the people themselves.'[90] The capacity to judge was the fault line of colonial politics.

With freedom of discussion and access to information, the people were capable of judging for themselves. Bidwell thought they had decided against primogeniture. As chapter 4 argued, by the early 1830s commentators increasingly invoked the concept of public opinion, but the retention of primogeniture graphically illustrated that the colony lacked a government responsive to it. In 1840, when a new governor promised the assembly that he would 'administer the government of these Provinces in accordance with the well understood wishes and interests of the people, and to pay to their feelings, as expressed through their representatives, the deference that is justly due to them,' David Thorburn, a moderate reformer, hailed the message as a revolution in colonial governance: 'What was the feeling of the people on the Intestate Estates bill, which passed this house several sessions? Was there any deference paid to the feelings and interests of the people?'[91] The debate about primogeniture helped convince those who were paying attention of two things: that decisions about the common good could be made by public deliberation among private individuals and that the constitution failed to heed those decisions.

---

89 *Substance of Mr. Bidwell's Speech*, 1, 29
90 *Mr. Bidwell's Speech*, 6
91 Thorburn, *Christian Guardian*, 22 Jan. 1840

In 1825, Charles Fothergill agreed that the Intestate Estates bill 'was universally desired by the people' and quoted Dr Johnson to the effect that 'the universal voice of the people could not be mistaken.' Earlier in the same debate Bidwell laid down the democratic axiom that, notwithstanding a few exceptions, 'every bill that was anxiously desired by the people ought to be adopted.'[92] Four years later, Peter Perry contended that the repeated majorities in the assembly reflected popular conviction. This extra-parliamentary verdict 'was not a transient feeling, produced by any sudden excitement, but a deliberate, though strong desire, founded on a conviction of its justice and necessity.' This was public opinion and when the people reached such a consensus, 'their wishes ought to be consulted, and were ... a sufficient reason, if no other could be adduced, for the adoption of the bill.' By making the public sphere the authoritative decision-making arena, Perry and Bidwell implied that the existing constitution, based on the balanced institutions of mixed monarchy, was inadequate, if not illegitimate. Public opinion and its servants, not a mixture of monarchy, aristocracy, and democracy, grounded legitimate constitutionalism.

Bidwell soon generalized from his experience with the intestate estates bills and other measures supported by the assembly but blocked by the governor or legislative council. During a debate on judicial independence in 1834, he concluded that 'public opinion does not have that influence here as it does in England ... The government of England is a government of public opinion; but if the whole government of Upper Canada was opposed to public opinion it would nevertheless go on if supported by the Executive, which plainly showed it had not that weight or force that it had in England.'[93] As already discussed, for the next two decades, the potential of and the institutions required for 'a government of public opinion' dominated constitutional debate in Upper Canada.

On the specific question of primogeniture, at least, there was much to lend credence to Bidwell's claim that non-legislators were capable of judging. As noted earlier, the issue came up so repeatedly in the assembly that on one occasion there was no debate. This was not typical. To a remarkable degree, both sides were committed to providing lengthy and reasoned justifications, even when the outcome was foreordained. One of the best speeches against equal partibility was given by John Beverley Robinson at third reading in 1825 – just after the measure had

---

92 Fothergill and Bidwell, *Kingston Chronicle,* 2 Dec. 1825
93 Bidwell, *Christian Guardian,* 18 Dec. 1834

passed second reading and was about to pass the third with only three other members dissenting. Likewise, some of the most forceful critiques of primogeniture came from Bidwell and Perry when they knew that their bill had no hope of becoming law.

Nor were these efforts limited to the assembly. Barnabus Bidwell's original motion in 1821 coincided with the beginning of regular reports of parliamentary debates. Subsequently, colonial newspapers provided their readers with arguments from both sides, regardless of their own editorial position. Thus the attorney-general's 1825 speech was not only carried by the *Kingston Chronicle* but also by such reform organs as the *Observer, Upper Canada Herald,* and the *Canadian Freeman,* where it occupied more than a page and a half of close type. The legislative council's report was published not only by such sympathetic organs as the *Patriot* and *Chronicle,* but also by one of Bidwell's strongest supporters, the *Christian Guardian,* at the behest of 'A Subscriber,' who wanted to demonstrate that the council had 'reasons to justify their determination.' Bidwell's 1831 speech, copied and judged 'able' by the *Kingston Chronicle,* was also available as a pamphlet.[94] Bidwell's speech the next year was likewise republished as well as being serialized over several months in both the *Colonial Advocate* and the *Christian Guardian.* Colonial newspapers made no claim of objectivity. Most were party organs, but active readers could learn much about the nature and extent of the opposing position from a single major paper. As discussed in two previous chapters, the accelerated growth of the colonial press in the 1830s and the development of public spaces and voluntary associations in which private individuals could reason in public only added to the credibility of appeals to public opinion.

Not surprisingly, supporters of primogeniture remained unconvinced. One of the *Brockville Gazette*'s readers denounced Bidwell's enlistment of public opinion on primogeniture as 'democratic cant.' Given the absence of petitions, his rhetoric entailed 'the extreme nonsense of deriving majesty and power from the people, by the authoritative mandate of their *silence.*' The relative absence of petitions was often used to deny that the majority of the people desired the abolition of primogeniture. In 1845, John A. Macdonald contended that 'there were but two legal and Parliamentary means of learning what were the opinions of the people – petitions and public meetings, and there had been

---

94 A Subscriber, *Christian Guardian,* 28 Mar. 1832 and *Kingston Chronicle,* 26 Feb. 1831

neither of these in its [the Intestate Estates bill's] favour.' This restricted, legalistic view of the mechanisms of public opinion, isolating parliamentarians from all but the most formal expressions of local opinion, was already antiquated by 1845.[95]

Twenty years before, John Beverly Robinson had made the more serious charge that Upper Canadians were poorly informed and failed to appreciate all the implications of the proposed change. 'It was the duty of the Legislature to look at every consequence.'[96] Even if, as Bidwell and others later contended, public opinion had reached a decision, it did not follow, as they would insist, that the law ought to be changed. The people were free to deliberate, but they were neither always right nor always to be heeded. Robinson was committed to a substantial degree of autonomy for the assembly from extra-parliamentary pressure. Moreover, as an adherent of mixed monarchy, he insisted that other legislative institutions, the governor and legislative council, should be largely immune to such pressure. As appointed bodies, they were free to disregard public opinion without fear of electoral sanction. That was, after all, in large part why they existed. The claims made for public opinion by Peter Perry and Marshal Spring Bidwell during debates on primogeniture in the 1830s were incompatible with the then still widely accepted axiom that Upper Canada's constitution was a form of mixed monarchy. They grew only more insistent.

It may be banal to conclude that an explanation incorporating political, social, economic, cultural, and intellectual factors is superior to a more limited one. Nonetheless, it is important to emphasize that, as a case study of deliberative democracy, the debate about intestacy laws in Upper Canada involved more than an all-too-predictable articulation of social and political 'realities' or the 'self-interest' of a speaker or class. Equal partibility was chosen, but was not widely practised. The legislative council ensured the persistence of primogeniture, but most of its members failed to apply it to their own families. Legislators made decisions that bore little relationship to their own testamentary behaviour. What precisely the 'social and political realities' of inheritance in Upper Canada were was itself subject to debate and rationalization. The long-term implications of those realities and the normative value to be assigned to each added to the contested domain and to the need for public debate.

---

95 Anon., *Brockville Gazette*, 5 Apr. 1832 and Macdonald, *Debates*, 30 Jan. 1845, 1236
96 Robinson, *Canadian Freeman*, 1 Dec. 1825

To argue that ideas merely reflect social, economic, or political reality to such an extent as to deprive them of independent explanatory weight risks implying that there is only one, correct way to read those realities and long-term implications. From the debate about primogeniture, it is evident that all the good arguments were not on one side; the answer was not obvious. Under conditions of imperfect information, scarce resources, and value pluralism, this was probably true of all serious public problems. Two yeomen farmers similarly situated might disagree about intestacy laws in good faith. There is no need to call upon such a poten-tially arrogant explanatory vehicle as 'false consciousness' to suggest that one got it right and the other got it wrong because he didn't see his 'true' interests as a property-owner or citizen. The immediate self-interest of most members of the public was unaffected by whether the land of those dying intestate descended to the eldest son or to all children. The conse-quences of either of these rules of descent and how they related to the interests, values, and aspirations of this public or a segment of it were not matters of social fact but of interpretation and argument. What was in any individual's self-interest was as much an intellectual construct as theories of the constitution. Both required public debate to sort out.

Barring resort to physical force, only the attempt to persuade through a process widely accepted as fair offered true resolution (rather than a temporary truce or the victory of one side that some refused to concede was legitimate). That process – the ordeal of prolonged public debate – elicited more information and honed argument and counter-argument, example and counter-example. It had the potential to educate and inform – to provide reasons for changing one's mind. Amidst all the ver-bal garbage, the ordeal tested both sides' case. Arguments that proved ineffective or even counter-productive fell into disuse, while others were taken up, refined, and evaluated. For instance, arguments derived exclusively from national identity proved problematic and so were eclipsed by appeals at least formally open to all who might listen. Politi-cal debate was a form of action. Which arguments to make and which ones to avoid – how to advance a cause with words – were as much forms of behaviour as dispensing patronage or purchasing property. Like all actions, they shaped the ones that followed.

The audience for these words extended beyond entrenched political operators or the economic elite. It incorporated an expanding, though far from universal, public buttressed by the mechanisms of the public sphere and increasingly addressed by political leaders. Commentators would not have bothered to mount such extensive efforts in the public sphere – to argue and persuade – if they thought it pointless. They behaved as if arguments mattered and expected their opponents to do likewise. Ultimately, contemporaries believed that, under certain circumstances, arguments did matter: they informed, persuaded, shamed, and motivated.

None of this means that the debate was somehow disembodied or disengaged. Competing intellectual constructs emerged, but they were not hermetically sealed. They were attempts to observe, understand, and shape the same material world. Contemporaries did not see this world in precisely the same way, but they still understood each other. Such viewpoints included rational arguments thought capable of persuading others, and thus vulnerable to being ignored, dismissed, refuted, or ridiculed. In short, some arguments were more credible than others; some were not accepted as reasonable interpretations of shared reality. What contemporaries meant by a given argument and how others may have understood it cannot be fully understood outside its specific, multiple contexts.

The arguments, assumptions, and language used by opponents of primogeniture eventually won out. Marshall Spring Bidwell's glorification of independent rural families had considerable appeal for an electorate dominated by the male heads of such families. His distrust of the wealth and political influence gained by other forms of economic activity; his emphasis on the desire of fathers to provide for each of their children; his commitment to equality between actual and potential heads of households without questioning inequalities within those households; his suspicion of lawyers employed by the government and of appointed legislators who thought the people incapable of judging for themselves; and his conviction that Upper Canada could be a more liberal, egalitarian, and free society than Britain must have resonated with his audience. After all, the desire for a family independence most often rooted in property-ownership and a secure future for one's children were prime motives for coming to and remaining in Upper Canada. Finally, those who were told that they constituted the most independent and reliable part of this society might easily conclude with Bidwell that primogeniture was a part of feudalism, where 'everything was derived from the lord ... But the true principle of a free government is the very reverse ... It is this, that everything is derived from the people, and held for their benefit.'[97]

---

97 Bidwell, *Christian Guardian*, 29 Feb. 1832

Thomas Jefferson translated this ideal into an agrarian republic sustained by independent yeomen actively exercising virtue, including the military defence of their republic. Bidwell and others held a comparable social ideal, but translated it into a political vision owing far less to classical republicanism. The capable would engage in critical public debate about the common good to solve concrete problems.[98] Male household heads should own sufficient land or command sufficient skills to render them relatively independent of oppressive material want, regular market fluctuations, political patronage, and other forms of dependence. Such independence allowed them to participate in public debate as equals, to speak for themselves and those dependent upon them, and to be guided primarily by argument and reason rather than the dictates of creditors, employers, or customers. Bidwell thought that amending inheritance laws would increase the ratio of 'independent' to 'dependent' households – increase the number capable of acquiring information and reasoning in public free from illegitimate constraints. The public sphere, not the *res publica* or city state of ancient philosophers, was the political manifestation of a truncated society – a society idealized to exclude those extremes of rich and poor that perverted democratic communication and provided the social basis for tyranny. For primogeniture's leading opponents, the social archetype of the public sphere was the sturdy yeomanry and independent artisans, not the bourgeoisie.

The arguments to retain primogeniture had less resonance, especially for rural voters most interested in the issue. Farmers' inheritance practices bore little immediate resemblance to primogeniture. Robinson had a point when he contended that the people were fixated on 'one single proposition – is it reasonable that one son should get the whole?'[99] To deny land to younger sons was not merely to deny them compensation for their contribution to the family economy, but to jeopardize their chances of attaining the same status as their fathers – independent competency. The importance placed on such status is evident: heads of households partitioned land only to the extent that it could support at least one son and his dependents as an independent farm household, and most went to considerable lengths to try to ensure that

---

98 For the differences between ancient and modern publics see Jürgen Habermas, *The Structural Transformation of the Public Sphere: An Inquiry into a Category of Bourgeois Society*, trans. Thomas Burger (Cambridge, Mass.: MIT Press, 1989), 52.

99 Robinson, *Canadian Freeman*, 1 Dec. 1825

all or most of their sons had the same opportunity. The burden of proof rested on primogeniture's supporters.

The argument that primogeniture was in the best interests of these same farmers was too long-term and not sufficiently convincing. Constitutional arguments appeared forced when the issue was 'only' intestacy law. Talk of aristocracy, British supremacy, alternatives to landed independence, and the limited amount of agricultural land proved a difficult sell. This did not make such arguments more or less self-interested or more or less true, but it probably helps explain why elected conservatives, many representing newly established or less-developed rural constituencies, often deserted Robinson and the legislative council.[100] On other issues or at times of crisis, such arguments had considerably more success in rallying elected conservatives and a broader segment of the public.

Conservative arguments lost much of their credibility when applied to intestacy law. This loss of power was ultimately tied to the decline in the belief that a healthy society and constitution comprised a mixture of the monarchical, aristocratic, and democratic elements. Deprived of this supportive context, many conservative arguments had to be recast or abandoned. The increasingly widespread conviction that the best society was dominated by independent families and that a heathy constitution reflected the political equality of the heads of those families undercut the resonance of conservative arguments on primogeniture and much else.

Membership in the assembly, an elected deliberative body, with a colonial press free to publicize and comment on its deliberations, forced supporters of primogeniture, however great their social standing, political influence, or executive office, to provide reasons and arguments. In the long term, to remain silent, to dismiss opponents, or to hurl abuse undermined their credibility. It also struck at their self-image as upright benefactors of their community who deserved to be respected and emulated. Moreover, they believed they were right. They believed that there were reasons why primogeniture should be retained that were independent of their own (or anyone else's) private self-interest or social position. Such reasons were capable of persuading those who were open-minded, honest, and sufficiently informed and rational. Before the 1840s, many conservatives believed that the majority

---

100 J.K. Johnson, *Becoming Prominent: Regional Leadership in Upper Canada, 1791–1841* (Kingston and Montreal: McGill-Queen's University Press 1989), 148–54

of non-legislators failed to meet this standard. Thus, they rejected republicanism and were sceptical about 'public opinion.' As long as the theory of mixed monarchy remained paramount, supporters of primogeniture were not entirely dependent on the outcome of public debate. The theory provided alternative sources of legitimacy. Once mixed monarchy was replaced by 'government by discussion,' no such alternative existed.

The abolition of primogeniture represented more than the triumph of assembly over legislative council, reformers over 'Tories,' egalitarianism over aristocracy, or social practice over antiquated law. There were elements of each, but something more fundamental had happened. The pre-rebellion debates about primogeniture helped to develop the concept of public opinion while highlighting the degree to which the existing constitution grew out of an older, competing set of assumptions. Public opinion developed in a constitutional and political order that failed to give it the authority that, by its very definition, was its due.

In 1845, Robert Baldwin admitted to serious reservations about equal partibility. He quite rightly 'saw no danger of the vast accumulation of property in a few hands arising from the existence of the present law.' Nonetheless, 'the opinion of nine tenths of the people of Upper Canada was in favour of a change; that opinion had been growing for years, and, instead of retrograding, was still advancing ... Then it became a question, with him, whether, sooner or later, it would not be necessary to introduce that measure; and if, sooner or later, it must be done, then let it be done at once.'[101] Something called public opinion had been created. Subject to further deliberation, it had rendered its verdict. It decided public questions and provided the basis for the new constitutional order. The abolition of primogeniture was the triumph of public opinion.

---

101 Baldwin, *Debates*, 30 Jan. 1845, 1233

Conclusions and Speculative Questions

Upper Canadians believed in the power of ideas and their expression. Words mattered. Living in a relatively new and rapidly developing society, they searched for ways to govern and understand themselves that best reflected the lessons of the science of politics, their diverse experiences, and their hopes and fears for Upper Canada and the broader North Atlantic world. The intellectual and political life of the colony, no matter how derivative it frequently was or how often it breached the ideals it proclaimed, was more reflective and dynamic than we have sometimes given it credit for. This was not an intellectual backwater devoid of important questions, serious debate, or individuals able to rise to the occasion. So much remained to be settled: the type of society Upper Canada was, could be, or ought to be; the principles of legitimate authority; and the best mechanisms for reflecting them. With so much at stake, is it any wonder that contemporaries cared passionately about politics?

Chief Justice John Beverley Robinson chose the November 1852 opening of the Normal School's permanent building to expound the two great constitutional experiments entrusted to his audience: constitutional monarchy and deliberative democracy. While 'it is common for us to hear of that great experiment in government in which the best republic near us is engaged ... we have an experiment of our own going on ... and an experiment of no light interest to our glorious mother country, or to mankind. We occupy a peculiar and a somewhat critical position on this continent ... to demonstrate that all such freedom of action as is consistent with rational liberty, with public peace, and with individual security, can be enjoyed under a constitutional monarchy as fully as under the purest democracy on earth.' Upper Canada was the principal testing ground for constitutional monarchy in the 'new world.'

Those concerned with the fate of governments and their connection to liberty had a second reason to look to Upper Canada. During its early years, the colony's experiment with constitutional monarchy had largely been conducted by gentlemen, who, like Robinson, united a knowledge of the science of politics with social and political leadership. By the time Robinson helped to open the school's new home, the experiment depended on citizens. Thus, the province's constitutional history was also a laboratory 'to prove that in proportion as intelligence increases what is meant by liberty is better understood, and what is soundest and most stable in government is better appreciated and more firmly supported.' Upper Canada was a test case for one of the most pressing problems of nineteenth-century political theory: could popular self-government sustain itself? There was a certain logic in marking a milestone in public education with a lecture on the constitution.

If constitutional monarchy was to survive, the public had to believe that it was the best form of government. On no other grounds should it be preserved. 'Monarchy,' continued Robinson, 'is not blindly preferred among us from a senseless attachment to antiquated prejudices, nor reluctantly tolerated from a sense of duty or a dread of change: but that on the contrary it is cherished in the affections and supported by the free and firm will of an intelligent people, whose love of order has been strengthened as their knowledge has increased – a people who regard with loyal pleasure the obligations of duty which bind them to the Crown, and who value their kingly form of government not only because they believe it to be the most favourable to stability and peace, but especially for the security it affords to life and property, the steady support which it gives to the laws, and the certainty with which it ensures the actual enjoyment of all that deserves to be dignified with the name of freedom.'[1] Robinson spoke of the knowledge of liberty increasing in tandem with the love of order. More typically, conservatives had feared that the demand for liberty from the 'vulgar masses' spelt the end of the very order that made liberty possible.

Regardless, the conviction that constitutional monarchy promoted both liberty and order was older than Upper Canada. Its proponents

---

1 Robinson, *North American*, 2 Dec. 1852. Privately, Robinson took a more jaundiced view of recent constitutional history. See his letter to Strachan cited in chapter 6.

had always insisted that it was the best form of government, a superiority that could be demonstrated to the rational and open-minded. Of more recent origin was Robinson's recognition that only 'the free and firm will of an intelligent people' could sustain it. Constitutional monarchy could endure only if it rested on the settled convictions of public opinion. The most privileged could no longer claim a monopoly on the norms and information required by public deliberation. They could no longer monopolize the right to judge. Government by gentlemen had been replaced by government by public opinion.

Yet there was something disingenuous about Robinson's emphasis on the continuity of 'constitutional monarchy' – a label as apt for Lieutenant-Governor John Graves Simcoe's promise that Upper Canada had 'the very image and transcript' of the British constitution as for the declaration of the *British North America Act* (1867) that Canada was to have 'a Constitution similar in Principle to that of the United Kingdom.' The first referred to an alternative to democracy; the second to one of its forms. Much had changed since 1791.

The original understanding of Upper Canada's constitutional monarchy as a mixed or balanced form of government and its grip on the political imagination of a wide range of commentators were the subjects of the first chapter. That understanding did not lead to a mindless, parrot-like recitation of the analogy between the Constitutional Act of 1791 and the British constitution. Rather, it provided a rich, nuanced idiom open to multiple strategies that cut across numerous political and intellectual traditions. It proved compatible with forms of opposition that criticized different offices and institutions, and could be used to advance both radical and reformist remedies. This flexibility helps explain its longevity, but the dynamics of public debate ensured that mixed monarchy was ably defended as the system of government most suited to Upper Canada. As the best form, mixed monarchy could, if necessary, be defended without using the analogy to Britain at all. The claim that it was the best, no matter how self-serving, also required evidence and argument and was thus vulnerable to counter-evidence and argument.

The question was really who could judge those claims. Justifying an appointive legislative council and governor, mixed monarchy guaranteed a legislative role for those relatively insulated from the general population. It did so, in part, because the science of politics was thought to be beyond the grasp of most. An adequate understanding of that science required the education, leisure, and access to books for study, sense of public service, and experience of leadership denied to all but the gentlemanly few. Claims that the nineteenth-century 'march of the mind' had rendered the basic axioms of political science few, more readily intelligible, and, by way of the printing press, available to an increasingly educated, informed, and numerous public undermined the salience of mixed monarchy. Once the many joined the few in the effective exercise of public reason, mixed monarchy lost much of its utility as an understanding of good government. Its insistence on political hierarchy, an intellectual division of labour, and the inability of the people to govern alone grew increasingly suspect.

As the radical Scottish Whig John Millar had understood, 'when a people at large employ themselves in discussing the advantages arising from different political arrangements, they must feel a bias in favour of that system, which tends to the equalization of ranks, and the diffusion of popular privileges.'[2] When non-legislators were appealed to as if they were capable of informed, rational political judgment – and when they saw themselves as such – the foundations of mixed monarchy were gradually, painfully, unevenly, but also inevitably, undermined. A simplified or less mixed system of government grounded in an egalitarian social ideal beckoned as it became more feasible. But how did those who were neither legislators nor gentlemen come to discuss 'different political arrangements?' How did they come to see themselves as a public capable of sound decision-making by deliberation? These questions push us beyond constitutional debate to the forces that lent credibility and value to the 'public sphere' as a space where private individuals could reason in public.

Chapters 2 through 4 examined the three most crucial contributors: voluntary associations, the periodical press, and the dynamics of political conflict. The expansion in the number and range of voluntary associations brought diverse Upper Canadians together to further common ends outside the purview of state, congregation, family, or work. They were mini-republics. Participants were equal members who imposed rules upon themselves and elected their leaders. Voluntary associations offered social recognition and an alternative platform to those who felt otherwise slighted. Some, like Freemasonry, instilled norms of mutual respect and individualism by attempting to create environments conducive to conversation and conviviality. Debating societies were premised

---

2 Millar, *Historical View of the English Government*, v. 4, 307

on the belief that such environments could also render intellectual controversy safe and beneficial for participants and a free society. By defining their potential membership and by diffusing key expectations and experiences, voluntary associations helped to define the parameters – indeed the very possibility – of a public sphere. They were among the colony's most important political institutions.

Likewise, the expanding and decentralized nature of the periodical press diffused the requisite information upon which to base political judgments. Access to newspapers, particularly as subscribers, was not universal, but still widespread. Most copies had multiple readers within the home or in taverns, reading rooms, voluntary associations, and elsewhere that encouraged reading aloud and discussion. The circulation of substantial quantities of print also reinforced the notion that scattered, anonymous readers belonged to the same community of enquiry, were able to adjudicate competing claims, could hold the claimants – whether newspaper editors, elected representatives, or government officials – accountable, and had the right to be informed and consulted by a government whose transparency was guaranteed by an expansive definition of the freedom of the press. The regular publication of parliamentary intelligence demystified law-making by laying it open to the prying eyes of newspaper readers in ways that redefined the roles of reader, legislator, and non-elective institution. Politics itself was redefined as the public exchange of reasoned claims. The idea that the ability to reason in public was the primary benchmark of citizenship was reinforced.

As evident from efforts to influence early parliamentary reporting, the acceptance of 'public opinion' was more than just a recognition of societal pressures or the inevitable consequence of developments in voluntary associations and the press. By appealing to and trying to manipulate 'the public,' political actors acknowledged its existence and invested it with authority. Early appeals to public judgment by government critics were typically met with disdain and an anger born of fear – a fear that those incapable of sound political judgment were being politicized. Mounting political opposition in the form of active participation in the emergent public sphere could not, however, be effectively silenced or safely ignored.

Conservatives began to call for a more robust and reasoned exercise of public judgment against their opponents – initially only to silence them, but eventually to legitimize their own standing and the constitution itself. Increasing efforts were made to shape that judgment and to distinguish it from popular enthusiasm. In the wake of armed rebellion, widely blamed on the misuse of the public sphere, self-styled moderates integrated the concept of public opinion into their constitutional theory as the very basis of good government. The routes by which various political groupings and individuals came to this point were products of particular political struggles – further evidence of the dangers of divorcing the history of political concepts from the concrete contexts within which they were deployed.

In trying to harness the power of public reason, political actors shaped the contours of the public sphere. They helped determine what counted as public opinion and who counted as full participants. Public opinion emerged from broad developments in voluntary associations and the press before 1840, and from the political polarization of the 1830s, as both an idealized form of collective decision-making and a sociological entity whose reality contemporaries no longer doubted.

The difficult questions posed by the Metcalfe crisis and the responses they elicited were discussed in chapter 5. They made it abundantly clear that mixed monarchy no longer offered a viable framework for understanding the constitution or its relationship to society. Gone were assumptions about the necessity of social hierarchy and a rigid division of intellectual and political labour. In its place, contemporaries embraced deliberative democracy and a vision of their social structure seemingly without those extremes of wealth and poverty that most threatened such a democracy. Socio-economic inequalities were not so great as to render political equality in public debate impossible. No class of public actors independent of 'the people,' requiring special representation, or able to thwart public opinion was recognized. Political and social forms were idealized and exaggerated, but contemporaries did not invent or completely falsify. Otherwise, claims about public opinion and political equality would not have resonated. They would have found no audience.

After the Metcalfe crisis, Upper Canadians embarked on a new constitutional experiment to bring the persisting institutional forms of governor, legislative council, and assembly into line with the newly established fount of public authority. How was a societal force like public opinion to be transmitted to government institutions? What did an accurate barometer look like? How did it function? How, in turn, did it shape public opinion? Chapters 7 and 8 dealt with the major alternatives and their advocates: American republicanism by a minority of conservatives; and government by popular delegates or the British parliamentary system by a larger, more diverse, amalgam of reformers and radicals.

Constitutional structures were not the passive product of habit, membership in the empire, or a hegemonic political culture, but were actively fashioned by the contest of alternatives. Moreover, just as mixed monarchy had been grounded in particular views about authority, forms of sociability, and a heathy social structure, so too was government by discussion.

Frustrated politically and certain that ministerial government was undemocratic and tyrannical, an articulate conservative minority championed the republican model of checks and balances as first developed by the American Federalists. From mixed monarchy, the idea that it was dangerous to concentrate power in a single institution, even if it was chosen by and represented the people, was retained. Gone, however, was the notion that there were social classes or a political hierarchy independent of 'the people.' Thus the separation of legislative, executive, and judicial functions eclipsed the tripartite balance of legislatures. Proposals for a written constitution, an elective governor and upper house, a federal union with American states or other British North America colonies, and imperial representation were designed to strengthen and stabilize democratic institutions while guarding against their inherent tendency towards anarchy and tyranny.

At the same time, electoral victory in 1848 gave reformers both control over existing institutions and the opportunity to implement new constitutional principles. The two alternatives to republicanism, parliamentary government and a more direct, fully elective democracy, were defined by struggle among reformers over how best to translate the ideals of the public sphere into the realities of law-making. The struggle was engaged on nearly every element of the latter process: the legislative council, executive-legislative relations, party cohesion, representation, and the franchise. Parliamentary government emerged victorious despite attacks from both conservatives and those reformers who found it insufficiently responsive to public opinion. Repeated criticism, however, revealed that some of the principles of parliamentary government had failed to take hold. Requiring almost unmitigated faith in the public sphere, parliamentary government seemed unable to distinguish itself fully from populist government by a committee of elected representatives. After 1854, the very meaning of 'responsible government' contracted until it was equated with the procedural platitude that ministers of the Crown command a majority of elected legislators.

The final chapter elaborates many of the themes of previous chapters. It also demonstrates that an adequate understanding of the replacement of the common law of primogeniture with equal partibility must take account of the content of the public debate it generated and the importance contemporaries attached to that debate. The significance of the issue, the options available, the consequences, and the interests thought to be at stake were all, in part, a function of what contemporaries said. The prolonged process of verbal exchange honed arguments and altered discursive strategies. It created the opportunity and resources for individuals to form, alter, or find better grounds for their beliefs and their assessment of their own and others' interests. It was also thought to demonstrate that, collectively, these individuals could reach informed decisions. The law ought, therefore, to reflect such decisions. Otherwise, the pressure on government would only mount, risking an explosion of those more dangerous forms of political behaviour that had been marginalized by the emergence of the public sphere.

Together, these chapters also reveal strains of nineteenth-century liberalism often overlooked, especially by critics quick to ridicule it as hyper-individualism corrosive to community and public life or rampant utilitarianism blind to non-material interests and notions of a common good. Private individuals, rather than family, government, or nation, were certainly centre stage. They were deemed capable of self-government, able to express and defend their opinions, and ultimately the best and safest judge of their own interests. Such individuals were, however, largely the product of their relations with others. Prejudices were worn off, manners polished, the value of tolerance learned, the desire to know stimulated, and the tools with which to listen, participate, and evaluate fashioned through interactions with others. Far from being isolated or alienated atoms, only such individuals could build meaningful and mutually beneficial bonds in public life.

Rather than abandoning any notion of the common good, liberalism found new ways for private individuals to define it. Rather than crude majoritarianism, liberalism valued attempts to explain, understand, and build consensus. Likewise, liberal government was not weak government. In fact, a secondary reason to ground the state in a process of social communications open, in principle, to all willing and able to participate, was to give the state the stability and legitimacy required for more concerted action. To the extent that state actions reflected citizens' collective decisions, or at least were generated by a process modelled on their deliberations, the problem of manufacturing or mobilizing consent once those actions had been taken evaporated. State formation did not occur in spite of liberalization; it was part of the same process. Even with its imperfections and contradictions, public deliberation, rooted in expansive definitions of the rights of free speech and assembly, seemed the best means available to respect individuals as capable, equal agents while empowering strong, effective government to coordinate their collective endeavours.

Even within the parameters of this study, however, there is much that remains to be done. In emphasizing how much more there was to colonial democracy than voting, the electoral process has escaped detailed attention. Petitions and petitioning could also be further mined.[3] Placards, handbills, the lesser-known examples of the religious and literary press, and the theatre of government and the law might also repay closer attention. Moreover, we should investigate the range of issues deemed amenable to collective decision-making as the authority of public opinion grew. The capacity to judge what?

This study has also focused on rational-critical forms of political behaviour. It is the story of how those forms came to be valued and how ordinary Upper Canadians came to see themselves as capable of participating in them. Other forms of participation, more broadly conceived, such as riots, effigy burning, and graffiti, were made increasingly suspect and even drained of some of their political content. They no longer counted – or at least not in the same way – as politics. The nuances of the relationship between public opinion and other forms of political behaviour require more study. If there were costs involved in the trade-offs between expanding membership in the public sphere and narrowing the range of what counted as optimum political participation, who paid the price? Why did many feel it worth paying?[4]

One can imagine circumstances where other forms of political behaviour might not be so divorced from the enlightenment conception of public opinion. By way of example, such behaviour might be the only means by which systematically silenced groups or causes could be heard.

---

3 Such work is under way with J.I. Little, *State and Society in Transition: The Politics of Institutional Reform in the Eastern Townships, 1838–1852* (Montreal and Kingston: McGill-Queen's University Press 1997) and J.K. Johnson, '"Claims of Equity and Justice": Petitions and Petitioners in Upper Canada, 1815–1840,' *Histoire sociale/Social History* 28, no. 55 (May 1995), 219–40.

4 By starting from an expansive conception of 'participation,' James Vernon, *Politics and the People: A Study in English Political Culture, c.1815–1867* (Cambridge: Cambridge University Press 1993) is able to argue that nineteenth-century England became increasingly less 'democratic.' There is something faintly odd about scholars who appear almost nostalgic for physical violence, riots, and mass illiteracy.

We must be careful, however, not to confound definitions of public opinion. As historians we may want to know how everyone reacted to a given issue or event. Riots or whatever else contemporaries denigrated as unreasoning, ill-informed, or illegitimate would be central to such a project.[5] This was not, however, the dominant definition of public opinion during the period of this study. To charge that mid-nineteenth-century public opinion was incomplete because it did not include everything that might now be construed as political 'speech' is to revert anachronistically to our own concept of public opinion.

Finally, this study comes to a chronological end in 1854 with the coalition of moderate reformers and conservatives. The coalition can be portrayed as a success story: the triumph of moderates over extremists and a victory for the politics of accommodation, the British constitution, and membership in the empire over republicanism and annexation. The coalition can also be used to mark failure. For moderate conservatives, it was the failure to fashion their own constitutional program. They returned to office only by accepting the constitutional principles of their former opponents. For moderate reformers, it was the failure to win whole-hearted support from their fellow partisans for key principles of parliamentary government. For more radical reformers and conservative republicans (and some might be tempted to add, for future Canadians), it was the failure of the on-going process of constitutional self-discovery. It is probably neither productive nor safe for constitutional first principles to be subject to constant interrogation, but, by 1854, had the relationships between public-opinion formation and law-making or between public deliberation and naked majoritarianism been fully explored? Had the resulting political institutions been sufficiently adapted to the Canadian context?

The years preceding the coalition formed a unique period of constitutional debate. Issues were relatively unclouded by imperial membership. The divisive battles of the 1830s over the merits of monarchy and democracy had been fought. The bipartisan annexation movement swept aside taboos against what could be considered publicly. There was also broad agreement that, whatever its precise mechanisms, government was to be responsible to public opinion. The constituent convention advocated by both conservatives and reformers was intended to

---

5 For riots as contributors to public opinion, see Mary Ryan, *Civic Wars: Democracy and Public Life in the American City during the Nineteenth Century* (Berkeley: University of California Press 1997), esp. 129–31.

create a forum, partially insulated from ordinary politics, where each constitutional position could be articulated, discussed, compared, and judged. It would be the ultimate exercise of the public sphere. The desired outcome was a widely understood, made-in-Canada constitution capable of finding a secure place in the hearts, as well as in the minds, of Canadians.

No such convention materialized, but a variety of constitutional models were canvassed. The debate petered out, cut short by politics and fear. Immediately after the coalition, the range of public voices narrowed. Among coalition opponents, the *Globe* swallowed the *North American, Examiner,* and *Mackenzie's Weekly Message.* Other reform organs, such as the *Daily Leader,* supported the coalition. Most conservative organs either supported the coalition or disappeared. Perhaps this reflected consensus, but, if so, the consensus may have been premature. The basic forms of parliamentary government were established, but Grit criticism had exposed both the fragility of support behind some of its principles and the preoccupation of many of its champions with the institutional forms inherited from Britain. How it might have been further adapted to reflect Canada's changing circumstances was left hanging. Parliamentary government withstood frontal attacks from conservatives and reformers before and after 1854, but it proved increasingly unable to distinguish itself from government by a single legislature elected by the people but controlled by a committee of its own members. Perhaps Lord Metcalfe had the ultimate revenge.

Over the longer term, parliamentary government atrophied in both Canada and Britain. Ironically, even as Walter Bagehot published his classic defence in 1867, it was probably entering a period of decline. The creation of party machines to manage an ever-increasing electorate and, later, the development of vast bureaucracies to administer complex programs, distorted parliamentary government in both countries. Between elections, ministries were increasingly less likely to be defeated in the House of Commons. Straight party votes became more frequent; attempts to persuade fellow representatives increasingly futile. The premiums on reasoned debate were reduced while the incentives for spectacle and partisanship mounted. In an important ruling on free speech in 1938, Canada's chief justice argued that parliamentary institutions still 'derive their efficacy from the free public discussion of affairs, from criticism and answer and counter-criticism.' Vestiges of parliamentary government's original meaning had survived, but power continued to shift from parliament to a much less publicized, much less accountable, web of cabinet, bureaucracy, and party.[6] The connections between these developments and the broader public sphere await its historian.

Bagehot's *The English Constitution* and the explanation of parliamentary government offered by Robert Baldwin, George Brown, and others still account for much of the form and appearance of the Canadian constitution. They no longer describe, explain, or justify the exercise of public power. Deprived of an overarching justification, the uses of state power can only breed public cynicism. By the early 1840s, the theory of mixed monarchy had reached a similar fate, but, unlike mixed monarchy, the theory of parliamentary government has yet to find its replacement.

As Bagehot and his contemporaries understood, far more important than the fate of particular political institutions was the continued vitality of the principles and practices that sustained them. Bagehot's exposition of parliamentary government was firmly rooted in his assessment of the public sphere. The connection was more fully explored in his *Physics and Politics or Thoughts on the Applications of the Principles of 'Natural Selection' and 'Inheritance' to Political Society*. As the subtitle suggests, Bagehot tried to apply to politics recent scientific theories that emphasized how competition transformed organisms from the simple to the complex. A society's political history was best understood as the movement from an early stage of permanence – an emphasis on status and a 'thick crust of custom' – to later stages of variability, choice, and tolerance for difference. Competition among options in the later stages produced optimum results and prevented the development of new customs that might reimpose uniformity or stasis.

These options were arguments about common interests; competition was public deliberation. Bagehot called the final historical stage 'The Age of Discussion.' Public deliberation was 'the root of change and progress.' It broke 'the yoke of fixed custom ... The mere putting of a subject to discussion, with the object of being guided by that discussion, is a clear

---

6 For Britain, see Crossman, 'Introduction,' in Bagehot, *The English Constitution*, 35–9. For Canada, see Thomas A. Hockin, 'Flexible and Structured Parliamentarism: From 1848 to Contemporary Party Government,' *Journal of Canadian Studies* 17, no. 2 (Summer 1979), 8–17 and Eugene Forsey, *Freedom and Order: Collected Essays* (Toronto: McClelland and Stewart 1974), esp. essays 6–10. For Justice Duff in the Albert Press Case see Janet Ajzenstat, 'Reconciling Parliament and Rights: A.V. Dicey Reads the Canadian Charter of Rights and Freedoms,' *Canadian Journal of Political Science* 30, no. 4 (December 1997), 561.

admission that the subject is in no degree settled by established rule, and that men are free to choose in it. It is an admission that there is no sacred authority.' Perhaps optimistically, Bagehot contended that once a subject had been submitted to the 'ordeal' of public discussion, 'you can never again clothe it with mystery, or fence it by consecration; it remains forever open to free choice and exposed to profane deliberation.'

Government based on such discussion blasted dead tradition and propelled progress. It rewarded intelligence over force, habit, or social status. It demonstrated the necessity of toleration and its virtues. In Britain (and Upper Canada), 'the discussion about this [English] constitution and the discussions within it, the controversies as to its structure and the controversies as to its true effects, have mainly trained the English political intellect, in so far as it is trained.' Constitutional history and the history of public discussion were one.

Despite this progressive story, Bagehot remained cautious. First, he understood that all 'arguments are produced under conditions; the argument abstractly best is not necessarily the winning argument. Political discussion must move those who have to act; it must be framed in the ideas, and be consonant with the precedent, of its time, just as it must speak its language.' Public deliberation was the best form of collective decision-making, not because it produced some transcendental or timeless truth, but because the best possible outcome emerged from intellectual competition among available arguments. Toleration for opposing views and a willingness to reopen questions ensured that these outcomes did not harden into 'fixed custom.'

Bagehot's insistence on the conditional nature of any discursive consensus highlighted a second note of caution. Since there was no sacred text, no scientific theory, and no great legislator capable of superseding public opinion, the constitution and public policy had to be subjected to regular public scrutiny. As Stefan Collini, Donald Winch, and John Burrow argue, 'nineteenth-century theories of human history, in Comte, Spencer, Marx, characteristically culminate in a supersession of politics; its antagonisms and uncertainties are marks of imperfections to be overcome. Bagehot's is the only notable one which ... actually culminates in the emergence of full political life, in the Age of Discussion, and sets nothing beyond it.'[7] No salvation – no 'quick-fix' – lay outside politics.

---

7 Stefan Collini, Donald Winch, and John Burrow, *That Noble Science of Politics: A Study of Nineteenth-Century Intellectual History* (Cambridge: Cambridge University Press 1983), 180–1

Finally, Bagehot recognized that, despite progress, government by discussion was 'a plant of singular delicacy.' Before mass printing and the concept of political representation, states had to be compact enough for people to gather to listen to orators. Such small states were vulnerable to external aggression and those passions and prejudices more easily ignited in face-to-face communication. Even with printing, representation, and the safeguards of parliamentary government, public discussion could still excite passion and prejudice. For Bagehot, the ultimate requirement of government by discussion was moderation: an openness to opposing arguments, a willingness to admit the possibility of one's own error, a desire to debate without abandoning civility, an eagerness to inquire into and criticize the actions of legislators without forsaking discretion, and, above all, a commitment to continue deliberating. Bagehot was cautiously optimistic in the early 1870s because he thought government by discussion inculcated the very moderation it required. 'A strong idiosyncratic mind, violently disposed to extremes of opinion, is soon weeded out of political life, and a bodiless thinker, an ineffectual scholar, cannot even live there for a day. A vigorous moderateness in mind and body is the rule of a polity which works by discussion.'[8] Vigorous moderation nicely encapsulates the empowerment and constraints of public opinion.

There was, however, little sense in Upper Canada that government by discussion was 'a plant of singular delicacy.'[9] Its promoters emphasized the strength and potential of public opinion. Equated with reason, liberty, and equality, how could it fail? Often compared to a physical force, it would crush the pretensions of institutions, officials, and 'aristocrats' who refused to acknowledge its authority. It was the ultimate form of enlightenment, an elixir for all the ills of government. Important truths lurked in the inflated language, but it also obscured difficult questions.

First, what about minorities within the public sphere? During the Metcalfe crisis, the *British Colonist* insisted on the need to restrain 'those petty conquerors, the representatives of temporary majorities, from riding rough-shod ... over the minority for the time being.'[10] Clearly the *Colonist* had *political* minorities in mind. They were a minority only 'for the time being.' By posing new questions, confronting new circum-

---

8 Bagehot, *Physics and Politics*, esp. 114–48
9 I am grateful to A.B. McKillop for pushing me to think harder about these issues and to A.I. Silver for keeping me on track.
10 *British Colonist*, 12 Nov. 1844

stances, altering their judgment, or persuading their current opponents, ongoing deliberation could transform them into the majority.
Restraints on a majority, whether in the form of specific institutional
arrangements or safeguards for those rights that made ongoing public
debate possible, were fully consistent with, even required by, deliberative democracy. After the Metcalfe crisis, the details of the relationship
between public opinion and law-making were just being worked out.

But what about more entrenched groups whose minority status arose
from something other than their failure to persuade? An important
measure of political equality had been achieved across such divisions as
occupation, religion, and national origin. Full participation was denied
to those deemed incapable of being equal. But (leaving aside the contested boundary between the capable and incapable), could problematic cases not arise *within* a public? One can imagine groups who either
systematically fail to gain a hearing despite internalizing the norms of
public deliberation or whose point of view and interests others are
unwilling or unable to appreciate and therefore cannot consider in
good faith. As the public sphere continued to expand after mid-century,
wasn't it increasingly likely to incorporate members from identity
groups with potentially rival sets of deeply held moral values not suscep-
tible to compromise and rational adjudication? The public sphere had
overcome several older assumptions about difference and inequality,
but it still operated against a backdrop of relatively similar assumptions
and values. How might it fare under conditions of deeper moral and
epistemic pluralism? Yet today several scholars champion deliberative
democracy precisely because they argue that it is actually the best means
to deal fairly with such pluralism.[11] More challenging are groups who
either claim that, or are treated as if, internalizing the norms of public
deliberation would itself be incompatible with their differences or identity; that is, for whom the norms of the public sphere are inescapably
imperialistic and discriminatory.[12] If such groups exist, the equality
offered by the ideals of the public sphere is also, in part, a demand for
some degree of cultural assimilation.

---

11 For a cogent case that pluralism requires deliberative democracy, see Amy Gutman
    and Dennis Thompson, *Democracy and Disagreement* (Cambridge, Mass.: Harvard Uni-
    versity Press 1996).
12 For the implications of such a theoretical stance for constitutionalism, see James Tully,
    Strange Multiplicity: Constitutionalism in an Age of Diversity (Cambridge: Cambridge Uni-
    versity Press 1995), esp. chap. 2.

Second, was reason always enough? Had the modern state no need for settled habits, customs, or even prejudices? If they conflicted, could the good of stability ever trump the good of critical judgment? Was it ever rational for a community to forgo rational dialogue? When such dialogue occurred, was reason sufficient to rouse and activate the community? The classical art of rhetoric was premised on the belief that 'even an orator who provides his fellow citizens with good reasons for acting in a particular way can never hope by force of reason alone to motivate them so to act.'[13] As the amount of scurrility in newspapers of the period attest, to excite and motivate a large audience required work on the senses as well as the mind. Yet too much work on the former could render deliberation impossible. The lessons of rhetorical art risked raising the old fears of a populace swept along by demagoguery.

As part of its defence of political parties during the Metcalfe crisis, the *Canada Inquirer* was almost alone in acknowledging the potential tension: 'Many men I fear would abandon their opinions and their principles for a public employment while the same men would not desert a party to which they were attached by affection as well as reason ... There are persons indeed who are of the opinion that pure intention and the force of argument may govern the world. But let us hear Mr. Wilberforce when he speaks of religion: – "Man is not a purely intellectual being."'[14] (But enthusiasts of public opinion were never so naive as to see every individual as a super-rational adjudicator. Prolonged, collective discussion was necessary precisely because no individual or clique could conceive of all possibilities, assess all arguments, know all information, weigh all interests, or detect and counter all prejudices.) Much hung on the *Inquirer*'s 'affection *as well as* reason' construction. Supporting a political party only (or even mostly) from affection rather than reason was just another form of dependence; espousing positions and arguments one did not believe. Once accepted as a useful glue binding individuals to a set of principles they otherwise endorsed on rational grounds, how could 'affection' be prevented from distorting the deliberative process? How could others be certain that partisan speakers did, in fact, endorse their principles on rational grounds? At what point did the notion of legitimate affection permit, even encourage, a gap

---

13 For Hobbes's illuminating engagement with these issues see Quentin Skinner, *Reason and Rhetoric in the Philosophy of Thomas Hobbes* (Cambridge: Cambridge University Press 1996), quotation at 93.

14 *Canada Inquirer*, 4 Oct. 1844

between individuals and the arguments they espoused in public –
between private belief and public pronouncement? Was such a gap
always dangerous?

In his study of parliamentary government, Earl Grey found another
use for 'passions and feelings.' Would politics garner so much attention
if it could ever display cold rationalism alone? Grey thought not. 'If
men's passions and feelings were not so much excited by political struggles, it is not likely they would read, as they do, the debates in parliament.' Here 'passions and feelings' compensated for predictable
deficiencies and lapses in rational will. They motivated people to pay
attention to a forum where 'the keen encounter of intellects seldom
fails in the end to lead to the discovery of truth.'[15] Enough emotion or
heat was required to encourage reading, but not so much as to cloud
the merits of competing arguments. (Grey seems to have assumed that
the less rational elements of politics had positive effects on the broader
public without significantly negative effects on parliamentarians or their
ability to educate the public.) Collective reason would determine outcomes even if it alone could not arouse interest or move people to act.

In this more permissive ideal of motivation in the public sphere, passions could be crucial adjuncts to reason. Distinguished by their function in public deliberation, there were good and bad affections, good
and bad appeals to prejudice and passion. But could their use to stimu-
late interest or to keep individuals loyal to principles they endorsed on
rational grounds be so easily distinguished from their use to cloud the
adjudication of competing arguments? Was there not a danger of flirt-
ing with the starkly non-deliberative and anti-democratic notion that so
long as there were reasons for a position, it didn't much matter how
individuals were brought to assent to it?

Like so much of the discussion of public opinion, Grey's argument
also hinged on the assumption that the very process of deliberation
separated out misinformation, prejudice, emotional appeal, personal
attack, and weaker argument from more substantive reasons. Once each
case was shorn of its impurities, the best answer 'seldom fails in the end'
to emerge from an ordeal among them. Even if that were true, what
happened when it did fail or when action had to be taken before the
best answer emerged 'in the end'? Indeed, did the clash of arguments
always reveal and negate (rather than entrench and magnify) the emo-

---

15 Grey, *Parliamentary Government*, 34

tions and passions that the *Inquirer* and Grey thought might play a useful, though subordinate, role in public debate? As we have seen, the
ongoing debate about intestacy laws honed arguments on both sides.
Many of the developments traced in previous chapters also show that
Grey's assumption was credible. They cannot show the extent of its
validity or how to govern when it seemed inadequate.

Third, didn't other, non-enlightenment definitions of 'public opinion' become more prevalent among mid-nineteenth-century liberals
elsewhere? From the introduction, recall Dr Robert Douglas Hamilton's
rousing speech at Scarborough in 1832: 'Do not trust either my propositions or conclusions, examine for yourselves ... Let me admonish you
never to place implicit confidence in any man, however commanding
his talents may be, for authority is not proof, and assertions are not
arguments, never therefore surrender your own reason to that of
another man.'[16] (Of course, trust was not so easily banished. Hamilton
offered reasons for shifting trust – at least conditionally – from authorities and the talented few to the assumptions and mechanisms of public
criticism.) But what if people began to trust or defer to public opinion
itself? Of course, in a restricted sense, they were supposed to. Dissenters
had to accept, within limits, the right of the public verdict to govern.
They did not have to accept that it was right. In fact, common goals were
advanced if they continued to offer dissenting arguments. Only the
ongoing ordeal of public discussion ensured that there were still good
reasons for that verdict, not just inertia, habit, force, or unadorned
majority will.

But what if many found it politically advantageous or just easier to
nod towards what the collective inclination seemed to be? How could
individuals be prevented from abdicating their responsibility to participate honestly in public deliberations rather than just acquiesce to
'whichever way the wind was blowing'? Just as Hamilton insisted that you
should not surrender your reason to that of another individual, so too
you shouldn't surrender it to that of the public. By becoming so powerful, did public opinion encourage increasing numbers to defer to it for
the wrong reasons – intellectual laziness, moral cowardliness, a craven
desire for applause, or an immobilizing fear of scorn? Instead of encouraging people to offer reasonable grounds for their opinions and interests so they could be tested or used to persuade others, perhaps public

---

16 Hamilton, *Western Mercury*, 22 Mar. 1832

opinion offered powerful incentives to adopt opinions and interests that *others* appeared to espouse.

Mirroring this problem, might not voluntary associations undermine the very individualism and democratic sociability they had helped to create? Some might become vehicles for leaders to control their members and manipulate rather than reflect their values and interests. Some might devalue individuality by making combinations and groups indispensable for public recognition. Some might foster a kind of 'group think' or a cult-like, all-encompassing, loyalty potentially hostile to the mutual exchange of arguments and the impersonal rule of law. Thus, searching for contradictions in democracy to explain the extremes of French Jacobinism, Augustin Cochin found them in pre-revolutionary philosophical societies. There 'each submits to what he believes is believed by all. Opinion follows its own shadow, and from illusion a reality is born.'[17] In short, could public opinion undermine the very process of individual reasoning that created it?

By the second half of the nineteenth century, several prominent European and American liberals came to just such a dispiriting conclusion. Compare Hamilton's faith in the future of individual reasoning with Walter Bagehot's anxiety about its eclipse in an essay on Sir Robert Peel (1856): 'Public opinion is a permeating influence, and it exacts obedience to itself; it requires us to think other men's thoughts, to speak other men's words, to follow other men's habits.'[18] Hamilton's 'never surrender' cry was part of public opinion in the heady days of battle against its foes – it was oppositional, individualistic, rational, predominantly political, and full of emancipatory promise – the public opinion of this study. The second was only one, but an increasingly common, reading of public opinion as dictatorial, not only in politics, but also in morality, manners, and art. John Stuart Mill was not alone in fretting that the individualism upon which public opinion had been built threatened individuality. Such a collective force appeared to foster a dull, plodding, herd mentality capable of imposing conformity – yet another

---

17 Cochin in Daniel Gordon, *Citizens without Sovereignty: Equality and Sociability in French Thought, 1670–1789* (Princeton: Princeton University Press 1994), 31. The closest approximation of this critique in Upper Canada was *Kingston Spectator*, 2 July 1835, responding to material copied from the U.S.

18 I am much indebted to John Burrow, *Whigs and Liberals: Continuity and Change in English Political Thought* (Oxford: Oxford University Press 1988), esp. chap. 3 for this and subsequent paragraphs. The quotation from Bagehot's essay is at 75.

source of tyranny rather than the force to overcome it. Ways had to be found for the artist, the genius, the statesman, and the otherwise different to thrive and be able to stand against such 'public opinion.'

'England has done one thing,' quipped Oscar Wilde; 'it has invented and established Public Opinion, which is an attempt to organize the ignorance of the community, and to elevate it to the dignity of a physical force.'[19] Whatever one makes of the claimed parentage, Wilde captured the renewed emphasis on non-enlightenment definitions of public opinion. They bore a close resemblance to longstanding notions of 'the public mind' or 'popular sentiment' – a confused jumble of ill-digested information, rumour, fragments of arguments, instincts, and prejudices open to manipulation by the self-interested few. This re-evaluation was far from universal and the term 'public opinion' had always had multiple meanings. Yet it does appear that the enlightenment definition, so pervasive in earlier decades, was losing ground to its competitors. With the negative connotations of Wilde's definition, it is not surprising that arguments re-emerged about the need for balance and special representation for minorities. Thus, John Stuart Mill considered multiple votes for university degree holders and a panel of experts to draft legislation. As we have already seen, Bagehot chose a big white lie about the constitution to distract most people from how power was exercised. Government should only listen to those he thought had something worth saying. The political and intellectual division of labour once central to mixed monarchy and the gentlemanly science of politics was being refashioned. Likewise, disenchanted liberals like Sir Henry Maine and Goldwin Smith found parliamentary government wanting, requiring as it did such confidence in the self-regulating nature of the public sphere. As an alternative, they rehearsed many of the arguments already advanced by Upper Canada's 'Tory republicans' in favour of American republicanism with its written constitution and institutionalized separation of powers.

In Upper Canada by mid-century, there had been no such re-evaluation of public opinion. While a few might fret about its strength, 'public opinion' continued to refer almost exclusively to a positive force arising from rational, informed discussion. Who could seriously oppose such a thing? At no time were political actors forced to concede that more information and more reasoning might not eventually solve the prob-

---

19 Wilde, 'The Critic as Artist,' in Michael S. Foldy, *The Trials of Oscar Wilde: Deviance, Morality, and Late-Victorian Society* (New Haven: Yale University Press 1997), 51

lems they diagnosed. So long as they believed in progress (that more people were getting more informed, more educated, more reasonable, and more tolerant, or at least that it was possible to imagine future conditions under which such progress could occur),[20] public opinion was not only a positive force, but its power would continue to grow. It would continue to be politically useful.

It is natural to think that one's own opinions are informed and rational and so remain confident that the 'thinking public' will agree with you. It follows too easily that those who don't are ill informed, ill willed, or irrational. Thus, the rationality and positive definition of public opinion are preserved by distinguishing it from popular clamour. While one can hold onto the ideal without believing that it will work every time, are there not limits to how much one can shrink the size of the public relative to that of the community as a whole? If public opinion was to be effective and if it was safe to ground the state in it, then it must, in most instances, triumph over popular clamour. As its Upper Canadian champions had understood, the public must be large and powerful, not just rational. Setbacks could only be aberrations.

For instance, several of those champions were defeated in the election of 1836. As we saw, they blamed misinformation, corruption, and violence – not the value of their own cause. Defeat did not, therefore, undermine their confidence that they would have won if everyone had collectively reasoned through the arguments and been able to vote accordingly. They did not have to face two ugly possibilities: first, that even with this sought-after decision-making process, they might still have lost. Once belief in progress was shaken – perhaps history wasn't moving in the 'right' direction – it became harder to remain so sure that a well-functioning public would never come to conclusions one found politically or morally abhorrent. Of course, a willing decision to exchange reasons in public implied the admission that one might be mistaken. Nonetheless, it seems likely that the enthusiasm with which such exchange was promoted in the 1830s and 1840s would have been dampened had political notables really thought that their most cherished beliefs could be discarded.

The painful possibility that the defeat of the rational public might not be temporary was also avoided. Again, a generalized belief in progress ensured ultimate vindication since, while currently stymied, public opin-

---

20 Burrow, *Whigs and Liberals*, esp. 71–2

ion would continue to develop. For the reform generation of 1836, the assumption of political power after the 1848 election served precisely this function; but what if the dynamics of future political conflict had worked out differently? Perhaps future defeats, like those of 1836, meant that a large and decisive segment of the population was not *yet* participating according to the dictates of the public sphere, but how far into the future could the happy day be projected? Once heroic efforts had been made to disseminate information and arguments, once contestants had appealed to and participated in public deliberations, and once at least some had proved competent, all the rationalizations about the eventual triumph of public opinion might wear a bit thin. Perhaps defeat wasn't an aberration after all. Perhaps it was evidence of deep-seated values or prejudices that 'reason' couldn't touch. Perhaps a decisive portion of a given community refused or were not able to do what the enlightenment ideal of public opinion demanded of them. It would remain an abstract ideal, but it would cease to be a workable political reality or a guide to political action. Even more disconcerting, perhaps its assumptions about the power of reason and value of intellectual exchange were grossly exaggerated or just false.

None of these sobering thoughts took hold in Upper Canada by mid-century. Most weren't even conceived of. The enlightenment definition of public opinion remained dominant. The point of all these questions and conjectures is not to suggest that deliberative democracy was a sham or incoherent or incapable of meeting future challenges. Some, in fact, were relatively easy to overcome. For example, the paradox of a community valuing public deliberation but deciding not to deliberate is more apparent than real. It might be prudent to voluntarily forgo public discussion of some topics, such as certain religious principles, that are not subject to compromise or rational adjudication and whose airing threatens to undermine the basis for societal cooperation.[21] Constitutions of the colony's early debating societies had already pointed the way by prohibiting certain classes of questions. Moreover, it bears repeating that espousing the enlightenment ideal of public opinion and the desire to work towards it were compatible with a frank acknowledgment of reversals and hostile circumstances. In Upper Canada, both ideal and desire were products of practical politics and an assessment of concrete social and cultural developments, not abstract theorizing.

---

21 Stephen Holmes, *Passions & Constraint: On the Theory of Liberal Democracy* (Chicago: University of Chicago Press 1995), chap. 7

Highlighting what had not been thought through or even confronted does, perhaps, bring the contours of public opinion as both an idealized construct and social reality into sharper focus. Such informed speculation also underlines the continued importance of well-designed institutions and laws. No amount of confidence in a social force like public opinion should divert attention from the mechanics of government and their role in protecting and fostering public criticism, acting in the absence of a clear public verdict or defying an inappropriate one, limiting the exercise of power, and managing conflict.[22] In turn, properly designed institutions help create citizens better able to participate in the public sphere. Again, debating societies had already made the point. Supremely confident that intellectual controversy had positive individual and social consequences, far from dispensing with procedures and rules, they adopted elaborate constitutions. Self-regulation required more than the desire and ability to partake. It also required a framework of accepted norms and institutions – a framework that, in turn, encouraged the development of more and better debaters. Finally, it is clear that public opinion as understood in Upper Canada entered the second half of the nineteenth century having vanquished its original foes and full of revolutionary promise, but incomplete – its ideals of inclusion and reason often betrayed and some of its internal tensions and potential pitfalls unforeseen.

Significant changes in the conditions under which public opinion had first developed and gained credibility also lay ahead. Informed by the fortunes of democracy in twentieth-century Germany, Jürgen Habermas devotes the second half of *The Structural Transformation of the Public Sphere* to the eclipse of its liberal phase. Indeed, the concept of the public sphere 'cannot be applied to the actual conditions of an industrially advanced mass democracy organized in the form of the social welfare state.' To sketch Habermas's argument: the public expanded to include social classes that he assumes had incompatible interests that generated selfish demands in welfare policy and taxation. The state, forced to regulate items once left to the private market, became the battleground for competing interest groups in a zero-sum game. State decisions appeared to reflect the balance of power among classes preoccupied by their own material benefit rather than rational deliberation among citizens seeking the common good. A print culture that fostered critical exchanges

---

22 For an overstatement of this point, see Gordon, *Citizens without Sovereignty*, 243.

of information and opinion was also replaced by the mass media or 'public relations work' designed to entertain and to market a variety of consumer goods ranging from dishwashers to political leaders.[23]

Minko Sotiron finds similar trends in Canada's newspaper industry after 1890. Increasing capital costs of production and distribution meant greater barriers to entry for new or independent voices and gave predominant influence to big business as advertisers rather than to citizens as subscribers. The importance of the editorial page declined. Lengthy reports of parliamentary intelligence disappeared to make way for more advertising, better graphics, sensationalist coverage, and new sports and other entertainment features. Fear of offending large advertisers or any segment of the papers' mass audience further diluted political content. Finally, increasing market concentration empowered a handful of metropolitan papers to gain control of or displace local organs.[24]

Regular public opinion polling did not arrive in Canada until the 1940s, although consumer marketing surveys, driven by many of the same forces reshaping the press, had established their assumptions and methodology by the end of the 1920s. Such polling provided political notables with a more effective means to gauge and exploit the aggregated opinions, prejudices, aspirations, and fears of a sampled (though not necessarily representative) public. As polls redefined public opinion, so too democracy was modelled more on the buying and selling of the economic market than on the uncoerced communications of public deliberation.[25] Increasing interest in human psychology had already led Graham Wallas to sound the alarm in *Human Nature in Politics* (1908). If new marketing and advertising tools could manipulate a mass market, they could manipulate a mass electorate. The distinction between consumer and citizen was blurring. Nor was Wallas alone in shifting attention to the irrational, emotional, and group character of collective decision-making. The contrast between public and crowd also lessened. Walter Lippmann's sceptical *Public Opinion* was followed in 1925 by his *The Phantom Public*, expounding the need for experts to compensate for

---

23 Jürgen Habermas, 'The Public Sphere: An Encyclopedic Article,' *New German Critique* 1, no. 3 (Fall 1974), 54–5 and *The Structural Transformation of the Public Sphere: An Inquiry into a Category of Bourgeois Society*, trans. Thomas Burger (Cambridge, Mass.: MIT Press 1989), chap. 5–7

24 Minko Sotiron, *From Politics to Profit: The Commercialization of Canadian Daily Newspapers 1890–1920* (Montreal and Kingston: McGill-Queen's University Press 1997)

25 Daniel J. Robinson, *The Measure of Democracy: Polling, Market Research, and Public Life, 1930–1945* (Toronto: University of Toronto Press, 1999), 6–8, 10, 64–93, 162–3

the public's inability to grapple with the increasingly technical questions of public policy. H.D. Lasswell's *Propaganda Technique in the World War* (1927) drew attention to yet another twentieth-century phenomenon that cast doubt on the ability of the public to withstand manipulation. Behaviouralist studies of the American voter that highlighted voters' limited knowledge of and interest in politics, and the centrality of partisan identity rather than policy issues, had further sobering effects despite lingering echoes of the enlightenment definition of public opinion in democratic theory and political rhetoric.[26]

The findings of such studies and Habermas's chart of the eclipse of the liberal public raise a number of questions. For instance, Upper Canada's public sphere drew additional credibility from the widespread belief that the colony lacked those extremes of wealth and poverty most dangerous to unfettered democratic communication. Even though the majority of its households were represented in the colonial public sphere, they expressed a narrower range of interests and experiences than a similar proportion of households would in a more class-ridden or class-conscious society. What adjustments were required if the liberal public sphere was to outlive industrialization? In 1854, at the end of this study, many of the forces identified by Habermas and others as especially corrosive to that sphere remained in the future. As well, only later developments would reveal the degree to which the tensions and pitfalls identified above were inherent in the concept of public opinion as it had developed by the mid-1850s or could be avoided.

Barring future work, such questions must remain open. P.B. Waite's justly classic study of Confederation shows the continued vitality of newspapers and public debate in the mid-1860s. The movement had 'a vital public existence' outside parliamentary and official circles. It is, however, difficult to know whether A.I. Silver's work should hearten or discourage enthusiasts of the public sphere. Silver demonstrates that both French Canadians and Ontarians had rational and coherent grounds for their conclusions, even on such an explosive issue as the appropriate punishment for Louis Riel in 1885. Their judgments were based on the

---

26 Burrows, *Whigs and Liberals*, 74, Paul A. Palmer, 'The Concept of Public Opinion in Political Theory,' in Carl Witke, ed., *Essays in History and Political Theory in Honor of Charles Howard McIlwain* (Cambridge, Mass.: Harvard University Press 1936), 231–2, 251–3, and J.A.W. Gunn, '"Public Opinion" in Modern Political Science,' in James Farr, John S. Dryzek, and Stephen T. Leonard, eds., *Political Science in History: Research Programs and Political Traditions* (Cambridge: Cambridge University Press 1995), 103–4, 107–8

public discussion of the information at hand, alternative arguments, and their previous experience with each other, analogous cases, and Riel himself. Yet the result was considerable misunderstanding, distrust, and group-based hostility.[27]

Moreover, it cannot simply be assumed that the norms and ideals of classical public opinion were impossible outside the socio-economic and cultural circumstances in which they developed; that they cannot be translated to other environments. Thus, the concept of deliberative democracy is enjoying something of a renaissance among theorists and political scientists well aware of current conditions.[28] As well as trying to challenge some of the stock portrayals of Upper Canada by bringing new questions and perspectives to now-neglected constitutional topics, this book has also tried to equip us to better interrogate current definitions and manifestations of public opinion and parliamentary government in light of what they once meant and promised. We would do well to guard against undue optimism for their future as well as undue nostalgia for their past.

As Immanuel Kant insisted, enlightenment was not a body of doctrine or an event. It was a process – a process of intellectual maturation. By 1854, a liberal public sphere existed in Upper Canada. Its ideals and claims were integrated into the province's constitutional and social self-understanding. The acceptance of public opinion and deliberative democracy was something of a revolution. Pre-democratic concepts and assumptions were exploded in ways that remind us why contemporaries expended so much effort in public debate and why they sought to invest it with more authority. Yet the process had not reached its conclusion. One of its greatest achievements was to insist on the irrelevance to political standing of most differences arising from such characteristics as occupation, religion, and national origins. This achievement seemed to point towards seeing other sources of difference as equally irrelevant, but by not making them so it also seemed to reinforce them as especially

27 P.B. Waite, *Life and Times of Confederation, 1865–1867* (Toronto: University of Toronto Press 1962), esp. 6, 106, 141, and 323–4 (quotation at 323), and A.I. Silver, *The French Canadian Idea of Confederation, 1864–1900* (Toronto: University of Toronto Press 1982), chap. 8 and 'Ontario's Alleged Fanaticism in the Riel Affair,' *Canadian Historical Review* 69, no. 1 (March 1988), 21–50

28 E.g., Gutman and Thompson, *Democracy and Disagreement,* James Bohman and William Rehg, eds., *Deliberative Democracy: Essays on Reason and Politics* (Cambridge, Mass.: MIT Press 1997), and Jon Elster, ed., *Deliberative Democracy* (Cambridge: Cambridge University Press 1998)

problematic. Nonetheless, a few already saw where the logic of their arguments led.

In subsequent decades, marginalized groups demanded incorporation into the public sphere on many of the same grounds that advocates had used to insist that public opinion govern the state: first, that their perspectives were not voiced by others and, second, that they not only had something important to offer, but had the information, rationality, and sociability to offer it effectively in the deliberations of their community. Positive political participation had been redefined as participation in the public sphere – politics as dialogue – but what counted as sufficiently 'reasonable,' 'informed,' or 'moderate' and who could participate in these ways was determined by the public sphere itself. These were more porous standards, more open to challenge than claims to citizenship based on the arbitrary whim of the few, physical characteristics, membership in a group, birth, or prescription. The uneven and contested inclusion of other voices, the nature and consequence of their participation, the impact of external forces on the public sphere, and the relationship between that evolving social space and persisting political institutions mark Canada's engagement with liberal democracy in this century. There is much here for citizens to ponder and historians to study.

The diffusion of the Kantian definition of enlightenment freed the community from older ways of conceptualizing knowledge, power, and society, even as it developed its own definitions and mechanisms and even as its ideals were often breeched. To see only triumph would be to lapse into a linear, progressive narrative, but to emphasize only incompleteness and restriction would be to underestimate the shift that had occurred and to forget that some costs are worth paying. To write the history of enlightenment public opinion as one of either unmitigated progress or the mere substitution of one form of regulation for another is to limit ourselves to either utopian hope or dystopian despair. Both breed cynicism and excuse apathy. Neither do justice to the anonymous Kingston mechanic with whom we began. In the spring of 1834, he could no 'longer remain a mere idle spectator' in the constitutional, political, and intellectual history of his community. Declaring, 'I will not remain silent,' he joined his fellow citizens in shaping that history, for, as Thomas Carlyle put it a few years later, 'the nation is governed by all that has tongue in the nation.'[29]

---

29 'A True Irishman,' *British Whig*, 11 Mar. 1834 and Carlyle, 'The Hero as Man of Letters,'
   142

Bibliography of Printed Primary Sources

Newspapers and Periodicals

Brockville: *The Brockville Gazette* (1828–32) and *Brockville Recorder* (1830–40, 1843–4, 1849–55).

Chatham: *Canadian Freeman* (1848) and *Chatham Journal* (1843–4).

Cobourg: *The Cobourg Star* (1831–44, 1848–53) and *The Reformer* (1832–5).

Cornwall: *The Cornwall Constitutional* (1850–1) and *The Freeholder* (1850).

Hamilton: *The Canadian Casket* (1831), *Hamilton Gazette* (1848–54), *Hamilton Spectator* (1848–55), *The Provincialist* (originally Cobourg, 1848–50) and *Western Mercury* (1831–4).

Kingston: *The British Whig* (1844, 1848–52), *Canadian Loyalist and Spirit of 1812* (1843–4), *The Kingston Chronicle / The Chronicle and Gazette* (1819–44), *The Kingston Gazette* (1810–18), *The Kingston Spectator* (1834–40), *The News* (1844), and *The Upper Canada Herald* (1826–40).

London: *Canadian Free Press* (1849–52), *Canada Inquirer* (1840–4), *London Gazette* (1837), *London Herald* (1843), and *The Upper Canada Times* (1836).

Niagara: *The Canada / Canadian Constellation* (1799–1800), *The Niagara Argus* (1844), *The Niagara Chronicle* (1838–44), *The Niagara Gleaner* (1818–33), *The Niagara Herald* (1801–2), and *The Niagara Spectator* (1816–20).

St Catharines: *British American Journal* (1834–5), *British Colonial Argus* (1833), *The Farmers' Journal* (1826–33), *St Catharines Constitutional* (1851–3), and *St Catharines Journal* (1835–40, 1843–4, 1848–54).

St Thomas: *The St Thomas Standard* (1844) and *The St Thomas Liberal* (1833–6).

Sandwich: *Canadian Emigrant* (1832–5) and *Western Herald* (1838–40).

Woodstock: *British American* (1848–52), *The Monarch* (1842–4), and *Woodstock Herald* (1844).

York/Toronto: *The Artisan* (1848), *The Banner* (1843–4), *The British Colonist* (1838–44, 1848–54, org. *The Scotsman*), *Canadian Correspondent / Correspondent & Advocate* (1833–7), *Canadian Freeman* (1825–34), *The Christian Guardian* (1829–44), *The Church* (org. Cobourg, 1837–44), *Colonial Advocate* (org. Queenston, 1824–34), *The Constitution* (1836–7), *The Courier* [*of Upper Canada*] (1830, 1832–6), *The Daily Leader* (1853–5), *The Examiner* (1840–4, 1847–55), *The Globe* (1844, 1847–55), *The Independent* (1849–50), *Mackenzie's Weekly Message* (1852–5), *The Mirror* (1837–44, 1848–55), *The Monthly Review* (1841), *The North American* (1850–5), *The Palladium of British America* (1838), *Patriot* [*and Farmer's Monitor*] (org. Kingston, 1829–44, 1848–54), *Provincial Freeman* (org. Windsor, 1853–5), *The Royal Standard* (1836–7), *The U.E. Loyalist / The Loyalist* (1826–8), *The Upper Canada* [*York*] *Gazette* (org. Newark, 1793–1820), *Weekly Register* (1822–5), and *York Weekly Post* (1821).

Other: *Bathurst Courier* (Perth, 1834–40, 1843–4, 1848–54), *The Bytown Gazette* (1836–44), *The Dundas Weekly Post* (1834–6), *The Elora Backwoodsman* (1852–4), *The Gore Gazette* (Ancaster, 1827–9), *The Guelph Advertiser* (1848–54), *Hallowell* [Picton] *Free Press* (1830–4), *Huron Signal* (Goderich, 1848–54), *The Port Hope Watchman* (1850–1), and *The Whitby Reporter / Ontario Reporter* (1850–2).

Contemporary Publications

Address of the Hamilton Branch of the British American League, with the By-Laws, For the Guidance of the Association. Hamilton: Spectator Office 1849.
The Addresses Presented to His Excellency The Right Hon. Sir Chas. T. Metcalfe, Bart., G.C.B., Governor-General of British North America, &c., &c., On The Occasion of the Resignation of His Late Advisors; with His Excellency's Replies. Toronto: H.&W. Rowsell 1844.

Anon. *Arguments Against an Elective Legislative Council.* Toronto: Leader and Patriot Office 1856.

Anon. *Responsible Government for Canada: An Enquiry as to the Causes and Consequences of the Late Ministerial Resignations.* Montreal: Armour & Ramsay; Kingston: Ramsay, Armour & Co.; Hamilton: A.N. Armour & Co.; Quebec: T. Cary & Co.; and Toronto: Hugh Scobie 1844.

Anon. *To the Right Honorable Lord Castlereagh one of His Majesty's Principal Secretaries of State, &c., &c., &c.* Quebec 1809.

Bagehot, Walter. *The English Constitution.* Ed. R.H.S. Crossman. London: Fontana/Collins 1963 [1867].

– *Physics and Politics or Thoughts on the Application of the Principles of 'Natural Selection' and 'Inheritance' to Political Society.* Ed. Hans Kohn. Boston: Beacon Press 1956 [1867–72].

Bentham, Jeremy. *A Fragment on Government.* Ed. Ross Harrison. Cambridge: Cambridge University 1988.

Bidwell, Marshall S. *Mr. Bidwell's Speech on the Intestate Estate Bill, in the Provincial Assembly of Upper Canada, January 24, 1831.* York 1831.

– *Substance of Mr. Bidwell's Speech on the second reading of his Intestine [sic] Estates Bill, in the Session of 1832.* York 1832.

Bird, Isabella Lucy. *The English Woman in America.* Ed. Andrew Hill Clark. Toronto: University of Toronto Press 1966 [1856].

Blackstone, William. *The Commentaries on the Laws of England.* Ed. Robert Malcolm Kerr. 4th edition. London: John Murray 1876.

Bonnycastle, Sir Richard Henry. *The Canadas in 1841.* East Ardsley: S.R. Publishers, Ltd. and Toronto: Johnson Reprint Corp. 1968 [1841].

Bridges, John George. *A Digest of the British Constitution; Complied by Dr. Bridges, and Delivered by Him as a Lecture at Many of the Principal Towns in Upper Canada.* Montreal: John Lovell 1839.

– *The Every Boy's Book, or a Digest of the British Constitution. Compiled and Arranged for the Use of Schools and Private Families.* Ottawa: Ottawa Advocate Office 1842.

Brown's Toronto City and Home District Directory, 1846–7. Toronto: George Brown 1846.

[Buchanan, Isaac]. *First Series of Five Letters, Against the Baldwin Faction, by An Advocate of Responsible Government, and of the New College Bill.* Toronto: British Colonist Office 1844.

By-Laws of the Western District Literary, Philosophical and Agricultural Association ... Together with The Discourse Delivered by the President of the Occasion ... Sandwich: Henry C. Grant 1842.

Carlyle, Thomas. 'The Hero as Man of Letters. Johnson, Rouseau, Burns.' In Michael K. Goldberg, Joel J. Brattin, and Mark Engel, eds., *On Heroes, Hero-*

Worship, & the Heroic in History. Berkeley: University of California Press 1993 [1841].

[Cartwright, Richard]. *Letters, from an American Loyalist in Upper-Canada to His Friend in England.* Halifax 1810.

The City of Toronto and the Home District Commercial Directory and Register with Almanack and Calendar for 1837. Compiled and arranged by George Walton. Toronto: T. Dalton and W.J. Coates.

Clarke, James. *An Address to a Large and Respectable Body of Freemasons, on their Laying the Corner Stone of St. George's Church, St. Catharines: July 29, 1835, Published at the Request of the Members of St. George's Lodge, no 15 and of Several Other Lodges.* St Catharines: British American Journal Office 1835.

Confederation Debates of the Province of Canada. Ed. P.B. Waite. Toronto: McClelland and Stewart 1963.

Constitution and By Laws of the Wilberforce Lyceum Educating Society for Moral and Mental Improvement. Amherstburg: I.B. Boyle 1850.

The Constitution of the Canadas, Adopted by the Imperial Parliament in the Thirty-First Year of the Reign of His Majesty, George III., and, in the Year of Our Lord, 1791, Together with the Debates Thereon. Hallowell: Joseph Wilson 1833.

Constitution and Laws of the Hamilton Literary Society. Hamilton: The Canadian Conservative 1837.

Constitution of the Midland District Agricultural Society. Kingston: Chronicle 1837?

The Constitutions of the Antient Fraternity of Free and Accepted Masons. Part the Second. Containing the Charges, Regulations &c. &c. Published by the Authority of the United Grand Lodge, by William Williams, Esq. Provincial Grand Master for the County of Dorset. First Canadian Edition. Republished by Order of the Provincial Grand Lodge of Upper Canada. Kingston: H.C. Thomson 1823.

Creen, Thomas. *Two Discourses, Delivered in St. Mark's Church, Niagara, ... for a Day of Public Fasting and Humiliation ...* Niagara: Simpson and Menzies 1838.

Davis, Robert. *The Canadian Farmer's Travels In the United States of America, in which remarks are made on The Arbitrary Colonial Policy Practiced in Canada and the Free and Equal Rights, And Happy Effects of the Liberal Institutions and Astonishing Enterprise of the United States.* Buffalo: Steele's Press 1837.

De Lolme, J.L. *The Constitution of England; or, An Account of the English Government; in which it is compared both with the republican form of government and the other monarchies of Europe; a New Edition, with Life and Notes by John Macgregor.* London: Henry G. Bohn 1853.

Duncombe, Charles. 'Report on Education.' In J. George Hodgins, ed., *Documentary History of Education in Upper Canada.* Vol. 1, 289–308. Toronto: Warwick Bros and Rutter 1894.

Dunlop, Dr. *An Address Delivered to the York Mechanics' Institution, March 1832.* York: W.J. Coates 1832.

The Federalist Papers. Ed. Isaac Kramnick. London: Penguin Books 1987.

A Form of Prayer, to be used ... for a Day of Pubic Fasting and Humiliation ... Toronto: R. Stanton 1838.

Fuimus. *Letter to His Excellency the Right Honorable Lord Elgin, On Responsible Government, As applied simply to the Province of Canada; Together with his Lordship's Celebrated Speech Delivered in the House of Commons as Lord Bruce, in 1841, Deprecating in the Strongest Terms, All Appointments to Office by a Tottering Ministry, Not Enjoying the Confidence of the People.* Montreal: Donoghue & Mantz 1847.

Gourlay, Robert. *Statistical Account of Upper Canada ...* East Ardsley: S.R. Publishers Ltd. and Toronto: Johnson Reprint Corp. 1966 [1822].

Gowan, Lieutenant-Colonel. *An Important Letter on Responsible Government.* Toronto: Examiner Office 1839.

Grey, Earl. *Parliamentary Government Considered with Reference to a Reform of Parliament: An Essay.* London: Richard Bentley 1858.

Haliburton, Thomas C. *An Historical and Statistical Account of Nova Scotia in Two Volumes.* Belleville: Mika Publishing 1973 [1829].

Head, Sir Francis Bond. *A Narrative with notes by William Lyon Mackenzie.* Ed. S.F. Wise. Toronto: McClelland and Stewart 1969 [1839].

Herchmer, W.M. *Love, The Spirit of Masonry: An Address Delivered in St. George's Kingston, on the Festival of St. John the Evangelist, December 27, 1847.* Kingston: Argus Office 1848.

Howard, John Henry. *The Laws of The British Colonies; in The West Indies and other parts of America, Concerning Real and Personal Property and Manumission of Slaves; with a View of the Constitution of Each Colony.* Westport, Conn.: Negro University Press 1970 [1827].

Howison, John. *Sketches of Upper Canada, Domestic, Local, and Characteristic: to which are added, Practical Details for the Information of Emigrants of every class; and some recollections of the United States of America.* [East Ardsley:] S.R. Publishers Ltd. and Toronto: Johnson Reprint Corp. 1965 [1821].

Humphreys, J.D. *The Junior Warden's Toast.* The Music Composed and Dedicated to F.W. Barron, Esq. W.M. and the Brethren of St. Andrew's Lodge No. 1 Toronto, 27 Dec. 1854. N.p.

J.K. *Plain Reasons for Loyalty: Addressed to Plain People.* Cobourg: R.D. Catterton 1838.

Jackson, John Mills. *A View of the Political Situation of the Province of Upper Canada, in North America in which her physical capacity is stated; the means of diminishing her burden, increasing her value, and securing her connection to Great Britain are fully considered, with an appendix.* London: W. Earle 1809.

Jameson, Anna Brownell. *Winter Studies and Summer Rambles in Canada.* Toronto: McClelland and Stewart 1990 [1838].

Jarvis, Samuel P. *Statement of Facts Relating to the Trespass on the Printing Press in the Possession of Mr. William Lyon M'kenzie, in June 1826, Addressed to the Public Generally, and Particularly to the Subscribers, and Supporters of the Colonial Advocate.* York: R. Stanton 1828.

Journals of the House of Assembly and *Journals of the Legislative Council of Upper Canada.*

Kant, Immanuel. *Kant: Political Writings.* Trans. Hans Reiss, 2nd edition. Cambridge: Cambridge University Press 1991.

[Lachlan, R.] *Address of the Directing President of the Western District Agricultural and Philosophical Society.* Sandwich: Henry C. 1838.

Laws for the Constitution and Government of the York Literary and Philosophical Society in Upper Canada. York: Robert Stanton 183?.

Legion [Robert Baldwin Sullivan]. *Letters on Responsible Government.* Toronto: Examiner Office 1844.

Leith, Alexander. *Commentaries on the Laws of England: Applicable to Real Property by Sir William Blackstone, Knt. Adapted to the Present State of the Law of Upper Canada.* Toronto: W.C. Chewett 1864.

Lord Durham's Report: An Abridgement. Ed. G.M. Craig. Ottawa: Carleton University Press 1982.

MacGill, Robert. *The Love of Country, A Discourse.* Niagara 1838.

Mackenzie, William Lyon. *Catechism of Education. Part First.* York: Colonial Advocate Press 1830.

– 'Draft Constitution.' In H.D. Forbes, ed., *Canadian Political Thought*, 38–42. Toronto: Oxford University Press 1985.

– *Sketches of Canada and the United States.* London: Effingham Wilson 1833.

MacKinnon, William A. *On the Rise, Progress and Present State of Public Opinion in Great Britain and Other Parts of the World.* Shannon, Ireland: Irish University Press, 1971 [1828].

Millar, John. *An Historical View of the English Government, from the Settlement of the Saxons in Britain to the Revolution of 1688.* London: J. Mawman 1803 [1786].

Minutes of the Proceedings of the Second Convention of Delegates of the British American League. Toronto: Patriot Office 1849.

Moodie, Susanna. *Roughing It in the Bush.* Toronto: McClelland and Stewart 1989 [1852].

– *Life in the Clearings versus the Bush.* Toronto: McClelland and Stewart 1989 [1853].

Morleigh. *Life in the West: Back-wood Leaves and Prairie Flowers: Rough Sketches on the Borders of the Picturesque, the Sublime, and Ridiculous, Extracts from the Note Book of Morleigh in Search of an Estate.* London: Stanley and Otley 1842.

Paine, Thomas. *Political Writings.* Ed. Bruce Kuklick. Cambridge: Cambridge University Press 1989.

Paley, William. *The Works of William Paley, D.D. with a Biographical Sketch of the Author ...* Ed. Rev. D.S. Wayland. Derby: Henry Mozley 1825.

Reform Association of Canada. *'The Globe' Extra. Proceedings at the First General Meeting of the Reform Association of Canada, Held at the Rooms of the Association, Toronto, on Monday, 25th March, 1844.* Toronto: The Globe 1844.

Reform Association of Canada [John Macarer?]. *Address to the People of Canada by the Reform Association; Adopted at a General Meeting, held at the Association Rooms, at Toronto, the 16th Day of May, 1844.* Toronto: Examiner Office 1844.

Report of the Commissioners appointed to enquire into the affairs of the Post Office in British North America, 1841. Reprinted in *Journals of the Legislative Assembly of the Province of Canada,* 1846.

Report, from the Select Committee of the Legislative Council of Upper Canada on the State of the Province, Feb. 1838.

The Revised Statutes of New Brunswick, 1854.

Ross, Dunbar. *The Seat of Government Question ... Also The Composition and Functions of the Legislative Council ...* Quebec: E.R. Fréchette 1856.

Rowsell's City of Toronto and County of York Directory for 1850–1. Ed. J. Armstrong. Toronto: Henry Rowsell 1850.

Russell, Lord John. *An Essay on the History of English Government and Constitution, From the Reign of Henry VII. To the Present Time.* 2nd edition. London: Longman, Hurst, Reees, Orme and Brown 1823.

Ryerson, Egerton. *Civil Government - the Late Conspiracy. A Discourse, Delivered in Kingston, U.C. December 31, 1837.* Toronto: Conference Office 1838.

– *Sir Charles Metcalfe Defended against the Attacks of His Late Counsellors.* Toronto: British Colonist Office 1844.

– *The Hon. R.B. Sullivan's Attacks upon Sir Charles Metcalfe Refuted by Egerton Ryerson; Being a Reply to the Letters of 'Legion.'* Toronto: British Colonist Office 1844.

– *'The Story of My Life': Being Reminiscences of Sixty Years' Public Service in Canada.* Ed. J. George Hodgins. Toronto: William Briggs 1883.

The Seventh Report from the Select Committee of the House of Assembly of Upper Canada on Grievances. Toronto: M. Reynolds 1835.

Sherwood, Henry. *Federative Union of the British North American Provinces.* Toronto: Hugh Scobie 1850; reprinted with additions, Toronto: Lovell and Gibson 1851.

Simpson, John. *Essay on Modern Reformers; Addressed to the People of Upper Canada to which is added A Letter to Mr. Robert Gourlay.* Kingston: Stephen Miles 1818.

Smart, W.M. *An Address Delivered Before the Provincial Grant Royal Arch Chapter of*

Upper Canada, at York, on the 8th of July 1823. Published by order of the Chapter. Kingston: H.C. Thomson 1823.

Strachan, the Rev. John. *A Discourse on the Character of King George the Third: Address to the Inhabitants of British America.* Montreal: Nahum Mower 1810.

Swift, Patrick [W.L. Mackenzie]. *A New Almanack ... 1834.* York: Colonial Advocate.

Talbot, Edward Allan. *Five Years' Residence in the Canadas ...* East Ardsley: S.R. Publishers Ltd. and Toronto: Johnson Reprint Corp. 1968 [1824].

Thompson, Samuel. *Reminiscences of a Canadian Pioneer For the Last Fifty Years [1833–1884], An Autobiography of Samuel Thompson.* Toronto: McClelland and Stewart 1968 [1884].

Tocqueville, Alexis de. *Democracy in America.* Trans. George Lawrence, ed. J.P. Mayer. New York: Harper & Row 1969.

Wollstonecraft, Mary. *A Vindication of the Rights of Men with A Vindication of the Rights of Woman and Hints.* Ed. Sylvana Tomaselli. Cambridge: Cambridge University Press 1995.

York Commercial Directory, Street Guide and Register, 1833–4; with Almanack and Calendar for 1834. Compiled and arranged by George Walton. York: Thomas Dalton 1833.

Zeno [Ross Dunbar]. *The 'Crise' Metcalfe and The Lafontaine-Baldwin Cabinet Defended. Letter of Zeno to the Legislative Assembly of Canada.* Quebec: W. Cowan & Son 1844.

Printed Documents

The Arthur Papers Being the Canadian Papers Mainly Confidential, Private, and Demi-Official of Sir George Arthur, K.C.H. Last Lieutenant-Governor of Upper Canada In the Manuscript Collection of the Toronto Public Libraries. Ed. Charles R. Sanderson. Toronto: Toronto Public Libraries and University of Toronto Press 1957.

The Child Letters: Public and Private Life in a Canadian Merchant-Politician's Family, 1841–1845. Ed. J.I. Little. Montreal and Kingston: McGill-Queen's University Press 1995.

Debates of the Legislative Assembly of United Canada. Ed. Elizabeth Nish et al. Montreal: Presses de L'École des Hautes Études Commerciales 1970–93 and, from 1856, Province of Canada, scrapbook debates.

The Elgin-Grey Papers, 1846–1852. Ed. A.G. Doughty. Ottawa: Public Archives of Canada 1937.

'Letters of 1844 and 1846 from Scobie to Ryerson.' Ed. C.B. Sissons. *Canadian Historical Review* 29, no. 4 (Dec. 1948), 393–411.

'"Neither Radical Nor Tory Nor Whig": Letter by Oliver Mowat to John Mowat, 1843–1846.' Ed. Peter Neary. *Ontario History* 71, no. 2 (June 1979), 84–131.

O'Brien, Mary. *The Journals of Mary O'Brien, 1828–1838*. Ed. Audrey Saunders Miller. Toronto: Macmillan 1968.

The Papers of the Prime Ministers. Volume 1. *The Letters of Sir John A. Macdonald, 1836–1857*. Ed. J.K. Johnson. Ottawa: Public Archives of Canada 1968.

Public Archives of Canada. 'Political State of Upper Canada in 1806–7.' In *Report on Canadian Archives 1892*. Ottawa: Queen's Printer 1893.

The Records of the Federal Convention of 1787. Vol. 1. Ed. Max Farrand. New Haven: Yale University Press 1966.

The Town of York, 1793–1815: A Collection of Documents of Early Toronto. Ed. Edith G. Firth. Toronto: The Champlain Society and University of Toronto Press 1962.

The Town of York, 1815–1834: A Further Collection of Documents. Ed. Edith G. Firth. Toronto: The Champlain Society and University of Toronto Press 1966.

Illustration Credits

Index

Abraham, Nelles, 378
agricultural societies, 92, 93–7
Agricultural Society of Upper Canada, 94
annexation to the United States, 280, 284–5, 294, 420
aristocracy. *See* legislative council; social structure
assembly, the: compared to House of Commons, 35–6; parliamentary reporting and, 151–74; representation in, 336–42, 348–50

Bagehot, Walter, 350, 357, 429, 430; *The English Constitution*, 272, 312n21, 313, 316, 324, 342n105, 354–5, 421–2; *Physics and Politics*, 422–4
Bagot, Charles, 215
Baker, G. Blaine, 84, 383
Baker, Keith Michael, 176
Baldwin, Augustus, 376
Baldwin, Robert, 43, 136, 214, 351; on the British Empire, 250, 257, 296; on the cabinet, 325; on the legislative council, 312–13, 317, 320; on the liberty of the press, 141; on the Metcalfe crisis, 214–15, 223; on primogeniture, 360, 369, 409; on responsible government, 45, 213, 243, 306; on representation in the assembly, 336
Baldwin, William Warren, 43, 186, 369n22, 388
ballot, secret, 69, 301–2, 341
Barry, John, 91
Beales, Captain, 260
benevolent and religious societies, 103, 109–10
Bentham, Jeremy, 26
Bethune, A.N., 79, 204
Bethune, Donald, 81, 387
Bidwell, Barnabus, 385, 403
Bidwell, Marshall Spring: freemasonry and, 81; on the legislative council, 33; on the liberty of the press, 143; as a newspaper agent, 123, 128; on primogeniture, 170, 369n22, 371, 381–2, 390, 391–3, 394, 395, 398, 400–1, 402, 403, 406, 407; on public opinion, 168, 186; temperance and, 103
blacks, 80, 104n115, 266, 345–7
Blackstone, William, 25–6, 53, 138, 362–3
Blaquiere, Peter Boyle de, 379